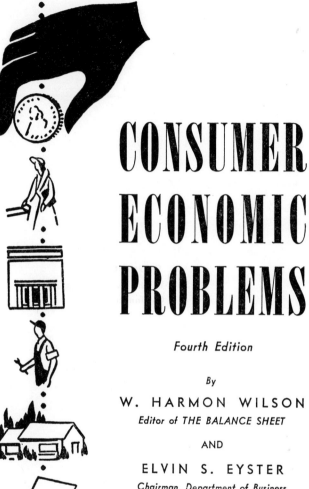

CONSUMER ECONOMIC PROBLEMS

Fourth Edition

By

W. HARMON WILSON

Editor of THE BALANCE SHEET

AND

ELVIN S. EYSTER

*Chairman, Department of Business
Education, Indiana University*

SOUTH-WESTERN PUBLISHING CO.

CINCINNATI 2   CHICAGO 5   SAN FRANCISCO 3   DALLAS 2

NEW ROCHELLE, N. Y.

G15

H554

*Printed in the
United States of America*

PREFACE

The fourth edition of CONSUMER ECONOMIC PROBLEMS reflects the philosophy of consumer-economic education that has emerged as a result of fifteen years of active interest in this phase of education on the part of businessmen, educators, and consumers. While many characteristics of the previous editions have been retained, the fourth edition differs in that new topics have been added, factual data have been brought up to date, and many changes in subject matter and methods of presentation growing out of the suggestions of teachers and students have been made.

Economics is considered to be primarily a study of how the wants of people are satisfied through business activity. It deals not only with the natural laws and principles of business but also with man-made regulations that govern business activity. Consumer education, which in the early stages of its development dealt primarily with specific commodity information, is relatively new but has become increasingly popular since the depression years following 1929. In a popular sense it has been limited primarily to wise selection and buying practices with only incidental attention being given to the basic principles of economics. The more comprehensive consumer-economic education that is evolving is not primarily concerned with the historical development of economic theories and principles nor is it limited to information on products and services. Its purpose is to help people acquire sufficient understanding—a layman's understanding—of those economic principles that affect their opportunities to earn a living and that regulate and govern the management of their personal business affairs. Further, it is a goal of consumer-economic education that people should be able to apply basic economic principles and efficient business practices in the performance of their own consumer-business activities. These purposes of consumer-economic education are complementary to the motives of business institutions; for the wiser a person is as a consumer, the better he is as a customer or client of business. Thus consumer-economic education serves the needs both of consumers and of business.

To summarize the current, popular definitions of consumer-economic education, it is that phase of education which enables the individual——

(1) To understand the minimum economic principles and the common business practices that are essential for the wise management of one's personal business affairs and that are generally helpful in the pursuit of one's occupation or profession;

(2) To get the most value and the most satisfaction out of the time, effort, and money that are expended for food, clothing, shelter, personal services, and all other economic goods and services;

(3) To plan and operate a well-balanced financial program, considering needs and wants on the one hand and income and expenditures on the other;

(4) To work toward a higher level of living for all the people in a democratic society;

(5) To understand fully one's responsibility to be constantly alert to the economic problems confronting consumers, business firms, and government and to participate actively in their solution.

In this textbook the basic principles of economics and the practices of business considered to be of importance to everyone have been introduced in the discussions of specific problems encountered by consumers. The emphasis is placed upon the application of an economic principle to the solution of a consumer problem rather than upon the theory. Many economic principles and concepts thus are discussed more than once in their relationship to several different problems. To illustrate, the effect of the division of labor or occupational specialization is introduced in the treatment of marketing and is discussed in a later chapter in its relationship to sharing income and wealth. The legal aspects of consumer buying and credit, likewise, are discussed several times in their relationships to specific consumer problems.

Though it is not the primary purpose of this book to provide training in business practices and procedures, some of this type of information is presented because of its indispensability to the conduct of personal business affairs. Guides and principles for solving consumer problems are given in summary form for the convenience of the reader. The responsibility to study and understand the economic problems of consumers and to contribute to their solution is stressed.

The economic problems of consumers are divided into ten areas or groups in CONSUMER ECONOMIC PROBLEMS, each of which is one of the major parts of the book. The sequence of these problem areas has been carefully planned, but the order may be changed to fit special conditions. In Part I, the student is introduced to the general nature of the problems that consumers encounter. In the chapters in Part II, an understanding is provided of the interests of consumers in the services of business firms and of government. Part III deals with the services of government and private agencies for the protection of consumers. The general principles of buying are presented in Part IV, and guides to the wise buying of particular kinds of goods that are commonly purchased by all consumers are given in Part V. Bank services, the use of credit, installment buying, and borrowing are presented from the point of view of the consumer in Part VI. In Part VII, the managing of personal finances, with special emphasis on personal and family budgets, records, and savings and investments, is discussed. Part VIII deals with the protection afforded by insurance and social security. Information on considerations involved in obtaining a home is provided in Part IX.

When the student has gained an understanding of the problems of consumers, he is properly conditioned to appreciate the broader economic problems common to the interests of business firms and government and hence of consumers. A comprehensive study of these economic problems is presented in Part X.

It is hoped that through the use of this textbook those who study it may not only become more efficient in handling their personal business affairs but that they also may participate in solving the economic problems of business and government through intelligent voting on economic issues.

The authors take this opportunity to thank the many teachers who have offered suggestions and criticisms.

W. HARMON WILSON
ELVIN S. EYSTER

TABLE OF CONTENTS

PART I. GETTING WHAT YOU WANT

PART II. BUSINESS AND GOVERNMENT SERVICES

PART III. CONSUMER PROTECTION

PART IV. PRINCIPLES OF BUYING

PART V. PROBLEMS IN BUYING

PART VI. HOW BANKS AND CREDIT SERVE YOU

PART VII. MANAGING YOUR PERSONAL FINANCES

PART VIII. BUYING INSURANCE PROTECTION

PART IX. OBTAINING A HOME

PART X. ECONOMIC PROBLEMS OF THE CONSUMER

PART I
GETTING WHAT YOU WANT

Chapter 1
How Can the Consumer Live Better?

Purpose of the Chapter. It is natural for you to want things. As a consumer or user of such things as clothing, food, equipment, and different services, you have varying degrees of success in getting what you want. Many factors help to determine what you get. Some of these factors that are very important to you are discussed in this chapter.

You Are a Consumer. Every individual is a *consumer* because he uses or consumes goods and services. Even the businessman who employs a trained specialist to buy goods and services for his business is an ordinary consumer when he buys food, clothing, medical care, recreation, and other goods and services for himself and his family. Therefore, when we speak of consumers, we have in mind every individual engaged in the daily process of spending money and using goods and services.

Economic Problems of the Consumer. The subject of *economics* deals with the problems of making a living and of satisfying our wants as consumers. To understand how we can best be served by our economic system, we must know something about production, marketing, money, banking, interest, profits, government, social security, and other related topics. With this knowledge we can then learn how to manage our affairs better.

Your Level of Living. If you live in a home with modern heating and plumbing, and good furniture; if you are able to buy all the food you want; if you can buy an ice cream soda without worrying about spending the money; if you own a car and can travel and take vacations regularly; if

1

DETROIT, MICHIGAN: AVERAGE MONEY INCOME, EXPENDITURES, AND SAVINGS, BY NET INCOME CLASS, 1948

ITEM		ALL FAMILIES: ANNUAL MONEY INCOME AFTER PERSONAL TAXES								
	UNDER $1,000	$1,000 TO $2,000	$2,000 TO $3,000	$3,000 TO $4,000	$4,000 TO $5,000	$5,000 TO $6,000	$6,000 TO $7,500	$7,500 TO $10,000	$10,000 AND OVER
Per cent of families in each class	1.4	5.7	17.6	29.4	21.5	9.6	8.8	4.0	2.0
Average family size	2.6	2.9	3.1	3.1	3.4	3.7	4.5	4.9	4.1
Average number of earners	0	1.0	1.2	1.4	1.4	1.8	2.2	3.1	2.4
Expenditures for current consumption	$1,768	$2,119	$2,819	$3,473	$4,276	$5,348	$6,382	$8,147	$13,697
Food	641	723	1,043	1,182	1,421	1,588	1,941	2,196	3,192
Housing, fuel, light, and refrigeration	437	476	539	566	780	681	720	712	2,756
Household operation	62	109	97	134	162	205	206	265	895
Furnishings and equipment	30	34	154	201	250	396	581	564	1,040
Clothing	138	173	330	408	561	713	1,017	1,470	2,210
Automobile	161	266	212	309	430	728	757	1,562	1,351
Other transportation	9	28	61	85	64	83	101	173	102
Medical care	62	145	135	218	208	302	242	329	656
Personal care	25	44	63	73	93	104	127	146	219
Recreation	28	30	81	137	164	349	436	462	735
Tobacco	5	44	52	70	69	86	92	100	110
Reading	18	22	29	39	44	51	51	55	104
Education		1	6	15	7	35	39	57	132
Other	152	24	17	36	23	27	72	56	195
Gifts and contributions	47	74	121	150	237	360	382	463	1,509
Insurance	19	38	86	123	152	207	165	278	610
Net surplus	0	0	0	0	0	0	11	0	8,027
Personal taxes	0	36	114	230	340	461	639	862	4,773

From the *Monthly Labor Review* (December, 1949) of the U. S. Labor Department; Bureau of Labor Statistics.

you have insurance and investments to protect you in your old age; and if you have money laid aside for a rainy day, your level of living is high. In many countries the level of living is low. The people have poor homes or no homes at all; they seldom get enough food or clothing; many of them are cold and sick; and they have nothing laid aside for a rainy day. Even in our own country we have various levels of living; but by comparison with levels in some other countries, ours are very high, even for the poor.

The *level of living* consists of the goods and services that an individual or family regularly obtains. The level of living is often referred to as the standard of living. A *standard of living* is something similar to a goal or a guide. Many of us set standards that we should like to attain. There really is no standard in the true sense of the word; but when we use this term, we usually are thinking in terms of a certain degree of success in satisfying our needs and wants.

How We Spend Our Money. The way you spend your money will not only depend upon economic factors but also upon your ability to manage your income. It will be interesting to take a look at what other people do. The table on page 2, based on government figures, shows how families with different incomes spend their money in one city.

Observe that families with the lower incomes did not receive enough to break even. They actually went into debt or they did not have the food, shelter, clothing, and other things necessary for good health and comfortable living. Perhaps in some cases a little more careful management and the elimination of certain luxuries, including an automobile, tobacco, and certain recreations, would have enabled these families to break even.

All of these families had to make choices. They had to decide how much money should be spent for food, clothing, an automobile, recreation, life insurance, and other goods and services.

Studies such as this one supply us with information that enables us to start a budget plan. Budgeting and financial planning are taken up in later chapters.

This table helps to give a picture of the levels of living
and shows what the average family is able to buy with its
income. To raise these standards families must be able to
buy more at lower prices with the same income or to get
more income without a similar increase in prices.

How Can We Raise Our Level of Living? As individuals,
we often set our own standards and strive to accomplish
them. The degree of success in obtaining our own standard of living is often dependent upon our personal abilities,
the extent to which we use our abilities, the degree to which
we follow a plan, and the breaks that we get in life. We can
raise our level of living in other ways, but these are dependent upon many factors over which the individual concerned
does not always have control.

Let us assume, for example, that each group of 100 people
working at different tasks could supply the group with the
goods and services needed. If they all work slowly and only
a few hours a day, the total produced by the group will be
very little. If they all work fast and efficiently, production
will be high and they will all have more goods and services
to enjoy. If they use no tools, production will be low. If
they use modern tools and equipment with gasoline, electric,
or steam power, their production will be higher; each person will turn out more goods or render more service.

Let us assume that each one of these 100 people performs
one job or service and has complete control over what he
does. If one cuts down his production of a vital product
or service, the supply will not meet the demands of the
group. The other 99 will beg for it, plead for it, and bid for
it. In terms of what they are willing to trade for it or pay
for it in money, the price will be high. Thus one person
who restricts his production may benefit himself by getting
as much or more total income by charging a higher price
for less goods or services, but all the other persons in the
group suffer. By restricting his production, he is not helping to raise the level of living for all people and actually
may contribute to lowering it.

As the result of the scarcity or shortage of the product or
service created by this one individual, the efficiency of the

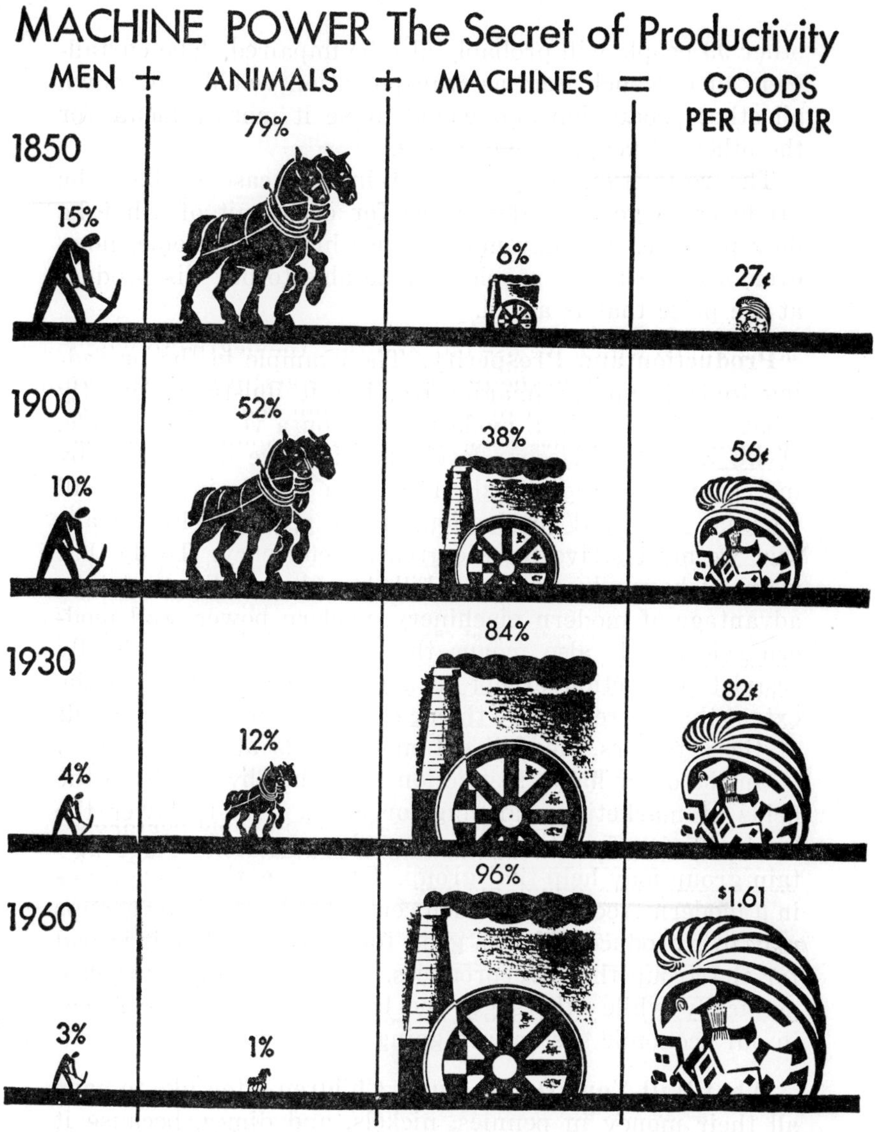

MACHINE POWER The Secret of Productivity

MEN	+	ANIMALS	+	MACHINES	=	GOODS PER HOUR

1850
- 15%
- 79%
- 6%
- 27¢

1900
- 10%
- 52%
- 38%
- 56¢

1930
- 4%
- 12%
- 84%
- 82¢

1960
- 3%
- 1%
- 96%
- $1.61

Back in 1850 men and animals supplied most of the energy for our work. By 1960, with machine power supplying 96 per cent of the energy we use, we can turn out six times as much per man-hour of work. Future progress lies in raising our output per man-hour through increasing use of machine power.

From U. S. A., Measure of a Nation, The Twentieth Century Fund

Machines and power increase our productivity.

other 99 people will probably also be impaired. The curtailment of one such item as transportation would slow down all other production and would make it more difficult for the other 99 people to get along.

The restriction of production in this case enables the producer to get a higher price for each unit of what he does produce. He may not increase his total income, however, because fewer people may be able to buy his product at the price that is asked.

Production and Prosperity. The example in the preceding topic is purely imaginative, but it illustrates exactly what can happen in a modern world on a very large scale. If we want to raise our level of living, we must do it by increasing our individual production which in turn will increase the total production of all people. This means that we must strive for the greatest efficiency. To do that we must have educated and skilled workers. We must take advantage of modern machinery, modern power, and modern science. It also means that we must not artificially restrict production except to avoid overproduction to the extent that there is more than can be consumed. As a result of these factors, we will get more goods at lower prices.

On the other hand, restrictions, whether by people in the fields of marketing, farming, or labor, tend to lower the level of living for everyone although a restriction by a certain group may help that group. Of course, there are times in a modern free system when certain individuals or groups may overproduce. This is good for all others, but it is bad for the group that overproduces. Somebody gets hurt economically while others get the benefit. These experiences in our economic system are going on regularly.

What Will Your Dollar Buy? Children often like to have all their money in pennies, nickels, and dimes, because it seems like a lot of money. An older child often prefers five single bills instead of one $5 bill. A typical question that Joe will ask Frank is, "How much are you earning?"

We are all very conscious of the money we have or the money we are earning. The amount of money that we have

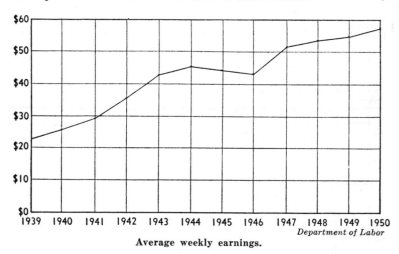

Average weekly earnings.

Department of Labor

or earn, however, is not so important as what it will buy. That is one of the most important of the fundamentals affecting our prosperity.

Let us assume that Jack Cook graduates from high school and starts earning $30 a week. He finds that he can buy his food, clothing, shelter, personal services, and amusement and still have $5 left that he can save.

Ten years later Jack Cook has advanced in his work. He is a more valuable man; and so far as money income is concerned, he is doing well because he is now earning $60 a week. He is still single, but something has happened that affects Jack. A law of economics has been at work.

Although he is earning $60 a week and has a more important job, Jack is not getting along as well. He is just as careful as ever in his spending. He eats as economically as possible and is not extravagant in the buying of clothing or anything else, but now Jack is still able to save only $5 a week because the prices of what he buys have increased. In other words, Jack is worse off than he was ten years ago because, even though he has had more experience, is a more valuable worker, and is getting more cash income, it requires $55 instead of $25 a week to live. His money will buy less. Even the $5 that he saves may buy less when he wants to spend it.

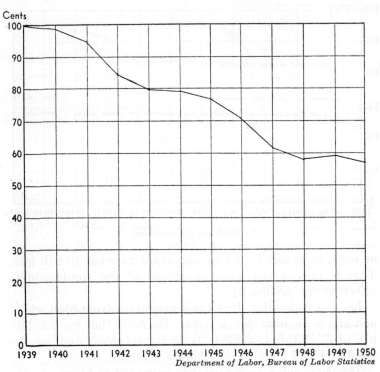

Cents

1939 1940 1941 1942 1943 1944 1945 1946 1947 1948 1949 1950

Department of Labor, Bureau of Labor Statistics

Purchasing power of the dollar (1939 = 100 cents).

Prices do not always go up, causing the purchasing power of the dollar to decrease. There are times when prices of goods and services go down. Under such conditions the purchasing power of the dollar increases, and as a result one can maintain his level of living on less money than when prices were higher.

Some simple examples of what has happened to the value of the dollar are illustrated in the table on page 9.

From the figures in this table you can clearly see that the amount of money that one earns is not so important as what that money will buy. The buying power of a dollar (the buying power of one's income) is sometimes referred to as *real income.*

The first part of this table (A) means that an income of $1,318 in 1948 was no better than an income of $1,205 in

A	The average income of every man, woman, and child in the United States at the end of 1948 was ...... $1,318 On the basis of the purchasing power or value of the dollar in 1947 this amount of income would provide a purchasing power in 1948 of $1,205
B	Assume that the *average* purchasing power of the dollar in 1935 to 1939 was .... 100 % The purchasing power of the dollar in 1948 was.. 60.6% The purchasing power of the dollar in 1933 was.. 112.9%

Purchasing power of earnings.

1947. Although the total average earnings were greater, each dollar bought less. In the second part of the table (B), if we take for comparison the average purchasing power of the dollar in the years 1935 to 1939, a dollar earned in 1948 bought only 60.6 per cent of the amoun that it would have bought in the previous period.

Economic Voting. Throughout your life you will be call upon to vote in terms of economic choices. Everything y buy or fail to buy is an economic choice. You are decidi first whether it is better to keep your money for so future use or to spend it immediately. You are mak choices between two different brands or types of goods between one type of article and another. You have to de for instance, whether a scarf or a pair of gloves wi more useful to you.

In this choice of economic voting you are serving a of the final judges as to whether some business firn succeed or fail. The highly skilled businessman tr determine what customers will buy, but he may wrong. If you, with many others, choose his prod succeeds; but if his product is not chosen by enough he will fail. This example illustrates the fact th sumers have the power to determine the success of ness. If it does not serve the consumer satisfact will fail because there are other competitors who v satisfactorily.

In government you also have economic choices. ernment collects money from you and from ever

to provide services for you or for others. Even though you may not pay taxes directly to Federal, state, or local governments, you are still being taxed through the goods and services you buy. Throughout your lifetime you must help to make decisions as to whether it is better to buy services through government taxes, to buy services from private business enterprise, or to perform these services yourself. The question of what you get as a consumer will depend a lot on the decisions you and everyone else will make in your economic voting. As you study further in this course, you will discover very real ways in which your choices can improve your level of living.

In labor unions and many other types of organizations, such as groups of manufacturers, groups of merchants, and farmers, the freedom to exercise a vote or a choice helps to determine how we all shall live. Each individual and each group has a responsibility not only to himself and to his group but also to the whole nation. If all individuals and all groups act unwisely or too selfishly, we all suffer because of the bad choices and bad decisions that are made.

Let the Buyer Beware. Under the old principles of law, the buyer was expected to protect himself. In other words, it was all right to cheat a person if he did not know it or failed to discover it. "Let the buyer beware," was the general rule.

A closely related term was *laissez faire.* The general meaning of this term is "let a businessman do as he wishes without interference." Much of our early business history of the United States was carried on under this principle, along with letting the buyer beware.

Today, however, we live under a different set of rules. Businessmen can no longer do as they wish if what they do injures a competitor or a consumer. They must be honest in their dealings. Their advertising must tell the truth and must not mislead. Products must be what they are supposed to be, and some products cannot be sold at all if they are harmful or useless.

We have gradually developed a system of government under which business is controlled and consumers are pro-

tected. We still operate under a relatively free enterprise system, but it is a system that is regulated and controlled. We try to prevent honest people from getting hurt in business dealings, and our aim is to prevent unethical or dishonest practices.

We need to know some of the rules of our economic life so that we will know how to play the game and deal with other people. As you study further in this course, you will learn some of these rules.

How You Can Exercise Your Free Choice. In some countries people do not have free choices, because the limited few who run the government make the decisions controlling everyone. People are told what to do. Goods and services that are to be produced are decided by the government. In these countries, if you go to a store to buy food or clothing, you find only what the state has decided you should have, and you take what is available. However, in a free country such as the United States, you have many free choices as to what you buy and where you buy it.

Freedom means allowing one to do as he wishes as long as he does not hurt others; it means that he has a right to choose and a right to vote. In a free enterprise system businesses may do largely as they wish provided they abide by the rules. Since you live in a free enterprise system, you must know how to deal with it. Most businessmen are smart. In order to survive they must make a profit, and to do that they must sell their goods and services to us. If you are going to be able to exercise a *free choice* in this kind of world, you must have the knowledge that it requires to make intelligent selections and to deal intelligently with business. Otherwise, you are at the mercy of misleading advertising, high pressure selling, and propaganda.

Planning Helps You Get What You Want. To get the most out of life it is necessary to set up a plan that will include an education, recreation, health, savings, protection, and buying the things that seem necessary under the plan. To accomplish all of this it is desirable to have a budget that will serve as a guide. Planning your economic life in all its aspects will be developed in detail as you complete this course.

As you study further, you will learn many ways in which you can improve your own level of living, and you will discover ways in which the level of living of everyone can be improved.

TEXTBOOK QUESTIONS

1. Is a businessman a consumer? Why or why not?
2. With what does the subject of economics deal?
3. What is meant by the "level of living"?
4. Do we all have the same standard of living?
5. Why do some people have low levels of living even with good incomes?
6. What are some of the ways in which we can raise our level of living?
7. Since 1850 what has gradually happened to production in terms of men, animals, and machines? See page 5.
8. What would happen to our level of living if everybody slowed down production?
9. What effect would the serious curtailment of any one factor of production, such as transportation, have on all of us?
10. How does individual productivity affect our level of living?
11. Why was Jack Cook, in the illustration in this chapter, less favorably situated when he was earning $60 a week than he was when he was earning $30 a week?
12. Based on the tables or illustrations in this chapter, what happened to the purchasing power of the average income between 1947 and 1948?
13. What do we mean by "economic voting"?
14. What is the difference between the old system of *laissez faire* as contrasted with our present situation in business?
15. Name some ways in which you have a free choice as compared with people in some countries under rigid governmental control.

DISCUSSION QUESTIONS

1. A professional economist probably would choose to give technical definitions of the level of living and the standard of living. Explain in your own words what you feel to be the differences between these terms.
2. Can you pick out any one item in the table on page 2 showing the expenditures of families in Detroit and suggest how a change in these expenditures could raise the general healthful level of living of the family?

3. Discuss the problems of the individual and the nation in raising the general level of living of everyone, and point out some of the handicaps.
4. Explain why an increase in real prosperity cannot be measured in terms of wages.
5. One politician has held out the hope to all wage earners that by 1960 the average wage of a worker would be $5,000. What does this mean? What is the rest of the story?
6. Name some ways in which your family can vote economically.
7. What controls prevent businessmen from doing whatever they may wish to do?
8. Do you feel that we are or are not gradually drifting away from a system whereby we have free choices? Is that good or is it bad?

PROBLEMS

1. In the table below are some imaginary examples to illustrate the relations between wages and the cost of living. The first year (No. 1) is the base year used for comparison and is therefore 100 per cent. The second year (No. 2) is worked out for you as an example.

   In this example the increase of $5 in the average wage, as shown by the figures for Years 1 and 2 in column (2), has been recorded in column (3). The per cent of increase (14.3%), as shown in column (4), was determined by dividing the increase in the average wage, $5, by the average wage in the first year, $35. The per cent of increase in the Cost of Living Index (8%), as shown in column (6), was determined by subtracting the Cost of Living Index for Year 1 in column (5) from that index for Year 2.

   (a) Complete the figures in the table.

(1) YEAR	(2) AVERAGE WAGE	(3) AMOUNT OF INCREASE OR DECREASE IN WAGES	(4) PER CENT IN- CREASE OR DECREASE IN WAGES (COMPARED TO BASE YEAR)	(5) INDEX OF COST OF LIVING	(6) INCREASE OR DECREASE IN INDEX OF COST OF LIVING (COMPARED TO BASE YEAR)
1	$35 (Base)	0	0	100 (Base)	0
2	$40 (Example)	$5	14.3%	108	8
3	$45			120	
4	$50			121	
5	$45			130	
6	$40			120	
7	$35			110	

   (b) Explain what has happened to wages, what has happened to the cost of living, and how well off is the worker in the seventh year as compared with the first year.

2. Part of the story of wages and prices is illustrated in the previous problem, but there is another way to analyze wages and prices as shown in the table below. The first year is used as a base year with which other comparisons can be made. The purchasing power of the dollar in this particular year is considered to be 100 per cent. The second year is used as an example. In this case each dollar is worth 95 cents, which means that it is worth 95 per cent of what it was worth the previous year in terms of what it will buy. Therefore, how much will $38.00 in wages buy? Answer ($38 × .95 = $36.10).

(a) Complete the rest of the table.

YEAR	AVERAGE WAGES	DOLLAR PURCHASING POWER	BUYING POWER OF WAGES
1	$35.00 (Base)	100% (Base)	$35.00
2	$38.00 (Example)	95%	$36.10
3	$40.00	92%	
4	$42.00	90%	
5	$45.00	85%	
6	$55.00	80%	
7	$60.00	60%	
8	$65.00	50%	

(b) Explain what has happened in these eight years to wages and their purchasing power.

COMMUNITY PROBLEMS AND PROJECTS

1. From governmental sources, the library, banks, local newspapers, or any other reliable sources, collect information in regard to prices and wages and make analyses, if possible, similar to those in Problems 1 and 2 in this chapter. Study these figures and prepare your own interpretation.

2. In order to evaluate the level of living, prepare a table so that you can compare what you consider to be the goods and services available to the person who, in your opinion, in this country enjoys an *average* level of living. Then pick some other country for which you can obtain similar information and make the same analysis for the average level of living in that country.

3. As explained in this chapter, we once operated pretty largely under a system of "let the buyer beware." Make a list of ways, from your own observation and experience, in which this situation is now changed to the extent that the buyer has some means of protection.

Chapter 2

Major Factors Affecting
What You Get

Purpose of the Chapter. If a small group of people lived together on an island and produced everything they consumed but did not have any tools or equipment, life would be rather simple; but these people would not have much in terms of the goods, services, and modern conveniences that people in the United States are accustomed to enjoying. In the world in which we live, however, the pattern of life has become rather complicated. Most of us are working at special jobs. We have power and modern machinery to help us. We depend upon other people for what we eat, wear, and use. In this modern world even the poorest people have more things than the people on a primitive island could have.

In earlier times families made their own clothes and produced their own food. They were very nearly independent. Today we know very little about most of the things we eat, wear, and use. In order to buy them and use them intelligently we must study them.

In this modern world of specialization, power, modern machinery, and mass production there are many problems over which we as individuals have very little influence, but which we must understand. This chapter will help you as a consumer to understand some of the major influences affecting what you get.

Let Us Look Back for a Moment. If we could take a glimpse at the average family in 1700, we would see a family larger than the average family today working together as a producing unit and as a consuming unit. Most of the people lived on farms or in small communities. They raised the food they ate and produced many of the things they used.

15

Yesterday	*Today*
1. Built his own home.	1. Earns money and buys what is needed.
2. Made his own clothes.	
3. Raised and preserved his own food.	2. Buys amusements.
	3. Is a specialist to a degree.
4. Made home remedies.	4. Lacks first-hand consumer knowledge.
5. Created his own amusements.	
6. Developed wide consumer knowledge.	5. Has to gain consumer knowledge by study and observation.

Very little trading was carried on with other people because other people also largely produced everything they needed. In those days the main problem was getting enough to eat and storing food for the winter. Every individual spent a major part of his time in those processes. Those same people made their own tools, built their own houses, made their own clothing; they even made their own soap, cut their own hair, and were pretty independent.

Production in those days required a tremendous amount of time and energy because people produced by hand, were without tools or had only crude tools, and had no modern power. Before the day of modern machinery the total amount of time required to make one shirt, including spinning, weaving, and sewing, was about two weeks of labor

on the part of one member of the family. Since the people
in those days were both producers and consumers, however,
they all gained expert knowledge about the things they
used.

History Has Changed Our Problems. You and I live in
a new kind of world as compared with the one in which
our great-grandparents lived. It is a rich world compared
with the world of fifty or one hundred years ago. It is rich
in opportunities and rich in the things that enable us to
live well.

This new world has been brought about partly by the so-
called Industrial Revolution and partly by our own individual prudence and abilities. The *Industrial Revolution* was
the change from home production by hand labor to machine
production in factories on an economical and larger scale.
As a result, today very little production is done in the home.
Farms have become mechanized, and factories are equipped
with the most efficient machinery.

Except during times when war has created scarcities,
we live in a world in which the problem of producing enough
has been virtually conquered. We can have a high level of
living, therefore, if we conquer the problem of distribution
and if we do not place artificial restrictions on what we
produce. Our problems today are largely consumer
problems.

This new type of world requires more intelligent individuals. We must focus our attention on the problems of
getting and using the goods and services that will give us
the most satisfaction and the highest degree of prosperity.
Highly skilled technicians are taking care of production and
scientific development for us, but it is only as we become
highly skilled in handling our own affairs that we can
obtain the best use of the goods and services available.

Specialization Helps Us Get What We Want. All of us
together make up what is called our society. As a large
group of individuals, we have problems, because we sometimes cannot sell to ourselves as much as we can produce.
The result sometimes is a national or even a world-wide

depression—yes, and even a war, because wars are some-times caused by economic problems.

Some of the problems of our society and some of the problems of individuals are brought about by the same con-ditions that have given us the great advantages of plenti-ful production. Specialization has led to mass production, which in turn has led to low cost of production. *Specializa-tion,* in simple terms, means that each individual performs a particular task or job while others are doing something else. Each receives his compensation in money and spends it for the goods and services that he wants. Specialization represents a progressive step, but it has led us to a depend-ence upon a money income. Even farmers, who years ago were largely independent so far as food products were con-cerned, have become dependent upon a money income. They sell their products for money and then purchase at least some of their food for their own consumption. It is com-mon for farmers to sell their wheat and buy flour and to sell milk and buy butter.

In the cities individuals are almost totally dependent upon a money income. For example, a stenographer is a specialist. Let us assume that she has to raise her own food, grow her own fibers for cloth, prepare the fiber, spin the yarn, weave the cloth, and make her own clothes. Let us suppose that she also has to do all her own cooking, baking, and laundering. Let us go a step further and assume that she has to obtain her own fuel and provide a place in which to live. Obviously she would be spending all her time doing these tasks and would not have time to serve as a stenographer. However, by specializing and serving as a stenographer and earning wages, she may then spend those wages for the goods and services that she needs. By specializing, each of us becomes efficient, and through this specialization we can serve each other more effectively.

Specialization Causes Conflicts. One hundred years ago most family units were producers and consumers. As we have become more highly specialized, we have developed group interests. Sometimes various groups appear to be opposed to each other, but actually we all have common

E. I. du Pont de Nemours & Company

Every person in this group represents a different kind of specialized
worker in the Chemistry Department of a modern business.

interests because no society can be totally prosperous unless all elements of the society are prosperous.

Some of the major group interests are those of farmers,
factory laborers, merchants, manufacturers, bankers, and
professional men. Among these various groups there are
numerous types of organizations. For instance, the farmers are organized into federations, bureaus, granges, and
unions to protect themselves, to gain laws and regulations
to their own advantage, to control prices, and, in general,
to improve the position of the farmer in relation to other
groups. Labor groups, manufacturers, bankers, merchants,
professional men, and other groups are all seeking advantages for themselves. Some activities of all these groups

are totally selfish, but others are generally beneficial to society.

Usually labor unions want higher wages, shorter working hours, and better working conditions. They sometimes restrict labor and production. Merchants want to eliminate as much competition as possible. Generally speaking, they do not like sales taxes. Manufacturers want tariffs on competing foreign goods to protect themselves, but they do not want tariffs on things that they import. Some of them want to pay low wages and are often opposed to legislation favorable to labor. Likewise, bankers and professional groups have their special interests. These conflicts of group interests lead often to regulations, laws, and practices that are detrimental to consumers. The consumer is often the common victim of the battle among these groups for a selfish advantage. Since everyone is a consumer, it is important that he know how to protect his special interests as a consumer.

Machines, Power, and Mass Production. As we have learned to specialize, we have found it profitable to use machinery to help us. The average home of one hundred years ago certainly could not have had a complicated weaving machine as we know it today or an elaborate machine on which to make shoes. In our specialization, however, we have found these machines useful in developing mass production and in reducing cost. Machinery and power to operate the machinery have multiplied our productive capacities so that all of us have available more materials to use and to enjoy. Increased productivity is one main goal of economic society.

Science has also helped us in an industrial way. Certain persons have specialized in the study of science. They have improved our products and processes. They have developed new machinery. They have discovered new uses for old raw materials. They have really put nature to work for us. This was seldom possible in the home, but in our modern division of labor the scientist has made a great contribution that has helped all of us.

Spinning in a modern factory contrasted with spinning by hand in colonial times.

Specialization in factories has meant a division of labor that has led to mass production. There was a time, for instance, when an automobile was made in a small machine shop by only one or two men. Now under mass-production methods and straight-line assembly procedure, more than a hundred men may help in the final assembly of each automobile, each man performing only one or a few related tasks. One man may do nothing but insert and tighten certain bolts; another may put the two wheels on one side of a car; another may connect only certain of the electrical wires; and so on down the production line.

These truck tires on a conveyor line tell the story of machines, power, and mass production.

Modern automatic machinery is used to speed up the production process and to save physical labor. The specialization, the use of power, and the use of modern machinery have all led to mass production, which in turn has resulted in efficiency and low cost of production.

Each new machine serves to produce a higher degree of specialization. For instance, in the early days of the manufacture of cloth, each worker in the mill knew all the processes and could operate all the machines. Now nearly every employee in such a mill knows how to operate one machine and only that machine, but in his work he becomes efficient. As we all become more efficient, we profit from the efforts of each other.

What Mass Production Means to You. What have been our benefits from specialization and mass production? Mass production has created greater human comfort, less fatigue, more leisure, and an average longer life. The farmer may work hard, but with his modern tractor and the electrifica-

		1914	1950
VACUUM CLEANER		88.1 hours	45.2 hours
MEN'S WORK SHOES		12.8 hours	5.8 hours
ANTHRACITE (one ton)		31.3 hours	14.3 hours
DINING ROOM SUITE		239.1 hours	113.8 hours

Courtesy, Friends Magazine

This chart shows the hours of labor the average factory worker had to give in 1914 to earn some typical products, compared to hours required in 1950.

The purchasing power of labor.

tion of his equipment, he can produce many times what the same man could have produced a hundred years ago.

The same thing is true in factories where specialization has developed mass production. Even thirty years ago the owning of an automobile was an extreme luxury to be enjoyed only by the wealthier people. That was because the automobile was produced largely by a mechanic or a group of mechanics who made the castings, machined the parts, and fitted them together in a relatively slow and inefficient process. As further specialization took place, mass production became possible. Mass production of automobiles, however, required tremendous plants and tremendous quantities of machinery, with an entirely new conception of a plan of specialization. It was through this process that you and I today are able to buy an automobile that we could not have afforded to buy thirty-five years ago. Today an automobile costs a much smaller percentage of our earnings.

Mass production has also brought many improvements in the materials that we use. Some items could not be made

GETTING WHAT YOU WANT

24   GETTING WHAT YOU WANT   [Part 1]

in small quantities at a price that you and I could afford to
pay. It is only through mass production that we can get
many things that we need. Take, for instance, aluminum
ware. Do you think that you could develop a small plant in
your home to make aluminum ware? Assuming that it
might be possible for you to produce raw aluminum, would
it be worth while for you to spend your time making an
aluminum platter or any other article needed in the home?
If you counted the cost of your time, the article would probably be expensive and undoubtedly would be inferior to
the product you could buy.

Mass production has lowered the price that consumers
must pay for nearly everything that we use. This does not
mean that you and I can pay for everything that we want,
but on an average we all have more than our grandparents
and our great-grandparents had. From an economic point
of view, we have more goods and services to enjoy. Money
prices have gone up, but a day's work will pay for more
than ever before, and that is the real measure of prices.

It is evident that specialization and mass production have
tremendously increased the total quantity of goods and services and have also improved the quality while cutting the
cost. If we all work together as specialists, we can have
much more than we could if we did not have this high degree of specialization. One of the major results of mass
production is a general high level of living for everyone.

Problems of Choice. Why should there be a consumer
problem when we admit that we have more goods and services available at lower cost than people in most other
countries? Where have the difficulties crept in? Undoubtedly you can begin to see what has happened to the consumer in the changing process. The average consumer does
not know much about automobiles because he does not
produce them. Most girls do not know much about cloth
because they have not made any cloth. Often the housewife
cannot distinguish one cut of beef from another because she
has never seen a side of beef cut into its various parts. All
along the lines of our activities we have lost touch with
the direct sources of information that were common to our

grandparents. In the process of specialization each of us has learned to know his own task well. We have become efficient producers, but we have become poor consumers. We know less and less about what the other fellow produces.

Our lack of firsthand knowledge is not the only problem facing the consumer. Goods have changed also. In fact, they sometimes change so rapidly that experts and specialists have difficulty keeping themselves familiar with all new products and the changes in old products. Consequently, the process of determining quality has become a difficult one. While your grandmother could distinguish the grades of plain woolens, cotton goods, or silks, today you have to contend with numerous grades and weaves of woolens, new combination fabrics, entirely new cotton goods that grandmother never knew, and new synthetic yarns that are woven into many types of new fabrics.

In the food lines there have also been many changes. Your grandmother bought sugar and crackers out of a barrel, and beans out of a hundred-pound sack. She judged her coffee by its taste and aroma. Today goods are put up in attractive cans and beautiful packages of all sizes and shapes. There are many brands, many grades, and many advertising claims. Not only many types of standard products are on the market, but also many processed foods add to our confusion and make it more difficult for us to make a wise selection. We recognize the fact that products today are cleaner, more durable, and in many ways more satisfactory than the older products, but the difficulty is that we often do not know whether *Grade A* is better than *Grade AA* or whether *Fancy* is better than *Supreme*. We do not know whether cloth with a bright finish is better than one with a dull finish. We do not know whether one kind of synthetic yarn is better than another. We certainly have to develop a new means of judging the merchandise, since we have had no experience in producing all these items.

This matter of choice is a part of the whole problem of economic voting. You as an individual, along with millions of other people, have a tremendous power in your possession in controlling what you get and how you get it. In order to

exercise your power of economic voting, you must have the
knowledge that will enable you to make wise choices.

Organized Marketing Helps Us. Specialization has
brought with it a marketing system that makes it possible
for each of us to do our specialized tasks while somebody
else sells the things we make. Perhaps you may think the
marketing system costs too much, and it is wasteful in some
instances; but the functions performed are essential. Since
the field of marketing is competitive, only the most efficient
firms can survive in the long run.

Our marketing system makes it possible for you to buy
almost anything you want if you have the money to pay
for it. This magic has been brought about by a complicated
system that will be discussed in detail in Chapter 3.

Of course we can all perform some of the functions of
marketing if we have the time to do so. We can go directly
to the farm and buy eggs if we have the time and the means
of transportation. For the average family, however, it is
more expensive to get the eggs in that way than it is to buy
them at a store.

Sometimes the farmer and other producers give up some
of the specialization in the hope of making more profit. For
example, the farmer may decide to try to peddle vegetables,
eggs, and poultry from door to door in the city. As a result,
he will get a higher price than if he sold them to a wholesaler. On the other hand, selling his goods may take so
much time that he has little opportunity to work on his
farm. He may find, therefore, that he can make more
money if he spends all of his time at production and lets
somebody else do the selling.

Interdependence Creates Problems. In this period of
specialization a great chain of interdependence has developed—interdependence between individuals, between communities, between states, and between nations. One man
repairs shoes for a barber. The barber cuts the hair of the
shoemaker. The people in a city in the East specialize in
making hats, and people in the West raise fruit to sell in
the East. The coal miners in Pennsylvania, West Virginia,

If a farmer takes time to peddle his own products to consumers, will he have time to produce; or is it more profitable for him to let someone else perform the functions of marketing?

and Kentucky dig coal for people in Missouri. Some of the people in Missouri spend their time in raising food products for sale to the people who produce the coal. The chain of interdependence is endless and hard to trace, for each person who receives money for his work or his goods uses this money to buy what is produced by many others.

In this latest stage of civilization it has become highly necessary for every individual to be a good manager of money income. The management of money income relates to the handling of expenditures for necessities, savings, and protection. In the stage of independent subsistence a person was assured of a living provided he could produce enough to fill his wants. If he produced enough grain and meat, made enough cloth and shoes, and had comfortable living quarters, he was satisfied and was protected. Families grouped themselves together and took care of the older members.

We cannot have a prosperous society unless all of us who are dependent upon each other receive the goods and the services that we need. For instance, the farmer can be prosperous only if people in the city pay satisfactory prices in sufficient quantity for the goods produced on the farm. Manufacturers can prosper only if the farmers and the city dwellers buy their machinery and other goods. Manufacturers can therefore be prosperous only if the farmers and the city dwellers earn enough to buy the products that are manufactured. The interests of consumers should be essentially the same as the interests of farmers, laborers, and manufacturers if we consider the whole program from the point of view of interdependence. Our interests are common.

In the last fifty years many people have discovered the pitfalls of specialization when they have moved from the country to the city. Some people who found it possible to make a living under simple conditions in the country have become destitute after moving to the city where they have to depend entirely upon a money income. Before moving to the city, they could take care of themselves during unproductive seasons by using some of the food they had raised. In the city, when wages are no longer received, there is no way of existing unless money savings have been accumulated; charity comes to their assistance; or aid is obtained from unemployment compensation, old-age insurance, or other sources.

In a society in which a money income is of major importance, it is necessary to look ahead and to plan the use of the income. For this reason many persons become interested in life insurance and other forms of income that will be available when they can no longer continue in their occupations. Pension plans and savings for old age are relatively much more significant in the kind of economic life in which we live than they were in previous times.

What Have We Learned? Up to this point you have learned some very fundamental but relatively simple principles of economics. You have learned that efficient production by everyone at a high level and at a low cost raises our level of living. You have learned that money wages are not so important as what they will buy and that you, along with millions of other people, have within your hands the power of economic voting to help determine how well you can live.

Our society has become quite complicated, and we are dependent upon each other. We have all become specialists; and by specialization, mass production, the use of machines, the use of power, and modern distribution, we are able to enjoy a higher level of living than has been possible under any other economic system.

If you have studied this chapter and the preceding chapter carefully, you have also observed that because of our interdependence and our specialization the matter of economic voting, or choice making, becomes increasingly important because what each of us does affects somebody else and may affect the total welfare of all of us. Increased prosperity must come from efficient production on the part of all specialists, and efficient production is helped by machines and power.

TEXTBOOK QUESTIONS

1. Explain briefly the difference between the consumer of yesterday and the consumer of today.
2. Explain briefly in your own words what you consider the Industrial Revolution to be.
3. Explain in your own words what is meant by specialization.
4. Explain how a farmer is a specialist.
5. How do specialized groups sometimes come into conflict in their economic interests and goals?
6. How do machines and power help us to get what we want?
7. What is meant by mass production and how has it contributed to helping us get what we want?
8. Why does the consumer have such a problem of making choices in buying goods and services?
9. What benefits or lack of benefits may there be to the farmer if he does his own producing and marketing directly to the consumer?
10. Explain some ways in which there is geographic interdependence.
11. Explain briefly how the farmer and the city worker are dependent upon each other.

DISCUSSION QUESTIONS

1. Explain some of the advantages of specialization.
2. It is still possible for an individual to make cloth and to prepare some of his food. For instance, one could buy a bushel of oats and make rolled oats for breakfast cereal. Rolled oats that you buy in a package in a store cost about ten times as much as the raw oats from which it is made. Would you recommend that every family prepare its own rolled oats? Why?

3. Explain the changes in our society that have come about from the practice of saving money instead of saving goods to take care of us during times when we cannot produce.

PROBLEMS

1. List and describe the changes that have taken place in some particular goods in your lifetime.
2. This chapter includes a brief discussion of the conflicts that arise among certain groups of specialists, such as farmers, city workers, manufacturers. Write a theme according to the instructions of your teacher, developing further all the group conflicts that you can think about. Show how some of these conflicts can be detrimental to all of us but how compromises of their aims could help all of us.
3. Write a theme showing in detail how the farmer, the laborer, the manufacturer, and the consumer are interdependent and therefore have common problems and common interests.

COMMUNITY PROBLEMS AND PROJECTS

1. Over a period of a week develop a list of all the different kinds of specialists that you can think of within your community.
2. Give several examples of mass production factories that require so great an investment that ordinarily no single individual could organize one.
3. Make a list of specific examples of modern machinery that have made it possible to increase production and lower costs.

PART II
BUSINESS AND GOVERNMENT SERVICES

Chapter 3
How Modern Marketing Affects You

Purpose of the Chapter. How would you, as a consumer, like to go to a farmer to get the wheat you need for your bread, invest your money in enough wheat to last you for a year, store the wheat in your basement, take the wheat to a mill as you need it made into flour, and then use the flour to make bread? If you contemplate these problems, you will realize the valuable functions performed by the marketing system. The marketing system is just one further evidence of the advantages of specialization.

Entirely too few people know anything more about the marketing system than they have learned through their experience in buying goods in retail stores. Since marketing affects every consumer directly, he should know what functions it performs and how it operates so that he may get the most benefits from the marketing system. As has been pointed out, modern mass production has reduced costs; but unless we have an efficient distribution system, these savings in production cannot be passed on to the consumer. A good marketing system is one that enables us to get things that we want or need, surely and conveniently, when we want them, and at the lowest possible price. The purpose of this chapter is to describe the economic functions of marketing, the methods and channels of distribution, the weaknesses of the distribution system, and the economic problems of marketing.

Functions of Marketing. The marketing process is sometimes called *distribution* or *the distributive system*. This system includes all of the functions that have to do directly

with satisfying the wants and needs of individuals; but it
does not include the productive or manufacturing process.
Some of the functions of the system involve the actual
physical handling of goods and others involve services.
These functions are as follows:

\ı   *Functions of Marketing*

1. Assembling
2. Storing
3. Grading and standardizing
4. Advertising and selling (stimulating demand)
5. Merchandising
6. Transporting and communicating
7. Financing
8. Risk bearing

The exact channels of distribution for various products
are not the same, but the functions are always the same.
Certain middlemen may be eliminated by combining some
functions, but it is not possible to eliminate any of these
basic functions.

Assembling. The assembling of goods is one of the first
steps in marketing. _Assembling_ means accumulating or
gathering goods from various sources. Many individuals
and businesses are engaged in assembling goods. For example, manufacturers assemble raw materials for manufacture. Wholesalers assemble many types of manufactured
goods from many different manufacturers located in many
different places and make these available for the retailer.
The retailer assembles a considerable variety of goods from
different wholesalers and makes these goods available for
the consumer. Creamery stations, grain elevators, and
stockyards are also important agencies in the assembling of
products for consumers.

Storing. Storing is a function that is performed during
many stages of the process of delivering goods from pro-

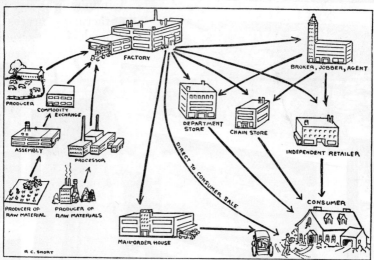

Several routes are followed by the raw materials that go from producers to a factory and by the finished goods that go from a factory to consumers. Transportation, communication, financing, advertising, risk bearing, and the other functions of marketing contribute to all these activities.

ducers to consumers. The businesses that assemble goods in large quantities hold them for the demand of those to whom they sell. We ordinarily think of cold-storage plants, commercial warehouses, and grain elevators as places of storage.

In all stages in the distribution process, goods must be stored, either temporarily or for a long period of time. The manufacturer, the wholesaler, and the retailer, however, must have on hand a supply of goods to serve those to whom they sell.

Many people fail to realize the extremely important function of storage. Without storage many products could not be enjoyed. This fact is especially true of such products as meat, eggs, and fresh vegetables. Fresh meat is available in practically every community at all times of the year. Eggs are stored during seasons of high production for use in seasons of low production. Fresh vegetables are available during the twelve months of the year in most cities and towns. These foods are available as the result of cold storage. The introduction of quick-freezing methods of

Quick freezing brings fresh foods to the consumer.

storage brings to our tables fresh fruits and vegetables in all seasons, preserved with their original flavors.

Grading and Standardizing. Grading is rapidly becoming one of the most important functions of distribution. Tobacco, wheat, corn, and other agricultural products are carefully graded as they are assembled and marketed. They are sold in large lots on the basis of grade. Meat especially is marketed on the basis of inspection and grading. Grading determines the differences in value.

The Federal Government and many associations organized to promote standards are performing an important function for the consumer. Many products can now be bought to meet standard specifications and are marked as to grade. Canned food products—as will be discussed in more detail later—are now being graded for the protection of the buyer. Grading and standardizing save time and money in buying.

Advertising and Selling. The preceding functions deal with the accumulation and the preparation of goods for dispersion through the various channels of trade. Those who have collected goods, graded them, and stored them cannot always rest assured that people who want these goods will seek them. Advertising and salesmanship are therefore used in stimulating a demand for the goods.

The functions of advertising and selling are closely correlated. They have either one or the other of the following objectives:

(a) Stimulating a demand for a particular product.
(b) Stimulating a demand for one class of product as opposed to another class.

Advertising performs the function of telling prospective buyers about a product in the hope that they will want to buy it. Advertising is carried on through newspapers, magazines, radio programs, billboards, and a variety of other means.

Salesmanship is a personal means of obtaining orders for a product, either with or without the assistance of advertising. In our form of economic system selling and advertising are necessary. They have helped to create a large demand, have stimulated mass production, and have helped in many cases to decrease cost. The best forms of advertising from the consumer's point of view are those that are informative. They help the consumer to get what he wants and what he needs.

There are two general methods of stimulating demand. The first method is to pass on to each member in the distributive system the responsibility of selling the product at a particular stage in distribution. Under this method the manufacturer may sell to the wholesaler, the wholesaler sells to the retailer, and the retailer sells to the consumer. The retailer has the final responsibility of selling the product to the consumer.

The second method is to create consumer demand. Under this plan the manufacturer buys advertising space in newspapers and magazines, uses time on the radio, and employs various other means of mass advertising to tell consumers about his goods, thus causing them to want his goods in preference to others. Under this method the function of selling is partially reversed. The consumer demands the product from the retailer; the retailer buys it from the wholesaler; and the wholesaler buys it from the manufacturer.

In actual practice the two methods are almost always intermingled; the manufacturer advertises to the public, but he also has salesmen to call on wholesale dealers. The wholesaler or manufacturer, in turn, may advertise to the public; but he will also send salesmen to call on retailers. In recent years, however, manufacturers have tended to go directly to the consumer with a mass advertising message to create direct consumer demand. Creating consumer demand gives the manufacturer better control over his distributive system, provided he is successful in his advertising efforts. Great sums of money are expended annually for advertising.

Merchandising. After demand has been created, it must be satisfied. Merchandising is the actual process of filling demands for products. It is particularly important in retail stores, and in such cases includes the following:

1. Systematic credit policy.
2. Delivery service.
3. Window displays.
4. Arrangement of counters and other store facilities.
5. Display of goods.
6. Procedure and personnel for showing and demonstrating goods to prospective customers.
7. Installation and repair service.

Not every retailer performs all these functions, but he must perform some of them. For instance, a retailer may have no delivery service, and he may not require installation and repair service; but he probably does have to perform the other functions.

A very important function in the merchandising of household equipment is installation and repair service. For instance, if a person buys an electric refrigerator, he wants to be assured that it will be installed properly, will operate properly, and can be repaired if the need presents itself.

Transporting and Communicating. Transporting and communicating represent indispensable services in the distributive system. Such means of transportation and communication as railroads, boats, airplanes, trucks, telephones, and telegraph and postal service help each person obtain the goods that he needs.

The outline map on this page indicates the main sources of the fresh fruits and vegetables consumed in the metropolitan area of New York during the winter and spring months. The transportation costs take an average of 18 cents from each dollar that the consumer spends for these foods.

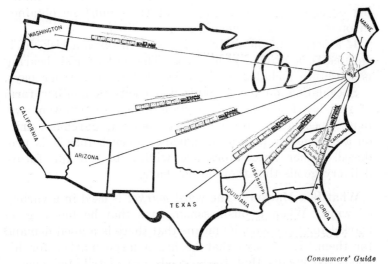

Consumers' Guide

New York City's sources of fresh fruits and vegetables during the winter and the spring months.

Financing. Whenever goods are assembled, stored, or graded, or any of the other functions of distribution is performed, money or credit is needed. Suppose, for example, that a farmer stores his wheat in a grain elevator until he can sell it. He will have to pay for the storage and will probably need to borrow some money until he can sell his wheat. On the other hand, if the operator of the grain elevator buys the wheat to hold for future sale, he must have the cash with which to pay the farmer, or he must borrow the money.

When a product such as wheat is stored, a receipt is given to the person who has stored the product. This receipt can be left with a banker or an individual as security for a loan. If the loan is not paid, the product that is stored becomes the property of the person who has lent the money.

Risk Bearing. Taking a risk means bearing the chance of a loss. Constant risks occur all along the line of distribution. These risks include theft, fire, breakage, spoilage, shrinkage, and a drop or a rise in prices. Insurance can be obtained to provide protection against most risks. Limiting or eliminating other types of risks must be obtained through good management.

If a person in the distributing system takes a risk, he is entitled to a profit for his risk. The cost of risk bearing is therefore included in the price that the consumer pays.

Speculation on our organized markets is another form of risk bearing that is important in our distribution system. Speculators are willing to offer a purchase price on a commodity months in advance, even before it is produced. Other speculators are willing to sell for future delivery goods that they do not have.

What Is a Market? The word *market* is used in a variety of ways. When a businessman says that he has a good market for his goods, he means that there is a good demand for them. If he says that he has a large market for his goods, he means that these goods are distributed over a wide geographical area.

The word *market* is also used to refer to a place used for buying and selling. In many cities there are public market squares where produce merchants and farmers gather to sell to people who are seeking their products. Exchanges are markets. The New York Stock Exchange, for instance, is a security market. The Chicago Board of Trade is a grain market.

The word *market* is used in still another way. For instance, if a person says, "How is the stock market today?"

he has reference to the trend of prices and conditions in the entire United States, although most transactions are centralized in New York City.

Wholesale Markets. A *wholesale market* is distinguished by its practice of trading only in large lots. A large lot may be one hundred cases, a carload, or an entire shipload of goods. Wholesale markets are classified as (a) general wholesale markets, (b) commission markets, and (c) auction markets. Dealers and brokers operate in all types of markets. A *dealer* buys with the hope of selling goods at a profit. The *broker* acts as an agent in buying for someone else. He does not take the title to the goods, but assists in the transaction between the buyer, whom he represents, and a seller.

Dealers are ordinarily the principal operators in general wholesale markets. A dealer takes the title to goods and sells the goods in smaller lots to other wholesalers, to retailers, or directly to consumers. For example, dealers may buy hogs and cattle that have been brought to a central marketing place and sell them to packing houses, who are the wholesalers. These wholesalers sell the meat to retail stores and the retail stores sell the meat to consumers.

Commission markets are ordinarily operated by merchants who take possession of goods but do not take the title. In some commission markets, however, the merchants, for all practical purposes, take possession of the goods and also take the title. The commission markets in such cities as New York, Cincinnati, and Chicago are highly organized. Fresh vegetables and poultry are common commodities sold in such markets. The *commission merchant* acts merely as an agent in handling products. He usually sells the products entrusted to him at the highest price he can obtain, although he is sometimes subject to special instructions from his client with regard to the price to be obtained. For his service he obtains a commission.

Suppose, for example, a farmer brings to a commission merchant in Cincinnati fifty sacks of potatoes. In the absence of specific instructions with regard to the price at which the potatoes must be sold, the commission merchant

will sell them at the highest price that he can obtain on the
basis of bids offered by buyers. For his services he will
charge either a percentage of the sale or a fixed amount.

An *auction market* is one in which buyers congregate and
bid for products that are offered for sale. Fruits, tobacco,
and furs are frequently sold in this manner. Important
tobacco auction markets are located in Lexington and Louis-
ville, Kentucky. Important fur markets are located in St.
Louis and New York.

The wholesale markets of the United States are concentrated in sections where they can serve most effectively the
concentrated areas of population.

Retail Markets. A retail market is the final outlet in the
distributing system—the final link in the chain between the
producer and the consumer. There are more retailers than
there are business proprietors of any other type. Grocery
stores, department stores, filling stations, meat markets,
shoe stores, and clothing stores are representative types of
retail markets. These are places to which consumers may
go in order to obtain the goods they want.

Organized Markets. An organized market is a place
where buyers and sellers can congregate for the purpose of
trading in securities or products. Such a market is commonly referred to as an *exchange.*

Organized commodity markets are located in many parts
of the country. Some of the smaller exchanges maintain
close contact with the larger exchanges. Canned food,
cottonseed, grains, feed, eggs, hides, lard, lead, potatoes,
rubber, silk, minerals, sugar, tobacco, wool, and many other
products are sold on organized exchanges in various parts
of the country. Products are sold on the basis of grades and
frequently by samples.

Organized markets or exchanges provide a nationwide
means of buying and selling. They benefit the seller by
providing an assured market of a wide scope so that he does
not have to depend upon selling his products locally. They
benefit the buyer by providing a relatively sure and constant
supply of goods. They also tend to establish and to stabilize

Trading on an organized market.

prices. For instance, one can determine very quickly the price of a commodity by looking at the latest market quotations. These quotations are published in the newspapers and are often broadcast over the radio.

Organized markets also provide a means of speculation that is used by businessmen to hedge their operations. *Hedging* is a system whereby businessmen can buy raw materials sold on an organized market and yet avoid the usual risks of fluctuating prices.

Scope of Markets. In general, markets are considered to be (a) *local,* (b) *national,* or (c) *international.* International markets are frequently referred to as *world markets.*

The large geographical area of the United States has enabled many businesses to develop large national markets. There is an interesting contrast between a manufacturer's potential market in the United States and a manufacturer's potential market in one of the small European countries. The manufacturer in a small European country must face a barrier of tariff between his country and other countries. A large national market encourages production in large quantities. As this type of production is usually economi-

41

cal, the consumer benefits. For instance, if an automobile manufacturer were limited to a market the size of Michigan, the company could not produce automobiles in large numbers. Both the cost of production and the price to the consumer would therefore be high. Many automobile manufacturers have national markets, and some have international markets. A few of the latter make their products in foreign countries in order to avoid the tariff barrier.

Not all products or services can reach out into the national market. The nature of the product or the service and various other influences tend to restrict the market. Laundries, for instance, are usually confined to local communities. Without establishing branches, a laundry seldom finds it profitable to solicit business at greater distances than twenty or thirty miles. A single retail meat market is necessarily confined to its own neighborhood. It sometimes enlarges its territory by delivery service.

The marketing of vegetables at one time was confined to areas close to the points of production. The marketing areas for these products have, however, been extended to almost every point of the United States through the use of transportation and storage facilities. Nevertheless, the market for seasonal fresh vegetables is usually confined to relatively small areas around producing regions. For instance, during the producing season, it would be foolish for a person who raises beans in Missouri to attempt to sell fresh beans in New York City if beans are produced economically within a few miles of New York City. Certain regions, such as the South and the West Coast, have national markets for fresh fruits and vegetables during the seasons when other regions cannot produce these foods.

Place of the Middleman. A *middleman* is one who performs a marketing service between the producer and the consumer. Criticism of the middleman may be attributed largely to a lack of understanding of the functions he performs. Many buyers fail to realize that after goods are produced many additional services are required before consumers can enjoy these goods. These services are performed by the middlemen. Some of the most common types of middlemen are wholesalers, jobbers, commission merchants, and retailers. The term *jobber* arose out of the custom of certain dealers to buy from producers in quantities called "job lots." Jobbers and wholesalers are now almost indistinguishable because they serve essentially the same purpose. If middlemen perform useful services at reasonable cost, their existence is justified.

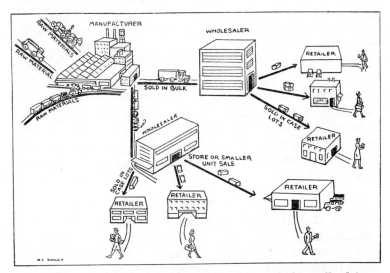

The distribution system involves sales in progressively smaller lots.

Whenever the services of a legitimate middleman are discontinued, his function must be taken over by someone else. The services may be consolidated, but nevertheless they are still performed. A wholesale grocery company, for example, collects a wide variety of food products and other grocery items from all parts of the United States and even from various foreign countries. These goods may be obtained in large lots from canneries, jobbers, commission merchants, manufacturers, and importers. Buying in these large quantities is economical. The goods are transported to the warehouses of the wholesaler, are stored, and are then sold in smaller lots to retailers. During all this time the wholesaler has his money invested in the goods going in and out of his warehouses. Without the assistance of a middleman, such as this wholesaler, the small retailer would not have access to this wide variety of products, or he would have to assume the function of collecting a large variety of goods.

There are various attempts at times to make the distributive system more economical or at least more advantageous to some persons who are interested in the marketing system. For instance, farmers have organized numerous co-operative marketing associations, which perform some of the functions of buying, assembling, storing, transporting, financing, risk bearing, and selling. None of the processes are eliminated, but some of the benefits go to the farmers. In a sense, the farmer invests in a business by becoming a member of a co-operative. A specialist takes over the functions of operating the co-operative in his behalf. The farmer then spends more of his time in producing his crops and therefore gains a personal advantage. If by his action the whole process becomes more efficient, the consumer also receives a benefit.

Direct and Indirect Marketing. Distribution through the wholesaler and the retailer is frequently referred to as *indirect marketing*. Indirect marketing has acquired its title because products pass through several hands in going from the producer to the consumer.

Conversely, *direct marketing* or *direct selling* is the process by which the producer sells to the consumer directly or through his own representatives. Well-known manufacturers sell directly to the consumer.

We can eliminate certain individual middlemen, but we cannot eliminate the fundamental economic functions of marketing. Therefore, the whole question of our marketing system is one of efficiency, not one of eliminating functions. The same functions have to be performed regardless of who does them or how they are done. For example, the chain store eliminates the wholesaler, but it performs the wholesale functions itself.

How Much Does Distribution Cost? Studies made by the Twentieth Century Fund, an unbiased organization for the

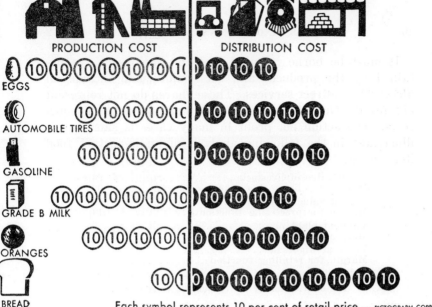

| | PRODUCTION COST | DISTRIBUTION COST |

EGGS

AUTOMOBILE TIRES

GASOLINE

GRADE B MILK

ORANGES

BREAD

Each symbol represents 10 per cent of retail price   PICTOGRAPH CORPORATION

study of economic problems, report that, out of every dollar which the consumer spends for goods and services, an average of about 41 cents goes for production and 59 cents goes for the services of distribution. The difference between the 41 cents, which is the cost of production, and the final selling price is referred to as the *spread*. In this case it is 59 cents, which represents the cost of distribution. Not all of this is profit. In fact, net profit is usually only a small part of this amount.

The price spread between the actual original production cost and the final retail price is not the same for every product. This fact is shown in the preceding illustration, which shows the cost of production and the cost of distribution for six different items. At first glance one might assume that there is a tremendous amount of profit made in the distribution of oranges, but actually the percentage of net profit made in the distribution of eggs, automobile tires, or gasoline might be greater. In the case of oranges the high distribution cost is due to a great extent to the fact that oranges are hauled long distances to reach the large markets where most of them are consumed. Other factors will be discussed later.

45

It must be borne in mind that the various shares obtained by the producer and each middleman include all direct and indirect services. These shares do not represent net profit. Out of his share each must pay for his own costs. The actual net profit in many cases is small, as is illustrated in the following analysis of an important food item, meat.

Farm value of livestock	$ .64
Margin for livestock marketing function	.02
Market value of livestock	.66
Margin for processing function	.14
Value at plant	.80
Margin for wholesaling function	.04
Value at wholesale	.84
Margin for retailing function	.16
Value at retail	$1.00

The distribution of the consumer's meat dollar.

The margin in each case covers all the expenses and the profit of the particular middleman. Although the margin shown for the retailing function in this example is 16 cents, not all of this is profit because the retailer must pay the wages, rent, and other store expenses.

A Summary of Effects on You. Just what have you learned from the study of this chapter? Obviously, any improvements in marketing from the consumer viewpoint must come from increased efficiency in performing the various functions of marketing. No function can be eliminated. Each function of marketing provides a fundamental service and each person performing one of these services is entitled to a fair compensation. The consumer could perform some of the functions himself and some consumers do perform some of these functions. By doing so they may

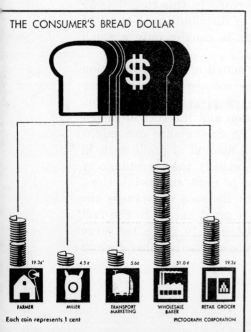

THE CONSUMER'S BREAD DOLLAR

FARMER 19.3¢   MILLER 4.5¢   TRANSPORT MARKETING 5.6¢   WHOLESALE BAKER 51.0¢   RETAIL GROCER 19.3¢

Each coin represents 1 cent   PICTOGRAPH CORPORATION

be able to create some savings for themselves. But if a consumer performs very many of these functions, he will not have time to make a living at his regular occupation so he can buy the other things he needs. Marketing is part of our system of specialization. It enables us to go about our regular duties while other people help us get the things we need, which we buy with the money that we earn as specialists.

TEXTBOOK QUESTIONS

1. What are the main economic functions of marketing?
2. What is meant by (a) assembling goods? (b) storing goods?
3. How does the function of grading and standardizing goods aid in the distributive system?
4. What function is performed by advertising?
5. What activities are included in the merchandising function of retail stores?
6. Why are banks necessary in the distributive system?
7. If a person says, "There is a good market for this product," what does he mean?
8. What distinguishes a wholesale market from a retail market?
9. Name some products that can be bought in organized markets.
10. How does a large national market help American enterprises to expand their business?
11. What functions of distribution enable people in most parts of the United States to enjoy fresh foods of practically all kinds during the twelve months of the year?
12. What is meant by direct marketing or direct selling? Does it eliminate any fundamental function of distribution?
13. Give some reasons why the cost of distribution of oranges is high.

DISCUSSION QUESTIONS

1. (a) Are there any advantages to the consumer in allowing farmers to peddle products without restriction in cities? (b) Are there any disadvantages?
2. Do you think we could get along without the services of the wholesaler? Explain your answer.
3. "The commission market helps the farmer to make more money." Is this statement true? Explain your answer.
4. Explain in what way storage may have aided in distributing the food that you consumed in your morning meal.
5. What happens to the distributive system if farmers become bankrupt in great numbers?

6. If manufacturers could no longer make profits, what would happen to the distributive system?
7. How do the transportation and storage functions reduce the profits of producers in some regions?
8. A manufacturer of fountain pens sends an agent to your door to attempt to sell a pen to you. Does the manufacturer perform distributive functions in addition to the functions of manufacturing and selling?
9. Name some mail order houses that sell in large areas directly to the consumer, and explain in what way you feel they eliminate certain functions of distribution.

PROBLEMS

1. From the point of view of economic functions performed in marketing, make a list of those that you believe are performed by a local drugstore.
2. What has refrigeration done for distribution, particularly as it affects the consumer?
3. State the advantages of the storage of wheat in large elevators from the point of view of (a) the grower and (b) the consumer.
4. List as many as possible ways in which risk is involved in distribution.

COMMUNITY PROBLEMS AND PROJECTS

1. If any products (such as lumber, machinery, canned goods, clothing, farm produce, or the like) are produced locally, find out the various channels of distribution through which a particular product goes from the time of its production until the time of its final use. Make a report on the process of distributing this product. List specifically the types of outlets through which the product is sold; and, if possible, use a map to indicate the area in which it is sold.
2. List various local businesses within a radius of your school that is designated by your teacher and consider four types of businesses that you select, such as bread manufacturers, drug stores, automobile dealers, and manufacturers of shoes. Classify them according to the markets that are available to them, such as local, national, or international; and in the case of local markets, try to define how far you feel their local markets extend.
3. Select some product with the approval of your teacher and make a study of it with the aid of any library material or information that you can obtain from that business. Write a report as to how it is produced or distributed and where it goes.

Chapter 4

How Business and Government Serve You

Purpose of the Chapter. Many of the things we want are provided for us by business firms and government agencies. As individuals, we make or produce very little of the food, clothing, household articles, or other things we use. We buy these things from business firms primarily because, by specializing in the production of the things we want, they can produce them more efficiently and economically than we can.

In addition to material things we also use many services. These services range all the way from getting our shoes repaired or our clothes laundered to having our physician call on us when we are ill or the fire department come to put out a fire in our home. If we made a list of the services we use in a day or a week, we probably would be surprised at the number of them. We buy services just as we buy items of food and articles of clothing. Some of these services are available through business firms and some through government agencies.

The greater portion of our income is spent in buying the commodities and services that we want. The remainder, if any, is invested in savings. It is important that we understand how business firms and government agencies provide the commodities and services we want and need. Many of these services we would find it difficult, if not impossible, to provide for ourselves. Business and government are both important to us in providing for our wants.

Why Business Firms Are Organized. Business firms earn their income by specializing in making a product or in rendering a service that others want and will buy. While they are organized and operated to make a profit, they do so by providing commodities or services used by consumers.

49

Armstrong Cork Company, Makers of Armstrong's Linoleum

The retailer is organized to make a profit by providing a variety of products for the convenience of the consumer.

Some business firms are started when it is believed that there is a commodity or service that can be more efficiently and economically provided by a business firm than the consumer could provide that commodity or service for himself. For example, a man may decide to start a factory to make lawn mowers. By the use of tools and machinery, he may make a better lawn mower and at a lower cost than each consumer could make one for himself. Another person may observe that all families use bread and, therefore, decide to start a bakery. He believes he can make bread in large quantities both better and at less cost than the bread could be made at home. Still others buy merchandise of various kinds from many wholesalers and assemble it in their retail stores where consumers may select the goods they want without traveling long distances to the wholesalers or other suppliers of the merchandise. These are examples of products that a consumer may provide for himself but which he finds it is not convenient or economical to do.

Other business firms make products or render services that would be wholly impossible for consumers to provide for themselves. Gasoline is an example of such a product.

50

One could not make his own gasoline because of the great amount of special equipment needed in its manufacture. Very few people would have automobiles if each one had to make his own gasoline. Likewise, the services of professional men, such as the physician and the lawyer, cannot be provided by each person for himself. One could make a list of many products and services that he would have to do without if they were not provided by business firms that specialize in them. Thus business firms exist to provide for the wants of consumers.

Classes of Business Firms. Business provides thousands of different products and many kinds of services for consumers. The business firms providing these services may be classified broadly according to the nature of the products and services in which they specialize.

> ### Classes of Business Firms
>
> Mining, extracting, and lumber industries
> Agriculture
> Manufacturing, construction, and building
> Wholesaling, storing, and retailing
> Finance
> Transportation
> Personal and professional services
> Public utilities

Relation Between Business Firms and Consumers. Business firms and consumers are dependent upon each other. The consumer looks to business to supply his wants not only more completely but more efficiently and economically than he can provide for those wants himself. The long-range success of a business firm is dependent upon its ability to provide a product or a service for consumers at a cost that is reasonable and at the same time yielding a profit for the firm. Consumers could not get along without the products and services that are made available to them by business firms, and business firms could not remain in operation without consumers to buy and use their products and services.

Consumers want many different kinds of products and services. In fact, the variety of their wants is almost unlimited. Each of these wants potentially is an opportunity for some business firm to make a product or to provide a service that satisfies the want. As the products and services used by consumers increase in kind and in quantity, the opportunities for business firms increase correspondingly. When the volume of business increases, the opportunities for employment increase. To be employed either by one's self or by a business firm is essential for most of us. We must earn an income in order to buy the products and services we want.

The consumer's primary interest is to obtain the products and services that best satisfy his needs at a price he can afford to pay. Therefore, when a consumer wants some commodity or service, he first determines whether it is available at a satisfactory price. If more than one commodity or service fulfills his requirements, he next decides which one of those available is the most economical and the best for his purposes. By making these decisions the consumer is really casting an *economic vote*. Thus, the consumer, by making his choices, really determines the kinds of products and services that business firms offer, for those products that receive fewer votes yield little profit and will be discontinued by business.

Business firms are interested primarily in making a profit by providing products and services for consumers. Business firms continue to make profits only as long as they continue to satisfy consumer needs and wants. Whenever a business fails to satisfy consumer needs and wants, that business will fail to make a profit.

Business firms are entitled to make a fair profit because of the risk they incur when they undertake to serve consumers. A farmer is entitled to a greater return than his farm hand. Both the farmer and the farm hand may do equal amounts of labor. However, the farmer in addition risks his investment in land, machinery, seed, and fertilizer. In a year when poor crops are harvested, a farmer may suffer a loss; but the farm hand will be paid for his labor.

Individual consumers could not provide petroleum
products for themselves.

In years of good harvest a farmer may earn a profit beyond
the return for this labor while the farm hand is paid only
for his labor. <u>The risk of losing money invested with the
hope of satisfying consumer needs and wants is the justification for a business making a profit.</u>

If prices for a product or service are high, consumers
may not buy because they cannot afford to do so. If a product or service does not serve the needs of consumers well,
they may not buy at all or they may select the products or
services of another business firm that meets their needs
more completely. Business firms are vitally affected by
the decisions made by consumers. The success of business
firms is dependent upon the economic votes cast by consumers. Consumers' interests and the profit objective of
business firms do not conflict. Both are legitimate. They
are interrelated. Many of the wants of consumers can be
provided only by business firms that specialize. To earn
profits consistently year after year, business firms must
supply at reasonable prices the products and services that
consumers need and want.

Common Forms of Business Organization. Not all business firms are owned or managed in the same way. The
form of the organization of a business firm is determined

primarily by the laws under which it exists and operates and how and by whom it is owned and managed. The three most common forms of business organization are single proprietorship, partnership, and corporation.

A *single proprietorship* is a business enterprise owned by one person and usually managed by that person. A *partnership* is a business firm owned by two or more persons, all of whom usually share in the responsibilities of management and all of whom usually share in profits and losses in proportion to their share in the ownership. In most states, specific laws regulate the ownership, operation, and management of partnerships. The laws governing this form of business organization usually are to protect the rights and to prescribe the responsibilities of the partners. The laws also protect those persons who loan money to the partnership or who do business with it.

Another common form of business organization is the *corporation*. It is given the right to exist and operate by the laws of the state in which it is organized. The conditions under which a corporation is organized and may operate are stated in its *charter*, which is the legal evidence of its right to exist and to do business. The charter is issued by the state. Ownership in a corporation is represented by *shares of stock* which, for any one corporation, may be owned by many different persons. Ownership of one or more shares of stock in a corporation entitles the owner to help elect members of the board of directors and to vote on certain other issues, depending upon the provisions in the charter. The *board of directors* is charged with the responsibility of managing and operating the business of the corporation although usually it delegates much of the responsibility for management to the *officers* of the corporation whom it elects. A distinct advantage of a corporation over a partnership is that the owners of a corporation are not responsible personally for the debts of the corporation; however, they may lose what they invested in shares of stock if the corporation fails. In a partnership, each partner is personally responsible for all of the debts of the firm if his partners are unable to pay their shares.

The form of business organization has little or no effect upon the products or services that a business firm offers to consumers. However, the stability of the business firm and the judgment used in the management of the business may affect prices and the quality of the products and services offered to the consumer. Consumers like to buy from reputable business firms that are managed efficiently and that are able to sell at reasonable prices.

Two Special Forms of Business Organization. Two special types of business organizations to serve consumers have been developed, the consumer co-operative and the public utility. The ownership and management of consumer co-operatives and public utilities are dissimilar, yet the two forms of business organization have one common objective, and that is to satisfy the wants of consumers.

Consumer Co-operatives. Some consumers believe that the amount of profit taken out during the process of distribution is unjustified and unnecessary. Consumers who are willing to perform some of the functions of distribution themselves may band themselves together in a co-operative association, commonly known as a *consumer co-operative* or a *retail co-operative*. The objective of this type of co-operative is to pass on to the members of the co-operative any savings that result from the enterprise.

A co-operative enterprise may be operated either as a large or a small business. Some of them are relatively small, the members (owners) being confined to a certain group of people, such as the postal employees in a city. Consumer co-operatives are frequently organized as retailing establishments or as credit unions. Some deal only with their own members; however, some also transact business with the general public.

In a consumer co-operative the owners of the business are also consumers of the product or users of the service provided by the business. The owners are known as members of the co-operative enterprise. Sometimes they buy the commodities they want from the co-operative firm at a lower price than nonmembers can purchase them. They

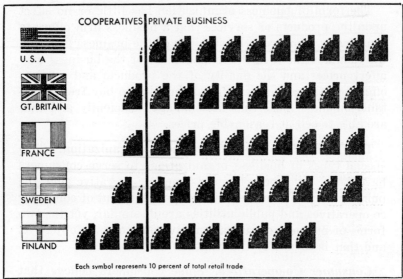

COOPERATIVES | PRIVATE BUSINESS

U. S. A

GT. BRITAIN

FRANCE

SWEDEN

FINLAND

Each symbol represents 10 percent of total retail trade

Pictograph Corporation, for Public Affairs Committee, Inc.

Retail trade handled by co-operatives and private businesses.

have a voice in the management of the business by electing a board of directors, and they share in the profits and losses.

Public Utilities. Such services as telephone, gas, water, electricity, and transportation are often provided by business firms that are known as *public utilities.* These companies usually are given the exclusive right to provide a service to the consumers of a certain geographical area. This right is granted to assure the utility company that no other company will be permitted to compete with it in providing the same kind of service to consumers in its territory. This protection is necessary because of the exceedingly high cost of building water and gas mains or electric and telephone lines by which such services are made available to the consumers. Pipe lines and telephone or electric lines are permanent, and the investment in them cannot be recovered by removing them if they are no longer used. Uncontrolled competition might force the abandonment of such equipment or make it unprofitable for the public utility to remain in operation.

The public utility company usually is given the privilege to operate and to provide a particular kind of service in a given territory by the state and sometimes by the Federal Government. This privilege or right to operate is known as a *franchise*. In accepting a franchise, the public utility company assumes certain responsibilities and agrees to abide by certain regulations relative to its management and operation.

American Telephone and Telegraph Company

A public utility has an exclusive right to provide a consumer service.

When conditions are such that it is not advisable or economical for more than one public utility to provide a service for a given territory, the firm to which the right to provide the service is granted is said to have a *monopoly*. Though many public utilities are virtually monopolies because they may be free from competition in a particular territory, the rates charged for their services are regulated and controlled by the state or the Federal Government. The rates are regulated to insure consumers the services at a fair and reasonable cost. Rates also are established to produce sufficient income to pay all expenses, to provide for proper maintenance and repair, and to provide a reasonable profit for the owners of the company if it is one that is privately owned. Some public utilities are owned by a governmental unit, such as a town, township, or city. These are said to be publicly owned. Usually provision for profit is not made in establishing the rates of public utilities that are publicly owned. Thus the consumer is given the benefit of the potential profit through lower rates for the service he uses.

Public utility companies provide many essential services for consumers at rates that consumers can afford to pay. Most services of public utilities would be impossible for the consumer to provide for himself. Thus public utilities are important factors in meeting the wants and needs of consumers in modern life.

Government Serves Consumers. Some services may be considered as public services because they are "for the good of all of the people." Because all of the people of a town or other governmental unit may use these services and benefit from them, the cost usually is paid from public funds. Common examples of public services are the benefits we derive from schools, libraries, roads and bridges, police and fire protection, traffic direction and control, and national defense. You could list many other things that are provided as public services and paid for from public funds.

Public services are provided and controlled by governmental agencies. Some are under the control of local government, some under the state government, and others are provided by the Federal Government. Education is an example of a service that is provided by all three levels of government—local, state, and Federal. Elementary and secondary schools usually are provided by local units of government, state colleges and universities by the state government, and the stimulation of education in local communities and states is provided through funds by the Federal Government. Police protection and road construction are other examples of public services that are planned by local, state, and Federal agencies.

The services that are planned for the general good of all of the people at public expense are increasing. We demand good roads and bridges for our convenience and use; we want hospital service; we ask for old-age benefits and unemployment insurance; we seek new public buildings and roads and dams for our local communities and states; and we would be reluctant to abandon the postal service. These are just a few examples of the public services that now are provided primarily at public expense. You could easily make a list of many more services performed by governmental agencies for the benefit of consumers.

Two trends may be observed in studying the services provided by governmental agencies. The one is that there

Services provided by government are paid by consumers
through toll charges and taxes.

is a notable increase in the number and extent of the services that people want to have provided for them at government expense. The second trend is that services for the
benefit of all people are gradually shifting from local units
of government to state and Federal Government agencies.

Several governmental agencies supply consumers with
reliable information that is useful in wise buying. They
also provide for the inspection, grading, and labeling of
many products, thus protecting consumers from unsanitary
and inferior quality merchandise.

Because of the importance of the services provided by
governmental agencies, consumers should understand them
and know how to use them in the most effective manner.
Some of these services will be discussed in detail in later
chapters.

The Cost of Government Service. There is practically
no activity of government that does not affect consumers
in some way. The benefits derived from some governmental
activities are more tangible and, therefore, more easily
seen than others. Though some consumers may not realize
it, everyone pays the cost of all governmental activities
through direct and indirect taxes. The more services we

GOVERNMENT INCOME AND EXPENDITURES

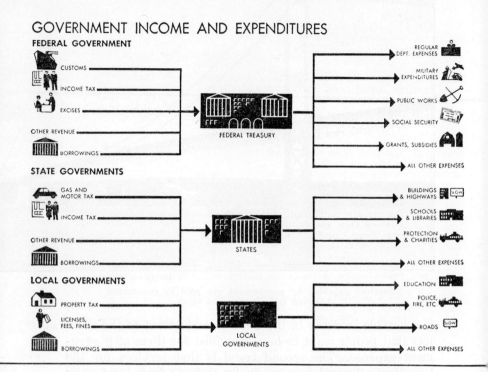

FEDERAL GOVERNMENT

CUSTOMS
INCOME TAX
EXCISES
OTHER REVENUE
BORROWINGS

FEDERAL TREASURY

REGULAR DEPT. EXPENSES
MILITARY EXPENDITURES
PUBLIC WORKS
SOCIAL SECURITY
GRANTS, SUBSIDIES
ALL OTHER EXPENSES

STATE GOVERNMENTS

GAS AND MOTOR TAX
INCOME TAX
OTHER REVENUE
BORROWINGS

STATES

BUILDINGS & HIGHWAYS
SCHOOLS & LIBRARIES
PROTECTION & CHARITIES
ALL OTHER EXPENSES

LOCAL GOVERNMENTS

PROPERTY TAX
LICENSES, FEES, FINES
BORROWINGS

LOCAL GOVERNMENTS

EDUCATION
POLICE, FIRE, ETC
ROADS
ALL OTHER EXPENSES

demand at public expense, the higher the cost of government; and the higher the cost of government, the more taxes we pay. High taxes not only increase the amounts we pay directly in property and income taxes, but they are reflected in the price of every commodity or service that we buy. When we buy a dozen of oranges for sixty cents, that price includes not only the fifteen or twenty cents that goes to the grower of the oranges but some of it is to pay for the taxes, which are a part of the costs of doing business that were paid by the trucker, the wholesaler or jobber, and the retailer who handled the oranges.

Some people erroneously assume that services provided by the government are free. The cost of these services must be paid from public funds, which come either directly or indirectly from consumers. In other words the services and benefits, such as price supports, subsidies, and public works, are not free; they are paid out of the taxes we pay and are included in the cost of every article or commodity that we buy. When we are considering buying some article

GUIDES TO AN UNDERSTANDING OF
HOW BUSINESS AND GOVERNMENT SERVE CONSUMERS

1. Many commodities and services used by consumers can be more economically and more satisfactorily provided by business firms than by the consumers themselves.

2. Business firms are organized to make a profit by providing goods and services that consumers want and buy. In the long run the profits made by a business firm are determined by how well consumers' needs are satisfied.

3. Consumers and business firms are dependent upon each other. Consumers could not get along without the products and services that are available through business firms, and business firms could not remain in operation without consumers to buy and use their products and services.

4. Business firms are entitled to make a fair and reasonable profit, just as a laborer is entitled to enough wages to enable him to save. Consumers have a right to expect from business firms products and services that will effectively meet their needs at a reasonable price. There is no conflict between the profit motive of business and the primary interests of consumers.

5. The form of organization of a business enterprise does not materially affect the consumers who buy products or services from a business firm, except that efficiency of the management may affect prices of the products and services offered. The consumer co-operative and the public utility are two forms of business organization designed to serve the special needs of consumers.

6. Services provided for consumers by governmental agencies at public expense are tending to increase both in extent and in kind. Many services can be provided more economically and more efficiently by governmental agencies than by individuals themselves if, indeed, they could provide them at all.

7. Government services and benefits, such as price supports, subsidies, and public works, are not free but are paid for primarily from public funds, which are derived from direct and indirect taxes paid by consumers.

8. In requesting more governmental services at public expense, the consumer should consider not only whether the services are necessary but whether he and other consumers are able and willing to pay for the services requested through higher taxes and prices.

9. The consumer uses the services provided by governmental agencies, and he pays for them through direct and indirect taxes. Therefore, the consumer should understand how these services are provided and how to use them in the most effective manner.

for our personal use, we ask ourselves whether we can afford it, whether our budget will stand it. However, many people when requesting their legislators to vote for another service or for a new building or bridge do not consider the question whether they and other consumers are willing and able to pay for it by paying higher taxes.

Consumers benefit greatly from services and from public buildings, roads, dams, and similar conveniences that are provided by governmental agencies at public expense. Public services are essential for good living and good business. The consumer uses the services, and he pays for them. Therefore, it is important that you understand the nature of these services and how they are provided. Bearing the cost of these services will be discussed in detail in a later chapter.

Relation of Consumers to Business Firms and Governmental Agencies. Most of the goods and services that we want as consumers are provided by business firms and governmental agencies. Some are provided by the consumer by making the articles or goods that he wants or by doing things for himself that he might get others to do for him. An example of the former is a homemaker who makes a dress or who bakes a cake. By his own labor, the man who mows his own lawn really has performed a service for himself. Consumers should understand their relationship to business enterprises and to governmental agencies that serve them. A summary of a few basic facts may help in understanding that relationship.

TEXTBOOK QUESTIONS

1. Why are business firms organized?
2. Why do consumers buy the products they want and need rather than make them for themselves?
3. Why do most business and professional firms specialize in only one class of commodity or kind of service?
4. What are the major classes of business firms?
5. What does the consumer expect from business?
6. The primary interest of business firms is to make a profit. What effect does consumers' acceptance of the product or

service have on the profits of the business or professional firm?

7. Why is a merchant entitled to a fair profit?
8. What are the most common forms of business organization?
9. How may the prices and the quality of products and services provided for consumers by business firms be affected by the form of organization of the business firm?
10. What is a consumer co-operative enterprise?
11. What is the primary purpose of a consumer co-operative?
12. What is the nature of the services provided by public utility companies?
13. Why is the exclusive right to provide service to the consumers in a certain geographical area granted to a public utility company?
14. What is a franchise?
15. Why are the rates for services provided by public utility companies regulated by the state or Federal Government?
16. What kinds of services are provided by governmental units at public expense?
17. Is the trend toward asking for more or fewer services and benefits at government expense?
18. How are the costs of governmental services paid?
19. Why are governmental services important to consumers?

DISCUSSION QUESTIONS

1. Why is it possible for a manufacturer to make some products that serve better and more efficiently than if they were made at home?
2. What are some of the products that a housewife could make for her home but which may be more economically and conveniently purchased from a business firm?
3. What are some of the services that many homes would have to do without if they were not available from business and professional firms that specialize in them?
4. Explain how business firms and consumers are dependent upon each other.
5. How does the consumer really determine the kinds of products and services that business and professional firms offer?
6. What are the advantages of being a member of a consumer co-operative enterprise?
7. What are the disadvantages of being a member of a consumer co-operative enterprise?
8. How do public utilities serve consumers?
9. Make a list of the ways government provides services and benefits for consumers.

PROBLEMS

1. Compile a list of the products that usually are purchased rather than made at home because of the time required in making them.
2. In your school library, locate books on business law, business organization, or bookkeeping in which are given the characteristics of single proprietorships, partnerships, and corporations. Prepare a report on the advantages and disadvantages of each of these three forms of business organization.
3. What public utilities provide service to the consumers of your community or city?
4. Many years ago the wants of people were fewer in number and much simpler in nature than they are now. It is said that every new commodity or service wanted by consumers provides another opportunity for a business firm to serve people. Make a list of commodities that in the last 25 to 40 years have become almost universally demanded by consumers, thus providing opportunities for business firms to make a profit.

COMMUNITY PROBLEMS AND PROJECTS

1. Make a list of business firms in your community or city that specialize in (a) making a product that is used by individuals or families as consumers, (b) making a product that is used by other business firms in the making of their products, and (c) rendering a service to individuals and to families.
2. Ask three businessmen in your community or city the reasons or motives why they operate their business firms. Discuss the reasons they give.
3. Interview one of the officers, preferably the president, of a consumer co-operative enterprise in your community. Prepare a report giving the nature of the co-operative enterprise, number of members, requirements for membership, how the co-operative is managed, the volume of business and the savings for consumers during the past year and the basis for distributing the savings to the members.
4. Make a study locally to determine the services for consumers that are given by local and Federal Governmental agencies and paid for from public funds.
5. From local government officials and from any other sources available to you, prepare a list of the buildings, bridges, roads, and other public works in your community that were paid for, at least in part, from Federal funds. Also give on the list the names of the local, state, and Federal agencies that co-operated in the construction of the project and the amounts each contributed.

Chapter 5

Legal Relations Important to You

Purpose of the Chapter. To be an effective consumer, you need to know your legal rights and responsibilities and how to protect yourself if difficulties arise. An important aim of this chapter is to help you conduct your affairs so that legal difficulties will not arise.

What Is a Contract? A _contract_ is an agreement between two or more competent parties that creates an obligation enforceable by law. If one of the parties does not carry out his part of the agreement, the other party may resort to a court action.

When you buy goods in a store on account, you make a contract with the store to pay the cost of the merchandise. If you leave shoes in a repair shop to be fixed, a contract is made on the part of the repairman to fix the shoes and on your part to pay the prescribed charges. When you rent a house, you enter into a contract to pay the rent; and the owner obligates himself to let you have possession of the property. Many other situations exist in everyday life that involve contracts. Buying life insurance, buying fire insurance, shipping merchandise, or accepting a position, all involve contracts.

The basis of a contract is an agreement between the parties. But not all agreements are contracts because some agreements do not have all the essentials of contracts. Ashworth agrees to go hunting with Stillwell; but if Stillwell changes his mind and decides not to go, he is not breaking a contract. On the other hand, if Ashworth and Stillwell make arrangements to go on a hunting trip together and arrange for a professional guide to provide them with hunting equipment, food, and lodging, they have entered into a contract with the guide. They are both responsible to the guide for

65

carrying out the contract or for settling it in some satisfactory manner if they change their minds.

A contract must have the following elements: (a) mutual assent, (b) competent parties, (c) legal bargain, (d) consideration, (e) required form.

Elements of a Contract

1. Mutual assent.
2. Competent parties.
3. Legal bargain.
4. Consideration.
5. Required form.

Offer and Acceptance (Mutual Assent). Mrs. Burton bought a stove and had it sent out to her home. She used it for two weeks; and when the store asks for payment, she insists on returning it although she has no complaint as to its performance. She insists that she has never accepted it because she has not paid for it. Courts would undoubtedly hold that there was an offer and an acceptance. On the other hand, if she had ordered it sent out on approval, an acceptance would not have been indicated until she had signified her approval or had kept the stove an unreasonable length of time without expressing dissatisfaction or a willingness to return it. *Mutual assent* in simple terms means the making of an offer on the part of one person and the acceptance of the offer on the part of another.

The essential characteristics of an offer are: (a) the proposal must be definite; (b) the proposal must be made with the intention that the *offeror* (person making the offer) be bound by it; (c) the proposal must be communicated by words or actions. For instance, if you were to offer to work for an employer for "all that you are worth," the offer would be too indefinite to be the basis of an enforceable agreement. If an offer is made in obvious or apparent jest, it is not a real offer. Most advertisements are not offers. They are usually merely invitations to buy or invitations to make an offer to buy. For instance, if you

A cash purchase at the grocery store is an example of a simple contract.

see something advertised and you send your money but the order cannot be filled because the merchant is sold out, you have not entered into a contract. Likewise, if one walks into a store and finds goods on display with a price marked on them and the goods are obviously offered for sale at that price, the proposal has been communicated and he has made a contract when the money is accepted for the purchase of those goods.

Generally speaking, the acceptance of goods is indicated by (a) specific indication that the buyer accepts the goods; (b) use of the goods; or (c) detention of the goods for an unreasonable length of time. Under the principles of law, it is not considered that there is mutual assent unless both parties have freely, intentionally, and apparently assented to the same thing.

It can be seen from the requirements of an offer that acceptance has much to do with the way that the offer is made and terminated. If acceptance is required to be made in a special manner, it must be made in that way. For instance,

acceptance may be requested by mail or by a certain dead-
line. If it does not conform to these requirements, it is not
a legal acceptance. However, if the acceptance is later
approved by the offeror, the agreement becomes binding.

As in the case of an offer, the acceptance must be indicated by some word or act. For instance, one cannot be
bound against his will by an offeror who states in his offer,
"If I do not hear from you by ten o'clock, October 10, I
shall consider that you have accepted this offer." The acceptance must also be made by the party to whom the offer
was made. If someone has made an offer to you and you
tell a friend about it, the person who made the offer does
not have to recognize an acceptance by your friend. The
acceptance may be in the form of a definite promise that
completes the mutual agreement, or it may be made in the

form of some act. For instance,
if a boy is offered $1 for cutting
a lawn, the act of cutting the
lawn is evidence of accepting the
offer.

As a general rule, when offers
are made by letter with the acceptance to be made by mail, the
offer is considered to be accepted
when the acceptance is deposited
in the mail. Likewise, if the
acceptance is to be made by tele-
gram, the agreement is considered to be completed when the
message is given to the telegraph company.

When an offer is made by mail,
the contract is formed when
the acceptance is mailed.

Termination of an Offer. An offer can be terminated in
many ways. It may be terminated at a definite time stated
in the offer. If no definite time is stated, it will be terminated in a reasonable amount of time, which often has to
be determined by the court if a dispute arises. Definite
refusal of the offer or a counteroffer (a new offer by the
person to whom the original offer was made) will terminate

the original offer. The withdrawal or revocation of the offer before it is accepted is a clear termination. Other unusual circumstances that terminate offers are death or insanity of the offeror.

Ordinarily, if an offer is made for a specified length of time, it may still be revoked before the expiration of that time if proper notice is given of the withdrawal. However, if a general offer is made to the public, such as a reward published in a newspaper, it is still in effect unless it is withdrawn in the same way that it is offered.

Keeping an Offer Open. Offers are sometimes kept open for specified periods of time by a special contract that is known as an *option.* If the offeror receives cash or something of value as an inducement to keep an offer open for a certain specified time, the offer cannot be withdrawn for the period of time covered by the option. This is an important type of offer that is used in large transactions. For example, a person considering buying a home or a company considering buying a new factory would want time to consider the matter with the assurance that if a decision is made to buy the property, the original quotation of the price would be accepted.

Competent Parties. The Ridge Hardware Store accepted a properly signed order for a bicycle for $40 from Bob Hansen, age 12. When the bicycle arrived from the factory, the price had risen and the dealer insisted on getting $50 for the bicycle or canceling the contract. He argued that the original agreement was not binding because Bob Hansen was a minor and was, therefore, incompetent to contract. This agreement is binding, however, on the dealer. Bob could cancel the contract if he wished. A situation such as this and many others are involved in contracts with minors and certain other types of people.

The question of competence of parties determines who is legally qualified to make contracts. Anyone who is not otherwise prevented by law from making enforceable agreements may make a contract. In many cases children (minors, or those who are not of legal age) are not competent to contract

Ewing Galloway

A minor's contract to buy a bicycle may be voidable.

and may not be required by law to carry out agreements. There are, however, some exceptions to this rule, such as contracting for necessaries. When a minor makes an agreement with an adult, the adult is required to fulfill the contract if it is legal; but if the minor chooses to rescind (cancel) the contract, he can, in most cases, escape his responsibility.

Usually contracts made by a minor are voidable (that is, they may be broken) by the minor. He may break them while he is still a minor or within a reasonable time after he becomes of age. If he reaffirms the agreement after he becomes of age, it becomes a binding contract. The voidability of a contract applies generally whether it has been fully performed or only partially performed.

Contracts made by minors to acquire reasonable necessaries are binding upon the minor. A contract by a merchant to furnish jewelry, tobacco, or sporting equipment to an ordinary minor is voidable, but a contract to furnish necessary clothes or food is not voidable if the amounts charged are reasonable and the goods are needed and are actually delivered. On the other hand, if all these necessaries of life are provided by the parents, any contract made by the child to obtain them is voidable. A contract by a poor child to buy expensive clothing beyond his means would be voidable also.

Howard Martin, age 20, signed a contract for the purchase of an automobile. The dealer questioned him as to his age, and he assured the dealer that he was 21 years old on his last birthday. When the dealer notified him that he was ready to deliver the car, Howard refused to accept it, asserting that he misrepresented his age at the time of making the contract and, therefore, he could not be held responsible. In some states a minor is held responsible if he deliberately misrepresents his age; but if a child, age 12, were to misrepresent his age, the dealer might find it difficult to hold the child responsible because of his obvious young age.

Other persons who are not competent to contract under certain conditions are intoxicated persons and insane persons. The reason for making voidable all contracts made by these persons, except those for the reasonable value of necessaries actually furnished, is obvious: it is considered that they are not capable of exercising their own judgment. In certain states there are special laws applying to contracts that may not be made by convicts, foreigners, or married women, but there is a wide variation in these laws.

Legal Bargain. A contract is not legal unless the subject of the agreement is legal. In fact, in most cases when the subject of the contract is not legal, there is not even a contract.

Some examples of illegal bargains are those involving agreements to steal, to accept stolen goods, or to commit any other crime. All agreements to wager or gamble are illegal except in the cases of certain states in which betting on horse racing has been legalized. For instance, if you make a bet with somebody, you have not made a legal

An agreement to commit a crime is not enforceable.

contract; but in a state where betting on horse races is legal, your placing of a bet is a legal contract.

In all states there are so-called usury laws that establish the highest contract rate of interest that may be charged. If a contract is made and interest is charged at a higher rate, the contract is an illegal contract. Exceptions to these laws are the small loan regulations that permit licensed small loan organizations to charge higher rates.

It is always illegal to enter into any contract to obstruct justice, such as an agreement to give false testimony or an agreement to avoid giving testimony.

Generally speaking, when a certain type of business or professional man is subject to licensing, any contract made with one who is unlicensed is void. For instance, in most cities electricians and plumbers are licensed. If you make an agreement with an unlicensed electrician or plumber, the agreement is not a legal contract.

In almost all cases, agreements that restrain trade unreasonably are void. Examples of such agreements that are void are those involving control of prices, limiting production, creating a monopoly, creating an artificial scarcity, or causing unreasonable injury to competitors or to consumers.

Anyone buying stolen goods does not get a valid title to the goods. They must be returned to the rightful owner if the ownership can be proved.

Consideration in Contracts. J. R. Jackson, a wealthy member of Summit Hills Country Club, offered to give his old set of golf clubs to a caddy at the end of the golf season. He changed his mind and did not give them to the caddy. The caddy insisted that a contract had been made. Mr. Jackson insisted that there was no consideration on the part of the caddy in the nature of goods, money, services, or promises. If the caddy can prove that the clubs were promised him as a reward for caddy service or any other favor to Mr. Jackson, he probably can consider that there is a contract; but in the absence of such proof, there is no contract. It is simply in the nature of a promise to make a gift.

Ordinarily the promise made in an agreement is not enforceable unless something of value is received for the promise. The value may consist of goods, money, services, refraining from doing something that one has a right to do, or giving up a privilege. A common example of a consideration is the down payment made to a merchant when an agreement has been reached for the delivery of a piece of furniture. When one takes a job, the employer promises to pay for the services and the employee promises to perform the duties required in the job. A landlord may pay a tenant a certain sum of money to give up his lease and vacate the property. The amount paid is the consideration for the giving up of a legal right on the part of the tenant if the lease has not expired.

Proper Form of Contracts. Mr. and Mrs. Waltham bought a house from the Oval Realty Company for $10,000 on an oral agreement. This is not a regular contract because the law requires that agreements of this type must be in writing. However, they can make other purchases orally that are legal contracts.

Generally speaking, there are two main types of contracts, (a) *oral* and (b) *written*. Most contracts may be made informally merely by the exchange of a few words or the performance of certain acts. Certain contracts must be made in special form specified by law.

AGREEMENT.

Articles of Agreement *entered into this* first *day of* February *A. D. 19*51 *at* Columbus, Ohio *by and between* James A. Keegan
of Columbus *in the County of* Franklin
and State of Ohio *party of the first part and* Ralph R. Stevens
of Columbus *in the County of* Franklin *State of* Ohio
party of the second part, witnesseth:

The said party of the first part in consideration of the promises and agreements of said party of the second part herein set forth hereby covenants and agrees

To vacate the property he now occupies located at 210 Main Street and to relinquish all rights under the unexpired lease now in existence on said property. Party of the first part is to vacate said property on or before March 1, 1951.

In consideration whereof said party of the second part hereby promises and agrees

To pay $1,000 by certified check upon vacation of the property and to assume all obligations under the lease.

And it is agreed by and between the parties hereto upon the considerations aforesaid, that in case of the failure of either party to perform the things covenanted by him
[Here state what shall be the penalty or forfeiture for such failure.]

None

In Witness Whereof, *the said parties have hereunto set their hands to duplicates hereof the day and year first above written.*

James A. Keegan
Ralph R. Stevens

Witness Howard A. Holms
Marie J. Alfred

A written contract.

The following are some types of agreements that must be in writing:

(a) An agreement to answer for the debt, default, or obligation of another person. For instance, one may sign a note or sign an agreement to pay an account if someone else does not pay it.

(b) An agreement that is not to be executed or performed within a period of one year after it is made. For example, a guarantee to provide free service on a piece of household equipment for a period of two years should be in writing.

(c) An agreement to sell real property. Real property includes land, buildings, minerals, or trees.

(d) In most states an agreement to sell goods for more than a specified amount unless there is a receipt and acceptance of at least part of the goods or unless part payment is made. Ordinarily, oral evidence of a sale is sufficient when the price does not exceed the amount set by the Statute of Frauds in a particular state. If it exceeds this amount, it must be in writing. The table on page 76 shows the maximum for oral evidence in each state. Note that in two states written evidence is required in all sales. In six states no written evidence is required. If the requirements are not met, the oral agreement to sell goods is legal, but it is voidable by either party. It may be carried out by mutual agreement.

Contracts for work and labor, including materials, are generally not covered by the Statute of Frauds because that statute pertains to contracts for merchandise, goods, wares, or other materials. For example, contracts for medical or dental services need not be in writing regardless of the amount involved. A contract for the painting of a house need not be in writing, although it should be to avoid any misunderstanding.

Contracts may be classified in another way. They are said to be either *express* or *implied*. An *express contract* is one that arises out of an agreement expressed by oral or written words. If you orally agree to buy a refrigerator

Maximum Amounts for Which Sales May Be Proved in the
Various States, Alaska, the District of Columbia,
and Hawaii Without Written Evidence

Alabama	$500	Montana	$ 200
Alaska	50	Nebraska	500
Arizona	500	Nevada	50
Arkansas	30	New Hampshire	500
California	500	New Jersey	500
Colorado	50	New Mexico	50
Connecticut	100	New York	50
Delaware	500	North Carolina	none required
District of Columbia	50	North Dakota	500
Florida	all sales	Ohio	2,500
Georgia	50	Oklahoma	50
Hawaii	100	Oregon	50
Idaho	500	Pennsylvania	500
Illinois	500	Rhode Island	500
Indiana	500	South Carolina	50
Iowa	all sales	South Dakota	500
Kansas	none required	Tennessee	500
Kentucky	500	Texas	none required
Louisiana	none required	Utah	500
Maine	500	Vermont	40
Maryland	50	Virginia	none required
Massachusetts	500	Washington	50
Michigan	100	West Virginia	none required
Minnesota	50	Wisconsin	50
Mississippi	50	Wyoming	50
Missouri	30		

at a specified price and the dealer agrees to sell it to you at that price, you have made an express contract that is legally binding. An *implied contract* is one that is made through an agreement implied by the acts or the conduct of the parties involved. If you pick up an article in the store and hand the required amount of money to the clerk, who wraps up the article and hands it to you, you have made an implied contract. If you board a streetcar or a train, you imply by your act your willingness to pay the proper fare, and the carrier implies that he will transport you as a passenger.

A great many contracts do not have to be in writing because the offer, acceptance, payment, and delivery of goods often occur within a short space of a few seconds or a few minutes. In general, a contract should be written instead of oral when there is any chance for misunderstanding or disagreement between the parties and when a written contract is required by law.

When a written contract is required by law, both parties are not bound until the contract is signed properly by both parties. Evidence of an agreement signed by one party binds that party to the agreement. The primary essentials of a written contract are: (a) the date and place of the agreement; (b) the names and the identifications of the parties entering into the agreement; (c) a statement of the purposes of the contract; (d) a statement of the money, services, or goods given in consideration of the agreement; (e) a statement of the acts to be performed, the refraining from any acts, or the relinquishing of any privileges by each party; and (f) the signatures of both parties or the signatures of legal agents. In the case of some contracts witnesses are required, and in such cases the witnesses must sign in accordance with the provisions of the law.

A *bill of sale* is a written contract with which many consumers are acquainted. It is required in most states for the transfer of ownership of such items as automobiles or refrigerators. Even in states where a bill of sale is not required for these items, it is often desirable to obtain one because it provides evidence of ownership after the transaction has been completed.

In states where the bill of sale is used, it is usually necessary to register the bill of sale with the proper county authority so that the ownership of the property can be established.

√ *Reasons for a Written Contract*

1. To prevent misunderstanding.
2. To prevent the terms from being forgotten.
3. To provide an exact agreement.
4. To avoid litigation.
5. To prevent fraud.
6. To provide evidence in the case of the death of either party to the contract.

Defective Agreements. From the foregoing discussion you have learned what constitutes a *valid or enforceable contract*. When an agreement fails to include all the essentials, it is not a contract. If James Hirsh orally agrees to buy a car for $2,600 from the City Motor Company, the contract is not enforceable because it is not in writing.

Agreements that are not enforceable may be classified as void or voidable. When an agreement is *void,* it has no legal force or effect. In other words neither party can enforce the agreement. A *voidable* contract is one that may be avoided by one or both of the parties. Such an agreement is enforceable if the party or parties having the option to reject it choose not to do so.

Ordinarily a mistake made by one party, such as the quoting of the wrong price, does not make the contract void or voidable. Mistakes that make a contract void include mutual mistakes as to the existence of the subject matter or a mistake as to the indentity of the parties. For instance, a man agreed to sell a certain dog at a definite price, but later it was found that the dog had died before the agreement was made. The agreement was void because of mistake as to the existence of the subject matter. Let us assume as a second example that you call a telephone number and make an agreement over the telephone but learn later that the person to whom you were talking was not the person to whom you thought you were talking but instead was a person with whom you had no intention of forming a contract. The agreement thus made would be void because of the mistake as to the identity of one of the parties.

The following are examples of voidable agreements:

(a) If fraud in the form of misrepresentation is present. Consider the following example: Mr. Allen intentionally misrepresents to Mr. Smith that he is acting as an agent for a certain producer of clothing. When the merchandise is delivered, Mr. Smith discovers that Mr. Allen is acting as the agent of an entirely different producer. Mr. Allen is guilty of fraudulent representation; therefore the contract is voidable by Smith but not by Allen.

(b) If one person makes an agreement as the result of a threat or an act of violence. For instance, Mr. A induces Mr. B to sign a contract for merchandise under the threat that Mr. B's daughter will be abducted if he does not sign the contract. This contract is not enforceable, for it has been obtained by means of a threat of violence.

An agreement signed under threat is voidable.

(c) If there has been undue influence to the extent that one person has not reached the agreement through the free exercise of his own judgment. For instance, consider the case of an aged woman who has inherited a small sum of money. A favorite nephew, after prolonged pressure and argument, induces her to spend a major portion of her inheritance for a farm. Such a case would probably represent undue influence.

Preventing Fraud and Misunderstanding. Never sign a contract in blank or with part of the figures or conditions left to be filled in. If someone hurries you or suggests that you sign the contract with the rest of the information to be filled in later, your suspicion should be aroused.

Some contracts are printed in very small type in the hope that they will not be read. The type, in fact, is so small in some contracts that it can scarcely be read. Many old forms of contracts are printed in this manner, although the businesses that use them are entirely honest. A person should not be misled by a contract that is printed in small type. He should insist upon taking time to read it.

Every contract should be examined carefully before it is signed. An honest and legitimate business will encourage the buyer to read the contract before signing, whereas an unscrupulous business may try to induce the buyer to sign before reading. An invitation to read a contract should always be accepted. The document may be presented in the hope that it will not be read. If there is any indication that an attempt is being made to prevent the reading of the contract, one should insist upon reading every detail.

Do not sign a contract with the understanding that supplementary agreements will be made later. Be sure that all agreements are in the contract. In the absence of substantial proof with regard to oral agreements or supplementary written agreements, only the agreements stipulated in the contract are enforceable.

Read What You Sign

Reading a contract may prevent mistakes, misunderstandings, or fraud. For the following reasons every contract should be read before it is signed.

1. To ascertain the exact responsibilities that are about to be assumed.
2. To prevent misunderstanding concerning what is being offered, what the costs will be, and when payment is to be made.
3. To ascertain the responsibility of the seller.
4. To protect oneself against a few merchants who sell by fraud and misrepresentation.
5. To assist honest businesses in detecting intentional or unintentional misrepresentations on the part of salespeople.
6. To ascertain whether merchandise that is purchased may be returned.

Warranties. Under an old principle of law of "Let the buyer beware," it is assumed that the buyer must be pretty largely responsible for knowing what he gets. However, when a seller, in making a sale, makes promises that an article will operate in a specific way or that it has a certain specific quality, he makes statements on which the buyer has a legal right to rely in regard to the quality of the goods. These promises or representations are called *warranties*.

There are two types of warranties: (a) *express* and (b) *implied.* For example, if a merchant states definitely that cloth is pure virgin wool, that is an express warranty. An example of an implied warranty is one in which the buyer has a right to expect that the article purchased will serve the purpose for which it is sold, although there is no definite statement in regard to it. For instance, if one buys a stove, he has a right to expect that the stove will operate; if it does not operate, the buyer has a legal recourse. If one goes into a restaurant and orders food, there is an implied warranty that the food is fit to eat. If you become poisoned, the restaurant owner is liable. If it can be proved that the manufacturer or processor of the food was responsible because of improper processing or handling of the food, that person may also be liable for any damages resulting from the sickness.

Generally speaking, when a buyer has an opportunity to inspect the goods, there is no implied warranty that the goods are of a particular quality; but there is an implied warranty that they will serve the purpose for which they are intended. If the buyer does not inspect the goods but relies largely on the judgment and honesty of the seller, there is an implied warranty that the goods are of a certain quality. When a sample is used to indicate the kind and quality of the goods, the seller impliedly warrants the goods to correspond with the sample shown in kind and in quality. When merchandise is purchased by description, such as by specifications, the seller impliedly warrants the goods to correspond to the description.

"Trade puffs" or "trade talk" are not warranties and should not be relied upon by the buyer. A *trade puff* is a general claim, such as "This is the best merchandise you can buy," "This is the most popular item on the market," or "This suit is very becoming to you."

Remedies for Breach of Warranty. In the case of misrepresentation or if goods do not fulfill the reasonable expectations of a warranty, there has been a *breach of warranty.* Several different remedies are available in case

of a breach of warranty. The following general recourses
are open to the buyer: (1) to keep the goods and to deduct
from the price the amount of the damages; (2) to keep the
goods and to bring an action against the seller for damages;
(3) to refuse to accept the goods and to bring an action
against the seller to recover damages; (4) to rescind the
contract and to refuse to receive the goods or, if the goods
have been accepted, to return them to the vendor and to
recover the price that has been paid.

Passing of the Title. When a cash sale is made, the title
passes immediately. When a sale on credit is made, the

title passes immediately; the
buyer merely has an agreement as to the time when he
will pay for the goods. Ordinarily C.O.D. sales result in
a transfer of the title at the
time the goods are shipped;
the seller merely does not give
possession of the goods until
the charge has been paid.

When one buys something
on approval, the title does not
pass to him until the article
has been approved and an
acknowledgment of its accep-

The buyer need not accept delivery
if the seller violates his contract.

tance has either been given or implied.

In the case of installment sales in which the conditional
contract is used, there is really not a sale until all provisions of the contract have been fulfilled. The seller has a
right to reclaim the goods. If payments are not kept up,
the buyer may in that case lose what he has paid and may
even have to pay something extra if he does not fulfill the
provisions of the contract. When the provisions of the contract are fulfilled, the title then passes to the buyer.

In a sale subject to return, the title passes at the time
of the sale; but if the goods are returned, the title reverts
to the seller.

Remedies of the Seller. If the buyer of merchandise fails to perform his part of the contract, the seller may select any one of the following remedies:

(a) _Sue for payment_ (if the title has passed). When the buyer refuses or neglects to pay, the seller may sue for the price of the goods.

(b) _Sue for damages_ (if the title has not passed). When the buyer wrongfully refuses or neglects to accept and pay for the goods, the seller may sue for damages. The amount of damages will usually be the difference between the contract price and the market price.

(c) _Rescind the contract._ When the buyer repudiates the contract, or when he cannot perform the contract or fails to perform it, the seller is allowed, under most laws, to rescind the contract.

Remedies of the Buyer. If the seller fails to perform his obligations, the buyer has the choice of one of the following remedies:

(a) _Possession of the goods or the value of the goods_ (if the title has passed and payment has been made). When the seller wrongfully refuses or neglects to deliver the goods, the buyer may sue for the possession of the goods, for the recovery of the value that has been paid, or for damages.

(b) _Sue for damages_ (if the title has not passed). If the seller wrongfully refuses or neglects to deliver the goods, the buyer is entitled to damages for nondelivery. The amount of the damages is ordinarily the difference between the contract price and the market price at the time and the place of delivery. The amount may also include any other damages for loss resulting from the failure to fulfill the contract.

(c) _Insist upon the fulfillment of the contract._ The buyer has the right to sue for specific performance if damages will not be adequate compensation or if they cannot be computed. When the buyer sues for specific performance and wins the case, the seller is ordered by the court to carry out the original contract.

(d) *Refuse to accept goods.* If the seller has broken his part of the contract or in any way has failed to carry out his part of the contract, the buyer may refuse to accept delivery of the goods or may return them if delivered. If damages have resulted, he may also sue for damages.

Goods Not Ordered. You do not have to accept goods that you have not ordered. Some firms and other organizations follow a practice of sending unsolicited merchandise in the hope that persons receiving them will send a remittance. If you receive such a package, you may refuse to accept it, you may return it, or you may hold it subject to whatever the sender wishes to do with it. However, you must not use the merchandise or in any way indicate an acceptance of it unless you intend to pay for it. On the other hand, if you are in the habit of receiving and accepting such merchandise, you may be responsible unless you return it or notify the sender that you do not accept it.

Goods Entrusted to Other Persons. If you leave an automobile with the City Garage for repairs, the City Garage may hold the automobile if it wishes until you have paid the bill. This claim against the car is referred to as a *mechanic's lien.* If you send clothing to a laundry and it is damaged, you have a claim against the laundry for the damage. If an automobile is entrusted to a garage or a parking lot for safekeeping, the garage or parking lot is responsible for its safekeeping. This is especially true if you are given a parking ticket that is a receipt for your car and if you are required to leave the keys in the car so that it can be moved. However, if you regularly place your own car in a lot without an attendant and take the keys with you, the operator of the parking lot is generally not liable.

If you rent or borrow an article, such as a lawn mower, you are responsible for taking reasonable care of it to prevent damage or theft. Likewise, if you take a lawn mower to a repairman and he damages it in the process of repairing it, he is liable because he is expected to exercise reasonable care and skill.

The operator of a parking lot is responsible for the safekeeping
of your automobile.

Generally speaking, people who accept the property of
others are responsible for it. On the other hand, if a neighbor brings you some jewelry and asks you to keep it while
he is gone on a vacation, you are not responsible for its
loss or theft if you exercise reasonable care over it.

Use Legal Advice. In this world of specialization it is
sound practice for one to go to a doctor when he is ill. Likewise, it is sound business procedure to obtain competent legal
advice on important problems. Some of the problems on
which an individual should consult a lawyer are the writing of an important contract, the writing of a will, and
protection against law suits. In selecting a lawyer, one
should be careful to avoid the so-called shyster who is often
too eager to take a case or who solicits a case. It is a practice among reputable lawyers to wait for the client to request legal counsel. Only lawyers who are members of the
local or state bar association should be considered. When
in doubt, ask the advice of some reputable businessman or
consult a member of the local legal aid society.

85

TEXTBOOK QUESTIONS

1. What is a contract?
2. Give the essential elements of a contract.
3. What are the three essential characteristics of an offer?
4. What evidence may there be that the buyer has accepted the goods?
5. How may offers be terminated?
6. What is an option?
7. Name some items that can serve as the basis for a valid contract with a minor.
8. Name some types of persons who are generally not competent to make a contract.
9. Give an example of a bargain that is not legal because of the subject of the contract.
10. Explain the difference between a promise and a consideration in relation to a contract.
11. What types of contracts usually must be written to be enforceable?
12. What is meant by an implied contract?
13. Give at least three good reasons for putting important contracts in writing.
14. Give an example of a voidable contract.
15. What is a warranty?
16. If there is a breach of warranty, what recourses are open to the buyer?
17. If a buyer of merchandise fails to perform his part of the contract, what possible remedies does the seller have?
18. If a seller fails to perform his obligations, what may the buyer do to protect himself?
19. If you are sent merchandise on approval which you have not ordered and which you do not want, what may you do with the merchandise?
20. What is your responsibility if you borrow something from a friend?
21. If a repairman loses or damages an article left with him for repair, what is his responsibility?

DISCUSSION QUESTIONS

1. Why will a court not enforce an agreement that has an unlawful purpose?
2. When is an oral contract as binding as a written contract?
3. From the study of this chapter why is it apparent that one should consult a lawyer to handle important legal problems?

4. Mr. Jacobs insists that he will not fulfill a contract because he did not know all the terms of the contract when he signed it. His reason for not having read the contract carefully is that he finds it difficult to read fine print. He admits, however, that the signature on the contract is genuine. Is there anything he can do to avoid fulfilling the contract?

5. You are given a sales demonstration in a store. During the demonstration the salesman tells you many ways in which his product is better than some other product. Later you find that what he has told you is not true. (a) Do his statements constitute fraud? (b) Have you any legal basis for returning the merchandise and demanding your money?

6. You received through the mail some literature with samples of cloth from which shirts are made. You test the cloth in various ways, including washing it and counting the threads in each square inch. You keep these samples and order five of the shirts for $12.50. When the shirts are delivered, you find that they are poorly tailored and that the cloth does not seem to be like that in the samples. One of the shirts is worn and then washed. It fades badly. Then you count the threads in each square inch and find that the cloth is actually inferior to that in the samples. What recourses have you?

7. Besides the examples given in your textbook, can you describe an agreement that is void?

PROBLEMS

1. Write a simple contract between you and someone else, in which you agree to perform some task.

2. Mrs. Smith bought a dress in Mr. Jones's store on the strength of his statement that it was colorfast and would not shrink. There was no label on the garment to this effect and no written agreement; but when she first laundered the dress, the color faded and the garment shrank. She took it back and demanded her money. Did Mrs. Smith receive a warranty from Mr. Jones and had she any basis for a legal claim?

3. On April 3, Mr. Ladley made a legal offer by mail to sell Mr. Moore a house and lot for $7,000, $4,000 to be paid in cash upon the acceptance of the offer. On April 6 Mr. Moore mailed a letter to Mr. Ladley and enclosed a certified check for $4,000. The letter was delivered on April 10. On April 7 Mr. Ladley decided to withdraw the offer because he thought that the value of the property had increased. He wrote Mr. Moore withdrawing the offer. When Mr. Ladley received the check, he refused to accept it and returned it, claiming that the offer had been withdrawn. Mr. Moore brought a suit

for breach of contract. Do you think Mr. Ladley had broken a contract?

4. Mrs. Allison bought a dress from the Elite Dress Shop on the assurance of a salesperson that the dress would make her look slender. She was satisfied with it when she tried it on in the store; but when she got home, other members of her family assured her that it did not make her look slender. Was the statement of the clerk a warranty and does Mrs. Allison have any legal basis for damages or can she force the store to accept the return of the goods?

COMMUNITY PROBLEMS AND PROJECTS

1. An insurance policy is a contract. Obtain a policy at home, study it, and report on some of the agreements that you find in the contract.

2. Obtain one or more textbooks on business law and read all you can about warranties. Then write a report in your own nontechnical language as to your interpretation of different kinds of warranties and all their applications.

3. From some merchandise obtain a warranty or a guarantee and report on your findings as to how good it is and just what the agreement is.

PART III

CONSUMER PROTECTION

Chapter 6

Government Agencies That Aid and Protect You

Purpose of the Chapter. A prime purpose of any government is to protect its people from exploitation and to secure their maximum welfare. Any government does this to some extent, if only through laws against fraud. But as specific problems arise to plague consumers, our government also adds special provisions to help solve the problems. Hence, there are many Federal laws, state laws, and local ordinances that have been established for the primary purpose of protecting the consumer. Some laws have been established primarily to assure fair trade practices in business; these also protect the consumer. You cannot put out a fire with a modern fire extinguisher unless you know how to use it; likewise, government services and protection will not be of much benefit to you unless you know how to use them. The purpose of this chapter is to explain the various laws and agencies that aid and protect the consumer and also to help you use these services intelligently.

United States Department of Commerce

Benefits to the Consumer. The primary purpose of the United States Department of Commerce is to serve business. It publishes regularly information on production, sales, and prices. This information is of interest also to the consumer because it keeps him informed about the supply, the consumption, and the prices of the items that he needs. One of the most important activities of the Department is, however, the operation of the National Bureau of Standards, the functions of which are explained in the following paragraphs.

89

National Bureau of Standards. The functions of the Bureau of Standards that are of particular interest to the consumer are those that pertain to (a) the making of tests, (b) the establishment of standards, and (c) the control of weights and measures. The Bureau helps the consumer indirectly in many ways.

Federal Specifications. One of the first functions of the Bureau of Standards has been to establish minimum requirements for goods bought in various Federal departments. These are called Federal Specifications; they are prepared for hundreds of commodities. This function in itself has had an influence on the general standard of products offered for sale to the public. Most of the important national associations in industry co-operate with the Bureau of Standards in drawing up the specifications. The standards established by the Bureau do not necessarily correspond to those established by national associations, although they usually do.

The Bureau publishes a list of producers who are willing to certify that their goods meet the Federal specifications. This list is not distributed widely but is sent to anyone upon request. The manufacturers whose names appear on the list signify their willingness to certify to purchasers, upon request, that the goods offered for sale by them are guaranteed to comply with the minimum standards and the tests established by the National Bureau of Standards. These manufacturers have the privilege of mentioning this certification in their advertising and of using it on their trade-marks and labels. The Bureau encourages manufacturers to adopt a distinguishing mark by which the purchaser will know that he is obtaining a product that measures up to the standards of the Bureau.

The standardization phase of the Bureau's activities may be summarized as follows:

(a) To bring commodity specifications of the United States Government to the attention of producers.
(b) To list the "willing-to-certify" producers for the benefit of the producers and for the benefit of consumers who request the list.

National Bureau of Standards
The Bureau of Standards tests paints.

(c) To furnish all tax-supported institutions with copies of the list of "willing-to-certify" producers.

It is therefore possible for a prospective purchaser, large or small, to obtain from the Bureau of Standards an analysis of the standard specifications for most products and a list of producers from whom products with these specifications can be obtained. However, this arrangement is more useful to large buyers than to ordinary consumers, for writing for the lists and finding out which products meet the standards involves considerable work.

Tests. The Bureau of Standards will make tests of products submitted by individual manufacturers and associations. It will also co-operate with manufacturers and associations in conducting research designed to establish standards and better processes of manufacture.

The following classes of testing activity are within the scope of the National Bureau of Standards, but are subject to the judgment of the director:

(a) Fundamental tests for the National Government and state governments, or such tests to aid science, industry, or the general public.

National Bureau of Standards

The Bureau of Standards tests hosiery.

    (b) Routine tests including the certification of weights, measures, materials, and devices, provided the work does not compete with that of commercial laboratories.

    (c) Referee tests or investigations to settle disputes when private laboratories are unable to agree.

    (d) Co-operative tests, the results of which are desired by the Bureau and other government agencies.

    (e) Tests of products submitted by individual manufacturers and associations.

    (f) Tests in conducting research, designed to establish standards and better processes of manufacture in co-operation with manufacturers and associations.

Under the policies of the Bureau the following tests are not permissible:

    (a) Investigations of secret processes.

    (b) Tests of inadequately described materials.

    (c) Assays, analyses, and tests of methods already standard, for which private laboratories are equipped.

(d) Unnecessary tests that cause duplication of work.
(e) Tests that have as their primary object sales promotion.

Simplification. Another important function in the establishing of standards has been to eliminate unnecessary variations in size, grade, color, shape, and nomenclature of products. The standardization of the sizes of bricks and bolts is a good example.

Labels. To carry the benefits over to the ordinary consumer, the Bureau of Standards is encouraging the use of self-certifying labels. On these labels the manufacturer states that his goods meet the Federal specifications or commercial standards. The use of such labels is entirely voluntary. The values that accrue to the consumer as a result of this labeling are as follows:

(a) It identifies a product that has been manufactured under recognized standards.
(b) It gives the over-the-counter buyer the same advantages as large-quantity buyers, who have their own laboratories and trained purchasing staffs.
(c) It encourages other producers to comply with these specifications and standards.

How the Consumer Is Benefited. As a final summary of the activities of the Bureau of Standards, let us see how the consumer is benefited. The consumer is benefited by the standards that are set up, because products are improved and high-grade products are made easier to identify. The consumer is benefited through testing and research, which result in improvement of products. Since standardization and simplification cut the costs of production and distribution, consumers benefit by lower prices.

United States Department of Agriculture

Standard Grades for Canned Foods. The Secretary of Agriculture has the right to designate the grading standards for canned foods above the minimum standards. These standards are generally designated as Grade A, Grade B, Grade C. Standards have been established for such farm products as corn, peas, beans, and tomatoes, and they are being extended to other foods. As standards are established for additional canned foods, the information can be obtained from the United States Department of Agriculture. The use of these grade designations is voluntary; but if they are used, the canned foods must conform to the standards established by the United States Department of Agriculture.

It should be observed that packers of canned fruits and vegetables may independently grade their own products A, B, or C; but if they do, their products must measure up to the standards. A food product may bear the "official" Federal grades only if it has been packed under the continuous inspection of the Agricultural Marketing Service. The packer is then entitled to use a seal such as that shown in the illustration at the left, which states: "Packed under continuous inspection of Agricultural Marketing Service U. S. Dept. of Agriculture."

Part of a label showing an official Federal grade.

Individual consumers may obtain a more direct advantage of this grading service on any can of fruits or vegetables. Under this plan the consumer may submit a can of food for grading for a stipulated fee. Specific buying guides in regard to packaged foods are discussed in Chapter 12.

Milk Grading. There are a great many grades of milk on the market. There may sometimes be as many as five or six in one city. The same quality of milk may even be sold at different prices, because consumers are not aware of the difference. As the handling cost of low- and high-grade milk is exactly the same, the difference in cost should be only the additional amount paid the producer for better milk. Milk of the highest grade should be lowest in bacterial content and highest in percentage of butter fat. The housewife has a right to demand that milk be labeled to show the bacterial content and the percentage of butter fat. The Department of Agriculture has authority, under the Food, Drug, and Cosmetic Act, to establish a single basic standard of quality of milk. The use of grade designations for milk is voluntary; but when they are used, they must conform to the standards of quality established by the United States Department of Agriculture.

There are four grades of raw milk. The highest grade of raw milk is *certified raw*. The three most common grades of raw milk are A, B, and C. The highest grade of pasteurized milk is *certified pasteurized*. The most common grades are designated as A, B, and C. The main functions of grading milk are performed by the United States Public Health Service of the Department of the Treasury. The use of these grades is promoted by encouraging local communities to adopt a milk ordinance based upon the standards recommended by the United States Public Health Service.

Meat Inspection and Grading. From the previous discussion it is evident that the United States Department of Agriculture protects the consumer from unfit, adulterated, and misbranded goods when these are sold in interstate commerce. The grade labeling of some foods is optional; but as there is a tendency on the part of consumers to demand grade labeling, they eventually can obtain more foods with grade labels.

In the case of meats there are two possible types of labeling performed by Federal inspectors of the United States

Consumers' Guide

A product inspected by the U. S. Department of Agriculture.

Department of Agriculture. The first is an inspection stamp. All meat coming from a plant that sells in interstate commerce must bear the meat inspector's purple "Inspected and Passed" stamp to indicate that the meat is safe for consumption. This certificate does not, however, indicate whether the meat is tender or tough, old or young.

In addition, meat may be graded by Federal graders on a quality basis. Grading is optional on the part of the packer. If he uses the service, he must pay for it. The quality stamps are used in addition to the meat inspector's purple stamp. Turkeys and some other poultry are graded and marked when they are packed. Tags are put on the box or on the leg of the fowl in such a manner that they cannot be removed and changed. This service is being used in many of the large cities, and its use is being extended.

Butter. The Federal Government, through the United States Department of Agriculture, controls the minimum quality of butter that is sold in interstate commerce. The Federal law requires that, besides being pure and unadulterated as under other food regulations, butter must contain at least 80 per cent butter fat.

Even with this minimum standard for butter, it is natural that butter will differ widely in quality. Therefore, a producer or distributor of butter may use the optional Federal grading standard. Butter with a score of 92 or 93 is considered top grade. When a producer or distributor does not sell in interstate commerce, he may use different standards for the butter and a different means of grade labeling.

Eggs. Standards have also been established for eggs. Eggs are graded on the basis of type, size, color, and freshness. The table on page 162 (Chapter 9), illustrates the various grades of eggs. The inspection and grading of eggs are not so general as those for meat, but if they carry a Federal grade marking, they have been inspected by a representative of the United States Department of Agriculture.

Grading of eggs can be made more widespread if consumers insist upon it. Various states also have many different grading systems for eggs. It is because of this diversity of grading systems that the Federal standards are about the only ones that have an understandable meaning.

Margarine. There are Federal laws governing the manufacture and the sale of margarine, which is technically referred to as oleomargarine. Margarine is made principally from vegetable or animal fats, usually in combination with skim milk, and fortified with not less than 9,000 U.S.P. units of Vitamin A a pound and sometimes with Vitamin D added. Manufacturers are permitted to use a certain specified amount of harmless preservative, but it must be indicated on the label. It may be colored, either through the natural color of the oil or by artificial coloring (except in states that prohibit artificial coloring). Salt is added as in butter. The finished product must contain not less than 80 per cent fat.

As a food product, margarine has been discriminated against by certain agricultural groups, although its food value is unquestioned by technical experts. It is subject to Federal inspection in manufacture to a greater extent than is butter. It can be reasonably assumed that any margarine that is sold meets the minimum standards established for this product.

Fresh Fruits and Vegetables. The Agricultural Marketing Service maintains an inspection and grading service for fresh fruits and vegetables sold in wholesale lots. The grades are marked on the wholesale packages and sometimes appear on the individual retail cartons. Because most fruits and vegetables are sold in small quantities in retail stores, there often is little opportunity for the consumer to observe government grades. However, if the foods are still in the original shipping containers, grades will often be found marked on the containers.

Even though the consumer may not have access to grade designations on fruits and vegetables, the government grading procedure helps the consumer by helping the wholesaler and retailer. Since the wholesaler and retailer are in a position to buy intelligently by grades, packers and shippers are inclined to be more careful in shipping these foods so that they do meet government standards.

Other Functions. The United States Department of Agriculture administers several other acts that are of particular interest to the consumer.

The Tea Act and the Import Milk Act are concerned mainly with the wholesomeness of tea and milk. Standards of quality regulate the importation and the sale of these foods. The Insecticide Act is concerned mainly with the quality and the effectiveness of insecticides, fungicides, turpentine, and resin. When these products are sold in interstate commerce, they must meet the requirements of the Act and must be labeled accordingly.

Under the annual Appropriation Act, the Department of Agriculture is granted the authority to provide grading standards for various farm products, such as cotton and wheat, that are sold in interstate commerce. This grading of farm products refers to large-scale marketing.

Federal Trade Commission

Functions. The Federal Trade Commission Act is the outgrowth of a demand for protection of competitors by the prevention of unfair methods of competition. The protection of the consumer was not originally the express purpose of the Act, although the consumer did benefit indirectly. An analysis of the decisions of the Commission shows that the consumer, as well as business, is protected. The original Federal Trade Commission Act provided only "that unfair methods of competition in commerce are hereby declared unlawful." Subsequent revision of the law and additional acts pertaining to the Federal Trade Commission provide that "unfair methods of competition in commerce and unfair or deceptive acts or practices in commerce are hereby declared unlawful." Hence it is not necessary for competition to be involved in order for an act or practice to come under the jurisdiction of the Federal Trade Commission.

Complaints. Any person, partnership, corporation, or association may apply to the Federal Trade Commission with a request for that body to act in respect to any violation of law over which the Federal Trade Commission has jurisdiction. Such an application, in the form of a complaint, must be in writing and signed by or on behalf of the person making the complaint. It should contain a short and simple statement of the facts in regard to the alleged violation of law, giving the name and the address of the person making the complaint and of the person against whom the complaint is being filed. Some of the causes for complaint are adulteration, mislabeling, false advertising, misleading selling schemes, selling refinished goods as new, selling imitations of products, or otherwise misrepresenting an article to the extent that an individual or a competitor has been misled or damaged.

Assume, for instance, that Mrs. Jackson buys at her drugstore a cosmetic that makes some claims on the label or in the advertising which she feels are misleading. She has the right to register a complaint with the Federal Trade Commission and to ask for an investigation.

Reports. A study of the weekly releases and the annual reports of the Federal Trade Commission will give an idea of the unfair trade practices that have come to the attention of the Federal Trade Commission. The reports of action taken by the Federal Trade Commission are published annually. They cover misbranding, false advertising, unfair competition, and many other violations that affect not only consumers but also competitors in business.

Federal Control of Advertising. The Wheeler-Lea Act, which became effective on March 21, 1938, as an amendment to the Federal Trade Commission Act, provides for Federal jurisdiction over false advertising. Among other forms of control, that amendment provides for the following, which are significant to the consumer:

(a) In general, all unfair methods of competition in commerce, as well as unfair or deceptive acts or practices, are declared unlawful.

(b) It is unlawful to disseminate false advertising in order to induce purchases of foods, drugs, devices, or cosmetics.
(c) Publishers, radio broadcasters, advertising agencies, and other advertising mediums are relieved from liability under the Federal Trade Commission Act unless they refuse to furnish the Commission with the name and the address of the manufacturer, packer, distributor, seller, or advertising agency that has caused the dissemination of such advertisements.
(d) False advertising is defined as being "misleading in a material respect," including the failure to reveal facts as to consequences that may result from the use of the advertised commodities.

Disapproved Advertising. The preceding discussion has mentioned various types of unscrupulous advertising. The following represent types of advertising that are reported by the Federal Trade Commission as meeting with its disapproval:

Patent medicines for incurable diseases.
Appliances for the correction and the cure of bodily deformities.
Anti-fat remedies.
Hair restorers.
Lotions, creams, and various other toilet preparations, advertised as capable of making impossible improvement in personal appearance.
So-called puzzle advertisements that offer valuable inducements.
Advertisements soliciting manuscripts and articles on which a copyright or a patent may be obtained.
Lottery schemes disguised in countless ways.
Matrimonial advertisements.

Wool Products Labeling. Under a law passed in 1939, entitled Wool Products Labeling Act, the Federal Trade Commission was given jurisdiction over the labeling of all wool products sold in interstate commerce. Under this specific law it is unlawful to misbrand wool products. Each wool product must be identified with a stamp, tag, or label giving specific information as to the actual fiber content of the materials used in the garment. The term *wool product* means any product or any portion of a product that contains or is represented to contain wool, reprocessed wool, or re-used wool. The specific definitions of terms that must be used on the label are as follows:

(a) The term *wool* means the fiber from the fleece of the sheep or lamb or hair of the Angora or Cashmere goat (and may include the so-called specialty fibers from the hair of the camel, alpaca, llama, and vicuna) which has never been reclaimed from any woven or felted wool product.

(b) The term *reprocessed wool* means the resulting fiber when wool has been woven or felted into a wool product which, without ever having been utilized in any way by the ultimate consumer, subsequently has been made into a fibrous state.

(c) The term *re-used wool* means the resulting fiber when wool or reprocessed wool has been spun, woven, knitted, or felted into a wool product which, after having been used in any way by the ultimate consumer, subsequently has been made into a fibrous state.

The label must also indicate whether the fabric has been loaded or weighted with a chemical or adulterated in any way. It must bear the name of the manufacturer or the name of the distributor or retailer.

Codes of Fair Practice. The Federal Trade Commission has authority to organize conferences within industries for the purpose of establishing rules of fair trade practice. More than one hundred fifty industries are now operating under sets of rules established in this manner. The conference is usually called at the request of the industry, but it may be called by the Federal Trade Commission. Consumers are included in the conference. After rules have been set up and approved by the Federal Trade Commission, they, in a sense, become a sort of law of that industry pertaining to fair competition. The rules are of two types: (a) Those that become the basis of legal action and that the Federal Trade Commission will enforce; and

(b) those that members of the industry agree to follow but that remain optional. It will be seen that those in the first group really become laws. Those in the second group are not really laws, but they are very influential in the industry.

Robinson-Patman Act. In 1936 an act was passed by the Federal Congress entitled the Robinson-Patman Anti-Discrimination Act. This law supplements the Federal Trade Commission Act by specifically making unlawful certain trade practices. Under this act it is unlawful for a manufacturer, wholesaler, or any other type of distributor to discriminate among his customers as regards price, discount, or services. For instance, it is not lawful for a manufacturer to sell to one distributor at a lower price than he does to another, provided the conditions of the sale are the same. One of the purposes of this law was to prevent unusual discounts from being given to one customer when another might be required to pay the standard price.

Fair Trade Laws. Various attempts have been made by the Federal Government and by the various state governments to establish laws that would prevent retailers from cutting prices on popular merchandise for the purpose of attracting people into their stores to buy this well-known merchandise at bargain prices. The practice of price cutting on popular branded merchandise has been injurious to the manufacturer because some stores will not sell such merchandise.

The Miller-Tydings Act of 1937 (Federal) and special laws in all but three states permitted retail prices to be fixed and maintained by manufacturers under certain conditions. Many nationally-known brands of merchandise were sold at these so-called "fair trade" prices. In May, 1951, the United States Supreme Court declared one of these state laws unconstitutional. The result has been to make all similar laws ineffective or void. Therefore, retail prices of manufacturers are generally being ignored. Certain types of price-cutting, however, are illegal as explained in the next topic.

Unfair Trade Acts. Approximately thirty states still have laws that prohibit merchants from selling at or below cost as a means of bait advertising to attract customers.

Some Prohibited Activities. The previous discussion has pointed out in a general way certain types of acts that are prohibited under the laws administered by the Federal Trade Commission. Most of these prohibited acts can be summarized as follows:

(1) Any act that restrains trade.

(2) Any monopolies except those specifically authorized by law, such as public utilities.

(3) Horizontal price fixing, such as agreements among competitors to fix prices.

(4) Agreements among competitors to divide territory, earnings, or profits.

(5) Gaining control over the supply of any commodity in order to create an artificial scarcity.

(6) False or misleading advertising.

(7) Imitation of trade-mark or trade name.

(8) Price discrimination.

(9) In some states, selling goods below cost as bait advertising.

(10) Pretending to sell at a discount when actually there is no reduction in price.

(11) Offering so-called "free" merchandise with a purchase when actually the price of the article sold has been raised to compensate for the "free" merchandise.

(12) Misrepresentation as to the quality, the composition, or the place of origin of a product.

(13) Selling secondhand or reclaimed merchandise as new merchandise.

The Federal Food and Drug Administration

Food, Drug, and Cosmetic Act. As the Federal Food, Drug, and Cosmetic Act is a Federal law, it is effective only when products sold cross state lines. It is the most important single law benefiting consumers.

The law specifically prohibits the following acts that are of particular interest to the consumer:

(a) The introduction or the delivery for introduction into interstate commerce of any food, drug, device, or cosmetic that is adulterated or misbranded.

(b) The adulteration or the misbranding of any food, drug, device, or cosmetic in interstate commerce.

(c) The receipt in interstate commerce of any food, drug, device, or cosmetic that is adulterated or misbranded, and the delivery or the proffered delivery thereof.

(d) The giving of a guarantee that is false.

(e) The alteration, mutilation, destruction, obliteration, or removal of the whole or any part of the labeling of, or the doing of any other act with respect to, a food, drug, device, or cosmetic, if such act is done while the article is held for sale after shipment in interstate commerce and results in the article being misbranded.

Under this act poisonous cosmetics may be barred from interstate traffic; but certain cosmetics, such as hair dyes, that contain coloring that may cause irritation may be sold if they are marked with the proper warnings.

Any food that is injurious to health is barred from interstate commerce. Unsafe amounts of harmful ingredients may not be added to any food product. The Law makes it mandatory that harmful sprays on fruits and vegetables be thoroughly washed off before shipments of the products may cross state lines. Any type of food that may be contaminated during the process of manufacture or packing may be subjected to regulation and licensing by the Secretary of Agriculture in order to assure its wholesomeness.

The Law permits the Food and Drug Administration to set minimum "standards of identity" for foods after conducting public hearings. That is, for each commonly named food, it can write a definition with minimum standards. Only foods meeting these standards can be marketed under that name. Foods that do not meet the standards, but that are clean and wholesome, may be marketed but must be labeled "substandard." Even these must meet all standards of sanitation and nutrition.

Strict control is granted over all forms of drugs and healing devices so that they will be labeled properly and

Dough for bread that will be sold in another state is subject to inspection by the Food and Drug Administration.

will be free from false and fraudulent claims. All drug labels must bear adequate directions for use, as well as adequate warnings. The label on a nonofficial drug (a patent medicine) must declare the common name of the drug if there is one, the name of each active ingredient, and the quantity or proportion of each of a specified list of ingredients named in the Law. A drug that may be subject to deterioration must be marked accordingly on the label. New drugs intended for interstate sale must be examined and approved by the Federal Food and Drug Administration before the drugs can be sold.

Judgments. The Food and Drug Administration of the United States Department of Agriculture regularly issues Notices of Judgments against manufacturers and distributors. These judgments are issued as a result of inspections that disclose misbranding, adulteration, or impure foods. For instance, tomato catsup may be condemned if it contains excessive mold or if it is found to contain artificial coloring that is not indicated on the label. Anyone may have his name placed on the mailing list to receive these Notices of Judgment.

Other Public Agencies

United States Department of Labor. The Bureau of Labor Statistics collects and publishes regularly data in regard to retail prices, wholesale prices, employment, wages, hours of work, and cost of living. It also publishes information that is helpful in the operation of consumer co-operatives.

The Children's Bureau is of particular interest to parents. It provides literature on the health and the care of the family and is in a position to give advice on the problems of parents.

United States Post Office Department. The inspectors of the United States Post Office Department are constantly checking fraudulent schemes that operate through the mail. Certain classes of mail may be opened for inspection, but first-class mail may not be opened except with the authority of a search warrant issued by a court. If fraudulent letters are sent through the mail, the complaint must therefore be taken to court to provide authority for searching through any other letters of a similar kind. You may, for instance, be invited through the mail to get in on the ground floor of some new business venture. You may be offered an opportunity to invest your money so that you will earn five times your investment in the first year. If you are confined to your home because of a physical handicap, you may be invited to do work at home and thus "get rich quick." Such schemes as these are investigated by the postal inspectors.

The Federal postal laws prevent lotteries through the mail. *Lottery* is a scheme or game of chance. For example, it is illegal to sell horse race betting tickets through the mail or to sell chances on any merchandise, whether the profits are for charitable purposes or for private profit.

The protection of the United States Post Office Department is limited because (a) much damage can be done before someone complains and the post office inspectors investigate a particular case, and (b) slowness and tediousness mark the procedure before post office inspectors can open mail. Furthermore, this protection does not cover any frauds except those that go through the mail.

However, the system is sure, even if slow, and the penalties are high. In the fifty-odd years of its operation, the Postal Frauds unit has saved consumers billions of dollars.

Securities and Exchange Commission. The most important Federal legislation with regard to security transactions consists of three laws: the Securities Act of 1933, the Securities Exchange Act of 1934, and the Public Utility Holding Company Act of 1935. These are administered by the Securities and Exchange Commission. The general purposes of the legislation are:

(a) To require the public disclosure of information indicating the true worth of securities offered for sale to the public.
(b) To penalize those who offer securities for sale through fraud and misrepresentation.
(c) To place definite duties upon persons who sell securities.

A company that wishes to register a security and offer it for sale must file an application with the Securities and Exchange Commission. The general statement that is filed must provide the following information:

(a) Name of the company.
(b) State and county under the laws of which the company was organized.
(c) Address of the main office.
(d) Names of the directors and officers.
(e) Character of business actually transacted.
(f) Articles of organization.
(g) Complete information on capitalization.
(h) Complete information on indebtedness.

In addition to this information, the applicant must file specific answers to detailed questions about the particular security that is to be offered for sale. The information must cover the amount and the kind of stock, the various provisions and stipulations in the stock, the sales price, the commissions, the expenses of issuing the stock, the financial statements, and detailed information with regard to all contracts and legal obligations of the company.

The Federal Registration Law places limitations on a prospectus that may be used in making sales through interstate commerce or through the mails. A *prospectus* is a notice, circular, letter, or radio communication that offers a security for sale. The Securities and Exchange Commission has the right to pass upon any prospectus that a company proposes to use. For the public interest or for the protection of investors, it may order the omission of any information or statements that are considered not necessary or not appropriate. The Commission, on the other hand, may require information to be added that it thinks is necessary or appropriate to the public interest or for the protection of investors.

Federal legislation does not, however, apply to securities that are not sold on registered exchanges or in interstate commerce. These securities are therefore subject only to the laws of states in which they are issued and sold. They are not even subject to the regulations of local stock exchanges unless they are registered on those exchanges.

State Regulation of Securities. The laws of the various states with regard to selling securities are not uniform, but the provisions in many cases are the same. These laws, designed to protect investors from fraudulent schemes for selling securities, are commonly referred to as *blue-sky laws*.

Some states require a public listing of security announcements, whereas others do not. The laws of some states are similar in various respects to the Federal laws regulating the issuing of securities. The laws of every state have provisions against fraud. The Federal and state laws are supplemented by the rules and regulations of local stock exchanges and brokerage concerns.

In each state a designated state officer or department handles applications for the listing of securities. When securities are submitted for state listing, the same general information is required as in submitting them for Federal listing. To ensure the safety of the investment, some states stipulate what percentage of the proceeds from the sale of securities must go to the company that issues the securities. For instance, the state of Ohio stipulates that not less than 85 per cent of the proceeds from the sale of securities must go to the issuer.

Many states require dealers of securities to submit prospectuses and advertisements for approval before distribution. Others require merely the official listing of a sample of all promotional literature. For instance, some states specify that a copy of every prospectus or advertisement regarding a security must be sent promptly by registered mail to the state officer or department in charge of securities. If any piece of literature is not approved, the dealer can be restrained from using it, and in case of fraud is subject to prosecution and the loss of his license. This provision is for the protection of investors.

Public Health Service. The Public Health Service is a part of the function of the Department of the Treasury. The principal activity is the prevention of disease and the protection of health. Close co-operation is provided with medical, dental, nursing, and other social service groups, and with schools and governmental bodies of states, counties, and cities. For instance, one of the activities of the Public Health Service has been to set up standards for milk and to promote the adoption of a standard milk ordinance in cities. This Service deals largely with groups rather than with individuals.

State and City Protection. In some states laws have been set up for grading the quality of such items as fruits and vegetables. Many states and cities have set up regulations for controlling the quality of milk and other foods sold in local markets. The health departments of those states and cities require products to measure up to specified standards. Most cities require the regular inspection of scales and measures. Many other local regulations tend to protect the consumer.

CITY OF CINCINNATI
DEPARTMENT OF SAFETY
PUMP
EXAMINED AND SEALED
I. VAN CLEEFF,
Supt. Markets, Weights, Measures
Office, Sixth and Plum Sts.   Market House
Phone CHerry 5300, Line 303   Cincinnati, O.

A city inspector's seal.

Public Testing Departments. The testing departments of cities, counties, states, and universities provide an important means of protection to the consumer, even though this means of protection may be rather indirect. Any agency that makes tests and sets up standards usually causes producers to attempt to meet those standards, even though there is no law requiring such action. In some cities, counties, and states there are definite testing departments that are used to judge the quality of goods which, being sold locally, do not come under the jurisdiction of the Federal Government. Local laws and ordinances frequently place restrictions on such perishable foods as milk, fruit, and eggs. If a dealer does not live up to the standards of the law, the consumer has recourse to the proper local authority, to whom he may complain.

Many of our leading colleges and universities maintain laboratories that are used for testing materials and foods brought to them by consumers and by business concerns. Most of the reports are confidential and are available only to the person or the business that requested the test on a product.

State Control of Advertising. There are numerous state laws that represent barriers against dishonest advertising. Probably the most famous law is the *Printers' Ink* Model Statute. The following is the Model Statute:

Any person, firm, corporation or association who, with intent to sell or in any wise dispose of merchandise, securities, service, or anything offered by such person, firm, corporation or association, directly or indirectly, to the public for sale or distribution, or with intent to increase the consumption thereof, or to induce the public in any manner to enter into any obligation relating thereto, or to acquire title thereto, or an interest therein, makes, publishes, disseminates, circulates, or places before the public, or causes, directly or indirectly, to be made, published, disseminated, circulated, or placed before the public, in this State, in a newspaper or other publication, or in the form of a book, notice, handbill, poster, bill, circular, pamphlet, or letter, or in any other way, an advertisement of any sort regarding merchandise, securities, service, or anything so offered to the public, which advertisement contains any assertion, representation or statement of fact which is untrue, deceptive or misleading, shall be guilty of a misdemeanor.

A public testing laboratory.

The following twenty-six states and the District of Columbia have adopted it:

Alabama	Iowa	Nebraska	Oregon
Colorado	Kansas	Nevada	Rhode Island
District of	Kentucky	New Jersey	Virginia
Columbia	Louisiana	New York	Washington
Idaho	Michigan	North Dakota	West Virginia
Illinois	Minnesota	Ohio	Wisconsin
Indiana	Missouri	Oklahoma	Wyoming

The following seventeen states have substitute laws patterned after the *Printers' Ink* Model Statute:

Arizona	Maryland	North Carolina	Tennessee
California	Massachusetts	Pennsylvania	Texas
Connecticut	Montana	South Carolina	Utah
Florida	New Hampshire	South Dakota	Vermont
Maine			

Generally there are qualifying phrases in the laws enacted in the various states. Furthermore, a survey made by *Printers' Ink* reveals that enforcement of the law is weak in many states and is almost totally lacking in some states.

A revision of the Model Statute has been prepared and is recommended to states as a substitute for the original. The revision is clearer in certain respects than the original and is more difficult to evade but has not yet been adopted widely.

TEXTBOOK QUESTIONS

1. What is meant by the list of manufacturers "Willing to Certify"?
2. What testing service is performed by the National Bureau of Standards?
3. What are the advantages that the consumer derives from the self-certifying labels?
4. Give a summary of all the benefits the consumer gets from the activities of the National Bureau of Standards.
5. (a) What are some of the canned farm products for which grades have been established? (b) What are these grades?
6. Does all milk conform to the standards recommended by the United States Public Health Service and bear the corresponding grade marks?
7. What two services does the Department of Agriculture perform in connection with meat that aid the consumer?
8. What is the minimum amount of butter fat that butter must contain if it is to be sold in interstate commerce and is to conform to government standards?
9. What is considered a good score for a high grade of butter?
10. On what factors are eggs graded?
11. How many units of Vitamin A and what percentage of fat must margarine contain?
12. (a) Why is it difficult for the consumer to take advantage of Federal grades on fresh fruits and vegetables? (b) How is it possible to detect these grades?
13. Is competition necessary in order for the Federal Trade Commission to take action in regard to unfair trade practices?
14. Who may file a complaint with the Federal Trade Commission?
15. In what way does the Federal Trade Commission have control over advertising?
16. Under the Wool Products Labeling Act, what does the term *wool* mean?
17. Name the two types of rules that are a part of the Codes of Fair Practice sponsored by the Federal Trade Commission.
18. What is the Robinson-Patman Act?
19. What is the Miller-Tydings Act?
20. What does the Federal Food, Drug, and Cosmetic Act specifically prohibit?
21. In what way does the United States control the sale of poisonous cosmetics?
22. What is meant by the setting up of "standards of identity" by the Food and Drug Administration?
23. How does the Federal Food, Drug, and Cosmetic Act affect the labeling of drugs?

24. Give an example of how the Food and Drug Administration may issue a judgment against a manufacturer or distributor.
25. What are the two functions of the United States Department of Labor that are of interest to consumers?
26. What is one of the main ways in which the United States Post Office Department protects consumers?
27. Do the regulations of the Securities and Exchange Commission apply to all security sales?
28. What are the so-called *blue-sky laws*?
29. What is the *Printers' Ink* Model Statute?

DISCUSSION QUESTIONS

1. How do the tests that are made by the National Bureau of Standards for individual manufacturers help all consumers?
2. In what way does the standardization program of the National Bureau of Standards help you as a buyer?
3. (a) How do the grading and inspection services of the Department of Agriculture aid the consumer? (b) How can you as an individual benefit from these services?
4. Do you think the standards set up by the Department of Agriculture for grading milk will help a local consumer of milk, even though there are no local laws with regard to milk? How?
5. Many local packers of meat utilize the inspection service of the Department of Agriculture although they are not required to do so. Why do you think they use this service?
6. On which would you place more reliance: an advertisement of a particular product, or the label on the product?
7. Assuming that you buy a product sold in interstate commerce on the basis of an advertisement in a magazine and find that the article does not conform to the quality or the description given in the advertisement, what means of protection do you have?
8. If a manufacturer of an article tells completely truthful facts in radio advertising of an article offered for sale but the article proves injurious to the consumer, is there any action that the consumer may take for his protection?
9. Formerly there were many advertisements of remedies that claimed to cure cancer and epilepsy. What do you think is the status of such advertising under recent laws?
10. (a) Is a garment labeled properly if the label on it states "100% wool" and it is made partly from reclaimed wool? (b) Is a garment labeled properly if the label states truthfully that it is made from 50 per cent reprocessed wool and 50 per cent re-used wool, but the lining is of rayon?

11. If you were a manufacturer, could you sell the same item to one customer for $1.50 and to another for $1.00 under the same conditions of sale?
12. In order to eliminate competition and cut down costs, two large wholesale hardware companies agree between themselves to divide the territory into two parts, one company covering one part and the other covering the second part. Is this permissible?

PROBLEMS

1. Read the labels on foods that are purchased during one entire week for use in your home. (a) List the specific information on the labels that indicates quality and contents. (b) Find out which foods measure up to government standards, and tabulate the standards that are indicated on the labels.
2. Examine the products in your medicine cabinet at home. Study the labels and find out whether the products comply with the regulations of the Federal Food, Drug, and Cosmetic Act. List under the name of each product the contents and the quality; whether or not artificial coloring or adulteration is present; and other similar facts.
3. From a magazine or a newspaper obtain an advertisement giving a rather complete description of a food, drug, cosmetic, or device. Analyze the advertisement to see whether it, in your opinion, violates the Federal law.

COMMUNITY PROBLEMS AND PROJECTS

1. Investigate the regulations in your community for maintaining the quality of milk. Write a report on the information that you have obtained and indicate how the consumer is aided by these regulations.
2. Investigate to see whether your state has any laws or regulations pertaining to the grading or labeling of eggs, and then check in local stores to see whether packaged eggs are sold under these grades or under Federal grades.
3. Obtain a copy of a report of a judgment rendered by the Food and Drug Administration of the Department of Agriculture. (a) Make a summary of the findings in a particular case involving a violation of the Food, Drug, and Cosmetic Act. (b) Report the benefits that accrued to businessmen and to consumers from this judgment.

Chapter 7

PART III _____

Private Agencies That Aid and Protect You

Purpose of the Chapter. Besides the government agencies that have been organized to serve the consumer, there are many private agencies. It is impossible to discuss in the short space of one chapter all the functions performed by such agencies. Nevertheless, every buyer should know something about the more important private agencies that can be relied upon for protection and guidance in buying. The purpose of this chapter is, therefore, to point out some of these agencies and to discuss their functions.

Better Business Bureau. The better business bureaus of the United States were originally organized to improve the quality of advertising by fighting unethical advertising. Today they are concerned with all unfair trade practices, but still concentrate their main efforts on advertising and promotional schemes. At one time they were more concerned with unfair competition, but now they fight against the unfair treatment of consumers.

One function of a local better business bureau is to check carefully the practices of local businesses in order to prevent any unfair trade practices. Standards are usually specified for truthful advertising and fair public relations. The local bureau also investigates the various promotional schemes of new businesses that enter the community. Some local better business bureaus conduct newspaper campaigns to warn people against fraud and deception. The illustration on page 116 shows examples of some of the warnings that are published regularly in local newspapers by the Cincinnati Better Business Bureau.

Many of these bureaus investigate soliciting schemes and promotional schemes. Anyone has the privilege of calling the local better business bureau for information and advice.

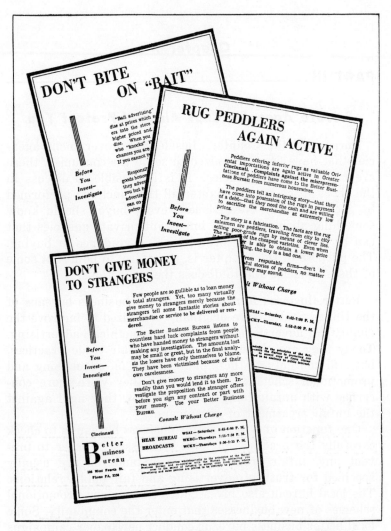

Warnings published by the Cincinnati Better Business Bureau.

In many communities the members of the bureau will not contribute to any soliciting scheme until it has been approved by the bureau. Consumers can protect themselves if they will get in touch with the bureau immediately whenever there is any question of an unfair trade practice. Even after a person has been injured or swindled by an unfair trade practice, he should get in touch with the better business bureau. This serves two purposes: first, to acquaint the better business bureau with what is going on in the community; and second, to get a possible adjustment through the assistance of the bureau.

The National Better Business Bureau publishes various pamphlets specifically for the benefit of the consumer. These pamphlets provide warnings and information with regard to specific types of commodities and lending institutions. These pamphlets were developed by the Boston Better Business Bureau. They are distributed through the National Better Business Bureau and can be obtained at a small cost through any local bureau.

The National Better Business Bureau, located in New York City, conducts campaigns for better standards and practices in advertising and selling. It issues a long list of subjects and organizations on which reports have been prepared. A list of the reports and copies of them can be obtained from the Bureau. Some of the reports are distributed to publishers of newspapers and periodicals; others are for general distribution.

Legal Aid Societies. Under the belief that getting justice should not depend upon one's ability to pay fees and hire a lawyer, organizations that are generally called *legal aid societies* or *legal aid organizations* have been formed throughout the various states. These organizations are found principally in the larger cities. They are often sponsored by lawyers in order to provide an organized method of handling cases for persons who cannot afford to obtain legal assistance. Therefore, if a consumer does not have the money to fight his own legal battles to protect himself, legal assistance is often available to him if a real need for it exists.

American Medical Association. The American Medical Association is probably one of the most respected non-public agencies for the aid and the protection of the consumer. This association maintains a Council on Phar-

macy and Chemistry, a Council on Physical Medicine and
Rehabilitation, a Council on Foods and Nutrition, and a
Committee on Cosmetics; it also has a staff of laboratory
investigators. Products are submitted to this association
for consideration with a view to acceptance in accordance
with certain rules. The first types of products to be accepted by this association were mainly of a medicinal nature.
The original purpose was "to protect the medical profession
and the public against fraud, undesirable secrecy, and
objectionable advertising in connection with proprietary
and medicinal articles." The association issues annually a
book, *New and Nonofficial Remedies,* containing descriptions of proprietary articles that have been accepted as
conforming to the rules of the association.

Each of the three councils and the committee established
by the American Medical Association issues its own seal of
acceptance. The four seals are illustrated below. When one
of these seals appears on the label of a product or in the
advertising of the product, it indicates that the product has
been approved and accepted as meeting the rules of the
respective group. No remuneration in any form is accepted
for this work; the expense is borne entirely by the American Medical Association.

Manufacturers whose products are accepted by one of
the groups of the American Medical Association are allowed to advertise them as "accepted by the Council on
Foods and Nutrition of the American Medical Association"
if the product is food. Similar acceptances may be indicated
for products accepted by the other groups. In the case
of foods, the current policy is to rate only the foods that
claim special health values.

Seals of the American Medical Association.

The American Medical Association issues reports on its investigations. These reports are available to anyone who subscribes to the publications of the association. The accepted foods and drugs are announced in the journal of the American Medical Association.

Another service of the American Medical Association that is of interest to consumers is the publication of a magazine entitled *Today's Health.*

American Dental Association. The Council on Dental Therapeutics of the American Dental Association publishes a list of accepted dental remedies and dentifrices. This list contains descriptions of proprietary articles that seem to be of sufficient importance to warrant their inclusion. The Council has established rules and regulations for observance in examining and accepting dental remedies and dentifrices. Not only the remedy or the dentifrice itself must be acceptable, but the advertising also must be approved. A manufacturer whose remedy or dentifrice is accepted may use the seal of acceptance of the council in his advertising and on the label of his package. Several tooth pastes and tooth powders have been accepted, but it is significant to know that not a single mouthwash has been accepted.

The seal of the American Dental Association.

National Board of Fire Underwriters. The National Board of Fire Underwriters maintains laboratories that are operated on a nonprofit basis for the purpose of giving information on the merits of materials and appliances that may involve hazards of life, fire, theft, or accident. The laboratories are known as the Underwriters' Laboratories, Inc. They operate somewhat independently on a self-supporting fee basis.

Tests are conducted in the laboratories on the basis of predetermined standards. Information on these standards may be obtained by writing to a testing laboratory of the

National Board of Fire Underwriters. The major work of the laboratories consists in inspecting various materials and appliances to ascertain whether they meet the minimum standards of safety. The board publishes annually a list of important appliances and materials, such as electrical appliances, fire-protection appliances, oil and gas appliances, and automotive appliances, that have been approved by it.

The consumer can profit from the services of the underwriters' laboratories by purchasing only equipment or material that has been approved. Approved equipment and material can be determined from the published lists and

also from the labels on the products. A product that bears the label of the Underwriters' Laboratories has been inspected and approved in the factory in which it was pro-

A sample label of the Underwriters' association.

duced. The seal appears in various forms, sometimes merely with "U. L." stamped into or impressed on the article.

American Gas Association. Manufacturers of gas-operated equipment and appliances have the privilege of sending their products to the American Gas Association laboratories, which are located in New York City and in Cleveland. These products are tested for safety, durability, and efficiency. If they meet the standards set up for each type of equipment,

Seal of the American Gas Association.

the manufacturer is permitted to use a seal of approval. This distinguishing mark of approval has become so important in marketing gas appliances that over 95 per cent of the gas-operated appliances that are manufactured bear this seal of approval. It must be borne in mind that this seal of approval indicates only that the product meets a certain minimum standard of quality. There will naturally be a difference in quality among the products that bear this seal of approval.

Illuminating Engineers' Society. The seal of approval of the Illuminating Engineers' Society is one that has become commonly known to many buyers of portable lamps. It is distinguished by the letters I. E. S. found on the label attached to the lamp. In order to be permitted to use this label, a manufacturer must have had his product tested by an official testing laboratory designated by the society. This testing has resulted in a great saving of eyesight. Probably the most

Seal of approval of the Illuminating Engineers' Society.

common product that the consumer may have observed bearing this label is the table lamp used for reading.

American Standards Association. The American Standards Association includes in its membership practically all the standardizing agencies, associations of manufacturers, associations of producers, and private laboratories, as well as a great many educational organizations and private business concerns. Membership is open to anyone who is interested in standardization. The association is founded upon the principle that "commercial contracts transferring the ownership of commodities must be based on dimensional standards and quality specifications that are mutually satisfactory to the buyer and seller. National recognition of such standards will remove misunderstandings and expedite commercial standards." It is evident from this statement that the functions of the association are closely related to the consumer as well as to the producer.

The American Standards Association has organized an Advisory Committee for Ultimate Consumer Goods. This committee co-operates with various interested groups, such as the American Home Economics Association and the National Retail Dry Goods Association, to develop reliable standards and the use of informative labels.

The American Standards Association publishes a year-book and a monthly bulletin. The yearbook contains a report of the activities of the association and lists of new standards that have been developed. The monthly bulletin provides current information with regard to progress in the standardization, the certification, and the labeling of products.

Although the activities of the American Standards Association are somewhat far removed from consumers, the consumer may purchase the literature of this association. Specification of the standards for any product that has been standardized by the association can be obtained at a nominal cost.

American Institute of Laundering. The American Institute of Laundering is a research center maintained by the laundering industry. Any garment or fabric bearing the seal of this association is certified that it can be laundered well and safely. The tests upon which this seal of approval is based cover shrinkage, tensile strength, color fastness, and general launderability of the entire garment, including buttons, snaps, and slide fasteners.

Two special seals for fabrics and garments.

National Association of Dyers and Cleaners. The National Association of Dyers and Cleaners maintains a research and testing laboratory similar to that maintained by the laundry industry. In order to bear the seal of approval of this association, fabrics and garments must meet certain standards that are similar to those of the laundry industry.

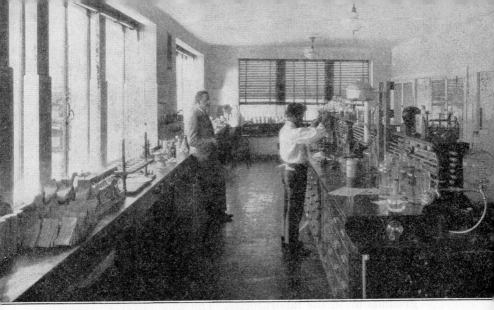

A private testing laboratory.

Private Laboratories. In a discussion of private agencies for consumer protection, it is desirable to include various types of laboratories that test foods and other merchandise. Such laboratories may be classified as follows:

(a) Laboratories maintained by private companies for testing their own products and purchases.

(b) Laboratories of some schools and universities that will conduct a test for anyone who is willing to pay a fee for the service.

(c) Private laboratories that will do testing on a fee basis for anyone who submits a product.

(d) Laboratories retained by or owned and operated by associations such as the Better Fabrics Testing Bureau, Inc. of the National Retail Dry Goods Association.

A company laboratory is organized primarily for the benefit of a particular company and its customers. For instance, one large chain-store grocery company has a completely equipped laboratory that is used to test all merchandise before it is bought. Upon the basis of its test the laboratory authorizes or rejects any proposed purchase. Some of the great corporations operate scientific laboratories for testing their own products. This in itself is a service to consumers. However, some stores and mail-order

123

houses go further; through detailed information on labels, they pass on to consumers facts discovered by their laboratories.

The proving grounds and the testing laboratories of our large corporations indirectly affect the consumer, for they tend to raise standards of quality. For example, the automobile manufacturers have large proving grounds used to test new devices and new models of automobiles before they are offered for sale. If this testing were not conducted, the consumer in many cases would not get his money's worth. He would do the experimenting rather than the producer. Producers usually feature in their advertising certain tests that have been made on the proving grounds or in the laboratories. The wise buyer will weigh the results of such tests.

Fabric quality seals.

The laboratories of some schools and universities are operated only for the benefit of the institutions, but occasionally the facilities of such a laboratory are available to any client who is willing to pay an established fee.

Numerous laboratories are open to individuals or organizations for the purpose of testing various types of products, ranging from foods to chemicals, clothing, and heavy machinery. The National Bureau of Standards of the United States Department of Commerce publishes a directory of commercial testing laboratories and college research laboratories. This directory indicates the types of commodities that can be tested by each laboratory. Some of these laboratories will test items such as clothing, shoes, or food for a fee ranging from one dollar to ten dollars.

The Electrical Testing Laboratories, Inc. is a privately operated laboratory that tests and awards seals of approval on electrical apparatus. One of the most common products that a consumer will find carrying this label (ETL) is the portable electric lamp, including the lamp shade. Certificates are awarded on the basis of safety, durability, effectiveness, convenience, and absence of objective features. Some lamps may bear both the ETL and IES labels.

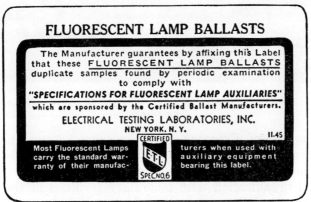

Certification label of ETL.

Consumers' Research Organizations. There are at least two organizations that solicit membership on a fee basis and furnish members with bulletins and buyers' guides. These organizations are as follows:

> Consumers' Research, Inc., Washington, New Jersey.
> Consumers Union of U. S., Inc., 38 East First Street, New York, New York.

Such organizations are operated on a nonprofit basis for the benefit of their members. The membership fee is reasonable. Their services are within the reach of most consumers.

The direct benefit of these organizations is limited largely to the subscribers. As these organizations are operated largely for members, however, they have greater freedom in making tests and in reporting the information to their members.

Machine for testing abrasion resistance of smooth-surfaced floor coverings.

Consumers' Research, Inc. Consumers' Research is the outgrowth of what was originally a small club for the study of consumers' goods. Consumers' Research is now a national organization with laboratory facilities at the headquarters in Washington, New Jersey, and elsewhere.

Consumers' Research tests products that are most widely distributed and most inquired about by those who use its services. *Consumers' Research Bulletin,* issued monthly, presents in nontechnical language reports on products that have been tested or studied in the laboratory or by other means by experts and consultants. These bulletins are not confidential and anyone or any organization may subscribe. The *Annual Cumulative Bulletin,* which furnishes a convenient summary of a wide range of findings in one volume, is issued in September and is available to individual subscribers at an additional charge. Those who wish to obtain this book alone for personal individual use without the other part of the service may do so.

Products that have been examined and reported on are classified on the basis of quality as (a) recommended, (b) intermediate, or (c) not recommended. The fact that a particular product is not listed in a bulletin usually means that the product has not yet been examined.

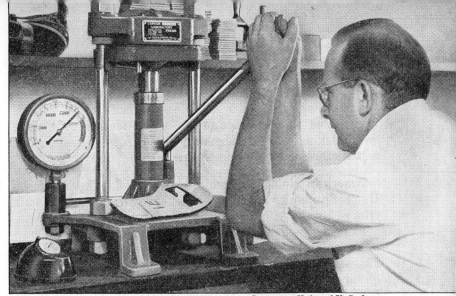

Machine for testing shoes.

Consumers Union of U. S., Inc. This nonprofit testing organization, with offices and laboratories in New York City, reports on consumer goods and services through its monthly publication, *Consumer Reports.* The annual subscription includes eleven issues of the *Reports* and the annual Buying Guide. In addition to serving more than a quarter of a million subscribers, *Consumer Reports* goes into public and special libraries, schools, and colleges.

Most of the product ratings are based on tests made in Consumers Union's laboratories, but tests are also made by more than 200 technical specialists in university, government, and private laboratories, acting as consultants on special projects. In addition to product information, the magazine also contains many special departments and sections, including topics on health, consumer economics, legislation affecting consumers, product design, gardening, phonograph records, and a movie poll.

The *Reports* carries general buying information and brand name ratings. Products rated as "Best Buys" should give greater return per dollar; products rated "Acceptable" are usually listed in order of estimated over-all quality. Products rated "Not Acceptable" usually receive this rating because of low quality or potential harmfulness.

127

In arriving at ratings many characteristics are considered. For example, in a project on men's shoes, ratings were based on resistance of the upper leather to scuffing and cracking, and of the sole leather to compression, and on the other materials and workmanship found in the shoes.

American Home Economics Association. The American Home Economics Association has devoted some of its main efforts to the education and the protection of the consumer by furnishing buying information and by encouraging suitable legislation and the use of proper standards. The association publishes a monthly magazine and bulletins on buying and the protection of the consumer. Most of the information pertains to such topics as food, clothing, health, and legislation.

Magazines and Newspapers. Magazines and newspapers have been performing a great amount of service for the average consumer. Some of the publishers maintain testing laboratories, and others have an advisory or consultation service for the benefit of consumers. Much advertising is rejected because the goods fail to meet the claims. In some cases products are tested and are given seals of approval that may be carried on the labels and in the advertising. Some of the testing is conducted with a view to aiding the advertisers and developing editorial material for the articles that are published.

Good Housekeeping magazine and *Parents' Magazine* maintain testing services, as a result of which any product that is accepted for advertising is guaranteed by the magazine. The seal indicating approval may be carried on the label and in the advertising.

In the case of *Parents' Magazine,* there is a Commendation Seal and a Guarantee Seal that may be used under stipulated conditions. The seal of *Good Housekeeping* is used with the legend "Replacement or refund of money guaranteed by *Good Housekeeping* if defective or not as advertised therein."

In some cases, such as *Parents' Magazine* Consumer Service Bureau, products are sent out to technical testing

Magazine seals of approval.

laboratories for neutral, unbiased tests, and the products are then assigned to consumer advisors who use the products in order to give them a practical test.

National Canners Association. The National Canners Association has been responsible for setting up certain minimum standards for sizes of cans, quality, fill, and description of the product. Members of this association are encouraged to pack their products in accordance with these standards.

National Consumer-Retailer Council. The National Consumer-Retailer Council was originally recommended and organized by the American Standards Association. The membership of the council includes the American Association of University Women, American Home Economics Association, General Federation of Women's Clubs, American Retail Federation, National Association of Food Chains, National Better Business Bureau, National Retail Dry Goods Association, and National Shoe Retailers Association.

The purposes of the council are as follows:

(a) To promote the use of informative labeling.
(b) To promote the use of informative advertising.
(c) To promote informative salesmanship.
(d) To encourage practices that will tend to reduce abuses of such privileges as customer accounts, returns, deliveries, and similar services.
(e) To foster local co-operation between stores or groups of stores and local consumer groups.

(f) To promote the use of adequate standards for consumer goods.

(g) To promote the use of uniform terminology in describing consumer goods and services.

(h) To develop and promote the use of suggested codes of ethics for both retailers and consumers.

Advantages of Research Laboratories. In this chapter you have studied examples of the principal testing laboratories that are of most benefit to the consumer. A word of caution is important: Not all so-called scientific laboratories or tests are authoritative, and not all seals of approval are meaningful. Research laboratories, however, have directly and indirectly given the consumer two advantages, as follows:

(a) When an authoritative seal or guarantee is involved, it furnishes the buyer one more way of distinguishing quality.

(b) When laboratories analyze goods, they stimulate improvements by the manufacturers.

TEXTBOOK QUESTIONS

1. What are some of the functions performed by the better business bureaus in promoting fair trade practices?
2. Who may utilize the services of a better business bureau?
3. In most large cities how can a person without money obtain legal advice or assistance?
4. What are the four groups of the American Medical Association that examine products?
5. When a product has been accepted by one group of the American Medical Association, how can a consumer distinguish this product from others?
6. What is the significance of the fact that a dentifrice bears the seal of approval of the American Dental Association?
7. What two main functions are performed through the tests conducted in the laboratories of the National Board of Fire Underwriters?
8. What does the seal of the American Gas Association mean?
9. What products are tested and may bear the seal of the Illuminating Engineers' Society?
10. On what principle is the American Standards Association founded?
11. What factors are tested to determine whether the American Institute of Laundering will issue a certifying label?

12. What are some of the factors that determine whether the National Association of Dyers and Cleaners will approve a garment or fabric?
13. Name three of the types of private laboratories that test foods and other merchandise.
14. What kinds or classes of products are tested by Consumers' Research, Inc.?
15. Under what classifications are products rated by Consumers Union, Inc.?
16. How does the American Home Economics Association benefit the consumer?
17. (a) What statement appears on the seal of *Good Housekeeping*? (b) What are the two kinds of seals of *Parents' Magazine*?
18. To what extent has the National Canners Association contributed to the protection of the consumer?
19. (a) Who organized the National Consumer-Retailer Council? (b) What are some of the groups in the Council? (c) Name at least three purposes of the Council.

DISCUSSION QUESTIONS

1. Assume that a large store in your community advertises an article for a special sale on Monday. You are within the store ten minutes after opening time requesting the purchase of the item, but it is not available. As you feel that you have been misled, to what agency would you go for some advice and protection?
2. How does the American Medical Association help to protect consumers, even though only a small percentage of products is approved by this association?
3. On which would you place the greatest reliance: a test by the American Medical Association, the testimonial of a user, or a laboratory test made by the manufacturer? Why?
4. How do the laboratories of the National Board of Fire Underwriters save money for all of us?
5. "The activities of the American Standards Association save many thousands of dollars each year." Do you think this statement is true? Why?
6. Why do you think some manufacturers organize an association and use a seal indicating that products of the members of that association meet certain requirements?
7. Some manufacturers oppose such organizations as Consumers' Research, Inc., and Consumers Union, Inc., whereas others approve them. How do you account for the difference in attitude?

8. It is not likely that, at the time of purchasing any ordinary product, the consumer will use the service of a testing agency. How might he, however, use such a service to his advantage?
9. Some of the reports issued by consumer research organizations are often a year old and sometimes older. Are these reports valuable? Discuss.
10. Some people assert that the scientific laboratories maintained by periodical publishers are operated for the benefit of manufacturers and therefore render little service to buyers. Do you think this assertion is true? Why?

PROBLEMS

1. Prepare a complete list of the products that are advertised in a current issue of some popular magazine. Opposite the name of each product indicate whether there is any seal, label, certified test, or testimonial used to indicate the standard of quality of the product. Indicate the specific proof that is given.
2. Make a list of food products and drugs that you find bearing seals or labels of approval. Indicate the particular seal or label for each product. If you find any seal or labels with which you are not acquainted, inquire about the conditions under which these are awarded.
3. Study a daily newspaper and cut out all advertisements (a) that may violate the principles under which better business bureaus operate, and (b) that conform to standards set up by the American Dental Association, the American Medical Association, or any other agency mentioned in this chapter. Paste these advertisements on sheets of paper, and submit them with your comments.

COMMUNITY PROBLEMS AND PROJECTS

1. If you are in a community where there is a better business bureau, contact the bureau and find out some of the activities in which it has engaged recently, and obtain a description of some of the latest examples of frauds about which consumers in your community should be warned.
2. Obtain all the information you can on the services of the American Medical Association in aiding the consumer. Write a synopsis of your findings in the form of a report.
3. Investigate the services that are performed by some periodical publisher in testing and approving products and in issuing information for the benefit of consumers. Write a report on your findings, and evaluate the services performed.

PART IV
PRINCIPLES OF BUYING

Chapter 8
How to Interpret Advertising

Purpose of the Chapter. In our modern society advertising is essential because producers and consumers are usually so far apart that there must be some means of communication between them. Because we consumers need the information to be found in the advertisements, we should learn how to interpret and to use advertisements intelligently; but, because we may also be unduly influenced against our best interests by clever advertisers who know how to influence our emotions and by some who would mislead us, we must also learn to protect ourselves by analyzing advertising carefully and critically. The purpose of this chapter is to help you analyze buying motives, to explain the sales appeals that are used in advertising, to illustrate good advertising and bad advertising, and to point out how advertising can serve you as a buying guide.

Advertising serves as a means of communication.

Then and Now in Advertising. When our country was young, production and distribution were very simple. Before production in factories, most consumers produced the goods they consumed, or they traded with nearby acquaintances. Stores often traded goods across the counter, and very little money changed hands. The first common form of advertising was the sign of the doctor, the merchant, the blacksmith, and other business establishments. In those days no means of mass production was known; therefore, there was no need for mass distribution.

Now we have mass production with producers and con-sumers widely separated. A complicated system of trans-portation and communication is needed to help producers reach the consumer. Advertising has become the means of telling the consumer in distant places what the producer has to sell. Under our present system of economics advertising is essential.

Of course in a completely controlled society, advertising would not be so useful because producers would be told what to produce, and consumers would be able to buy only the goods placed at their disposal. We would have very few kinds of goods from which to make a selection.

Purposes of Advertising. Advertising performs certain useful business and economic functions. However, there have been some criticisms of the wastefulness of adver-tising in some particular cases. From an economic point of view, the following are the purposes and the functions of advertising:

(a) *To provide a necessary means of widespread com-munication from the producer to the consumer in a democratic and capitalistic type of society.* Unless there were some means of advertising, a producer would never be able to communicate with customers on a wide scale. Without advertising, consumers in San Francisco might never learn of a product manu-factured in New York.

(b) *To create a demand for a particular product or type of products.* This function might be considered as a part of the first function. Advertising has edu-cated us to accept and to use new products or im-proved products. It has educated us to demand certain types of foods, and in many ways it has changed our eating habits. In this respect it has performed a useful social function.

(c) *To get a premium price on brands over and above the average price of unbranded goods or of competing brands.* By establishing in the minds of buyers a preference for a particular brand, it has been possible in many cases to get a higher price for that brand of merchandise. In some cases this function works to the disadvantage of the consumer when the price is higher than that of other goods of equal quality. Some consumers, however, are willing to pay a premium price to be able to identify a brand of established quality.

(d) *To get wide distribution, mass production, reduced costs of distribution, reduced costs of manufacture, and therefore reduced prices to the consumer.* This process of obtaining mass distribution and lower prices is often used to compete with other companies. At the same time, it tends to push prices down for the consumer and to force other competitors to operate equally efficiently or to go out of business.

(e) *To speed the process of distribution.* It is a well-known fact in business that advertising helps to move goods off the shelves of individual merchants. It therefore reduces the time that the goods are held on the shelves, it reduces the amount of money that the merchant has tied up in merchandise, and it reduces the time that he has his money tied up. In business terminology, advertising increases the turnover of merchandise. By increasing the turnover, there is lower cost for the merchant, and the consumer gets fresher goods. The merchant will either make a greater profit, or the consumer will enjoy lower prices. It is a well-established fact in business that a merchant must charge a higher margin of profit on goods with a low turnover than he charges on goods with a high turnover. The consumer therefore always profits by speeding up the distribution process, because by speeding up the process every individual in the whole distribution system has his money invested in the merchandise for a shorter length of time and can afford to take a lower rate of profit.

Could you buy as confidently if no goods were branded and advertised?

Does Advertising Really Help You? Have you ever stopped to study advertising long enough to discover whether you really get any helpful information from it? If it is of no value to you, then it is wasteful. If it is of some value, you should learn how to get the greatest value from it. Answering some of these questions will help to determine whether advertising is of any value to you.

What Are Your Answers to These Questions?

1. If you were a farmer, could you get all the information you want about the latest farm equipment without referring to advertisements?
2. Does advertising give you any information about the latest developments in household equipment?
3. Has advertising educated you in regard to television?
4. If all refrigerators were sold without trade-marks and trade names, would you feel safe in picking a good refrigerator?
5. If all canned foods were prohibited from carrying labels and trade-marks, do you think you could select foods wisely?
6. Do you ever read the newspaper to see what is offered for sale in your local stores?
7. Did you ever buy from a mail-order catalog?
8. Do you use advertising (posters, leaflets, or announcements) in your school to promote attendance at a school play or athletic event?

How You Are Influenced. The professional seller is a trained psychologist. He understands human behavior and the workings of the human mind. He presents his product so that it will attract attention, create desire, convince the consumer of its worth, and cause him to act by purchasing it. The following steps therefore constitute the psychology of selling: (a) attracting attention, (b) creating desire, (c) causing conviction, and (d) obtaining action. These steps are followed in both advertising and personal selling.

Appeals That Open Your Purse. There are two general types of sales appeal. The first is known as the *emotional,* or *human-interest, appeal*; the second, as the *rational,* or *reason-why, appeal.* Professional sellers refer to these respectively as the *short-circuit* and the *long-circuit appeal.*

Experience has proved that, in the selling of many commodities, the emotional appeal is more effective than the reason-why appeal. The emotional appeal influences the buyer through suggestion. He is not invited to deliberate or compare; he is made to feel that the article that is advertised will please his senses or satisfy his desires.

The reason-why appeal is referred to as the long-circuit appeal because it requires a careful presentation of facts that appeal to conscious deliberation. This type of appeal must present logical reasons why the product should be purchased.

Within these two general classes of sales appeal, there are numerous appeals used by advertisers to stimulate sales. The following is a list of fourteen that are commonly used in advertising all general types of products:

(a) Health.	(h) Beauty and appearance.
(b) Maternal affection.	(i) Efficiency.
(c) Appetite and taste.	(j) Vanity, pride, and
(d) Attraction of the sexes.	fashion.
(e) Economy.	(k) Safety.
(f) Comfort, pleasure, and	(l) Sympathy.
luxury.	(m) Envy.
(g) Ambition.	(n) Fear.

The way in which the advertiser utilizes an appeal depends upon whether the appeal is emotional or rational. For instance, if clothing is sold purely for the sake of beauty or appearance or with the purpose of enabling the buyer to imitate someone else, the appeal is highly emotional. On the other hand, if the advertiser of men's clothing points out how attractive clothing and a good appearance will help a man in business, the appeal is somewhat rational.

The illustration on page 139 shows an advertisement with an emotional appeal and one with a reason-why appeal. Compare the two. Determine which one actually tells enough to enable the reader to determine the merits of the product.

Experts in selling and advertising study very carefully the appeals that are most effective in selling products. They find that some appeals are satisfactory for men, whereas they cannot be used satisfactorily with women; and vice versa. Style, for example, is an important consideration in selling shoes to women, whereas it is not so important in selling them to men. Many tests will show that men consider the quality of shoes before style, whereas women make style the paramount consideration. In choosing an appeal to be used, the seller or the advertiser must therefore consider the prospective buyer.

Results of Advertising. Does advertising pay? It certainly does. The fact that advertising does pay is proved by the successful selling of advertised products and by the fortunes that have been built as the result of good advertising programs. It can also be proved by an analysis of the effects on consumers. For instance, the following analysis [1] shows the partial results of an examination of one thousand college students. When the test was administered, students were requested to associate a particular product with a trade name. The table shows the results.

880 out of 1,000 mentioned "Eastman" for camera.
771 out of 1,000 mentioned "Singer" for sewing machine.
757 out of 1,000 mentioned "Campbell" for soup.
748 out of 1,000 mentioned "Arrow" for collars.
436 out of 1,000 mentioned "Life-Savers" for 5-cent mints.
430 out of 1,000 mentioned "Sunkist" for fruit.
396 out of 1,000 mentioned "Gillette" for razors.
389 out of 1,000 mentioned "Ivory" for soap.

Who Pays the Cost of Advertising? Some critics contend that all advertising is wasteful because it influences people to buy when they should be allowed to make their

---

[1] Adapted from *The Leadership of Advertised Brands* by George Burton Hotchkiss and Richard B. Franken. Doubleday, Page & Company, 1923.

A Maiden's Dream

NEW SPRING SUIT
$49.50

Definitely new, sensational, and excit-
ing. A designer's dream! For a
thousand and one hours of blissful
spring wear. Tailored for a slenderiz-
ing effect. In green and blue pastels.
You will get a real thrill from one of
these suits.

THE BATES STORE

An emotional appeal.

New Tweeds

SELECTIONS FOR SPRING
$49.50

We have just received a new shipment
of tailored tweed suits made of virgin
wool fabrics in a wide range of colors
and patterns. The lining is guaranteed
for two years. Excellent for street or
office wear. Alteration charges on any
suit will not exceed $2.00.

THE BATES STORE

A reason-why appeal.

own choices without such an influence. It is true that some advertising is wasteful; but, on the other hand, if one makes an honest analysis of the situation, he will see that without advertising it would be impossible to have mass distribution. Without mass distribution it would be impossible to have mass production. Without mass production it would be impossible to have manufacturing processes improved to the high degree to which we now are accustomed. Without improved manufacturing processes it would be impossible to have many of our commonly accepted necessities produced at a low cost. For instance, in 1922 a few thousand people with radio sets costing from $100 to $500 could make their friends envious by receiving radio programs. There are now more than 42,000,000 homes equipped with radio sets, which have cost in some cases as low as $10 or $20 a set. Advertising and mass production have brought about this change.

Sometimes critics cite examples of manufacturers who are able to produce and sell an item, such as a razor, for $5, $10, or $15. These critics attribute the high cost to advertising. One of the reasons for the high cost is patent protection, which enables the producer to get the price he wants. Lack of competition is another factor. Furthermore, during the early stages in the introduction of a product, it is necessary to charge a higher price to carry the burden of advertising until mass production results in lower production costs. Without advertising, a large market would not be created; low production resulting in high production costs would therefore tend to keep the price at a high level. In normal, unrestricted advertising and trade, however, when new competing products come onto the market, additional advertising causes wider use; and, through competition and mass production together, a lower price is made available to the consumer.

It is true that, in the case of luxuries such as exclusive clothes and cosmetics, advertising costs may run unusually high; but when one buys a luxury, he is not necessarily looking for economy. When one analyzes commonly advertised commodities, he finds the advertising cost rather low.

For instance, in the case of a well-known shirt, only 64/100 of a cent goes into public information about it. In the case of a well-known brand of soup, only 36/1000 of a cent on each can is spent for advertising.

In the final analysis, it is not a question of who pays for advertising, but rather it is a question of the total cost of merchandising and whether this total cost is too high. It is frequently a choice between using more advertising or more direct selling. One of the best defenses of advertising is that, when it is well done, it is the cheapest way of selling. When this is true, it is to the advantage of the consumer. In the case of some products, it has been shown that the advertising costs are high because of pressure that is needed in selling those products. In the case of many other products, it has been proved conclusively that advertising has served an important economic function by gaining widespread distribution, low costs of production, and therefore the lowest possible price to the consumer. If it were not for this function of advertising in our distributive system, it can easily be seen that we would not enjoy some of the benefits that we enjoy today. It cannot therefore be said that advertising is either entirely good or entirely bad.

Honest and Dishonest Advertising. Every buyer must recognize the fact that, although the majority of advertisers are honest, some are unscrupulous. Substantial and well-established business concerns recognize the fact that honesty, in advertising as well as in other relationships with consumers, must be the basis of permanent success. The publishers of magazines and newspapers recognize the fact that dishonest advertising reacts unfavorably against their publications as well as against the products advertised. Because of the importance of advertising, the Federal Government and also state governments have passed laws on this subject. The most important government agency in the supervision of advertising is the Federal Trade Commission. One of the most effective promoters of honesty in advertising is the National Better Business Bureau and its affiliated organizations.

Misleading Advertising

The National Better Business Bureau publicizes various advertising schemes that are considered misleading and unethical. A few of the schemes are as follows:

1. Fire sales that are really not fire sales.
2. Puzzle contests that are so difficult and long that most contestants drop out after paying a fee and never have a chance of winning.
3. Work-at-home schemes that require applicants to pay for a course of instructions which they seldom complete.
4. Help-wanted advertisements that are really advertisements for the enrollment in a training program.
5. Bait advertising that attracts people to stores because of a bargain when only a few of the bargain items are available.
6. Advertisements of pure gold jewelry that has a very low gold content or which is gold-plated.
7. Wholesalers that advertise for retail trade.

Some Absurdities of Advertising. Let us consider some of the tactics of those who write advertisements that are supposed to educate consumers and to induce them to buy. Demands are placed upon the writers of advertising copy to use devices that will build up the maximum amount of emotion. Note just a few of the irrational appeals that are used: Turn to a page

Fire sales are not always legitimate.

of a popular magazine and you will find the picture of a beautiful young woman with a statement that Miss So-and-So uses Such-and-Such face powder; turn to another page and you will see pictured an attractive young woman who is supposed to convey the idea that, if a particular product is good enough for her, it is good enough for you; turn to another page and you will find a grotesque picture warning you against dire results if you do not use a certain disinfectant or mouthwash. In advertisements you should search for statements relating to performance, quality, ingredients, and actual results.

Testimonials. It is common knowledge that debutantes, society leaders, political figures, film stars, and many other people prominently before the public eye have been guilty of selling their names and photographs for use in the testimonial advertising of various products. They have been paid in money, publicity, or other forms. In fact, there are agencies that make a business of arranging contracts with clients who are willing to sell their names and photographs for such purposes. Obviously, testimonials that are obtained and used promiscuously cannot be sincere. In evaluating testimonials, one must therefore take this common practice into consideration. If a consumer is going to judge a testimonial upon its merits, the testimonial should come from a person qualified by experience, training, and integrity.

Testimonials influence many buyers.

Meaningless Statements. Pictures are not the only devices used to convey certain emotional impressions. Headings, slogans, verse, and humorous quotations also serve that purpose. Here are some examples of slogans:

> "The Standard of the World"
> "The Most Beautiful Car in America"
> "It's the Best"
> "It Can't Be Beat"
> "The Perfect Dentifrice"
> "The Best Shoe Available"
> "The Unusual Watch"
> "Our Product Is Recognized as the Best"
> "Better Than Any Others"

Do any of these statements convey definite assurance of quality, performance, or value? The answer is definitely "No."

Headings are interesting. Slogans sometimes catch the eye. Verse and humorous statements are frequently amusing. But these should not be allowed to influence buying. One should read the advertisement carefully, and then learn something about the quality of the product, the contents, the cost, and the performance.

It has been said that the public likes to be fooled. Most buyers are influenced by tradition, and many lack the incentive to investigate for themselves. Instead of taking the initiative, they wait until the seller does so. Flattery and the appeal to envy often induce a prospective purchaser to buy without consideration of quality, cost, or utility.

Food Advertising. The American Medical Association, through its Council on Foods and Nutrition, has been instrumental in developing higher standards in the advertising of foods. The principles laid down by this association can be applied in general to all forms of advertising. The following is a brief summary of the general criteria of good advertising advocated by the Council on Foods and Nutrition of the American Medical Association:

(a) The common name of the food should be used in the advertising; or if the product is sold under a trade name, the ingredients should be identified properly in the order of their decreasing proportions.

(b) Any statement of the physical, chemical, nutritional, or physiological properties or values of the food should be truthful and should be expressed in simple terms that the public can understand.

(c) Good advertising is free from false implications.

(d) It does not create incorrect or improper inferences with regard to foods, or lead to such comparisons between foods.

(e) It attempts to promote sales solely on the merits of the food article itself.

(f) It discusses nutritional values, but avoids specific claims concerning health.

Informative Advertising. For many years advertisements for goods purchased by manufacturers have been phrased in terms giving exact descriptions of those goods. At present some advertisers of consumers' goods are featuring in their advertisements pertinent statements on standards, specifications, and performance.

It is now common practice of certain stores to give exact descriptions or sizes of dresses available, the name of the cloth, and the quality of the cloth. In advertising furniture, some stores give an exact description of the type of frame that is used, the type of springs, the kind of padding in the cushions, the kind of covers, the finish, and sometimes additional information. Others sometimes go a step farther and provide additional information in regard to the materials that are used. Some of the advertisements of merchants are backed up by tags and labels on the merchandise providing detailed information as to quality.

From a consumer's point of view, an advertisement may be considered primarily good if it provides facts in regard to quality, standards, specifications, and performance. It can be generally considered not good if it fails to provide this information but instead appeals only to the emotions.

It is true that much advertising is far from being educational. The publishers of reliable newspapers and magazines scrutinize the advertisements that they accept and attempt to eliminate obviously fraudulent statements. The better business bureaus in some cities give publicity to stores that deliberately misrepresent their wares. In spite of these activities, however, the buyer must learn to read advertising critically if he expects to obtain information that is worth while.

How to Read Advertisements. Advertisements should be read from two points of view: (a) to learn everything possible from the advertisements, and (b) to try to detect if there is any deception or misleading information. Some advertisements are neither informative nor deceptive. They are simply evasive or general, or they merely appeal to the emotions. The intelligent consumer will look for helpful information. Learn to distinguish between emotional appeals and rational appeals. Learn to evaluate testimonials and to discern the facts that are included.

Follow These Guides in Analyzing Advertisements

1. What does the product contain and how is it made?
2. Is it beneficial?
3. How long will it last?
4. How economical is it?
5. How does its price compare with the prices of similar products?
6. Do I need it?
7. What proof is used to back up the statements?
8. Does it carry any seals identifying quality or any evidence of authoritative scientific tests?
9. It it harmless?
10. Are any of the advertising statements evasive or misleading?
11. Does the advertisement appeal to your intelligence?
12. Does the advertisement make you feel confident that, if you buy, you will be a satisfied customer.

Every large business has at least one buyer who is a specialist. Some concerns, such as wholesale grocers, have several buyers. Professional buyers devote all their time to buying. They sometimes have difficulty in distinguishing a good product through its advertising, and in the final analysis they must examine the product. The average consumer is an amateur when it comes to buying. His emotions are easily influenced in buying. Often he buys emotionally rather than rationally because the professional advertiser knows how to appeal to the emotions of the individual. One can become more than an amateur buyer if he learns to interpret advertising and to look beyond the advertising.

If you believe that advertising can be improved and ought to be improved, you should co-operate with the advertisers that give you the information that you want and need. Have you ever analyzed your own buying habits to see how you are influenced? Check yourself on some of these points to see how wisely you are using advertising. From what you

have learned in this chapter you should be able to evaluate
your own answers.

Check Yourself

1. Do you buy on a basis of emotional or a reason-why
   appeal?
2. Are you influenced by facts and information or by high-
   sounding generalities?
3. Do you ever compare one advertisement with another and
   one product with another?
4. Do you buy the most advertised brand without further
   thought of quality or economy?

Some Legal Protections. In Chapter 6 you studied governmental protection, which includes the regulation of
advertising. Chapter 7 introduced you to some private
agencies that are interested in helping the consumer to get
honest advertising. A knowledge of the information in
these chapters will help you to evaluate advertising and to
guard against unethical and dishonest advertising.

Some Legal Implications of Advertising. An advertisement of goods is not necessarily a legal binding offer in
terms of a contract. It may be withdrawn at any time and
becomes a contract only when it has been accepted according to the legal requirements of a contract. For that reason
prices that are quoted in advertisements are not necessarily
binding upon the seller; therefore, an advertiser has the
right to change his prices without notice. For example, a
store advertised a washing machine for $45. When Mrs.
Jones went to the store to buy one, the store refused to sell
it, contending that the price had risen and the new price
was $50. There was no contract because an advertisement
is considered merely an invitation to trade.

However, ethical advertisers are very careful in quoting
prices, for goodwill is lost when such situations arise. Although merchants have a legal right to increase prices, it
is undesirable to do so if an offer to purchase is made soon
after the publication of the advertisement.

TEXTBOOK QUESTIONS

1. State briefly the five economic functions of advertising.
2. How does advertising sometimes speed up the processes of distribution and benefit the consumer?
3. What four fundamental steps constitute the psychology of the selling process?
4. (a) What are the two general types of appeal that advertisers and sellers use in encouraging people to buy? (b) What are the differences between them?
5. Name at least five specific appeals.
6. Show how the fact that advertising pays has been proved through a test based upon the memory of trade names.
7. Who pays the cost of advertising?
8. (a) What jurisdiction does the Federal Government have over advertising? (b) By what agency is control over advertising administered?
9. Give at least two examples of advertising that the National Better Business Bureau considers misleading.
10. Why is testimonial advertising often frowned upon?
11. Give some examples of shallow, meaningless statements used in advertising.
12. Give at least two of the criteria of good advertising advocated by the Council on Foods and Nutrition of the American Medical Association.
13. What are some of the characteristics of advertising that you would consider to be genuinely informative?
14. What suggestions do you offer as a guide in helping you to read advertisements?
15. Name some ways that you can check yourself to see how you are influenced in reading advertising.
16. If a price of an article is advertised, is this a legal binding contract?

DISCUSSION QUESTIONS

1. Explain the necessity of advertising as a communication medium.
2. If advertising is used by producers or distributors to get a premium price on branded merchandise, is this purpose of advertising ever advantageous to you?
3. Give two examples of how advertising may force prices down.
4. Discuss some of the advantages and the disadvantages of brands or trade names from the point of view of the buyer.
5. "Advertising has converted many luxuries into necessities." Explain this statement.
6. "An uneducated person is a toy in the hands of an advertising expert." Explain this statement.

7. When you buy clothes, what appeals influence you most?
8. When an advertiser is trying to sell a piece of mechanical equipment to women, he finds that emotional appeals are rather effective; but when he sells the same equipment to men, he finds in general that rational appeals are more effective. How do you account for this difference?
9. Select some article, such as women's shoes, and think of some statements that might be made in advertising them that might be (a) emotional and (b) rational.
10. More than a billion dollars is spent each year for advertising. If advertising were discontinued, could we expect to buy the same goods in the same quantities for one billion dollars less?
11. Why is the question of who pays for advertising not important?
12. How may testimonial advertising of athletes sometimes serve a useful purpose?
13. What do you think of a statement such as this in an advertisement: "Used by the best families"?
14. What information do you gain from superlative terms, such as "best," "greatest," and "most modern," that you find in advertisements?
15. What may be one of the objectives of advertising cigarettes on the comic-strip pages of Sunday newspapers?
16. Try to recall and describe a recent advertisement that you feel was informative. Give your reasons.

PROBLEMS

1. In magazines or newspapers in your home find advertisements that contain appeals to (a) health, (b) beauty, (c) economy. Paste these on a sheet of paper, and write opposite each advertisement a brief notation indicating how the appeal is emphasized.
2. In this chapter you were given some examples of how trade or brand names become so well known that consumers immediately identify products by their brand name. Make a list of at least ten additional brands, trade names, or slogans that are well known to you and that you believe are also well known to others.
3. Bring to class two advertisements of similar products, one giving few or no specific facts and the other containing several facts. List for each advertisement the specific facts that are given with regard to the product. If none are given, indicate accordingly. If it is impossible to find two advertisements of similar products, select advertisements of different products and then complete the same work.

4. Bring to class an advertisement containing a testimonial that, in your opinion, is not sincere and that probably has been purchased. Give your reasons for your opinion.
5. Pick out the best advertisement that you can find in some recent popular magazine. Submit it with a written statement as to why you think it is the best advertisement from a consumer's point of view.

COMMUNITY PROBLEMS AND PROJECTS

1. (a) From five magazines or newspapers make a list of all the high-sounding titles and terms used in advertising products. This list should include meaningless, but attractive, slogans and descriptive terms. (b) After listing these terms, analyze their truthfulness, their intent, and their usefulness from the point of view of the buyer.
2. If your community has a better business bureau, find out exactly what functions it performs in regard to maintaining the ethics of advertising locally. If possible, obtain some examples to report to the class.
3. Learn from a magazine or a newspaper publisher what regulations are placed upon the acceptance of advertisements. Ask specific questions with regard to how the truthfulness of advertising is judged and investigated. Write a report of your findings.

Chapter 9

_____

How to Interpret Standards, Grades, and Labels

Purpose of the Chapter. One of the most obvious examples of size standards is evident in electric lamp bulbs. Any standard bulb bought for the home will fit any standard socket because all manufacturers follow the same specifications. However, not all bulbs are of the same quality standard. Quality standards and grades are not so easy to interpret. For example, do you know whether or not a can marked *Grade A* is the best in vegetables? Do you know whether *fancy* is the best grade in canned fruits? Do you know what *preshrunk* means in regard to fabrics? These and many other questions will be answered in this chapter. A study of this chapter will point out how the consumer can use standards, grades, and labels as guides in intelligent buying.

The Importance of Standards. In this modern world can you imagine buying without standards? Without standards one pound of coffee would not be the same weight as another pound of coffee; one yard of cloth would not be the same length as another yard of cloth; shoes of a certain size made by one manufacturer would not necessarily be the same size as those made by another manufacturer, although the indicated size might be the same.

We have many standards that are very helpful to us. We have standards as to size, quality, and performance; but much still needs to be done in standardization. Standardization enables us to talk the same language. It also permits a considerable amount of work simplification and the saving of money. A good example is in the case of typewriters. All regular typewriters take the same size sheet of paper; the amount of spacing is the same between lines of typewritten pages; the elite type on typewriters will permit the same number of characters to be typed for each line, regardless of who made the typewriter.

The Problem of Standards, Grades, and Labels. Let us assume that Mrs. Jones goes to the store to buy a can of lima beans and finds on the shelves various brands and types, some marked "Superior," some marked "Select," some marked "Superb," and some marked "Supreme." Others may be marked with A, B, or C grades, and some may be marked "Below standard." There may be descriptions on the labels, such as "Green and white" (which, if the consumer is aware of the fact, means that at least 50

per cent of the beans are green) or "White and green" (meaning that at least 25 per cent of the beans are green). Nearly every label will contain some kind of information in regard to standards, grades, or description. Just what do these various bits of information mean on the different cans? Unless the consumer has some idea in regard to standards,

Labels on canned goods are sometimes confusing or meaningless.

grades, and inspection processes, the labeling information does not mean much. It is therefore important for the consumer to have some knowledge of standards, grades, and labels.

A *standard* is a measuring stick that serves as a definition of quality. A *grade* is a means of identifying a standard. A *label* is the information on a wrapper that carries a message in regard to the contents.

All grades are informative if the person knows what the grades mean and on what standards they are based. So-called descriptive labels are also informative, at least in a general way, although some descriptive labels do not give exact information in regard to precise standards and grades. Each bit of information is useful if the consumer knows how to use it. A consumer should familiarize himself with standards and grades; he should then look for these on the labels.

Standardizing Agencies

Standards of U. S. Department of Agriculture. The U. S. Department of Agriculture has the power to establish standards for both raw fruits and vegetables and canned fruits and vegetables. At present the standards for such items as fresh fruits and vegetables are used chiefly in wholesale markets, but many of these can be useful in retail markets where the products are still available in their original containers.

In order to arrive at a grade classification, which will be explained later, certain standards must be established for every item. A scoring table is therefore arranged that is used as a guide in determining grades. For instance, in the case of canned tomatoes the following are the points that are considered:

Drained weight (solids without juice) .. 20 points
Wholeness (percentage of whole
    tomatoes) .... 20 points
Color .... 30 points
Absence of defects .... 30 points
      Total .... 100 points

Products marketed under these standards may or may not be inspected by Federal agents, but if they purport to measure up to the standards, they must adhere to the standards.

In order for butter to be sold in interstate commerce, it must contain at least 80 per cent butter fat and must be wholesome. In order for meat to be sold in interstate commerce, it must be inspected and passed by a Federal inspector. This assures its wholesomeness but not its specific quality.

The Federal Food, Drug, and Cosmetic Act is administered under the Food and Drug Administration. Under this particular law provision is made for establishing standards for canned fruits and vegetables as well as drugs and cosmetics. After standards have been established for a canned fruit or vegetable, every food of that type entering into interstate commerce must measure up to the minimum standards or must be marked in some such manner as "Below U. S. standards," "Not high quality," "Below U. S. standard. Low quality but not illegal." If a food is not wholesome, it cannot be sold legally in interstate commerce.

The Food and Drug Administration also sets up standard fills for containers. For instance, the standard fill for many fruits and vegetables is 90 per cent of capacity of the can. If it is below this standard, it must be marked appropriately, such as "Below standard in fill."

If no standard has yet been established for a fruit or vegetable entering into interstate commerce, the common name of the food and the ingredients, if there are two or more, must be indicated. The ingredients must be named in the order of their predominance by weight.

Special dietary foods, such as those advertising vitamin concentrations, must indicate on the label the amount of the vitamin content. Foods fortified with vitamins by adding vitamin content must indicate this content.

When artificial coloring, artificial flavoring, or preservatives are used, the label must state this fact. Butter, cheese, and ice cream are exempt from this provision. However, in some states the coloring of margarine is prohibited entirely by state law.

If any food is an imitation, the label must be marked "Imitation."

For many compound food products there are also so-called "standards of identity." For instance, jam is defined as containing not less than forty-five parts of fruit by weight and fifty-five parts of sugar or other sweetening agents. If it contains less than forty-five parts of fruit, it is not considered jam and may not be labeled as such. Similar standards of identity have been established for other foods.

Standards of Federal Trade Commission. The Federal Trade Commission has specific authority over maintaining standards for wool products, as explained in Chapter 6. Under this law all wool products sold in interstate commerce must identify not only the fiber content, but also the quality of the fiber. If fiber other than wool is included, it must be so indicated.

Probably the greatest contribution of the Federal Trade Commission in serving the consumer is through the trade practice rules that are the outgrowth of conferences in all the major industries, including the hosiery industry, the silk industry, the fur industry, and approximately one hundred fifty others. When various standards of identification and standards of quality are established for an industry, the Federal Trade Commission recognizes these as standards for the determining of unfair trade practices. If any producer or distributor in interstate commerce violates one of these standards, the Federal Trade Commission can take action to prevent the practice. For instance, let us assume that a manufacturer of silk hosiery sells a product that is inferior in quality as based upon the standards that have been established. When this fact is discovered by the Federal Trade Commission, it will, through so-called stipulation, request the offender to sign an agreement to stop the practice. If he stops the practice, the case is not prosecuted; if he does not sign the agreement and stop the practice, hearings are held; and if he is judged guilty, the Federal Trade Commission issues a *cease and desist* order. This order has the effect of becoming law. If the order is ignored, the Commission may bring a court action to force the manufacturer to stop the unfair trade practice and the violation of the order.

Standards of U. S. Bureau of Standards. An important function of the National Bureau of Standards is to develop "Federal Specifications." These are specifications used by governmental agencies in purchasing. When the goods are received, the Bureau may test them to see if they meet the standards.

The Bureau also works with trade groups and helps them
to set up "commercial standards." This activity is voluntary on the part of producers; but if a set of standards
meets general acceptance, the Bureau publishes it and gives
it a number. Then any manufacturer who is willing to
make goods that meet these standards may, upon application, have his name placed on the "Willing to Certify" list
for that article. Buyers can get this list on request from
the U. S. Bureau of Standards.

As this system is rather inconvenient for the ordinary
consumer, the Bureau now encourages the "Willing to Certify" producers to go one step farther. These producers
may put a "Self-Certifying" label on the goods, which
usually states something like this: "The manufacturer

guarantees this wallpaper
to meet requirements of
U. S. commercial standard
CS 16-29 issued by the
U. S. Department of Com-
merce." This plan shows
the consumer immediately
that the manufacturer
guarantees that the goods
meet the standards. The
National Bureau of Stand-
ards, however, does not
guarantee that they do. It

A self-certifying label.

does not check up on the manufacturer. In fact, it has been
known that names of manufacturers have been kept on the
list after the goods ceased to meet the standards. However,
the use of the "Self-Certifying" label in such cases is misrepresentation that can be prosecuted as an unfair trade
practice.

Standards of U. S. Pharmacopoeia. The Food and Drug
Administration accepts the minimum standards of identification established by the U. S. Pharmacopoeial Conven-
tion. Every ten years various medical authorities representing the U. S. Public Health Service, the Department of
Agriculture, the U. S. Army, the U. S. Navy, and various

medical societies and colleges meet to draw up standards of quality and purity for all known types of drugs and medicines. These are then published in a book called *U. S. Pharmacopoeia*, which is referred to as "U. S. P." No new remedy can be added to the official list until it has been properly tested and tried out under special supervision. This book is recognized by Federal and state governmental agencies and by manufacturers as the basic guide as to standards for these products. If a drug or medicine is described as to strength on the basis of U. S. P. standards and fails to measure up to these standards, the producer or the distributor is subject to prosecution by the Federal Trade Commission or the Food and Drug Administration. When a consumer buys any drug or medicine with its contents described on the label on the basis of U. S. P. standards, he can therefore have reasonable assurance as to the quality and purity.

Standards of American Pharmaceutical Association. Another agency that establishes standards for drug products is the American Pharmaceutical Association, which meets every ten years to establish standards for formulas and prescriptions of physicians that are compounded by druggists. These standards are published in the *National Formulary*. When the letters "N. F." appear on a drug product, the consumer may have reasonable assurance of quality and purity.

Standards of American Institute of Homeopathy. This institute publishes annually a *Homeopathic Pharmacopoeia* of the United States, which sets standards of identification for certain drug products. When the letters "H. P." appear on a drug product, they carry an assurance of standards similar to those previously mentioned.

Standards of American Standards Association. The American Standards Association has been primarily concerned with the establishment of industrial standards. It has served two functions. One is to simplify sizes, shapes, and gauges so that there will be a greater uniformity in the products that we buy. After many years of work by this

association, one may now buy a machine bolt of a certain
size with the assurance that it is standard. One may buy
a stove bolt of a certain size with the assurance that it is
standard. Besides these standards that have resulted from
simplification, the association has established standards of
quality that are recognized in industry and are used by
some Federal and state agencies in identifying quality.
These are referred to as "American Standards." If any
manufacturer or distributor claims that a product conforms to American Standards, it will be considered unfair
if the product does not meas-
ure up to these standards.

**Standards of Illuminating
Engineers' Society.** As was
described in Chapter 7, the Illuminating Engineers' Society
has established various standards by which portable lamps
are judged as to quality.
Any product that meets these
minimum standards may, upon
inspection, carry the I. E. S.
identification.

The label of a certifying agency
is a guide to quality.

Standards of Underwriters' Laboratory. The National
Board of Fire Underwriters sets up certain minimum
standards of safety for materials and appliances that
might involve hazards of life, fire, theft, or accident. The
Underwriters' Laboratory maintained by this organization
passes judgment on a product before it is permitted to
carry the U. L. label.

Other Standards. There are other specialized agencies
that set standards. The American Institute of Laundering
sets standards in regard to the washability of fabrics.
The Better Fabrics Testing Bureau issues a "color tested"
seal for fabrics that meet its standards of color fastness.
Other agencies, including the Federal Trade Commission,
have also been developing standards for the fastness of
colors in fabrics. Many states have laws establishing stand-

ards for such items as foods, drugs, and bedding. Many of these are the same as the standards established by the Food and Drug Administration, the U. S. Bureau of Standards, the U. S. Department of Agriculture, the Federal Trade Commission, or the American Standards Association.

Some states, however, have established their own particular standards. For instance, there are several states that have grading and labeling laws applying to fruits and vegetables. Several have laws pertaining to bedding, including blankets, mattresses, and springs. These laws particularly apply to new and secondhand materials used in padding mattresses and upholstery. In some states it is mandatory that the labels used to identify the quality must not be removed from the product.

In order for a consumer to know what protection is afforded by state laws, it would be necessary to investigate the standards established in the state in which he lives.

It will be seen from the previous discussion that many of the standards are voluntary; some, however, are mandatory. When voluntary standards have been established by private agencies and are so marked on the label, the consumer may be reasonably certain that the commodity at least meets those minimum standards. When minimum standards for such commodities as goods have been established under the agencies of the U. S. Department of Agriculture and the Federal Trade Commission, they become mandatory for those products covered by the standards that are sold in interstate commerce. If these products do not measure up to the minimum standards and are sold in interstate commerce, they must be labeled in some manner as "Below U. S. standards, a good food, not high grade," or "Below U. S. standards, low quality but not illegal."

Misbranding. Under the specific laws developed by the Food and Drug Administration, an article may not enter into interstate commerce if it has been adulterated or if it contains an ingredient that is harmful or dangerous. Poisonous articles must be so labeled. If foods contain preservatives, this fact must be indicated on the label and no preservative may be used that is harmful for human consumption. Any food that contains decayed or decomposed matter is not allowed to be sold in interstate commerce.

Any food or drug item that fails to measure up to the minimum standards of identification is considered to be misbranded. For instance, if a fruit salad that illustrates on the label a certain proportion of cherries, peaches, and pears fails to contain all these ingredients in the approximate way in which they are shown on the label, it is considered to be misbranded.

Grading Based on Standards

Government Grades Versus Private Grades. What are the grades? The previous discussion has shown how standards are developed. In order to identify these standards and make them meaningful to consumers, it is necessary to have some kind of grading plan. Now let us examine the various means of grading.

In the past many manufacturers and many producers of foods have used their own grades, such as superb, fancy, extra fancy, top grade, superior, and many others. As a

result the consumer has never been able to depend upon such indefinite grade designations. It is for this reason that governmental agencies and many organizations of consumers and producers have insisted upon a more definite use of grade terminology. On page 153 the bases for the standards set up for canned tomatoes were indicated. These standards for tomatoes are converted into grade designations as follows:

Grades are helpful if you understand the standards on which they are based.

A total score of 90 to 100 is Grade A
A total score of 75 to 89 is Grade B
A total score of 60 to 74 is Grade C

Failure of a product to rate a specified number of points for any one factor may determine its grade regardless of the total score. For example, if a can of tomatoes contains some that are undercolored, they cannot be given a Grade A rating regardless of the total score. It must be borne in mind, however, that all three grades of tomatoes are thoroughly wholesome or else they would not be permitted to be sold in interstate commerce. Information in regard to the standards and grading scale for canned foods can be obtained from the Processed Products Standardization and Inspection Division, U. S. Department of Agriculture, Washington, D. C.

The U. S. Department of Agriculture also has the power to establish grades for such additional food items as butter, eggs, milk, and cream, besides many other products that are of primary interest to the consumer.

Government Grades of Farm Products. At present, farm products such as fruits, vegetables, and dairy products are not sold by official grades except in wholesale markets. In most wholesale markets, however, the burlap potato bags, the boxes and barrels of apples, crates of strawberries, and other similar containers carry the official grade markings. Some of the individual packages sold in retail stores also contain these grade markings and can be observed by the consumer in retail stores either by examining the original wholesale carton or the small retail carton. The official government grades vary for some products, but those for potatoes will serve as an example.

U. S. Fancy
U. S. Extra No. 1
U. S. No. 1
U. S. Commercial
U. S. No. 2

In the case of every product there is a definite scale by which the grades are determined. The table on page 162 shows how the grades for eggs are determined.

It must be borne in mind that these grades do not take into consideration the size of eggs. The best way to buy

eggs is by weight if one wants to be assured of getting the
proper value. Grades of eggs are often indicated on the
shipping cases used by wholesalers and sometimes on individual packages.

QUALITY FACTORS	SPECIFICATIONS OF EACH QUALITY FACTOR			
	AA GRADE OR U. S. SPECIAL	A GRADE OR U. S. EXTRA	B GRADE OR U. S. STANDARD	C GRADE OR U. S. TRADE
Shell	Clean ; sound ; normal.	Clean ; sound ; normal.	Clean ; sound ; may be slightly abnormal.	Clean ; sound ; may be ab-normal.
Air cell ...	One-eighth inch or less in depth ; regular.	Two-eighths inch or less in depth ; regular.	Three-eighths inch or less in depth ; may show move-ment not in excess of one-half inch.	May be over three-eighths inch in depth ; may show movement in excess of one-half inch ; may be bubbly or free.
Yolk	Well centered ; outline indis-tinct ; motion sluggish ; free from visible germ develop-ment and other defects or blemishes.	Fairly well centered ; out-line moder-ately defined ; may be slightly mobile ; free from visible germ develop-ment and prac-tically free from other defects or blemishes.	Outline well de-fined ; may be mobile ; may show slightly visible germ development and other definite but not serious defects.	May be plainly visible ; may be freely mo-bile and cast dark shadow ; and show clearly visible germ develop-ment but no blood ; may show other serious defects.
White	Firm ; clear.	Firm ; clear.	Reasonably firm ; clear.	May be weak and watery.

Summary of United States standards for eggs.

Many eggs are perfectly wholesome and are otherwise
of high quality except that they are dirty. They sell at
lower prices and if a person is willing to accept dirty eggs,
they represent the most economical purchase. Grades are
also established for dirty eggs, such as "U. S. extra, dirty,"
"U. S. standard, dirty," and "U. S. trade, dirty."

Government Grades of Canned Fruits and Vegetables. Under the Federal Food and Drug Administration, standard
grades have been established for canned fruits. The grade
markings do not appear on the labels of all canned fruits,
but they do appear on the labels of many. The purchaser
has a right to demand canned fruits that have such markings; in fact, he should insist upon them as a protection.

The table on this page provides an explanation of the grades for canned fruits. This method of indicating grades is commonly known as the ABC method of grading. Other methods have been established by various associations, canners, and distributors; but there is no particular uniformity among the standards set up under these methods.

GRADE	QUALITY	COLOR	FORM	SIZE	SIRUP WHEN PACKED
A (fancy)	Very best	Very high	Free from blemishes; mature but not overripe	Very uniform and symmetrical	From 40 to 70 per cent sugar, depending on acidity of fruit
B (choice)	Fine	High	Free from blemishes; mature but not overripe	Uniform, symmetrical, usually smaller than A	From 30 to 55 per cent sugar
C (standard)	Good	Reasonably good	Reasonably free from blemishes; reasonably uniform in ripeness	Reasonably uniform and symmetrical	From 14 to 30 per cent sugar, or water pack
Substandard	Second	Below standard	Below standard; not uniform	Below standard; not uniform	Below standard for sirup or water pack

Quality grades for canned fruits.

The United States Department of Agriculture has established standards for such products as canned corn, peas, beans, and tomatoes. The following table describes various grades. New standards are being established constantly.

GRADE	QUALITY	COLOR	FORM	SIZE	LIQUOR
A (fancy)	Finest; of uniform quality	Uniformly good	Uniform; very tender	Uniform	Clear or only slightly turbid
B (extra standard)	Sound; of good stock	Practically free from under-colored parts	Practically uniform; tender	Practically uniform	May be some discoloration
C (standard)	May be field run of good stock	May be slightly discolored	Some may have been broken in processing	Need not be uniform	May be somewhat turbid
Substandard	Second	Below standard	Below standard; not uniform	Below standard; not uniform	Below standard; not clear

Quality grades for canned vegetables.

Many canners are voluntarily labeling their products according to these designations.

Canned fruits and vegetables of the fancy grade are uniform in size, color, and texture. They represent the perfect portion of the crop. The choice fruits and the extra-standard vegetables are next best, while the standard products rank third. The better grades are usually packed in better juice. Additional designations are used in grading such products as asparagus, corn, and peas.

The ABC grading may be used on canned fruits and vegetables in the following manner:

(a) The canner or distributor may do his own grading; but if he does, the grades must meet government standards.

(b) On the payment of a fee, a government grader will check sample lots and award grades for the entire lots, which permits the label to carry the statement "This grade officially certified by the U. S. Department of Agriculture."

(c) On the payment of a fee, an inspector will be stationed in the cannery for continuous inspection of every lot, in which case the label may bear the statement "Packed under continuous inspection of the U. S. Department of Agriculture."

Informative Labeling

What Is Informative Labeling? There are two opposing ideas in regard to identifying merchandise. One is that there should be fixed standard grades, as previously explained. It is contended that when consumers learn to recognize these grades, definite information will be provided on labels to guide them in buying.

Canners, producers, and distributors have contended, and possibly rightfully so, that an absolutely uniform system of grading is difficult to carry out and does not give the consumer the maximum amount of information. Many of these individuals have proposed instead certain information on labels, referred to as descriptive labels, containing the kind of information that might be useful to the consumer. Other groups, notably a group of canners organized as U. S. Inspected Foods, Inc., have argued for a combination of grade labeling and descriptive labeling.

Individual canners and distributors may use their own grading system; but unless the consumer knows what this

Packed under continuous inspection of the U. S. Department of Agriculture.

GRADE B (EXTRA STANDARD) EARLY VARIETY PEAS
This means that they meet the following standards:
1. Reasonably tender.
2. Reasonably uniform in color and size.
3. Surrounded by liquor which may be somewhat cloudy.
4. Reasonably free from skins, broken peas and other defects.
5. Must possess a good pea flavor.

GENERAL DESCRIPTION

Type	Early Variety
Size	No. 4 Sieve
Size of Can	No. 2
Contents	1 lb. 4 oz.
Servings	4 to 5
Cups	Approx. 2¼

Packed under continuous inspection of the U. S. Department of Agriculture.

GRADE C (STANDARD) TOMATOES
This means that they meet the following standards:
1. Small or large pieces.
2. Fairly red in color.
3. Fairly free from defects.
4. Possess a normal tomato flavor.

GENERAL DESCRIPTION

Type	Slightly Salted
Size of Can	No. 2
Contents	1 lb. 3 oz.
Servings	4 to 5
Cups	Approx. 2¼

Portions of labels showing both grade and description.

grading system means, it will not be helpful to the consumer.

Informative labeling applies to many products, including appliances, clothing, and fabrics. In the case of fabrics, there are various terms used to indicate shrinkage, such as "preshrunk." If this term is used, the fabric should not shrink more than 2 per cent. Other information on fabrics and clothing may indicate the type of fiber used, the weave, the water repellency, the finish, the crease resistance, and other special features.

Descriptive General Labels. Some canners and distributors have used and promoted a type of labeling that they contend is better for the consumer. It is often referred to as descriptive labeling. Descriptive labels for foods, for instance, would contain such information as: (a) style of the pack; (b) degree of maturity of the food; (c) number of units in the can, such as the number of slices of peaches; (d) the quantity in terms of cups if the units are small, such as cherries; (e) the quantity in terms of servings; (f) the size of the can; (g) the description of the raw product and the method of processing; (h) the suggested methods or ways of serving. It will be seen that this type of label has many advantages over the kind used with strictly grade labeling.

Progress in Informative Labeling. It is obvious that the use of fixed grades or general descriptive labels all provide a certain amount of helpful information to the consumer. The National Consumer-Retailer Council has been active in the development of the so-called informative labeling practice. In developing informative labels, this organization—composed of consumers, producers, and distributors—attempts to find out the kind of information that will be most useful to the consumer in determining quality. The following illustration is the master outline for all such labels. Such labels have now become quite generally used, particularly in the textile field. Many chain stores, large department stores, and mail-order houses are using informative labels of their own development or those sponsored by the National Consumer-Retailer Council. A part of such a label is shown at the left.

On page 168 is an example of an informative label that provides a guide in the selection of materials.

What You Can Do in Regard to Informative Labeling. The National

---

COUNTRY CLUB
FANCY LARGE SWEET PEAS

Large, tender, sweet peas of the fancy variety, grown and packed in the best producing area. Delicious natural full flavor, uniform size and color make them a popular favorite. Ready to heat and serve direct from the can. This can contains 6 to 8 average servings.

BAKED PEAS AND BACON

1 No. 2 can Country Club Large Sweet Peas

6 slices bacon	1 teaspoon grated onion
½ teaspoon salt	2 tablespoons melted butter
⅛ teaspoon pepper	½ cup soft bread crumbs
1 cup coffee cream or thin white sauce	

Cook the bacon until crisp, and then dice. Add the bacon to the peas, together with 2 tablespoons of bacon fat, the salt, pepper, cream and onion. Turn into a greased casserole and top with the crumbs which have been combined with the melted butter. Bake in a hot oven (400° F.) for 20 minutes.

Yield: 6 average servings.

Recipe prepared and tested by The Kroger Food Foundation

Part of a label showing a description
of the product.

OUTLINE FOR INFORMATIVE LABELS

It is understood, of course, that labels should conform to local, State or Federal regulations where such exist.

WHAT IT WILL DO (Performance)

Degree of color permanence; shrinkage or stretchage; breaking strength; seam slippage; resistance to water, perspiration, wind, wear; light, heat and power tests; power consumption; cost of upkeep; etc.

WHAT IT IS MADE OF (Composition)

Kind and quality of fiber, metal, wood, leather, ceramics, cement, rock, fur, plastics, petroleum products, rubber, paper, bone, chemicals, drugs; ingredients of food products; etc.

HOW IT IS MADE (Construction)

Size, weight, number of yarns per inch, weave, number of stitches per inch, finish, ply, cut, hand or machine made, pressed, molded, stamped, inlaid; etc.

HOW TO CARE FOR IT

Detailed instructions for washing and/or cleaning; precautions to be observed in cleaning or in storage; refrigeration; oiling and greasing; polishing; etc.

RECOMMENDED USES

Purposes for which it is most suitable; recipes; etc.

NAME OF MANUFACTURER OR DISTRIBUTOR

Name and address of the manufacturer or distributor.

A model outline for an informative label.

Consumer-Retailer Council suggests four ways in which the consumer can obtain increasing benefits from informative labels. These are as follows:

1. Read labels carefully.
2. Patronize the firms that label their merchandise informatively. To be maintained, improved business practices such as better labeling must be profitable to the firms employing them. Firms will use these labels if they know that buyers read them and want them.

Pepperell
Peeress Sheet

An exquisitely smooth percale, made of combed yarns. One of the finest, most luxurious cotton sheets you can buy.

This Pepperell product has been tested and approved by the Better Fabrics Testing Bureau.

PEPPERELL MANUFACTURING COMPANY
Boston, Massachusetts

WHAT IT IS MADE OF

Fibre Content: 100% American Mississippi Delta cotton.

HOW IT IS MADE

Thread count (after bleaching) averages: 202 threads to the square inch—103 lengthwise, 99 crosswise.
Weight averages 3.92 ounces to the square yard.
Finishing materials: less than 1%.

This luxurious sheet is made of the finest cotton yarns, combed to remove short fibres. Only the silkiest, longest fibres are used.
3/8-inch Tape selvage is tightly woven to offer extra protection against cracking and tearing.
4-inch hem at top, 1-inch at bottom. Stitched with small stitches, and the ends firmly caught.
Tellmark tab, in corner of sheet, makes it easy to tell the size without removing sheet from shelf.
Inspected 28 times during manufacture. Samples tested weekly to check quality maintenance.

WHAT SERVICE IT WILL GIVE

Breaking strength: Sheet fabric will withstand a pull of 79 pounds lengthwise, 87 crosswise. (Average figures.)
Shrinkage tests made on the rotary ironer basis show approximately 6% lengthwise and 1.75% crosswise.

This exquisite sheet provides the utmost in sleeping comfort. But the fine yarns and tight weave, which make it so smooth and even-textured, also give it extreme strength and durability.
Its lightness makes it easy to handle, and cheaper to launder at pound rates.

3. When you find a label that is helpful, "think out loud" about it:

   (a) Comment on it to the salesperson.

   (b) Write a note to the store president, thus assuring that your recommendation reaches top executives.

   (c) If the label is a manufacturer's label, write him about it.

   (d) Send your comments to the National Consumer-Retailer Council, 8 West 40th Street, New York, N. Y. The Council will pass on your comments to the manufacturer or distributor.

4. File the labels you find helpful. Instructions as to care may be needed throughout the life of the article. When it is necessary

An informative label.

to replace the article, you can refer to your label file as a buying guide.

TEXTBOOK QUESTIONS

1. Give at least one good example of why standards are important to you in buying some of the things that you need.
2. In what way does the Federal Trade Commission enter into the establishing of standards?

168

3. How does the Federal Trade Commission enforce the trade practice rules in regard to standards?
4. Distinguish the difference between the "Federal Specifications" and the "Commercial Standards" that were developed by the U. S. Bureau of Standards.
5. What is the "Willing to Certify" list?
6. What is the significance of the "U. S. P." found on some drug products?
7. On what products are you likely to see the letters "N. F." and what do they mean?
8. What do the letters "H. P." mean on a product?
9. How is the American Standards Association affecting the consumer directly?
10. If you see the letters "I. E. S." on a tag on an electric reading lamp, what do the letters mean?
11. What is the significance of the "U. L." label, and on what kinds of products are you most likely to find it?
12. Is there any standard by which you can identify the washability of fabrics?
13. Give an example of how standards are converted into grades. Use tomatoes as an example.
14. What is the highest grade of potatoes?
15. What is the highest grade of eggs?
16. Under what three plans may a producer or a distributor use the ABC grading on canned fruits and vegetables?
17. What are some of the helpful items that might be found on a good descriptive label on a food product?
18. What function is the National Consumer-Retailer Council trying to perform?

DISCUSSION QUESTIONS

1. Name some grades and descriptions of products that you have seen which have meant nothing to you.
2. Name some grades that you can identify.
3. Is it possible to sell an imitation catsup in interstate commerce?
4. Is a jar labeled as jam legal if it contains 40 per cent fruit, 20 per cent starch, and 40 per cent sugar?
5. How is it possible for you as a consumer to take advantage of the functions of the U. S. Bureau of Standards?
6. Let us suppose that a standard is set by an industry and one member of that industry does not choose to meet this standard. Is there anything that can be done about it?
7. Name some articles on which you have found the "U. S. P." standard on the label.

8. Can a canner or a distributor sell any food product that is below standard?
9. How would you attempt to take advantage of Federal grades in buying potatoes?
10. Discuss the question of wholesomeness and value as concerned with grades in regard to eggs.
11. Discuss some of the advantages and disadvantages of the ABC labeling advocated by the Federal Government.
12. Give some of the arguments for and against descriptive labeling without fixed standards for grades.
13. State your final opinion and summary of the question of the use of fixed grades as compared with descriptive labels without grades. What would be your choice?

PROBLEMS

1. Make a list of food, medical, and clothing products in your home on which you find indicated any of the standards that are described in this chapter. Indicate on which different items you found these standards given.
2. Make a list of all products used in your home on which you can find any of the grades described in this chapter, or which give other grades.
3. Give your own description of an ideal food label, either by a list of information that you would want on it or by drawing a model of a food label.
4. Present your idea of an ideal clothing label either by making a list of information that it should contain or by drawing a model.

COMMUNITY PROBLEMS AND PROJECTS

1. Find a label that you think is either (a) helpful or (b) not helpful in buying merchandise. Write your commendations or your criticisms to the National Consumer-Retailer Council as indicated on page 168 of this chapter and submit these to your teacher.
2. File for future reference all labels that you find helpful. Paste these up in the form of a scrapbook with divisions for different classes of products, such as foods, clothing, drugs, furniture, and other items. At a time fixed by your teacher, submit this scrapbook for grading.
3. Obtain from the U. S. Department of Agriculture a set of standards for some food product. With this scale before you, establish a grade for a can of this food that you have available in your home.

Chapter 10

PART IV _____

The General Principles of Buying

Purpose of the Chapter. In preceding chapters you have learned how government and private agencies aid in protecting the consumer. You have learned specific sources of information and should have a rather definite idea of how you can depend upon advertising, labels, standards, and grades as guides in buying. Before taking up the study of buying specific products, there are certain other guides in buying with which you should be familiar. The purpose of this chapter is to discuss these additional general principles of buying.

A Plan for Spending. Very few people earn so much money that they can buy all they want without considering whether or not they have enough money to pay for their purchases. Therefore a plan of buying is necessary. Although budgeting is presented in detail in Chapter 23, it is desirable to emphasize it at this point because of its relationship to buying. A budget is a plan of spending and saving. The plan will help you to determine how much to spend and how much to save. When the spending program is broken down into months and weeks, it should be checked periodically with the original plan to be sure that overspending is not taking place. It often must be revised and adjusted to take care of unforeseen problems as they arise.

Advantages of a Budget Spending Plan

1. It will help you to live within your income.
2. It will help you to save.
3. It will help you to determine what you can and must have so that you will not recklessly spend your money for foolish things and deprive yourself of things you really need.

Intelligent shopping
is one of the best
means of buying.

Ewing Galloway

'   **Methods of Buying.** Most people have a choice of several methods of buying. They may buy by telephone, from house-to-house salesmen, by mail from a catalog, or by shopping in stores. These methods have their advantages and disadvantages.

Buying by telephone is convenient, but it deprives you of the privilege of careful shopping and comparing the merchandise. Usually buying by telephone is more expensive because it involves delivery service.

Buying from house-to-house salesmen is an easy way to obtain what you need, but it is not always a satisfactory way. Unless you take the trouble to make comparisons with other products, you may not be getting the best merchandise in this manner; and you may be paying more than is necessary. However, the convenience of buying in this manner is often an important advantage to some buyers.

Buying by mail is convenient because it can be done in the home; but it is also inconvenient because of the neces-

172

sity of sending a remittance or paying for the package when it comes C.O.D. Waiting for the package to be delivered is another inconvenience. Selecting suitable merchandise is difficult by this method because you have to depend upon pictures and descriptions.

Buying in stores, although it may be inconvenient, is generally the most satisfactory method of buying. Buying in stores permits you to see what is available and permits you to make comparisons within a particular store and among several stores. You have an opportunity to choose as to quality and price. Often you may either pay cash or charge it, and in many cases you have a choice of taking the merchandise with you or having it delivered.

Shopping Procedures. At the time of purchase the buyer seldom has an opportunity to make comparisons. When

---

Hints for Shopping

What to Do

1. Take a shopping list with you.
2. Do your shopping before you buy; avoid having merchandise sent on approval.
3. Make use of all buying information available, such as advertising, the salesclerk, labels, tests, and specifications.
4. In making comparisons, check not only the price but also the quality.
5. Watch scales and measuring devices.
6. Avoid rush periods in stores so you can shop with greater ease.

Where to Buy

1. Select a store with a reasonable range of varieties, sizes, and qualities.
2. Select a store that has labels and standards that aid in making intelligent selections.
3. Select a store with shopping conveniences that save time and energy.
4. Select a store with fair prices based on the quality and the service.
5. Select a store with services, such as credit and delivery, if you need them.
6. Select a store that is reliable.
7. Select a store that gives courteous service.

there is opportunity for it, comparison may be made casually and hastily, or it may be well thought out and reasonably scientific. The more scientific the procedure, the more chance the buyer has of getting value for his money.

Intelligent buying demands the development of a consciousness of differences between products. One of many products may be good. Two products may be very similar. It is frequently difficult to determine the better of two products even under the most careful scrutiny. When such is the case, there is little danger of making an unwise selection.

Legitimate Bargains. The following paragraphs explain types of bargain sales that are conducted by reputable stores. The buyer must learn from experience what stores really offer bargains when such sales are conducted.

Remnants are merchandise, usually yard goods, that a merchant is anxious to sell to avoid a loss. A remnant is a bargain if the total price paid for the piece is less than the cost of the actual quantity of goods needed. Buying a large remnant that cannot be used is not a bargain. *Mill ends,* short lengths of goods purchased by the merchant from a mill, are sometimes included in such sales.

Soiled goods placed on sale may be returned goods, shelf-worn goods, or sample merchandise. Such goods may represent true bargains; but if the merchandise requires dry cleaning or repairing, this additional cost should be taken into consideration.

Preseason sales usually give the customer the advantage of obtaining seasonable merchandise in advance of the regular season. The merchandise is offered at a reduction in price in order to encourage the consumer to buy a little earlier. This type of sale should not be confused with the practice of giving preferred customers a chance to buy new merchandise at regular prices before it is offered for general sale.

Preinventory sales are conducted by merchants to reduce their stocks so that merchandise can be converted into cash and need not be carried over into a new season. Such a sale also helps to reduce the work of checking the inventory. Bargains can usually be obtained at these sales.

Out-of-season sales are sales of merchandise at the close of a season. For instance, summer clothing is often put on sale in July and August so that the merchant can clear out his stock and need not carry it over into the next summer season. Genuine bargains can be obtained at these sales if the clothing is of a color, a design, and a style that can be worn satisfactorily during the following summer. Extreme styles, however, will probably go out of date by that time.

Odd-lot sales are sales of odd sizes and irregular merchandise, such as seconds. The odd lots may consist of apparel of unusual sizes that the merchant cannot sell. A person can usually get a bargain at such a sale if the clothing is suitable in size. Irregular clothing or seconds should be examined carefully to see whether the flaws materially affect the value of the merchandise.

Sales of *surplus stock* sometimes result from the overproduction of mills or the overbuying of the merchant. The merchant may buy a special lot of merchandise from a mill at a low price and offer it for sale, or he may attempt to unload his shelves to stimulate business during the regular season. Such sales usually provide bargains if the merchandise is what the buyer needs.

Anniversary sales of legitimate merchants with good reputations are usually important events. Such events frequently offer unusual bargains.

Special or seasonal sales, when conducted by reputable stores, usually offer good bargains. Some stores hold annual furniture sales in August at which they offer good merchandise at attractive prices. Other stores hold linen sales at certain times of the year. Food stores sometimes hold sales of canned goods in the fall or in the spring at which bargains are available.

The reputation of the store is usually the best guide in determining whether or not sales provide real bargains. In order to check on bargains it is important to keep yourself informed regularly as to prices and quality so that, when merchandise is put on sale, you are in a position to judge its value in relation to its price.

Remember that merchandise bought on sale is not a bargain at any price unless it is needed or will be needed at a definite time in the future.

When to Buy. The preceding discussion of various types of sales gives some ideas as to when to buy. For instance, it is easy to observe that seasonal goods usually run through a definite cycle in price level. When offered in advance sales, they are usually sold at reduced prices. The buyer who is especially interested in the style of his clothing can frequently take advantage of such sales. At the beginning of a season style goods sell at the highest prices. As the season progresses, the prices are gradually lowered, for merchants hope to dispose of their goods before the end of the season.

There are important price cycles for many other products. For instance, in cities in which coal is used for heating purposes, it is usually sold at its lowest price in April and May and at its maximum price during the winter months. It sells at a low price in the spring and the summer because then the rate of consumption is low and dealers are anxious to make sales and deliveries during the slow season.

Fresh fruits and vegetables usually sell at the cheapest prices during the summer. The prices of canned goods are lowest soon after the canning season. The illustration on page 177 shows the seasonal trends in the prices of some of the most common food products. As one might suspect, products that are most difficult to store have wide fluctuations in price.

During periods of generally high prices the wise consumer will avoid buying everything that he does not really need. He will save his money and wait until prices are lower. Of course, certain things must be purchased regularly, such as food. Because the prices of different kinds of food fluctuate during the year, the wise consumer will avoid foods when they are at their highest prices and will substitute other foods that are available at lower prices. These policies in buying not only will save money for the consumer immediately but will also tend to bring prices down so that the consumer can buy what he wants at a

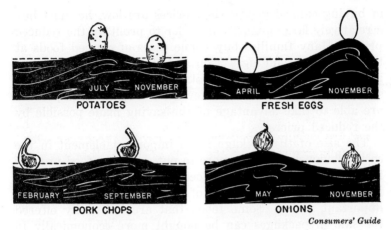

Consumers' Guide

Seasonal price trends of common foods.

lower price. This might be called consumer resistance. In
a competitive market, consumers can control the prices of
commodities by the way they buy them. If consumers refuse
to buy a particular product, it is sure to come down in price.

Some Policies in Buying. In determining how to buy, let
us think in terms of shopping procedure. The saving of
time, energy, and money are the points to be considered
in shopping procedure. The saving of money may be the
primary consideration of one buyer, whereas the saving of
time may be an important consideration of another. For
instance, the buyer may save time and energy by ordering
by telephone, but he may pay extra for delivery service
and may not get the benefit of personal selection.

Buying in large quantities rather than in small quantities
usually is desirable, provided the large quantities are needed.
People who buy small lots of groceries from day to day, or
even several times a day, are causing an economic waste of
time and are paying more per unit than persons who buy in
larger quantities. A housewife will, however, find it desirable to buy food in small quantities if larger quantities
would spoil before they could be used.

Seasonal buying and quantity buying go hand in hand.
In other words, if a person decides to enjoy the advantage

of buying canned goods when prices are low, he must buy
a relatively large quantity in order to profit by the reduced
prices. Many families buy whole cases of canned foods at
the end of the canning season and store these for use during the winter. Others buy potatoes in large quantities and
store them in a place where they will not spoil. Such persons
are able to take advantage of the saving made possible by
the reduced prices.

The size of the package is an important element in the
cost. Obviously, it costs more to put a certain food product
into ten small cans than it does in one large can. In some
instances, therefore, the cost of the package is an extremely
important factor. Some foods that are ordinarily offered
for sale in packages can be bought more economically in
bulk. The wise buyer will learn to shop as infrequently as
possible to save time and energy. He will also learn to buy
in packages of a size that will be economical for his family.
If one finds it necessary to buy a small package, it is often
cheaper to buy three packages at a time. This factor will
be studied in detail in a later chapter.

Guides in Buying Foods and Household Supplies

1. Buy in as large quantities as can be stored conveniently
   and used without waste from spoilage.

2. Keep informed of the regular prices of staple foods and
   household supplies in order to gauge the savings that will
   be possible through taking advantage of special sales.

3. Watch market conditions and know whether the general
   price trend is upward or downward. Take advantage of
   seasonal low points and of rising markets for quantity
   buying.

4. Consider the value of time and effort, as well as money,
   a. When deciding between charge-and-delivery and cash-
      and-carry stores.
   b. When deciding whether to buy in large or small quan-
      tities.
   c. When deciding whether to buy in bulk or in packages.

5. Keep on hand an emergency supply of foods that will provide at least one meal on short notice. A larger supply,
   however, is usually advisable.

No definite rules can be laid down for buying, because there are many variables. Different quantities must be bought for families of varying sizes. The quantity to be bought will depend upon the amount of money available and upon the peculiar needs of the family.

Trade Names and Terms. There are many trade names and terms used in connection with various products. Most of these are not intended to be deceptive or misleading, but they are confusing unless a person knows what they mean and knows something about the differences in quality. For instance, stainless steel is a general term used to identify a steel alloy that will not tarnish so easily as ordinary steel, but there are many qualities of stainless steel.

Let us consider a few other common examples. Wool cloth may be made from all virgin wool, reprocessed wool, re-used wool, or a mixture of these with some other fibers. The dictionary defines parchment as the skin of a sheep. Parchment paper and parchment lamp shades, however, are very seldom made of skin; they are usually made of paper. Chinaware usually does not come from China;

When buying woolen products, read the labels.

the word designates a type of clay from which the pottery is made. The product may or may not be better than a similar product made in China. Silverware is not sterling silver, but usually plated ware. Sterling silver is solid silver. For examples of trade names of furs and fabrics, refer to Chapter 14.

How to Read the Label. The buyer should read labels carefully to obtain information with regard to (a) the weight or the volume, (b) the grade or the quality, and (c) an analysis or a description of the contents. The labels of some private agencies have been discussed previously.

Until uniform grade standards have been established and are used for a particular product, it is impossible to rely upon the existing grade designations without knowing what those grades mean. Much of the terminology in use means one thing to the seller, but a different thing to the buyer. If the buyer takes the words at their face value, he is frequently misled into believing the goods to be of a grade higher than they actually are. Furthermore, the terminology is made confusing by the wide variation in its use. In other words, buyers and sellers do not speak the same language. When this situation exists, grade designations are of very little value.

For instance, one would suppose that the *first* grade of butter is the best grade, but as a matter of fact it is the third grade when compared with government standards. To get the best grade of butter, one has to buy the *extra* grade. Similar confusing grades are used for other products.

As was explained in a preceding chapter, the Federal Food and Drug Administration protects the consumer from obtaining adulterated and misbranded products. Under the Federal law the labels on foods and drugs must not mislead consumers. For instance, if an article is artificially colored, this fact must be indicated on the label. All imitations must be definitely indicated. Ingredients in imitations must be declared. Although an imitation product may be wholesome, it may be inferior to the genuine product. If the consumer is to realize the full benefit of such protection, however, he must learn to read labels accurately.

Read the label on a package or a can before buying.

Suppose, for example, that you ask for a bottle of vanilla and are handed a bottle marked "Vanillin Extract." What does this name mean? It really means that the bottle contains a flavoring material that is a synthetic coal-tar product, whereas the genuine product is made from the vanilla bean. If the extract is colored to imitate genuine vanilla extract, this fact should be indicated on the bottle. The names of some other products are also misleading.

If you ask for egg noodles and are given a package merely labeled "Noodles," you are not getting what you requested. Egg noodles must contain egg solids to the extent of 5½ per cent by weight. Plain noodles contain no egg products.

When you buy jams, jellies, and preserves, do the labels on the containers mean anything to you? Do you expect to get pure fruits and sugar? If you wish to be sure to obtain a product containing nothing but pure fruit and sugar, you should buy one that has a label indicating what you desire.

The partial label below on this page illustrates the type of information that a consumer may find on a good label. If one learns to use such labels in buying, he will find that they not only serve as helpful guides, but also

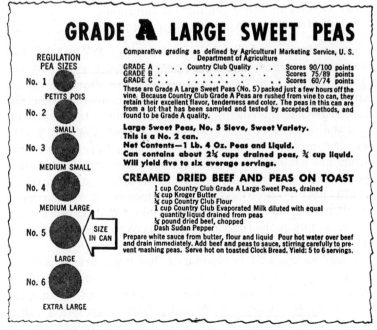

An example of specifications and information on a food label.

encourage other producers and distributors to use equally informative labels.

Many of the products, including food products, sold in stores today do not carry information in regard to standards or grades; but many labels, particularly on foods, do contain certain helpful information. This information can be relied upon to be generally truthful and accurate, because if it were not truthful or accurate, the producer or the distributor would be guilty of misbranding under Federal and state laws.

The contents indicated on labels are also important, for the size of the container is frequently misleading. Deceptive containers are now illegal if the products are sold in interstate commerce. In examining a label, one should look for the following information:

(a) Specific descriptive statements.
(b) Facts regarding quality.
(c) Facts regarding quantity.
(d) Grades or other similar designations.
(e) Certificate or other mark of approval.

Trade-Marks and Trial Use. A trade-mark is used for one purpose only: to encourage people to ask for the product again after using it the first time. The manufacturer of an established brand therefore usually strives to fulfill certain standards that the consumer will expect to obtain when he buys the product. In the absence of information that would permit comparison, the recognized brands of reputable producers are usually more reliable than other brands. If other information is available, however, the brand on a product should not be used as the only means of comparison. Furthermore, the branding of a product may cause a purchaser to pay more than he would have to pay for another product of an equivalent quality.

Trade names and trade-marks, however, are important guides for a consumer, because after a person has tried a certain product, he can ask for the same brand again with reasonable assurance that he will get the same quality that he has used before. Reputable manufacturers attempt to follow standards on products carrying their brand names. However, in the case of some lesser known food products, the standard of quality is not always maintained.

Trial use is an important means of buying any product, whether it is trial use from a sample, trial of merchandise bought by a friend, or trial use from a small purchase before making a large purchase.

Testing. A previous chapter has disclosed that the U. S. Bureau of Standards makes tests of products, but does not make any tests for individuals. You can profit by these tests and standards only through the fact that manufacturers voluntarily label their products if they measure up to these standards.

Food products packed under the supervision of Federal agencies have been properly inspected and tested so that you have the assurance of protection. If the products have been inspected or tested, this information is indicated on the label.

There is constant scrutiny on the part of the Federal Government of the food, drugs, and cosmetics that are sold in interstate commerce, so in a general way you have protection from dangerous or harmful products; but unless there are state laws to protect you adequately, you have no assurance that products made and sold within a particular state are of satisfactory quality.

As has been pointed out, one may send a product for testing to the Agricultural Marketing Service of the U. S. Department of Agriculture. This kind of testing service is useful only in buying in relatively large quantities or in attempting to establish a conclusion as to the quality of a certain brand.

There are many private testing agencies that will test any kind of product for a stipulated fee. Anyone may use these agencies, but their principal advantage to the consumer is through the fact that individual manufacturers and retailers use these testing agencies in determining the quality of their merchandise and indicate this quality on informative labels. The table on page 184 provides an analysis of the various types of testing agencies.

ORGANIZATION	TYPE OF ORGANIZATION	IS ORGANIZATION CONCERNED WITH SALE OF THE PRODUCT?	PRODUCTS USUALLY TESTED	USE AND LIMITATIONS
U. S. Dept. of Agri. Marketing Service	Federal	No	Foods	For packers and processors, but available on a fee basis to consumers.
U. S. Dept. of Agri. Meat Inspection Service	Federal	No	Meat	On meat sold in interstate commerce.
U. S. Bureau of Standards	Federal	No	All types	Testing and standards for government purchase; manufacturers may have products tested; "Willing to Certify" use of labels.
Federal Food and Drug Administration	Federal	No	Foods, drugs, cosmetics	Testing done to enforce standards. Service not directly available to consumers.
American Medical Association	Professional members	No	Foods, drugs, medical appliances	Some products carry seal of approval but reports not easily available.
American Dental Association	Professional members	No	Dentifrices, mouthwashes	Some products carry seal of approval but reports not easily available.
Consumers' Research, Inc.	General members	No	Many types	Service available to members, limited facilities.
Consumers Union, Inc.	General members	No	Many types	Service available to members, limited facilities.
American Gas Association	Trade association	No	Gas appliances	Products tested and approved carry informative labels for consumer.
Underwriters' Laboratories, Inc.	Trade association	No	Electrical and safety devices	Products tested and approved carry informative labels for consumer.
Better Fabrics Testing Bureau	Trade association	Yes	Fabrics	Products tested and approved carry labels certifying specifications.
American Institute of Laundering	Trade association	No	Fabrics	Labels certify color fastness, shrinkage, and laundering qualities.
National Association of Dry Cleaners	Trade association	No	Fabrics	Labels certify color fastness, shrinkage, and cleaning qualities.
Manufacturers	Manufacturing	Yes	Many types	Test control aids, consumers, but detailed information not always available.
Retail Stores	Sales	Yes	Mainly textiles, clothes, foods	Tests used in purchasing; information and standards made available to consumers on labels.
Independent Laboratories	Independent	No	All types	Service available to anyone willing to pay fee, but cost is high.
Public Laboratories	Cities, states, etc.	No	Food, water, measures, weights	Used largely to enforce health and other local laws; tests available to consumers.
Magazine Publishers	Publishers	May be	Mainly foods, cosmetics, textiles, and household equipment	Testing for approval and standards for production guarantees; tests not directly available to consumers.

Testing services.

There are certain simple tests that any individual may use when he is buying merchandise, and other slightly more complicated tests that may be performed in the home. Some of these means of identifying quality will be discussed in succeeding chapters pertaining to various types of goods.

Using Salespeople and Advertising. Demonstrations were formerly considered to be applicable only to mechanical products; but they are now applied to food products, pharmaceutical products, and cosmetics. In watching the demonstration of a cosmetic, one should ask oneself, "What will be the effect?" rather than merely, "How is it done?" In watching a demonstration of a food product, such as baking powder, the buyer should ask himself, "In what way does this product differ from other products?"

In observing demonstrations of mechanical appliances, it is usually possible to make comparisons. No wise purchaser will select the first make that he has examined. He should watch the demonstration of more than one make. The more demonstrations he observes, the greater chances there are that he will get his money's worth. Through a demonstration of a mechanical appliance, for instance, he gets specific information with regard to original cost, performance, cost of operation, length of life, amount of service, guarantee, workmanship, finish, and chance of obsolescence. If possible, the information obtained from a demonstration should be supplemented by that obtained from unbiased users of the product being considered.

A person may not be sufficiently familiar with workmanship and finish to be able to judge a single product, but a comparison with other similar products will give some basis for judgment. The free service furnished with an appliance can be evaluated definitely. The cost of extra service is very important. The amount that other users of the product have had to pay for service is measurable.

Obsolescence is one of the important elements to be considered. In many cases obsolescence occurs when the manufacturer of the product has gone out of business. Under such circumstances it usually becomes difficult or impossible to obtain replacements or proper service for the product. Such a product is referred to as an "orphan."

The prospective buyer should remember that the primary objective of a salesperson is to sell something. Before he buys, he should therefore have a reasonable conception of what he wants. He should not buy the first article he sees unless it measures up to his expectations in every detail. Furthermore, he should know clearly the distinction between high-pressure selling and courteous, considerate selling.

Intelligent salespeople can and will give information if it is demanded. Sales propaganda should, however, not be

Some Typical Mistakes in Buying

1. Habitual bargain hunters often buy goods they do not need just in anticipation that they may need them.
2. Goods bought at auctions or other types of sales are not necessarily bargains.
3. Claims by agents that house-to-house selling eliminates the middleman's profit and therefore offers the greatest bargain are not necessarily true.
4. Consumers who buy at "wholesale" often pay just as high prices as at retail and may not get the choice merchandise they need.
5. "Bait" advertising that draws people into stores may lead them to purchase other merchandise that is not a good bargain.
6. People who buy in small quantities on a day-to-day basis are not getting the best bargains.
7. The person who insists on being the first to get seasonal fruits and vegetables or the first to get new styles will usually pay the highest prices.
8. Following a blind rule that all advertised merchandise is the best will cause a buyer to overlook good bargains in nonadvertised merchandise.
9. The cheapest is often not the best bargain.
10. People who buy household equipment from unknown manufacturers and retailers may have difficulty getting repair parts and service.
11. Buying all that merchants will sell the consumer on the installment plan often leads to financial disaster.
12. Habitual returning of merchandise bought on approval increases costs for everyone.

confused with real sales information. One should distinguish between glowing terms
that paint a beautiful picture
without telling what the product will do for the prospective
buyer and facts that show
what it has done for others.

The prospective buyer
should ask questions and see
that his questions are not
avoided. If, in examining a
product, a person does not

An item bought at an auction may
not be "cheap" unless it is actually needed.

readily observe what he wants to know, he should ask the
salesperson. The failure of the latter to give a satisfactory
answer will be based on lack of knowledge or on unwilling-
ness to tell the truth.

In Chapter 8 you learned something about advertising.
If you learn to read advertising properly, you can use the
knowledge gained from advertising in the actual buying of
merchandise. The reading of good advertising should
therefore gradually build your buying information.

TEXTBOOK QUESTIONS

1. What should be the relationship between budgeting and
   buying?
2. Why is personal shopping in a store ordinarily a better way
   to buy than by telephone, from a catalog, or from a house-to-
   house salesman?
3. What types of hints can you offer in regard to good shopping
   procedures?
4. (a) What kind of special sale is advantageous to the person
   who is interested in style? (b) What kind of sale is advantageous to the person who is not interested in style?
5. As a season progresses, why do merchants gradually reduce
   the price of their seasonal merchandise?
6. Are the price cycles for various products the same?
7. What is the result of buying frequently and in small quantities?
8. Under what circumstances is it desirable to buy food in small
   quantities?

9. How can the person who has surplus funds take advantage of the price cycle in buying foods?
10. Give some examples of trade names or terms that are confusing.
11. What information besides grades on a label is helpful in buying?
12. Why are trade-marks used?
13. Name some products that can be bought on the basis of trial use.
14. If you want to test some article, such as canned peaches, to get an authoritative answer in regard to its quality, what testing agency do you think would be most helpful to you?
15. Give some examples of testing services that are most directly available to consumers.
16. If you feel that some food you have purchased is not wholesome and is misbranded, to what agencies could you turn for testing as to its wholesomeness?
17. Are goods sold directly from the producer to the consumer always sold more cheaply than through other means?
18. What might be some of the difficulties and risks of buying an item from a legitimate wholesale source?
19. Are advertisers and salespeople helpful in buying? If so, how?

DISCUSSION QUESTIONS

1. What are some of the advantages and disadvantages of buying by telephone?
2. Name some of the reasons why you should expect to pay less when you deal at cash-and-carry stores.
3. To what extent does experience in buying and using commodities serve as an adequate guide in making the following purchases: (a) Suppose an article is expensive and will normally last many years. Will the consumer's experience in buying that article be of any value to him? (b) Suppose an article of a relatively low price is used frequently and bought rather often. Will the consumer's experience in buying that article be adequate as a guide? (c) Suppose an article such as tooth paste is bought frequently. Will the consumer's experience in buying that article be a suitable guide in making purchases?
4. What are some of the limitations to the benefits derived from buying in order to take advantage of low prices during price cycles?
5. Mrs. Jones prides herself on buying only nationally advertised goods. (a) What do you think of her practice? (b) Is she following good judgment? Why?

6. If you went into a strange grocery store for the purpose of buying peas, and found on the shelf two brands of peas, one of which was well known to you and the other was not known, what procedure would you follow in buying? Why?

7. (a) Name some products that do not lend themselves to trial use before the purchase is made. (b) Why do they not?

8. (a) In what ways do you think you could rely on the opinions of your friends and neighbors in buying? (b) In what ways do you think it would be unwise to rely on their opinions?

9. What guides can you suggest as to policies in buying in small or large quantities?

10. Discuss how consumers may contribute to the injury of good merchants in the case of a price war.

11. For a family of six, what would you think of the policy of buying in quantities of (a) a bushel of fresh sweet corn, (b) a year's supply of potatoes, (c) two small cans or one large can of peaches?

12. (a) What articles do you think are most likely to be safe to buy by mail? (b) Which are least likely to be safe to buy by mail?

13. Explain some of the bad features of the privilege of returning goods.

PROBLEMS

1. Analyze the reasons why you and your family buy from the places where you are accustomed to buy (a) groceries, (b) drugs, (c) clothing. Give a list of reasons for each classification. If you buy in more than one place, give the reasons.

2. From your local newspaper, over a period of a week, make a list of different kinds of special sales that, in your opinion, come under the classification of legitimate bargain sales as described in this chapter.

3. Compare prices of foods in different sizes of cans in the same store, and figure the percentage of saving if a family can justify buying the larger size.

4. Compare prices on one-half peck, one peck, and one bushel of potatoes, and indicate for what size of family you think the different sizes of purchases would be most appropriate without running the risk of spoilage.

5. Compare prices on one-half peck, one peck, and one bushel of oranges (or in terms of pounds or dozens, depending upon the way they are sold), and determine which is the most economical quantity for your own family to purchase without running the risk of spoilage.

COMMUNITY PROBLEMS AND PROJECTS

1. As a class project, select some canned fruits or vegetables and send them to the Marketing Service of the U. S. Department of Agriculture for testing. The usual fee should be sent along. Identify the cans and remove the labels before sending them for testing.
2. Start to collect all of the buying guides that you can find for individual products. Make a written alphabetic list of products in one column and of buying guides in the second column. Prepare this with the intention of keeping it for permanent reference.
3. Investigate the return privileges of your local stores and write a report as to the fairness and the abuses on the part of the stores and the customers.
4. Select some article that is sold from house to house, by mail-order houses, and by local stores. Compare prices and quality and give your opinion as to the best bargains.
5. Investigate some so-called "wholesale" prices that are charged consumers, and ask the local better business bureau or a reliable retailer to give you facts in regard to whether the prices are below usual retail prices for goods of the same quality.
6. Make a list of at least six items (not more than four foods) and state the time for each when you think it is at its lowest seasonal price.
7. Arrange with your parents to let you buy three different brands of some canned food at the same or approximately the same price. Set up a rating scale of your own, and as you open each of these cans, form a conclusion as to which is the best bargain.

PART V
PROBLEMS IN BUYING

Chapter 11
Getting the Most for Your Food Dollar

Purpose of the Chapter. Buying food is such an important consumer problem that it deserves more than just a casual treatment. Before a person is ready to select individual foods, he must understand the functions that various foods perform and the kinds and quantities of various foods that should be consumed. In other words, the spending of money for foods involves a practical diet or nutrition problem. The purpose of this chapter is to explain the functions of various foods and to suggest the quantities and types of food that will make up a balanced diet for families on various levels of income.

Types of Foods. From the point of view of nutrition, there are three types of foods, as follows: (a) foods that provide fuels or energy for the body, which include *carbohydrates* and *fats*; (b) body-building foods, which are *proteins*; and (c) the regulatory foods, which include those that furnish *minerals, vitamins,* and the proper amount of *bulk* and *water* in the daily diet.

What Functions Do Foods Perform? Each type of food has a definite function to perform in the human body. Since the body is a human machine, it must have *fuel* to provide energy just as any other machine has to have fuel. The *carbohydrates* and *fats* provide fuel in the form of what is known as *calories*. A calory is a unit by which fuel energy is measured.

Since *proteins* are the *body builders*, we need them to build muscles and tissues and to take care of the necessary repairs of the body. Our blood, our hair, our nails, and all

	WHAT THEY DO	MAIN SOURCES	DEFICIENCY MAY CAUSE
CALORIES	GIVE ENERGY	WHOLE WHEAT, SUGAR, BUTTER	FATIGUE
PROTEIN	BUILDS MUSCLES	MEAT, EGGS, BEANS	FLABBY MUSCLES
CALCIUM	BUILDS BONES AND TEETH	MILK, CHEESE	SOFT BONES AND TEETH
IRON	BUILDS RED PART OF BLOOD	MEAT, LIVER, EGGS	ANEMIA
VITAMIN A	HELPS GROWTH, KEEPS EYES HEALTHY	GREEN & YELLOW VEGETABLES	STUNTED GROWTH, NIGHT BLINDNESS
VITAMIN B₁	HELPS DIGESTION & NERVES	PORK, PEANUT BUTTER	POOR APPETITE
VITAMIN B₂	BUILDS RED PART OF BLOOD	LIVER	CRACKS IN SKIN
NIACIN	KEEPS SKIN HEALTHY	GREENS, WHOLE WHEAT	PELLAGRA
VITAMIN C	KEEPS BODY CELLS TOGETHER	ORANGES, STRAWBERRIES, TOMATOES	SCURVY
VITAMIN D	KEEPS BONES AND TEETH HEALTHY	SUN, FISH-LIVER OIL	RICKETS

WHAT KEEPS OUR BODIES GOING

GRAPHIC ASSOCIATES FOR PUBLIC AFFAIRS COMMITTEE, INC

Functions, sources, and effects of deficiencies of various foods.

parts of our body require proteins for building and maintenance. Without sufficient proteins, children would stop growing normally. Their muscles would become soft and many of their organs would fail to function normally.

The most important *regulatory* foods may be roughly classified as (a) *minerals* and (b) *vitamins*. Of course, the body must take in a certain amount of bulk foods and water, but the bulk may be provided by any one of the types of food. There is usually no problem in taking water into the body because, besides the liquids that one drinks, water is taken into the body through many foods. For instance, a high percentage of fresh fruits and vegetables is water. Likewise, a high percentage of meat is water.

The most important minerals from a body-building and maintenance point of view are *calcium* and *iron*. Calcium builds bone and teeth and helps to keep one in good physical condition. Iron is an important part of our blood and must be constantly provided through food. Iron serves to build and maintain vigor. Lack of iron causes people to tire easily.

Probably the third most important mineral is *phosphorus*, although *copper* is also considered essential in small amounts. *Iodine* and other less important minerals are considered essential in small amounts. They all have a general regulatory effect on the body in maintaining it in its normal healthful state.

There are many types of known vitamins, and new ones are being identified by science. The principal vitamins, however, are: Vitamin A; Vitamin B$_1$ (thiamine); Vitamin B$_2$ (riboflavin or Vitamin G); Vitamin C (ascorbic acid); Vitamin D; and niacin.

Vitamin A is especially important for normal growth of children, and it is needed by adults to keep their eyes, skin, and body linings in a healthy condition. Some of the indications of the lack of Vitamin A are night blindness and lack of resistance to colds, sore throat, and pneumonia.

Vitamin B$_1$ is also important to help in the normal growth of children. It contributes to a good appetite and calm nerves. It assists the body in digesting sugars and

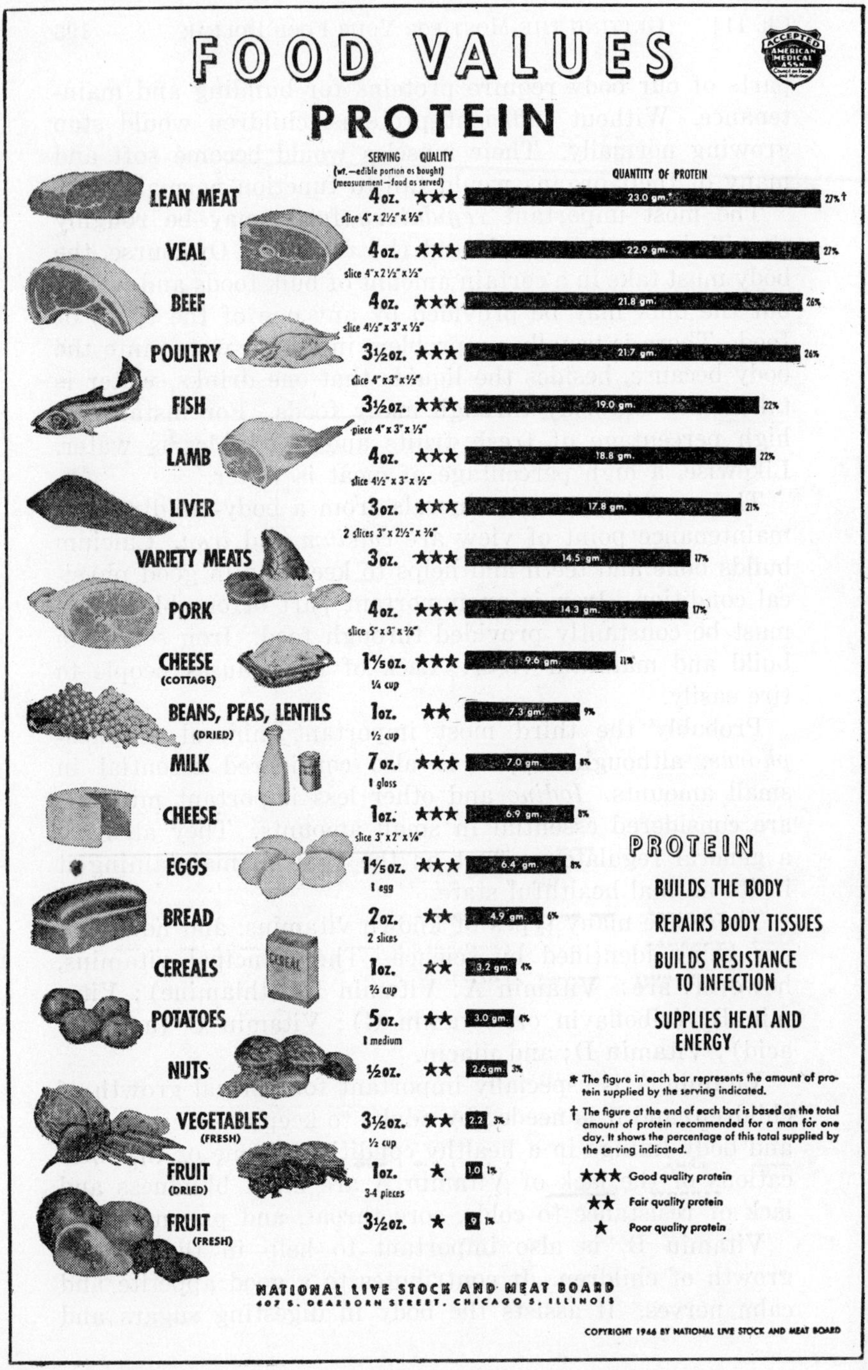
FOOD VALUES
ACCEPTED AMERICAN MEDICAL ASSN. Council on Foods and Nutrition
PROTEIN
SERVING
(wt.—edible portion as bought)
(measurement—food as served)
QUALITY
QUANTITY OF PROTEIN
LEAN MEAT 4oz. ★★★ 23.0 gm.* 27%†
slice 4" x 2½" x ½"
VEAL 4oz. ★★★ 22.9 gm. 27%
slice 4" x 2½" x ½"
BEEF 4oz. ★★★ 21.8 gm. 26%
slice 4½" x 3" x ½"
POULTRY 3½oz. ★★★ 21.7 gm. 26%
slice 4" x 3" x ½"
FISH 3½oz. ★★★ 19.0 gm. 22%
piece 4" x 3" x ½"
LAMB 4oz. ★★★ 18.8 gm. 22%
slice 4½" x 3" x ½"
LIVER 3oz. ★★★ 17.8 gm. 21%
2 slices 3" x 2½" x ⅜"
VARIETY MEATS 3oz. ★★★ 14.5 gm. 17%
PORK 4oz. ★★★ 14.3 gm. 17%
slice 5" x 3" x ⅜"
CHEESE (COTTAGE) 1⅘oz. ★★★ 9.6 gm. 11%
¼ cup
BEANS, PEAS, LENTILS (DRIED) 1oz. ★★ 7.3 gm. 9%
½ cup
MILK 7oz. ★★★ 7.0 gm. 8%
1 glass
CHEESE 1oz. ★★★ 6.9 gm. 8%
slice 3" x 2" x ¼"
EGGS 1⅘oz. ★★★ 6.4 gm. 8%
1 egg
BREAD 2oz. ★★ 4.9 gm. 6%
2 slices
CEREALS 1oz. ★★ 3.2 gm. 4%
⅔ cup
CEREAL
POTATOES 5oz. ★★ 3.0 gm. 4%
1 medium
NUTS ½oz. ★★ 2.6 gm. 3%
VEGETABLES (FRESH) 3½oz. ★★ 2.2 3%
½ cup
FRUIT (DRIED) 1oz. ★ 1.0 1%
3-4 pieces
FRUIT (FRESH) 3½oz. ★ .9 1%
PROTEIN
BUILDS THE BODY
REPAIRS BODY TISSUES
BUILDS RESISTANCE TO INFECTION
SUPPLIES HEAT AND ENERGY
* The figure in each bar represents the amount of protein supplied by the serving indicated.
† The figure at the end of each bar is based on the total amount of protein recommended for a man for one day. It shows the percentage of this total supplied by the serving indicated.
★★★ Good quality protein
★★ Fair quality protein
★ Poor quality protein
NATIONAL LIVE STOCK AND MEAT BOARD
407 S. DEARBORN STREET, CHICAGO 5, ILLINOIS
COPYRIGHT 1946 BY NATIONAL LIVE STOCK AND MEAT BOARD

FOOD VALUES
VITAMINS
PROMOTE GROWTH AND PROTECT HEALTH

	SERVING e.p. as bought	food as served	A international units	B THIAMINE milligrams	B RIBOFLAVIN milligrams	B NIACIN milligrams	C milligrams	D international units
LIVER	3 oz.	2 slices 3"x2½"x⅜"	17,820	.24	2.45	12.41	15.5	29
HEART	3 oz.	¼ heart 3"d.x3½"lg.	31	.32	.82	5.64	.9	
KIDNEYS	3 oz.	slice 4½"x2"x½"	705	.21	1.73	6.45	6.2	
BEEF	4 oz.	slice 4½"x3"x½"	0	.09	.16	5.59	0	
LAMB	4 oz.	slice 4½"x3"x½"	0	.15	.26	5.93	0	
VEAL	4 oz.	slice 4"x2½"x½"	0	.14	.31	7.18	0	
PORK	4 oz.	slice 5"x3"x⅜"	0	.63	.17	3.65	0	
FRANKFURTERS	2 oz.	one 5"lg.x¾"d.	0	.11	.14	1.41		
PORK SAUSAGE	2 oz.	three 3"lg.x½"d.	0	.12	.09	1.31		
POULTRY	3½ oz.	slice 4"x3"x½"		.11	.17	6.44	1.8	
OYSTERS	3½ oz.	5 medium	—	.19	.23	1.25	—	5
FISH	3½ oz.	piece 4"x3"x½"		.04	.07	3.99	1.0	
EGGS	1⅘ oz.	1 egg	570	.04	.13	.02	0	46
MILK	7 oz.	1 glass	300	.07	.34	.22	2.6	4
BUTTER	⅓ oz.	1 pat	312	—		.01	0	4
BREAD (ENRICHED) [2]	2 oz.	2 slices	0	.14	.09	1.32	0	
CHEESE	1 oz.	slice 3"x2"x¼"	782	.01	.15	.16		
OATMEAL	1 oz.	¾ cup	—	.22	.03	.32	0	
APPLES	5 oz.	one 3" d.	135	.06	.03	.30	6.0	
ORANGES	5⅓ oz.	one 2¾" d.	304	.13	.05	.32	80.0	
BANANAS	3½ oz.	one 6" long	430	.09	.06	.60	10.0	
GRAPEFRUIT	3½ oz.	one-half 3½" d.	21	.04	.02	.20	40.0	
PRUNES	1 oz.	4 medium	482	.03	.05	.51	.9	
SPINACH	3½ oz.	½ cup	6,580	.09	.18	.50	32.5	
POTATOES	5 oz.	1 medium	30	.13	.05	1.42	11.3	
TOMATOES	4½ oz.	one 2¾" d.	1,441	.08	.05	.76	30.1	
PEAS	3 oz.	½ cup	468	.23	.12	1.36	12.7	
CARROTS	3½ oz.	two 5" long	10,680	.03	.02	.40	4.6	
COD LIVER OIL [3]	⅙ oz.	1 teaspoon	4,016					402

Figures in heavy type represent the amount of the vitamin retained after cooking.

— (Dash) present but in negligible quantity (too little to appear on this table).

Abbreviations: oz.=ounce d.=diameter lg.=long e.p.=edible portion

[1] Evaporated milk diluted with an equal amount of water has essentially the same food value as pasteurized whole milk. Most evaporated milks are fortified to contain 100 I. U. vitamin D in one quart of milk so diluted.

[2] Whole wheat bread is higher in niacin than enriched bread; other vitamins are approximately the same.

[3] Minimum required by U. S. Pharmacopeia

NATIONAL LIVE STOCK AND MEAT BOARD
407 S. DEARBORN STREET, CHICAGO 5, ILLINOIS

COPYRIGHT 1946 BY NATIONAL LIVE STOCK AND MEAT BOARD

starches. A lack of the proper quantity of Vitamin B₁ sometimes causes a poor appetite and nervous ailments.

Vitamin B₂ assists the body in using the fats and carbohydrates and helps the body to use the oxygen carried through the blood. A lack of Vitamin B₂ sometimes causes skin disorders and other discomforts and low vitality.

Vitamin C strengthens the muscles and teeth and is a safeguard against infections. Sometimes a lack of Vitamin C in the body is made evident by bleeding gums, aching joints, and a general feeling of discomfort. The absence of the proper supply of Vitamin C in one's system will eventually cause scurvy, which is a dread disease of people who have inadequate diets of fresh fruits and vegetables.

Vitamin D is the sunshine vitamin. It is absorbed through the skin from the sun's rays and may be taken internally through certain foods. It helps our bodies to assimilate calcium and phosphorus, which are so necessary to the well-being of our bones and teeth. It is therefore especially important to children, but adults also need it. One of the most common results of Vitamin D deficiency on the part of children is the serious disease of rickets.

Niacin is similar to Vitamin B₁ in that it helps to keep our nerves, skin, and digestion in a healthy condition. A prolonged absence of niacin in the diet will eventually cause the serious disease of pellagra.

Other less common vitamins have been identified or partially identified by scientists. Vitamins, other than those obtained in food, should be used only on the advice of physicians.

How Much of Each Food Do We Need? Doctors and dietitians are not wholly agreed on the exact amount of food that should be taken into the body daily. It is probably seldom that any one individual will eat exactly the proper quantities of each kind of food daily, but over any long period of time it is important that a proper balance be maintained. The illustration on the opposite page shows the approximate daily quantities of foods that should be taken into the body.

Where Do We Get Our Food Values? Now that we know what types of food and the approximate quantities of food we should have, the next question to decide is through what food sources we are going to get the various food values. The tables on pages 194 and 195 show the main sources of proteins and vitamins.

	MAN MODERATELY ACTIVE	WOMAN ACTIVE	BOY 13-17 YEARS	CHILD 4-6 YEARS
A NUTRIENT YARDSTICK				
CALORIES	3,000	2,500	3,200	1,600
PROTEIN IN GRAMS	70	60	85	50
CALCIUM IN GRAMS	0.8	0.8	1.4	1.0
IRON IN MILLIGRAMS	12	12	15	8
VITAMIN A IN INTERNAT. UNITS	5,000	5,000	5,000	2,500
VITAMIN B₁ (THIAMINE) IN MILLIGRAMS	1.8	1.5	1.6	8
VITAMIN B₂ (RIBOFLAVIN) IN MILLIGRAMS	2.7	2.2	2.4	1.2
NIACIN IN MILLIGRAMS	18	15	16	8
VITAMIN C (ASCORBIC ACID) IN MILLIGRAMS	75	70	90	50

GRAPHIC ASSOCIATES FOR PUBLIC AFFAIRS COMMITTEE, INC.

Food requirements of adults and children.

Spending the Food Dollar. The problem of acquiring sufficient quantities of the proper types of food is not difficult for families with adequate incomes. The only problem for such families is buying the proper food. A family with a moderate, a minimum, or a restricted income, however, must attempt to get the greatest maximum food values out of every food dollar that is spent.

The following table shows the approximate satisfactory division of the food dollar into various proportions for the items that are purchased.

TYPE OF FOOD	FOR FAMILY WITH CHILDREN (How to spend each dollar)	FOR FAMILY WITHOUT CHILDREN (How to spend each dollar)
Milk and cheese	25 cents	15 cents
Vegetables and fruit.	25-20 cents	30-25 cents
Flour, wheat, corn meal, oats, rice, grits, bread, other grain foods	15-20 cents	15-20 cents
Butter, lard, other fats, sugar, molasses	20-15 cents	20 cents
Meat, fish, eggs	15-20 cents	20 cents

A suggested division of the food dollar.

197

FAMILY FOOD PLAN AT LOW COST

FAMILY MEMBERS	Milk¹ (Qt.)	Potatoes, sweet potatoes (Lb. Oz.)	Dry beans and peas, nuts (Lb. Oz.)	Citrus fruit, tomatoes (Lb. Oz.)	Green, yellow vegetables (Lb. Oz.)	Other vegetables and fruit (Lb. Oz.)	Eggs (No.)	Meat, poultry, fish (Lb. Oz.)	Flour, cereals² (Lb. Oz.)	Fats and oils (Lb. Oz.)	Sugar, sirups, preserves (Lb. Oz.)
Children:											
9-12 months	7	0 8	......	2 0	1 8	0 8	5	0 2	0 8	0 1	0 1
1-3 years	5	1 0	......	1 12	1 8	1 0	5	0 8	1 8	0 4	0 2
4-6 years	5	1 8	0 2	1 8	1 8	1 8	5	1 0	2 0	0 6	0 8
7-9 years	5	2 8	0 2	1 8	1 8	2 8	5	1 8	2 8	0 10	0 8
10-12 years	6	3 0	0 2	1 8	1 8	2 8	5	2 0	3 4	0 12	0 10
Girls:											
13-15 years	6	3 8	0 4	1 12	1 8	2 8	5	2 0	4 0	0 14	0 10
16-20 years	5	3 0	0 4	1 12	1 8	2 8	5	2 0	3 8	0 12	0 10
Women:											
Moderately active	4 ½	3 0	0 6	1 8	1 8	2 8	4	2 0	3 8	0 12	0 12
Very active	5 ½	4 0	0 12	1 8	1 8	2 8	4	2 0	4 12	1 0	0 12
Sedentary	4 ½	2 0	0 4	1 8	1 8	2 8	4	2 0	2 8	0 12	0 12
Pregnant	7	2 0	0 6	2 0	2 0	2 8	6	2 5	3 0	0 12	0 10
Nursing	10 ½	4 0	0 6	3 0	3 0	3 8	6	2 5	3 0	0 12	0 10
Boys:											
13-15 years	6	4 0	0 8	1 12	2 0	3 0	5	2 0	5 0	1 2	0 12
16-20 years	6	5 0	0 12	1 12	2 0	3 0	5	2 0	7 0	1 6	0 12
Men:											
Moderately active	5	4 0	0 12	1 8	1 8	2 8	4	2 0	4 12	1 0	0 12
Very active	6	7 0	1 0	1 8	1 8	2 8	4	2 0	9 0	1 10	0 12
Sedentary	5	3 0	0 6	1 8	1 8	2 8	4	2 0	3 8	0 12	0 12

FAMILY FOOD PLAN AT MODERATE COST

FAMILY MEMBERS	Milk¹ (Qt.)	Potatoes, sweet potatoes (Lb. Oz.)	Dry beans and peas, nuts (Lb. Oz.)	Citrus fruit, tomatoes (Lb. Oz.)	Green, yellow vegetables (Lb. Oz.)	Other vegetables and fruit (Lb. Oz.)	Eggs (No.)	Meat, poultry, fish (Lb. Oz.)	Flour, cereals² (Lb. Oz.)	Fats and oils (Lb. Oz.)	Sugar, sirups, preserves (Lb. Oz.)
Children:											
9-12 months	7	0 8	......	2 0	1 8	0 8	5	0 2	0 8	0 1	0 1
1-3 years	5	0 8	......	1 12	2 0	2 0	6	0 8	1 4	0 4	0 2
4-6 years	5	1 4	0 1	1 8	2 0	2 0	6	1 0	1 12	0 6	0 8
7-9 years	5	2 0	0 1	1 8	2 0	3 0	6	1 8	2 4	0 10	0 8
10-12 years	6	2 8	0 2	1 12	2 0	3 0	6	2 0	3 0	0 12	0 12
Girls:											
13-15 years	6	3 0	0 2	1 12	2 0	3 0	6	2 8	4 0	0 14	0 12
16-20 years	5	3 0	0 2	1 12	2 0	3 0	6	2 8	3 0	0 12	0 10
Women:											
Moderately active	4 ½	2 8	0 4	2 0	3 8	4 0	5	2 8	3 0	0 12	0 12
Very active	5 ½	3 8	0 6	2 0	3 8	4 8	5	2 8	4 0	0 14	0 12
Sedentary	4 ½	2 0	0 2	2 0	3 8	4 0	5	2 8	2 4	0 10	0 12
Pregnant	7	2 0	0 2	2 8	4 0	4 0	6	2 12	2 8	0 12	0 12
Nursing	10 ½	3 0	0 4	3 0	4 0	4 8	6	3 0	2 8	0 12	0 12
Boys:											
13-15 years	6	3 8	0 4	2 0	3 0	4 0	5	2 8	4 8	1 0	0 12
16-20 years	6	4 8	0 8	2 0	3 0	4 0	5	2 8	6 0	1 4	0 12
Men:											
Moderately active	5	3 0	0 4	2 0	3 8	4 0	5	3 0	4 8	1 0	0 12
Very active	6	5 8	0 8	2 0	3 8	5 0	5	3 0	8 8	1 10	0 12
Sedentary	5	2 8	0 4	2 0	3 8	4 0	5	2 8	3 0	0 14	0 12

Bureau of Human Nutrition and Home Economics
U. S. Department of Agriculture

¹ Or its equivalent in cheese, evaporated milk, or dry milk.
² Count 1 ½ pounds of bread as 1 pound of flour.

Low cost and moderate cost food plans.

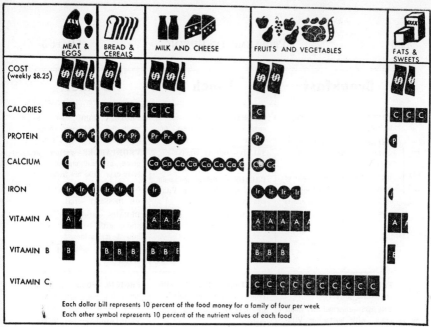

	MEAT & EGGS	BREAD & CEREALS	MILK AND CHEESE	FRUITS AND VEGETABLES	FATS & SWEETS
COST (weekly $8.25)	$ $ $	$	$ $ $	$ $	$ $
CALORIES	C	C C C	C C	C	C C C
PROTEIN	Pr Pr Pr	Pr Pr Pr	Pr Pr Pr	Pr	P
CALCIUM	Ca	Ca	Ca Ca Ca Ca Ca Ca Ca Ca	Ca Ca	
IRON	Ir Ir Ir	Ir Ir Ir	Ir	Ir Ir Ir Ir	Ir
VITAMIN A	A A		A A A	A A A A A	A A
VITAMIN B	B	B B B	B B B	B B B	B
VITAMIN C				C C C C C C C C C C	

Each dollar bill represents 10 percent of the food money for a family of four per week
Each other symbol represents 10 percent of the nutrient values of each food

Pictograph Corporation, for Public Affairs Committee, Inc.

Example: If 20 per cent of the food dollar is spent for fruits and vegetables, these will provide the entire supply of Vitamin C. They will also provide 10 per cent of the calories needed, 30 per cent of Vitamin B, and so on.

Relation of food cost to nutrient values.

If one follows this monetary budget in buying foods, it should be checked periodically with the tables on pages 197 and 198, showing the proper quantities, because the prices of particular items will fluctuate periodically and one may find that on a monetary basis he is not getting a satisfactory portion of a particular food.

Another way of showing the relative cost of obtaining various food or nutrition values is illustrated in the chart at the top of this page.

Examples of a Balanced Diet. The final goal of this chapter is to present for study some satisfactory meals that are appetizing and adequate. The table on the following page shows how three meals a day can be planned from these various food sources to provide for light, medium, and heavy diets. A person working at a desk or doing other light work should use a light diet. A person on his feet and reasonably active daily should use a medium diet. A person who follows an active life, such as a factory worker or a farmer, will require a heavy diet.

	Breakfast	Lunch	Dinner
LIGHT	FRUIT — orange, grapefruit, or tomato juice BREADS—enriched or whole grain, with butter or Vitamin A margarine OR CEREAL—whole grain or restored—with whole milk BEVERAGE—coffee for adults —milk for children	NUTRITIOUS SOUP—cream soup or vegetable soup, for instance SALAD—fruit or vegetable OR DESSERT—fruit BREADS—enriched or whole grain, with butter or Vitamin A margarine BEVERAGE—milk, in greater quantities for children	PROTEIN FOOD, such as meat, fish, fowl, eggs, cheese, dried beans, soybeans, etc. VEGETABLES—yellow or green, at least one of each every day. Use raw frequently SALAD—fruit or vegetable OR DESSERT—fruit BREADS—enriched or whole grain, with butter or Vitamin A margarine BEVERAGE—milk and coffee or tea
MEDIUM	FRUIT — orange, grapefruit, or tomato juice BREADS—enriched or whole grain, with butter or Vitamin A margarine OR CEREAL—whole grain or restored—with whole milk EGGS—or some other protein food BEVERAGE—coffee for adults —milk for children	VEGETABLE PLATE, with yellow or green vegetables OR SALAD—fruit or vegetable BREADS—enriched or whole grain, with butter or Vitamin A margarine DESSERT—fruit, pudding, or some other simple dessert BEVERAGE—milk	PROTEIN FOOD, such as meat, fish, fowl, eggs, cheese, dried beans, soybeans, etc. VEGETABLES — one cooked, one or more raw, perhaps as a salad BREADS—enriched or whole grain, with butter or Vitamin A margarine DESSERT—fruit, custard or pudding, or some other simple dessert BEVERAGE—milk and coffee or tea
HEAVY	FRUIT—orange, grapefruit or tomato juice BREADS — enriched or whole grain, with butter or Vitamin A margarine CEREAL—whole grain or restored—with whole milk EGGS—or some other protein food BEVERAGE—coffee or milk	PROTEIN FOOD, such as fish, eggs, cheese, dried peas or beans, soybeans, peanut butter VEGETABLE—yellow or green OR SALAD — fruit or vegetable BREADS — enriched or whole grain, with butter or Vitamin A margarine DESSERT — fruit, or some simple dessert BEVERAGE—milk	PROTEIN FOOD, such as meat, fish, fowl, eggs, cheese, dried beans, soybeans, etc. VEGETABLES—at least two cooked vegetables, one yellow or green SALAD—fruit or vegetable BREADS — enriched or whole grain, with butter or Vitamin A margarine DESSERT — fruit, custard, pudding, or other simple dessert BEVERAGE—milk and coffee or tea

Home Economics Institute
Westinghouse Electric and Manufacturing Co.

Menus for different types of people.

An examination of these diets will disclose that they provide for both balance and variety. Due consideration is given to quantities of calories, proteins, minerals, and vitamins needed by persons doing light, medium, and heavy work.

The menus on page 200 can be used as models from which to construct additional menus with variations that appeal to individual likes and dislikes.

TEXTBOOK QUESTIONS

1. Name the three different types or classes of foods.
2. What are the functions of the three main types or classes of foods?
3. (a) What is the function of Vitamin A? (b) What are some of the indications of a deficiency?
4. (a) What is the function of Vitamin B_1? (b) What are some of the indications of a deficiency?
5. (a) What is the function of Vitamin B_2? (b) What are some of the indications of a deficiency?
6. (a) What is the function of Vitamin C? (b) What are some of the indications of a deficiency?
7. (a) What is the function of Vitamin D? (b) What are some of the indications of a deficiency?
8. (a) What is the function of niacin? (b) What are some of the indications of a deficiency?
9. Name important natural sources of (a) protein and (b) Vitamin A.
10. (a) How many calories does an active woman need daily? (b) How much protein does a boy 13 to 17 years of age need daily? (c) How many units of Vitamin A does a child 4 to 6 years old need daily? (d) How much iron does a man who is moderately active need daily?
11. (a) Of every dollar that is spent for food in a family with children, about how much should be spent, at normal prices, for milk and cheese? (b) How much for a family without children?
12. Through what natural food sources can you get the greatest number of calories at the lowest cost?
13. From what natural food source can you get the greatest amount of iron at the lowest cost?
14. From what natural food source can you get the greatest amount of Vitamin B at the lowest cost?
15. Give an example of a recommended light breakfast.

DISCUSSION QUESTIONS

1. If you are seeking an energy food, what kind of food will you need and from what source can it best be obtained?
2. If you are susceptible to colds and sore throat, what kind of vitamin may help you and from what natural food sources can it best be obtained?
3. If one has a poor appetite and is nervous, giving an indication of a deficiency of a certain vitamin, what vitamin is it and from what source can it best be obtained?
4. On the basis of food and vitamin requirements, what particular foods would you strongly recommend for children?
5. If a person has the following ailments, what vitamin deficiencies are indicated: (a) low vitality, skin irritations, and discomforts; (b) bleeding gums, aching joints, and general feeling of discomfort?
6. Many primitive people have strong bones and teeth. Can you give any possible reason for this fact?
7. Why does a factory worker need more calories than an office worker?
8. Can you give any reasons why manual workers usually require considerable meat?
9. Why do women usually avoid diets high in calories?

PROBLEMS

1. Suggest a diet for a child of a certain specified age.
2. On the basis of the general suggestions for a lunch for a heavy diet for an active worker, plan a specific lunch menu.
3. Plan a dinner menu that you think is appropriate for a woman office worker who sits at a desk each day. Give reasons for your selections.

COMMUNITY PROBLEMS AND PROJECTS

1. On the basis of Vitamin A and B daily requirements, obtain information in regard to the cost of obtaining these requirements entirely from commercial vitamin concentrates.
2. Keep a record of what you eat for an entire week without discussing the matter with your parents. Estimate the quantities that you eat. Then, on the basis of the facts you have studied in this chapter, determine whether you have been following a balanced diet.

Chapter 12

How to Buy Packaged Foods

Purpose of the Chapter. In previous chapters you have learned about standards, grades, and labels that provide helpful information in buying. You have also studied the general principles of buying. The purpose of this chapter is to give you some more specific guides in buying some of the most important packaged goods, particularly canned fruits and vegetables. It is not possible in the space of a single book to make a detailed study of all kinds of packaged foods; therefore this discussion will be confined to the more important items, which will be used as examples.

Standards and Grades of Canned Foods. In Chapter 9 there was a more detailed discussion of how the Federal Government sets up standards and grades for canned fruits, vegetables, and other items. It must be remembered that the use of standard Federal grades on foods going into interstate commerce is voluntary, not required. However, it is mandatory that all the foods covered by Federal regulations must measure up to the minimum standards or must be marked to show how they fail to meet minimum standards. None of these regulations applies when a food is produced and distributed within a single state, but in those cases the food must conform to state requirements.

In the case of interstate shipments, a food must be wholesome, but it may be below the minimum standard in quality provided it is marked in some such manner as "Below U. S. standard. Low quality but not illegal." It may also be below the standard in fill provided it is marked "Slack fill" or "Substandard. Not completely filled."

Adulterated Foods. In general, the Federal Food, Drug, and Cosmetic Act prohibits the sale of foods that contain a poisonous or otherwise harmful substance, or that contain any decayed substance. Some foods naturally contain a certain amount of harmful substance; but if such foods

Food and Drug Administration

The can on the right is "slack fill."

are ordinarily not injurious to health, they may be acceptable. Manufacturers are prohibited from abstracting a valuable constituent from a food and substituting partially or totally some other substance. If a product has been damaged or if it is inferior, that fact must be disclosed. If any substance has been added or mixed to increase the bulk or the weight, or to reduce the quality or the strength so as to make the food appear of greater value, that food is considered to be adulterated. In general, a food may not contain a coal-tar coloring unless that fact is certified according to the law. There are also other minor regulations.

Misbranded Foods. Under the Federal Food, Drug, and Cosmetic Act a food is considered to be misbranded under any of the following conditions:

(a) If its labeling is false or misleading in any particular.

(b) If it is offered for sale under the name of another food.

(c) If it is an imitation of another food and its label does not bear in type of uniform size and prominence the word *imitation* with, immediately thereafter, the name of the food imitated.

(d) If its container is so made, formed, or filled as to be misleading.

(e) If it is in a package that does not bear a label (1) showing the name and the place of business of the manufacturer, the packer, or the distributor, and (2) containing an accurate statement of the quantity of the contents in terms of weight, measure, or numerical count. Under clause (2), however, reasonable variations may be permitted, and exemptions as to small packages may be established, under regulations prescribed by the Secretary of Agriculture.

(f) If any word, statement, or information that is required, by or under authority of the Act, to be placed on the label is not prominently shown thereon.

Food and Drug Administration

The label must tell the whole story.

(g) If the food purports to be one for which a standard has been established, but fails to conform to that standard.

(h) If the food is one for which a standard of quality has been established, but it falls below that standard and does not bear a label indicating the substandard grade.

(i) If the label fails to bear the common or usual name of the particular food.

(j) If the food is fabricated from two or more ingredients, and the label fails to indicate these ingredients.

(k) If the food purports to be or is represented to be for special dietary uses, but its label fails to provide such information as the Federal Food and Drug Administration prescribes as necessary to inform purchasers concerning its vitamin, mineral, and other dietary properties.

(1) If the food contains any artificial flavoring, artificial coloring, or chemical preservative, but its label does not state that fact.

Mandatory Labeling Information. Although the Federal ABC grading system is not mandatory on foods going into interstate commerce, there is certain information designated for various types of foods that is mandatory for descriptive purposes on the label. For example, the style of pack of asparagus must be indicated as follows:

"Spears" or "Stalks"—3¾ inches or more of the upper end of the sprout.

"Peeled Spears" or "Peeled Stalks"—3¾ inches or more of the upper end of the sprout, peeled before canning.

"Tips"—Not less than 2¾ inches but less than 3¾ inches of the upper end.

"Points"—Less than 2¾ inches of the upper end.

In the case of green and wax beans, it is mandatory to indicate the style of pack as to whether it is whole, cut, or sliced lengthwise (shoestring, French style, or julienne). The style of pack must be indicated for nearly every fruit or vegetable. In addition, it is mandatory to indicate the variety of such foods as peas, peaches, and cherries, and to indicate the type of syrup for fruits. In order to buy intelligently, therefore, one must know something about the style of pack, the varieties of fruits and vegetables, and the standards for syrup.

Voluntary Labeling Information. It has been contended by the Labeling Committee of the National Canners Association that Federal grades are not sufficient in themselves because they are not completely informative. This committee has therefore set up for the industry a voluntary labeling practice that every member of the industry is requested to follow. The following are the five requirements of this labeling practice:

1. The terms must be simple and understandable by ordinary people, for when so, the label is self-explanatory.
2. The terms must be specific. Generalizations permit

too much latitude in use and allow too much variation in consumer interpretation.

3. The terms must be standardized and used alike by all canners and distributors.

4. The terms must be readily enforceable under the misbranding section of the Food, Drug, and Cosmetic Act.

5. In order to achieve the third and fourth points, the terms must be based upon objective definitions and standards.

SEMPO BRAND

YOUNG   WHOLE GRAIN
GOLDEN SWEET CORN

Your own description of raw product and method of processing. Must be honest, factual, brief, unpuffed.

COLOR	GOLDEN
STYLE	WHOLE GRAIN
MATURITY	. YOUNG
2½ CUPFULS . .	5 SERVINGS
NO. 2 CAN . .	I LB. - 4 OZS.
SEASONING .	SALT AND SUGAR

ALREADY COOKED - HEAT ONLY

DIRECTIONS: Pour liquid into a sauce pan. Boil down to about one-half. This saves flavor and food values. Add corn. Heat only a few minutes. Add butter, salt and pepper to taste.

It can also be used in preparing many other appetizing dishes. Either use the liquid for such dishes or save it for soups and gravies.

Part of a label in the form recommended by the National Canners Association.

As a result of these recommendations, many canners now provide additional information on labels in regard to (a) quantity in terms of cupfuls and servings, (b) size, (c) maturity, (d) seasoning, (e) color, and (f) uses and directions for serving. An example of these voluntary standards for indicating the approximate size of asparagus is as follows:

"Size 1, Small," approximately ⅜ inch in diameter.
"Size 2, Medium," approximately ½ inch in diameter.
"Size 3, Large," approximately ⅝ inch in diameter.
"Size 4, Extra Large," approximately ⅞ inch in diameter.
"Assorted Medium and Large," Sizes 2 and 3.
"Assorted Medium and Small," Sizes 1 and 2.
"Mixed Sizes," any wider range of size groups.

The way in which this labeling information is put into practice is shown in the illustration on this page.

Meaningless Designations. Consumers should not be misled by such designations as Extra Special, Exquisite, Superb, Supreme, Superior, Our Best, or any other designation that has no recognized meaning. These are terms selected by packers or distributors. Consumers should look for standard designations, such as Grades A, B, and C, or Fancy, Extra Standard, Choice, or Standard. In the absence of standard grades, look for intelligible descriptive labels. If the contents of the can have been graded according to size (as in the case of beans or peas), the size number should be observed. The size number (1, 2, 3, or 4) will indicate the relative size but not the specific size.

If a canner or a distributor marks foods according to the governmental grades, the foods must conform to the governmental standards for these grades.

Price and Value. *Consumers' Guide,* a former Federal publication, reported a survey to answer the question, "Does the price mark on canned foods tell the quality of the product?" The survey was based on an examination of about one hundred and fifty cans of peas, corn, and tomatoes, which had been purchased at different stores in the regular manner. The cans did not bear grade markings of the Federal Government; some of them bore various meaningless grade designations. The cans were opened, and the vegetables were examined on the basis of governmental standards. The study disclosed definitely that paying a high price for a canned food that is not graded according to governmental standards does not necessarily ensure obtaining a good product. Another investigation by *Consumers' Guide* disclosed the fact that canned green beans of almost uniform quality were distributed by the same company in two different cans of the same size, and were sold in the same stores in Washington, D. C. One can was priced at thirteen cents, whereas the other was priced at only eight and a third cents. In all fairness it must be recognized that after foods have been packed for some time and shipped long distances, they may not measure up to the same grade standard as when packed.

The following table is an analysis of forty-seven cans of peas that were purchased at prices ranging from eight cents to twenty cents a can.

CANNED PEAS—SIZES AND QUALITIES

PRICE CLASS	SUB-STANDARD	GRADE C	GRADE B	GRADE A
17½ to 20 cents	......	4 cans	3 cans	......
15 to 17½ cents	......	7 cans	4 cans	......
12½ to 15 cents	2 cans	3 cans	8 cans	1 can
8 to 12½ cents	8 cans	6 cans	1 can	......

The price does not indicate the grade.

It is evident from this analysis that price was no definite indication of quality. There was only one Grade A can of peas out of the forty-seven, this particular can having been bought for thirteen cents. In the higher-priced groups there were no cans of Grade A.

Furthermore, the labeling of the cans provided no guide to quality. Six of the cans were marked Fancy, but four of these were of Grade B and two of Grade C. Brand names were also unreliable. For example, four cans were branded in identically the same way; but one was of Grade A, two were of Grade B, and the fourth was of Grade C. Although brand names proved unreliable in this case, they are not, however, disqualified as guides in all cases. If a person learns to depend upon a particular brand name as indicative of good quality, purchasing under that name is probably more satisfactory than attempting to follow miscellaneous grade designations that are meaningless.

A similar study made in Washington, D. C., disclosed the wide range of prices paid for various quantities and qualities of tomato juice. The table at the top of the following page shows the results of this study.

Determining the Quality of Canned Foods. The average buyer of canned foods finds it difficult to rely upon his own judgment in determining quality. Some large buyers of canned foods employ experts to perform this function for

TOMATO JUICE—SIZES AND PRICES
(In one Washington store)

NO.	SIZE *	FLUID VOLUME		PRICE	PRICE PER 10 OZ.
				CENTS	CENTS
1	211 x 315		10¼ oz.	2 for 0.09	4.4
2	211 x 411		12 oz.	.07	5.8
3	211 x 413		12 oz.	.07	5.8
4	211 x 414		12½ oz.	3 for .25	6.7
5	300 x 407		14 oz.	.07	5.0
6	300 x 407		14 oz.	2 for .17	6.1
7	300 x 408		14 oz.	3 for .19	4.5
8	Bottle		1 pt.	.12	7.5
9	303 x 509	1 pt.	4 oz.	2 for .17	4.2
10	307 x 512	1 pt.	8 oz.	.10	4.2
11	307 x 512	1 pt.	8 oz.	.08	3.3
12	Bottle	1 pt.	10 oz.	.17	6.5
13	Bottle		1 qt.	.21	6.6
14	404 x 615	1 qt.	14 oz.	.21	4.6
15	404 x 708	1 qt.	18 oz.	.19	3.8
16	502 x 505	1 qt.	18 oz.	.25	5.0
17	502 x 505	1 qt.	18 oz.	.22	4.4
18	502 x 510	1 qt.	20 oz.	.25	4.8
19	Bottle		2 qt.	.27	4.2
20	603 x 700		3 qt.	.39	4.1
21	603 x 700	3 qts.	3 oz.	.39	3.9

* 211 x 315 means a can 2¹¹⁄₁₆ inches in diameter and 3¹⁵⁄₁₆ inches in height, outside measurements.

The price per ounce should be considered, not the price per can.

them. Nevertheless, a person has an opportunity to determine quality largely by comparison.

There are positive characteristics that distinguish quality, and there are negative characteristics that distinguish lack of quality. These simple observations can be made at home. In trying to establish brands that are of a good quality, it is desirable to try different brands until adequate comparisons can be made.

In determining Federal grades, only a few characteristics are taken into consideration. In the case of canned creamed corn, there are six: color, 5 points; consistency, 25 points; lack of defects, 20 points; cut, 5 points; maturity, 25 points; flavor, 20 points. Grade A is awarded to corn with a score of 90 points or better; Grade B, 75-89 points; and Grade C, 60-74 points.

An individual may take advantage of the Federal grading service; but for one who buys only a can at a time, this is not a very useful service. The person who buys a can at a time can make comparisons and determine brands that have the highest quality for the price charged. If the

Quality Characteristics of Canned Fruits and Vegetables

Positive Characteristics

1. Fullness of can
2. Gross weight of contents
3. Volume of juice
4. Weight of juice
5. Net weight of food
6. Absence of defects
7. Clearness of liquor or juice
8. Character of liquor or juice
9. Color of food
10. Consistency
11. Crispness
12. Flavor
13. Aroma or odor
14. Maturity
15. Percentage of whole food
16. Tenderness
17. Uniformity of size
18. Uniformity of color
19. Nature of blemishes
20. Units per can

Negative Characteristics

1. Lack of uniformity in size
2. Lack of uniformity in texture
3. Overmaturity or undermaturity
4. Discolored liquor
5. Too much liquid
6. Poor color
7. Broken pieces
8. Poor flavor
9. Foreign particles

consumer is a member of a buying group or a co-operative, he has an inexpensive method of getting official information in regard to a canned fruit or vegetable. For a relatively small fee, canned foods may be sent for testing and grading to the nearest office of the Agricultural Marketing Service. These offices are located in the principal cities. The following is the rate of fees charged for this type of service:

NUMBER OF CANS	NO. 3 SIZE CAN (OR SMALLER)	CANS LARGER THAN NO. 3 SIZE	NUMBER OF CANS	NO. 3 SIZE CAN (OR SMALLER)	CANS LARGER THAN NO. 3 SIZE
1 can	$0.35	$0.65	9 cans	$2.25	$4.80
2 cans	.70	1.30	10 cans	2.50	5.40
3 cans	1.00	1.90	11 cans	2.75	6.00
4 cans	1.30	2.50	12 cans	3.00	6.00
5 cans	1.50	3.00			
6 cans	1.50	3.00	For each additional can in the sample, per		
7 cans	1.75	3.60			
8 cans	2.00	4.20	can	.25	.50

Fees for testing and grading by the Agricultural Marketing Service.

Sizes of Cans. When canned goods are bought, the size of the can and the quality of the contents must be considered. There is so much variation in the sizes of cans that the buyer should familiarize himself with them. Even though he is acquainted with the sizes in general, unusual shapes of cans may sometimes mislead him. Cans ordinarily used for fruits and vegetables are listed below.

The average weight of content and the number of cupfuls are based upon the average standard fill. There is always a certain amount of open space in a can. The exact weight

NUMBER OR NAME OF CAN	AVERAGE NET WEIGHT	APPROXIMATE CUPFULS
Buffet or Picnic	8 oz.	1
No. 1	11 oz.	1½
No. 300	14 oz.	1¾
No. 1 tall	16 oz.	2
No. 303	16 oz.	2
No. 2	20 oz.	2½
No. 2½	28 oz.	3½
No. 3	33 oz.	4
No. 3 cylinder	46 oz.	6
No. 5	3 lb., 8 oz.	7
No. 10	6 lb., 10 oz.	13

Contents of cans of various sizes.

will vary according to different kinds of fruits and vegetables because they do not have the same density.

Some foods may be advertised at "three cans for 35 cents." This statement does not mean anything unless one knows the exact size of the can. If a can appears not to be of standard size, it should be compared with a can of standard size on the merchant's shelf.

Usually the larger the can, the less one pays proportionately for the quantity of goods bought. For instance, if a person buys a vegetable in No. 2 cans, he probably pays from two to four cents a pound less than if he bought the same food in No. 1 cans. If he buys fruit in No. 2½ cans, he probably pays three or four cents a pound less than if he bought the same fruit in No. 1 cans.

One should watch for cans of unusual sizes, for they are sometimes misleading. For instance, a special can used by some companies appears to be much the same as the No.

2 standard-size can. The average person cannot discover the difference because the can is just slightly shorter and a little less in diameter than the No. 2 can. It holds, however, three or four ounces less. In spite of its smaller capacity it is often advertised at the same price as the No. 2 can. The can is known to the trade as No. 303. It is, of course, labeled correctly according to the weight of the contents.

Food and Drug Administration

Consider the contents, not the size of the can—an example of how the Food and Drug Administration required a producer to avoid deception in the size of the container.

Relative Values According to Sizes of Cans. Another important consideration in buying canned foods is the amount that should be purchased. It is not economical to buy a large can if part of the contents will spoil before they can be used. The table below, which is based upon a study made in a large city, shows the relative price a pound for canned goods bought in cans of different sizes. This

ITEM OF FOOD	COMMERCIAL GRADE AS INDICATED BY DISTRIBUTOR	PRICE PER POUND (CENTS)			
		8- OR 9-OUNCE CAN	NO. 1 CAN	NO. 2 CAN	NO. 2½ CAN
Vegetables:					
Beans, cut	Extra standard		9.1	6.6	
Beans, cut	Standard		8.7	5.0	
Beans, Lima	Extra standard		14.0	10.0	
Corn	Fancy		10.9	9.2	
Corn	Extra standard		9.1	6.6	
Corn	Standard		8.2	5.0	
Peas	Extra standard		14.0	10.0	
Tomatoes	Fancy			10.1	
Tomatoes	Extra standard		10.0	7.0	
Fruits:					
Apricots	Choice	16.0	12.5		12.3
Cherries	Choice		12.5		12.3
Fruit salad	Choice		17.0		14.4
Grapefruit	Fancy	12.5		10.0	
Peaches	Fancy	14.0	12.5		9.1
Pears	Fancy		15.0		11.2
Pineapple, sliced	Choice	22.2			8.9
Pineapple, sliced	Fancy		13.0		9.6

The price per pound of foods in cans of various sizes.

table can be used as a guide in determining the fairness of prices in comparison with the sizes of cans. For instance, if cut beans in No. 1 cans cost 9.1 cents a pound, the price should be 6.6 cents a pound when the beans are purchased in No. 2 cans. The absence of figures in some of the columns indicates that products are seldom packed in those sizes.

The buyer usually chooses a No. 1 can or a No. 2 can. He should pay approximately 25 per cent less a pound if he buys the larger can. As the difference between sizes becomes greater, the percentage difference in the price per pound becomes greater.

Packaged Foods Versus Bulk Foods. When buying certain types of groceries of a staple or semistaple variety, the consumer must choose between bulk and packaged goods. In recent years there has been a definite trend toward selling goods in packages, although many of the same foods are still available in bulk. Such foods as dried fruits, dried beans, butter, lard, crackers, tea, and coffee are still available in bulk. Packaged foods have the advantage of greater sanitation, convenience in handling, and ease of identification. On the other hand, bulk goods usually cost somewhat less. Their quality is often as good as that of the packaged foods, but the quality may deteriorate more quickly.

If the consumer does not wish to buy bulk goods, his problem is to decide what size of package to purchase. If the contents of a large package can be consumed before they spoil, the large package is often more economical than a small one. In a comparison of purchases made in the same stores on the same days over a period of two years, the saving that resulted from buying in large packages ranged from 8 to 38 per cent, depending upon the quantity purchased and the difference in size of the packages.

Guides in Buying Canned Goods. Depend to some extent upon a brand that you have learned gives you the quality and value that you expect for a particular purpose. If you buy a new brand, make some evaluation to determine its quality and value.

Note whether the label bears any indication of government standards or failure to meet government standards.

Note whether the label bears any seal of approval, such as that of the American Medical Association or any other agency.

Read the labels carefully. Note the designation of size, weight, and grade, and any descriptive or informative terms used. Compare the product with other similar products to determine value.

Ewing Galloway

A careful buyer reads all labels.

Evaluate the cost by comparing the product with two or more similar ones after the specifications of each product have been determined.

Shop in more than one place, and compare products at home. Learn where the best values can be obtained.

Determine how much canned food should be bought at a time. If your requirements at any one time can be filled by one large can, do not buy two small ones, for the cost in the latter case will be greater. If your budget will permit the purchase of a number of cans at one time, buy at special sales in dozen lots or in case lots.

Watch the appearance of the can. If the can is dirty, discolored, or rusty, examine it carefully. If the can has a small hole in it, do not accept it. If the ends are flat or slightly drawn in, but there is no noticeable flaw, the can is probably all right. If the ends are bulged, however, or if one end bulges out when the other is pressed, the food has probably spoiled.

When the can is opened, note the condition of the food and observe whether the quality is what you expected. If there is any doubt as to whether the food is good, return it to the merchant as soon as possible.

Decide what use you wish to make of the food. Lower grades of canned foods are often suitable for combination dishes, whereas the better grades may be more desirable for other purposes.

Summary of Buying Guides

For Quality:

1. Learn brands of high quality by comparison.
2. Check the labels for standards.
3. Check labels for seals of approval.
4. Check the labels for informative descriptions.
5. Compare the costs.
6. Shop in more than one place.
7. Buy in economical amounts.
8. Select the quality and grade to fit your particular needs.
9. Watch for damaged containers.
10. Return food in original container if it is unsatisfactory.

For Personal Preference:

1. Look for the variety.
2. Look for the style.
3. Look for the sizes.
4. Look for the seasoning.
5. Look for the kind of syrup in the case of fruits.

How to Read Labels. One may have a fair knowledge of canned goods in terms of the previous discussion; but unless a person knows what he wants, he may not get it. Besides grades and other marks of quality, there are other very important factors.

Be sure to get the variety that you want. For instance, there are early June peas and Alaska peas, each of which has certain characteristics that may or may not appeal to you. Peaches may be freestone or clingstone.

Foods are packed in different styles. You should know the difference between whole kernel and cream style corn. You should be careful to note whether the peaches are sliced, whole, or halved.

Sizes often make a difference, particularly as regards peas, cherries, plums, and other fruit items. Sometimes labels show actual life-sized drawings or pictures of the contents, but in many cases the illustrations are exaggerated both as to size and to color. You can learn something about the sizes. For instance, peas may be tiny, small, or medium.

Nearly all canned foods are seasoned only lightly so that the consumer may add seasoning to suit the taste. Read the labels to discover whether salt, sugar, or some other seasoning has been added. Some foods for special dietary conditions are canned without seasoning.

In the case of canned fruits, one of the quality guides is the kind of syrup that is used. Most fruits are canned in sugar syrup. Some fruits are canned in water to which no sugar has been added. In order to understand the designations in regard to syrup content, the following table is given in terms of ordinary household measurements:

SYRUPS % SUGAR	CUPS WATER	CUPS SUGAR
70 (extra heavy)	1	2¾
60	1	1¾
55 (heavy)	1	1½
50	1	1¼
40	1	¾
30	1	½
25 (medium)	1	⅓
20	1	¼
10	1	⅛

Quality guides for syrup.

What Is Vacuum Packing? All canned foods that are cooked have a partial vacuum in the open space in the can. This is accomplished by heating the food to expand it and drive out the air. The full can is then sealed and sterilized. When it cools, the can then has an empty space.

The so-called *vacuum packing* now used in the food industry indicates that the can is filled and sealed with a special sealing machine with a vacuum attachment that withdraws the air without heating. The can is then sterilized as in the regular process. Since air in contact with the food causes it to deteriorate or will eventually change its flavor, vacuum packing for such items as coffee, peanuts, and other similar items will preserve these for a much longer time than if they were in packages that admit air.

Frozen Foods. A frozen food is neither a canned food nor a fresh food in the real sense. It is a packaged food. At the same time, it is a fresh food because it has not been completely cooked.

Most frozen foods that are sold on the market are blanched, which is usually done with steam. The secret of preserving the texture and flavor of frozen fruits and vegetables is in *quick freezing*. After the food has been prepared and packaged and mildly cooled, it is then put in a freezing compartment approximately 20 to 40 degrees below zero. This quick freezing creates tiny ice crystals that do not destroy the tissues. In the slow-freezing process, large crystals would be formed that would destroy the tissues.

After a food has been frozen, it must be kept at a low temperature until it is ready for use. This temperature is usually about zero. When the frozen food is taken home, it should be kept in a frozen state until immediately before cooking. If it is thawed out and is frozen again, it no longer is a satisfactory food. Although frozen foods will keep an indefinite length of time without spoiling, some of them do deteriorate through evaporation, particularly if they are not kept tightly sealed.

Some standards and grades have been set up for frozen foods. If these are used, they will be indicated on the label.

TEXTBOOK QUESTIONS

1. Do the standards established for canned foods by the Federal Government appear on the labels of all canned foods?
2. Give examples of how foods are considered to be adulterated under Federal law.
3. Name at least three ways in which a food may be considered to be misbranded under the Federal Food, Drug, and Cosmetic Act.
4. Give some examples of kinds of information that are mandatory under the Federal labeling system for canned foods.
5. Give some examples of voluntary labeling information that the National Canners Association requests its members to place on canned foods.

6. Name some meaningless grade designations.
7. How much difference in price for each ten ounces of tomato juice was found in a certain store in Washington?
8. Name at least five positive characteristics that determine the quality of canned fruits and vegetables.
9. Name at least three negative characteristics that determine the quality of canned fruits and vegetables.
10. What is the approximate average weight of canned fruits or vegetables that one should expect to find in a (a) No. 1 can, (b) No. 2 can, (c) No. 3 can, (d) No. 3 cylinder can?
11. Why should the consumer be familiar with the sizes of cans?
12. What are the advantages of buying packaged goods?
13. What is usually a disadvantage of buying packaged goods?
14. What is meant by buying in economical amounts?
15. Although variety, style, size, seasoning, and the syrup may be no indication of quality, why should these be considered in buying?
16. What is vacuum packing?
17. To get the best results, at what temperature should foods be frozen originally? At what temperature should they be stored?

DISCUSSION QUESTIONS

1. (a) In your opinion how useful are the standards established by the United States Department of Agriculture? (b) What will determine their future usefulness?
2. Do you think a store has any advantage in selling merchandise that is marked according to standard grades?
3. What do you think is meant by Grade AA, which appears on the label of a canned food?
4. Explain a procedure that you would suggest for comparing canned foods on the basis of quality and value.
5. Why should a person beware of cans that have unusual sizes or shapes?
6. One advertiser announces, "Three cans for 25 cents." Another announces, "Three large cans for 28 cents." What do these advertisements mean?
7. Some maple syrups that do not contain pure maple syrup are sold on the market. Is it legal to make such sales?
8. Which would you rather have on canned fruits and vegetables: (a) A regular ABC grading system, or (b) all of the voluntary information recommended by the National Canners Association?
9. If a label on a can indicates that the food is packed in a 40 per cent syrup, what grade of syrup is this?

PROBLEMS

1. If a No. 1 can of food sells for 20 cents and a No. 2 can sells for 30 cents, what is the price of a pound in each case?
2. Canned tomatoes were advertised by one store as selling at 20 cents a "large can." Another merchant advertised a "large can" for 25 cents. The tomatoes were of approximately the same quality. Investigation disclosed, however, that those advertised in the first case were packed in No. 1 tall cans, whereas those advertised in the second case were packed in No. 2 cans. Was there any difference in the price of a pound? If there was, which can was the cheaper?

COMMUNITY PROBLEMS AND PROJECTS

1. Make a list of the various grades used to designate the quality of canned foods sold in a local grocery store. Indicate which foods bear unrecognized Federal grades.
2. Compare the contents of two or more cans of beans or of some other product. Note the price, volume, weight, taste, and other factors that can be used in determining the quality and the value. Make a comparative report on the quality and the price. Use the brand names to distinguish the products that you compare.
3. Collect a variety of labels from cans of similar products. Make a list of the information shown on the labels, and report your conclusions as to what criteria can be followed in evaluating these foods on the basis of the information given on the labels.

Chapter 13

How to Buy Perishable Foods

Purpose of the Chapter. In previous chapters there have been discussions of standards, grades, labels, and other guides that may be used in buying. There has also been a discussion of Federal and state agencies and the protection that they provide for the buyers of food. Buying perishable foods, such as meats, butter, eggs, fruits, and vegetables, however, presents certain specific problems. The purpose of this chapter is to point out more specifically the guides in buying the most common types of perishable foods. Space limitation makes it impossible to cover all foods.

Grades of Beef. The grading of meat has been gradually extended, although what has been done applies largely to the grading of beef. Packers are not required to have their meat graded by the United States Department of Agriculture. The grading of meat is therefore entirely voluntary on their part. If consumers are not obtaining graded meat, however, they have the privilege of indicating a preference for it from local dealers. If graded meat is demanded, packers will be more likely to furnish this service.

The official grades of beef established by the United States Department of Agriculture are listed as follows in their order of excellence: U. S. Prime, U. S. Choice, U. S. Good, U. S. Commercial, U. S. Utility, U. S. Cutter, and U. S. Canner. The first four grades are the most common.

The consumer should remember that government inspection of meat is not grading of meat. While inspection is mandatory for all meat coming from plants that sell in interstate commerce, the grading is voluntary. Meat inspection was discussed in Chapter 6.

There are also different classes of beef. Steer is generally considered to make the best class of meat; heifer is considered second in choice; cow is considered third in choice.

How to Judge the Quality of Beef. Choice beef is difficult to distinguish from prime beef. Good beef is very desirable. Most beef sold is, however, of the medium (U. S. Commercial) grade. This grade has a large amount of bone and a small amount of fat in proportion to flesh. Furthermore, the flesh and the fat are inclined to be less firm than those in other grades.

The characteristics that are desirable in beef are (a) light cherry red color; (b) velvety appearance; (c) firmness and fine grain; (d) absence of excess connective muscle tissue; and (e) evenly distributed fat that is brittle, creamy white,

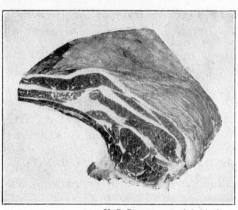

U. S. Department of Agriculture

Good beef has a marbled appearance.

and flaky. The picture at the left shows the desirable way in which fat is distributed in high quality beef. The surface should not only be covered evenly with firm fat, but the fat should be distributed throughout the flesh. This distribution of fat, as shown in the illustration, is called "marbling." In the case of beef this is the best indication of quality.

A consumer can never get the most value and satisfaction out of meat without knowing something about the proper cuts of meat. Unless the consumer knows what cuts to request for certain purposes, he should depend upon an ethical dealer to recommend the proper cuts for specific purposes.

The chart on page 223 is provided to illustrate briefly the various cuts of beef.

Meat Cuts and How to Cook Them
BEEF CHART

Retail Cuts

Ground Beef **Heel of Round**
—Roast or Broil — Braise or Simmer—

Hind Shank
—Soup or Simmer—

Rolled Flank **Flank Stew**
— Braise — *— Stew—*

Flank Steak **Flank Steak Fillets**
— Braise —

Plate Boiling Beef **Rolled Plate** **Short Ribs**
— Simmer or Braise —

Beef Brisket **Corned Beef**
— Simmer —

Knuckle Soup Bone **Cross Cut Fore Shank**
— Soup or Braise —

English Cut **Arm Pot Roast** **Arm Steak**
— Braise —

Wholesale Cuts

ROUND
RUMP
LOIN END
FLANK
SHORT LOIN
PLATE
RIB
BRISKET
SHANK
CHUCK

Retail Cuts

Round Steak **Top Round** **Bottom Round (Swiss Steak)**
— Braise —

Rolled Rump **Rump Roast**
— Braise or Roast —

Sirloin Steak **Pin Bone Sirloin Steak**
— Broil or Panbroil —

Porterhouse Steak **T Bone Steak** **Club Steak**
— Broil or Panbroil —

Standing Rib Roast **Rolled Rib Roast** **Rib Steak**
— Roast — *— Broil —*

Blade Steak **Blade Pot Roast**

Triangle Pot-Roast **Boneless Chuck Pot-Roast** **Shoulder Fillet**
— Braise —

Rolled Neck **Boneless Neck**
— Braise or Stew —

Ten Lessons on Meat, National Live Stock and Meat Board

A good buyer should know the cuts of meat and how to cook them.

How to Judge the Quality of Veal. *Veal* is the name applied to the meat of a young calf not more than twelve weeks of age. The meat of an older animal, for instance, from three to ten months in age, is referred to as *calf meat.* The principal grades of veal are Prime or No. A1, Choice or No. 1, Good or No. 2, Commercial or No. 3, and Utility or No. 4. There is very little Prime veal sold.

Good veal is finely grained, firm, somewhat moist, and light pink. The lighter the flesh, the better the meat. The exterior of the better grades of veal is covered with a thin layer of white fat. A good quality of calf meat is firm, finely grained, velvety, and light tan or reddish in color. The exterior should be covered with a generous amount of creamy white fat. Calf meat is graded in the same manner as veal except that none is classified as Prime or No. A1.

How to Judge the Quality of Lamb and Mutton. Lamb comes from animals that are from twelve to fourteen months old. The meat of an animal that is more than fourteen months old is considered mutton. Lamb is sold principally during April, May, and June. Practically no mutton is sold in this country. The grades of lamb are Prime or No. A1, Choice or No. 1, Good or No. 2, Medium or No. 3, Common or No. 4, and Cull or No. 5.

Lamb and mutton are firm and finely grained if the quality is high. The color varies from pink to dull red according to age. The fat of a young lamb is creamy and slightly pinkish. It becomes white as the animal grows older. Lamb is graded with the same quality designations that are used for beef and veal. The same grade designations used for lamb are also used for mutton.

How to Judge the Quality of Pork. Pork is inspected in the same way as beef and is marked with the same type of Federal inspection stamp. Although there is no governmental grading of pork, packers usually have their own grades, which are numbered one, two, and three; some use names to designate grades.

Most pork comes from hogs that are from seven to twelve months old. Pork of high quality has a grayish pink color.

The flesh is firm and finely grained, and the fat is firm and white. Smoked ham and bacon of high quality are firm, have a thin layer of fat, and have a smooth skin.

How to Judge Poultry. Practically all dressed turkeys and a great many dressed chickens and ducks are graded by the Federal Government. This grading service is available to any producer at a cost of only one cent a bird. The governmental grade mark is put on each box in which the dressed fowl are packed and is printed on a tag attached to each bird. Each tag also states whether the bird is young or old. The grades for dressed poultry in general are:

GRADE	CHARACTERISTICS
U. S. Special or AA	A commercially perfect specimen. The supply of this is very limited and the price is correspondingly high.
U. S. Prime or A	Well-fleshed and fattened, and practically free from pinfeathers, skin tears, and other defects. Approximately 60 per cent of the graded chickens sold are of this quality.
U. S. Choice or B	Fairly well-fleshed and fattened and may show slight defects such as skin tears or discoloration. Not more than three such defects may appear on the breast of birds of this grade.
U. S. Commercial or C..	Less well-fleshed and fattened and shows more defects. It is the lowest grade of edible poultry.

Grades for dressed poultry.

Dressed chickens are sold in wholesale lots by grade, but they are seldom tagged. The crates in which they are packed are, however, tagged according to grade. The quality of dressed chickens can be judged as follows:

(a) If the bird is young, the breastbone is flexible, the feet and skin are soft, and the claws are short and sharp.

(b) If the bird is old, the breastbone is brittle and frequently rough. The skin is coarse, and the claws are long and usually dull. The presence of long hairs also indicates age.

(c) The female fowl is usually more tender than the male. The fowl that is plump and well rounded is of good quality.

(d) Fresh poultry of a high quality is plump, fat, and firm. Storage poultry is frequently flabby and dull in color.

A mark like this shows that the meat has been inspected and passed as wholesome food.

U. S. Department of Agriculture

Inspecting and stamping poultry.

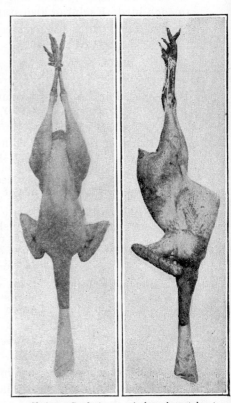

Choice or Grade A turkey.   A sharp breast denotes low quality.

High and low grades of poultry.

Since most of the turkeys are graded, except those killed and sold locally, the consumer has a little better chance in having a guide in buying. Generally speaking, hen turkeys are better than gobblers (or Toms). The age of a turkey can be most easily judged by its size. Ordinarily a dressed hen turkey weighing 12 pounds or less is a young one. A dressed gobbler weighing 16 pounds or less is a young one. The same general characteristics suggested above for testing the quality of chickens will also apply for turkeys.

Milk. Dairy products include milk, cream, butter, eggs, and cheese. The consumer may choose from among several grades of raw or pasteurized milk. The price of milk varies according to the grade, the grades usually being designated as A, B, and C. However, certified milk is of a higher grade. These grades are approved by the United States Public Health Service. Milk sold in cities is usually pasteurized. Grade A pasteurized milk is produced under more sanitary conditions and has a lower bacterial count than Grade B. Grade C milk must be labeled "cooking milk."

Departments of health in most cities have established rigid systems for controlling the inspection and the grading of milk. The standards set up by these communities are usually patterned after those of the Federal Government.

Cream. There are four classes of cream: heavy cream, whipping cream, medium cream, and light cream. They rank according to their content of butter fat, which may test from 36 per cent to 18 per cent.

Butter. The United States Department of Agriculture maintains a service for grading butter. Butter is classified as follows: dairy butter, which is made on the farm; creamery butter, which is made in the creamery or factory; packing-stock butter; ladled butter; process or renovated butter; and grease but-

U. S. DEPARTMENT OF AGRICULTURE
Bureau of Agricultural Economics

WASHINGTON, D.C.

★ MAY 22 19 ★

92 SCORE

A government grade mark
for butter.

SCORE	GRADE
93 or above	AA or Special
92	A or Extra
90 to 91	Standard
89	B
84	D

Grades of butter.

ter. In the scoring of the first three classes, maximum ratings are given to various factors in the following manner: flavor, 45 points; body, 25 points; color, 15 points; salt, 10 points; package, 5 points; total, 100 points. Butter that scores about 93 or 94 points is fine, sweet, fresh, mild, and clean. Any butter that scores below 75 points is classified as grease butter and is considered unfit for food. Only butter scoring 92 points or above may be marked with the certificate of quality issued by the United States Department of Agriculture. Except in case of butter that is sold under certification, the score of the butter sold in most retail stores is not easily available for the consumer. Any butter that contains less than 80 per cent of butter fat is an adulterated product and cannot be sold legally. Butter may be colored without indicating it on the label.

Butter is also designated by grades in addition to scores.

Margarine. Margarine, which is technically referred to as oleomargarine, is a spread that is similar in characteristics to butter. When it is properly fortified with vitamins according to regulations, it contains essentially the same nutritional value as butter. All margarine, regardless of whether it is sold locally or in interstate commerce, is under government supervision in its manufacture. It is not sold by grade, but it must measure up to minimum standards.

Margarine is made either from animal fat or vegetable fat. Most of it is made from vegetable oils such as soybean oil, cottonseed oil, peanut oil, or cocoanut oil. These oils are refined and hydrogenated so that they are converted from liquids to a spreadable solid with a suitable melting point. Skimmed milk, whole milk, or powdered milk is usually added along with the required vitamins and salt. Anyone buying margarine has assurance that it is wholesome.

Eggs. On page 162 there is a table illustrating the standards and grades of eggs set up by the U. S. Department of Agriculture. In many markets eggs are sold in cartons bearing the grade markings and the Federal seal of inspection. Even though a consumer may not buy eggs in cartons, it is sometimes possible to determine the quality by examining the wholesale carton from which they are taken.

Official U. S. grade label for eggs in carton.

Eggs may vary in weight from about 30 ounces to 17 ounces a dozen. There are five different classes of eggs by weight: The jumbo or largest size has a minimum net weight of 28 ounces a dozen; the extra large, 26 ounces; the large, 24 ounces; the medium, 21 ounces; and the small, 18 ounces. It is to the consumer's advantage to buy eggs by weight or by size. The following table gives some indication of the relative value of eggs:

WHEN LARGE GRADE A EGGS COST	MEDIUM GRADE A EGGS ARE AS GOOD OR BETTER VALUE AT	SMALL GRADE A EGGS ARE AS GOOD OR BETTER VALUE AT
$0.40	$0.35	$0.30
.45	.39	.33
.50	.43	.37
.55	.48	.41
.60	.52	.45

Relative value of different sizes of eggs.

Eggs are classified both as to quality and size. In many retail stores Federal-state graded eggs are available, bearing a label on the carton similar to the one illustrated below. The date of grading will indicate the freshness of the eggs.

Cheese. American cheese is classified on several bases. On the basis of flavor it may be classified as fresh, mild, or aged; on the basis of texture, as close, medium close, or open; on the basis of color, as uncolored, medium-colored, or highly colored. The final scoring represents the combined ratings on the basis of the various factors. For instance, a particular cheese may be scored as follows: flavor, 30 per cent; texture, 40 per cent; finish and appearance, 20 per cent; color, 10 per cent; total, 100 per cent. The grades and corresponding scores established by the Federal Government are as follows: U. S. Extra Fancy, a score of 95 or more; U. S. Fancy, a score of 92 to 94; U. S. No. 1, a score of 89 to 91; U. S. No. 2, a score of 86 to 88; U. S. No. 3, a score of 83 to 85.

Great quantities of cheeses sold in American markets are so-called processed cheeses. These are made from natural cheese after the natural cheese has matured. Natural cheese is mixed and blended to obtain a uniform fat content, flavor, moisture, and acidity. It is then pasteurized, molded into the proper form, and packaged. The pasteurization of cheese is essentially the same as that for milk.

All the special types of cheeses are purchased by persons who learn to evaluate them for particular flavor, texture, and age. Some types of cheese are not good until they reach a proper age. Since the regular American cheese is the kind sold in greatest quantity, the following simple test of quality is suggested: Rub a crumb of it between the thumb and finger. It should feel velvety, like cold butter or paraffin. If it is pasty, sticky, or crumbly, it is not of the best quality or age.

Grades of Fresh Fruits and Vegetables. Although the number and the names of grades established for the different varieties of fresh fruits and vegetables differ somewhat, the classification is, in general, as follows: best grade, U. S. Fancy; next grade, U. S. No. 1; third grade, U. S. No. 2. Many states have adopted their own grades, but most of these conform to the standards established by the United States Department of Agriculture.

Many fruits and vegetables, especially berries and green vegetables, are so perishable that their desirability decreases rapidly. Hence it is often not possible for the retailer to offer such products for sale according to grades. If, however, such fruits and vegetables have been graded and the original grading is known, the consumer can judge the quality by considering the degree of freshness. Less perishable products, such as potatoes, apples, and citrus fruits, are sold in some retail markets according to grades.

How to Judge the Quality of Fruits and Vegetables. The following are brief guides that can be used by the consumer at the point of purchase:

Peaches

Quality in peaches is indicated by the general appearance and firmness of the flesh. A peach of fine quality should be free from blemishes, should have a fresh appearance, a ground color that is either whitish or yellowish and sometimes combined with a red color or blush depending on the variety. The red color or blush alone is not a true sign of maturity. The flesh should be firm or fairly firm.

Peaches are very perishable and for long-distance shipment are picked when slightly immature. They are sometimes picked when so immature that they cannot ripen. They may arrive on the market either too green or too ripe for immediate use. If the ground color is green and shows none of the mature whitish or yellowish color, it is an indication that the fruit may be too immature to ripen satisfactorily. Immature peaches may develop a pale weak color and will shrivel, and generally the flesh becomes tough and rubbery and lacking in flavor.

Overmature or soft peaches should be avoided unless for immediate consumption. They bruise easily and soon break down. Bruised fruit is wasty and undesirable. The outer skin of a bruise may not be discolored, but the bruised flesh is usually soft and discolored.

Worm injury may often be detected by the unevenness of the form of the peach, and the small punctures from which gum exudes. Generally a wormy peach has an appearance of premature ripeness and is usually softer than the average sound peach in the same container. Decay usually appears in the form of brown circular spots of varying sizes; it spreads very rapidly, frequently causing the complete loss of the fruit. Peaches that have growth cracks usually soften quickly and are wasty.

Strawberries

Quality in strawberries is indicated by the general appearance. Strawberries should be fresh, clean, and bright in appearance; should have a full solid red color; should be free from moisture, dirt, and trash; and should have the cap attached. Small misshapen berries or nubbins usually are of poor quality and flavor, and often they have a small, hard, green area.

Overripe strawberries, or those that are not fresh, have a dull lusterless appearance, are sometimes shrunken, and are likely to be wet or leaky. Such berries are wasty. The presence of leaky or damaged strawberries is often indicated by a stained container. Decay is easily detected through the presence of mold on the surface of the berries. It may be found anywhere in the container and is not always evident in the top layers.

Strawberries without the caps should be carefully examined. They may have been roughly handled, or they may be overmature. Such berries are likely to break down rapidly and be wasty.

Asparagus

Asparagus ages rapidly after it is cut; the tips spread and the stalks become tough and woody. Hence, to buy fresh stalks lessens the risk of buying tough asparagus.

Two kinds of asparagus are found in the markets, blanched or white and green. The blanched or white is used largely for canning. The green is most popular and is seen most commonly.

Asparagus grows from root crowns that are covered with several inches of earth. The depth depends upon the kind of asparagus to be produced. The blanched or white is covered or ridged more deeply than the green. After the growing spear breaks through the ground, the tip turns rapidly from white to green. Blanched or white asparagus is usually cut as soon as the tips appear above ground and is cut deeply below the surface. Green asparagus is cut a few inches below the surface of the ground after the spear has developed the desired length above the ground. If growth is rapid, a green shoot, 6 to 10 inches long, may be obtained before any part of it has become tough. After a few inches of the tip are green, the white portion below the ground begins to toughen. Thus, spears that show 4 or 5 inches of green tip and an equal length of white butt have usually been cut well below the surface, and the white part may be tough or woody. Green asparagus should be green for almost its entire length. White or blanched asparagus is said to be somewhat milder in flavor than green asparagus.

Beans, Lima (Fresh)

The pods of the best unshelled lima beans should be well filled, clean, bright, fresh, and of dark green color. The shelled lima beans should be plump, with tender skin of good green or greenish-white color.

Dried, shriveled, spotted, yellowed, or flabby pods of unshelled lima beans may be old or may be affected by disease. Usually beans contained in such pods are of poor quality; they may be tough and of poor flavor. Decay may appear on the pods in the form of irregular sunken areas in which mold may appear.

Shelled lima beans are very perishable. They heat quickly and if kept under ordinary conditions soon become moldy or slimy. Shelled limas should be examined closely for damage and tested for tenderness by puncturing the skin. Those with hard, tough skins are overmature and usually lack flavor.

Examine fruits and
vegetables for the
characteristics of
quality.

Ewing Galloway

Beans, Snap

The best snap beans should be clean, fresh in appearance, firm, crisp, tender, free from blemish, and all in a lot should be of the same stage of maturity so that they will cook uniformly. Firm, crisp, tender beans will snap readily when broken. Pods in which the seeds are very immature are the most desirable. Generally, length is unimportant if the beans meet the other requirements for quality.

If the seeds are half grown or larger, the pods are likely to be tough, woody, and stringy. Stringiness is very undesirable. This characteristic can be detected by breaking the bean and gently separating the two halves. Beans age rapidly on the vine and develop toughness as rapidly as they age. A dull, dead, or wilted appearance may indicate that the beans were picked several days before and are no longer of the best quality. Decay is shown by mold or a soft watery condition.

Cabbage

Prime heads of cabbage should be reasonably solid, hard, or firm, and heavy or fairly heavy for their size. They should be closely trimmed, that is, the stems should be cut close to the head, and all except three or four of the outer or wrapper leaves should be removed. Early or new cabbage usually is not so solid or firm as cabbage of the late or winter crop.

The defects of cabbage are readily detected. Worm injury, decay, yellowing of the leaves, and burst heads are the most common. Cabbage that is badly affected by these defects should be avoided; but if only slightly affected, cabbage may be trimmed and utilized to advantage. Heads of cabbage that have yellow leaves or that are otherwise discolored are generally wasty. They may be past their prime or may be affected by some form of

233

injury. Sometimes examination of a head of cabbage will reveal that the base of some of the outer leaves has separated from the stem and that the leaves are held in place only by the natural folding over the head. Such cabbage may be strong in flavor or coarse in texture when cooked.

Soft or puffy heads, although edible, are usually of poorer quality than those that are hard or firm.

Celery

The most desirable celery is that of medium length, thickness, and solidity, with stalks or "branches" that are brittle enough to snap easily. Such celery usually has good heart formation.

Pithy or stringy celery is undesirable. Pithy stalks are those of open texture with air spaces in the central portion. Pithiness may be caused by freezing or may be due to a hereditary defect present during the entire life of the plant. Plant breeders have developed methods of eliminating this trouble. Pithiness can be detected by pressing or twisting the stalks, and stringiness can be detected by breaking.

Freezing injury may cause a browning and drying of the tops, which may later decay. Celery is also subject to a trouble called blackheart, which is usually followed by rots that attack the heart of the stalk. The rot, if present, can be seen by separating the branches and examining the heart. The presence of insects or insect injury can be detected in the same way.

Celery that has formed a seed stem has poor flavor and may be more or less bitter. The seed stem can be seen by separating the stalks or branches—the typical heart formation is replaced by the development of a solid roundish stem of varying size depending on the stage of development.

Corn (Green)

A good ear of corn is one that has a fresh green husk and a cob that is well filled with bright, plump, milky kernels that are just firm enough to offer slight resistance to pressure.

Dry, yellowed, or straw-colored husks are an indication of age or damage. Corn heats rapidly when packed for shipment. Heating causes the yellowing and drying out of the husk as well as the toughening, discoloration, loss of flavor, and shriveling of the kernels.

Corn that is too immature is unsatisfactory. The kernels on cobs of immature corn are very small and very soft, and when cooked they lack flavor. Corn should be cooked as soon as possible after being picked, as it loses flavor very rapidly.

Worm injury is not serious when confined to the tips, since the injured portion usually can be removed with little waste, but it is more objectionable if it occurs along the side of the ear.

Quality can best be determined by pulling back the husk and examining the kernels.

Peas

Peas of the best quality are young, fresh, tender, and sweet. Quality is indicated by the color and condition of the pod, which should be bright green, somewhat velvety to the touch, and fresh in appearance. Some varieties of peas have large puffy pods that stand out away from the peas so that they never appear to be well filled even though the peas are well developed. The pods should be well to fairly well filled, and the peas contained therein should be well developed.

Pods of immature peas are usually flat, are dark green in color, and may have a wilted appearance. Pods that are swollen, of poor color, or more or less flecked with grayish specks, may be in an advanced stage of maturity. The peas may be tough and of poor flavor. A yellowish appearance indicates age or damage. Generally peas with such an appearance are poor in flavor or too tough for satisfactory table use. Water-soaked pods should be avoided as well as those that show evidence of mildew, for the peas are likely to be wasty and may prove to be very poor in quality.

Sweet Potatoes

Good sweet potatoes are smooth, well-shaped, firm, and of bright appearance. The most common defects of sweet potatoes found upon the markets are decay, misshape, and growth cracks. Badly misshapen potatoes and those with growth cracks are undesirable only from the point of view of waste in preparation.

Sweet potatoes affected by decay are objectionable, because the decay usually spreads rapidly and usually imparts a disagreeable flavor to the potato even if the decayed portion is removed before cooking. Decay may appear either as a soft wet rot or as a dry, shriveled, discolored, sunken area, usually at the ends of the potato, but it may appear anywhere on the surface. Another form of decay may appear as greenish (almost black) circular spots, varying from small to large. At times the spots are irregular, occurring in bruised and injured places.

Sweet potatoes sometimes are marked with small, dark, clay-colored spots that may unite and form large dark blotches. These spots are only skin deep and affect the appearance but not the flesh. Sweet potatoes that appear damp should be carefully examined—they may have been badly handled or frozen, or decayed specimens may be present.

Tomatoes

Good-quality tomatoes are mature, firm but not overripe, fairly well formed, plump, smooth, of good color, and free from blemish.

There are many defects in tomatoes that are serious only from the standpoint of waste in preparing for table. Catfaces or scars around the blossom end are typical of the defects within this class. Tomatoes that are rough or irregular in shape may not be attractive in appearance; yet for certain purposes they can be used with little waste.

Tomatoes that have been attacked by worms are very objectionable, especially if the worm has bored deeply. Those having growth cracks will seldom keep long but are fit for immediate consumption. Puffy or watery fruit is usually of poor flavor and is wasty. Puffy tomatoes are usually angular in shape. Decay is usually indicated by a soft watery spot.

Citrus Fruits. As graded citrus fruits are likely to be found in retail markets, they can be discussed in more detail. Citrus fruits are graded for quality and also for size. Oranges, for example, run in size from 80 to 324. The number indicates how many are in a crate. The table on this page shows the number of oranges in a crate, the approximate diameter of each orange, the approximate weight of a dozen, and the volume of juice in each dozen.

A pound of Florida oranges usually yields about one cup of juice. Navel oranges, however, ordinarily yield less juice. As a general rule, citrus fruits that have smooth, thin skins have more juice than the varieties that have rough, thick skins.

The relative economy of buying different sizes of oranges depends upon the price according to the most important

SIZE OF ORANGE AND NUMBER IN CRATE	APPROXIMATE DIAMETER OF FRUIT [1]		APPROXIMATE WEIGHT PER DOZEN [2]		APPROXIMATE VOLUME OF JUICE PER DOZEN [3]		
	FLORIDA ORANGES	CALIFORNIA ORANGES	FLORIDA ORANGES	CALIFORNIA ORANGES	FLORIDA ORANGES	CALIFORNIA NAVEL ORANGES	CALIFORNIA VALENCIA ORANGES
	Inches	*Inches*	*Pounds*	*Pounds*	*Cups*	*Cups*	*Cups*
Large:							
80	...	3¾	...	10.4	...	8.5	...
96	3⅝	3⅝	10.0	8.8	...	...	...
100	...	3½	...	8.4	...	7.1	...
126	3¼	3⅛	7.6	6.7	9.9	...	7.1
Medium:							
150	3⅛	3	6.4	5.6	7.1	5.7	...
176	3	2⅞	5.4	4.8	5.9	4.2	...
200	2⅞	2¾	4.8	4.2	...	...	...
216	2¾	2⅝	4.4	3.9	4.8	3.4	4.0
Small:							
250	2⅝	...	3.8	...	4.2	...	...
252	...	2½	...	3.3	...	2.9	3.5
288	2½	2⅜	3.3	2.9	3.5	...	...
324	2⅜	2¼	3.0	2.6	2.8	...	...

[1] The data for Florida oranges have been obtained from the Bureau of Agricultural Economics, United States Department of Agriculture; those for California oranges, from the California Fruit Growers Exchange.
[2] The approximate net weight of 1 crate of Florida oranges is 80 pounds; that of a crate of California oranges, 70 pounds.
[3] These data have been obtained from the Food Utilization Section of the Bureau of Home Economics.

Juice content of oranges of various sizes and weights.

element to be considered in buying. For instance, if the quantity of juice obtainable is the most important element in buying oranges for a specific purpose, the No. 126 Florida oranges would be cheaper at 50 cents a dozen (9.9 cups for 50 cents) than the No. 250 oranges at 25 cents a dozen (8.4 cups for 50 cents).

How to Judge the Quality of Oranges. The following is a brief guide that can be used by the consumer at the point of purchase:

Oranges of the best quality are firm and heavy, have a fine-textured skin for the variety, and are well-colored. Such fruits (even with a few surface blemishes such as scars, scratches, and slight discolorations) are much to be preferred to oranges that have a badly creased skin, or are puffy or spongy, and light in weight.

Puffy oranges are likely to be light in weight, lacking in juice, and of generally poor quality. Exceptions occur in the tangerines (of which Dancy is the principal variety), satsumas, King, and mandarin types and varieties. These oranges are usually thin-skinned, and are usually oblate or decidedly flattened at the ends. The skin is easily removed; there is little coarse fibrous substance between the skin and the flesh; and the segments of the fruit separate readily. The flavor is distinctive, and the aroma is pungent and pleasant. Because of the looseness of the skin, these oranges are likely to feel puffy; therefore, judgment as to quality should be based mainly on weight for size and deep yellow or orange color of the skin.

The fruit is sound when shipped, but sometimes decay develops before the fruit reaches the consumer. When present, decay is usually in the form of soft areas on the surface of the fruit that appear to be water-soaked. These areas may be covered by a mold. In the early stages of development, the skin in the affected area may be so soft and tender that it breaks easily under pressure. Oranges that have been mechanically injured should be carefully examined. Decay may be present at the point of injury, and decay organisms may easily find entrance to the flesh of the fruit. Wilted, shriveled, or flabby fruit is sometimes found. Age or injury may cause these conditions. Oranges so affected are not desirable.

Oranges are received in bulk on many markets, many bulk oranges being shipped by motor truck. Such fruit is usually not graded or sized and is known as "grove or orchard run." Frequently considerable saving can be made by buying such fruit if the quality is suited to the use for which the fruit is intended.

All citrus fruits that are marketed wrapped in paper and packed in boxes are first put through a mechanical washing and polishing process. This improves appearance and increases the cost, but it does not improve the flavor.

How to Judge the Quality of Grapefruit. The following is a brief guide that can be used by the consumer at the point of purchase:

Grapefruits of good quality are firm but springy to the touch; not soft, wilted, or flabby. They are well-shaped and heavy for their size. Fruits heavy for their size are usually thin-skinned and contain more juice than those that have a coarse skin or are puffy or spongy. Generally speaking, most of the defects found on the grapefruit in the markets (such as scale, scars, thorn scratches, and discoloration) are minor in nature; they affect appearance only and not eating quality.

Decay is sometimes evident and should be avoided, since it usually affects the flavor, making the taste flat and somewhat bitter. Decay sometimes appears as a soft discolored area on the peel at the stem end or "button" of the fruit; or it may appear in the form of a water-soaked area, much of the natural yellow color within the area being lost and the peel being so soft and tender that it breaks easily on pressure of the finger.

Sometimes a fruit is somewhat pointed at the stem end; it is likely to be thick-skinned, particularly if the skin is rough, ridged, or wrinkled. Judgment in selecting this kind of fruit should be based on weight for size.

Grapefruit is called "bright" when the surface of the fruit shows very little russeting, and "russet" when most of the surface of the fruit shows considerable russeting. The choice between fruits showing varying amounts of russeting is a matter of personal preference. In most markets the russets are cheaper, but a few markets pay a premium for such fruit. Russeting does not affect the flavor.

Potatoes. The most economical time to buy potatoes is, of course, in the fall. If sufficient money is available and if the potatoes can be stored so as to keep properly, a considerable saving can be effected by purchasing a large quantity. Most city buyers, however, find it more economical to purchase potatoes in small quantities, for then there is less chance of shrinkage and decay.

After the variety that is most suitable for a particular need has been determined, the next step is to select the grade. In many markets potatoes can be purchased according to grade, especially if they are still available in their original containers. The grade is often indicated on the container. The desirable grades are U. S. No. 1 and U. S. No. 2. The finest grade, of course, is U. S. Fancy. Potatoes of inferior grades may be more economical if they are to be used for certain purposes or if they can be purchased at exceptional bargain prices. The important thing to remember, however, is that not only the price and the variety of the potatoes, but also the purpose for which the potatoes are intended, determine the relative economy.

Very few people can recognize potatoes by name. When the names are known, however, the following information can be used as a guide in selecting potatoes according to use:

NAME	USE
Triumph (Red Bliss or Bliss Triumph) .	For steaming and for salads.
Rose (Spaulding Rose or Early Rose) .	For steaming, for salads, and for French frying.
Irish Cobbler	For most cooking purposes.
Early Ohio	For all general purposes, including baking.
Rural	For all general purposes, including baking.
Green Mountain	For all general purposes, including baking.
Russet Burbank (Idaho)	Especially good for baking or frying.

How to Judge the Quality of Potatoes. The following is a brief guide that can be used by the consumer at the point of purchase:

Potatoes that are sound, smooth, shallow-eyed, and reasonably clean are usually of good quality. Dirty potatoes are unattractive, but the presence of dirt does not injure the eating quality.

A mixture of varieties that are not similar as to cooking quality is undesirable. It is often economical to buy and cook a small sample before buying in quantity. Medium-sized potatoes are usually the most desirable for general use, but selection on the basis of size should be governed by the use for which they are intended.

Wilted, leathery, discolored potatoes should be avoided. They may have been dug too early or injured by some other means. Occasionally both new and old potatoes show a green color on some part of the surface. This condition is known as sunburn. It is usually caused by long exposure to light, which may have occurred in the field or in storage. Sunburned potatoes should be avoided, as they usually have a bitter taste that makes them largely inedible.

Hollow heart and blackheart are defects that can be detected only by cutting. Hollow heart is more likely to be found in large potatoes, but it may be present in potatoes of smaller sizes. Blackheart is very objectionable, particularly in potatoes used for baking.

Potatoes injured by freezing are sometimes found on the market during the winter. Bad cases are indicated by the potato being wet and leaky; or when cut across, it may show a black ring just within the outer surface. In such potatoes the flavor is usually affected, and the flesh turns dark in cooking.

Decay is one of the most serious defects. It may appear as either a wet or a dry rot, which may affect both the surface and the interior flesh. Sometimes the decay is so slight that it can be cut away with little waste. Another defect is caused by wireworms. Affected potatoes show numerous small perforations, which may be so deep as to cause appreciable waste.

In the late spring or early summer, old potatoes may have a shriveled appearance, may be soft and spongy, or may even be sprouted. They are very wasty and may not cook satisfactorily. Badly formed or misshapen potatoes are sometimes offered for sale. They should be considered from the standpoint of the possible quantity of waste in preparing them for use.

Buying Rules That Will Save Money

1. Make your own selection; do not order by telephone. Buy in small quantities unless you have a cool, dark place for storage.

2. Fruits and vegetables that are in season in the nearest marketing area are cheapest in price and often best in quality.

3. Do not handle fruits and vegetables unnecessarily. Handling increases spoilage and the retailer's overhead, both of which represent costs that must be passed on to consumers.

4. Avoid the purchase of foods that show decay. Distinguish between blemishes that affect only appearance and those that affect eating quality.

5. Whenever possible, buy by weight instead of by measure.

6. Do not always buy the best; but buy the grade that is wholesome, economical, and suitable for the purpose for which the food is intended.

7. Buy from more than one merchant. Compare prices and quality.

8. Determine the relative values obtained from a particular merchant, or from various merchants, by testing the foods at home.

TEXTBOOK QUESTIONS

1. What means are used to protect the buyer of meat that is sold in interstate commerce?
2. What are the official grades of beef?
3. Name the characteristics of a good piece of beef.
4. What are the characteristics of good veal?
5. During what months is lamb principally sold?
6. What are the characteristics of good lamb and mutton?
7. Is pork inspected and graded in any way?
8. What are the characteristics of good pork?
9. What grading service is provided for dressed poultry?
10. Is U. S. Prime or A the best grade of turkey?
11. How can the quality of dressed chickens be judged?
12. Explain the grades of milk.
13. What are the four classes of cream?
14. What are the factors by which butter is judged?
15. What percentage rating must butter have before it may bear the certificate of quality issued by the United States Department of Agriculture?
16. What percentage of butter fat must butter contain in order to avoid being classified as an adulterated product?
17. From what is margarine made?
18. (a) What is the range of weight of eggs? (b) What is the largest size called?
19. What factors are considered in rating cheese?
20. What grades of fresh fruits and vegetables are recognized by the United States Department of Agriculture?
21. Name some defects that are an indication of poor quality of (a) celery, (b) cabbage, (c) corn.
22. Give some indications of quality of (a) fresh peaches, (b) fresh snap beans, (c) fresh peas in pods.
23. Give some indications of decay in (a) fresh lima beans, (b) sweet potatoes, (c) tomatoes.
24. In addition to the variety, what are some of the other points to consider in buying potatoes?

DISCUSSION QUESTIONS

1. If a piece of beef has a dark, dull red color and is very lean, how would you classify it according to quality?
2. Some buyers insist upon obtaining lean pork. What do you think of this demand?
3. How do you think you could distinguish a young dressed fowl in a meat market?
4. Explain some of the dangers of relying on grade marks on packages of eggs.

5. Should one always attempt to buy Grade A jumbo eggs because they are the largest and best? Explain.
6. Why do you think it is difficult to enforce the use of quality standards for fresh fruits and vegetables?
7. On what basis should one buy citrus fruits: weight, juice, size, price?
8. If you were given an opportunity to handle green snap beans, what would be one of your first tests of freshness and quality?
9. Potatoes must be known by variety in order to be judged. Why is this knowledge necessary? Explain your answer.
10. Why do some people contend that the top grade of beef is not always the best for every purpose?
11. In the general rules for buying it is suggested that whenever possible one should buy by weight. Why is this important?
12. Would you recommend, under any circumstances, the buying of fruits or vegetables that show decay or damage?

PROBLEMS

1. Assume that Grade A eggs weighing 24 ounces a dozen cost 48 cents. (a) What is the price per ounce? (b) In order to pay the same price, what should one pay for a dozen eggs weighing 20 ounces?
2. If Florida oranges are packed 216 to a crate and sell for 30 cents a dozen, what should be the price of California navel oranges of the same size if they are bought on the basis of juice content? (Use the table on page 236.)
3. If California oranges that are packed 150 to a crate sell for 40 cents a dozen, what should be the price of a pound of these oranges? (Use the table on page 236.)

COMMUNITY PROBLEMS AND PROJECTS

1. In your local stores see what information you can find in regard to grades of fresh fruits and vegetables. Write a report of the information you obtain and indicate how you obtained it.
2. Investigate to see whether your state has any state laws pertaining to the grading and marketing of fruits and vegetables and give a report to the class.
3. Visit a local meat-packing plant and report on the grading and inspection procedures.

Chapter 14

PART V _____

How to Buy Clothing, Fabrics, and Shoes

Purpose of the Chapter. Next to food, we spend more for clothing and other items of apparel than for any other commodity or service that we buy. In addition to being a substantial item in our budgets, the purchase of clothing and apparel is important to us because of comfort and personal pride. Furthermore, we purchase a great variety of fabrics for the household. Several volumes would be required to present a detailed analysis of the procedure involved in buying these various products scientifically. The purpose of this chapter is, however, to present (a) guides for use in buying clothing, (b) information for use in analyzing and judging cloth, (c) simple tests that can be performed in the procedure of buying fabrics, (d) simple chemical tests that can be performed in the home, and (e) helpful guides for buying shoes.

Kinds of Cloth. A *fabric* is cloth woven or knit from fibers. The manner in which the cloth is woven is known as the *weave*. Sometimes the weave is loose, sometimes tight; and sometimes it makes patterns, such as the herringbone weave. The selection of a particular weave will depend largely on taste and style. As a general rule, tightly woven cloth is more durable than cloth that is loosely woven.

A knowledge of fabrics is important in buying clothing and household materials. Not only is it desirable to be able to identify the kinds of fibers of which a fabric is made, but also you will be a wiser buyer if you can judge the quality and value of the cloth.

Wool. Yarn or thread from which woolen fabrics are woven is made from the soft, curled fibers of the coat of sheep and some other animals. A characteristic of cloth made from wool fiber is that it holds its shape well and has a tendency to resist wrinkling much more than cotton and better than some but not all of the fibers made by chemical processes.

Fabrics are sometimes referred to as *all wool, pure wool,* and *part wool.* All wool or pure wool fabrics may be made either of wool that has not been used before, which is known as *virgin wool,* of wool that has been spun or woven before, but which has been *reprocessed,* or of wool that has been reclaimed from previously used cloth, *re-used wool.* Virgin wool cloth is usually considered more desirable because it is more durable.

Wool fibers are made into two types of yarn, one of which is known as woolen yarn and the other as worsted yarn. Ordinary *woolen yarn* is usually spun from a mixture of short and long fibers; *worsted yarn,* from fibers two or more inches in length that are combed so they will lie parallel when spun. Fabrics made from worsted yarns are hard surfaced and long wearing, while fabrics made from ordinary woolen yarns are fuzzy and somewhat uneven in appearance. Though they may be as warm, they do not wear as long as fabrics made from worsted yarn.

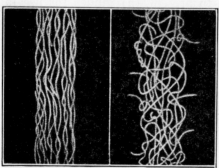

Forstmann Woolen Company

WORSTED YARN   WOOLEN YARN
(Enlarged)   (Enlarged)
A single worsted yarn   A single woolen yarn
spun from long fibers   made of short and long
combed into a parallel   fibers mixed together
position.   and then spun.

Examples of worsted and woolen yarns.

Cotton. Cloth made from the fibers that grow on the cotton plant is known as *cotton.* It is the most commonly used fabric in making clothing. Cotton in its natural state is nonabsorbent, but it may be treated chemically to make it absorb moisture readily. It is more inflammable than wool, and ordinarily it does not have the luster or the body that wool and linen have.

Linen. Cloth made from the fibers in the stems of the flax plant, which is a kind of tall grass, is called *linen.* It is a very durable cloth and is characterized by its smoothness, crispness, and luster. Though cotton is sometimes substituted for it, women especially like linen for summer dresses.

Silk. Silk worms make a very fine fiber that they wrap tightly around the cocoons in which they spend part of their lives. The silk fiber is very strong and has a high luster. When made into cloth, it wears very well unless it is damaged by chemicals in the dying process. If a piece of "silk" cloth splits or breaks after brief wear, this fact is a definite indication that the cloth is not pure silk.

Rayon. *Rayon* fabric is made from synthetic fibers of which there are two types, cellulose and acetate. Rayon has a higher luster than silk and, although heavier, it is weaker. Its fibers are also coarser than those of silk. Rayon feels stiffer and is less elastic than silk. Cloth made of it is usually cheaper than silk cloth.

Regular rayon yarns are made from the natural long synthetic fibers. Spun rayon is made from cut rayon fibers that are spun into yarn in the same manner as wool. Spun rayon fabrics feel somewhat like wool fabrics. Rayon is a popular cloth for women's dresses, curtains and drapes, table coverings, and decorative fabrics used both in wearing apparel and in the home.

Nylon. *Nylon* is a synthetic fiber derived from coal, air, and water and in the near future may also be made from natural gas and petroleum. It can be made to possess varying degrees of toughness, resistance to abrasion, elasticity, hardness, solubility, and moisture absorption. Thus nylon is a term that does not refer to a single fiber but to a group of similar fibers which may vary considerably in physical properties.

Nylon fibers, carefully selected for the purpose the cloth is to serve, are woven into fabrics for parachutes, curtains and drapes, and wearing apparel. It is a popular fiber for

PROPERTIES	WOOL	SILK	COTTON	LINEN	RAYON CELLULOSE	RAYON ACETATE	NYLON *
Tensile strength.	Comparatively weak. Weaker when wet.	Strongest of textile fibers. Weaker when wet.	Stronger than most wools. Weaker than linen. Stronger when wet.	Stronger than cotton. Weaker than silk. Stronger when wet.	Fairly strong. Weaker when wet.	Fairly strong. Weaker when wet.	Very strong.
Conductor of heat.	Good for cold weather.	Fairly good for cold weather.	Fairly good for hot weather.	Good for hot weather.	Fairly good for hot weather.	Fairly good for cold weather.	Good for hot weather.
Absorbency of moisture.	Not readily absorbent, but holds moisture without feeling damp. Does not lose moisture rapidly.	Not readily absorbent.	Very absorbent. Loses moisture rapidly, and produces a cooling effect on wearer.	Very absorbent. Loses moisture rapidly, and produces a cooling effect on wearer.	Very absorbent. Loses moisture rapidly, and produces a cooling effect on wearer.	Not very absorbent.	Not absorbent except when especially treated in manufacturing.
Resiliency (resistance to wrinkling).	Good.	Fairly good.	Poor.	Poor.	Poor—can be improved by use of chemical finishes.	Poor.	Exceptionally good.
Resistance to alkalies (such as strong soaps).	Readily damaged.	Readily damaged.	Not harmed.	Not harmed.	Not readily damaged but withstands less than cotton or linen.	Damaged more easily than cellulose rayon.	Not easily damaged by soaps, synthetic detergents, or dry cleaning solvents.
Resistance to acid (such as perspiration).	Not readily damaged.	Easily damaged.	Fairly easily damaged.	Fairly easily damaged.	Easily damaged.	Easily damaged.	Not easily damaged by perspiration.

* The degree of strength, absorbency, and other properties of nylon can be controlled in the manufacturing process.

Characteristics of fabrics.

making hosiery. In addition to serving for personal and household purposes, nylon is being used for many industrial purposes, such as making ropes and transmission belts.

Characteristics of Fabrics. Every fabric has definite characteristics that make it especially useful for certain purposes. Those characteristics for the principal fabrics are explained in the table on page 246. It must be borne in mind, of course, that there are various grades of wool and other fabrics and that some fabrics are mixtures of two or more different fibers. The characteristics of the different types of fabrics given in the table are based upon a good grade of each type.

Simple Tests for Fabrics While Shopping. Many complicated tests of fabrics can be conducted in laboratories, and simple tests can be made in the home; but most buyers have to depend upon a casual examination while shopping. Tests of the last type must be simple and easy to perform. The following are a few tests that may be used in a store:

(a) *Creasing fabrics.* If a fabric is folded lengthwise and crosswise, the sharpness of the crease indicates the kind of fiber present. Creasing the fabric also provides an opportunity to examine it more closely to determine if one kind or more than one kind of fiber was used in weaving. Linen folds more readily and holds creases longer than cotton. Cotton creases more readily than wool or silk, which will spring back into its original form. When nylon is creased, it quickly goes back to its original form. Rayon creases readily and tends to hold the crease. The scratching of the edge of the fold will frequently disclose whether the cloth has been *weighted,* that is, impregnated with a substance to fill the pores and to add weight.

(b) *Examining yarns.* The labels of yard goods and garments usually identify the fabric, but you can conduct your own yarn tests. If a piece of fabric has a rough edge, some of the threads may be raveled from the cloth and untwisted to determine whether there is a mixture of fibers. Silk or wool may be combined with any one of several other fibers.

If the threads are raveled, it is easy to distinguish the silk or the wool from the other fiber.

Frequently cotton and linen are woven together, as, for example, in materials for towels. The linen threads may run in one direction and the cotton threads in another; they are rarely twisted together. Another test to distinguish linen from cotton is to note the relative stiffness and luster. Cotton is limp and dull; linen is stiff and lustrous.

Rayon is frequently combined with cotton or silk. Rayon and cotton are easily distinguishable because of their relative luster. Rayon and silk can be distinguished easily by the degree of fineness. Nylon fiber, like silk, is usually fine and, therefore, not easily distinguished from silk, but garments made of nylon usually are labeled.

(c) *Examining fibers.* The kind of fiber in a yarn made of wool, cotton, or linen is rather easily determined by untwisting it and examining separate fibers of which it is composed. Woolen fibers when untwisted from a piece of yarn appear kinky and have a resiliency that cotton and linen do not have. Cotton fiber is softer and more pliable than wool or linen when rubbed between the fingers. Both wool and linen fibers have a higher luster and they usually are longer than cotton fibers. Cotton fiber has more tensile strength than wool but less than linen.

Rayon, nylon, and silk fibers are somewhat more difficult to identify than wool, cotton, and linen fibers. However, with experience you can learn to distinguish them from each other. Rayon and nylon fibers have higher luster than silk. A silk fiber will stretch slightly before breaking; rayon and nylon fibers have very little elasticity. Rayon fibers are not as strong as silk, and usually nylon is stronger than silk. Rayon and most nylon fibers are somewhat coarser than silk.

Some yarns may be made of two or three different fibers. Fibers from mixed yarns are sometimes difficult to separate so they can be examined. Untwisting will enable you to identify the kind of fiber better than breaking the yarn abruptly or attempting to compare yarns. This test is most practicable for examining the yarn in a garment. A piece of yarn can usually be obtained, for instance, by taking a thread from the inside of the pocket or from along a seam.

When there is considerable nap on cloth that is a mixture of cotton and wool, the wool nap can be distinguished from the cotton. If a moistened finger is passed over the nap, the cotton will absorb the moisture and lie flat, whereas the wool will spring back into its original position.

Rayon can be distinguished from silk by untwisting the yarn to see if there is a difference in the fineness, the softness, and the strength of the fibers.

Linen can be distinguished from cotton by untwisting the yarn and pulling it apart slowly. The linen will usually come apart in long pointed strands, whereas the cotton will break more abruptly with brushlike ends.

These tests usually are not applicable in the case of some novelty or highly decorative cloths, in which there is a mixture of several kinds of fibers. For them the statements of the manufacturers may be necessary in order to determine their characteristics such as strength, durability, and resistance to cleaning agents.

(d) *Determining weighted cloth.* The finish of a piece of cloth determines not only how pleasing it is to the eye, but

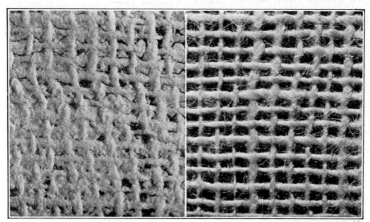

Consumers' Guide

A filled cloth before washing.   A filled cloth after washing.

Weighted fabric before and after washing.

Many weighted fabrics lose their luster and body after the first washing because the filler washes out.

it may be an important factor in how well it retains its original appearance and how well it wears. Many fabrics, especially cotton fabrics, are weighted to improve the appearance. In weighted cloths, the thread is impregnated with starch and with another filler, such as chalk, China clay, or magnesium. When the cloth is finally pressed between rollers, it will not be substantial although it may appear to be so. It will lose its beauty when it is washed and worn. The filling in cotton cloth can be detected by rubbing a piece briskly to dislodge the filler.

The substances used for weighting silk cloth are usually added to the filling (the crosswise yarns) so as not to impair the lengthwise strength. Weighted silk will stay creased lengthwise better than it will crosswise. In fact, the continued lengthwise creasing of weighted silk may cause the cloth to split.

It is too much to expect that the ordinary buyer will make a close examination of every fabric during the process of buying. However, it is suggested that one learn to recognize various fabrics by "feel" and appearance. For instance, after one has examined carefully a number of fabrics to determine the thread count, it is possible to feel a piece of cloth and at least determine whether it has a low thread count or a high thread count. It is also possible

---

Guides for the Selection of Fabrics
When Shopping

1. Read the labels on garments and on bolts of fabrics to determine the kinds of fibers in the cloth.
2. Determine the amount of shrinkage to be expected.
3. Inquire if the fabrics are resistant to the soaps and detergents used in laundering and dry cleaning processes.
4. Consult the standards division or customer's information service in stores having such services relative to the suitability of the fabric for your purpose.
5. Apply the simple tests of creasing the fabrics, examining the yarns for the kinds of fibers used in them, examining the fibers for uniformity and for mixtures in weaving, and determining whether the cloth is weighted.

to determine reasonably accurately the kind of fiber by casual examination.

Testing Fabrics at Home. Tests of fabrics at home may supplement those performed in the store while shopping. The most satisfactory tests that can be performed at home are as follows:

Lye test. Wool and silk are animal fibers; cotton and linen are vegetable fibers; and rayon and nylon are synthetic fibers made by chemical processes. Animal fibers (wool and silk) may be distinguished from vegetable fibers in the following manner: Place a sample of the cloth in a granite pan or a porcelain cooking dish, and pour over it a solution of one tablespoon of lye to one-half pint of water. Cover the container and boil the contents for fifteen minutes. At the end of that time animal fiber will be completely destroyed, but vegetable fiber will remain. This test reveals the presence of such vegetable fibers as cotton or linen. Inasmuch as a lye solution of this strength is very strong, considerable caution and care should be used in conducting this test.

Acid test. The acid test reveals the presence of vegetable (cotton and linen) fibers. It requires the use of a hot iron and a 2 per cent solution of sulphuric acid. It is as follows: Place a drop of acid in the center of the sample, and then place the sample between layers of heavy paper. Press the cloth with a hot iron. If cotton or any other vegetable fiber is present, the cloth will burn black and become brittle. Rub the cloth between the fingers. The cotton or other vegetable fiber will disintegrate and leave merely the wool or the silk.

The presence of rayon or nylon fibers may not be determined positively by either the lye or the acid tests.

Counting the threads. The closeness of the weave, that is, the number of threads lengthwise and crosswise through the cloth, is an important factor in the durability of different grades of cloth. The threads running lengthwise through the cloth are the *warp* and those running crosswise are the *woof,* sometimes referred to as filling threads. The

U. S. *Bureau of Home Economics*
Making a thread count.

thread count or closeness of the weave is determined by counting the number of warp and woof threads in each inch. The counting can be done best with the aid of a microscope. A special instrument is sometimes used. Anyone can make a count, however, by laying off a one-quarter inch of the cloth and, with a magnifying glass, counting the number of threads in each direction.

A relatively expensive cloth may prove to be cheaper, in the long run, than a cloth that costs less. For instance, in the case of muslin, the warp (or lengthwise yarns) has been found to range from 44 to 109, while the filling (or crosswise yarns) ranges from 47 to 97. A cloth with a warp count of 80 and a filling count of 55 might be only 10 per cent cheaper than one with a warp count of 109 and a filling count of 97, but the more expensive cloth might last almost twice as long as the cheaper.

The American Standards Association has classified sheets by types, such as Type 200, Type 180, Type 140, and Type 128, in which the numbers represent the number of threads in the warp per inch plus the number of filling or crosswise threads per inch. It would be desirable if the minimum thread count in each direction were specified; however, it is assumed that it is best when the number is equal in each direction. A fabric with a high thread count is usually smoother, firmer, more even, and has more luster than one with a low thread count; although many fabrics, such as those used for sheets, are loaded with starch or some other compound that is washed out in the first laundering. In buying fabrics such as sheets the weight of the yarn is important in addition to the thread count. The weight of sheets usually runs from 3¼ ounces a square yard to 5¼ ounces a square yard. After examining fabrics a few times, one can usually determine the approximate thread count by looking through the cloth toward a light, regardless of whether or not it is loaded.

Information on desirable thread counts can be obtained for nearly every fabric, including those used in sheets and other garments. One should familiarize himself with this information and then look for it on tags and labels. If this information is not available, ask for it. The standards divisions or customer information services in many large stores have this information available.

Burning test. If cotton yarn is woven with woolen yarn, it is easy to ravel the cloth and burn the separate pieces of yarn for comparison. Cotton burns with a flash and leaves no deposit. Wool burns more slowly and gives off an odor similar to that from burning hair or feathers.

Combinations of silk and cotton yarns are easy to identify. The yarns should be burned separately. The cotton will burn with a flash, leaving no deposit, whereas the silk will burn more slowly and will form a bead at the end. Weighted silk, however, acts differently in some cases.

Unweighted silk burns like wool, whereas weighted silk usually retains its form. Rayon burns like cotton. It is therefore possible to distinguish good silk from weighted silk or imitation silk.

Test of tensile strength. Tensile strength is important and is used frequently as a selling point, but it should not be taken as the sole measure of quality. Many fabrics, such as muslin or percale in sheets and madras or broadcloth in shirts, first break or split lengthwise, indicating that the filling or woof threads were not as strong as the warp. Thus, it is important that strength both crosswise and lengthwise should be considered. It is difficult to obtain a suitable test of tensile strength without some kind of equipment. Special scales are available for measuring the amount of weight required to break threads. Crude scales can sometimes be constructed. One can, however, make a rough test by stretching the cloth till it breaks, or by breaking one of

the threads in the hands. Several different threads should
be tested in measuring tensile strength.

Washing test. The laundering test is one of the most
important, especially in the buying of wash clothes and
household fabrics. A careful check should be kept on the
length of life of a particular brand of sheet, shirt, or other
item. The brands that wear longer should be given favor
in future purchases.

Sun test. One way for a consumer to protect himself
from unsatisfactory dyes is to take a sample of the fabric
home and to submit it to conditions similar to those under
which it will be used. A very satisfactory test is to place
the fabric where it will be exposed to the sunlight and then
to cover part of it with a piece of cardboard. The cardboard should be removed occasionally, and the change in
the color of the exposed part should be observed. A portion of the fabric should also be washed to determine
whether the cloth fades or loses its original luster. For the
average individual a more practical guide is a tag or label
of the Better Fabrics Bureau that provides a reasonable
guarantee of color fastness.

Test for slippage. Some fabrics do not wear well in garments because the threads slip at the seams. This is particularly true of such fabrics as satins, rayons, nylons, and
crepes. The only practical test for slippage is to sew samples together in a seam, then stretch both sides away from
the seam to see if any slippage occurs.

Microscope test for uniformity. With the aid of a microscope another test may be made to determine whether yarns
are of uneven size, lumpy, or fuzzy. Smooth, uniform yarns
are desirable except in novelty cloth. In this test several
samples of the cloth should be used and the threads in the
yarns counted so that the average quality of the cloth can
be determined.

Fabrics with imperfect weaves will wear out faster than
those that are woven perfectly. In an item such as a sheet
an imperfect weave is characterized by a lump or a loose
thread. In examining bath towels for thread count, push
aside the loops and note how closely the cloth in the

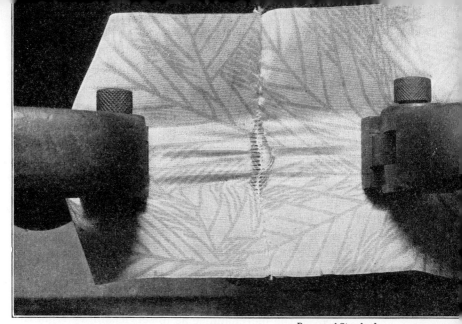

A test for slippage.

Although the tension on the cloth is not heavy, the seam is rapidly pulling apart.

"ground work" is woven. The loops in a bath towel must be firmly caught or they will pull out easily.

Look for Tags and Labels. Some manufacturers of clothing and fabrics use labels indicating the standards set up by the United States Bureau of Standards. Some of the trade associations require their members to use tags and labels indicating the quality of the clothing and the working conditions under which the clothing was manufactured. A truly informative label will provide information on such points as fibers used in the fabric, yarns per square inch, weight per square yard, sizing, finish, size of the garment, seams, how seams are made, strength of fabric, resistance to slippage, shrinkage, washability, resistance to sunlight and perspiration, and suggestions for laundering and dry cleaning.

Look for the following specific information on tags and labels:

(a) Under the rules of fair trade practices of the Federal Trade Commission terms, such as "preshrunk," "will not shrink," "completely shrunk," or "fully

255

shrunk," may not be used unless no further shrinkage will occur. If such a statement is used, it must
be qualified as in the following example: "Preshrunk; will not shrink more than 2 per cent under
Commercial Standard CS 59-41." Such a statement
on a garment gives assurance of adequate protection.
The so-called Texturized process for woolen fabrics
and the Sanforized process for cotton and linen
fabrics have proved reliable.

(b) The seals or tags of approval of the American Institute of Laundering and the Better Fabrics Bureau
are important guides in determining color fastness,
shrinkage, and construction.

(c) The label of the National Association of Dyers and
Cleaners indicates whether that association has approved the merchandise as to serviceability from the
point of view of cleaning.

(d) The fabric identification labels on garments provide
valuable information for a purchaser. As was explained in Chapter 6, every garment made in whole
or in part from wool and sold in interstate commerce must be labeled to indicate the percentage of
wool and the type of wool. Under the trade practices rules of the Federal Trade Commission, all
rayon products must be labeled "rayon." The trade
name or blend name may not be used alone. For instance, celanese must be labeled "celanese rayon."
Fabrics and products containing rayon and other
fibers must disclose the kinds of fibers present, each
being named in the order of the predominance by
weight.

(e) Brand names may be helpful to a buyer in identifying merchandise especially after he has had experience using it. Brand names fall into two classes:
those well known through advertising and wide
distribution and those that may be considered private
brands. Merchandise ranging from poor to high
quality may be found under both well-known and
private brands.

(f) Special labels with regard to workmanship may disclose the types of seams, the method of sewing, the
inner construction, the type of hem, or other features.

(g) Many buyers consider it important to look for union
labels or other labels indicating the working conditions under which the clothing was manufactured.

(h) Many manufacturers, department stores, and specialty stores are making an increasing use of informative and descriptive labels and tags on clothing.
Besides the information mentioned above, look for
information pertaining to tensile strength, tearing
strength, and instructions in regard to cleaning.

(i) Any other kind of so-called protective label is meaningless unless the label indicates definitely what protection is provided.

How to Judge the Quality of Clothing. In buying clothing it is always advisable to consider first the use for which
the garment is intended and the amount your budget will
permit you to spend. Having decided whether the article

Guides in Determining the Quality of Clothing

1. Read the labels and ask questions about the garment as
to the kind of fabric, shrinkage, color fastness, permanence
of finish of cloth, method of laundering or dry cleaning,
and resistance to wrinkling.

2. Inspect the inside to determine width and stitching of
seams, hems, and bindings.

3. Test the strength of the seams and note the quality of
thread used in sewing the garment.

4. In dresses, lingerie, and garments made of light weight
fabrics, note the quality of the workmanship. In good
quality garments, the length of the stitches will not be less
than fourteen to the inch, and allowances will be made
for hems and alterations.

5. Try the garment on. Stretch, bend, reach, move about, and
sit down to be sure the garment will be comfortable when
worn for normal physical activity. A try-on is especially
important in purchasing an inexpensive garment to make
sure it was not skimped in material.

6. Examine sleeves, collars, pockets and exposed seams to
see that there is no objectionable matching of plaids or
stripes.

7. Look at the lining to determine if it is made of substantial
material, securely sewed in, and lies flat and smooth.

NAME OF FUR	DURABILITY			COST		
	LOW	MEDIUM	HIGH	LOW	MEDIUM	HIGH
Beaver			x			x
Ermine		x				x
Fox		x			x	
Hare (rabbit)	x			x		
Kid	x			x		
Lamb		x		x		
Lamb, Broadtail	x			x		
Lamb, Mouton			x	x		
Lamb, Persian			x	x		
Leopard			x			x
Marmot	x			x		
Marten			x			x
Mink			x			x
Muskrat			x		x	
Opossum		x			x	
Opossum, Australian		x			x	
Otter			x			x
Rabbit	x			x		
Raccoon			x	x		
Seal			x			x
Sheep		x			x	
Skunk			x		x	
Squirrel		x			x	
Weasel		x			x	

Durability and cost of furs.

of clothing is for sportswear, street wear, work, or for dress-up occasions and the amount that you can afford to spend, there are certain guides that may help you.

How to Buy Furs. Many different kinds of furs are used in making coats and scarfs, but not all of these are common enough to be found in most stores. Several types of fur have been sold in previous years under names that did not distinguish the kind of fur. However, a law effective August 9, 1952, forbids the misbranding or false advertising of furs sold, advertised, offered for sale, or transported in interstate commerce. Each fur must be labeled by its true name as established by the Federal Trade Commission. The names of many furs are given in the table at the left with an indication as to their durability and cost. Any fur or fur garment must be labeled to indicate whether it is composed of used fur; has been bleached or dyed; or is composed of paws, tails, or other undesirable parts of the skin. There may be little relationship between the price paid for a fur garment and its wearing quality. For instance, Chinchilla is a very expensive fur, but its wearing quality is rather low. A garment made of squirrel fur is medium in cost, but its wearing quality is low.

In the days when there were no regulations as to using trade names on furs, there were many fur garments sold as lapin, coney, and beaver, which were actually dyed rabbit fur. It is quite possible that for some time after the passage of the Federal law there may be furs with these old labels still available in stores.

Determining the Right Size of Hose. Hose that are either too small or too large not only are uncomfortable and may cause foot injury but also may not wear well. The chart on page 260 is recommended as a guide.

How to Judge the Quality of Hose. The quality of hose is determined largely by (a) the type and quality of fiber and (b) the method of manufacture. In one method of manufacturing the hose are knit in a flat piece, then sewed

CHILDREN'S		WOMEN'S		MEN'S	
SIZE OF SHOE	HOSE SIZE	SIZE OF SHOE	HOSE SIZE	SIZE OF SHOE	HOSE SIZE
6 - 7	6	1 -2½	8½	5½- 6	9½
7½- 9	6½	3 -4½	9	6½- 7	10
9½-10	7	5 -6	9½	7½- 8	10½
10½-11½	7½	6½-7	10	8½- 9	11
12 -13	8	7½-8	10½	9½-10	11½
		8½-9	11	10½-11	12
				11½-12	13

Hose sizes.

together forming a seam up the back to fit the form of the
foot and the leg. These hose are known as *full-fashioned*
and usually fit well.

Another method of making hose is to knit them in a
circular manner, then shaping them to fit the foot and the
leg by drying them on a form. These hose are *seamless* or
circular knit hose. Sometimes an imitation seam is placed
on the back. A circular knit hose can be distinguished by
the fact that all lengthwise stitches run parallel the full
length of the hose. Seamless or circular knit hose are likely
not to fit so well as full-fashioned hose.

Practically all sheer hose for women are now made of
nylon. The sheerness and the serviceability of nylon hose
are determined by two factors, the denier and the gauge.
Denier refers to the size (diameter) of the thread used in
knitting nylon hose and is indicated by numbers usually
ranging from 15 to 70; the heavier the thread, the larger
the number. The *gauge* of hose refers to the number of
threads in each inch (the closeness of the stitches) and is
indicated by numbers usually ranging from 39 to 52 and
occasionally as high as 66. Thus denier and gauge are important in buying hose, for they determine not only sheerness and fineness but serviceability as well.

The strength of cotton yarns used in hose is determined
by the number of ply. For instance, in men's hose if two
yarns are twisted into one it is known as two ply. Hose
made from yarns that are at least two ply are more serv-
iceable than hose made from single-ply yarns.

Mercerized cotton is a fabric that has been put through a certain process which makes it more lustrous and usually stronger. Lisle is a very high grade of smooth cotton yarn made from long fibers tightly spun and with the fuzz removed. It is also mercerized and is therefore considered the finest and smoothest type of cotton fabric for hose.

Hose made from long fiber worsted wool yarns will be longer wearing than hose made from shorter fibers or from loosely spun yarns.

Regular nylon will make a finely knit hose with a luster similar to silk. Spun nylon is soft and has a dull luster.

Types of Shoes. There are five principal types of construction for shoes: the *welt,* the *McKay,* the *turned,* the *Littleway,* and the *stitchdown.* The difference between them lies in the process by which the sole is attached to the upper. This process is the manufacturer's most important problem and has an important relation to the quality of the shoe. There are still other types of construction, which may be classified according to the process of attaching the sole to the upper. These are the *standard screw,* the *pegged,* the *nailed,* and the *cemented.* The nature of each of these four types of construction is obvious from the name. The five principal types that have been mentioned previously are briefly described in the table on the following page.

Kinds of Leather. The average person is not in a position to judge the specific quality of leather. Furthermore, there is no mark on shoes to indicate the grade of leather. It is advisable, therefore, to deal only with reputable shoe merchants.

The general quality of leather can, however, be detected by examination. Good leather is closely fibered, flexible, and firm. Poor leather is loosely fibered, stretches much, and is inclined to break when bent. The finish on poor leather sometimes cracks when the shoe is bent. Rough edges on soles and a rough finish on uppers are also indications of poor leather.

The uppers of shoes are made from many qualities and kinds of leather. Calfskin is probably the best kind for the

WELT. The **welt** construction is especially good for shoes that are subject to heavy wear, such as school shoes and work shoes. In this type of construction the sole and the upper are joined by being stitched to a narrow strip of leather called the welt. The welt shoe can be identified by examining the inside and lifting the lining, if there is one. The inside should be smooth. If tacks or thread can be felt or seen, the shoe has not been made by the welt construction.

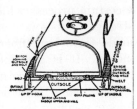

McKAY. The insole and the outsole are fastened together with tacks and are then stitched. The stitches on the inside are covered by a thin lining. The stitching on the outside is hidden in a channel that is made by splitting the insole. McKay shoes are made generally for women and children. Such a shoe may be identified by lifting the lining. The sewing and the tacks near the edge will then be evident. In some cases the stitching and the tacks may hurt the feet.

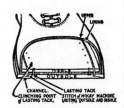

TURNED. This type of construction is used especially in the manufacture of high-grade boots, shoes, and slippers for women and children. No insole is used. The outsole is channeled and sewed to the upper. When the lining of a turned shoe is lifted, the seam should be evident in the groove at the edge of the sole. This type of shoe can be distinguished from the McKay type because the sewing in the former case is farther from the edge of the sole.

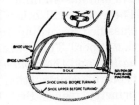

LITTLEWAY. The **Littleway** method is somewhat similar to lower grades of construction, although the staples do not come through the insole. It is used in the manufacture of shoes for women and children and also for athletic wear. Work shoes are sometimes manufactured by this method. The Littleway process can be distinguished from the McKay process by the absence of tacks or staples on the surface of the insole.

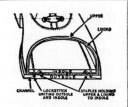

STITCHDOWN. Many children's shoes are made by the **stitchdown** process. In this process the upper is stitched to the insole and the outsole. This method produces a satisfactory shoe for small children. Shoes made in this way can be identified by the smooth insole and by the inner edge of the welt, which shows on the outside of the sole when the upper is pushed back.

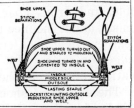

Shoe construction.

uppers of dress shoes. Various other heavy skins are used as substitutes. Many varieties of special leathers are coming into use. These include the skins of reptiles, deer, ostrich, and kangaroo, and many substitutes for them. The buying of shoes made of novelty and special leathers also presents difficulties. Again, the only safe method is to buy from reputable dealers.

Comfort versus Style and Cost. Shoes should be fitted to the foot in both length and width. The numerals refer to length and the letters to width. For example, men's shoes vary in length from 6 to 14 and in width from Triple A (very narrow) to Triple E (very wide). In addition to the right length and width, the shape of the shoe is also important. The arch, the lining, the size, and the shape are far more important than style. Failure to buy properly fitting shoes may cause not only great discomfort but also ill health and physical deformity. Wise buyers realize that shoes cannot be bought like other clothing, but must be bought with the advice of a capable shoe-fitter.

Rapid changes of style in women's shoes often have an important influence on price. Style also influences the price of men's shoes. Comfort should never, however, be sacrificed for cost or style, even though comfortable shoes may cost more and may be less stylish than other shoes.

The price of a shoe is governed largely by the process of manufacture, the quality of the leather, and the style. If a manufacturer has given special attention to style, it is possible that the buyer may be attracted by a shoe that has been made by a cheap process and of low-grade material. In general the higher-priced shoes are constructed better and are made of better leather than lower-priced shoes. However, it is not always possible to determine quality or to predict comfort from the price paid for shoes. Probably it is more difficult to select shoes from the middle-price range with confidence as to their construction and quality than from the high- and low-priced ranges.

Evaluation Guide for Buying Shoes. Even experts admit that it is difficult to detect poor leather and substitutes for leather in shoes. For many years American buyers have demanded style in preference to comfort. It has been estimated that only 14 per cent of the women and 40 per cent of the men wear shoes that are correctly fitted. In buying shoes, it is therefore important to consider more than style

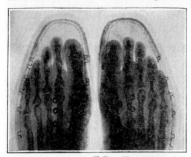

X-Ray Shoe Fitter, Inc.

X-ray shoe fitting.

and appearance. By the use of X-ray shoe fitting machines that some shoe stores have, the fit of the shoe as to width, length, and shape can be easily seen. A warning has been issued, however, that exposure of the foot to the X-rays through the use of this machine either too long at a time or too frequently is injurious.

In the selection of shoes, design is the most important consideration, for it regulates comfort. A person can sometimes afford to sacrifice quality in order to get a shoe of the proper design to give him comfort. Because of the importance of this consideration, a person should buy shoes only from a merchant who is qualified to fit his feet properly.

Workmanship and materials are sometimes given less consideration than design. Style may have a greater influence than workmanship and materials in determining cost. In determining the value of a shoe, however, quality should never be forgotten.

One of the greatest mistakes made in buying shoes is to choose them without regard to the purpose for which they are needed. For instance, school children may look better in lightweight calfskin shoes with thin soles; but a more durable leather will give longer wear, and a thicker sole will ensure greater comfort. If a woman is to be on her feet much during the day, she will not want to wear shoes with extremely high heels. Climate and type of occupation often must be taken into consideration in deciding between shoes that are cut low and those that have higher tops.

TEXTBOOK QUESTIONS

1. What is a fabric?
2. What is meant by the weave?
3. What are the different types or grades of wool that may be used in a garment?
4. Explain the difference between worsted and woolen yarns.
5. Explain briefly the general characteristics of (a) cotton, (b) linen, (c) silk, (d) rayon, (e) nylon.
6. What are good fabrics for clothing in hot weather?
7. Name two fabrics that do not absorb moisture readily.
8. Name two fabrics that are especially resistant to wrinkling.
9. Explain the creasing test.
10. Explain how yarns may be tested.
11. What is meant by weighted cloth?
12. What simple rules may be followed when buying fabrics?
13. Explain each of the following tests to determine the kinds of fibers of which yarn is made: (a) lye, (b) acid, (c) burning.
14. What tests can be used to determine whether cloth will hold its color?
15. Explain the characteristics of a fabric with a low thread count as compared with one with a high thread count.
16. What is the meaning of Type 140 when applied to sheets?
17. After one has become familiar with a thread count by conducting several tests, how can one, when buying in a store, determine in general the thread count without having specific information or without making definite tests?
18. What kind of information should one expect to find on tags or labels of fabrics and garments?
19. What does "preshrunk" or "will not shrink" mean as applied to labels according to the rules of the Federal Trade Commission?
20. Name at least three old trade names of furs that are dyed rabbit fur.
21. Which is likely to be the higher in cost, Squirrel or Seal?
22. Which fur is likely to be the higher in durability, Muskrat or Ermine?
23. From the point of view of the manufacturing process, what is generally considered to be the best type of knit for women's hosiery?
24. What is meant by denier and gauge in hosiery?
25. How does the two-ply differ from the single-ply cotton yarn used in making men's hose?
26. Name the principal types of shoe construction.
27. By examining shoes, how can the average person determine the quality of the leather?

28. What are the most important factors as to the fit of shoes?
29. What is the relation between price and quality of shoes?

DISCUSSION QUESTIONS

1. Why is it important for a consumer to know the characteristics of the various kinds of fibers of which fabrics are made?
2. (a) Should you always buy clothing of the best grade? (b) How can you determine which is the best grade? Discuss your answers to these questions.
3. What attitude may salespersons in stores take about your making tests of fabrics before buying?
4. Why are some fabrics weighted? How is this done? How may it be detected? What effect does it have on the fabric?
5. On the basis of the discussion in this chapter, explain the steps that you feel are practicable in buying your own clothing.
6. A list of five guides for the selection of fabrics when shopping is given in the chapter. Discuss the meaning of each of these principles and how they may be applied when purchasing articles such as a skirt for girls or trousers for boys.
7. Even though some of the tests explained in this chapter cannot be conducted in a store at the time a purchase is to be made, how are they helpful to the buyer?
8. What do the heat-conducting qualities of a fabric have to do with its seasonable use? Explain your answer.
9. From your study of this chapter, explain the importance of knowing something about fabrics and clothing before you go into a store to buy.
10. What, in your opinion, provides you the safest guides in regard to shrinkage?
11. What are the factors of primary importance to consider before going to a store to select clothing of any kind?
12. Discuss the seven guides for determining the quality of clothing that are given in this chapter.
13. Name at least one fur you would buy if you wanted one among the lowest in cost but highest in durability.
14. If a woman is attempting to get the greatest amount of wear out of hose, what would be your recommended guides in buying?
15. Women are generally considered to have more trouble with their feet than men. Why do you think this condition exists?
16. From your observations, what is your opinion of the effect of style on the price and the wearing quality of shoes?
17. State some advantages of buying all your shoes at the same place.

PROBLEMS

1. Secure pieces of thread or yarn that are known to be wool, cotton, linen, silk, rayon, and nylon. Untwist each piece and examine the fibers of which it is made especially to determine resiliency, tensile strength, luster, and body. Prepare a report giving the characteristics of each type of fiber.

2. A person buys two summer suits. One suit can be laundered, but the other must be dry cleaned. The suit that can be laundered costs $20 and is expected to last two years. It will have to be laundered eight times during each summer at a cost of $1 each time. The other suit costs $30 and is expected to last three years. It will have to be dry cleaned four times during each summer at a cost of $1.50 each time. Figure the yearly cost of each suit, considering that the original cost in each case is divided equally over the number of years during which the suit will be worn.

3. If a broadcloth shirt sells at $3 and may be laundered 24 times before wearing out and another broadcloth shirt with fewer threads to the inch in the fabric sells for $2 and may be laundered 20 times, which is the more economical to buy? What other factors than the number of times a shirt may be laundered may influence your selection?

4. Bring to class a newspaper or magazine advertisement showing merchandise bearing some quality designation of a type mentioned in this chapter.

5. From some piece of clothing that you have purchased recently, check all the information you can find on the tags and labels which provide guides in buying. Write a report on the information that you have obtained. Try in particular to find information on yarns, fabric, construction, color fastness, and directions for care.

6. Bring to class an advertisement of a fur coat, and try to determine from the list given in this book the exact kind of fur that is being advertised.

7. Examine the shoes that you are wearing and determine, if you can, the kind of manufacturing process by which they have been made. Give the reasons for your decision.

COMMUNITY PROBLEMS AND PROJECTS

1. Obtain samples of three different kinds of fabrics. Cut them into squares of approximately one inch. Paste them on a sheet of paper, and opposite each classify the fabric and write an explanation of why you have classified the fabric as you have.

2. Obtain two different pieces of cotton fabric. Cut them into pieces approximately two inches square. Paste them on a sheet of paper, and opposite each give your opinion of the strength and the general quality of the fabric. Give an analysis of the thread count by marking off a one-inch square on each piece and counting the number of threads running lengthwise and crosswise.

3. Obtain samples of two pieces of cloth that are supposed to be all wool or to contain part wool. Conduct tests in your home to determine whether the cloths are made of wool. Submit a report giving the results and your conclusions.

4. Obtain samples of at least two pieces of cloth that are supposed to be silk. Conduct tests in your home to determine whether the cloths do contain silk. Report the results of the tests and your conclusions.

5. Compare four pieces of similar cloth by subjecting them to the sun test or the washing test. Submit the samples with a written report on your procedure and the results.

6. Take ten pieces of cotton fabric, number these with a pencil or a tag, make a thread count, and record in a table the thread count opposite the number of each piece of fabric. Then proceed as follows: (a) Turn the fabrics over and mix them up so that you will not remember them, feel them, and on the basis of your experience with these fabrics, try to judge the thread count; and as you guess it for each piece, identify it by number and record this information in a second column in your table. Do this for each piece. (b) Turn them over again and then take one at a time and look through it before the light and by this process attempt to judge the thread count. Record your judgment in a third column in your table.

7. Make a complete analysis of the quality of some garment you have purchased recently, such as a suit, topcoat, dress, or trousers. Use the seven guides given on page 257 as a basis for making the analysis. Include in the analysis all items listed in each of the seven guides so far as applicable and possible. Prepare a report on what you find, giving as complete information as possible on all items included in the seven guides.

8. At a specialty shop or department store that sells hosiery, ask the salesperson in charge for literature explaining serviceability, sheerness, denier, and gauge in stockings. The salesperson may also be willing to explain the various processes by which hose are manufactured and the advantages of each process. Study the literature obtained and prepare a report, including in it the important information you learned both from the literature and from the salesperson.

Chapter 15

PART V _____

How to Buy Appliances and Automobiles

Purpose of the Chapter. The purchase of home appliances, mechanical equipment for home and personal use, and automobiles is an important problem in the average home. Not only does the purchase of one of these items involve a major expenditure but in many instances operating and service costs are dependent upon the wisdom of the choices made. As such purchases occur less frequently than the purchase of food and clothing, the householder obtains relatively little practice in buying appliances and mechanical goods. It is important, therefore, to know in advance how to proceed wisely. In a book of this kind it is impossible to discuss all household appliances and mechanical products, but the more important types will be considered.

Buying a television set involves a major expenditure.

Ewing Galloway

Buying Home Appliances and Equipment

Some General Guides. Home appliances and equipment are found in the average home, and many of the items are considered necessities for modern living. Among the home appliances purchased for the average home are such products as ranges, refrigerators and home freezers, washing machines, ironers, dishwashers, garbage disposers, water heaters, heating units, vacuum sweepers, and lamps.

Even in homes where only a few of these appliances and mechanical devices are used, the selection of them is very important because of the amount of money invested in them and the service expected. Some principles of selection and

---

Guides in the Selection and Purchase of Home Appliances and Equipment

1. Is the product manufactured by a reliable company? Will the manufacturer continue to make repair parts available?
2. Does it carry any kind of seal of approval?
3. Can the dealer be depended upon for efficient and prompt installation and service?
4. Is it sturdily constructed to withstand the service you expect from it? Is its capacity for service satisfactory for your needs?
5. What is the experience of your friends and acquaintances in the use of this or a similar type of product? What experience have they had in regard to economy, dependable use, repair parts, service, and general length of life?
6. Does it have any special features that make it superior to competing products?
7. What is the cost of operation?
8. Is any guarantee in printed form issued by the manufacturer or the dealer? (No guarantee is satisfactory unless it is in writing.) If it is a written guarantee, does it cover specific operating parts and the finish or is it just a general promise of satisfaction? Read and save the guarantee.
9. What special care and service does the appliance require?
10. Is there an opportunity to try out the appliance or mechanical product in the home, or is a demonstration in the store possible?

buying apply generally to the purchase of all home appliances and mechanical equipment.

In addition to these general guides for the selection and purchase of home appliances and laborsaving equipment, some specific guides may be considered in the selection of each type of appliance, such as ranges, refrigerators and home freezers, and vacuum cleaners.

Guides in Buying Household Ranges. There are two major types of ranges for cooking purposes, electric and

---

Guides in Selecting and Buying Ranges

1. Does the range carry the seal of approval of the American Gas Association or the Underwriters' Laboratory?

2. Are the doors, sides, top, oven, and drawers made of heavy enough sheet steel and are they satisfactorily enameled? Are corners rounded for easy cleaning?

3. Is the oven a satisfactory size for the type of roaster and other cooking utensils that you expect to use? Is it sturdily lined with enamel with proper shelves? Does the oven contain a broiler, or is there a separate broiler on the range? Is there an automatic temperature control? Is the oven sufficient height from the floor for convenient use? Is the oven properly insulated to conserve heat and to prevent excess heating of the kitchen? Is the insulation moisture proof and resistant to settling?

4. Will the range fit into the space where you want to use it in your kitchen? Will the doors open properly if the range is placed there? Can the flue outlet be connected satisfactorily to your vent?

5. If you are considering an electric stove, what type of electric current is required; are the switches satisfactory; how durable and how efficient are the heating units; are special electrical wiring and special electrical outlets required; how well have other users liked the stove?

6. If you are considering a gas stove, does the stove give proper and complete combustion? A blue flame indicates complete combustion; a red flame indicates incomplete combustion. If you have an opportunity to see the stove in operation, you will have a chance to judge it in this respect.

7. Is the range available either with or without automatic timing devices, signal lights, and special burners or cookers?

---

gas. Both types are used in rural and urban areas; however, in rural areas if gas is used, it usually is dry or bottled gas. Of course, coal and wood are used as fuel for cooking in some places. The type of household range you buy depends not only upon the availability of gas or electricity but upon the relative cost per heating unit, which varies from one community to another. After you decide upon the type of range that you should buy, several other factors should be considered in making the selection.

A person buying a gas or an electric range cannot be expected to have the technical knowledge to make his own personal examination and to conduct tests to determine the exact quality. However, there are some general guides which are useful in selecting a range.

Buying Refrigerators and Home Freezers. The rapid change from preserved and canned to fresh and frozen fruits, vegetables, and meats has made a food refrigerator a necessity in the home. Mechanical refrigerators use electricity or gas, and nonmechanical refrigerators use ice. Mechanical refrigerators are of three types: (1) the conventional type for short-term storage of foods with a small freezing unit for ice cubes, desserts, and small quantities of frozen foods; (2) the home freezer for the freezing and storage of foods for several weeks or months; (3) the refrigerator-freezer, which combines the two. The home freezer, either as a separate unit or in combination with the conventional refrigerator, is especially applicable to the needs of people who have gardens or farms and is useful for people in cities who like to buy food in large quantities.

There are six points to be considered in the satisfactory performance of refrigerators and home freezers. They apply to both mechanical and ice refrigerators.

(a) Temperature. Tests disclose that the following temperatures are necessary to preserve particular types of food under average conditions for short-term storage:

Milk, milk dishes, butter, broth,
    desserts ....Not over 45° F.
Uncooked meats, poultry, covered
    jars of salad material ....Not over 47° F.

> Berries, cooked meats . . . . .Not over 48° F.
> Cooked vegetables, eggs, fats,
>   left-overs .Not over 50° F.
> Uncooked fruits and vegetables . .Not over 52° F.

The average temperature of a modern type of refrigerator should not exceed 45 degrees in the milk compartment and 50 degrees in the food compartment, when the outside temperatures average 80 degrees with occasional periods of 90 degrees or higher.

(b) Cost of operation. When one considers the cost of operation of a refrigerator, he must take into consideration the following factors:

(1) Actual tests that show the cost of ice, electricity, gas, or kerosene at a constant room temperature.
(2) The rate of depreciation of the refrigerator. (Five or ten per cent of the cost of the refrigerator can be considered the expense of each year.)
(3) Cost of repairs. (Warranties, guarantees, and service contracts should be considered carefully.)

Studies made in Washington, D. C., of different types of refrigerators, each with a six-cubic-foot capacity, indicated the various costs of operation:

> Electric refrigerator, 90 cents a month.
> Gas refrigerator (manufactured gas), $1.40 a month.
> Kerosene refrigerator, $1 a month.
> Ice-storage refrigerator, $4.20 a month.

The average cost of operating a six-cubic-foot home freezer has been estimated at approximately $1.20 a month, and the cost of a 25-cubic-foot home freezer of the type frequently used on farms at $2.10 a month.

(c) Storage space and freezing capacity. Manufacturers of ice-storage refrigerators construct them so that the ice compartment has a definite relation to the food-storage space. In better refrigerators the food-storage space is greater in proportion to the ice compartment than it is in refrigerators of lower grades.

In considering mechanical refrigerators, one should determine the amount of food-storage space, the amount of shelf space, the rate of freezing, and the capacity of freezing. The rate and the capacity of freezing should be measured at a definite room temperature. In some mechanical refrigerators, fast freezing will cause the freezing of certain foods in the refrigerator and therefore will spoil them. On the other hand, some of the refrigerators have a freezing compartment as an added feature for housewives who wish to freeze meats and other foods.

Studies indicate that a family of two will require approximately six cubic feet of refrigerator space. The minimum for a family of four is seven or eight cubic feet, and for each additional member of a family one additional cubic foot of space is desirable.

The cubic foot of space is not the only problem. The square foot of shelf space is important, because shelf space determines the practical, usable capacity. A refrigerator containing six cubic feet should contain from twelve to fourteen square feet of shelf space in order to make maximum use of the refrigerator.

(d) Construction and durability. Cabinets of mechanical refrigerators and home freezers should be made of steel that will resist rust. The frames should be rigid and strong, and the exterior finish either lacquer or baked enamel. In the refrigerators of good quality the lining usually is seamless and is coated with enamel. The bottom of the food compartment is sometimes made of porcelain to resist acids from foods that may be spilled. The racks should be of a good quality steel that will resist rust. Home freezers should be constructed of the same type of materials as conventional refrigerators; however, the bottom of the food compartment need not be porcelain because frozen foods seldom are spilled.

(e) Insulation. The insulation used in the walls, door, top, and bottom of the refrigerator or freezer is an important factor in operating cost. Several kinds of insulation are used in the construction of refrigerators and freezers. Testing agencies may be consulted for the relative efficiency of the different kinds of insulation materials. Insulation in home freezers is especially important because of the low temperature that must be maintained.

Insulation should be of an inorganic type that will not settle and that will resist moisture. Usually the insulation of good refrigerators is at least three inches thick and of good home freezers, four inches thick.

Guides in Buying Refrigerators and
Home Freezers

1. Is the refrigerator or freezer made of good quality, rust-resisting steel?
2. Are the operating parts of good quality and easily serviced?
3. If it is an electric refrigerator, is the motor quiet? If it is a gas or kerosene refrigerator, can you depend upon it for continuous, dependable service?
4. What temperature does the refrigerator maintain at various room temperatures?
5. What is the rate of freezing ice cubes? What is the capacity for ice cubes?
6. What is the cost of operation in order to maintain proper food preservation temperature?
7. If it is an electric refrigerator, what percentage of time does the motor run to hold the temperature at the proper level? Some studies indicate that a motor will wear out too fast if it runs more than 35 per cent of the time.
8. What kind of insulation is used? Is there a sample available to examine?
9. How many cubic feet of storage space and how many square feet of shelf space does the refrigerator contain?
10. What kind of finish is used on the exterior and the interior? Will fruit acid damage the interior?
11. Is the frame sturdy enough so that it will not be damaged in moving?
12. What is the experience of your friends in using the same or a similar refrigerator in regard to economy, dependability, repairs, and general length of life?
13. Is it the proper shape and size to fit where you want to use it? Do you have the proper gas, electricity, or other fuel available to operate it?
14. Is there any specific written guarantee indicating that it meets certain other standards? Does the guarantee cover the mechanism, the cabinet, the finish, or any other specific parts?

(f) Mechanical efficiency. All electric refrigerators and home freezers have several mechanical parts that are operated by a motor.

Quietness of operation is important in the mechanical refrigerator. Although it may be quiet when new, it may later become noisy. The experiences of others with the same make will aid the purchaser. Another consideration is the assurance of adequate service. Service will depend upon the reliability of the manufacturer and the distributor. A buyer should be assured that he can get adequate service.

Buying Vacuum Cleaners. Many appliances that can be demonstrated in the store or in the home should be tried out thoroughly before they are purchased. Most distributors of electric sweepers will give a home demonstration and will

---

Guides in Buying Vacuum Cleaners

1. Is a cleaner of the upright or tank type best suited to your cleaning needs?
2. Are special attachments for cleaning upholstery and drapes available?
3. Is the cord long enough to permit reaching all parts of your largest room?
4. Can the sweeper be moved with little effort?
5. Is the handle such that you can operate the machine comfortably? Will this handle stand erect in storage?
6. Will the cleaner go into corners and under beds and other low furniture?
7. Is the weight of the machine light enough to permit you to carry it and move it easily?
8. Can the nozzle attachment be quickly and easily operated?
9. Is the bag easy to remove and clean?
10. Is the belt easy to replace?
11. Is the brush easily adjustable so that when bristles are worn short the brush can be lowered?
12. Can the brush be easily removed, cleaned, and replaced?
13. Are repair parts available?
14. Is the cleaner made by a reputable manufacturer? Is there a written guarantee? If so, keep it.

$330

$260

$210

$145

$55

TELE- REFRIGER- FURNITURE WASHING RADIOS
VISION ATORS   MACHINES

U. S. COMMERCE DEPT.   GRAPHIC SYNDICATE

leave equipment on trial for at least a short period. This is one of the best means of determining whether a piece of equipment will fill the needs.

Buying Other Laborsaving Equipment. The general guides in the selection and purchase of home appliances given on page 270 apply not only to ranges, refrigerators and freezers, and vacuum cleaners, but to all kinds of mechanical equipment for home and personal use. Furthermore, many of the specific guides mentioned for the buying of ranges, refrigerators, and cleaners may be applied to the purchase of other equipment, such as food mixers, water heaters, garbage disposers, electric dishwashers, radios, fans, lawn mowers, bicycles, and cameras.

The principles of selection that may be applied to the purchase of such equipment as an electric washing machine are illustrative of the principles for the selection of other mechanical equipment.

A warranty may justify a
higher price.

Price should be considered as a relative matter. A machine that sells for $125.00 may be a bargain as compared with one that sells for $80.00. All the factors of quality, length of life, and cost of operation must be taken into consideration with price. Whenever possible, the choice should be based on comparison of all the factors.

Reports of testing laboratories, Consumers' Research, Consumers Union, and governmental agencies will be helpful when selecting mechanical equipment for home and personal use.

Guides in the Buying of an Electric Washing Machine

1. Is the machine made by a reliable manufacturer?
2. Is service assured through the local dealer?
3. What results have others obtained from using the same type of machine?
4. Are the mechanical parts safe, and is the operation of the machine simple?
5. Will the agitator injure the types of fabrics that will have to be washed in the machine?
6. Will the noise and the vibration be undesirable?
7. Can the machine be moved easily?
8. Can the tub be drained easily, and is the opening large enough to prevent clogging?
9. Is the tub durable, and can it be cleaned easily?
10. Is a wringer or an extractor preferable?
11. If the wringer is used, is there a safety device?
12. Is the motor made by a reliable manufacturer; is it of the proper voltage; and can it be operated on the current that is available?
13. Are the working parts enclosed to ensure safety?
14. Are there any special features?
15. Is the actual time required for adequate cleansing comparable to that required by two or more similar machines?
16. Is the machine of adequate size and capacity to handle the work for which it is being considered?
17. If the washer being considered is automatic, that is self-filling and emptying, how many gallons of hot water are required for each washer of clothes? Is the supply of hot water adequate for washing the amount of clothes usually washed at one time?

Buying Automobiles and Automobile Supplies

Types of Automobile Engines. As a general rule, an automobile with high power in proportion to its weight will give the better performance as to speed and acceleration, but will not operate so economically as an automobile with low power in proportion to its weight. Furthermore, a high-speed engine normally will not last so long as one with less

Factors for Evaluating Automobiles

Carefully examine and study each car in your price range. Considering the use that you will make of your car, use the following code to indicate your evaluation of each factor. Code: S—wholly satisfactory; A—acceptable; N. A.—inadequate or deficient.

	Car A	Car B	Car C
Engine and Power Transmission:			
Number of cylinders	S	A	A
Type of motor	S	S	S
Motor speed, revolutions per minute	A	S	S
Maximum horsepower at high speed	S	A	A
Taxable horsepower	A	A	A
Compression ratio	A	S	N. A.
Piston travel per mile	S	A	A
Relation of power of engine to weight of car	A	A	S
Clutch or kind of power drive	S	A	A
Transmission, standard, automatic, or semiautomatic	S	A	A
Device to reduce motor revolutions at high speed such as fourth gear and overdrive	A	S	N. A.
Chassis and Other Mechanical Features:			
Construction of frame	S	A	A
Ease of repair in case of accident	S	N. A.	A
Capacity of battery	A	A	A
Carburetor, automatic choke, fuel pump, and booster vacuum pump	S	A	N. A.
Generator, voltage regulator	A	A	A
Starter, starter control	A	A	A
Cooling system: radiator capacity, water pump, and temperature control	S	A	A
Provision for installing heater, defroster, radio, and other devices	S	A	N. A.
Windshield wiper	S	A	A
Type of brakes	S	S	S
Relation of brake lining area to car weight	A	A	N. A.
Type of springs and shock absorbers	S	A	A
Wheel suspension	S	A	N. A.
Size of tires considering weight	S	A	N. A.
Types of springs and shock absorbers	S	S	S
Safety Factors:			
Protection by frame and body from injury.	A	A	A
Adequacy of brakes	S	N. A.	A
Roadability, control of steering, effect of rough pavement, cross winds, etc.	S	A	S
Vision, location of windshield posts, height and size of windshield and side windows	A	S	N. A.
Vision, rear	N. A.	A	A
Distortion of vision by curved glass and by viewing an image at an angle	A	N. A.	A
Safety glass	A	A	A

	Car A	Car B	Car C
Safety Factors—(concluded)			
Reserve power for spurts of speed in emergencies	S	A	N. A.
Lighting system, ahead, dimmer control, direction signals, stop and tail lights ..	S	S	S
Bumpers, horn, car ventilation	S	S	A
Door handles, window controls, instrument panel	S	A	S
Body Features and Appearance:			
Width of seats, front and rear	S	S	N. A.
Head room, front and rear	A	S	A
Knee, leg, and foot room, front and rear ..	A	A	S
Shoulder room	A	A	A
Arm rests	A	A	A
Ease in getting in and out	S	N. A.	A
Close fitting of doors	S	A	A
Ease of opening and closing of doors	S	N. A.	A
Heat, steam or frost, and ventilation control	S	N. A.	A
Engine, tire, and wind noise	S	A	A
Comfort and durability of seats	A	A	N. A.
Vibration and sensitivity to road shock ..	S	A	A
Luggage and package space, amount and accessibility	A	A	N. A.
Rust-resisting steel in body and fenders ..	S	A	N. A.
Over-all width of body	S	A	A
Opening of doors at high curbs and in home garages	A	N. A.	A
Protection from excessive damage in case of collision or accident	A	N. A.	A
Durability of paint and finish	A	N. A.	N. A.
General appearance	S	A	A
Economy:			
Types of gasoline that may be used	S	A	A
Probable fuel mileage per gallon	A	A	N. A.
Oil consumption	A	A	A
Lubrication system, motor	S	A	A
Lubrication system, chassis	S	A	A
Probable service life of such parts as piston rings, fuel and water pumps, generator and starter, valves, and brakes	A	A	A
Relation of horsepower to weight of car ..	S	A	N. A.
Ease with which replacements and repairs of fenders, chassis parts, and body parts may be made in case of accident	A	N. A.	N. A.
Cost of labor for normal service and repairs according to the "Flat Rate Manual" published by "Automotive Digest" or a similar source	A	N. A.	N. A.
Cost of state license annually	A	A	A
Relative trade-in value	A	N. A.	A
Probable depreciation	A	A	A

	Car A	Car B	Car C
Ease of Control and Comfort:			
Maneuverability in parking and heavy traffic	A	A	N. A.
Responsiveness in emergencies	A	A	A
Ease of steering both when driving and in parking	A	A	N. A.
Relation of wheelbase to comfort and to maneuverability	S	A	A
Turning radius	S	A	S
Vision, driver and passengers	A	N. A.	N. A.
Legibility of instruments, speedometer, oil pressure, gasoline gauge, etc.	S	A	A
Foot controls	S	S	S
Gear shift and parking brake	S	A	A
Manipulation of controls for lights, ventilation, defrosting fans, heaters, radios, etc.	A	A	A
Door and rear compartment locks	A	A	A
Other Important Factors:			
Cruising speed	S	A	S
Rating by reliable testing agencies	S	A	N. A.
Frequency of change in design	A	A	N. A.
Reputation of manufacturer	S	A	A
Reputation of local dealer	S	S	S
Availability of service	S	N. A.	A
Availability of car with or without extra equipment, such as heaters, radios, and seat covers	A	S	N. A.
Guarantee	A	A	A
Price	A	A	A
Summary:			
Number of features evaluated as			
S—wholly satisfactory	47	14	13
A—acceptable	40	60	51
N. A.—inadequate or deficient	1	14	24
Total	88	88	88

A check sheet for evaluating automobiles.

power. In addition to the capacity or power and revolutions of the engine for each mile of travel, compression ratio and type of gasoline are two other factors to be considered when buying an automobile.

Comparison of Values. Prospective buyers should learn to weigh the value of one product as compared with that of another. It is true that a purchaser can virtually shut his eyes and buy any one of several automobiles and yet get one that will give satisfactory performance. On the other hand, he should not pay more than is necessary to get what he wants. Some analysis should therefore be made so that actual values can be compared. A prospective buyer should select the automobile that not only has the largest number of points that appeal to him but also will be of the greatest benefit to him.

Let us examine, for example, the check sheet prepared by Mr. Thompson, a prospective purchaser of an automobile. This check sheet is shown on pages 279-281. Forms such as this are made available by some automobile manufacturers, but they can be compiled by anyone. The danger of using a check sheet prepared by a producer is that it may be constructed with the idea of influencing a person to buy the product of that company without consideration of important features of competing automobiles.

Mr. Thompson used this check sheet in evaluating the desirable features of three automobiles that were within the range of price that he could afford to pay. He indicated his evaluation of each factor by using the code shown on the check sheet. For instance, for the use Mr. Thompson expected to make of the automobile he thought the number of cylinders in the engine of Car A was better than in Car B or Car C. In the case of an overdrive or fourth gear to reduce engine speed we may assume Car A was conventional, having neither an overdrive nor a fourth gear; and Car B had one type and Car C another type of device to reduce engine speed when traveling on the open road. Mr. Thompson considered Car A to be acceptable for his purpose but Car B, having an overdrive, to be better. Some other person may prefer a car with the three conventional speeds ahead and, therefore, rate Car A as superior.

The final summary on the check sheet shows that for the use Mr. Thompson intends making of the car he purchases, he rated Car A as "wholly satisfactory" on 47 factors; Car B, 14; and Car C, 13; Car A as "acceptable" on 40 factors; Car B, 60; and Car C, 51; and Car A as "inadequate or deficient" on 1 factor; Car B, 14; and Car C, 24. Of course, Mr. Thompson selected Car A as it obviously meets the requirements for the use he intends making of a car better than either of the other cars.

Some features outweigh others. One factor may be important to one person, but not important to another. For instance, if the gas consumption of Automobile C were much more economical than that of Automobile A, a person who was thinking largely in terms of economy would give favorable consideration to Automobile C.

This same type of evaluation can be used for all kinds of mechanical equipment and for many other products that are purchased by the average consumer. If the buyer does not follow a formal plan of checking various features, he can do so mentally.

Gasoline and Oil Consumption. The consumer should know that every automobile burns more gasoline at a high rate of speed than it does at a reasonable rate of speed. Furthermore, there is a difference among automobiles. Some will burn more gasoline than others at certain rates of speed. The chart at the right shows the quantity of gasoline burned by each of five different automobiles at varying rates of speed. For each of these automobiles the most economical rate of speed is between twenty and thirty miles an hour. When a person is selecting an automobile on the basis of economy, he will want to consider gasoline and oil consumption along with maintenance and service costs.

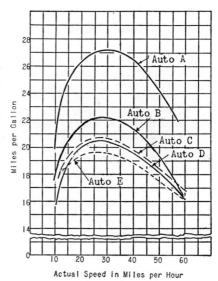

Actual Speed in Miles per Hour

Reprinted from *Consumers' Research Bulletin*, February, 1939, by special permission of Consumers' Research, Inc., Washington, New Jersey

Gasoline consumption.

Every automobile must consume a certain quantity of oil because oil lubricates the mechanism. Nevertheless, some automobiles consume excessive quantities of oil. For instance, the following table shows the quantity of oil consumed by each of five automobiles in the same price class:

Automobile A	1,670 miles on a quart of oil
Automobile B	1,180 miles on a quart of oil
Automobile C	990 miles on a quart of oil
Automobile D	880 miles on a quart of oil
Automobile E	830 miles on a quart of oil

Oil consumption of five automobiles.

General Factors to Be Considered. Although the engine of an automobile is the matter of first importance, there are many other important factors. The check list on pages 279-281 shows the points to be investigated in purchasing an

---

Nontechnical Factors in Selecting an Automobile

1. Considering horsepower, speed, weight, passenger and luggage space, and operating costs, is the automobile well adapted to the use you intend making of it?
2. What is the reputation of the manufacturer of the automobile? Has the car stood up well in past performance? What has been the experience of your friends who have driven it? What has been your own past experience with this or other cars?
3. Does the dealer have a reputation for fair treatment and good service?
4. Are there adequate facilities for obtaining service and repair parts where the automobile will be used?
5. Is there any danger that the automobile will soon become obsolete or that the manufacturer will go out of business?
6. What do repairs cost? What are the flat labor rates for common repairs?
7. Is the automobile within a satisfactory price range with reference to the budget?
8. Can the operating expenses of the automobile be afforded?
9. Are the body and fenders so constructed that they can be repaired reasonably well if damaged? Are they made of rust-resistant metal? Is the paint satisfactory?

automobile. Riding comfort, ease of driving as well as of starting and stopping, safety, and reasonable economy of operation are important factors. The average buyer of an automobile is not qualified to judge the technical advantages or disadvantages of an automobile. He must therefore depend to a very great extent on other guides in making a selection.

Besides these points one should take into consideration the trade-in allowance from several points of view. The highest trade-in allowance on an old car is not always the best guide in buying a new car. The particular make of new car that you are considering buying is one factor that will determine the trade-in allowance. The free services that are furnished with the new car are another consideration. The cost price and the model of the new car are still other considerations. For instance, one dealer might offer a trade-in allowance of $500 on an old car in consideration of the purchase of a new car for $2,100. A second dealer might offer a trade-in allowance of $600 on the same car on the purchase of a new car for $2,300. Generally speaking, if one has assured himself of the reliability of certain dealers and is making a comparison of prices on exactly the same new cars, then the dealer offering the best trade-in allowance is offering the best bargain.

Automobile Depreciation. For practical consideration, *depreciation* of an automobile and loss from *obsolescence* are the same. When a person drives a new automobile out of an agency and takes the title to it, he suffers a loss due to obsolescence, although the automobile has not depreciated because of wear or deterioration. If the automobile were to be resold immediately, the owner would have to accept a price lower than that he paid. Depreciation, on the other hand, results from wear.

Obsolescence is an important factor in the value of an automobile.

If an automobile is used exclusively for business purposes, the Federal Government will allow the owner, in computing his income tax, to deduct depreciation to the extent of one fourth of the cost during each of the four years after the purchase. In other words, the Federal Government recognizes that an automobile used for business purposes normally serves its useful life in four years.

Most people find that it is most economical to trade in a car at least every three or four years. Although an automobile may have been driven less in three years than another was driven in two, it is a common practice in the automobile industry to allow less for the automobile that has been driven three years than for the one that has been driven two. This practice is based on the fact that the older model has become more obsolete than the one that has been out only two years.

Two automobiles made by different manufacturers that were purchased at the same price may not have the same trade-in value because one of them may have a greater rate of depreciation. The greater rate of depreciation arises from the fact that cars of this make are not readily salable as secondhand or used automobiles. If one is interested in owning an automobile that has a relatively good trade-in or secondhand value, he should consider this fact when he purchases a new car. In general, the higher the purchase price of the car, the greater the percentage of depreciation and the greater the total amount of depreciation.

Delivery Cost. The actual cost to the purchaser is usually greater than the advertised cost although some dealers now quote delivery price in the advertisements in local newspapers. The advertised cost is ordinarily stated "f.o.b. the factory." This term means free on board at the factory; that is, the buyer is expected to pay the shipping costs.

A handling charge, usually charges for extra equipment, and in many instances a state tax must be added to the factory price to know the delivery price.

Sometimes it is difficult to determine what is included in the handling charge. This charge may range from 10 to 35 per cent of the factory price, depending to some extent upon where the automobile is delivered. Sometimes the price quoted on an automobile does not include the cost of spare tires, bumpers, and other equipment that the average driver considers necessary. All these additional charges should be investigated before an order for an automobile is signed.

New Features and Devices. Automobile manufacturers make it a practice to bring out a new model annually having a few new or different features and devices. This practice is followed not only to attract customers but to compete with other manufacturers. They hope that the new features and devices will be an improvement and that purchasers will want automobiles in which these new devices have been installed. Frequently so much emphasis is placed upon these relatively insignificant devices that the buyer overlooks other undesirable characteristics. The wise buyer will not be too eager to accept a new device and certainly will not allow a single new device to outweigh all other considerations in the choice of an automobile. The check sheet on pages 279-281 will help a person to weigh values without placing too much emphasis on a new device. Sometimes new devices prove to be unsatisfactory and are discontinued by manufacturers after one or two years.

Automobile Supplies and Accessories. Tires, oil, and gasoline represent the major operating costs of an automobile. The problem of buying automobile supplies, of which these are the chief items, is so important that technical information should be obtained from some authoritative source. Consumers' Research, Consumers Union, and other testing agencies are in a position to furnish such information.

The most expensive product is not necessarily the best; but cheap tires, oils, or gasolines are frequently not economical. Some cheap oils may damage the engine, and some cheap gasolines may cause the formation of carbon and a loss of power. A number of the more expensive gasolines, however, are not adapted to high-speed and high-compression engines. The only safe guide in buying automobile supplies is to learn from authoritative tests what products measure up to reasonable standards. Two or three of the better products should then be selected for regular use.

Every manufacturer wants his automobile to stand up well. It is therefore advisable to study carefully the recommendations of the manufacturer in regard to the type of gasoline and type or grade of oil to use. So-called high compression engines require a high grade of gasoline with a high octane rating.

There are various qualities and types of oils. They are rated as to their viscosity, which means the readiness with which they pour, sometimes referred to as lightness or heaviness. For passenger cars and light trucks the oils normally range from 10W to 40; the smaller the number, the lighter the oil. It is very important to follow the manufacturer's recommendations as to weight of oil for the various driving conditions and at various temperatures. To use the wrong weight of oil may result in excessive wear.

In order to be sure that you are getting the proper grade of oil, it is advisable to buy it in sealed containers labeled by the producer or to buy bulk oil only through some reputable distributor. There are some individuals who contend that it is not necessary to change oil frequently. The age of the car, the quality of the oil, driving conditions, and various other factors determine how often oil should be changed. A good filter will help keep oil in good condition and will help preserve the motor. Generally speaking, oil should be changed when it ceases to have a lubricating quality. A simple test of that is to put some oil between your fingers and see whether it has adequate body or lubricating quality.

TEXTBOOK QUESTIONS

1. Make a list of some of the home appliances and other equipment used in a modern home.
2. What general guides may be followed in the selection and purchase of home appliances and equipment?
3. What are some of the general guides that may be used in selecting a range?
4. What are the three types of mechanical refrigerators?

5. What is the maximum temperature that should be permitted in a refrigerator to preserve (a) milk, (b) cooked meats, (c) uncooked fruits and vegetables?

6. What did the study in Washington show in regard to the relative costs of operating electric and ice-storage refrigerators?

7. What is the minimum size of a refrigerator for (a) a family of two, (b) a family of four?

8. List six factors to consider in determining the satisfactory performance of refrigerators and home freezers.

9. What are some of the important construction features of a refrigerator or home freezer?

10. What are the characteristics of good insulation in a refrigerator or home freezer?

11. Make a list of as many guides for the buying of home refrigerators and home freezers as you can.

12. How do you recommend examining an electric sweeper before buying?

13. Make a list of as many guides applicable to buying a vacuum cleaner as you can.

14. Prepare a list of guides for buying an electric washing machine.

15. Name at least five factors to be followed in evaluating an automobile.

16. What are some of the nontechnical factors that may be useful in selecting an automobile?

17. Explain why the highest trade-in value of an old car does not represent the best bargain in purchasing.

18. Which cars usually depreciate more rapidly: (a) low-priced cars or (b) high-priced cars?

19. What usually accounts for the difference between the advertised price of an automobile and the delivered price?

20. Why should one give relatively little attention to the sales emphasis placed on a new device on an automobile?

21. What does a high octane rating of gasoline mean in terms of the power to be derived from the gasoline?

22. What do the various numbers of lubricating oil mean?

DISCUSSION QUESTIONS

1. Discuss how each of the guides listed on page 270 for the selection and purchase of home appliances may be applied when purchasing an ironer.

2. How would you determine if the manufacturer of a home appliance is reliable?

3. Discuss the importance of selecting a household appliance made by a reliable manufacturer and of purchasing it through a reliable dealer.

4. How much dependence should be placed on the statements of friends and acquaintances about their experiences in using a particular appliance?

5. How does the seal of approval of the American Gas Association protect a purchaser against inferior materials in a gas appliance?

6. Discuss the type of guarantee that you think would be acceptable if you were buying an electric refrigerator.

7. If a gas-burning appliance bears the seal of the American Gas Association, what can you assume with regard to the quality of the appliance?

8. If a gas-burning appliance does not bear the seal of approval of the American Gas Association, is that fact an indication that the appliance is of a poor construction?

9. When you try to investigate the performance of an electric refrigerator, you find that styles in refrigerators change so frequently that it is impossible to form any conclusions unless a comparison is made with older models of the same refrigerator. What are some of the factors that could be investigated in order that you might base some of your conclusions on the experience of those who are using older models?

10. What factors should be considered in the purchase of a home freezer?

11. A dealer advertises the sale of the electric refrigerator of a bankrupt manufacturer at 75 per cent of the cost. (a) Would you consider such an electric refrigerator to be a bargain? (b) Would you buy one? Give your reasons.

12. How would you obtain the answers to the guide questions given on page 276?

13. From your knowledge of copper, enamel, and aluminum, what do you think would be the advantages and the disadvantages of washing machines made from each of these three kinds of materials?

14. What major classes of factors should be considered in selecting an automobile to meet your needs?

15. Discuss repair service as a factor in buying an automobile.

16. Can you see any reasons why one dealer might offer as much as $100 more for a secondhand car on a trade-in than was offered by another dealer?

17. In proportion to the original cost of the automobile, a large secondhand automobile can be purchased for less than a small used automobile of the same age. Why is this true?

18. Why do automobile manufacturers introduce new devices and features on their cars every year? What cautions should the prospective purchaser observe relative to the statements about the merits of the new devices and features?

19. What information can you recall having seen in advertisements or in filling stations pertaining to the octane rating of gasoline? What does it mean to you in terms of values?

PROBLEMS

1. A family that has a savings budget of $15 a month wishes to buy an electric refrigerator. The payments will amount to $15 a month for twelve months. The increase in the electric bill will average 85 cents a month. Past experience discloses that the average amount spent for ice during the warm weather is $18 a year. The family does not want to withdraw anything from its savings fund to use in paying the monthly installments. (a) Can a plan be worked out satisfactorily? (b) If the refrigerator will cost $180 and can be used no more than twenty years, do you think it will be a wise investment? Under what circumstances?

2. The Williams family keeps a record of the costs of ice used during the warm weather in one year. These costs are as follows: April, $3; May, $3.25; June, $3.40; July, $4.50; August, $4.25; September, $3.15; October, 75 cents. Omitting any consideration of food savings, the Williams family tries to decide whether to buy an electric refrigerator. Investigation discloses that a family that has been using the type of refrigerator that is being considered paid an average monthly electric bill of $2.35 before buying the electric refrigerator, but has paid an average monthly electric bill of $3.45 since buying the electric refrigerator. From the point of view of costs of operation, would the purchase of the refrigerator result in a saving or an added expense for the Williams family?

3. Prepare a list of factors that may be considered in evaluating electric fans for home use.

4. A company that uses a large number of automobiles finds that the average costs per mile for the operation of each automobile are:

Gasoline and oil	$0.021
Garage rent	.003
Repairs	.01
Insurance	.003
Depreciation	.023

(a) What should be the annual cost of operating an automobile that is driven 30,000 miles during the year? (b) On the basis of the costs listed above, what should be the monthly cost of operating an automobile if the owner drives the car about 10,000 miles a year and trades it in on a new automobile at the end of three years?

5. How much would it cost for three years, for one year, and for each mile to own and operate an automobile, assuming the following conditions: The automobile cost $1,300; it may be traded in on a new one at the end of three years at an allowance of $450; the average cost of gasoline and oil is 2¼ cents a mile; repairs and maintenance service cost $72 a year; insurance including bodily injury and property damage costs $80 a year; license and property taxes cost $18 a year; the average mileage is 10,000 a year. What would be the effect on the cost a year and the cost a mile if the automobile were driven 20,000 miles a year?

COMMUNITY PROBLEMS AND PROJECTS

1. Assume that a young man who has a moderate income and who rides five miles to work every day is considering the purchase of an automobile. The automobile is also used for short shopping trips, pleasure, and some vacation travel. There are two adults and a four-year-old child in the family. Using the check sheet on pages 279-281, investigate three automobiles that may meet this young man's needs. You may need some information about the automobiles that is not listed on the check sheet. Write a report on your findings. In the report, reproduce the check sheet. Explain your procedures and justify your conclusions as to which is the better automobile for the young man to buy.

2. From two local businesses that sell competitive types of a household appliance, find out the installation service, the repair service, the adjustment service, and the guarantee offered by each. Without considering the quality of either make, write a report giving your conclusions as to the reliability of each make on the basis of the services and the guarantee.

3. Besides the points given in this chapter, add all additional points that you can think of and prepare a rating chart for electric refrigerators and home freezers. With this chart proceed to make a comparison of two refrigerators or two freezers to try to determine the best buy.

4. Obtain copies of the guarantees on two makes of some one type of home appliance, such as electric ironers, gas ironers, electric irons, steam irons, toasters, refrigerators and freezers. Analyze and compare items of protection to the consumer in each of the guarantees. Write a report on your findings, including a statement of your evaluation of the protection afforded the consumers in the guarantees.

Chapter 16

How to Buy Furniture and Floor Coverings

Purpose of the Chapter. The purchase of furniture and floor coverings is an important problem. These items are not purchased often; but when they are purchased, they deserve careful consideration, for they will be used a long time. The primary purpose of this chapter is to establish a few fundamental standards by which furniture and floor coverings can be judged without the necessity of a technical analysis.

Selecting the Right Furniture. The householder should *buy* furniture and not allow himself to be *sold* furniture. In furnishing a home, it is desirable to know in advance the space to be filled and the amount of money that may be used. Of course, the ideal situation is one in which the funds available will permit the furnishing of all the rooms adequately. In many cases, however, the budget must be stretched considerably to buy the bare necessities.

Deliberation will help to eliminate unwise buying. There are two extremes to be avoided. One is a disproportionate expenditure for a few pieces of furniture at the sacrifice of other necessary pieces. The other extreme is the buying of unsatisfactory furniture at a low price in order to obtain a full suite.

The suitability of furniture depends largely on personal taste. Good judgment can, however, be formed by studying color combinations, by considering the space that is available, by observing the furnishings in other homes, and by examining the furniture in several stores.

Except for the modern styles of furniture, most furniture of good quality and of good style is based on well-established patterns that, in most cases, were created centuries ago. Style books of furniture, which are available in libraries, may be used as guides in selecting attractive and harmonious furniture.

What Is a Good Furniture Wood? The type of wood has an important relation to the price of furniture. It also has an important relation to the quality and the wearing features. Some woods crack easily and show scratches readily. Those that are soft show marks easily. Others are subject to warping when exposed to moisture.

The ideal wood for furniture possesses enough hardness to resist normal wear, yet it is sufficiently soft to be worked with ordinary tools without splitting. It should also be subject to minimum swelling and shrinkage. The natural grains are attractive, although no wood is perfect in this respect. Some woods have one desirable feature, but lack some other. The problem resolves itself into getting the best wood one can afford at a reasonable price.

Walnut is almost an ideal wood for furniture because it combines beauty, strength, and durability. There are various grades of walnut, most of which are good. Oak is a good wood for furniture because it is solid and substantial. It is so hard that it is not subject to scratching, as are many of the other woods.

Gum is one of the most widely used of the American hardwoods. It is used frequently by itself and in many cases in combination with other wood. It is not so desirable as the two previously mentioned woods because it is softer and is subject to scratching and warping.

Birch, maple, beech, chestnut, and cherry are also good woods for furniture. Mahogany is excellent, but most of it is imported and is therefore costly, although it is often not so costly as walnut.

The softer woods, such as poplar, spruce, and pine, are not so desirable for furniture because of their relative lack of durability.

The average person who is not familiar with woods cannot rely upon his own judgment in distinguishing them. In selecting a piece of furniture, he should therefore be sure to observe whether it is made of more than one piece of wood, how much of it is solid, and what parts are made of veneer. Ask what kind or combinations of wood are used in its construction.

The table below shows a list of the most common woods that are used in furniture. Those that are most desirable are indicated. Some of those listed as undesirable are used for cheaper grades of furniture. Some of them may make furniture just as sturdy as the better grades, but the furniture will be lacking in beauty. Some of the desirable woods for indoor furniture are not satisfactory for outdoor furniture. Cypress, redwood, and cedar are recommended for outdoor furniture because they will withstand weather conditions.

WOODS USED IN FURNITURE

DESIRABLE AMERICAN WOODS	DESIRABLE IMPORTED WOODS	UNDESIRABLE AMERICAN WOODS
Walnut	Mahogany	Ash
Oak	Ebony	Cypress
Cherry	Primavera	Elm
Birch	Teak	Pine
Maple	Rosewood	Redwood
Chestnut		Cedar
Gum		Fir
Beech		Hemlock
Basswood		Poplar
Hickory		Spruce
Sycamore		

Types of furniture woods.

Veneer. As a general rule, but not always, furniture made of a solid wood is more expensive than a comparable piece made wholly or partially of veneer. Solid wood can be carved. If it is scratched or chipped, there is no danger, as in the case of veneer, that a thin surface layer of wood will be penetrated. The use of veneer, however, is not necessarily an indication of low quality. In fact, some of the best furniture today is constructed with veneer for the tops and panels.

Veneer consists of two or more thin layers of wood glued together. Veneer makes it possible to use a good piece of wood for the surface of furniture and a cheaper piece for those parts underneath the surface. Large panels and the tops of large tables are less liable to warp if they are made of veneer than if they are of a solid wood. Cheap veneer may blister, however, because moisture loosens the glue. It also may develop checks and cracks.

The mechanical construction of a piece of furniture may be perfect, but the beauty of the piece may have been lessened by carelessness in matching the grain of the veneer in a panel.

The beauty of the grain in the wood is one indication of quality, whereas the careful matching of the grain tends to indicate good workmanship. The illustration below shows how veneer is matched in creating attractive designs. Unusual designs may be created in this way. Drawer fronts, doors, and table tops made of veneer often have beautiful patterns.

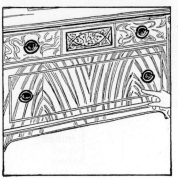

Well-matched veneer.

When examining a piece of furniture, the purchaser should look underneath and inside it if possible. He should notice ends that can be examined. A place that is not covered with varnish and stain is preferable for examination. It is easy to distinguish veneer from solid wood because veneer is composed of two or more thin layers of wood with the grains crossing. The purchaser should find out whether the furniture is made of just one kind of wood or of more than one kind.

The quality of veneer depends largely on (a) the care used in gluing, (b) the number of layers, and (c) the kind and the thickness of the veneer. The only way in which a casual observer can judge the quality of the gluing is to observe whether the veneer is coming loose in any place. This test is not absolute, however. It is often easy to determine the number of layers. When other factors are not considered, the veneer with the greater number of layers is the better piece of veneer. The illustration on page 297 shows five-ply and three-ply veneer. Although it is too much to expect the average person to be able to judge the quality of the wood used in a veneer, he can usually detect the thickness of the surface veneer. If this veneer is too thin, it will scratch easily or absorb moisture.

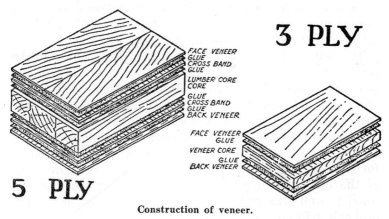

Construction of veneer.

Joints. A good piece of furniture cannot be judged from only the surface. Furthermore, good wood and a good finish should not be accepted as the only evidences of quality.

The back of any cabinet will give clues as to the quality of workmanship. The purchaser should notice whether it has been nailed or screwed and whether the work has been done poorly or neatly. The back posts of chairs and beds should be scrutinized carefully to determine how they have been put together. All points where there will be stress and strain should have been reinforced when the furniture was manufactured. Fastening joints together with glue, nails, or screws usually does not provide adequate strength. Corner blocks, which should have been fastened with screws and glue, are important because they add considerable strength.

In the illustration on page 299, the example designated as A shows the dowel type of construction; that designated as B shows the mortise and tenon type of construction. Both types are desirable, for they help to strengthen furniture. Sometimes a combination of the two is used. Example C below shows how a chair joint is frequently put together, and example D shows the assembled joint. Combinations of A and B are sometimes used by employing the dowel with the mortise and tenon. Examples E and F show a typical dovetail joint and dado joint used in the construction of drawers. These joints prevent drawers from coming apart provided they have been well glued. The best drawers will have dovetails at the front and the back.

The drawer is one of the best indications of care in the construction of a piece of furniture, for many things can be observed from the drawer but not elsewhere in the same piece of furniture. The purchaser should observe whether the bottom is strong and will stay in position. He should also determine whether the drawer slides easily. There should be a center slide for the bottom and special grooves for guiding the drawer. The relative ease in the movement of the drawer will give some indication of whether the wood is well seasoned. If it sticks or jams when new, it probably will be worse later.

Finish. The finish of a piece of furniture can be judged largely by its smoothness and its durability. The finish can be tested by scratching the varnish on an obscure part of the furniture with the fingernail to see whether it comes loose easily, becomes chalky, or rubs off. The varnish should also be pressed with the finger to see whether it is sticky. The finish is probably satisfactory if it reacts favorably to these tests and if it is smooth and unmarked.

Furniture is frequently advertised as having "walnut finish" or "maple finish." These terms do not indicate the kind of wood or veneer. They merely indicate the kind of stain that has been used. The wood may be, and probably is, entirely different. A walnut stain, for instance, may be given to furniture made of pine; but this treatment does not improve the quality of the wood.

Frames of Upholstered Furniture. The frames of upholstered furniture are usually made of wood. Although most wood that is used in these frames is of an inexpensive variety, it must be strong and free of knots and cracks to avoid breaking. Ash, birch, and hard maple are good woods for this purpose.

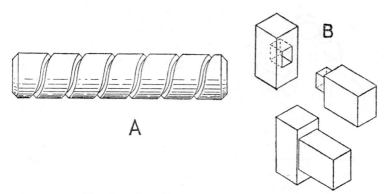

Dowel, and mortise and tenon construction.

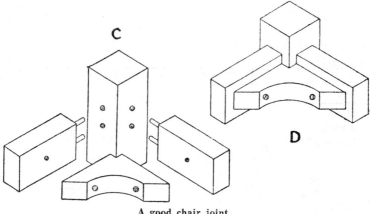

A good chair joint.

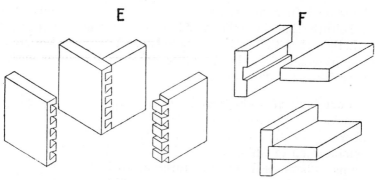

Good construction for drawers.

In buying furniture, look for sturdy construction.

The joints of upholstered furniture must be as carefully made as the joints of any other furniture, even though they may be covered. If possible, the purchaser should have the salesman display a cross section of the construction or have him turn the piece of furniture over so that the bottom construction can be seen and some of the joints can be felt.

Stuffing in Upholstered Furniture. The stuffing or padding that is used in cushions and over springs may consist of curly hair, short hair, moss, down, kapok, palm fiber, cotton, or excelsior. The first three are the most expensive. New cotton is also used in the upholstery of some of the better grades of furniture. Excelsior is the least desirable as well as the least expensive stuffing. Occasionally, in exceptionally low-grade furniture, shredded paper has been used. Before buying, therefore, it is wise to examine carefully any mattress or upholstered piece of furniture and to obtain some definite assurance of what has been used for stuffing.

Many states have laws pertaining to mattresses and other household furnishings containing padding or stuffing. On furniture that is upholstered, look for labels indicating whether the stuffing in the upholstery meets certain state requirements. This label will indicate the kind of material used for the stuffing or padding.

Coverings of Upholstered Furniture. The coverings of upholstered furniture are made of animal fibers, vegetable fibers, synthetic fibers, or leather. Woven fabrics may be a combination of animal, vegetable, or synthetic fibers. The animal fibers used for furniture covers include silk, wool, mohair, and horsehair. The vegetable fibers include cotton,

OFFICIAL STATEMENT	Space to Attach
Manufactured of All New Material MATERIALS USED IN FILLING: **COTTON LINTERS** ——— MADE BY **GOLD MEDAL FOLDING FURNITURE CO.** RACINE, WIS., U. S. A. VENDOR ADDRESS ——— This article is made in compliance with the laws of the State of California, approved June 7, 1915; of Missouri, approved May 26, 1919; of New Jersey, approved March 4, 1913; of Pennsylvania, approved May 1, 1913; as amended; and of all other states of the Union which have enacted sanitary bedding laws.	**DO NOT REMOVE THIS TAG** under penalty of law This article contains SECOND-HAND MATERIAL consisting of KAPOK . . . . 50% COTTON LINTERS . . 50% Registry No___Permit No___ Space for New York State Inspection Stamp / This tag is attached as required by law as a certification that this article is as represented CONTENTS STERILIZED Sold by **JOHN DOE and SONS CO., INC.** No. 567 Greene St. New York City

Upholstered, overstuffed furniture and bedding are required to carry informative labels in many states.

flax, hemp, and jute. The principal synthetic fiber used in upholstering fabrics is rayon. In general, any upholstering material made from an animal fiber will wear longer and will have a better gloss and color than a material made from a vegetable fiber.

Leather is used to a limited extent for upholstering. Good leather is relatively expensive. Some of the modern artificial leathers and plastics are very durable.

Generally speaking, fabrics that are firmly and closely woven from tightly twisted yarns are most likely to withstand heavy wear and the pulling that may result from catching the fibers on the surface. Loosely woven and soft fabrics are attractive, but they are subject to faster wear and pulling of the surface yarns.

The table on page 302 provides a list of fabrics rated according to their durability for coverings on upholstered furniture.

FABRIC	CHARACTERISTICS
Brocade Bracotel Tapestry Satin	Attractive, but long threads on the surface are subject to tear and abrasion. Not good for hard use.
Frieze Plush Velvet	Attractive; will give good wear if firmly woven. Uncut pile is subject to catching and pulling.
Chintz Cretonne Denim Taffeta Homespun	Cheaper grades; of this group denim will give longest wear. Others are not suitable for rough use.

Fabrics used for furniture coverings.

Types of Woven Rugs. The thickness of the pile, the closeness of the weave, the height of the pile, and the quality of the wool are more important than the type of weave. The types of weaves are as follows:

(a) *Cut-pile* carpets and rugs, including Oriental, Chenille, Wilton, Axminster, and Velvet.

(b) *Loop-pile* carpets and rugs, including Brussels and Tapestry weaves.

(c) *Flat-weave* rugs, such as those made of linen, cotton, wool, pulp fiber, and grass, which may be used either side up because both sides are alike.

Carpets and rugs in the first two groups mentioned above will stand the greatest amount of wear.

Another consideration is the particular quality of the rug that is being purchased. Still another is beauty. Some purchasers of rugs are willing to sacrifice a certain amount of quality for beauty.

Distinguishing Features of Rugs. The following discussion points out the characteristics and the merits of individual types of rugs.

Oriental rugs are the most costly of all floor coverings. The value of an Oriental rug can be determined only by an expert. A good Oriental rug will last a very long time. The so-called glossy Oriental rugs have been washed chemically to create the sheen on the surface. These will not wear so long as unwashed Oriental rugs, but some chemically washed rugs are permanently mothproof.

The quality of Persian rugs is measured in essentially the same way as that of other rugs. The lower quality rugs have only a few knots per square inch. Those woven with fine yarn with more knots per square inch are of higher quality. The design, color, perfection of the weave, and thickness of the pile determine the quality. Chinese rugs are either machine spun, hand spun, or Pekin Chinese. They are all handwoven, but the machine spun rug is made from yarn that is machine spun. The same characteristics of quality for all rugs govern the quality of these rugs. They are generally lower in price than Persian rugs. Turkish and Greek rugs may be judged in quality the same as other Oriental rugs, but they are generally lower in price than Persian rugs.

The *Wilton* rug used to be considered the standard for high-grade rugs and carpets, but such rugs are now produced in low grades as well as high grades. A genuine Wilton is a cut-pile fabric. The same basic construction with the pile left uncut is known as a Brussels rug. The color scheme in a Wilton rug is restricted because it may contain only five to six different colors of yarn. A real Wilton rug is made from dyed yarn. To determine whether the rug has been stamped with a design after being manufactured, look to see whether the yarns are covered evenly through the design. By looking at the reverse side of the rug you should see the different colors of yarn imbedded in the back.

The highest grades of Wilton rugs contain 95 to 128 tufts per square inch. The poorest grades have as low as 25 tufts per square inch and as few as two colors. A *worsted* Wilton is considered a better quality than a *wool* Wilton, although they are both made of wool. The most expensive Wilton rugs have a pile up to ⅝ inches in depth, while the pile on a lower grade carpet may be as short as ⅜ of an inch.

The *Axminster* is considered excellent for all purposes. Many of the better rugs on the market today are Axminsters. This type of rug has unlimited color possibilities. Its type of construction gives long wear. A genuine Axminster is made from dyed yarns. One with a stamped design can be detected if the various colors of yarns do not show through on the back. An Axminster can be distinguished from other types because it can be rolled only lengthwise. It is the only type of rug which cannot be rolled crosswise. This is because of the stiff back made of jute.

The quality of this type of rug can be judged by counting the number of tufts per square inch or by examining the back. The highest grade will have about 7¼ rows of tufts per inch, while the lower grades will have as few as 4 rows per inch. The higher grades will have as many as 50 tufts per square inch while the lower grades will have as few as 28 tufts per square inch. There are a few which have as many as 77 tufts per square inch.

The pile on the higher grades is about ⅜ inch in depth. That on the lower grades is sometimes not more than ⅛ inch in depth.

A *Velvet* rug does not require so much wool yarn as an Axminster because it is made by a more simple method of manufacture. Although Velvet rugs are cheaper to produce, the better grades are very durable. A Velvet rug of the best quality is difficult to distinguish from a Wilton rug. Many types of Velvet rugs are sold in plain colors and figured designs under the general term *broadloom*. This term may also apply to other types of large rugs that are seamless, but it most commonly applies to Velvet rugs.

If the type of yarn that is used is of high quality, one may determine the relative value of the rug in a manner similar to those described for other rugs. The finer grades have 80 tufts per square inch with a pile of approximately ⁵⁄₁₆ of an inch in depth. Lower grades may have as few as 50 tufts per square inch with a pile of only ³⁄₁₆ of an inch in depth. The better grades are soft and pliable.

Brussels carpets and rugs are seldom seen for sale in stores now. They have somewhat the same characteristics as Wiltons except that their pile is uncut. The surface is constructed of tightly looped wool. Some machine-made hooked rugs are manufactured in very much the same manner as the Brussels rug.

Tapestry rugs are made in a manner similar to Velvet rugs except that the pile is left uncut. Such a rug is sometimes referred to as a *Tapestry Brussels*. These rugs often resemble hooked rugs.

Some of the so-called *American Oriental* rugs are misnamed. They are often made in the same way as Wilton, Axminster, and Velvet rugs and are treated so that they have a surface sheen like that of washed Orientals. Many of the American Orientals have patterns copied from genuine Orientals. The value of an American Oriental rug is based upon its weave and not upon its name, Oriental.

Chenille carpets and rugs are not common among the better grades, but they are the most luxurious and will wear a long time because of the densely packed pile.

As *flat-weave* rugs are made of various types of materials, the quality of such a rug depends upon (a) the material used, (b) the thickness, and (c) the firmness of the weave.

Jute and hemp are used largely for the backing of cut-pile and loop-pile rugs and carpets. Jute is cheap and strong, but will decay if it becomes damp. Paper yarns are sometimes used. These are strong when dry but become weak when wet.

Standards for Carpets and Rugs. The National Bureau of Standards has set standards for some types of carpets and rugs. As an example, a summary of those standards for Axminster rugs and carpets is as follows:

Check the density and the depth of the rug pile.

(a) The fabric must be woven from the best quality of filling wools with a cotton warp and and a filling of jute. All weaving must be even and neat.

(b) The yarn must be elastic and uniform in diameter and strength.

(c) The pile must be evenly and thoroughly dyed with fast dyes.

(d) The weight per carpet yard (27 inches wide and 36 inches long) must not be less than 39.5 ounces, made up approximately as follows: 17.3 wool pile, 5.1 cotton, 17.1 jute. There must not be a variation of more than 5 per cent in the total weight, 5 per cent in the amount of wool, or 10 per cent in the amount of cotton or jute.

(e) The sizing in the rug or the carpet must not be greater than 10 per cent of the total weight.

A leaflet explaining standard specifications for some types of rugs and carpets can be obtained from the National Bureau of Standards and can be used as a guide in examining rugs.

Rug Cushions. The length of life of any rug or carpet can be prolonged through the use of what is called a *rug cushion*. Such a cushion, which is placed under the rug or the carpet, prolongs the life of the rug.

Fiber Rugs. Fiber rugs are usually made of a composition of paper pulp. The pulp is given special treatment so that the rugs will be hard and durable. Sometimes the pulp is combined with wool and other materials. The wearing qualities of a rug of this type depend largely upon the toughness of the fiber. In purchasing such a rug, one should therefore examine the fiber carefully with the fingernail to judge its toughness.

Another important consideration is whether the rug will hold its color under wear. Unless the color design has been stamped into the rug, it will probably wear off in a short time.

Linoleum. The use of such a wide variety of materials results in a great difference in quality. Some of the materials that go into the making of linoleum are cork, burlap, linseed oil, flax, cotton, rosin, and dyes. These materials in various combinations are mixed together and heated. They are then spread upon burlap by various processes. After aging or baking, they develop a hard, rubbery surface.

Guides in Buying Rugs

1. Is there a label certifying that the rug meets the minimum standards of the National Bureau of Standards?
2. Does the rug contain a label certifying that it conforms to the specifications of the Institute of Carpet Manufacturers of America?
3. Does it contain an informative or descriptive label indicating specific quality?
4. In the absence of one of these labels, check the rug yourself for the number of tufts per square inch, depth of the pile, and other characteristics briefly described for each type of rug. Tests disclose that these characteristics are the primary factors in determining length of wear.
5. What is the percentage of wool used in the yarn?
6. What kind and grade of wool is used? Wool products sold in interstate commerce must disclose these facts.
7. Investigate the selvage to see whether it will prevent the rug from unraveling on the ends and sides. Generally speaking, a rug without fringe will wear better than one with fringe because the fringe will tear off or wear off eventually.
8. What is the quality of the backing? Jute is better than a cord made from paper.
9. Has the pile been clipped evenly?
10. Is the design perfect or is it a second-grade rug because of a defect in design?
11. If a written guarantee is provided, what does it specifically warrant?
12. Is the manufacturer a known and reliable company?
13. Is the dealer reliable?
14. Does the rug lie smoothly on the floor? (Even a good Axminster rug, however, will curl at the ends until it lies on the floor for a while.)

The linoleum industry has rather generally adopted standard gauges of thickness. The price therefore usually varies in relation to the thickness and the pattern. The most expensive types of linoleum are inlays and special kinds resembling tile.

Most manufacturers of linoleum recommend that it not be installed on a cement floor. In a few cases the linoleum will be satisfactory, but in most cases it will absorb moisture through the cement and rot or will curl and peel.

Felt-Base Rugs. A kind of floor covering that is similar to linoleum is made of felt, asphalt, and paint. The asphalt is placed on a felt base, and durable paint is then applied. The final product is relatively inexpensive and can be obtained in a great variety of sizes. It is not so durable as linoleum. Unless the surface is preserved carefully, the paint will wear off. Some types of felt-base floor coverings are not much more durable than painted paper impregnated with tar. The quality of a felt-base floor covering can be judged by the thickness, the tearing strength, and the durability of the paint on the surface.

Tile. Ceramic tile was originally the only tile available and is still popular for bathrooms, sunrooms, and porches. In warmer climates it is often used for the floors of other rooms. Modern tiles today include asphalt, rubber, and plastic. All of these may be installed on cement floors, but asphalt tile is the most satisfactory for this purpose. Rubber and plastic tiles sometimes have the same disadvantages as linoleum when installed on cement floors.

TEXTBOOK QUESTIONS

1. What two extremes are to be avoided in buying furniture if it is necessary to budget the expenditures carefully?
2. What are the characteristics of a good wood for furniture?
3. (a) What is considered to be almost an ideal wood for furniture? (b) What is one of the most common American hardwoods? (c) What are some additional desirable woods for furniture?
4. Name some types of wood that are recommended for outdoor furniture.
5. Which is better for panels: solid wood or veneer?
6. What decorative advantage has veneer?
7. (a) Upon what does the quality of veneer depend? (b) In what way can one judge the quality of veneer?
8. What type of construction should be used to strengthen the posts of chairs and beds?
9. What type of construction should be used to fasten the corners of drawers in furniture?
10. What qualities should the wood in the frames of upholstered furniture possess?

11. (a) What are the most common types of stuffing used for upholstered furniture? (b) Which are the best? (c) Which is the least desirable?
12. Give some examples of cloth used in upholstering furniture that are (a) not good for hard wear, (b) good for hard wear.
13. Give the characteristics of the highest grades of Wilton rugs.
14. In a high-grade Axminster rug, how many rows of tufts is an indication of high quality?
15. What is the minimum standard for weight set by the National Bureau of Standards for Axminister carpets and rugs?
16. What labels on rugs may be used as buying guides?
17. (a) What are the most expensive types of linoleum? **(b)** What factors regulate the price of linoleum?
18. In what way do felt-base rugs differ from linoleum?
19. Name two types of floor coverings that should not be cemented to a concrete floor and give your reasons.

DISCUSSION QUESTIONS

1. What do you think would be a good policy to follow in buying furniture for a home in which there are children?
2. How would you judge the value of a piece of furniture if it contained (a) oak and poplar? (b) walnut and gum? (c) gum and pine?
3. "If a piece of furniture contains veneer, it is not of high quality." Discuss this statement.
4. As the first step in judging the quality of a piece of furniture, one expert on the selection of furniture advocates removing and examining the drawer. What information is disclosed in this way?
5. If you were asked to examine a piece of furniture and to pass judgment on the merits of the finish, on what would you base your judgment?
6. (a) What means may be used for determining the kind of stuffing used in furniture? (b) What are the best types?
7. Even if you are not able to identify types of fabrics, how would you judge a good fabric for covering upholstered furniture?
8. How would you distinguish an Axminster rug from another type of rug?
9. (a) Explain some of the characteristics by which you could judge any rug. (b) How would you detect these?
10. What kinds of floor coverings are most satisfactory for cementing to a concrete floor? Why?
11. Give some reasons why ceramic tile is not used to any extent in northern states for floor coverings in bedrooms, dining rooms, and kitchens.

PROBLEMS

1. If a living room is twenty feet long by thirteen feet nine inches wide and has no obstructions protruding into it, how much will be the cost of having a rug made from strips of carpeting that are twenty-seven inches wide and cost $8.90 a yard? A floor border of fifteen inches will be around the rug, and five strips of carpeting are to run lengthwise with the room. If a fraction of a yard is needed, the charge for a full yard must be used.

2. A kitchen is eight feet wide by eleven feet long and has no obstructions protruding into it. Linoleum is available in strips three feet wide. Compute the cost of linoleum for the kitchen if the price is $3.00 a yard and the strips are to run lengthwise with the room.

3. In order to judge furniture on the basis of modern style and harmony in the home, it is desirable to know something about furniture styles. From a library or from some source, such as a furniture store, obtain a book on furniture styles. Study these and select one type that you prefer for your own home. Give some of the reasons for your selection and give some of the history of this style of furniture.

COMMUNITY PROBLEMS AND PROJECTS

1. As a class project, gather samples of cuts of rugs. Identify these rugs and prepare a display giving the identification and, if possible, some indication of quality.

2. Make an analysis of the furniture in your home on the basis of (a) the kind of wood in the furniture, (b) the kind of construction used in the drawers and in strengthening the legs of chairs and tables, and (c) the use of veneer or solid wood. On the basis of the illustrations in the textbook, determine what kinds of joints have been used.

3. As a class project, obtain samples of wood from lumber companies, furniture stores, furniture manufacturers, and other sources. Separate the woods into those commonly used for furniture and those not commonly used. Stain part of the wood and varnish it. Leave part of it bare. Prepare a display with the proper identification of each wood.

4. Investigate through stores or through the proper authorities in your state to see what laws and regulations there are that apply to upholstering and bedding. Give a report on your findings.

Chapter 17

PART V _____

How to Buy Drugs and Similar Articles

Purpose of the Chapter. Although your major problems are those of obtaining food, clothing, and shelter, your personal welfare is affected by many other items that you purchase. Your health and happiness are also affected. Many of the items that you purchase are luxuries. Cosmetics, in many respects, are luxuries although—as will be seen later—some of them do serve useful purposes.

The purpose of this chapter is to discuss the problems relative to drugs, cosmetics, soaps, dentifrices, and similar items on the basis of available facts and from an unbiased point of view.

Dangers of Treating Yourself. Every year there are thousands of individuals who fail to obtain proper treatment because they attempt to treat themselves. Thousands of individuals make mistakes in using otherwise helpful drugs. One of the greatest dangers is the promiscuous use of prepared cures that are bought over a drugstore counter as casually as chewing gum. Any sensible person can keep on hand and can use a certain number of standard home remedies, such as those recommended for the home medicine cabinet by the Food and Drug Administration. In all serious ailments, however, and in the cases of diagnosis of the ailments, a doctor should be consulted. Since many drug and curative devices are bought by people who are not experts, the government seeks to protect them from exploitation. As explained in a previous chapter, the Federal Government has set up certain controls over drugs in regard to their advertising and labeling.

Federal Supervision over Drugs and Cosmetics. The Federal Food, Drug, and Cosmetic Act, which was enacted on June 25, 1938, represents the first instance of Federal control over cosmetics. It extends governmental control over drugs and curative devices sold or intended for sale in interstate commerce, although in some cases there had previously been a certain amount of state control over the manufacture and the sale of these items.

Under the provisions of the Act the term *drug* applies to articles recognized by the official United States Pharmacopoeia, the official Homeopathic Pharmacopoeia of the United States, the official National Formulary, or any supplement to any of them. The term also applies to (a) articles intended for use in the diagnosis, cure, mitigation, treatment, or prevention of disease in man or other animals; (b) articles (other than food) intended to affect the structure or any function of the body of man or other animals; and (c) articles intended for use as components of any articles specified in the other classifications.

The so-called health devices governed by the Act are instruments, apparatus, and contrivances for use in the diagnosis, cure, mitigation, treatment, or prevention of disease in man or other animals. The term also applies to devices that affect the structure or any function of the body.

The term *cosmetic* applies to articles intended to be rubbed, poured, sprinkled, sprayed on, introduced into, or otherwise applied to the human body for cleansing, beautifying, or altering appearance. In addition, the term applies to articles intended for use as components of such cosmetics. The Act does not, however, govern the sale of soaps.

Adulterated Drugs. Under the Federal Food, Drug, and Cosmetic Act, a drug is considered to be adulterated under any of the following circumstances:

(a) If the drug consists in whole or in part of any decayed substance.
(b) If it is prepared, packed, or held under unsanitary conditions whereby it may become contaminated or be rendered injurious to health.
(c) If the container of the drug is composed of any substance that may render the contents injurious to health.

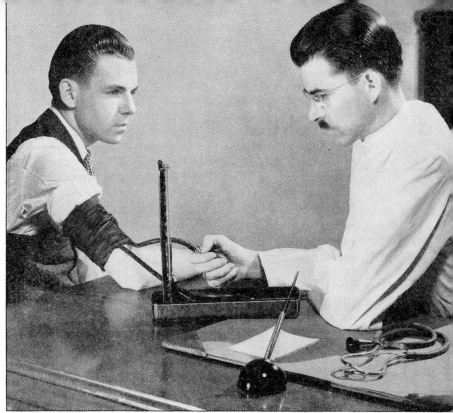

A doctor should be consulted about any serious ailment.

(d) If the drug contains coloring that has not been certified under the regulations of the Law.

(e) If the strength, the quality, or the purity of a recognized drug differs from the standard established for that drug.

(f) If the drug is mixed or packed with any substance that reduces its quality or strength.

Misbranded Drugs. Under the Federal Food, Drug, and Cosmetic Act, a drug is considered to be misbranded in any of the following cases:

(a) If the package fails to disclose the name and the place of business of the manufacturer, the packer, or the distributor.

(b) If the package fails to give an accurate statement of the contents in terms of weight, measure, or numerical count.

313

(c) If any statement required under the Act does not appear prominently on the label so that it is likely to be read and understood by the ordinary individual under customary conditions of purchase and use.

(d) If the drug may be habit-forming and does not bear on its label the statement, "Warning—May be habit-forming."

(e) If the drug is one not designated entirely by an official name and fails to bear the common name. If it contains two or more ingredients, the common or usual name, as well as the quantity, of each ingredient must be given.

(f) If the label fails to give adequate directions for use or warning against misuse.

(g) If the drug is a recognized one and is not packaged and labeled properly.

(h) If the drug is one liable to deterioration and is not packaged and labeled according to the regulations of the Food and Drug Administration.

(i) If the container is made, formed, or filled so as to be misleading.

(j) If the drug is an imitation of another or is offered for sale under the name of another.

(k) If the drug, when used according to the directions on the label, will be injurious to health.

The Food and Drug Administration not only attempts to prevent adulteration and misbranding, but also dictates how every remedy that is approved by the Pharmacopoeia shall be manufactured and packaged. This control covers the strength, dosage, instructions, and warnings. The approval of a new remedy is contingent upon a tryout under strict supervision before it may be offered for general sale.

Adulterated Cosmetics. Under the Federal Food, Drug, and Cosmetic Act, a cosmetic is considered to be adulterated in any of the following cases:

(a) If it contains any substance that is poisonous or injurious to users under the conditions prescribed on the label or under such conditions of use as are customary. This section of the Law does not apply, however, to coal-tar hair dye, the label of which

Guides in Buying Drugs

1. Rely upon a dependable doctor for prescribing drugs.

2. Learn from your doctor the names of manufacturers of dependable drugs and buy under brand names the drugs manufactured by those companies.

3. Be skeptical of new drug products until your doctor has assured you of their accepted use.

4. A drug clerk may be able to suggest some simple remedies, but a drug clerk or even a pharmacist is not a physician and is therefore not capable of making the same authoritative diagnosis and recommendation that a doctor would make.

5. Read the label for information in regard to dosage and warnings. If a drug is not sold in interstate commerce and is not covered by state regulations, sufficient information may not be given on the label. Buy only drugs for which the proper information is given on the label.

6. In determining the standard quality and reliability of a drug, check to see if it conforms to the standards of the United States Pharmacopoeia (USP), the official Homeopathic Pharmacopoeia (HP), or the National Formulary (NF).

7. Even though some drug preparations are more or less harmless for the purposes for which they are recommended, such drugs may be harmful if taken without the advice of a physician.

8. Some drugs may be harmless to certain individuals but harmful to others. Follow the advice of a physician in taking prepared medicines.

9. Beware of drugs with all-inclusive claims as to their uses.

10. Beware of any drugs that are to be taken internally to reduce weight. Most of these are injurious.

bears the following conspicuous warning: "Caution —This product contains ingredients which may cause skin irritation on certain individuals, and a preliminary test according to accompanying directions should first be made. This product must not be used for dyeing the eyelashes or eyebrows; to do so may cause blindness."

(b) If the cosmetic consists in whole or in part of any decayed substance.

(c) If it has been prepared, packed, or held under unsanitary conditions whereby it might have become injurious to health.
(d) If its container is composed in whole or in part of any poisonous or injurious substance that may render the contents injurious to health.
(e) If it is a cosmetic, other than a hair dye containing coal-tar coloring, that has not been certified according to the Act.

Misbranded Cosmetics. Under the Federal Food, Drug, and Cosmetic Act, a cosmetic is considered to be misbranded under any of the following circumstances:

(a) If its label is false or misleading.
(b) If the package fails to bear the name and the place of business of the manufacturer, the packer, or the distributor.
(c) If the package fails to provide an accurate statement of the contents in terms of weight, measure, or numerical count.
(d) If any statement required by the Act is omitted from the label.
(e) If any statement required by the Act is not printed prominently and in such terms as to permit it to be read and to be understood by the ordinary individual under customary conditions of purchase and under ordinary conditions of use.
(f) If the container has been made, formed, or filled so as to be misleading. For example, the contents of thick glass jars are sometimes very small.

Are Cosmetics Safe and Useful? On the whole, the cosmetic industry is legitimate and honorable, but it may get a bad reputation because of some unscrupulous manufacturers. Most of the products are of high quality and are safe to use.

The cosmetic industry also suffers disrepute because some people are allergic to various ingredients. In other words, some individuals are hypersensitive to substances that are not harmful in the least to the majority of persons. Such an ingredient may cause a skin irritation to a few persons, but may be used daily by others without injury. When one considers the great number of ingredients included in cosmetics, it can easily be seen how some of these ingredients may cause irritation to at least a few users.

The preparations that are most liable to contain dangerous ingredients are hair dye, hair tonics, dandruff removers, hair beautifiers, freckle removers, skin peelers, skin bleaches, depilatories, and personal deodorants. Many of these will cause the hair to fall out or the skin to become irritated.

To go into an elaborate discussion of the advertising and the labeling of cosmetics would be futile because most people buy these products regardless of the irrational claims in advertisements and on labels. Most people buy beauty preparations in the hope that they will become or will remain beautiful. Advertisements that contain testimonials of attractive women or photographs of glamorous persons merely add to the self-satisfaction of the individuals who buy those products. Such advertising has principally one purpose: to satisfy certain human emotions. As a result most cosmetic advertising appeals to the emotions rather than to the common sense of the buyer.

Advertisements of cosmetics usually have a strong emotional or glamor appeal.

Food and Drug Administration

The main value of facial creams is to moisten and soften the skin.

Function of Creams and Lotions. Price alone is not an adequate guide to quality or effectiveness in the purchase of cosmetics. Many preparations available at reasonable prices contain pure ingredients that are helpful. Unless a cream or a lotion serves a definite purpose as a drug, its real purpose is to keep the skin moistened. Any other purposes claimed for it are questionable.

A study of cosmetics involves many points of view. In this study there is no attempt to decide whether cosmetics should or should not be used. The lists on page 319 point out what creams and lotions will do and what they will not do. These statements are based upon available scientific facts.

Cautions About Cosmetics. When one studies the things that cosmetics will and will not do, he does not get the complete picture. The following is a summary of cautions on the use of cosmetics:

(a) Beware of preparations that contain a lead compound because such a compound may cause serious poisoning. Fortunately some preparations advertised as being radio-active do not have any radio-active substances in them. If they did, the preparations would be injurious.

(b) There are no creams or tonics that are known to grow hair.

(c) Nearly everyone is allergic to some kinds of preparations, usually resulting in skin irritation. To find out whether one is allergic to a certain cosmetic, apply it to a small area as an experiment.

What Creams and Lotions Will Do

1. A cosmetic preparation is primarily a protection for the skin from the ravages of weather and time. It may help to prevent defects and deficiencies, but it will not cure them.
2. The massage that accompanies the application of cosmetics is helpful in delaying the formation of wrinkles.
3. The application of a cosmetic has a temporary effect on the outer skin but has no permanent effect.
4. The skins of most people have excretions of fat that tend to lubricate the skin. These excretions are washed away by soap and water. A cosmetic will help to replace them.
5. Some lotions for the hands and the face will form a protective coating and help to retain natural oil and moisture, thereby encouraging the healing of chapped hands and face.
6. If astringent lotions are strong enough, they will temporarily keep pores from functioning.
7. Any make-up preparation that temporarily coats the skin will serve as a slight protection in addition to enhancing the appearance, provided it is applied properly.

What Creams and Lotions Will Not Do

1. No cosmetic will bring about a permanent change in the nature of the skin. The general nature of one's skin depends largely upon the health and the cleanliness of the individual and upon inherited characteristics.
2. Wrinkles in the skin are caused by the effect of emotions and expressions on the face. The folding of tissues gradually causes wrinkles that cannot be erased by the application of oils or creams. Wrinkles can be avoided or partially removed by prolonged rest and relaxation and by a conscious attempt to avoid frowning and other unusual facial expressions. Such treatment is effective only in the case of young persons, however.
3. No cosmetic can nourish or feed the skin.
4. An astringent lotion, although producing a slight contraction of cells, will not shrink the pores. Sometimes these lotions cause annoying irritation.

(d) Only those skin-bleaching compounds that bleach the surface are safe. Their effectiveness is slight and slow. Bleaches that loosen the outer skin cause irritation and possible poisoning. Many of them contain mercury, which is dangerous to the human body.

(e) Skin peelers or freckle removers that require the removing of layers of skin are considered very dangerous, especially when used by the average individual.

(f) There are several types of hair dyes that will cause irritation and possible poisoning to some individuals. The safest procedure is to consult a dermatologist or some other expert on the use of such dyes.

(g) Some so-called deodorants act as antiperspirant agents. Most deodorants are harmless, but some will cause an irritation to certain people. While most of them are harmless to the skin, they will injure many types of fabrics.

(h) Many of the so-called skin lotions or astringents have no particularly useful purpose except to provide temporarily an invigorating feeling and a pleasant odor. The danger of such lotions lies in the fact that many of them contain alcohol or mild acids or other astringent agents that may tend to dry the skin. In this respect they will serve the opposite purpose of a good facial cream.

(i) Many eye make-up preparations have potential dangers for individuals who use them. Those containing colors made from metallic salts or aniline dyes may cause permanent injury to the eyesight. Some dyes that may be used safely on the hair cannot be used safely on eyelashes.

(j) There are many good shampoos on the market, most of which are soaps in water solution. The lathering quality is not necessarily an indication of the effectiveness of the shampoo. A shampoo should be judged on the basis of its effectiveness and its failure to dry the scalp.

Bath Salts and Oils. Bath salts are usually nothing more than water softeners that have been colored and perfumed. They usually have no beneficial effect upon the skin; sometimes they may injure the skin by causing excessive dryness. Bath oils form an emulsion in water. The only real purpose of bath oils is to provide perfume and to prevent excessive drying of the skin.

Uses of Soap. While soaps have many specialized uses in the various industrial applications, their use in the home is primarily for cleaning—for washing the face, hands, dishes, floors, walls, and other articles. Some products are formulated to be all-purpose cleaners. This means that they can be used for all kinds of cleaning jobs, such as washing clothes and scrubbing floors. However, these types of all-purpose cleaners would usually not be satisfactory for washing the hands and face. Toilet soaps, fine fabric soaps, and shampoos are designed for more specific tasks.

Soaps used on the skin or the hair should be mild or neutral. Such soaps will prevent irritation of the skin and excessive drying of the skin. The most that a toilet soap can do is to cleanse efficiently. An inexpensive mild or neutral soap will serve the purpose; but if the family budget will permit, one may indulge in soaps that are perfumed and colored, and can be obtained in small bars or in unusual shapes. These soaps, however, do not have any additional advantage for the consumer.

There are numerous soaps, such as floating, castile, transparent, hard-water, grit, liquid, tar, and medicated. Grit soaps contain an abrasive for removing grease and stains. Hard-water soaps contain oils that lather well in hard water. Certain medicated soaps may have a slightly additional antiseptic value, but all soaps have a good antiseptic value because the lather washes away germs. In considering toilet soaps, one must bear in mind the two fundamental purposes of such soaps: (a) to cleanse and (b) to be mild or neutral. There are no other important considerations.

It is important for the housewife to become familiar with the various types of soaps that can be used for different purposes. For instance, silk, rayon, and wool require neutral soaps and careful handling. Laundry soaps, bleaches, and powders should be used with a full knowledge of their intended purposes.

Other Detergents. Soap is a detergent but not all detergents are soaps. A detergent is a cleansing agent that is usually combined with water. Several types of detergents are fundamentally different from soap but react like soap.

They are different from soap in that they do not form a scum in hard water. As a result, many people living in regions where there is hard water have found these special detergents preferable to soap; even in regions where there is soft water, these detergents are preferred by women for many uses.

Guides in Buying Soaps

1. An inferior brand of soap can easily be detected by comparison with one of the numerous good brands of soap on the market.
2. Avoid buying any soap in any class that is very much above the average price a pound.
3. A soap that is suitable for washing badly soiled garments in hard water is too strong for fine fabrics. In the laundering of a fine fabric, a relatively neutral and mild soap should be used, preferably one recommended by the manufacturer or the retailer of the fabric.
4. Use toilet soaps that are no stronger than is necessary to obtain the proper cleansing qualities. Strong soaps tend to dry out the skin and sometimes cause skin irritations.

Other Cleansing Agents. Other cleansing agents, such as naphtha, gasoline, and carbon tetrachloride, are used for cleansing surfaces. These are sometimes referred to as dry or waterless cleaners. Naphtha and gasoline are both explosive and extremely dangerous. Carbon tetrachloride is not explosive. Naphtha and gasoline are not only dangerous because of the possibility of being ignited by fire or electric sparks or static electricity, but they are also dangerous because of the fact that gases formed by them are highly explosive.

Buying Dentifrices and Mouthwashes. There are many good dentifrices on the market that are honestly labeled and advertised. It is true that one usually pays a pretty high price for a small tube of dentifrice. There are some people who claim that the price is exorbitant. By pointing out that certain ingredients can be obtained and mixed together to form a good dentifrice, they attempt to prove

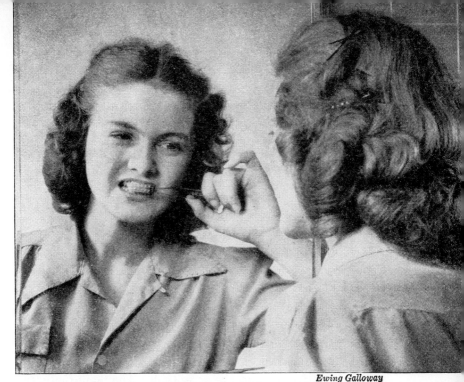

As a cleansing agent a dentifrice helps prevent tooth decay.

that the consumer is cheated. If one wishes to prepare his own dentifrice, he may use ordinary salt, soda, or magnesia. Any of these will make a satisfactory tooth powder. Nevertheless, if the consumer is willing to have the ingredients prepared and mixed for him, properly flavored and packaged, and finds that it is more advantageous to pay the price than to prepare his own dentifrice, no one can object to this procedure.

One should not expect too much of the dentifrice he uses. Tooth paste cannot do the work of a dentist in caring for the teeth. The *Journal* of the American Dental Association says: "On the basis of available evidence, the functions of a dentifrice are limited to its aid in mechanically cleaning the surfaces of the teeth when used with a tooth brush." No dentifrice can effectively clean the hidden areas of the teeth. As these are the real danger spots, the teeth should be inspected regularly by a dentist.

Authorities generally concede that almost any dentifrice will serve as a satisfactory cleansing agent and will, there-

323

fore, help to keep the teeth free from decay. However, for many years, medical and dental authorities have contended that there is no antiseptic or medicinal value in dentifrices. Some of the new dentifrices containing ammonium compounds, urea, fluoride, chlorophyll, or penicillin may tend to control tooth decay. Certain medical and dental authorities feel that still more ample evidence is needed in regard to some of these products before complete approval can be given to them.

Most dental preparations are composed of common ingredients, such as chalk, soap, salt, baking soda, borax, magnesia, glycerine, alcohol, saccharin, oils, water, flavoring, and color. Claims on the labels and in the advertising of dentifrices should be considered in the light of the latest medical knowledge.

As was explained in Chapter 7, the Council on Dental Therapeutics of the American Dental Association issues a list of dentifrices that are acceptable. The manufacturers of these products may use in their advertising and on their labels the seal of acceptance of the American Dental Association. The list is changed from time to time as new products are added or other products are dropped.

The Council does not approve so-called antiseptics that are recommended as mouthwashes. It feels that the general use of mouthwashes can be considered to serve no intrinsic purpose except to clean the mouth, largely through rinsing. Many doctors and dentists recommend a salt solution or a salt and soda solution as an effective mouthwash or gargle.

TEXTBOOK QUESTIONS

1. By what Federal law is the sale of drugs and cosmetics regulated?
2. What is the definition of a cosmetic?
3. Give at least two examples of the misbranding of drugs.
4. What restrictions are placed on the manufacturing and distribution of new drug compounds?
5. Give at least two examples of adulterations of cosmetics that are violations of Federal law.
6. Give at least two examples of misbranded cosmetics.

7. What are at least three of the things that a cream or a lotion will do for the skin?
8. What will a cream or a lotion not do?
9. Give at least three cautions that should be observed in using cosmetics.
10. What essentially is a bath salt?
11. What are the desirable characteristics of a good toilet soap?
12. How do some of the newer types of detergents differ from soap?
13. Give at least two guides in buying soap.
14. What basis is there for the contention that mouthwashes have an antiseptic value?

DISCUSSION QUESTIONS

1. Discuss your opinion of the advisability of attempting to buy with the aid of a drug clerk a remedy for (a) pneumonia, (b) heart trouble, (c) burns.
2. The Federal law governing drugs and cosmetics applies only to goods sold or intended for sale in interstate commerce. To what extent, however, are all consumers protected?
3. Do you think that ordinary cold cream comes under the regulations of the Federal Food, Drug, and Cosmetic Act?
4. Manufacturers of drugs and cosmetics have been blamed for diseases or ailments that resulted from the fact that certain persons were allergic to particular ingredients in the drugs or cosmetics. Discuss this situation.
5. In your opinion, may an advertisement for a cosmetic legally assert that the cosmetic will eliminate wrinkles in the skin?
6. Explain why some remedies and cosmetics are safe for some people but not for others. What do you recommend as a guide in such cases?
7. What are the advantages of some of the newer chemicals that are used in dentifrices?
8. Will mouthwashes tend to eliminate bad breath?

PROBLEMS

1. Remove the label from some cosmetic used in your home, or copy the information from the label. Submit the label or the information with a written report indicating to what extent you believe that the label conforms with the Federal law and to what extent it fails to conform with the law.

2. Obtain the label from an empty medicine container that you
find at home, or copy the information from such a container.
Submit the label or the information with a report on the
following: (a) ingredients, (b) quantity, (c) instructions,
(d) warnings, and (e) any other important information.
Point out any ways in which you think the label violates
the Federal law.
3. From among your family and acquaintances make a list of
the persons whom you know to be allergic to drugs or cosmetics containing certain ingredients. Explain the results.

COMMUNITY PROBLEMS AND PROJECTS

1. Investigate to see whether your own state has a law controlling the advertising, the labeling, and the selling of drugs
and cosmetics. Report the significant points of the law if
there is one.
2. As a class project, the girls in the class are to obtain and
bring to class for comparison different brands of the same
common type of facial cream. Keep a record of the brand
and the price and the results, bearing in mind that a cream
is primarily a moistening, massaging, and softening agent
for the skin.
3. As a class project for boys, bring to class different brands of
tooth paste or tooth powder. Keep a record of prices and,
after trying each brand, make a report on the relative values.

PART VI
HOW BANKS AND CREDIT SERVE YOU

Chapter 18
How Your Bank Operates

Purpose of the Chapter. Banks have an important influence on our lives. Because nearly everyone finds it necessary to use some of the services of a bank, banks have a direct interest to every individual. Because of their economic functions in the community, banks have a broader significance to every individual. In this chapter you will be given an understanding of how banks operate and how they may serve you.

Kinds of Banks as to Functions. Banks classified according to their function are (1) commercial banks, (2) savings banks, (3) trust companies, and (4) investment banks.

Some banks combine two or more functions. For instance, a commercial bank may have a savings department or a savings bank may have a trust department. Federal and state laws have forced national banks and state banks to separate the function of investment banking from the functions of commercial banking and savings banking.

A *commercial bank* derives its name from the fact that it confines its business largely to transactions with businessmen and business institutions. Loans made by commercial banks extend for short periods of time, ranging from thirty to ninety days.

Savings banks may be stock companies or mutual companies. A stock savings bank is one that is owned and operated by stockholders. Profits go to the stockholders. A mutual savings bank is one that is owned by the depositors and is operated primarily for their benefit. Mutual savings banks are explained in Chapter 25. Some commercial banks operate what they call savings departments.

327

Banks make loans to individuals and businesses.

The savings bank or the savings department of a commercial bank ordinarily will make loans for a longer period of time than a commercial bank. Loans may extend for one year or more. The following customs are relatively uniform among savings banks and the savings departments of commercial banks:

(a) Deposits are usually accepted for amounts as small as one dollar.
(b) Checks cannot be drawn against deposits.
(c) The bank reserves the right to demand several days' notice before the withdrawal of funds.

A *trust company* may be a separate company or a department of a commercial or a savings bank. Trust companies in many states are permitted to perform the functions of a commercial bank in addition to guaranteeing titles, operating trust funds, and managing real estate.

An *investment bank* is commonly a separate bank, although some of the large commercial banks operate investment departments. An investment bank is not a regular bank as the ordinary individual knows it; it is primarily interested in promoting the organization and the management of industrial concerns. As a result it deals in the securities of corporations. Large investment banks have not only marketed the securities of great corporations, but have also controlled these organizations. An investment bank may also deal in the securities of a corporation in which it has no control.

Kinds of Banks as to Organization. Banks classified according to their authorization are (1) state banks and (2) national banks. In addition to these types of banks, there are Federal reserve banks or bankers' banks. These banks deal largely with individual banks that are members of the Federal Reserve System, but they also have dealings with other banks.

A *state bank* is a bank that is organized as a corporation. It obtains its authority through a charter granted by the state in which it operates. It may be a commercial bank, a savings bank, a trust company, or an investment bank. A state bank may also be a member of the Federal Reserve System.

A *national bank* obtains its charter from the Federal Government and is subject to the regulations of the Federal Reserve System and the banking laws enacted by the Federal Government. A national bank is always organized as a corporation.

There are many other financial agencies that fit into the national plan of savings, investment, and the transfer of funds. Various mutual savings societies are organized under special laws and operate under particular rules. Building and loan associations, which are discussed on pages 453 and 454, are of a wide variety in different states. Two other important banking institutions are the Federal land bank and the home loan bank. These have been created to take care of emergencies. National banks and many of the state banks are not permitted to make loans for long periods of time to take care of the financing of farms and homes, and the production of crops. These special banking institutions are operated for the benefit of farmers and homeowners under the sponsorship of the Federal Government.

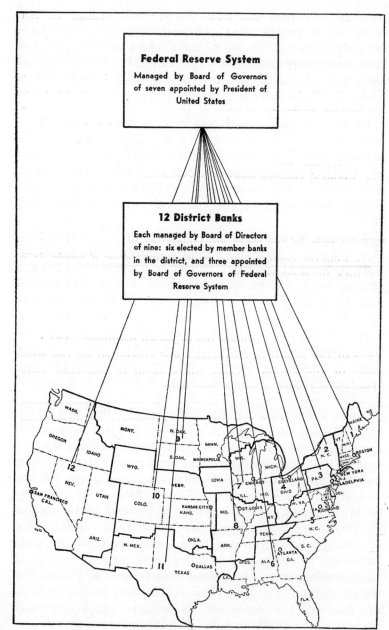

Federal Reserve System.

Organization of the Federal Reserve System. In 1913 the Federal Reserve Act was passed. It has been amended several times since, but it is still essentially in its original form. The banking system that is the outgrowth of the Federal Reserve Act is called the Federal Reserve System. Under the Federal Reserve Act the country was divided into the twelve districts shown on the opposite page. In each district there is a Federal reserve bank, which has a separate and distinct organization and is managed by a board of directors. Each member bank in the district in which the Federal reserve bank is located must subscribe to capital stock of the Federal reserve bank equal in amount to 6 per cent of its paid-up capital and surplus. In the past, however, a Federal reserve bank has called for payment of only a part of the stock subscribed for by a member bank.

A Federal reserve bank is operated under a board of directors of nine persons. Six of them are elected by the member banks in the district and three are appointed by the Board of Governors of the Federal Reserve System. The twelve Federal reserve banks are co-ordinated by this Board of Governors consisting of seven members. The members of the Board of Governors are appointed by the President of the United States for a term of fourteen years. The Federal reserve banks may rightfully be called bankers' banks for their stock is owned by the member banks. They do not accept deposits of individuals or businesses.

Functions of the Federal Reserve System. The Federal reserve banks deal largely with member banks, although under certain conditions they make certain types of loans to responsible business enterprises. The theory of the Federal Reserve System is that the funds of the entire United States should be organized so as to permit the rapid shifting of money and credit from one place to another to take care of supply and demand. This condition is especially necessary in times of emergency when there is an unusual demand in some particular place.

The three most important functions of the Federal reserve banks are as follows:

(a) Issuing notes (paper currency).
(b) Centralizing bank reserves.
(c) Rediscounting notes submitted by member banks.

The Federal Reserve System provides one type of note, the Federal reserve note, that is our main source of currency. It serves as credit money and is accepted in all business channels as legal tender. The Federal reserve banks act as the agent of the United States Government in issuing this type of note.

Federal reserve banks may buy from member banks ordinary notes signed by business concerns or individuals. This process is called *rediscounting*.

The function of rediscounting is an important one, for it helps each member bank to regulate the ratio between its cash and its deposits. If the proportion of cash to deposits becomes small, the bank may not have enough funds to pay depositors on demand. The Federal reserve bank, however, provides a means of relieving the situation. A member bank may sell to the Federal reserve bank in its district notes that have been purchased or notes that are held as security against loans. The Federal reserve bank will accept these and give in exchange either credit as a reserve deposit or Federal reserve notes. If credit as a reserve deposit is issued, cash can be made available quickly to the member bank; if Federal reserve notes are issued, they serve as cash. In other words, the member bank exchanges notes of its customers for cash (Federal reserve notes).

The *centralized reserves* of Federal reserve banks are the deposits of member banks. Member banks may create deposits or reserves in Federal reserve banks by depositing cash in these banks or by rediscounting notes at them. These reserves are held as a credit to the individual member banks. Each member bank is required, however, to keep in the Federal reserve bank in its district a reserve that is equal to a certain percentage of its own deposits. This percentage is governed by the Federal Reserve Board. The bank, of course, must also keep on hand a sufficient amount of cash to take care of the demands of its customers. The deposits in the Federal reserve banks make it unnecessary, however, for member banks to keep a great amount of cash on hand, for these deposits are practically the same as cash in that they are available quickly. This system causes a Federal reserve bank to act more or less as a financial reservoir for its district. Each member bank can draw upon the pool or reserves. The pooling of a portion of the funds of each member bank serves to strengthen every bank in the district.

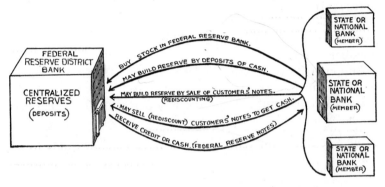

Relations of Federal reserve banks with member banks.

Regulating Business Expansion. Through the rediscounting process it is possible for individual banks to increase their quantity of currency and to increase their reserves. Whenever a bank has loaned all the money that it has available for that purpose, it may rediscount the notes of its customers and thus increase its available cash and reserves in the Federal reserve bank, which will enable it to make additional loans. When money is relatively scarce, the Federal reserve bank, therefore, makes it possible to stimulate expansion. If it is the desire of the Federal Reserve Board to restrict expansion, the rediscount rate is raised. If the Board wants to encourage expansion when money is scarce, it may reduce the rediscount rate until conditions improve.

The rediscount rate of the Federal reserve banks is usually lower than the discount rate of the member banks. For instance, a member bank might lend $1,000 at 5 per cent for thirty days. The discount on $1,000 for thirty days would amount to $4.17. The person or the business obtain-

ing the loan would actually get $995.83 in cash. Assume
that the bank then decided to rediscount this note at its
Federal reserve bank. If the note were discounted immediately and if the rediscount rate were 2 per cent, the member bank would get $998.33 for the note. It would make a
profit of $2.50 and would receive either a reserve deposit
in the Federal reserve bank or cash (Federal reserve
notes). If its total cash had a safe relation to its deposits,
the member bank could then lend more money to its customers. This operation would therefore be profitable to the
member bank.

Suppose, however, the Federal Reserve Board in Washington issued instructions to all Federal reserve banks to
raise the rediscount rate to 5 or 5½ per cent. This increase
in the rate would mean that member banks could not continue to make loans and to rediscount the notes profitably.
Individual member banks would therefore lend only what
they could on their own resources and would not rediscount
the notes. As the banks would be limited in the amount of
loans they could make, businesses would be limited in their
expansion. This process is referred to as the *control over
bank credit.*

Economists tell us that many of our depressions are
caused by overexpansion. The control over expansion is,
however, not so direct and so easily exercised as is indicated in this example. Because of uncontrollable influences
the action of the Federal reserve banks is not always as
effective as might be hoped. For instance, an individual
bank might raise the interest rate on its loans and still find
the rediscounting process profitable. In such a case, the
raising of the interest rate would tend to discourage customers from borrowing, because it would make borrowing
unprofitable. But if money is plentiful, the Federal reserve
banks have no means of controlling expansion through the
lending of individual banks, because the individual banks
do not find it necessary to rediscount their notes with the
Federal reserve bank. It is only when money is scarce that
the Federal reserve bank can restrict expansion by raising
the rediscount rate.

When money is scarce, the Federal reserve bank can in some cases encourage expansion by lowering the rediscount rate. Banks can lower their interest rates and rediscount their notes with the Federal reserve bank and obtain more reserves and cash to use as the basis for additional lending. For instance, if the rediscount rate in the preceding example had been lowered to 1 per cent, the bank would have made a profit of $3.34 on the $1,000 loan instead of a profit of $2.50. A profit of this kind on such transactions would have encouraged the member banks to continue making loans and rediscounting the notes. Business, in turn, would have been encouraged to expand.

Banks and Credit. The functions of the Federal Reserve System that have just been described are often referred to as credit functions. Money and credit have a very close relationship. A further discussion of the credit functions of banks will be taken up in Chapter 37.

Collection Between Banks. When there are only a few banks in a city, the process of exchanging checks among them is simple. Suppose, for example, there are only two banks in a particular city. Customers of Bank A will make deposits during the day. Some of the deposits may be in cash, but many of them will be in the form of checks. At the end of the day's business Bank A may have in its possession ten checks, amounting to a total of one thousand dollars, drawn on the funds of individual depositors in Bank B, besides those drawn on accounts in Bank A. A messenger from Bank A takes these checks to Bank B. Bank B accepts the checks, and either pays one thousand dollars in cash to Bank A or gives credit for that amount to Bank A. Credit may be issued at the time the checks are presented; but if Bank B finds that any particular depositor does not have enough money to pay his check, the check is returned to Bank A and credit for it is canceled. Bank B follows the same process with regard to checks it has that are drawn on Bank A. The average collections between the two banks will probably be about equal. Varia-

These checks are ready for delivery to a clearinghouse.

tions will not be large unless some unusual transactions are made during a particular day.

In large cities a system such as this would be cumbersome, slow, and costly. *Clearinghouses* have therefore been organized to facilitate collection between banks. A clearinghouse represents an association of banks. At a certain hour of each day, clerks from all the banks meet at the clearinghouse. In most cities two clerks represent each bank. One clerk delivers the checks that were received by the bank during the previous day and that are to be collected from other banks. With the checks is a list showing the amount due from each bank and the total amount due on all the checks. The second clerk receives from the other banks checks that are to be collected from his bank with statements showing the amount due each bank.

A clerk from each bank then quickly determines the amount his bank owes all the other banks and the amount that all the others owe his. If his bank owes more than the amount to be collected from other banks, it pays the difference to the clearinghouse. If the other banks owe his bank more than is due from the latter, the clearinghouse pays the difference to his bank. Under this system the collection between banks takes only a short time, and the banks are kept in balance daily. Small banks that do not belong to a clearinghouse association have their checks cleared through a bank that is a member of the association.

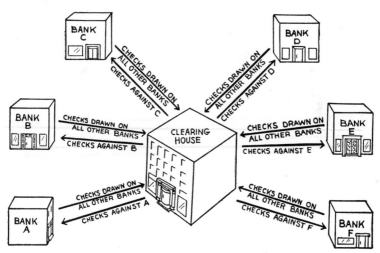

How a clearinghouse operates.

The Federal reserve banks perform an important function in the clearing of checks between one city and another. A Federal reserve bank or a branch will accept from the member banks in its territory all checks that are to be collected from banks in other cities. These checks are sent by the Federal reserve bank to the clearinghouses in the appropriate cities. Banks that are not members of the Federal Reserve System may, in some cases, have their checks cleared through the Federal reserve bank by a special agreement.

Some banks clear their out-of-town checks through *correspondent banks*. For instance, Bank A in Chicago may have arrangements with Bank A in New York for the exchange of checks. Bank A in Chicago may have a check for collection on Bank B in New York. Bank A of Chicago presents this to Bank A of New York. Through the clearinghouse procedure in New York City, Bank A of New York makes collection and either credits the proceeds to the account of Bank A in Chicago, or sends a draft, a check, or the actual funds to the latter.

The Citizen's Function in Banking. For the safety of our economic system the individual should understand the importance of his function in the banking system. In the first place, banks depend upon individuals and business concerns for deposits. On the basis of these deposits loans can be made. By making loans, banks earn a profit for themselves.

If all the money deposited in a bank were paid out as loans, there would not be any money left to pay to depositors. Such a situation does not, however, occur. When a loan is made, the borrower usually accepts a credit to an account. He can then write a check on this account. The borrower therefore becomes a depositor and also a debtor of the bank.

Through our system of credit there is not enough ready cash in the United States to pay in cash the amount that is represented by bank deposits. Our banking system works smoothly because not all depositors want their money at the same time. As some withdrawals are made, new deposits are also made. The withdrawals and the deposits therefore tend to balance one another.

If a bank is operated conservatively and makes loans that can be collected when they become due, each depositor is assured that he can obtain his money when he wants it. The experiences of the past prove, however, that sound banks are sometimes unable to pay when depositors become hysterical and attempt to withdraw all their money at the same time.

Deposit Insurance. In periods of normal business, people have little or no uncertainty about the safety of money deposited in banks. The possibility of loss to depositors

during periods of business recession has largely been removed through the insurance of bank deposits. This insurance is administered by the Federal Deposit Insurance
Corporation, which all national banks are compelled to join
and other banks may join voluntarily. Each individual account in a bank having this insurance is insured up to ten
thousand dollars.

A sign announcing that a bank's deposits are insured.

The Bank's Income. If a bank could not lend money, it
could not earn a satisfactory income. With the exception of
the amount of cash originally invested in the bank by the
stockholders, the bank has practically no money to lend
except what is deposited by individuals, business concerns,
and other institutions. When a depositor takes his money
to a bank, he expects a safe place of deposit and either a
service in checking or an income from the deposit. He
certainly expects to get his money when he wants it. The
problem of the bank is, therefore, to utilize its capital and
all the deposits either by lending to others or by investing
in securities and other assets that will produce an income.
Laws regulate the way the money may be used. A bank
must maintain a sufficient reserve of cash to pay out deposits when they are demanded.

Regulations on Loans. State and Federal laws limit
banks, according to their classification, in the types of loans
that they can make. State banks are governed by the laws

of their respective states. Members of the Federal Reserve
System are governed by the following restrictions:

(a) The Federal Reserve Board has power to fix the percentage of loans that the banks in any Federal reserve district can make with bonds and stocks as
collateral. In most cases a member of the Federal
Reserve System may not lend to any person an
amount in excess of 10 per cent of its capital and
surplus.

(b) Member banks may make loans secured by staple
agricultural products, goods, wares, or merchandise.

(c) Loans secured by direct obligations of the United
States, such as Government notes or bonds, may be
made to individuals, partnerships, or corporations.

(d) No member bank is permitted to lend money to an
affiliated organization or to individuals in an affiliated
organization. It may not accept securities of an affiliated organization as collateral for a loan if the loan
exceeds 10 per cent of the capital and surplus of the
affiliated organization.

(e) Loans can be made on improved real estate, including improved farm land. Such a loan must not, however, exceed 50 per cent of the actual value of the
real estate offered for security. Only a limited
amount of the funds of a member bank may be used
for loans on real estate.

TEXTBOOK QUESTIONS

1. How are banks classified according to their function?
2. What is the essential difference between a commercial bank
and a savings bank?
3. Are there any commercial banks that accept savings deposits?
4. Is there any difference between a trust company and an investment bank?
5. What are some functions performed by a trust company or
the trust department of a bank?
6. How are banks classified according to their authorization and
organization?
7. What is the difference between a state bank and a national
bank?
8. What is the supreme governing body of the Federal Reserve
System?

9. What are the three most important functions of the Federal reserve banks?
10. What notes are issued by Federal reserve banks and circulated as currency?
11. How can a member of the Federal Reserve System obtain cash or new currency?
12. How do member banks build up reserves in the Federal reserve bank?
13. Explain one way in which the Federal Reserve System may attempt to restrict business expansion.
14. Why are clearinghouses necessary?
15. Is there enough cash in the United States to pay in cash the amount represented by bank deposits?
16. Why is it possible for banks to lend more money than they have cash on hand?
17. What is the main source from which a bank obtains its income?
18. Name some ways in which the Federal Reserve System regulates the loans made by member banks.

DISCUSSION QUESTIONS

1. A member bank of the Federal Reserve System has notes that it has accepted from borrowers. The bank needs cash. What can it do?
2. Explain why you think it would not be possible to operate modern business under our present monetary system without the aid of banks as agents for pooling money and expanding credit.
3. Explain how loans made to business firms can serve as the basis for increasing the supply of currency.
4. Explain what you consider to be the main advantage of the centralized reserves of the Federal reserve banks.
5. The raising of the rediscount rate of the Federal Reserve Board is supposed to curtail business expansion. Can you think of any cases in which this would not be very effective? Explain your answer.
6. Theoretically the Federal Reserve System is in a position to encourage business expansion when it is needed by reducing the rediscount rate. Can you explain any situation when you think this would not be effective?
7. What would happen if every depositor in a bank wanted his money immediately and, when he demanded it, the bank attempted to furnish it?

8. Do you believe that deposit insurance justifies "shutting your eyes" in choosing a bank?
9. Can you see any reason for restricting loans of member banks to fifty per cent of the value of improved real estate?

PROBLEMS

1. Assume that money is scarce and a bank needs to rediscount some loans in order to get additional currency. It made a $1,000 loan at the rate of 3 per cent for 60 days. (a) What interest is collected by the bank in advance? (b) The bank rediscounts this note immediately with the Federal reserve bank at a rediscount rate of 1 per cent. How much currency or reserve credit would the bank receive? (c) How much profit would the bank make on the transaction?

2. From newspaper reports or banks learn the present rates that are being charged on commercial loans and the present rediscount rate of the Federal reserve banks. On the basis of the average existing rate on commercial loans and the present rediscount rate, compute the amount of profit that a bank can make by lending money and rediscounting the note, assuming that there are no miscellaneous service charges.

COMMUNITY PROBLEMS AND PROJECTS

1. One means of determining the banking activities of any community is through bank clearances, which means the monetary volume of checks cleared through the local clearing-house. From the financial page of your newspaper or any other source obtain information in regard to bank clearings for a recent month. Compare these with clearings for the same month in the year previous or in some other year, and give your conclusions as to the local business activity.

2. Make a list of the banks in your town, city, or county. Classify them according to the discussion in this chapter. If you find any special types of banks not discussed in this chapter, list them separately and describe them.

Chapter 19

PART VI ———————————————————————————

How to Use Your Bank

Purpose of the Chapter. Banks are business institutions dealing in financial transactions. They accept deposits, lend money, and provide additional services that are important to other businesses and to our economic system. You are certain to have some dealings with a bank because a bank is indispensable. The purpose of this chapter, therefore, is to explain the most important functions of the bank and to show you how to use a bank effectively.

Operating a Checking Account. Although there is some slight variation in the operation of checking accounts in different communities, the procedure is essentially the same everywhere. The instruments ordinarily used in maintaining a checking account are deposit slips, the bankbook, and the checkbook. The *deposit slip* should be made out by the depositor as evidence of a deposit. The deposit is then recorded in the depositor's *bankbook* by a clerk in the bank. Some people make a *duplicate deposit ticket*, which when signed by the bank clerk is kept as a record of the deposit, instead of using a bankbook.

A deposit slip is shown in the illustration. In the listing of the checks, the name of the bank (First National Bank)

MERCHANTS NATIONAL BANK

IN RECEIVING ITEMS FOR DEPOSIT OR COLLECTION, THIS BANK ACTS ONLY AS DEPOSITOR'S COLLECTING AGENT AND ASSUMES NO RESPONSIBILITY BEYOND THE EXERCISE OF DUE CARE. ALL ITEMS ARE CREDITED SUBJECT TO FINAL PAYMENT IN CASH OR SOLVENT CREDITS, WHICH SHALL HAVE COME INTO ITS POSSESSION. THIS BANK WILL NOT BE LIABLE FOR DEFAULT OR NEGLIGENCE OF ITS DULY SELECTED CORRESPONDENTS NOR FOR LOSSES IN TRANSIT, AND EACH CORRESPONDENT SO SELECTED SHALL NOT BE LIABLE EXCEPT FOR ITS OWN NEGLIGENCE. THIS BANK OR ITS CORRESPONDENTS MAY SEND ITEMS DIRECTLY OR INDIRECTLY, TO ANY BANK INCLUDING THE PAYOR, AND ACCEPT ITS DRAFT OR CREDIT AS CONDITIONAL PAYMENT IN LIEU OF CASH; IT MAY CHARGE BACK ANY ITEM, INCLUDING ITEMS DRAWN ON THIS BANK, AT ANY TIME BEFORE FINAL PAYMENT, WHETHER RETURNED OR NOT. IN DELIVERING ITEMS TO THIS BANK FOR DEPOSIT OR COLLECTION, THE DEPOSITOR AGREES TO THE FOREGOING CONDITIONS.
DEPOSITOR'S NAME

L. M. Sanderson

Cincinnati, O., *July 6* 19___

LIST CINCINNATI CHECKS BY NAME OF BANK AND FOREIGN CHECKS BY NAME OF CITY.

CURRENCY	23	—
SILVER	2	42
CHECKS *First Natl Bank*	160	—
Cheviot, Ohio	140	—
	325	42

A deposit slip.

is given because the bank is located in the city where the deposit is being made. When depositing a check drawn on a bank in another city, the name of the city and state (Cheviot, Ohio) is given.

Another method may be used to list checks on a deposit slip. Each bank has a number, which is referred to as an *ABA transit number* because the numbering system was established by the American Bankers' Association. An example of a transit number is 13-94 at the right of the bank's name in the illustration of a check on this page. The number below the line (420) is the sorting number used by the clearinghouse or bank. Some banks prefer to use the ABA numbers in listing checks, but others prefer giving the name of the bank or the city.

The depositor should record the deposit on a stub of his checkbook. Disbursements by check should also be recorded on the checkbook stubs. The illustration below is an example of an ordinary check. A *check* is a written order in

No._142_   Cincinnati_ July 7 _   19 _

Merchants National Bank $\frac{13\text{-}94}{420}$

PAY TO THE ORDER OF___ D. M. Mason ——————— $ 189 $\frac{65}{}$

One hundred eighty-nine and $\frac{65}{100}$ ——— DOLLARS

L. M. Sanderson

A check.

which one person directs a bank to pay to another person a certain amount of money. If a counter check is used to withdraw cash from the account, this withdrawal should likewise be recorded on a check stub. A *counter check* is a check without a stub that is available on the counter of any bank to be used at the convenience of a customer who may have forgotten his checkbook. It should be used in the same way that a person might borrow a blank check from a friend in order to write a check. He should make a note of the check and as quickly as possible record it on a stub

Keep your checkbook balance up to date.

Ewing Galloway

in his checkbook. Many people simply tear out and destroy a blank check in the checkbook and use the stub for recording a counter check. Checkbook stubs should be kept up to date so that the correct balance will be shown.

Using a bank for deposits is advantageous not only to the bank and its borrowers but also to the depositor. Although a checking account usually does not earn interest, the facilities provided by it are valuable. The following are some of the advantages:

No. *142*		
July 7 19__		
To *D. M. Mason*		
For *Painting house*		
	DOLLARS	CENTS
BALANCE BRO'T FOR'D	487	18
AMOUNT DEPOSITED	325	42
TOTAL	812	60
AMOUNT THIS CHECK	189	65
BALANCE CAR'D FOR'D	622	95

A checkbook stub.

(a) The money is in a safe place and can be transferred conveniently and safely simply by writing checks.

(b) The check stubs provide a convenient record of deposits, expenditures, and bank balances.

345

(c) The canceled bank check is valuable as a receipt and is evidence of the date, the manner, and the amount of payment.

(d) A checking account helps to enhance one's personal and business standing.

STATEMENT OF YOUR ACCOUNT WITH

MERCHANTS NATIONAL BANK
CLEVELAND, OHIO
REPORT PROMPTLY ANY
CHANGE IN YOUR ADDRESS
97-101

Walter A. Kline
236 Mt. Vernon Avenue
Cleveland 9, Ohio

CHECKS			DEPOSITS	THE LAST AMOUNT IN THIS COLUMN IS YOUR BALANCE	
			BALANCE FORWARD	Apr. 4	300.00
125.00	7.16			6	167.84
21.65	3.75	14.12		9	128.32
			184.75	12	313.07
46.20	18.40			13	248.47
			100.00	19	348.47
75.00	33.65		99.95	23	339.77
66.80	5.30			27	267.67
8.85	33.19	.21		30	225.42

PLEASE EXAMINE AT ONCE AND REPORT ANY DISCREPAN-
CIES OR ERRORS TO OUR AUDITOR WITHIN TEN DAYS.

VOUCHERS RETURNED 14
SHEET NUMBER

A bank statement.

Reconciliation of the Bank Statement. The above illustration shows a bank statement. The accuracy of this bank statement can be proved by the following procedure:

(a) Verify the checks recorded on the bank statement by comparing them with the canceled checks accompanying the statement.

(b) Verify all deposits by checking those listed on the bank statement with those recorded in the bankbook and on the check stubs.

(c) Determine from the checkbook stubs which checks were outstanding on the date of the bank statement.

(d) Subtract from the cash balance shown on the bank statement the total of the checks outstanding, and add the amount of any deposits made but not shown on the bank statement. This should give the adjusted bank balance.

(e) Subtract from the checkbook balance any charges, such as a service charge, made by the bank and not recorded on the check stubs. Add the amount of any deposits made but not recorded on the check stubs. The balance is the adjusted checkbook balance, and it should be equal to the adjusted bank balance.

In the case of (d), there usually is a lapse of a few days between the date of issuing a bank statement and the date of making a reconciliation. Therefore, the bank statement for the month of April will not show a deposit made on May 1, but after the reconcilation is made on May 10, the deposit of May 1 must be taken into consideration.

The bank statement shown on page 346 was reconciled as follows:

(1) The checks and deposits were verified. The outstanding checks were found to be for $10, $65.60, and $19.40, a total of $95.

(2) The checkbook balance was found to be $30.63, but a service charge of 21 cents had been made and a deposit of $100 had been made but not recorded on the check stubs.

(3) The reconciliation was then recorded in the manner shown below.

Cash balance indicated by the bank statement ...$225.42	Checkbook balance ......$ 30.63	
	Deduct service charge ... .21	
	$ 30.42	
	Add deposit made but not recorded in the checkbook 100.00	
Deduct total of checks still outstanding 95.00		
Adjusted bank balance ..$130.42	Adjusted checkbook balance $130.42	

The purpose of a reconciliation is to see whether the checkbook balance is correct on the date on which the reconciliation is made and to detect errors in the bank statement. If reconciliations are not made regularly, errors may be carried along for a long time and may then be hard to locate.

The Cost of a Checking Account. In selecting a bank for personal or family use, it is desirable to choose a bank that encourages personal checking accounts. Some large commercial banks are not especially interested in small accounts. The services of such banks are therefore not particularly suitable for individuals, and the cost of operating a checking account in such a bank may be rather high.

Most banks make a service charge on checking accounts, but there is no uniformity in the policy. Generally, however, one is allowed to write a certain number of checks without charge if a minimum balance is kept. For example, one might be allowed to write five checks without charge if the minimum balance is $200, but will be charged 5 cents for each check over five and on all checks if the average balance is less than $200. Other more complicated service charge plans are also used.

To minimize the cost of operating a checking account, one may use cash to pay bills that can be conveniently paid in this manner and write checks for those that must be paid by mail or for which a canceled check may be desired as a receipt.

Some banks provide a checking service without an account. One can go to the bank and buy a certain number of checks. The total amount of the checks plus a service charge is paid to the bank. These checks may then be used for payments in the same way that regular checks are ordinarily used.

One may wonder why it is necessary for a bank to make a service charge on checks. It is true that a bank has the privilege of using the depositor's money to lend to others at a profit; but if an account is small and many checks are written against it, the bank will lose money in handling the account. The bank provides many services, including a safe place to deposit funds, the bookkeeping records of the account, collecting for and paying checks, and rendering monthly statements. Unless a checking account balance is large enough, a bank cannot earn enough money on the deposits to pay for all the expenses involved.

Your Obligations as a Depositor

1. Keep an accurate record of each check on the check stub.
2. Keep a sufficient balance in your account; do not overdraw. (To overdraw an account is a criminal offense in most states.)
3. Reconcile your checkbook and bankbook balances once a month.
4. Keep all canceled checks for at least a year; keep important canceled checks indefinitely.

Joint Accounts. Often two persons will want to use the same bank checking account or savings account. Such an account, which is called a *joint* or *survivorship account,* is usually opened by a man and his wife. Each must fill out a signature card, and either person has authority to withdraw funds during the life of both parties. Upon the death of either party, the survivor has full right to the funds after furnishing the bank with proof that all state tax claims have been paid. In most states when one of the parties operating a joint account dies, the bank is forbidden by law to honor any further checks until any claims by the state are settled.

Stopping Payment on a Check. When a check is lost or stolen, the bank should be notified as soon as the loss is discovered. Notice may be given orally or in writing; but if it is given orally, it should also be followed by a written notice. Banks usually have a special form that may be used for this purpose. However, any written notice is satisfactory if you give the date of the check, the number, the amount, and the name of the payee (the person to whom the check was made payable).

You may also have occasion to stop payment on a check for other reasons. For example, let us suppose that you have written a check for payment to someone and have discovered that you have been cheated, or you have issued a check for merchandise that is found to be unsatisfactory. You may stop payment on the check.

Postdating Checks. The postdating of a check is legal and sometimes convenient, but the privilege should not be abused. For instance, on February 10 you might issue a check dated February 15. The check is not payable until February 15. Banks will not cash it before that date, although some banks will accept it for deposit if the difference in dates is not more than one or two days.

Postdating of checks usually arises out of two different situations. In one case, the person may not have a sufficient balance in his checking account, but he agrees to make a payment with a check dated to correspond with the time when he will deposit his monthly salary check. Another case is the making of a payment in advance of the time when the payment is due. Let us assume, for example, that one has a debt of $100 coming due on June 20, and he wishes to pay it on June 15 before going on his vacation. If he does not want the check cashed until June 20, he can postdate it.

Bank Drafts and Special Checks. Sometimes you may wish to make a payment to someone who will not accept your personal check. It could be an important payment in a distant city; it might be a deposit for the buying of a house; or it could be any one of several other situations. In such cases you may go to a bank and obtain a certified check, a bank draft, or a cashier's check, any one of which may serve your purpose.

A *certified check* is an ordinary check drawn by a depositor in the usual way but presented to the bank for certification by the drawer or by some holder. The bank stamps or writes a certification on the check as indicated in the illustration. This certification guarantees that, when the check is presented, it will be paid. The check is therefore acceptable to those who might otherwise hesitate to accept the check.

No._3 7 ✔_

The Public National Bank $\frac{37\text{-}64}{1113}$

CERTIFIED
PAYABLE ONLY AS ORIGINALLY DRAWN
AND WHEN PROPERLY ENDORSED _July 8_   19___

Pay to the order of___ _a. g. Bamburg + Co._ $ _43 ⁴⁰⁄₁₀₀_

Forty - three and ⁴⁰⁄₁₀₀

THE PUBLIC NATIONAL BANK
FT. WORTH, TEXAS   ——DOLLARS

R. d. Brown ASS'T CASHIER
DO NOT DESTROY _Anderson_

A certified check.

A *bank draft* is a check of a bank upon funds deposited
to its credit with some other bank. A bank draft is a convenient means of transferring money when the individual
who is making payment is not known in the part of the
country to which the money is to be sent. He may obtain
the draft by purchasing it from a bank. People will usually accept a bank draft provided the bank that has drawn
it is known. A certified check has practically the same
status as a bank draft, provided the bank is known and has
a good reputation.

City Bank & Trust Company $\frac{35\text{-}91}{1131}$

Houston, Texas,____ JULY 14 ____19 -- ___ No.___ 192 ____

PAY TO THE
ORDER OF   DONALDSON BROS. . . . .$1220.59____

REGISTERED $1220 AND 59 CTS
RA-2513   ___ Dollars

To CORN EXCHANGE NATIONAL BANK
$\frac{2\text{-}437}{710}$ CHICAGO, ILLINOIS   _Walter A. Hammond_
                                                        CASHIER

A bank draft.

One may buy a cashier's check in somewhat the same
way as a person buys a bank draft. The *cashier's check* is
a check on the bank that issues it, payable to the person
designated by the purchaser of the check.

Savings Account. Savings accounts may be maintained
in what are commonly known as savings banks or in the
savings departments of other banks. The bankbook is the

A cashier's check.

most important instrument in operating a savings account. In it are recorded all deposits and all withdrawals. Deposit slips are used as a record of deposits, and receipts as a record of withdrawals; but the bankbook must be presented each time money is deposited or withdrawn. Checks cannot be written on savings deposits, and many banks require advance notice of the withdrawal of savings.

A withdrawal slip for a savings account.

Savings accounts in banks usually pay interest. Saving by depositing money in a bank is a conservative means of investing, but it is usually a safe means as compared with investments in many types of securities. There is some difference in the yield of interest, depending upon the number of times a year the interest is calculated. Obviously, the income from a savings account is greater when interest is compounded semiannually than when it is computed annually at the same rate.

Trust Functions of Banks. The trust functions of banks have proved especially useful for people who wish to preserve their wealth for the benefit of dependents. Many wills include clauses that appoint certain trust companies or trust departments of banks to administer the estates left to wives and children. The trust officer, in a sense, becomes the business manager of the estate that is left in his care; but the trust officer does not guarantee a fixed rate of income from the estate.

Because of the close relation between wills and trusts, it is appropriate to consider wills. Some people believe that, if the necessity arises, they will make a will. They keep putting off the task, however, until it is too late. Laws in most states definitely prescribe the way in which property will be divided if there is no will.

As a matter of policy, a will should not be "homemade." It should be written with the aid of a competent lawyer and according to the legal requirements. In some states the law requires two witnesses to the signature of a will. If a will is made and property is left in trust, the trust agreement should be made at the time the will is drawn.

If the property that is willed to a beneficiary is left in trust, the person who administers the trust is the trustee. The powers and the duties of the trustee depend upon the wording of the agreement, although every trust agreement binds the trustee to look after the interests of the beneficiary. The trustee may be given great or little authority in investing and reinvesting the property that is entrusted to him.

Safe-Deposit Boxes. Safe-deposit boxes in the vaults of banks are provided on a rental basis. Such a box provides protection against burglary and fire, and should be used for valuables that are not safe in the home or in the business office.

A bank cannot open a private safe-deposit box except upon the order of a court. In most states, if a safe-deposit box is registered in the names of a man and his wife, the bank is legally required to seal the box upon notice of the death of either person. The box may not then be opened except on the order of a court. It is therefore frequently advisable to have the safe-deposit box registered in the name of the wife alone. Then, in case of the death of the husband, the widow has access to the box. Under this arrangement the husband may also have regular access to the box, authority being granted to him by his wife. When the wife, in such cases, gives written authority to the bank to permit her husband to have access to a safe-deposit box, the husband is referred to as a *deputy*. In case the wife dies without having transferred the title to the husband, the latter cannot gain access to the box except upon the order of a court. This procedure is recommended by most banks because, if the safe-deposit box were in the name of the husband, the widow, who often is not versed in financial affairs, would not have access to the box on the death of her husband. Under such an arrangement, if the wife dies first, it is assumed that the man, who is usually more versatile in business affairs, would not be greatly inconvenienced until the estate is settled in court.

Financial and Tax Advice. Most bankers have the problem of advising those who apply for credit. This advice must be given to individuals as well as to business owners. A wise banker will not make a loan to an individual if he believes that the loan cannot be repaid or that to repay the loan would place an undesirable hardship upon the borrower. Regardless of the character of the borrower or the security that would be pledged to the bank, the making of a loan in such a case might result in financial disaster.

Some banks maintain tax departments with a staff of lawyers and accountants who give advice on tax problems to the customers of the bank. These tax specialists, in some cases, will prepare income tax returns or assist in their preparation.

Other Bank Services. Miscellaneous services, such as those pertaining to travel, real estate, and foreign trade, are provided by banks in order to encourage business activity as well as to produce additional income for themselves.

Certain banks operate travel departments and collect a commission on the charges for steamer passage and on other

Your banker can give you advice and many kinds of help.

costs in connection with tours of foreign countries. They usually provide plans and complete information in connection with tours of various types. They may also sell foreign exchange and various credit instruments that can be used in foreign countries.

Real-estate departments are sometimes operated by banks in connection with trust departments. These departments function also as service departments for depositors by maintaining or disposing of property that has been taken as security on loans.

A bank will act as custodian of bonds and other securities that need attention from time to time. In return for a moderate fee, it will take charge of stocks, bonds, mortgages, and other negotiable papers and will collect the dividends, the interest, and the principal when they become due. The bank, for example, will clip the coupons on bonds, collect the interest represented by the coupons, and credit it to the account of the client. The bank will also assume responsibility for handling interest payments and principal

355

payments on the amounts borrowed by a client. In other words, the bank will act as an agent for the client and will take charge of his finances.

Protection of the Borrower and the Depositor. Many banks have a trained personnel to do nothing but decide upon the desirability of making loans to individuals and to business concerns. These persons analyze the assets, the liabilities, the financial condition, the business methods, and the future possibilities of the individual or the business requesting a loan. This analysis often enables the bank to be of service to the borrower by suggesting improvements in financial organization or changes in purchasing and production plans.

Obviously, the bank wants to protect its borrowers as well as its depositors. Its borrowers provide the source of its income, while its depositors provide the means of its income. Hence it is to the advantage of the bank to conduct its affairs so as to ensure the prosperity of the depositor, the borrower, and the bank.

Loans Made by Banks. A loan may be classified according to the basis on which it is made. It may be based (a) on the character of the borrower, in which case his own signature is sufficient; (b) on *security* or *collateral, in which case the borrower must turn over to the bank stocks, bonds, a mortgage on property, an insurance policy, or some other property or claim against property;* or (c) on the signature of the borrower plus the additional signature of a friend (*comaker* or *cosigner*), making both persons individually and jointly responsible.

If the conditions for a loan seem unusually favorable, the banker may not require security, but will rely upon the borrower's character and capacity to pay. Conservative commercial banks, however, usually require security in some form of property. This property can be taken over and sold by the bank to protect itself in case the borrower cannot pay the loan when it is due. In a sense, a comaker's signature is a form of security. If a person signs a note in order to aid a friend to borrow money, he is held responsible for the payment of the note in case the borrower is unable to pay.

Warehouse receipts and mortgages on real property are forms of securities. For instance, a farmer who wishes to borrow from a bank may have placed one thousand bushels of wheat in a grain elevator. If he has receipts for this wheat, he may turn these receipts over to a bank, thus transferring to the bank the right of ownership of the wheat in case he does not pay his loan when it becomes due. Likewise, a person may borrow money on real estate and grant a mortgage that gives the lender the right to take possession of the real estate if the loan is not paid.

Many banks, including those that are members of the Federal Reserve System, have installed personal loan departments. A discussion of the methods and sources of obtaining all types of personal loans is covered in detail in Chapter 22.

Negotiable Instruments. The legal relations of borrowing and lending center largely around a *negotiable instrument*. A negotiable instrument is a written evidence of some contractual obligation and is ordinarily transferable from one person to another by indorsement. It is frequently referred to as *negotiable paper* or *commercial paper*.

The most common forms of negotiable instruments are (a) promissory notes and (b) checks. A *promissory note* is an unconditional written promise to pay a sum certain in money at a certain time or on demand to the bearer or the order of one who has obtained the note through legal means. The one who executes a promissory note, that is, the one who promises to pay the amount specified in the note under the terms indicated, is the *maker*. The person to whom the note is payable is known as the *payee*.

The person who writes a check is the *drawer*. The person to whom the check is payable is the *payee*. The bank on which the check is drawn is the *drawee*.

The maker of a note or the drawer of a check is unconditionally required to pay the amount specified. This obligation assumes, of course, that the transaction relating to the use of the instrument has been proper and legal. The drawer of a check is required to pay the amount of the check if the drawee (the bank) does not pay it, but there are certain limitations on this rule in many states.

The person who indorses a negotiable instrument and transfers it to someone else is known as the *indorser*. The person to whom he transfers the negotiable instrument is referred to as the *indorsee*.

Transfer of Negotiable Instruments. Much of our money consists of notes that circulate as money without indorsement. The promissory notes issued by individuals and businesses may also circulate, although they usually require an indorsement.

A person who signs a negotiable instrument as an indorser is liable under varying conditions. For instance, if he indorses a note to help a friend obtain a loan from a bank, he must pay the amount of the note to the bank or to a subsequent indorser if his friend fails to pay it when it is due. The obligation of an indorser depends upon the type of indorsement used. Four principal kinds of indorsements are used in transferring negotiable instruments. These indorsements are as follows:

(a) *Indorsement in full.* An indorsement in full is frequently referred to as a *special indorsement*. It mentions the name of the indorsee. The indorser is liable only to the indorsee or to any person who subsequently takes title to the instrument through the indorsee.

(b) *Blank indorsement.* An indorsement in blank consists in merely the name of the indorser. A subsequent holder may add any stipulations to the indorsement that are consistent with the transfer.

(c) *Qualified indorsement.* A qualified indorsement is, as its name implies, one that limits the obligation of the indorser. Assume, for instance, that a person has a check that he wishes to transfer to another. He does not wish to assume responsibility for the payment of the check if the drawer cannot or will not pay it. He may therefore use a qualified indorsement with words such as "without recourse."

Although a person may make a qualified indorsement, he is not relieved from complete responsibility for the payment of the instrument. When a person signs a qualified indorsement, he implies or warrants (1) that the instrument is genuine and the facts stated in it are as they are represented to be, (2) that he has a good title to the instrument, (3) that all persons who have previously indorsed the instrument have been legally capable of making the indorsements, and (4) that he is not aware of any circumstances that impair the validity of the instrument.

Indorsement in Full

Indorsement in Blank

Qualified Indorsement

Restrictive Indorsement

Forms of indorsement.

(d) *Restrictive indorsement.* The restrictive indorsement is very common. It is one which specifies that the person to whom it is indorsed (the indorsee) may dispose of the instrument only in the manner indicated by the indorser. Checks, for instance, are frequently indorsed restrictively and mailed to a bank for deposit.

TEXTBOOK QUESTIONS

1. In filling out a deposit slip, indicate the two different ways of identifying a check drawn on a local bank that is being deposited.
2. What is the difference between a regular check and a counter check?
3. Name four advantages of a checking account.
4. Why is it that the checkbook stubs do not always show all the changes against the bank account that are shown on a bank statement?
5. Why will a monthly bank statement not always show all the money that has been deposited in the account?
6. Why is it necessary for banks to establish a charge for cashing checks?
7. Why is it sometimes necessary for a bank to charge for the facilities of a checking account?
8. Is it simply a matter of bad practice or is it illegal to write checks for more than the amount of your checking account?
9. Ordinarily what happens to a joint checking account when one of the parties operating the account dies?
10. If you have issued a check and then decide for some good reason that you should not allow the person to whom it was issued to cash it, what can you do?
11. How can you issue a check today to somebody for payment of a transaction and still be sure that the person to whom you have issued the check cannot cash it until the desired date?
12. What is a certified check?
13. What is a bank draft?
14. What is a cashier's check?
15. What is the distinction between a savings account and a checking account?
16. When money is left with a bank under a trust agreement, does the bank guarantee a definite income from the trust fund?
17. Why is it not desirable for a man and his wife to have their safe-deposit box registered in both names?
18. It is often said, "Your bank is your financial advisor." Name some of the ways that a bank can help you.
19. Why is a banker justified in refusing to make a loan to a person who cannot repay the loan under some definite plan?
20. (a) What is meant by security or collateral for a loan? (b) Are loans ever made without security?
21. What are some types of security for loans?
22. What is a comaker or cosigner?
23. In the case of a negotiable instrument, who is (a) the maker, (b) the payee, (c) the drawer, and (d) the drawee?

24. Who is (a) the indorser; (b) the indorsee?
25. What legal obligation or liability is involved in an indorsement of a negotiable instrument?
26. Give an example of and explain (a) an indorsement in full, (b) a blank indorsement, and (c) a restrictive indorsement.

DISCUSSION QUESTIONS

1. What would you recommend as a policy in regard to keeping the balance of your checkbook stubs up to date with the actual bank balance?
2. Some people are inclined to take the attitude, "Banks do not make mistakes; therefore why should I bother with reconciling my bank statement with my checkbook?" How do you feel about this matter?
3. Some people, because of mistakes and carelessness in keeping the records of the balances in their checking accounts, overdraw their accounts. In many states laws have been passed for the punishment of people who overdraw their accounts. Do you believe that these laws are justified?
4. Why is it a matter of good business to keep all canceled checks for at least a year?
5. What types of canceled checks would you recommend keeping indefinitely?
6. Can you give some advantages and disadvantages of a joint checking account maintained by a husband and wife?
7. Some people follow a practice of postdating checks when they do not have money in the account but expect to deposit the money before the check is cashed. Give your opinion of this practice.
8. What are the essential differences between a certified check and a bank draft?
9. Why do you think a cashier's check would be more acceptable for payment to a stranger 200 miles away than your ordinary personal check?
10. If the interest rate on savings deposits in banks drops from 2 per cent to 1 per cent, what do you think such a decrease indicates as to the condition of banks?
11. Why are funds frequently left in trust with a bank instead of in the care of the widow or the children?
12. Would you recommend putting cash in a safe-deposit box? Why or why not? Discuss.
13. A man who is known to be successful and thoroughly honorable feels highly insulted when he applies for a loan at a bank and is asked for considerable information on his assets, debts, and income. He believes that the bank has no right to

this confidential information. What is your opinion? Discuss the situation.

14. If you indorse a note for a friend in order to help him obtain a loan from a bank, what is your obligation?

15. What kind of indorsement would you recommend if you were away from home and were mailing a check to your bank for deposit? Why?

PROBLEMS

1. On the basis of the following information prepare a reconciliation of his bank statement for Mr. H. L. Jones: (a) Cash balance indicated by the statement, $236.10. (b) Checks outstanding: No. 103, $10.20; No. 104, $14; No. 105, $23.10.

2. Assume that a service charge of 50 cents was made for the month. Show the reconciliation of the bank statement mentioned in Problem No. 1.

3. Using your own signature, write models of the four different types of indorsements that you might use on a check or a note.

COMMUNITY PROBLEMS AND PROJECTS

1. Investigate the various types of services offered by the banks in your community. Summarize these services in the form of a table, indicating what services are available in each particular institution.

2. Go to your own bank or to a bank with which you believe you would like to deal and obtain the following: (a) All forms necessary for opening a checking account. (b) A list of the regulations governing a checking account. (c) Samples of all the forms used by depositors, such as a bank statement, a bankbook, a regular check, a counter check, and a deposit slip. Make a report on the method of opening a checking account, on the regulations governing such an account, and on the activities of depositors using such an account.

3. From your local banks obtain information in regard to personal loan privileges and regulations. Write a report of your findings, covering such important topics as interest rates, types of loans made, maximum size of loans, security required, repayment plans, and other important features.

Chapter 20

How to Obtain and Use Credit

Purpose of the Chapter. Credit is extended to people who can be relied upon to pay their debts when due. It is a convenience and an honored trust. It is also a great aid to our modern business system. The purpose of this chapter is to explain how the consumer may obtain credit, the procedures, the advantages, the disadvantages, and some of the obligations and legal problems involving credit.

What Is Credit? Credit, as we ordinarily use the term, means the privilege of buying merchandise without being required to pay for it until some future date. The consumer ordinarily has available to him two types of credit in making a retail purchase. One is short-term credit and the other is long-term credit.

Purchasing on account is the simplest type of *short-term consumer credit*. When the customer buys merchandise, the retailer charges it to his account. The retailer usually submits a monthly statement to his customer. In most communities the practice is to require the customer to pay his account by the tenth of the month following that in which the purchases were made. Some stores, particularily food stores that sell on credit, expect the customer to pay his account weekly.

Retail credit in rural communities is often handled differently. Crops are harvested once a year or only a few times a year. In the meantime, purchases are often made on account with the understanding that the accounts will be paid when the crops are harvested.

Long-term consumer credit is a term usually applied to special arrangements under which credit is extended beyond the usual period allowed on an open account. By special agreement a thirty-day account may sometimes be extended to ninety days or longer, but more often long-term credit takes the form of an installment contract. Often an extra charge is added when purchases are made on the installment plan or any other form of long-term credit.

The Need for Credit. Most of our business transactions are conducted on a credit basis rather than on a cash basis. Can you imagine a large corporation buying several carloads of raw materials and taking the cash along to pay for the order? Can you imagine a department store in St. Louis sending a buyer to New York with cash in his pockets to pay for the merchandise that he buys? Operating on a cash basis would be a very difficult procedure. Among consumers, credit is also a convenience. It enables people to go shopping without the risks of carrying large amounts of cash in their purses.

Consumers also use credit by necessity. Sometimes when consumers buy on credit, they do not have the cash available, but they expect to have it available when the payment becomes due. This kind of credit should never be accepted unless there is assurance that the amount can be paid when it becomes due.

Advantages of Charge Accounts. Some people openly boast, "We pay cash for everything." The ability to pay cash is commendable and desirable, but no one can predict when and under what circumstances he may need credit. Obtaining credit is not a reflection upon one's character or capacity to pay. Securing credit under proper circumstances is a good test of one's character. It is important to everyone who expects to attain prominence in business or to build up the standing of himself or his family in the community. A man with poor credit usually loses his self-respect. He almost invariably develops a feeling that he does not have a fair chance in life.

In addition to the advantage of buying merchandise without having to pay for it until a specified future time, the following are some of the advantages of using credit instead of paying cash:

   (a) The use of credit prevents loss. A person does not need to carry money with him when he goes shopping. He, therefore, is not so liable to lose money or to have it stolen. There is also less liability of mistakes in making change.

(b) Record keeping is facilitated by the use of credit. Statements rendered serve as a basis for maintaining records and keeping a budget. This method is simpler than attempting to keep daily and weekly records through cash purchases.

(c) The use of a charge account usually results in payments by check. The checkbook stubs can be used as a basis for entries required in keeping accounts and a budget.

(d) Clerks and store-keepers soon learn to know the name of a charge customer because the name must be recorded in connection with a charge sale. Therefore, a good charge customer will frequently get better consideration and better service than the person who buys only for cash.

(e) Charge accounts facilitate the ordering of merchandise by telephone.

(f) If credit is established when it is not needed, it will be available when it is needed.

Disadvantage of Credit. The only disadvantage of credit is for the person who has a tendency to spend money recklessly without regard as to whether he has enough income to pay his debts. Buying on credit will cause some people to purchase more than is actually needed just because they can get it. A few people have a feeling that they should buy on credit as much as anybody will sell them. A person with that point of view will soon destroy his credit.

Basis for Establishing Credit. Credit does not merely happen. It comes as the result of slow growth. It must be nurtured, fostered, strengthened, and improved. It is an asset of tremendous value to those who develop it over a long period of years. It can be destroyed easily; it is sensitive to abuse; and it usually continues only as long as it is justified. Credit is extended only to persons who deserve it and who have wisdom to protect it. It represents the willingness of others to accept a person's promise to pay under stipulated conditions.

Ewing Galloway

In arranging for credit, one is expected to give information about himself.

A commonly recognized formula for determining the credit of a person or a business consists of the "three C's"—character, capacity, and capital.

Character is the first consideration. J. P. Morgan, the famous banker, is reputed to have said that he would lend more on an individual's character than on his capital resources. Wealth alone cannot determine one's credit. Because of the importance of character, one's reputation must be guarded carefully.

Capacity is merely another term for earning power. It represents one's ability to earn and to pay obligations when they become due. An individual may have an honorable character and perfectly good intentions of paying an obligation; but unless he has the ability or capacity to pay, he cannot pay satisfactorily. It is often more difficult to judge character than it is to judge capacity. Capacity, or earning

366

power, can be measured reasonably accurately, but character is an intangible quality.

The third measuring standard, *capital*, applies only to people who have property. The amount of credit that individuals are entitled to receive varies greatly. A person with a temporary lack of earning power may be entitled to receive credit, provided he has good capital resources and a good character. Capacity and capital without character will, however, usually disqualify any credit applicant. The personal aspect of credit is extremely important.

How to Establish Your Credit. Every responsible family should establish its credit regardless of whether it is used extensively or not. By establishing retail credit you will take your first step in establishing bank credit because if you ever apply for a bank loan, your retail credit will be investigated.

To establish credit the usual procedure is to go to your favorite store and discuss the matter frankly with the credit manager or the owner. Every person who attempts to obtain credit must realize that the one who is to grant it must have some information that will serve as a basis

---

LEDGER RECORD	MEMBER OF RETAILERS CREDIT ASSOCIATION	DATE
ACCT. No. LIMIT	Application for Account	NOTIFIED

SPELL CORRECTLY. SURNAME FIRST, GIVEN NAME IN FULL. STATE IF SINGLE OR WIDOW

NAME OF HUSBAND Smith, Robert Allen		NAME OF WIFE Mary Ann
RESIDENCE ADDRESS 3948 Mission Street, San Francisco, California		HOW LONG 6 years PHONE None
FORMER ADDRESS 237 Holliston Street, Pasadena, California		
HUSBAND'S OCCUPATION Salesman Fuller Brush Co.	WIFE'S OCCUPATION None	
POSITION FIRM	BUSINESS ADDRESS	POSITION FIRM
BUSINESS ADDRESS 1512 Van Ness Avenue		
HOW LONG PRESENT EMPLOY 5 years HOW LONG IN CITY 6 years	HOME { ☒ OWN / ☐ RENT	OTHER PROPERTY
	COM. ☐ SAVGS. ☐	BANK SIGNATURE
BANK Merchants National Bank		OR NAME
BRANCH		
COMMERCIAL REFERENCES F. C. Nash & Co. Dept. Store, Pasadena, Calif.	COMMERCIAL REFERENCES	
"	"	
"	"	
PERSONAL REFERENCE Mr. F. L. Roth, Manager, Fuller Brush	NEAREST RELATIVE	
AUTHORIZED BUYERS Mary Ann Smith	ADDRESS	
SEND STATEMENTS TO { ☒ RESIDENCE / ☐ BUSINESS	TOTAL AMOUNT CREDIT REQUESTED $150.00 TERMS 30 days	SUBSCRIBER'S CODE No.

FOR THE PURPOSE OF HAVING CREDIT EXTENDED ME BY I CERTIFY TO THE ABOVE STATEMENTS AND AGREE TO PAY MY BILLS IN FULL IN SAN FRANCISCO DURING MONTH FOLLOWING PURCHASE.   *The Emporium*   SIGNATURE   *Robert Allen Smith*

APPLICATION TAKEN BY RMK

REMARKS

An application for credit.

for extending credit. Because the latter is contemplating giving merchandise in return for a promise to pay, he has a right to obtain the information that he needs to determine the applicant's character, capacity, and capital. This information is for credit purposes only and will be kept confidential.

Applying for credit is no disgrace. The applicant should approach the merchant with an open mind and with a willingness to give the information that is desired. Most merchants are pleased to have an opportunity to discuss credit relations and to open accounts if credit is justified.

The illustration on page 367 shows a typical application for credit for customers of a department store. In some cases the forms are more complicated, but in general they require the same types of information.

Protect Your Credit. Some people are too willing to buy on credit just because credit is available. Merchants sometimes make credit "too cheap." In other words, they are willing to grant credit even though the payment of the obligation is doubtful. The wisdom of buying an automobile on credit is doubtful when the payment of the obligation would mean the sacrificing of expenditures for food, clothing, and other necessities. The purchase on credit of an asset such as an automobile is, however, desirable if it will cause the family to avoid other wasteful expenditures. On the other hand, the dealer who encourages someone to accept credit in making a purchase but who does not consider the person's ability to pay is not fair to the purchaser. The user of credit should beware of the person who too willingly gives credit.

Many buyers are not good managers of their own incomes. They will accept just as much credit as will be extended to them. They do not look ahead and budget their incomes and expenditures. The wise credit manager will calmly and clearly give a prospective buyer reasons why he advises cautiousness and will give advice to his customers on the obligations that they should assume. The person who accepts credit should clearly understand his obligations.

Regardless of the credit policies of the store, it is the responsibility of the customer to study his own needs and his prospects of paying for what he wishes to buy. He should limit his use of credit according to his ability to pay. People commonly assume that they are going to have more money in the future than they have at present or have had in the past; therefore, unless they buy according to their budget plans, they may buy too recklessly. Many families are constantly harassed by old bills.

Good credit is something that money alone cannot buy because good credit involves character as well as the ability to pay. Even wealthy persons often do not have a good credit rating because of their abuse of the credit privilege. Your credit in your community will soon become well known; so guard it carefully.

Credit Rating Agencies. In general there are two types of credit agencies: (a) agencies that provide credit information with regard to businessmen and companies, and (b) agencies that provide credit information with regard to individual purchasers.

Banks sometimes give confidential credit information on individuals and businesses. It is therefore important for a person or a business to maintain satisfactory relations with a bank if a good credit rating is desired. Information can be obtained from the local Better Business Bureau as to whether there have been any complaints on the credit of a particular person or business.

Private credit agencies make a profit by collecting information and publishing confidential reports for the benefit of their subscribers, who are usually retailers. Each subscriber contributes to these reports by furnishing information and periodic ratings. Additional information is gathered from local newspapers, notices of change in address, death notices, and court records. Such information is valuable to the retailer in protecting himself from loss on accounts. If one of his customers moves, he will want to know of the change in address. If a customer dies, he will want to be sure that his claim is presented. If someone is taking

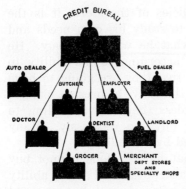

court action against one of his customers, he will want to protect his own claim.

The National Retail Credit Association is composed of local associations in various cities. These associations are organized to co-operate in furnishing credit information. Credit reports can be submitted promptly to any subscriber.

The twelve hundred credit bureaus of the Associated Credit Bureaus of America, an affiliate of the National Retail Credit Association, maintain credit records on sixty million persons. These records are kept up to date through the co-operation of local bureaus, which receive reports on delinquent accounts from local merchants. The information is quickly available to any member of a local bureau.

This huge network of credit-reporting agencies is beneficial not only to the merchant but also to the individual who seeks credit. Anyone who is honest and who desires to maintain proper credit should be perfectly willing to have a report submitted on him. With this system of reporting credit information, it is difficult for any person to establish a bad credit reputation without the information being made available to other merchants who may want to extend credit.

This nation-wide credit reporting system is an advantage to you if you have safeguarded your credit. You can move from one community to another, and your credit record will follow you or it can be checked upon very easily. However, a bad credit reputation also will follow you wherever you go.

There is another important source of information with regard to the credit of commercial houses and manufacturers. This agency is Dun and Bradstreet, Incorporated. A book of credit ratings is published regularly by this agency and sold as a service to subscribers. The service covers the entire United States. In addition, a subscriber can obtain a special report on any businessman or professional man in any part of the country. The reliability of this agency has been established through many years of effective service to all types of businessmen.

Cost of Credit to the Seller. Merchants who sell on open account may be classified as follows: (a) those who have uniform prices for credit and for cash sales; (b) those who charge more for credit than for cash sales.

The extending of credit adds extra costs to every sale. The principal extra costs result from (a) the clerical work necessary for recording credit sales and collecting accounts, (b) interest on the money that is invested in order to extend credit, (c) losses due to bad debts, and (d) the greater tendency of credit customers to return goods for exchange.

In stores that are not careful in their granting of credit, the losses from failure to collect debts are likely to be high. One may well expect to find inflated prices in stores that recklessly advertise generous credit terms to everyone. Stores that extend credit wisely, however, have practically no losses from bad debts. We need not assume, therefore, that a merchant who sells on credit must necessarily sell at higher prices than a merchant who sells for cash. If selling on credit increases sales, the total overhead cost of each sale may actually be decreased. On the other hand, stores that regularly grant credit often also supply delivery services and other conveniences. All of these services combined may cause the store to sell at higher prices than a cash-and-carry store.

Cost of Credit to the Individual. Any cost of credit is passed on either to the individual consumer on the basis of each sale, or to all buyers through generally higher prices.

Sometimes discounts are allowed to individuals in ordinary credit transactions. Common terms in such a case are "2% ten days, net thirty days." These terms mean that, if the purchaser pays the amount within ten days, he may deduct a discount of 2 per cent from the amount of the bill; but if he does not desire to take advantage of the 2 per cent discount, he may pay the net amount at the end of thirty days. The person who sells on this basis is willing to forego 2 per cent of the sale value in order to obtain his money promptly. If the purchaser chooses not to take the 2 per cent discount, he is paying 2 per cent for the use of the money for twenty days. In other words, if he buys on these terms goods amounting to $100, he may take a discount of $2 at the end of ten days and therefore pay only $98. Suppose, however, that he has enough money to pay the bill but believes that he can use the money better in some other way. He therefore prefers to wait until the end of thirty days before paying the bill. By doing so, he pays $2 for using $98 for twenty days. If interest is figured on the basis of 360 days, he is paying interest at the rate of 36.72 per cent a year to use this money.

Responsibility for Debts. A young married woman opened charge accounts in two stores. Her purchases amounted to one hundred and fifty dollars. The husband became very indignant and refused to pay the debt. The stores sued for collection and won the suits. In most states the wife has implied authority to pledge her husband's credit for the necessaries of a household. Necessaries may include domestic service, medical attention, supplies, and clothing. Under some circumstances jewelry and furniture may also be included.

Unless a husband has given legal written notice that he will not assume responsibility for his wife's debts, he must pay the debts that she incurs. In the absence of specific instructions or of the publication of a legal notice, a merchant therefore has a legal right to sell on account to a wife and to expect payment from the husband.

Parents are not ordinarily responsible for debts that their children have incurred, but they may be responsible if they have given their children permission to make purchases. For instance, if it has been customary for a child to use a charge account of the parents, the parents are responsible for the debts.

As mentioned in Chapter 5, minors are not always responsible for their contracts or agreements. A minor is responsible, however, for any debts that he incurs for things he really needs, such as food, necessary clothing, shelter, and medical care. Such items must be suitable and appropriate. For example, even though a child of a family with a moderate income has had the privilege of using the charge account regularly, the child or the parents could not be held responsible for an expensive mink coat sold by the store to the child. Of course, the store can insist upon having the coat returned.

A minor may legally contract for certain purchases.

Garnishment. If a debtor refuses to pay, the creditor may in some states bring a legal action to force the payment of the debt. By an order of a court the employer of the debtor is required to pay to the creditor a certain percentage of the debtor's wages until the amount of the debt or the amount specified by the court has been paid. This procedure is called the *garnishment,* or the *garnisheeing,* of wages. The laws on garnisheeing wages vary in the different states. In some states, only a certain percentage of a person's wages can be collected in this way. In other states a worker cannot be forced to pay small debts through this process.

Statute of Limitations. The unreasonable delay of a creditor in bringing an action for a claim may result in his loss of the right to take such action. The *statutes of limitations* in most states set a time limit after which a creditor cannot enforce a legal claim. For instance, in one state if an account is not collected within five years, the creditor cannot sue for the amount. If the debtor, however, makes a payment or promise to pay during the five years or at any time thereafter, the account is revived or reinstated. Under such circumstances the period of time during which the creditor has the right to collect the account is counted from the date of the last payment or promise by the debtor.

Attachment. If you owe a debt and refuse to pay or cannot pay it as agreed, you may be sued in court to force you to pay it. A common procedure in such a case is to ask the court for an attachment on some of your property until the case is settled. An *attachment* is simply a legal process whereby the property attached comes under the control of the court until the case is settled. If the case is decided against you, you are required to pay; and if you cannot pay, the courts in some states have the power to dispose of the attached property to pay the debt.

An attachment is ordinarily not used except when there has been some abuse of credit or when fraud is involved. For instance, if a person who owes money on a piece of household equipment attempts to move it to another city without permission before the debt is paid, the creditor may sue the debtor for an attachment.

Bankruptcy. Bankruptcy laws are Federal laws usually administered through the United States district courts. A debtor may become a *voluntary bankrupt* by applying to a court for a judgment of bankruptcy.

The purpose of bankruptcy laws is to let a person who has fallen hopelessly in debt throw off some of his obligations and get a new start. The court may discharge the debtor from further claims after all his assets that are not exempt have been utilized in paying his debts. The circumstances under which a person may apply for voluntary bankruptcy are regulated by law.

An *involuntary bankrupt* is one who has been forced into bankruptcy by his creditors. Most persons, partnerships, and corporations owing debts that amount to one thousand dollars or more may be forced into involuntary bankruptcy. There are, however, a few exceptions. The law specifically excludes farmers and wage earners. A wage earner is defined as an individual who works for wages or a salary and who earns not more than fifteen hundred dollars a year.

From this discussion it may be seen that voluntary bankruptcy is a means of protection for the buyer or debtor, whereas involuntary bankruptcy is a means of protection for the seller or creditor. Creditors often force a debtor into bankruptcy to avoid a greater loss that might result from allowing the debtor to continue in his former status. In this respect the creditor considers that it is better to accept a small loss than to wait and suffer a greater loss.

The latest Federal bankruptcy law provides an opportunity for debtors of various types to apply to the proper court for special arrangements whereby they can pay their debts. From the point of view of the individual the most important provision of that law is the one that permits any debtor except a corporation to file a petition for the acceptance of a plan for the alteration or the modification of the rights of creditors, whether those creditors are holding debts secured by real property or other assets or not secured by any assets. The court has authority to grant an extension of time or to rearrange a payment plan in view of future earnings. Therefore, a debtor who owes a debt secured by a mortgage on his home or on furniture may arrange a new plan of payment.

eck on
ourt yesterday
er, Collector of
enue. He claims $316.12 as
al security taxes for 1937 and 1938.

Man And Wife Bankrupts.

Albert W. Gerlaugh, coremaker, and his wife, Mrs. Mary L. Garlaugh, 6416 Chandler Street, Norwood, yesterday filed voluntary bankruptcy petitions. He lists indebtedness at $904.50, of which $300.98 is secured. Mrs. Gerlaugh reports the same secured indebtedness, plus $120.90 in unsecured claims. Joint assets are $100, representing household goods and an automobile.

Enter Bankruptcy Petitions.

Voluntary petitions in bankruptcy were filed in District Court yesterday by the following:

James Mark, last worker, Route 1, Portsmouth. Debts, $1,374; assets, $1,120, of which $1,100 represents value of real estate.

Ruford Vernon Moore, steel worker, 3702½ Rhodes Avenue, New Boston. Debts, $297.50; assets, $140.

Michael Parker, switchman, 710 East Pearl Street. Debts, $927.50; assets, $150.

Richard O'Brien, general pressman, 1010 York Street. Debts, $725.94; assets, $100.

Notices of bankruptcy.

TEXTBOOK QUESTIONS

1. Explain the difference between short-term and long-term consumer credit.
2. Why is credit so important in our business activities?
3. Name at least two advantages of buying on credit.
4. What is a main disadvantage of buying on credit?

5. What are the "three C's" in the formula for determining credit? Explain each.
6. List some of the information that an individual is required to give when he applies for credit.
7. What is the suggested procedure for establishing a retail credit in your community?
8. How may a merchant extend credit to you to such an extent that you may damage your credit?
9. What are some of the agencies through which credit information can be obtained?
10. In most communities how is it possible for all stores to know whether you have paid your account regularly at one store?
11. What are some of the extra costs involved in selling on credit?
12. Is a wife personally responsible for the debts she incurs, or is her husband responsible? Explain your answer.
13. What is meant by garnishment?
14. What is the Statute of Limitations?
15. What is an attachment?
16. What relief may an individual debtor obtain under the bankruptcy laws?

DISCUSSION QUESTIONS

1. Explain what you consider to be the most serious disadvantage of credit.
2. Why is character more important than capital in establishing credit?
3. Why has a creditor the right to know something about the income of a person who applies for credit?
4. From the point of view of (a) the creditor and (b) the debtor, discuss some of the evils of encouraging people to use too much credit.
5. Some merchants solicit customers to buy on account. (a) Why do you think they do so? (b) How do they plan this solicitation?
6. If you move to another city, how will a good credit rating that was established in your previous place of residence help you?
7. (a) Do you think you can open a charge account in the name of your parents and use the charge account? (b) Can you use the charge account of your parents if it has been established by them?
8. What do you think might happen to you if you owe $100 on a car and move to another city without notifying the lender?

9. If a person has become a voluntary bankrupt, why do you think it is difficult for him in the future to get credit?
10. Suppose that you owe $2,000 on a home and are six months behind in your payments. You owe a total of $200 on unsecured accounts in stores, and owe an additional $100 on household equipment on which there is a settlement mortgage. Your total assets amount to $1,200, including a $1,000 interest in the home. What relief can you obtain under the laws to straighten out your affairs and start over?

PROBLEMS

1. (a) If a department store doing a business of $500,000 a year has credit losses of $500, what is the percentage of credit losses on sales? (b) If the credit losses are $1,200, what is the percentage of loss?
2. Assume that you buy an article that is billed to you for $100 with the understanding that you may have a 1 per cent discount if you pay it within 10 days or that you have 30 days in which to pay the total net amount without the discount. (a) How much do you save by taking the discount? (b) If you consider the discount offered as interest for using the money for 20 more days, what annual rate of interest are you actually paying?

COMMUNITY PROBLEMS AND PROJECTS

1. Obtain a credit application blank used by some local store or a store in a neighboring city. (a) Fill in as much of the required information as you can, and (b) write a report explaining why each item of information is needed by the store.
2. Investigate the policies of local stores in selling for cash and on credit. Learn (a) which ones have variations in price, (b) how much the difference is, and (c) what additional carrying charges are added in the case of credit sales.
3. From local merchants, a local credit bureau, or some other local agency, obtain information with regard to (a) the percentage of merchandise sold on credit, (b) the average amount of credit losses, (c) the reasons for the credit losses, and (d) the local policies with regard to uniformity in granting credit.

Chapter 21

PART VI _____

Important Principles of Installment Buying

Purpose of the Chapter. Another type of credit that is often used by the consumer is installment credit. Buying on the installment plan usually permits an individual to pay for his purchases over a longer period of time than is possible under an ordinary credit account. It also involves additional legal relationships and responsibilities. These relationships are very important because they are commonly misunderstood by people who buy on this plan. The purpose of this chapter is to explain the responsibilities under various kinds of installment contracts and to emphasize the advantages and the disadvantages of this kind of credit.

What Is Installment Credit? Buying on the installment plan involves a type of credit that is different from open-account credit. *Installment credit* generally involves a formal contract, which in most states must be written. A down payment is required in most cases, and a certain amount of money must be paid regularly over a period of weeks, months, or years until the total amount owed is paid. Other characteristics of installment buying will be described later in this chapter.

Importance of Installment Buying. Estimates of the government and of various associations disclose the fact that about 60 per cent of the yearly retail sales are credit transactions. About one third of these credit sales are made on the installment plan. Installment business is therefore important. For instance, from 60 to 75 per cent of all new automobiles are sold on the installment plan.

Many other products besides automobiles are sold on the installment plan. Some of the common products sold thus are household appliances, musical instruments, and farm implements.

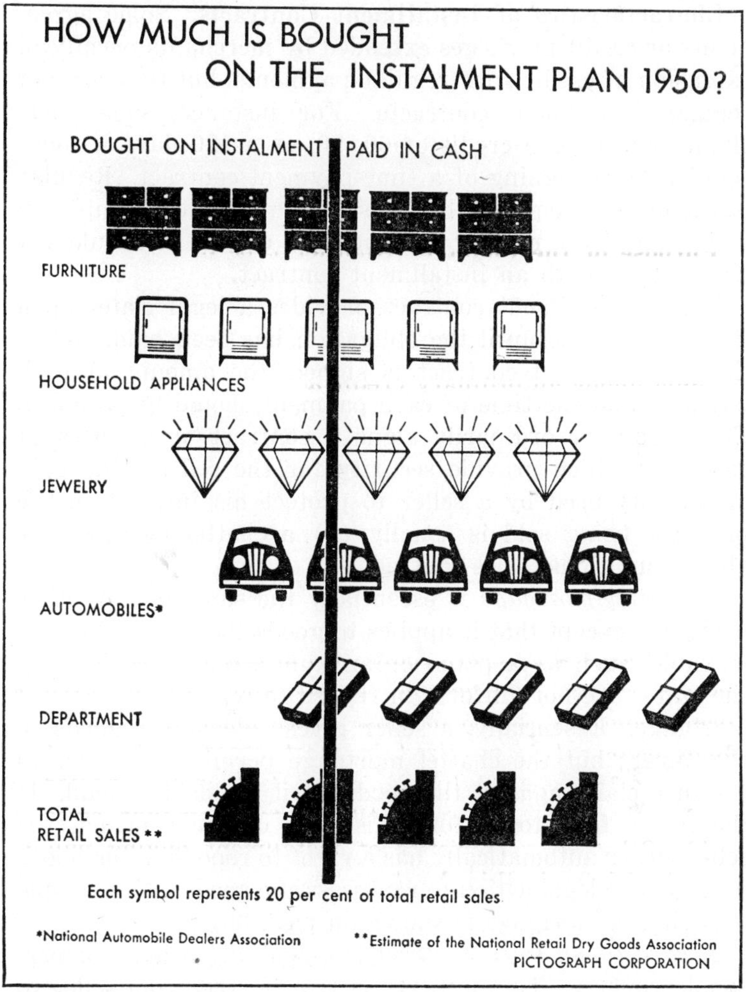

HOW MUCH IS BOUGHT ON THE INSTALMENT PLAN 1950?

BOUGHT ON INSTALMENT | PAID IN CASH

FURNITURE

HOUSEHOLD APPLIANCES

JEWELRY

AUTOMOBILES*

DEPARTMENT

TOTAL RETAIL SALES **

Each symbol represents 20 per cent of total retail sales

*National Automobile Dealers Association   **Estimate of the National Retail Dry Goods Association
PICTOGRAPH CORPORATION

The use of installment credit or any other type of credit serves as a means of temporarily increasing purchasing power and tends to stimulate buying. The more money or credit people have to spend for goods and services, the higher prices usually are. The extension of credit serves essentially the same purpose as increasing the amount of money available. The economic aspects of credit are discussed more fully in a later chapter.

Characteristics of Installment Contracts. Some agreements or credit privileges extended by merchants permit an extension of credit with regular payments, but they are not regular installment contracts. For instance, some merchants will extend credit of 60, 90, or a 120 days without requiring the signing of a time-payment contract. Regular payments are required, but this type of credit is simply an extension of the regular open-account credit. It should not be confused with an installment contract.

Every installment contract provides a legal claim upon the merchandise until the obligation has been paid. When the time-payment contract is signed, the amount of each payment and the time of each payment should be specified. The purchaser ordinarily signs a contract or a series of contracts which provide security for the seller. The type of security used by a seller to protect his interest in the property being sold is usually (a) a chattel mortgage or (b) a conditional sales contract.

A *chattel mortgage* is essentially the same as any other mortgage except that it applies to goods that are ordinarily movable, such as a piano or an automobile. The laws in the states are not uniform in regard to the use of a chattel mortgage. Essentially, a seller gives title of the goods to the buyer; but the chattel mortgage permits the seller to retain a claim against the goods until the debt is paid. If the buyer fails to perform his part of the contract, the seller either automatically has a right to repossess the goods or may take legal action to repossess the goods. An example of a chattel mortgage is shown on page 381.

A *conditional sales contract* is essentially a lease of personal property. The property is transferred from seller to the buyer, but the conditional sales contract permits the seller to retain title to the goods until the buyer has finished the last payment and fulfilled all other obligations under the contract. If the buyer fails to live up to his part of the contract, the seller can repossess the goods since they still belong to him. As soon as the buyer fulfills all terms of the contract, he becomes the full and legal owner of the property.

Motor Vehicle

CHATTEL MORTGAGE

Original and first copy for The Conference Bank
NO.

KNOW ALL MEN BY THESE PRESENTS, That the undersigned purchaser, of the City of _____ in the County
of _____, and State of _____, the MORTGAGOR, for the consideration of the balance of purchase money in the sum of
_____ Dollars ($_____) received to MORTGAGOR'S full satisfaction of
_____ of the City of _____, County of _____, and State of _____.

Dealer

MORTGAGEE, does hereby grant, bargain, sell, assign, transfer and set over unto the MORTGAGEE forever, the following described motor vehicle, together with any and all equipment, tires, accessories and parts, now or hereafter attached thereto and/or used in connection therewith, including such as may be added thereto and/or substituted therefor, all of which may be hereafter sometime referred to as "Chattel":

MAKE	Type of Body	Model	Manufacturer's Serial No.	Motor No.	If Truck Tons Capacity	Year	License No.

Statement of Items Covering Purchaser's Obligation

List Price of Car	$	Cash payment	$
Sales Tax			
Extra equipment—itemize		Trade in {Make ___ Year ___ / Serial ___ Model ___ }	$
		Balance in _____ equal successive monthly	
Freight and Delivery Charges		payments of $	
Cash Selling Price		Commencing the ___ day of ___, 19__ as evidenced by one Promissory Note bearing interest	
Add, per chart		from maturity at highest lawful rate, detachment of which is hereby authorized.	
Time Price	$	TOTAL (Total should agree with Time Price.)	

Said chattel will be kept at the following address: No. _____ Street _____ City _____

TO HAVE AND TO HOLD the chattel above granted, bargained and sold unto the MORTGAGEE forever, irrespective of any re-taking or re-delivery thereof to the MORTGAGOR or the granting of any renewals or extensions of the note secured hereby.

THE CONDITIONS OF THIS MORTGAGE ARE SUCH, That, WHEREAS, the MORTGAGOR has executed and delivered to the MORTGAGEE, his certain promissory note, dated the ___ day of ___, 19__, for the sum of ___

Dollars ($___), payable in ___ consecutive monthly installments of $___ each, commencing thirty days from date hereof and a final consecutive installment of $___ together with interest ...

[body of mortgage text partially obscured by magnifying glass]

... except temporarily, hires ...
... each and all of which acts ...
... in the event the MORTGAGEE ...
... balance remaining unpaid on the no... ...
...EE and MORTGAGEE may without ...
... without breaking into any premises ...
... actually covered by the lien of this m... ...
... damage caused thereby to MORTGA... ...
... time as MORTGAGEE may deem a... ...
..., the same being hereby expressly ...
... all be conclusively deemed a proper s... ...
... fees and expenses incurred in the ...
... the Chattel; second, shall pay a... ...
... charges touching the same; and ...
...d by reason of the violation o... ...
...nd remedies hereunder gi... ...GEE within twenty-... of repossession...

THIS ASSIGNMENT MUST BE EXECUTED BY DEALER

Date _____, 19__

For value received, the undersigned does hereby sell, assign, transfer and set over unto ... THE CONFERENCE BANK its successors and assigns...

By _____ (Signature of Owner, Officer and Title)

Signature of Dealer

From the pamphlet *Installment Selling—Pros and Cons*, by
William Trufant Foster, the Public Affairs Committee, Inc.

Read your installment contract carefully before signing.

An installment contract is a maze of legal technicalities, usually in fine print. If you are not sure what you are signing, take it home and study it and consult someone who knows.

The Uniform Conditional Sales Act has been enacted in only ten states. In all other states a certain amount of variation exists in the laws pertaining to installment contracts. In most states, however, the contracts must be in writing and must be signed by both the purchaser and the seller. In some cases the signatures must be witnessed. In most states the contracts must be written in triplicate. One copy is kept by the purchaser; another copy is filed in

A conditional sales contract.

some local recording office; and the third copy is kept by the seller. The purpose of recording an installment contract is to make the record public so that anyone can determine whether a claim has been made against the property. In most cases legal papers of this kind are recorded in the county courthouse or in a similar public building.

Installment contracts differ as to their wording and content, but a similarity is found between the conditional sales contract and the chattel mortgage contract. In each case the purchaser must agree to do certain things. For example, he must agree to make the payments as specified; he may not remove the property from the state without permission; he may not sell it to someone else without permission; and he has to keep it free from taxes, liens, and other claims.

Things to Check in Installment Contracts

1. What are the cost, the carrying charge, and the total cost?

2. What is the amount of each payment; what are the time, the place, and the conditions under which the payments are to be made?

3. What is the penalty if you fail to make a payment on schedule, and do you have any privilege of reinstating the contract if this happens?

4. If the goods are repossessed by the seller, under what conditions can you get them back?

5. Are there any other fees, such as legal or recording fees, besides the purchasing price and the carrying charge?

6. Before the regular payments are completed, do you have the privilege of paying the total amount due and settling the contract at a reduction in cost? If so, what are the conditions?

7. Besides the chattel mortgage or conditional sales contract, are you granting any additional security such as a wage assignment? (Wage assignment is an agreement to let the seller require your employer to take money out of your wages if you do not make payments as agreed.)

8. Is the merchandise insured by the buyer or the seller; if so, who pays the premiums? What happens if the merchandise is destroyed or stolen? Do you stand the loss or is the loss borne by the seller or an insurance company?

Read What You Sign. Sometimes oral promises may be made to the buyer. They may be made with perfectly good intentions; but when a written contract is made, the oral promises or agreements are worthless. The installment contract is often written with legal technicalities in very fine print, which is not only difficult to read, but which is also even more difficult to understand. Regardless of oral promises, read your installment contract very carefully before you sign it.

When to Use the Installment Plan. Installment buying has its advantages and disadvantages. Some plans are good, whereas others are unsound. The misfortune of a single person as the result of using the installment plan does not necessarily prove that the plan is fundamentally wrong. The misfortune probably did not result from the installment purchase, but from a blunder on the part of the purchaser or the seller.

In some cases installment buying is harmful. For instance, buying luxuries on the installment plan is not justifiable; such items should be bought with money especially saved for the purpose. No wise home-manager would purchase expensive clothing or elaborate jewelry on the installment plan. A railroad engineer, however, would be justified in buying a good watch on the installment plan if it were needed in his work. If a radio is needed to entertain a sick person or an automobile is required for business, installment buying is permissible and usually justified.

What constitutes a luxury is a debatable problem, for what may represent a luxury for one person may be a necessity for another. Circumstances must determine the case. For instance, an individual who has a mortgage on his home and is having difficulty in meeting all his obligations would be foolish to buy a radio or an automobile on the installment plan, for it is obvious that payments could not be made without sacrificing the well-being and the financial security of the family.

The age of a person and his expected income are vitally important in determining the advisability of buying on the

Will your budget allow for installment payments?

installment plan. If a person is sure that his income will not be reduced, and if, on the contrary, it may be increased, he has some basis on which to plan the installment buying of substantial assets that are needed. On the other hand, if there is a chance that his income may decrease, buying on the installment plan will be a very doubtful procedure. Young doctors starting in their profession frequently find it necessary to finance the purchase of equipment through the installment plan. The assets that they buy are necessary for the practice of their profession.

Installment buying can be used frequently as a means of saving. It should, however, be used carefully and with common sense. For example, if one is furnishing a home, the purchase of furniture on the installment plan will be justifiable if the payments can be made without jeopardizing the budget. Using the installment plan will be better than spending all available funds to buy cheap furnishings, which would soon wear out and then have to be replaced.

Some families do not accumulate savings rapidly because their regular incomes are spent foolishly. If persons of this type would acquire substantial assets by assuming obligations under the installment plan, they might be able to save. For people who have never acquired the habit of saving, the installment plan can be an aid. Anyone who admits that he is not able to save enough money to buy all he needs, but can force himself to pay on the installment plan, is admitting that he is a poor manager and has poor will power. A more economical handling of the problem would be to force oneself to save a certain amount weekly until a sufficient amount of money is available to make the purchase.

The seller of merchandise should be just as careful as the buyer in determining when the installment plan should be used. For instance, if Mr. Allen is contemplating buying an automobile from the Central Automobile Company, both the salesman and Mr. Allen should study carefully the latter's ability to pay for the automobile. Suppose that the automobile will cost $450. Mr. Allen has $100 that he can pay in cash. The most reasonable plan for the payment of the balance of $350 is $48 a month. Mr. Allen has been able, however, to save only $30 a month. It is obvious, therefore, that he cannot afford to buy the automobile unless he reduces his standard of living. If he makes the purchase, he will not only have to meet the payments of $48 a month, but also have to pay a license fee, repair bills,

---

Policies to Consider in Making
an Installment Purchase

1. Make a substantial down payment.
2. Pay the balance as quickly as possible.
3. Buy only durable goods that will be of value long after the final payment.
4. Don't use the full extent of your installment credit.
5. Budget your income and your expenditures to be sure that you can pay all obligations.
6. Leave a safety margin for unforeseen expenses and possible reductions in income.
7. Consider before you buy whether it is more profitable and more desirable to save your money and wait until you can pay cash.
8. Check other ways to get what you want that may be cheaper.

and other operating costs. If Mr. Allen were a salesman, however, and needed an automobile in his business, he would take into consideration any saving that would result from using his own automobile and any allowance that he might receive from his employer for using it.

Before You Buy. Before one buys an article on the installment plan and accepts the financing plan suggested by the seller, it is well to consider the following other alternatives: (a) buying from another seller who offers better terms; (b) paying cash from accumulated savings or waiting until one has saved enough money; (c) borrowing from a bank, a credit union, or another lending agency and paying cash; (d) borrowing on a life insurance policy and paying cash.

Advantages of Installment Buying. The following are some of the recognized advantages of installment buying:

(a) Savings result if installment purchases are made wisely by people who otherwise could not save money and accumulate enough to purchase for cash.

(b) Necessities may be enjoyed before the full price is available for payment.

(c) Better and more substantial merchandise can sometimes be obtained by utilizing the installment plan instead of paying cash for cheap merchandise.

(d) Without the aid of installment buying, many young married people would be unable to furnish a home and start housekeeping.

Disadvantages of Installment Buying. The disadvantages of installment buying arise, not necessarily out of the faults of the system, but often out of its abuses. The following are some of the disadvantages of installment buying:

(a) Some people buy assets because of false pride. They are encouraged to buy more expensive assets than they can afford.

(b) When the number of dealers allowing installment purchases is limited, the person who wishes to make an installment purchase may have to accept an inferior product because the grade of goods he wants is not sold where he can make purchases on the installment plan.

(c) The person who buys on the installment plan pays interest at a rate of from 6 per cent to 25 per cent on the unpaid balance. He therefore pays more than he would have paid if he had purchased the merchandise for cash. If one uses installment buying extensively, he will cut down his total purchasing power substantially.

(d) Some people may overbuy.

(e) "Credit competition" sometimes leads businesses to put customers under pressure in the hope of selling merchandise on "easy terms."

(f) Some merchants and dealers encourage buyers to use the installment plan because such a sale results in an additional income through the interest on the unpaid balance.

(g) Some users of the installment plan lower their standards of food, clothing, education, and environment in order to meet obligations on installment purchases.

(h) One of the greatest disadvantages is in committing oneself to future obligations. By promising to pay future income, one limits his freedom of action and cuts down his margin of safety in financial emergencies.

It is evident that installment purchases should be made only on the basis of necessity and convenience after a careful study of needs and ability to pay. In general, installment buying is recommended only for accumulating worth-while assets.

Terms of Payment. The percentage of down payment and the amount of time in which the debtor may pay vary according to the product, the amount of the down payment, and the policy of the finance company. The table on page 389 provides a summary of the usual percentages of down payment and the usual maximum periods for making payment for particular types of merchandise.

In times of national emergencies the Federal Government tends to increase the required down payment and shorten the length of time permitted for payment of installment

PRODUCT	USUAL PERCENTAGE OF DOWN PAYMENT	USUAL TIME ALLOWED THE DEBTOR (MONTHS) TO PAY
New automobiles	10 to 33⅓	12 to 24
Used automobiles	10 to 33⅓	6 to 18
Soft goods (textiles and perishables)	10 to 20	3 to 12
Furniture		
Department stores	10 to 20	6 to 18
Furniture stores	10 to 25	12 to 24
Refrigerators		
Department stores	5 to 10	12 to 36
Electrical appliance stores	5 to 10	12 to 36
Radios		
Department stores	10 to 20	12 to 24
Electrical appliance stores	10 to 20	12 to 24
Washing machines	5 to 10	12 to 24
Stoves	10 to 20	12 to 36
Jewelry	5 to 20	6 to 18
Men's clothing	10 to 25	3 to 12

Down payments and time allowed on installment sales.

purchases. Such tightening of credit reduces demand for products and retards inflation.

Charges for Installment Service. In making a decision with regard to buying on the installment plan, it is not a question of whether the cost of buying in this way is fair or unfair; it is a question of whether the merchandise is needed sufficiently to justify paying the amount that is charged for the privilege of buying on this installment plan. In some cases the charges may be exorbitant; and yet in most cases they are reasonable when the costs of the finance company are taken into consideration. The costs of operating one important finance company include: interest on borrowed money; banking costs; insurance on loans; credit investigations; office detail; collections; repossession of property from defaulting buyers; storing, advertising, and selling repossessed merchandise; losses on repossessed merchandise; legal expenses; and general office overhead. After all these operating costs have been given consideration, an additional 2 per cent is added for profit.

The preceding analysis of the costs that must be borne by a finance company provides some explanation of why the charge for installment buying seems excessive. The popular belief among buyers of automobiles and other equipment is that the finance business is largely one of banking. Because of the high charge the business appears to them to be simple and profitable. Competition has limited profit to a reasonably fair level. One should know what the real cost of buying on the installment plan will be, and then should decide whether he can afford to pay that cost.

The following table shows typical installment charges on automobiles.

AMOUNT FINANCED	TOTAL CHARGE	MONTHLY PAYMENT	LENGTH OF CONTRACT
$100	$15.32	$ 9.61	12 months
150	17.28	13.94	12 months
200	21.88	18.49	12 months
250	27.32	23.11	12 months
300	32.76	27.73	12 months

Computing Financing Charges. The financing charge on some installment sales is computed according to the following example: Mr. Jones makes a purchase of furniture amounting to $400 and agrees to pay $50 at the end of each month, plus interest at 6 per cent on the unpaid balance at the beginning of the month. At the end of the first month he pays $50 plus $2 interest. The unpaid balance is then $350. At the end of the second month he pays $50 plus interest amounting to $1.75, and he continues until all the payments have been made, which means it will take eight months to complete the payments.

The usual plan of financing is to charge in advance a certain percentage based on the unpaid balance and the length of time during which regular installments will be paid. Carrying charges vary in different states and communities. The tables on the following page show the typical carrying charges on installment contracts for new automobiles and household appliances. In the case of automobiles the charge may include life insurance on the buyer of the car. An example will show how these carrying charges apply. If an unpaid balance of $300 on the installment purchase of an automobile is to be paid in 15 months, the carrying charge would be $21.30. The total amount to be paid would be $321.30, which is the sum of the unpaid balance due and the carrying charges. The monthly payment would be determined by dividing $321.30 by 15, the number of months the installment contract is to run.

Carrying Charges on New Automobiles, Including Life Insurance on the Buyer

UNPAID BALANCE DUE	12 MONTHS	15 MONTHS	18 MONTHS	24 MONTHS
	CARRYING CHARGES			
$ 200	$13.96	$ 14.50	$ 17.26	$ 22.72
300	17.16	21.30	25.26	33.36
400	22.64	27.95	33.44	44.24
500	28.00	34.75	41.44	54.88
600	33.36	41.40	49.44	65.76
700	38.72	48.20	57.62	76.40
800	44.08	54.85	65.62	87.26
900	49.44	61.50	73.62	97.92
1000	54.80	68.30	81.80	108.80
1500	81.72	101.85	122.16	162.48

Carrying Charges on Household Appliances

100	10.76	15.05	xx	xx
150	14.52	18.15	21.72	29.04
200	17.68	24.25	28.96	36.40
250	22.76	28.55	34.22	45.68
300	19.23	32.10	38.58	51.36

NOTE: The carrying charge is added to the unpaid balance due to determine the total amount to be paid.

Carrying charges added to the unpaid balance.

Figuring the Cost of an Installment Purchase. There are numerous installment plans. Some of these reveal the true cost by making a charge, in the form of interest, on the unpaid balance. In such a case the actual cost of the merchandise to the purchaser is easy to figure. On the other hand, some plans involve discounts, fees, and carry-

ing charges in order to conceal the real interest rate. The following is an example of how to figure the actual interest rate on a typical installment purchase when the rate is concealed. The example is based upon a study made by the Pollak Foundation for Economic Research.

If you take time to figure the cost of installment purchases, you may decide to wait until you have saved the money.

A furniture store advertised a sofa on special sale at $79. The price could be paid at the rate of $9 down and $10 a month for seven months, with "no charge for the easy terms." A cash customer could get a $7 discount if he asked for it. The allowance of this discount meant, essentially, that an installment charge of $7 had been added on a sofa that was really priced at $72. One who purchased on the installment plan therefore had to pay an extra cost of $7. As the net price of the sofa was $72, the unpaid balance after the deduction of the $9 down payment was $63. The table below shows the basis on which the true interest rate was determined.

When one buys on the installment plan, he really borrows money because he owes a debt until it has been entirely paid off in installments. The table below shows that $63

MONTH	PRINCIPAL BALANCE	PAYMENT ON PRINCIPAL AT END OF MONTH	PAYMENT OF INTEREST AT END OF MONTH
1	$ 63	$ 9	$1
2	54	9	1
3	45	9	1
4	36	9	1
5	27	9	1
6	18	9	1
7	9	9	1
Totals	$252	$63	$7

Figuring the cost of an installment purchase.

was owed for one month, $54 was owed for one month, $45 was owed for one month, and so forth. A total of $252 was owed for one month. Seven dollars in interest was paid for the privilege of the installment purchase. The following is a step-by-step analysis of the formula for the computation of the actual yearly rate of interest:

(a) $252 was used for one month.
(b) This was the same as using $21 for one year ($\frac{252}{12}$).
(c) $7 interest was charged on $21 for one year.
(d) The rate of interest was .33⅓ or 33⅓% ($\frac{7}{21}$).
(e) The complete arithmetical formula for computing the rate is $12 \times 7 \div 252 = .33⅓$, or 33⅓% a year.

Finance Companies. In the field of installment credit a particular type of financial institution has developed. It is often referred to as a *finance company.* In a sense it is a dealer or a bank that purchases from merchants the contracts signed by customers who buy on the installment plan. These notes are purchased by the finance company at a discount. For example, a person may purchase an automobile on the installment plan and sign a mortgage contract. The dealer who sold the car may then sell the contract to a finance company. In such case the person who purchased the car will be required to make payments to the finance company instead of to the dealer.

Replevin or Repossession. When an article is sold under an installment contract and the buyer later fails to live up to his part of the con-
tract, the seller, in order to protect himself from loss, sometimes has the right to repossess the article. The legal action necessary is usually referred to as *repossession* or *replevin.* The law of replevin differs widely in various states. In some states the law permits

If a buyer on the installment plan fails to live up to the agreement, he may lose the goods.

the seller to repossess the property, and, regardless of the amount that has been paid, he need not compensate the

---

Warnings on Installment Buying

1. Do not allow yourself to be rushed into signing a contract until you know all the facts.
2. Refuse to sign any contract if you are not given an exact duplicate copy.
3. Do not sign any contract before all the blank spaces are filled in.
4. Do not pledge any security besides the article being purchased.

buyer for anything that the latter has already paid. Under the laws of many states, however, the person who repossesses an article must, according to a definite plan prescribed in the law, compensate the buyer for any interest that the latter may have had in the article. Laws on the right of replevin are important from the point of view of the consumer. The consumer should know not only that they exist, but also his rights under those laws.

TEXTBOOK QUESTIONS

1. What is meant by installment credit?
2. How does installment credit affect purchasing power and buying?
3. Two general types of contracts are used in selling merchandise on the installment plan. (a) What are they? (b) When does the title pass in each case?
4. How is the seller protected under each type of installment contract?
5. What types of products are most commonly sold on the installment plan?
6. In the case of a conditional sales contract or a chattel mortgage contract, what does the purchaser usually agree to do?
7. Give at least three things you should check when entering into an installment contract.
8. Why would you not recommend buying expensive luxuries on the installment plan?
9. How could the use of the installment plan result in a saving in buying furniture?
10. Before you buy on the installment plan, what are some other alternatives to consider?
11. What are some of the advantages of installment buying?
12. What are some of the disadvantages of installment buying?
13. When a new automobile is purchased on the installment plan, what is usually (a) the down payment required? (b) the time allowed for payment?
14. What is a typical carrying charge added to the price of a household appliance for a contract covering twenty-four monthly installments when the unpaid balance due is $200?
15. What is a finance company?
16. Explain briefly the regulations in regard to replevin or repossession.
17. Mention at least two warnings in regard to installment buying.

DISCUSSION QUESTIONS

1. How should installment buying be closely correlated with budgeting?
2. What effects do you think installment buying has in creating demand?
3. Do you see any dangers of installment buying in times of prosperity or in times of depression?
4. Name some of the important obligations assumed under an installment contract.
5. What do you think might be the privilege of a seller if the buyer of an automobile under a conditional sales contract moves to another state and takes the car with him without notifying the holder of the conditional sales contract?
6. Why do you think it might be advisable for a certain family to borrow money in order to buy a washing machine instead of buying it on an installment plan?
7. What do you think of the advisability of buying jewelry on the installment plan?
8. Can you see any possibility of economic evils in installment buying?
9. Some people are induced to buy refrigerators because of the slogan "25 cents a day will buy this refrigerator." What do you think of such a plan of buying?
10. A business advertises that it sells on the installment plan at no extra charge. (a) Is this practice fair to all customers of the business? (b) What should a cash customer expect?
11. If the law in your state or the contract that you sign requires the seller to compensate you for the financial interest that you have in an article when it is repossessed by the seller, how much would you expect to get back if you had paid $100 on a refrigerator and had used it two years?
12. Why would you recommend not signing an installment contract if the price and the information in regard to the finance charge and monthly payments are to be filled in later with the understanding that a copy of the contract will be mailed to you?

PROBLEMS

1. From the tables on pages 389 and 391, showing the terms of payment and the carrying charges for new automobiles, compute (a) the maximum usual down payment in terms of dollars and (b) the amount added to the original unpaid balance for a carrying charge if payments are to extend over eighteen months. Assume that the delivered price of the car is $2,250.

2. On the basis of the example given on page 392, compute the
annual interest rate on the purchase of a refrigerator that
is sold for $165 with a down payment of $15 and installment payments of $10 a month for fifteen months, "no charge
being made for the easy terms." Assume that a person paying cash could obtain the refrigerator for $150.
3. According to the model budget for a family of four on page
422, (a) how much can a family with an income of $75 a
week afford to pay on the installment plan for an electric
refrigerator if it wishes to continue depositing 5 per cent of
the income each week in a savings fund, if 10 per cent of the
allowance for food will be saved each week, and if a saving of
25 cents a week on a twelve months' basis will be made in substituting the cost of electricity for the cost of ice? (b) If
the balance due on the refrigerator is $172 plus a $28 carrying charge, how long will it take to make all the payments?

COMMUNITY PROBLEMS AND PROJECTS

1. Obtain the following information with regard to the purchase
of an automobile: (a) the price f.o.b. the factory, (b) the
delivered price, (c) the particular items and the amounts of
the items that add to the cost in delivering the automobile,
(d) the guarantee, (e) the service agreement, (f) the type
of bill of sale used, (g) the carrying charge on the unpaid
balance, and (h) the plan of paying the balance. Write a
report summarizing the information that you have obtained.
2. Obtain a copy of either a chattel mortgage or a conditional
sales contract (whichever is most commonly used and is
legally permitted in your state) and analyze this contract
by submitting your answers to the following questions:
(a) When does the title pass? (b) How may the title be
transferred? (c) What happens if there is a default of any
payment? (d) Are there any warranties? (e) What other
rights, privileges, or limitations of use are extended to the
buyer?

Chapter 22

_____

How to Obtain a Small Loan

Purpose of the Chapter. The consumer often finds it necessary to borrow money in small amounts. Most loans can be obtained from regular banks, as well as from other agencies. The ease in obtaining these small loans has often proved disastrous to many consumers. It is important, therefore, to understand various sources from which small loans can be obtained, the interest rates that are paid, and the obligations that are assumed. These problems are discussed in this chapter.

Need for Small Loans. Businessmen borrow money in periods of low income to help them continue to operate until higher periods of income when the loans can be repaid. They also borrow money to enable them to take advantage of opportunities that would otherwise not be possible. If it were not for borrowing on the part of businessmen, farmers, and others, there would be no particular need for banks except as a safe place to keep money. Banks and other lending agencies earn their income by lending money, and in this way they are able to pay interest to their depositors.

In some respects individuals and families are like businesses. They need to borrow money for emergencies. Small loans also enable families to buy necessary household equipment, to make permanent additions to the home, and to do other things that cannot wait until the money would be saved.

In order for you to be able to borrow money, you must establish a good credit rating in ordinary buying. If you have a good credit reputation, you can borrow the money you need when you need it.

Types of Loans. There are two types of loans as to the methods of repayment. One type of loan permits you to repay in a lump sum. The other type of loan permits you to repay in regular installments.

There are also two types of loans as to security. One type of loan is *unsecured.* In other words, you merely sign a contract, binding yourself to the terms of the contract. Your character and honor are sufficient to enable you to obtain the loan. If you fail to abide by the contract, you can be sued, of course, for the amount due. The other type is a secured loan. A *secured loan* means that you have to pledge or turn over to the lender some kind of property. The lender has a claim against this property until you repay the loan. If you fail to repay the loan, he can keep the property or sell it to satisfy his claim against you.

Another type of protection that a lender sometimes requires is the signature of an additional person who becomes jointly responsible with you and promises to pay if you fail to do so. As we learned in Chapter 19, this person is called a cosigner or a comaker. The illustration below shows a loan agreement signed by comakers.

15-1

$ 150.00 PERSONAL LOAN DEPARTMENT No. ____

THE FIFTH THIRD UNION TRUST CO
CINCINNATI, OHIO

CINCINNATI, OHIO ____ January 5, 19__

FOR VALUE RECEIVED, WE, THE UNDERSIGNED, JOINTLY AND SEVERALLY, PROMISE TO PAY TO THE ORDER OF THE FIFTH THIRD UNION TRUST COMPANY OF CINCINNATI, OHIO, THE SUM OF

____ One Hundred and Fifty ____ DOLLARS

AT ITS OFFICE IN CINCINNATI, OHIO, WITH INTEREST AT THE RATE OF EIGHT PER CENT PER ANNUM AFTER MATURITY UNTIL PAID, WAIVING PRESENTMENT, DEMAND FOR PAYMENT, PROTEST, NOTICE OF PROTEST AND NOTICE OF NON-PAYMENT OF THIS NOTE, THE FIRST OF THE UNDERSIGNED (NAMELY, THE BORROWER) HEREBY AGREEING TO PAY PROMPTLY $ 12.50 ON ____ March 6, 19__ AND AT REGULAR monthly (SEMI-MONTHLY OR MONTHLY) INTERVALS THEREAFTER FOR 11 INSTALLMENTS AND $ 14.50 AS THE LAST INSTALLMENT, AND THE OTHERS OF THE UNDERSIGNED JOINTLY AND SEVERALLY AGREEING TO MAKE EACH OF THE SAID PAYMENTS PROMPTLY IF THE SAID BORROWER SHOULD DEFAULT IN MAKING THE SAME. AS OFTEN AS THE MAKING OF ANY SUCH PAYMENT MAY BE DELAYED BEYOND THE DAY AS HEREIN AGREED TO BE MADE, THE UNDERSIGNED JOINTLY AND SEVERALLY PROMISE TO PAY TO THE HOLDER HEREOF AT OR BEFORE THE MATURITY OF THIS NOTE, A SUM CALCULATED AT THE RATE OF FIVE CENTS FOR EACH ONE DOLLAR OF SUCH DELAYED PAYMENT, BUT IN NO EVENT SHALL THE TOTAL CHARGE IN CONNECTION WITH ANY ONE DELAYED PAYMENT BE IN EXCESS OF FIVE DOLLARS ($5.00), AND TO MAKE SUCH PAYMENTS AS COMPENSATION FOR THE DAMAGE OCCASIONED BY SUCH DELAY.

UPON FAILURE TO MAKE ANY PAYMENT AS HEREIN AGREED, OR IN THE EVENT OF THE DEATH OF THE SAID BORROWER, OR IN CASE OF INSOLVENCY, BANKRUPTCY, OR FAILURE IN BUSINESS OF ANY OF THE UNDERSIGNED, THIS NOTE SHALL, AT THE OPTION OF ITS HOLDER, BECOME IMMEDIATELY DUE AND PAYABLE, WITHOUT DEMAND OR NOTICE. UPON THIS NOTE MATURING UNDER ANY OF ITS TERMS AND PROVISIONS, AND NOT BEING FULLY PAID AND SATISFIED ON THE DAY OF ITS MATURITY, THE TOTAL SUM THEN DUE HEREUNDER MAY FORTHWITH BE DEBITED TO ANY ACCOUNT OR ACCOUNTS MAINTAINED BY ANY OF THE UNDERSIGNED WITH THE HOLDER HEREOF, WITHOUT NOTICE TO OR FURTHER CONSENT FROM ANY OF THE UNDERSIGNED, THEY HEREBY AGREEING TO BE AND REMAIN JOINTLY AND SEVERALLY LIABLE FOR ALL INDEBTEDNESS REPRESENTED BY THIS NOTE IN EXCESS OF THE AMOUNT THEN TO THE CREDIT OF SUCH ACCOUNT OR ACCOUNTS.

EACH OF THE UNDERSIGNED HEREBY AUTHORIZES SAID TRUST COMPANY TO (1) PAY THE PROCEEDS OF THIS NOTE TO Mr. J. C. Murphy (2) DATE THIS NOTE AS OF THE DAY WHEN THE LOAN EVIDENCED HEREBY IS MADE; (3) COMPLETE ANY BLANK SPACES IN THIS NOTE ACCORDING TO THE TERMS UPON WHICH IT GRANTS SAID LOAN; AND (4) CAUSE THE SIGNATURE OF ONE OR MORE CO-MAKERS IN ADDITION TO THE ORIGINAL NUMBER, TO BE ADDED AT ANY TIME OR TIMES HERETO, AND TO DO SO WITH OR WITHOUT NOTICE TO ANY OF THE UNDERSIGNED, WHO HEREBY CONSENT THERETO AND ACKNOWLEDGE THAT SUCH MAY BE DONE WITH OUT AFFECTING THE JOINT AND SEVERAL OBLIGATION OF EACH OF THE UNDERSIGNED, AS HEREINBEFORE SET FORTH.

UNDERSIGNED, JOINTLY AND SEVERALLY, HEREBY IRREVOCABLY AUTHORIZE ANY ATTORNEY AT LAW, CLERK OF COURT OR PROTHONOTARY TO APPEAR FOR UNDERSIGNED, JOINTLY OR SEVERALLY, BEFORE ANY JUSTICE OF THE PEACE, OR IN ANY COURT OF RECORD, STATE OR FEDERAL, IN THE UNITED STATES OF AMERICA, IN TERM TIME OR VACATION, AND TO WAIVE ISSUE AND SERVICE OF PROCESS AND CONFESS JUDGMENT AGAINST THE UNDERSIGNED, JOINTLY OR SEVERALLY, IN FAVOR OF THE HOLDER HEREOF, FOR SUCH AMOUNT AS MAY APPEAR TO BE UNPAID HEREON, AFTER MATURITY, TOGETHER WITH INTEREST, AND TO RELEASE ALL ERRORS AND WAIVE ALL RIGHT OF APPEAL.

ADDRESSES (GIVE COMPLETE ADDRESS)	SIGNATURES (WRITE IN FULL AND IN INK)
528 Wakefield Drive, Cincinnati, Ohio	1. J. C. Murphy — BORROWER
528 Wakefield Drive, Cincinnati, Ohio	2. Catherine Murphy — CO-MAKER—WIFE OR HUSBAND OF BORROWER
2564 Williams Street, Norwood, Ohio	3. Carl A. Frederick — CO-MAKER
3151 Reading Road, Cincinnati, Ohio	4. Clifford Edwards — CO-MAKER

A personal loan agreement.

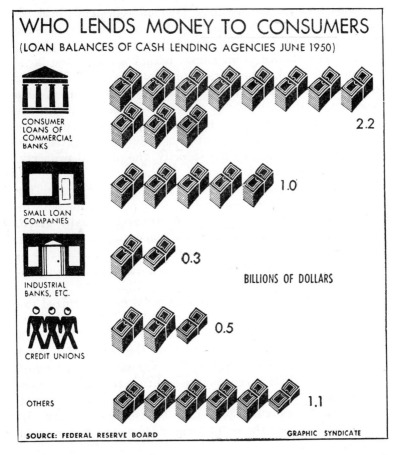

Borrowing on Security. An insurance policy can be used as the basis of obtaining a loan from the insurance company, usually at from 4 to 6 per cent interest. The policy must be given to the insurance company as security, and the loan can be repaid when it is convenient. If death occurs before the loan is repaid, the amount of it is deducted from the payment due the beneficiary.

The amount that can be borrowed on an insurance policy will depend entirely on the face of the policy and the length of time the policy has been in force. A bank will occasionally lend on an insurance policy.

Bonds and stocks are used frequently as collateral security for loans. The security may also consist of such items as furniture or livestock. Loans of this type can usually be obtained from banks, except some of the large commercial banks that are interested mainly in making loans for business purposes. When security loans of this type are obtained, bonds or stocks are usually turned over to the bank or other lending agency to be kept until the loan is repaid. An agreement is usually signed, giving the lender authority to keep the security, the pledged property, so that it becomes his property if the loan is not repaid. When money is borrowed from a bank or other agency for the purchase of some specific item, such as an automobile or household equipment, a chattel mortgage is usually given. This provides written evidence of the security. The lender can make you turn over to him the property if you fail to repay the loan. Chattel mortgages were discussed in Chapter 21.

Any stock or any bond that is traded on recognized exchanges will serve as collateral, provided there is evidence to indicate that the stock or the bond is good. A bank will ordinarily lend about 50 per cent of the value of a good stock or a good bond. Suppose, for example, that a loan of $200 is required for three months and that the bank charges 6 per cent interest. Good bonds or stocks with a market value of approximately $400 may be used as security. In making the loan, the bank will deduct the interest in advance as follows:

Amount given to borrower $197.00
6 per cent interest in advance for three
   months 3.00
Amount to be paid bank in three months...$200.00

In this example the interest charge is actually more than 6 per cent, for $3 is being charged for using $197 for three months. If the loan is not repaid in three months, the bank has the privilege of selling the securities to obtain the $200. Suppose that, at the end of three months, this loan has not been repaid. It may be possible for the borrower to have the loan renewed by paying $3 interest in advance and by signing a new note to take the place of the old one. Or he may pay $100 and sign a new note for $100 after paying $1.50 interest in advance on the new loan.

An ordinary note.

If the securities are sold to protect the bank, more or less than the amount of the loan may be obtained, depending upon the fluctuation of the market rate of the securities. Suppose that in the preceding example nothing is paid on the loan and the bank sells the securities at the end of the three months for $300. The additional $100 will go to the person who obtained the loan. If the securities were sold for only $175, however, the person who obtained the loan would still owe the bank $25.

Personal Loans from Banks. Two types of banks will lend money to individuals. One is the regular bank that has a personal loan department. A cosigner or a comaker may be required on a note to borrow money from such a bank, but some banks lend money to persons with high credit ratings on a single signature. Others will lend on a chattel mortgage or other types of security. It is a common practice for such banks to lend money to individuals who wish to buy an automobile or any other kind of equipment. It is also a common practice for persons with a good credit rating to borrow from such banks to pay doctor bills and to meet other emergencies.

In more than half of the states, banks commonly referred to as *industrial banks* have been organized. In many states

402   How Banks and Credit Serve You   [Part 6

they are better known under the name of *Morris Plan banks*. Such banks are regulated by the laws of the states in which they are located. The methods of operating banks of this type and the laws governing their operations are similar in the various states.

Industrial banks operate largely on the basis of making character loans. In obtaining a character loan from an industrial bank, the prospective borrower must have one or more, usually two, responsible people to indorse his note as comakers. If the person who obtains the loan does not pay the note, either of the other persons is liable for the amount of the note. Before making a loan, the bank investigates carefully the prospective borrower's character and capacity to pay. It also investigates the persons whose names are submitted as comakers.

Since the legal liability of a borrower and a comaker or cosigner is precisely the same, a responsible person will not ask anyone to sign for him unless he is sure that that person will not have to pay because of the borrower's default. A prudent person will be careful about becoming a cosigner of other people's notes, because he will have to pay if the borrower fails to pay.

Loans are made for as much as $5,000, although they are usually smaller. They ordinarily extend for one year, but they may cover a shorter or a longer period of time. Some banks accept mortgages on homes and on other property as a guarantee of the payment of loans.

The bank deducts interest in advance and usually charges a service fee. The following table shows the proceeds of a typical loan:

Amount of cash received by borrower $222.00
6 per cent interest for one year 14.40
Service charge 3.60

Amount of loan $240.00

Repayment of a loan must be made weekly or monthly. The interest is charged in advance on the total amount of the loan. The actual rate of interest on the loan mentioned above is, however, more than 6 per cent, because the borrower obtains only $222 and must repay $240 in weekly or monthly installments. Furthermore, the borrower will not have the use of $222 for a year.

There are several ways of figuring the actual yearly interest rate on loans of this type, but the simple formula explained in Chapter 21 for figuring the interest rates on installment contracts can also be used in figuring the actual interest rates on bank loans in cases when the interest is not charged on the unpaid balance at the time of each monthly payment. In this particular case, the actual interest rate would be 14.97 per cent if payment is made in 12 monthly installments.

Interest Rates. Interest rates vary according to the states and the types of lending institutions. Statutes in most states govern the interest rates of such institutions as pawnshops and loan associations. The state banking laws and the rules of the Federal Reserve System govern

STATES AND TERRITORIES	LEGAL RATE (PER CENT)	CONTRACT RATE (PER CENT)	STATES AND TERRITORIES	LEGAL RATE (PER CENT)	CONTRACT RATE (PER CENT)
Alabama	6	8	Montana	6	10
Alaska	6	8	Nebraska	6	9
Arizona	6	8	Nevada	7	12
Arkansas	6	10	New Hampshire	6	Any rate
California	7	10	New Jersey	6	6
Colorado	6	Any rate[1]	New Mexico	6	10[2]
Connecticut	6	12	New York	6	6
Delaware	6	6[4]	North Carolina	6	6[5]
District of Columbia	6	8	North Dakota	4	7
Florida	6	10	Ohio	6	8
Georgia	7	8	Oklahoma	6	10
Hawaii	6	12	Oregon	6	10
Idaho	6	8	Pennsylvania	6	6
Illinois	5	7	Puerto Rico	6	9[3]
Indiana	6	8	Rhode Island	6	30
Iowa	5	7	South Carolina	6	7
Kansas	6	10	South Dakota	6	8
Kentucky	6	6	Tennessee	6	6
Louisiana	5	8	Texas	6	10
Maine	6	Any rate	Utah	6	10
Maryland	6	6	Vermont	6	6
Massachusetts	6	Any rate	Virginia	6	6
Michigan	5	7	Washington	6	12
Minnesota	6	8	West Virginia	6	6
Mississippi	6	8	Wisconsin	5	10
Missouri	6	8	Wyoming	7	10

[1] When any rate is permitted for contracts, there usually is a limit for a small loan of approximately $300 or less, although this limit may be as high as 3 per cent a month.
[2] When a loan is unsecured by collateral, the contract rate may be 12 per cent.
[3] When the amount is more than $3,000, the maximum contract rate is 8 per cent.
[4] Any rate may be charged by a bank if it is in writing and loan is unsecured for more than $5,000.
[5] If the loan is for agricultural purposes, 10 per cent of the loan may be charged in lieu of interest.

Legal and contract rates of interest.

STATES	MAXIMUM SMALL-LOAN INTEREST RATES ALLOWABLE
Alabama	8% a year.
Alaska	8% a year.
Arizona	3½% a month.
Arkansas	10% a year (same as usury law).
California	2½% a month on first $100, 2% on remainder to $300; flat 2% if security insured. Rates on loans above $300 are not limited, but an administrative regulation requires consideration of rates charged in determining the lender's fitness.
Colorado	3½% a month on first $150, 2½% on remainder. Loans of more than $300 may be made at any rate of interest agreed to in writing.
Connecticut	3% a month on first $100, 2% on remainder; 12% a year after 20 months.
Delaware	8% discount on original loan including fees, plus fines for delinquency.
District of Columbia	1% a month.
Florida	3½% a month.
Georgia	1½% a month.
Hawaii	3½% a month on first $100, 2½% on remainder.
Idaho	3% a month.
Illinois	3% a month on first $150, 2% on next $150, 1% on remainder to $500.
Indiana	3% a month on first $150, 1½% on remainder.
Iowa	3% a month on first $150, 2% on remainder.
Kansas	No law.
Kentucky	3½% a month on first $150, 2½% on remainder.
Louisiana	3½% a month on first $150, 2½% on remainder; 8% a year 12 months after maturity.
Maine	3% a month on first $150, 2½% on remainder; 25 cents minimum charge. Loans of more than $300 may be made at any rate of interest agreed to in writing.
Maryland	3% a month.
Massachusetts	2% a month; 6% a year one year after maturity. Loans exceeding $300 by licensees are subject to the so-called Tender Act, which limits the charge on loans of less than $1,000 to 18% a year and $5 for expenses.
Michigan	3% a month on first $50, 2½% to $300, and ¾ of 1% on remainder to $500.
Minnesota	3% a month.
Mississippi	10% a year, fees.
Missouri	3% a month on first $100, 2½% on remainder.
Montana	No law.
Nebraska	36% a year on first $150, 30% a year on next $150, and 9% a year on remainder up to $1,000.

Maximum small-loan interest rates.

largely the interest rates of banks, although the demand for and the supply of money have important influences on interest rates on bank loans.

In nearly every state there is a legal rate and a contract rate of interest. In the absence of any agreement with regard to the interest rate, a bank may charge the *legal rate*. A special agreement may be made to permit a bank to charge the *contract rate*, which is limited in most states.

STATES   MAXIMUM SMALL-LOAN INTEREST RATES ALLOWABLE

Nevada ....3½% a month on first $100, 3% on remainder; $5 mini-
                mum charge, other charges.
New Hampshire 2% a month; fees of $1 on loans of $50 or less, $2 on
                larger loans up to $300. Loans of more than $300
                may be made at any interest agreed in writing.
New Jersey ....2½% a month on first $300, ½ of 1% on remainder to
                $500.
New Mexico ....3% a month on first $150, 2% on next $150, and 1% on
                remainder to $500; 10% a year 12 months after
                maturity and in certain other cases; step rate of 5%
                a month on loans of $50 or less; $1 minimum charge.
New York ......2½% a month on first $100, 2% on remainder.
North Carolina .No law.
North Dakota .. No law.
Ohio ....3% a month on first $150, 2% a month on next $150,
                ⅔ of 1% to $1,000, 8% a year on $1,000.
Oklahoma ..... 10% a year plus service charges not exceeding an ini-
                tial 5% and 2% (but not more than $2) a month,
                subject to various limitations.
Oregon ....3% a month.
Pennsylvania ..3% a month on first $150, 2% on remainder; 6% a year
                after 18 months.
Rhode Island ..3% a month. In general, loans of more than $300 may
                be made at a rate of 30% a year for interest and
                expenses.
South Carolina .No law.
South Dakota .. No law.
Tennessee .....6% a year, plus fee not to exceed 1% a month.
Texas ....10% a year (same as usury law).
Utah ....3% a month.
Vermont ......2½% a month on first $125, 2¼% on remainder.
Virginia ....2½% a month, can be reduced under certain circum-
                stances; 6% a year after 23 months, and under cer-
                tain circumstances.
Washington ... 3% a month on first $300, 1% on remainder to $500; $1
                minimum charge.
West Virginia . 3½% a month on first $150, 2½% on remainder.
Wisconsin .....2½% a month on first $100, 2% on second $100, 1% on
                remainder. Installment loans up to $2,000 are regu-
                lated by law which permits a discount of 8% a year
                on the first $300 and 7% on the remainder plus a
                fee of 2% but not exceeding $20.
Wyoming ..... 3½% a month on loans of $150 or less, plus service
                fee of $1 on loans of $50 or less, and a recording fee
                of $1.

Maximum small-loan interest rates.

The table on page 403 shows the maximum interest rates of the various states and territories. These rates are determined by law and are changed from time to time. If an individual wants to know the maximum rates in his state, he should consult the latest law. These rates should not be confused with small-loan rates.

Borrowing from Small-Loan Agencies. Individuals and businesses that have been accustomed to lending to the ordinary wage-earner agree that the average person of moderate means who is honestly earning a living will always pay his debts if he can and that he is thoroughly honest in his intentions. The Russell Sage Foundation, in conducting an investigation, found that there are many people who need to borrow amounts of $300 or less, but who do not have any securities that can be used as collateral to obtain such loans. Many people cannot find other persons to sign notes so that they will be able to borrow from industrial banks. Others do not care to have their friends obligated in this manner; they prefer to go to a place where money can be borrowed on a different basis.

As a result of findings of the Russell Sage Foundation, the Uniform Small-Loan Law was sponsored. It has been adopted in many states. On the basis of this law many *personal finance companies* have been organized. Several thousand are now in operation. No borrower should deal with any personal finance company that is not licensed by the state and is not under state supervision. If there is any question about a personal finance company, information can be obtained from such organizations as the better business bureau, the chamber of commerce, and the local welfare organization.

The costs of obtaining small loans of this kind are high. In states where there are laws controlling the rate, the common rate is 3 per cent or 3½ per cent a month on the unpaid balance. The table on pages 404 and 405 shows the maximum small-loan interest rates in various states. The loans usually run from ten to twenty months.

A loan can be obtained by giving a *chattel mortgage* on home furnishings. This type of mortgage gives the loan company permission, through legal proceedings, to obtain possession of the furnishings in case of default in payment of the loan, and to sell them to recover the amount of the loan. Actual practice discloses, however, that licensed loan companies do not foreclose on property unless there is definite evidence of fraud or a lack of desire to pay.

Although the rate of interest on the unpaid principal of the loan is usually 3½ per cent a month, the net interest

MONTH	AMOUNT PAID ON LOAN	INTEREST CHARGES	TOTAL PAYMENT
1	$ 8.33	$ 3.50	$ 11.83
2	8.33	3.21	11.54
3	8.34	2.92	11.26
4	8.33	2.62	10.95
5	8.33	2.33	10.66
6	8.34	2.04	10.38
7	8.33	1.75	10.08
8	8.33	1.46	9.79
9	8.34	1.17	9.51
10	8.33	.88	9.21
11	8.33	.58	8.91
12	8.34	.29	8.63
Totals	$100.00	$22.75	$122.75

Repaying a small loan.

charged on the original loan amounts to less than this because of the monthly payments. The table above shows how a loan of $100 at the rate of 3½ per cent a month is repaid in one year.

Many borrowers wonder why obtaining small loans costs more than the flat 6 per cent or less that is charged on larger loans. Let us take the case of a loan of $50 to a stranger who applies to the lending agency for the first time. Let us also assume that the interest on a loan of this size, to be paid in ten monthly installments, would be $2.75. The agency lending the money has to investigate the applicant, close the loan, keep bookkeeping records, collect the money, allow for a certain percentage of loss on bad loans, and earn something on the investment. When one takes this into consideration, it can be seen why rates are higher on small loans than on large loans. With the same amount of effort, the lending agency could handle a $5,000 loan.

Credit Unions. Credit unions arise out of a co-operative effort of people with common interests. No one can obtain a loan from a credit union unless he is a shareholder. To become a shareholder, he must buy shares in the credit union. He usually must also pay a membership fee. The earnings of the credit union are paid as dividends to the shareholders. Some credit unions accept deposits at a specified interest rate just as savings banks do.

The shareholder of a credit union can obtain a loan in the same way that a loan is obtained from an industrial

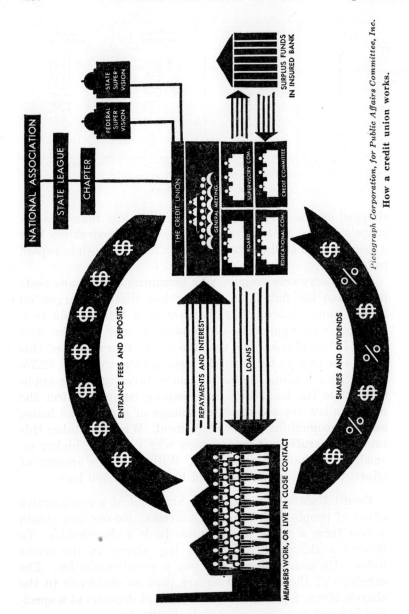

Pictograph Corporation, for Public Affairs Committee, Inc.

How a credit union works.

bank. Some unions permit the granting of loans on chattel mortgages and on second mortgages on real estate. The interest rate is usually about 1 per cent a month on the unpaid principal of the loan. It varies, however, in different states and is usually regulated by state laws.

Rates charged by credit unions often can be lower than those charged by other agencies because there is less difficulty in making the credit investigation. There are also lower costs of operation because the members operate the credit union with little or no compensation. Sometimes, however, the larger credit unions have a regular paid staff of employees.

Federal Credit Unions. Federal credit unions, supervised by the Bureau of Federal Credit Unions, Federal Security Agency, are co-operative thrift associations in much the same way as credit unions are organized under state laws. Membership in a Federal credit union is limited to persons having a common occupation or association, or to groups within a well-defined neighborhood, community, or rural district. Loans made by a Federal credit union must not be for periods exceeding three years in length. The interest rate must not exceed 1 per cent a month on the unpaid balance, including all charges incidental to making the loan.

Pawnbrokers. In most states, pawnbrokers are licensed by the cities in which they are located. The rate of interest charged on loans obtained from pawnbrokers varies widely, but it is usually extremely high.

To obtain a loan from a pawnbroker, one must turn over personal property, such as jewelry or tools, as security. The maximum amount of the loan is usually extremely low in proportion to the value of the property; it is seldom more than 50 per cent of the appraised value. Such a loan is seldom repaid in installments. It must be repaid in full before the pledged property will be returned.

Unlicensed Lenders. There are still some states that do not have any small-loan laws. In these states the unlicensed

---

Guides in Borrowing

1. Be sure you borrow from a company that is under state supervision.
2. Borrow no more than is necessary.
3. Borrow no more than you can repay according to your agreement.
4. Be sure that you understand your obligations and the obligations of the lender.
5. Be sure that you understand the amount of the loan, the cost of the loan, and the specific details with regard to repayment.
6. Read the contract carefully before you sign it.
7. Be sure that you get credit for every payment and receive a canceled contract when you have completed the payments.

---

lenders are the only sources of loans for many persons with low incomes who need an occasional loan. Unlicensed lenders also operate in states that do have regulatory laws. The person who patronizes an unlicensed lender is the one who needs credit the worst and who needs the most protection. Studies have shown that the lowest rate commonly charged by these illegal lenders is 120 per cent a year. It is common for the rate to be 240 per cent a year, and examples have been found of rates as high as 1,200 per cent a year.

The rates alone are not the only evils. Some of these unscrupulous lenders never allow their clients to get out of debt. The borrower is sometimes required to pay the whole loan at one time or no payment will be accepted. He is constantly in debt because he can never get enough money together to pay the whole loan.

The only sensible practice for a person who needs money is to patronize a regular lending agency. If he is being treated unfairly, he should seek advice from such an agency as the local better business bureau or the legal aid society if he cannot afford to obtain regular legal advice from an attorney.

TEXTBOOK QUESTIONS

1. What are the two types of loans classified as to security?
2. If an insured person borrows money on an insurance policy but dies before the loan is repaid, how do these circumstances affect the proceeds of the insurance?
3. What is a Morris Plan bank?
4. We sometimes speak of "uniform small-loan laws." Is there any uniformity in these laws in various states?
5. Why is there a need for small loan agencies?
6. In the selection of a personal finance company from which you want to obtain a loan, what factors should you investigate first?
7. If a person has no collateral security or insurance that could be used in obtaining a loan, and cannot find anyone to sign a note as a comaker, what are some of his other choices in obtaining a loan?
8. What is a credit union?
9. Distinguish a Federal credit union from other credit unions.
10. Give at least three of the guides that have been suggested for borrowing.
11. Why should one avoid patronizing an unlicensed lender?

DISCUSSION QUESTIONS

1. Why should one be careful in signing a note as a comaker?
2. What is one of the disadvantages of borrowing money on insurance?
3. What are some of the good features of borrowing on insurance?
4. Explain the difference between a character loan and a chattel mortgage loan.
5. If $1,000 is borrowed for a period of three years, which is the most advantageous plan of repayment (that is, the most economical): weekly installments, monthly installments, or payment in one amount at the end of the three years?
6. Why do you believe that it is necessary to have special small-loan laws?
7. Why is the interest rate on a small bank loan of $100 to an individual higher than the rate on a bank loan of $50,000 to a businessman?
8. Indicate two ways in which you could detect an unlicensed lender.
9. In what way do you think borrowing is related to budgeting?

PROBLEMS

1. Assume that you obtain a loan for $300 on your insurance policy at 6 per cent interest for one year. Compute the actual rate of interest that you pay, assuming that the interest is paid in advance and that the full amount of the loan must be repaid at the end of the year.
2. Mr. D. H. Collins borrowed from the Merchants' National Bank $500 on a 90-day note. The bank gave him cash for the face of the note less interest at 5 per cent for 90 days. (a) How much cash did he receive? (b) How much cash did he pay at maturity?
3. Assume that you obtained from a small-loan agency a loan of $100, to be paid back in ten monthly installments of $10 each. The interest of $6 and the loan service charge of $1 are deducted in advance. Figure the actual interest rate according to the formula given in Chapter 21.

COMMUNITY PROBLEMS AND PROJECTS

1. From your telephone directory or from some other source of information, make a list of all the places where small loans may be obtained in your community (not including regular banks). Classify them according to the types of lending institutions discussed in this chapter.
2. Find out whether there are small-loan laws in your state or your local community and make a study of the nominal and the actual interest rates charged by small-loan agencies. Write a report.
3. Investigate in your community to see whether the regular commercial banks have small-loan departments. Obtain information in regard to types of loans, sizes of loans, security required, terms of payment, and interest rates. Write a report setting forth this information.

PART VII
MANAGING YOUR PERSONAL FINANCES

Chapter 23
How to Keep Personal and Family Budgets

Purpose of the Chapter. We want many things for personal and family use. Some of the things we want are commodities and services that we could not get along without; others contribute to our comfort and happiness. The extent to which we are able to get the things we need and want depends largely on how carefully we plan our expenditures. Most people are able to save only a small percentage of their income because their actual expenses are almost as great as their income. Planning our expenditures so that they will not be greater than our income and so that we shall be able to buy as many of the things we want as possible is important for pleasant, satisfying living. The purpose of this chapter is to show how income can be estimated and how our wants can best be met by carefully planning how and for what we will use our income.

What Is a Budget? A *budget* is a systematic plan for using the money we earn to buy as many as possible of the things we want. It involves (a) estimating what our income will be for a certain period of time, and (b) planning our expenditures. *Income* includes not only what we receive in wages or salaries but also net profits from business, dividends on stocks owned, and interest received on investments. One must consider the total amount earned in wages and salaries and not just the take-home pay. *Expenditures* include in addition to the payment for items, such as food and clothing, withholdings from wages or salary; the amounts we pay for such permanent property as a radio, an automobile, or a home; payments on loans; and savings. Usually a budget is an estimate of income and a plan for expenditures for a year; however, it may be for a month or even a week.

Business firms and divisions of government prepare budgets to serve as guides for expenditures. Organizations such as churches and clubs also make budgets to govern their financial transactions. Family units and individuals whose incomes go the farthest in buying the things they want always have a financial plan for expenditures.

A budget need not be complicated. It is a device for keeping our expenditures within our income with some allowance, if possible, for savings. A budget gives one a sense of security. It makes living pleasant and successful because expenditures can be made as need for them arises. If we spend our money recklessly without consideration of income, we may deprive ourselves of the things we need and want most. Not only may we be unable to pay for our current expenses; we may also make it impossible to buy a home and to acquire major assets, such as an automobile or furniture. As a result, we find ourselves living from hand to mouth or even going into debt so deeply that it is impossible to find a way out.

In making a budget we need to know: (1) the factors upon which an estimate of income may be made, and (2) the factors upon which to base our estimates for expenditures and savings.

Factors upon Which Income Is Estimated. Wages or salary may be estimated fairly well for a year in advance by considering the wages or salary received in the past year and by making adjustments that may be anticipated either because of wage increases or decreases or because of anticipated overtime or unemployment. Probably the best indication of the amounts that may be received from dividends, interest, and similar sources are the amounts received from these sources in past years. Except in periods of abnormal economic conditions, such as inflation, war, or depression, or because of unforeseen conditions, as illness or accident, income for a family or an individual may be estimated with a fair degree of accuracy. If you plan to sell any property, the money you expect to receive from the sale of property must be included in the estimate of cash income.

Classification of Expenditures. Expenditures may be classified in many ways. Most of the methods, however, are reasonably uniform in the grouping of expenses under the various headings. A classification of the various types of expenditures for the purpose of keeping a budget is shown on the next page. This classification of expenditures should serve as a guide only. You may have expenditures that must be included in your budget that are not listed here, and some that are listed you may not have.

The largest items for which expenditures are made by a family or an individual are food, clothing, housing, and family operating expenses; other expenditures are for such items as education, recreation, and transportation. The basis for planning the amounts of these expenditures will be explained in a later section of this chapter.

The estimated expenditures for the budget period must include the payment of debts, such as monthly payments on a home or an automobile, interest charges on money borrowed, and payments that will fall due on charge and installment accounts.

If one is working for wages or a salary, certain deductions are usually made from his income. These deductions usually will include payments for social security and income taxes, which are required by law. In addition, the employee may voluntarily agree to deductions from his wages for insurance, union dues, savings, or other purposes. These are expenditures. One's income is considered to be the total stipulated salary or wage regardless of the number of deductions.

In the case of social security taxes (old-age benefits), the amount withheld is considered to be an asset because it accumulates to the credit of the individual. Although these deductions cannot be withdrawn as cash, they are eventually available at the time of retirement and therefore rep-

Essential

Food (include taxes)
  Food purchased
  Meals purchased
Clothing (include taxes)
  Clothes purchased
  Material used to make
    clothes
  Shoes
  Repairs and alterations on
    clothing
  Hats

Housing
  Rent or payments on home
  Taxes
  Insurance
  Repairs
  Painting
Payments on charge and
    installment accounts
Interest on money borrowed

Operating

Family (include taxes)
  Fuel
  Light
  Telephone
  Water
  Gas
  Expenses on the yard
  Cleaning clothes
  Cleaning house
  Household supplies
  Life insurance protection
  Income and other taxes
  Accident insurance

Personal (include taxes)
  Carfare
  Toilet articles
  Jewelry and other personal
    items
  Personal allowance
Automobile (include taxes)
  Gasoline
  Oil
  Repairs
  Insurance
  License fees
  Tax
  Storage and parking fees

Development

Health
  Physician's and dentist's
    fees
  Nursing
  Medicine, drugs, and surgi-
    cal supplies (include hos-
    pital care)
  Optical treatment
Recreation (include taxes)
  Theater tickets
  Vacations
  Hunting license
  Social club dues
  Concert tickets

Education
  Tuition
  Books
  School fees
  Traveling expenses in at-
    tending school
  Magazine subscriptions
  Lecture tickets
  Newspapers
Benevolence
  Church contributions
  Donations to charity

Savings and Other Assets

Savings funds
  Savings bank
  Building and loan association
Life insurance
  Cash value of policies

Social security
  Salary deductions
Assets (tangible)
  Furniture
  Automobile

Classification of expenditures.

Information Needed in Making an Annual Budget

Factors for Estimating Income

 (a) Wages or salary anticipated in the next year, considering the possibilities of increases or decreases, overtime, periods of unemployment, and time that may be lost through illness or accident.

 (b) Net profits from business ventures.

 (c) Dividends from shares of stock owned.

 (d) Interest from bonds, savings accounts, and money loaned.

 (e) Profit on sale of property.

Factors for Estimating Expenditures

 (a) Estimated cost of food, clothing, housing, and transportation, which comprise the major expenditures for most people.

 (b) Estimated cost of individual or family development, such as health, education, recreation and vacations, and personal needs.

 (c) Amounts needed to make monthly payments on a home, payments on charge and installment accounts, and interest charges on money borrowed.

 (d) Personal and income taxes; deductions or payments for social security.

 (e) Premiums on life insurance and annuities.

 (f) Contributions for religious and charitable purposes.

 (g) Amounts from income placed in savings of various kinds.

---

resent a specific type of saving. The deductions for hospital care represent expenses and are rightfully included as a part of one's health expense. Deductions for group insurance, which does not have a cash value, are expenses rightfully considered as a part of life insurance protection or family operating expenses. Deductions for union dues are also a part of the family operating expenses. Amounts withheld for savings bonds represent assets that accumulate to the credit of the individual; they should be recorded as one of the types of savings.

Average expenditure per family for—

Income level and size of family	All items	Food	Shelter			Clothing	Transportation		Medical care	Recreation	Personal care	Tobacco	Education	Reading	Other items
			Housing	Household operation	Furnish-ings		Auto-mobile	Other							
$2,000 to $3,000:															
2 persons	$2,557	$930	$552	$95	$153	$298	$125	$70	$105	$76	$58	$47	$1	$32	$15
3 persons	3,178	1,061	537	101	129	370	473	64	163	91	67	51	12	30	29
4 persons	3,105	1,198	534	83	286	454	135	38	189	83	82	49	16	25	31
5 or more	2,740	1,295	494	112	93	259	51	45	140	73	54	81	10	22	11
$3,000 to $4,000:															
2 persons	3,286	1,065	553	134	152	342	401	85	218	112	63	70	0	38	53
3 persons	3,430	1,262	567	135	190	399	231	85	198	136	77	65	19	40	26
4 persons	3,918	1,361	621	147	272	561	203	92	273	136	87	63	49	43	10
5 or more	3,679	1,220	522	100	347	478	244	65	158	290	86	103	15	27	24
$4,000 to $5,000:															
2 persons	4,096	1,190	678	166	231	578	639	75	170	139	83	66	3	38	40
3 persons	4,505	1,379	1,100	176	266	522	410	52	153	191	103	78	3	53	19
4 persons	4,139	1,473	747	158	237	500	299	78	265	160	95	67	6	42	12
5 or more	4,462	1,778	597	143	280	656	284	42	262	178	95	67	19	47	14
$5,000 to $6,000:															
3 persons	5,459	1,535	701	214	428	754	528	65	507	371	101	130	24	49	52
4 persons	5,472	1,684	825	297	430	771	532	72	198	373	98	91	35	46	20
5 or more	6,017	1,991	633	160	526	813	819	87	337	299	121	77	80	44	30
$5,000 to $10,000:															
2 persons	4,603	1,216	616	169	298	585	775	84	231	410	91	60	0	56	12
$6,000 to $10,000:															
3 persons	6,887	1,753	931	256	623	921	1,264	115	328	329	123	124	18	53	49
4 persons	6,901	1,940	655	228	550	1,115	1,086	120	261	565	138	55	94	52	42
$6,000 to $7,500:															
5 or more	6,563	2,315	658	201	608	1,285	308	111	249	372	134	93	57	55	117
$7,500 to $10,000:															
5 or more	8,106	2,283	647	239	532	1,471	1,600	178	237	492	153	120	24	52	78

Source: MONTHLY LABOR REVIEW, December, 1949.

Families of 2, 3, 4, and 5 or more persons in Detroit, Michigan:
Average money income and expenditures, by net income class, 1948.
Family expenditures.

Any other payments for insurance, contributions for religious and charitable purposes, and any other similar expenditure must be included in our budget plan for expenditures. Furthermore, money saved is not available for other purposes and is, therefore, really an expenditure of the income that has been received. It also should be included in the budget.

Factors to Be Considered in Estimating Expenditures. Estimated expenditures should be based upon (a) expenditures in preceding years, which may be obtained from personal and family financial records, (b) government reports of family expenditures, (c) model budgets and reports of how other families spend their income, (d) anticipated changes in cost of living, (e) payments coming due on a home, an automobile, or on charge and installment accounts, and (f) an anticipated irregular expenditure, such as replacement of the furnace. The precise circumstances that may be encountered during the year cannot be predicted although sometimes one can predict an expenditure, such as for school tuition, a change in taxes, a surgical operation, or some other unusual item. After including expenditures for these predictable items, the person who is making the budget may consider that the other expenditures will be somewhat in proportion to those in the past. The amount of each type of expenditure in the budget is determined after a careful consideration of each of the items that are included in this classification.

Guides in Budgeting. After the financial facts upon which income and expenditures are estimated have been assembled, the next step in making a budget is to find out what others have been doing. The Bureau of Labor Statistics releases statistics on individual and family income and expenditures that may be helpful as a guide in making your own budget.

The table on page 418 shows the actual expenditures of families in one large city. Other government figures show that in some of the lower income groups families often spend more than they earn.

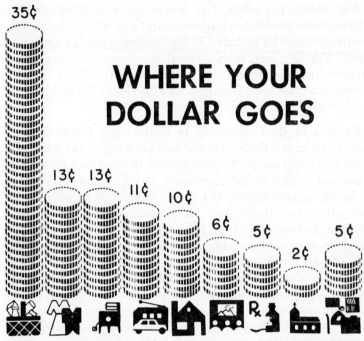

35¢ 13¢ 13¢ 11¢ 10¢ 6¢ 5¢ 2¢ 5¢

WHERE YOUR DOLLAR GOES

FOOD & TOBACCO   CLOTHING & ACCESSORIES   HOUSEHOLD OPERATION   TRANS-PORTATION   SHELTER   RECREATION   MEDICAL CARE   CHURCH, EDUCATION   PERSONAL BUSINESS

U. S. COMMERCE DEPT.   GRAPHIC SYNDICATE

Family expenditures for various classes of items, such as food, shelter, and clothing, vary according to the number of persons in the family and according to the income of the family. The figures show how families spent their income—not necessarily how they should have spent it. These figures include only expenditures for consumption and do not include gifts, savings, or personal taxes, which must be considered in every budget.

Government figures help to tell you what other people have actually been doing. These practices are not necessarily good. Therefore, another way to obtain a guide in budgeting is to consult some model budgets. In considering model budgets, one must first investigate the circumstances under which these budgets were prepared. For example, were they prepared at a time when both wages and cost of living were similar to those of the period for which the budget is being made, were they based upon urban or rural livings costs, and was the level of living in the areas upon which they were based similar to the level of living in the place you expect to live in the next year?

Model budgets should be used only for comparison. No one can prove that any particular budget is ideal. One that might be good for one person or family would not necessarily be good for another person or family. The tables on this and the next page are model budgets that have been prepared after a comparison of the expenditures of individuals and families in all parts of the country. Social security deductions are included in savings because they represent withholdings from salary that are held by the Federal Government and will eventually be available in the form of old-age benefits.

Notice that in every model budget provision is made for savings. As the income grows larger, savings increase more rapidly than most other items. The expenditure for food increases more slowly; in fact, the percentage spent for food may decrease, but the amount spent may increase. As

Suggested Budget for a Single Man

INCOME PER WEEK	$30	$37	$50	$62	$75
	%	%	%	%	%
Essential:					
Food	44	38	29	24	22
Clothing	10	12	13	11	10
Housing	15	13	12	11	10
Operating	13	16	18	18	20
Development	12	12	14	15	16
Savings	6	9	14	21	22

Suggested Budget for a Single Woman

INCOME PER WEEK	$30	$37	$50	$62	$75
	%	%	%	%	%
Essential:					
Food	40	34	27	23	21
Clothing	17	18	19	20	20
Housing	17	15	14	14	14
Operating	11	12	14	16	16
Development	10	11	12	13	13
Savings	5	10	14	14	16

Suggested Budget for a Man and His Wife

INCOME PER WEEK	$30	$40	$50	$60	$75
	%	%	%	%	%
Essential:					
Food	40	35	33	27	23
Clothing	7	8	8	10	12
Housing	25	20	20	18	16
Operating	15	19	19	21	21
Development	10	12	13	15	16
Savings	3	6	7	9	12

Suggested Budget for a Family of Three

INCOME PER WEEK	$40	$50	$60	$75	$90
	%	%	%	%	%
Essential:					
Food	37	34	27	23	20
Clothing	12	13	15	18	20
Housing	20	20	20	16	15
Operating	15	15	16	18	17
Development	10	11	13	14	14
Savings	6	7	9	11	14

Suggested Budget for a Family of Four

INCOME PER WEEK	$50	$60	$75	$90	$105
	%	%	%	%	%
Essential:					
Food	40	34	30	25	22
Clothing	15	15	16	16	16
Housing	20	20	20	20	16
Operating	13	15	16	16	15
Development	9	12	13	13	12
Savings	3	4	5	10	19

Suggested Budget for a Family of Five

INCOME PER WEEK	$50	$60	$70	$90	$105
	%	%	%	%	%
Essential:					
Food	42	35	32	26	23
Clothing	17	17	17	17	17
Housing	20	21	20	20	17
Operating	12	13	14	15	15
Development	8	10	12	13	13
Savings	1	4	5	9	15

the income increases, it is natural to expect that the provision for recreation and mental development will increase.
Expenditures for clothing, shelter, and operating should
also increase although the percentage spent for those items
decreases.

Example of Estimating Income. Let us assume that Mr. J. L. Murphy, who is married and has a son 12 years old and a daughter 8 years old, decides to make a budget to guide the family expenditures for the next year. One of Mr. Murphy's first problems in preparing a budget is to estimate his income for the year. His salary is $300 a month. He anticipates no changes in his salary. He receives two weeks' vacation in August with pay, but he plans to take a week of additional vacation without pay. In December last year Mr. Murphy received a dividend on some stock he owns in the company in which he works, amounting to $37. The balance of his savings account earns interest at the rate of 2 per cent, compounded semi-annually. An average of $40 in June, $75 in July, $75 in August, and $50 in September has been received in the past five years for small fruits and vegetables that Mr. Murphy has sold from his suburban home. The prospects for a similar income next year are good. The following table shows Mr. Murphy's estimated income:

Income	Jan.	Feb.	Mar.	Apr.	May	June	July	Aug.	Sept.	Oct.	Nov.	Dec.	Total
Salary	$300	300	300	300	300	300	300	225	300	300	300	300	$3,525
Interest						24						32	56
Dividends												37	37
Sale, fruits and vegetables						40	75	75	50				240
Total	$300	300	300	300	300	364	375	300	350	300	300	369	$3,858

Estimated income.

Although Mr. Murphy estimates that his income will be $3,858 for the next year, in some months he will receive more money than in other months. This fact should be considered when he plans his expenditures.

Example of Estimating Expenditures. Mr. Murphy and his family followed the principles outlined in the earlier pages of this chapter in estimating their various expenditures. They studied their previous expenditures, consulted government figures, and then used some model budgets to guide them in setting up their estimated expenditures as shown in the table on page 424.

	JAN.	FEB.	MAR.	APR.	MAY	JUNE	JULY	AUG.	SEPT.	OCT.	NOV.	DEC.	TOTAL
Essential:													
Food	$ 85.00	$ 85.00	$ 80.00	$ 80.00	$ 77.00	$ 77.00	$ 77.00	$ 77.00	$ 80.00	$ 80.00	$ 90.00	$ 91.00	$ 979.00
Clothing	38.00	38.00	39.00	30.00	30.00	30.00	30.00	30.00	60.00	37.00	35.00	35.00	432.00
Housing	45.00	45.00	45.00	45.00	45.00	45.00	45.00	45.00	45.00	45.00	45.00	45.00	540.00
Operating:													
Family (including tax) ...	46.00	46.00	46.00	43.00	43.00	43.00	50.00	46.00	46.00	47.00	50.00	75.00	581.00
Personal	5.00	5.00	5.00	5.00	5.00	5.00	5.00	6.00	6.00	6.00	5.00	5.00	63.00
Automobile ...	8.00	8.00	8.00	9.00	9.00	8.00	8.00	25.00	8.00	8.00	9.00	13.00	121.00
Development:													
Health	10.00	13.00	11.00	10.00	10.00	10.00	10.00	10.00	13.00	13.00	11.00	10.00	131.00
Education	4.00	4.00	4.00	4.00	4.00	4.00	5.00	4.00	4.00	4.00	4.00	4.00	49.00
Recreation	6.00	6.00	6.00	7.00	7.00	10.00	8.00	8.00	6.00	6.00	6.00	6.00	82.00
Benevolence	9.00	9.00	12.00	9.00	9.00	11.00	9.00	9.00	13.00	13.00	6.00	16.00	128.00
Savings and Assets:													
Savings Fund .	10.00	10.00	10.00	23.00	20.00	40.00	40.00	5.00	23.00	12.00	5.00	8.00	206.00
Savings Bonds.	25.00	25.00	25.00	25.00	25.00	25.00	25.00	25.00	25.00	25.00	25.00	25.00	300.00
Life Insurance (Cash Value)	.....	.....	.....	.....	.....	.....	30.00	.....	.....	.....	30.00	30.00	60.00
Social Security.	4.50	4.50	4.50	4.50	4.50	4.50	4.50	3.38	4.50	4.50	4.50	4.50	52.88
Other Assets ..	4.50	.....	4.50	5.50	1.50	31.50	18.50	8.50	16.50	.....	.....	.....	86.50
Total	$300.00	$298.50	$295.50	$300.00	$290.00	$344.00	$365.00	$301.88	$350.00	$300.50	$298.50	$367.50	$3,811.38

Estimated expenditures.

424

Their estimated income proved to be $3,858. They properly arranged their budget so that they would not spend as much as their income. Anything left over at the end of the year will be available in the form of cash or savings of some kind.

Comparison of Estimated Income and Estimated Expenditures. According to the plan outlined in this chapter, the expenditures represent the cash outlay of funds as the result of paying expenses, buying assets, or using the income for investment or savings. If a person always conducts his transactions on a cash basis, that is, pays cash for everything and does not buy on account, he will always be able to live within his budget. If purchases are made through charge accounts, the payment of the bills should be considered as a regular expenditure of cash and should be included as such in the budget. One should therefore not buy anything on account without taking into consideration the payment for the purchase and how it will affect the budget.

The estimated income and estimated expenditures should be compared for each month in the period covered by the budget to make certain that funds will be available for making expenditures as need for them arises. Most people plan to have some cash left at the end of each month. This cash balance may be added to the income of the month to determine the amount available for expenditures. An esti-

	ESTIMATED BEGINNING CASH BALANCE	ESTIMATED INCOME	ESTIMATED CASH AVAILABLE	ESTIMATED EXPENDITURES	ESTIMATED ENDING CASH BALANCE
January	$175.00	$300.00	$475.00	$300.00	$175.00
February	175.00	300.00	475.00	298.50	176.50
March	176.50	300.00	476.50	295.50	181.00
April	181.00	300.00	481.00	300.00	181.00
May	181.00	300.00	481.00	290.00	191.00
June	191.00	364.00	555.00	344.00	211.00
July	211.00	375.00	586.00	365.00	221.00
August	221.00	300.00	521.00	301.88	219.12
September	219.12	350.00	569.12	350.00	219.12
October	219.12	300.00	519.12	300.50	218.62
November	218.62	300.00	518.62	298.50	220.12
December	220.12	369.00	589.12	367.50	221.62

Cash estimate; comparison of estimated income and estimated expenditures.

mate of cash income and expenditures for the entire budget period should be prepared. Assuming that Mr. Murphy had $175 in his checking account, the illustration on page 425 is based upon his estimated income on page 423 and his estimated expenditures on page 424.

Economic Conditions Affect Budgeting. The person who plans his expenditures carefully year after year becomes acutely aware of changes in economic conditions that affect his income and expenditures. Economic factors that especially influence personal and family budgets are price changes that affect the cost of living by either increasing or decreasing it, ratio of personal and income taxes to total income, and deductions from income for social security. As taxes increase, smaller amounts remain from income for other expenditures and savings. An increase in income means little if there is a corresponding change in the cost of the commodities and services we need and want. The person who makes and operates a budget has an opportunity to observe the effects of inflation and deflation on his own personal life.

Summary of Steps in Making and Operating the Budget. A single person has only his own welfare to consider in

---

Steps in Making a Budget for a Family

1. Obtain the co-operation and consent of the members of the family in developing a plan for spending the income so that the essentials will be provided, as many as possible of the other wants of the family may be obtained, and a reasonable amount may be saved.

2. Prepare an estimate of income by months using a form similar to the table on page 423.

3. Prepare an estimate of expenditures by classes using a classification of expenditures similar to the one on page 416 and a form for monthly estimates similar to the one on page 424.

4. Compare the estimated income and estimated expenditures by preparing a table similar to the one on page 425.

---

making and operating a budget. A budget for a family affects the welfare of every member of the family and the happiness and comfort of the family as a whole. Successful budgeting of family income and expenditures requires both the help and the co-operation of every person in the family.

A budget may be perfectly prepared, but it can be no more successful in serving as a guide to our expenditures than the conscientious care and effort we use in operating it. Several principles must be observed in the successful operation of a budget.

Principles for Operating a Budget

1. Once the budget has been made and agreed upon, all members of the family must co-operate in keeping expenditures within the budget limits.

2. Revisions of the budget during the budget period may be necessary. These adjustments usually will reduce the expenditures for some items in order to provide more for other items. Hence, the family members should approve the revisions.

3. Accurate and complete records of all income and expenditures must be kept. Appropriate record forms should be used, and some member of the family should be responsible for making the entries.

4. When the major income for the month is received, the allocations should be made in the following sequence:

    The amount for savings should be deposited in the savings account or invested.

    Monthly payments for taxes, for purchase of the home, on charge and installment accounts, and on money borrowed should be made.

    Amounts budgeted for food and clothing should be set aside.

    Allowances for contributions, education, recreation, and personal expenses should be made.

5. Except in an emergency that could not be foreseen, no one should be allowed personal expenses or expenditures in any one of the classifications to overstep the amount budgeted for that purpose.

6. Periodically the actual expenditures should be compared with the estimated expenditures.

TEXTBOOK QUESTIONS

1. What is a budget?
2. What are some things included in income?
3. What items are included in expenditures?
4. In figuring one's cash income for budgeting purposes, is it necessary to take into consideration money received from the sale of property?
5. In considering wages in the budget, how is the deduction for social security handled? Explain the reason.
6. Why is money placed in a savings account considered an expenditure since it is still available to you when you want it?
7. Name at least three factors on which an estimate of expenditures may be based.
8. Under what classification in the budget would you include the cost of cleaning of clothes?
9. How would you classify magazine subscriptions in the budget?
10. In the budget of Mr. Murphy, how did he handle the expected sales of fruits and vegetables?
11. Does the budget ever provide for circumstances in which the expenditures for a particular month exceed the income for that month?
12. In the estimate of expenditures on page 424, the total of estimated expenditures is not the same as the total of estimated income. Why is this true and what happens to the difference?
13. How should buying on account or on the installment plan be correlated with budgeting?
14. In the planning of income and expenditures for budget purposes, what particular plan outlined in this chapter determines whether sufficient cash will be available for the expenditures that are planned?
15. When the income for the month is received, what allocations of expenditures are recommended first?

DISCUSSION QUESTIONS

1. What is the fallacy of contending that for budgeting purposes one's income is only the "take-home" income after deductions have been made for social security and all other items, which might include group insurance or hospital insurance?
2. Why do you think part of the expenditure for life insurance is recorded as a family operating expense rather than a personal expense?
3. Why does information gathered from past experience help in establishing a budget?

4. Explain the advantages and disadvantages of model budgets.
5. Explain some of the advantages of the cash estimate that is illustrated in this chapter.
6. (a) If, at the beginning of the year, Mr. Murphy had planned to buy a radio for $50 in December, how would this item have been shown in his budget? (b) How would this item have affected the budget?
7. If Mr. Murphy finds that, according to his budget, he is not going to have enough cash in his checking account to take care of expenses, what can he do to avoid this situation?
8. How do price changes affect a budget?
9. Why is it recommended that the essential operating expenses and the savings should be taken care of first?

PROBLEMS

1. Mr. H. A. Benson has a wife and two children. He earns $75 a week. On the basis of the percentages shown for a family of this size in the model budget on page 422, compute the expenditure for each item in the budget.
2. Mr. Hansen has $92.10 in cash in his checking account when he makes his budget. He estimates that his income will be $235 a month during the year. He also estimates that the following will be his total expenditures for each month:

January	$232.10	July	$240.52
February	260.15	August	232.43
March	213.25	September	230.31
April	230.23	October	231.37
May	222.42	November	220.26
June	225.36	December	252.93

Prepare a form similar to that on page 425, showing a comparison of the estimated income and expenditures.

COMMUNITY PROBLEMS AND PROJECTS

1. (a) List all your items of personal income and of personal expenditure. (b) Prepare a one-year budget of your income and your expenditures as described on pages 423 and 424. You will need this budget for your study of Chapter 24.
2. Make a study of the income and expenditures of your family. Either rule forms similar to those in this chapter for preparing a budget, or purchase a budget book in some store. On the basis of the information that you gain from your family and with the aid of the model budgets and suggestions in this chapter, prepare a budget of the income and expenditures for twelve months.

Chapter 24

_____

How to Keep Personal and Family Records

Purpose of the Chapter. Personal and family records need not be complicated. Any person with a high school education can keep the financial records needed by an individual or a family. However, the person who has had some training in bookkeeping will find the record keeping somewhat easier. A person who is really interested in keeping a record of financial matters either for himself or for his family may devise and operate a simple personal or family record plan. The purpose of this chapter is to point out the kinds of records that should be kept and some practical ways of keeping them.

Why Keep Personal and Family Records? Personal and family financial records are needed for several reasons:

(a) Records of income and expenditures are important elements in planning a budget for the future.

(b) A record of income and of some kinds of expense is needed for making Federal, state, and local tax reports.

(c) A statement of assets and liabilities (debts) at a particular time lets a person know what he is worth at that time.

(d) The income and expense statement for a particular period of time shows the net gain or net loss during that period.

(e) Miscellaneous records of such things as insurance policies, deeds for real estate, and items of value owned are desirable in case of loss of property through fire or other emergency.

Not all persons or families have need for all of these records, but most people have need for some of them.

Statement of Assets and Liabilities. The *assets* of an individual or family consist of property, such as money, savings accounts, cash value of life insurance policies, furniture, and an automobile. A *liability* is a debt that will require cash or some other asset to pay it. Examples of liabilities are amounts not yet paid on a home or an automobile, money borrowed and the interest due on it, and amounts yet to be paid on charge and installment accounts. You will recall that payments becoming due must be considered in estimating expenditures for a budget.

The following form is recommended for use in making a statement of the assets and the debts of a family. This form is used for computing the net worth of a person or a family. *Net worth* is determined by deducting the total of all debts from the total of all assets. For instance, if a person owns assets worth $100 and owes debts amounting to $30, his

Statement of Assets and Liabilities

ASSETS OWNED BY THE FAMILY		DEBTS OWED BY THE FAMILY	
Cash in Checking Account ..$	xxx.xx	Mortgage ....$	xxx.xx
Cash in Savings Account ...	xxx.xx	Loans on Insurance	xxx.xx
Bonds	xxx.xx	Loans Owed to Bank	xxx.xx
Cash Value of Life Insurance.	xxx.xx	Amount Due on an Installment Purchase	xxx.xx
Stocks	xxx.xx		
Notes	xxx.xx	Amount Owed to Stores	xx.xx
Real Estate	xxx.xx	Other Debts:	
Social Security	xxx.xx		
Household Equipment	xxx.xx	——————————	xxx.xx
Automobile	xxx.xx	——————————	xx.xx
Other Assets:		——————————	xxx.xx
——————————	xxx.xx	——————————	xxx.xx
——————————	xxx.xx		
——————————	xx.xx	Total Debts ....$x,xxx.xx	
——————————	xx.xx	Net Worth (Ownership) .... x,xxx.xx	
Total Assets ....$x,xxx.xx		Total Debts and Net Worth.$x,xxx.xx	

(Total Assets, $x,xxx.xx, — Total Debts, $x,xxx.xx, = Net Worth, $x,xxx.xx.)

net worth is $70. Notice that this summary disregards such items as clothing, which is worn out in a reasonably short time and must be replaced. Clothing, instead of being considered an asset, is charged off as an expense when it is purchased.

Let us take as a typical example the case of Mr. J. L. Murphy. Mr. Murphy decides to make a family survey of assets and debts to determine what the family is worth. He uses the model form for tabulating his assets and debts. It is easy for him to determine the amount he has in his checking account and savings account, for he can refer to his balances in these accounts. The cash value of his life insurance is determined by referring to the values indicated in his policies. He has no notes or stocks. The U. S. Bonds are listed at their present value. The amount listed for social security is the amount that has actually been deducted from his wages. His household equipment is valued by adding the cost of each of the more important items and disregarding miscellaneous items that are of little value and that will wear out in a short time. He sets the value of each article at less than the original cost because the equipment has been used several years and is partially worn out. He evaluates his automobile by obtaining an estimate of the trade-in value from an automobile dealer. He lists a vacant lot at the price it cost him.

He knows the amount of the loan that he owes on his life insurance. He determines the amount of a debt owed to a department store by referring to his monthly statement from that store. The following is his summary for January 1, based on these computations:

J. L. MURPHY
Statement of Assets and Liabilities, January 1, 195–

ASSETS OWNED BY THE FAMILY		DEBTS OWED BY THE FAMILY	
Cash in Checking Account .....$	175.00	Loan on Insurance ....$	100.00
Cash in Savings Account	200.00	Owed to Central Store	25.30
U. S. Savings Bonds	150.00	Total Debts	125.30
Life Insurance (Cash Value) ..	331.33		
Social Security	236.00		
Household Equipment	500.00		
Automobile	1,200.00		
Other Assets:			
Vacant Lot	250.00	Net Worth (Ownership)	2,917.03
Total Assets $3,042.33		Total Debts and Net Worth $3,042.33	

(Total Assets, $3,042.33, — Total Debts, $125.30, = Net Worth, $2,917.03.)

A person may possess a great many assets; but if he owes debts almost equal to these assets, his net worth is relatively small. The difference between what he owns and what he owes represents what he is actually worth. This difference was referred to before as net worth. Mr. Murphy's net worth on January 1 is $2,917.03, the difference between his total assets, $3,042.33, and his total debts, $125.30.

The statement of Mr. Murphy's assets and liabilities is also known as a *balance sheet.* Everyone should prepare a record of this kind at least once a year in order to determine his financial standing. Notice that the balance sheet prepared by Mr. Murphy omits not only items of clothing but also such items as fire insurance on the household equipment. In preparing a balance sheet for the practical use of an individual or a family, it is not necessary to list these items. It is simpler to consider them as expenses at the time they are purchased and to disregard them as assets. An insurance policy may have been purchased in order to provide fire insurance protection for three years. Until the policy expires it has an asset value, but for all practical purposes it constitutes an expense at the time it is purchased.

Life insurance is treated differently. Each premium payment consists partly of payment for protection of the family and partly of savings derived from the increase in the cash value of the policy. The expense element is recorded under family expense; the savings element, under life insurance.

The foregoing balance sheet for Mr. Murphy showed his assets, liabilities, and net worth on the first day of the year. During the year the value of the assets and the amount of the liabilities will change. Therefore, Mr. Murphy should prepare a balance sheet again at the end of the year to show his financial status.

J. L. MURPHY
Statement of Assets and Liabilities, December 31, 195–

ASSETS OWNED BY THE FAMILY		DEBTS OWED BY THE FAMILY	
Cash in Checking Account .....$	232.00	City Savings Bank ....$	100.00
Cash in Savings Account	305.70	(due on refrigerator)	
U. S. Savings Bonds	250.00	Owed to Central Store	25.00
Life Insurance (Cash Value) ..	391.33	Total Debts	125.00
Social Security	290.00		
Household Equipment	550.00		
Automobile	1,000.00		
Other Assets:			
Vacant Lot	250.00	Net Worth (Ownership)	3,144.03
Total Assets $3,269.03		Total Debts and Net Worth $3,269.03	

(Total Assets, $3,269.03, — Total Debts, $125.00, = Net Worth, $3,144.03.)

By comparing this balance sheet with the one prepared at the beginning of the year (page 432), it is possible to compute the increase in net worth for the year. This computation is as follows:

Net worth at the end of the year $3,144.03
Net worth at the beginning of the year 2,917.03
                                              ─────────
Increase in Net Worth .... $ 227.00

Statement of Income and Expense. We may recall that income includes wages or salary received, interest and dividends received, net profits from business ventures, and gifts. Expenditures include all expenses and all other ways in which cash is disposed of, such as the buying of furniture, payments on a home or on charge and installment accounts, or money placed in a savings account. It will be noted that there is a difference between expenditures and expenses. The difference between total expenses and total expenditures is the amount that has been put into furniture, bonds, savings, and similar items, or is available in some form of asset. The difference between one's income and his expenses for a given period of time is his net gain or loss. Part or all of the net gain may have been put in savings or some other asset. Actual income and expenditures for this year are good bases upon which to estimate income and expenditures when making a budget for next year.

If Mr. Murphy has kept records of the money he received and of the payments he has made during the year, he can easily determine the total for each class of income and expense. The statement of income and expense shown on the next page was prepared by Mr. Murphy at the end of the year.

You will observe that the Murphys earned less than they anticipated in their budget in Chapter 23 and paid more for rent, food, and clothing than they anticipated. Mr. Murphy was idle because the plant in which he worked was shut down for a while, and the family had to move into a house where they were required to pay more rent. Their planning still permitted them to have a net gain for the year.

J. L. MURPHY

Statement of Income and Expense for the Year Ending December 31, 195–

Income:			
Salary Income		$3,450.00	
Interest Income		56.00	
Dividends		37.00	
Income from Sales		240.00	
Total Income			$3,783.00
Expenses:			
Essential:			
Food $1,004.00			
Clothing 457.00			
Housing 740.00		2,201.00	
Operating:			
Family 581.00			
Personal 63.00			
Automobile 121.00		765.00	
Development:			
Health 131.00			
Education 49.00			
Recreation 82.00			
Benevolence 128.00		390.00	
Total Expenses			3,356.00
Net Gain			$ 427.00

Mr. Murphy's net gain of $427 for the year, as shown by his statement of income and expense, is $200 greater than the increase in his net worth of $227 (see page 434). The reason for this difference is the depreciation of $200 on his automobile, which was not included in his statement of income and expense because that statement includes only cash items.

Other Financial Records. In case of loss by fire or theft, an inventory of the items having value, such as furniture, appliances, books, jewelry, and silverware, should be kept. Dates of purchase, from whom purchased, and cost should be shown on the record.

Though deeds to property, stock certificates, bonds, and insurance policies should be kept in a safe-deposit box, a record of these items should always be kept. Most persons can devise a record plan for listing the items that may be classified as miscellaneous.

Correlating Record Keeping and Budgeting. It is necessary for the Murphy family to keep records so that, as they

CASHBOOK

Date	Explanation	Income	Essential Expenses			Operating Expenses				Development Expenses			Savings and Assets			
			Food	Cloth-ing	Hous-ing	Family	Per-sonal	Auto-mobile	Health	Educa-tion	Recrea-tion	Benevo-lence	Sav. Funds	Life Ins.	Social Sec.	Other Assets
	Budget for July	375	77	30	45	50	5	8	10	5	8	7	65	30	7.50	184.50
July 1	Life insurance													30		
2	Income for John															
4	Gasoline			6		20		3								
7	Dental bill for John							5								
8	Carfare Mary		12			18										
10	Accident insurance	150					2								2.25	
15	Payment Mr. Murphy					7				3			12.50			
16	Magazine subscription											5				
18	Concert tickets										6					
19	Paid grocery bill		39													
17	Gasoline							4								
23	Groceries Mr. Murphy			9							3					
25	Movie tickets								5							
26	Church dues															
26	Shirts for John			3												
27	Paid Dr. Smith				65											
30	Paid rent		41.50													
30	Paid grocery bills					7							12.50		2.25	12.50
30	Salary deductions	450											33.50			
30	Income from sales	75										6				
30	Installment payment on ...															
30	Savings account deposit															
30	Church dues															
30	Totals for July	375	80.50	30	65	32	2	7	10	3	9	11	58.50	30	4.50	12.50
30	Totals to date this year	2293	570.70	246.50	415	324.40	29.75	56	78	28	53	77	289.65	30	31.50	61.50
30	Budget estimate this year	2283	561	235	265	377	35	53	74	29	50	68	228	30	31.50	61.50

Cashbook record of income and expenditures.

go along, they can determine whether they are spending their money as they had planned. Transactions must be recorded daily, weekly, or monthly in accordance with a definite plan. There are many ways to keep a set of records, but the Murphy family chose a simple columnar cashbook with a column for each classification in the budget.

The illustration on page 436 shows a record of (a) income, (b) expenditures for expenses, and (c) expenditures for savings and assets. In other words, this record shows what the income is, its source, and how it is used. This type of business record is known as a *cashbook*. Items are recorded in this cashbook as they occur. In the part of the cashbook illustrated, the entries have been made for July. At the end of a month the various columns are totaled.

Observe that on July 15, Mr. Murphy recorded a salary income of $150. The amount of $7 recorded under family operating expenses is for a payroll deduction for Federal income tax. The amount of $12.50 recorded under savings funds is because of a deduction from his salary by the employer to purchase savings bonds. Likewise, the employer withheld an amount for social security old-age benefits. In other words, Mr. Murphy did not receive all his salary in cash because some of it was withheld for various purposes.

A total of $80.50 was withdrawn from the bank account during the month to pay for groceries. A check was written on July 30 to pay the rent, amounting to $65. Checks were written for clothing on July 1, 8, 23, and 26.

In recording an expenditure for life insurance, one must consider two elements: (a) the cost of the protection and (b) the accumulation of savings that results from the increase in the cash value. As will be explained in the chapter on insurance, most life insurance policies have a cash or loan value. This cash or loan value increases each time a premium is paid. The increases in the cash value are shown on the insurance policy. A definite portion of each premium payment (the increase in the cash value) should therefore be recorded as savings. The remainder should be recorded as a family operating expense (the cost of protection).

Having the proper cash balance available is important. The illustration on page 425 shows that the budget was planned so that there would be an adequate cash balance each month. It is appropriate to compare the income with the expenditures each month using a table similar to the following:

	BEGINNING CASH BALANCE	INCOME	CASH AVAILABLE	EXPENDI-TURES	ENDING CASH BALANCE
January	$175.00	$300.00	$475.00	$300.00	$175.00
February	175.00	300.00	475.00	298.50	176.50

Following the Budget. It will be observed that at the end of each month the columnar totals are added and the budget totals for the month are also inserted for comparison. This is important in order to see how the actual income and expenditures for that month for each classification compare with the estimated income and expenditures in the budget.

At the end of each month, total cumulative income and expenditures for each classification are included in the cashbook, together with the total cumulative budget figures up to date for the income and for each classification of expenditures. This arrangement makes it possible to compare the budget with the actual expenditures for the whole year ending on that particular date. If any expenditures are seriously exceeding the budget, it may be necessary to modify the budget or to change the spending habits. Sometimes it is possible to shift one type of expenditure to another in order to keep the total budget expenditures in line. For instance, let us assume that unusual medical expenses may arise far beyond the budget. Under such circumstances it may be necessary to reduce expenditures for recreation or clothing. It may even be necessary to reduce the amount put in the savings funds so that the total expenditures will not exceed the total income.

Unless some comparisons are made monthly, the expenditures may get out of control and one may end the year by spending considerably more than was planned. Failure to follow the budget is a common cause for using up savings and going into debt.

Recording from Checkbook Stubs. Some definite system must be followed in recording income and expenditures. Unless a definite plan is followed, some items of income and expenditure may be omitted through error. If a checking account is used, the following procedure is recommended:

(a) Deposit all income in the checking account, and record all deposits on the checkbook stubs. If a person's income is subject to payroll deductions, the amounts deducted on each payday can be recorded on the checkbook stub when the deposit is made.

(b) Withdraw only enough cash to take care of such items as food, clothing, and personal and automobile expenditures.

(c) When cash is withdrawn from the bank for a particular purpose, make a record on the checkbook stub to indicate the purpose for which the amount is withdrawn.

(d) Write checks for all major expenditures, such as rent, bills, charge accounts, insurance, and savings.

(e) At the end of the month verify the bank statement and use the checkbook stubs as the source of information for recording all income and expenditures.

The method described above is based upon the assumption that the checkbook stub will provide all the information from which entries can be recorded in the cashbook. However, some persons may wish to use a variation of this plan that will enable them to avoid certain additional service charges on checks. This may be done by cashing the pay check and depositing in the checking account only part of the salary. Sufficient cash can be withheld to make the deposit in the savings account and to take care of small bills and personal allowances which are not to be paid by check.

Recording without a Checkbook. If a checking account is not used, the following procedure is recommended:

(a) When the salary payment is received, keep out only what is allotted for essential, operating, and development expenditures.

(b) Deposit the remainder in a savings account.

(c) If rent or any other major payments are not due at the time the regular income is received, the amount needed may be laid aside until the payment is due.

(d) Record in the cashbook (1) the salary and (2) the deductions for social security and the amounts withheld for any other purposes, such as income taxes, savings, group insurance, or union dues.

(e) Record each expenditure at the time of each purchase for cash or when each bill is paid. If more money has been kept out than is needed during any period, a lesser amount can be kept for the next period. For instance, let us assume that each payday $35 is withheld for essential operating expenditures and that $4 is left over one period. On the next payday $31 could be withheld.

Checking accounts may not be economical for every family, but it is advisable for every family to have at least a bank savings account. Some families, however, do not have even a savings account in a bank. In such cases only the amount of cash necessary to take care of all anticipated expenditures during the month should be withheld on payday; the rest should be placed in Postal Savings, deposited in a credit union, invested in United States Savings Bonds, or put in some other safe place so that there is no temptation to spend it. The expenditures may then be recorded.

Other Methods of Keeping Records. There are hundreds of different plans of keeping records. In almost any stationery store you can buy satisfactory forms for keeping records, or you can design your own forms. Regardless of the system used, you should be sure that you have accurate records of income, expenses, assets, and liabilities.

In some families in which a fixed amount is allowed for each member of the family and a certain amount is allowed for the purchase of groceries and food, the main record is the checkbook, through which all other bills are paid. A supplementary record is kept of assets, and a file is kept of all bills due.

If one does not wish to use a columnar cashbook, such as is illustrated in this chapter, exactly the same plan can

A notebook is convenient for keeping personal and family records.

Harold M. Lambert

be followed by purchasing a notebook of an appropriate size and using it as follows:

(a) Use the first page as an index of expenditures. On this page list the classification of income and expenditures.

(b) Number the subsequent pages and place a title at the top of each page for each classification of income or expenditure. For example, page 2, Income; page 3, Food; page 4, Clothing; and so on through the entire list of expenditures.

(c) Record each transaction on the appropriate page in the same way that it was recorded in the cashbook in the illustration on page 436.

TEXTBOOK QUESTIONS

1. Give at least two reasons for keeping systematic personal and family records.
2. In the preparation of a statement of assets and liabilities (balance sheet), name at least two items that usually are placed in the left column.

3. From a statement of assets and liabilities, how can one determine his net worth or net ownership?
4. What are the two ways in which one can determine his net gain or increase in wealth at the end of a year?
5. In one year's time why is there a difference in the value of the automobile shown on the two statements of assets and liabilities of Mr. Murphy?
6. The statement of income and expenses on page 435 does not show all the expenditures. Why is this true?
7. What types of records should be kept in case of fire or theft?
8. What is a cashbook?
9. How did Mr. Murphy record all of the entries involving salary?
10. How should the purchase of a new suit be recorded?
11. If Mr. Murphy deposits $10 in a savings account, how will he record it in the cashbook?
12. How should Mr. Murphy record the purchase of gasoline?
13. How should Mr. Murphy record the payment of a dental bill?
14. Explain why two different amounts are recorded in two different columns for life insurance.
15. How is it possible for Mr. Murphy to make a careful comparison of his actual expenditures and his budget figures?
16. If a checking account is used, what recommendation is made in regard to depositing each salary check in the bank?
17. When a checking account is not used but a savings account is used, what policy is recommended in regard to depositing money in the savings account?
18. If a savings account in a bank is not used, what policy is recommended each payday in regard to money needed for expenditures and for the surplus fund?
19. Besides the columnar cashbook method of recording expenditures, what other method is recommended in this chapter?

DISCUSSION QUESTIONS

1. If a man's net worth at the beginning of the year was $1,900 and at the end of the year was $1,700, what was his net gain or loss?
2. Can you explain why the savings and assets are considered as part of the expenditures in the system explained in this chapter?
3. In the cashbook, the total of all expenditures equals the total of all income. Explain why the expenditures for savings and assets are not included in the statement of income and expense.

4. Suppose that sometime during the year Mr. Murphy's automobile had been stolen and he was not covered by insurance. How would you recommend showing this loss in his statements at the end of the year?

5. If Mr. Murphy gets $50 as a Christmas present from his employer, how will this amount be recorded in his cashbook?

6. In what column in the cashbook do you think Mr. Murphy would record such items as (a) a hunting license and (b) a parking fee?

7. What recommendations would you offer Mr. Murphy if he finds that his automobile expenses are running twice as much as planned in the budget?

8. If Mr. Murphy finds, by monthly comparisons, that expenditures for food are running over the budget, what would you recommend that he do?

9. If the income proves to be less than was originally expected, what must Mr. Murphy do?

10. What are some of the disadvantages of using a checking account?

PROBLEMS

1. Mr. Walsh has the following assets available: cash in a savings account, $150; U. S. Government savings bonds, $83; automobile, $350; cash value of life insurance, $460. He owes the following debts: account at grocery store, $15; account at department store, $23; due finance company for automobile, $100. Prepare a statement of assets and debts like the model in this chapter.

2. Mr. J. O. Jones has an insurance policy that has a cash value of $135.10. The annual premium is $46.20. After the premium for the current year has been paid, the cash value will amount to $161.20. How will Mr. Jones record the premium payment in his cashbook?

3. Assume that Mr. R. D. Malone's income was $1,819.47. Prepare his statement of income and expense for the year ending on December 31, 195-, using the following expenses:

Food	$382.15	Automobile	$52.20
Clothing	214.25	Health	28.00
Housing	490.00	Education	39.50
Family	96.20	Recreation	36.25
Personal	42.10	Benevolence	52.00

4. Mr. J. O. Mason found the following information on his checkbook stubs at the end of January. Rule a cashbook similar to the one shown on page 436, and record the transactions of Mr. Mason. Total and rule the columns of the cashbook after you have recorded all the transactions.

Jan.	2.	Clothing	$ 10.00
		Food	36.00
	5.	Personal allowance for Mr. Mason	5.00
		Personal allowance for Mrs. Mason	5.00
		Theater tickets	4.00
	10.	Food	34.00
		Magazine subscription	2.50
	15.	Salary (Less $2.40 for social security and $19.20 for withholding tax)	160.00
		Taxes on home	30.00
	20.	Telephone	3.50
		Light and gas	4.00
	22.	Gasoline	2.00
		Automobile repairs	5.00
	25.	Church contributions	4.00
		Dentist bill	6.00
	31.	Salary (Less $2.40 for social security and $19.20 for withholding tax)	160.00
		Savings deposit	15.00

COMMUNITY PROBLEMS AND PROJECTS

1. In Project No. 1 of the previous chapter you were required to prepare a budget for yourself. On the basis of the classifications of income and expenditures in that budget, prepare a cashbook for yourself in which you can record your income and expenditures. Keep an accurate record of your income and expenditures for at least two months, making comparisons at the end of each month with your budget, as Mr. Murphy did. At the end of two months submit this project to your teacher for checking.

2. Make a study of the income and the expenditures of your family. Rule a form for a cashbook or prepare a small notebook for keeping the records of your family. Record all the items of income and expenditure for one month.

Chapter 25

PART VII_____ _____

Planning Your Savings Program

Purpose of the Chapter. Successful management of personal and family finances includes not only earning an income and spending it wisely for the things we need and want but also maintaining a regular systematic plan of saving. Saving regularly is just as important in the financial management of a person's affairs as is the wise selection of commodities and services that we buy.

The amount of a person's income, of course, has something to do with the amount of his savings. Nevertheless, it is not how much he *earns* but how much he *saves* that eventually determines how much he is worth. Likewise, his program for savings is an important factor in determining how secure he is and, therefore, how happy he is. The purpose of this chapter is to point out some of the reasons why we save, the general principles to guide us in saving, and systematic plans for saving.

Guides to Personal and Family Saving. Four principles of saving for individuals and families are:

(a) Plan your income and expenditures by making a budget; keep accurate and complete records of income and expenses to make sure you live within your budget.
(b) Spend less than you earn.
(c) Invest these savings wisely.
(d) Reinvest the income from savings promptly.

Setting Goals for Savings. Most people have some definite goals in life, some things toward which they are striving. Some of these goals are really ideals and ambitions, and some are desires for material things that will add to the comfort and pleasantness of living. Regardless of the kind of goals we may have for ourselves, money is usually a factor in achieving them. Most of us have to set aside a

445

An education for a chosen occupation is one of the most important goals of a savings plan.

little at a time from our income in order to accumulate enough to realize our goals. Setting aside a part of our income regularly is *saving*, and investing the amount we set aside so interest may be earned is evidence of good money management. The following is a brief list of worthy goals for which one should be willing to save:

(a) Education.
(b) Marriage.
(c) Buying a home.
(d) Starting a business.
(e) Buying insurance for protection and future income.
(f) Investments in securities for future income.
(g) Buying major comforts and luxuries for better living.
(h) Emergencies.
(i) Retirement.

The time the money will be needed and the amount that will be needed for each of the goals we set for ourselves must be considered when we save for specific purposes.

446

When a savings fund has been established for some specific purpose, it should be used only for that purpose. One of the major goals of a student should be to acquire adequate education for a trade or profession.

After a person has established a savings program, he should not waver in carrying it out. If ten dollars a month is to be set aside for a certain savings fund, this amount should be taken out of the income first and only the remainder should be used for other purposes. In other words, a person should learn to live within the income that is allotted for living purposes. He should not penalize the savings fund by neglecting to contribute to it whenever some excuse arises. The program should be carried through to completion. If a person finds that he can save more money than he had anticipated, this fact is no excuse for his spending the surplus. It is an indication that more savings should be accumulated. If money is set aside for some purpose and is not needed, the best place to put it until there is some definite need is in a savings fund.

Retirement, a Goal for Saving. While many people receive old-age pensions and other forms of social security benefits when they no longer are able to work and earn for themselves, most people want a supplementary income of their own when they reach retirement age. They feel more independent and enjoy life more if they receive income from their own investments instead of depending entirely upon income from social security, even though they contributed to the fund from which their benefits may be paid. Therefore, during their best earning years many people set aside a certain amount of money each month that will be returned to them monthly with compound interest when they retire, usually at the age of 65 or 70 years. This amount received each month is known as *retirement income*.

In planning for retirement income, several factors should be considered:

(a) The amount of monthly income that is desired upon retirement.

(b) The amount of monthly savings invested at compound interest that will be required in order to produce that retirement income.

(c) The possible changes that may come about in a person's way of living. A modest home and ordinary comforts acceptable now may seem inadequate thirty or forty years from now. Therefore, plans for saving for retirement should be adjusted as permanent changes in standards of living become evident.

(d) The possibility of a decrease in the purchasing power of a dollar through a general increase in price levels (inflation). If in 1990 or when you reach retirement age, two dollars would be required to buy the same commodities or services that one dollar will buy now, you would need to save twice as much a month while you earn in order to live comfortably in retirement. As changes in economic conditions that appear to be permanent occur, you should, therefore, allow for them in your retirement saving plan.

Evaluating Expenditures. The judgment used in spending is an important factor in enabling us to save. If one's income is spent soon after each payday, the spending is probably not well planned.

The average family that spends its income as soon as it is received finds it impossible to take a vacation trip, or to purchase an automobile or any other items of comfort or luxury, without going into debt. If the same family were to forego certain trivial pleasures, however, and to establish a definite savings program, its members could enjoy more desirable comforts and luxuries, which require a reasonably large expenditure of money.

In making a decision with regard to buying a luxury, one should answer the question, "What will it cost me in terms of days of labor?" For example, if a stenographer earns $30 a week on the basis of a forty-hour week, she is earning at the rate of 75 cents an hour. Suppose she has enough to make a down payment on an automobile but finds that it will cost her $60 a month to pay for it, $6 a month for a garage, an average of $4 a month for repairs, and an average of $12 a month for gasoline and oil. The monthly

An adequate retirement
income is a savings goal
for everyone.

Ewing Galloway

cost will be $82. This calculation does not take into consideration that the tires will wear out and will have to be replaced, or that the automobile will wear out and that any accident will increase the maintenance costs. The minimum expenses therefore amount to $82 a month. As this stenographer is earning only $130 a month (four and one-third weeks in a month), it is obvious that the luxury of an automobile is not justified.

The following criteria should be observed in all spending:

(a) Refuse to buy anything that cannot be afforded.
(b) Do not buy anything that is not needed.
(c) No purchase is a bargain at any price unless there is a definite need for it.
(d) Buying the best is often right if you are sure that you get the best.

Paying as One Goes. One should not go into debt for things that will have been used or consumed before they are paid for. It is frequently desirable to go into debt for a major investment, such as a home, but the same thing is not true of going into debt for current purchases. The latter practice will soon lead to the destruction of the savings program.

Making a Plan for Saving. It is easy to spend all of our income and save none of it unless we have a goal or a reason for saving. The reason many people save is to have money at a future time to go to college, to establish or to buy a home or a business, or to invest to provide for a future income. Savings to meet these and similar goals must be planned in the budget of expenditures. Individuals and family units, like business firms, can never operate successfully financially without a plan. The plans for savings for special purposes usually involve planning for a sum of money to be available at some definite time in the future.

Anticipated needs can be calculated reasonably closely. For instance, the purchase of a home can be planned years in advance. A certain amount of money may be required as a down payment on the home. Money for this purpose can be saved under a definite plan. Money accumulates rapidly when a specific amount is deposited each month at compound interest. For example:

$5 deposited each month at 2 per cent interest grows to $665 in 10 years or at 4 per cent interest to $737.45 in 10 years.
$10 deposited each month at 2 per cent interest will be $1,330 in 10 years or at 4 per cent interest, $1,474.90.

These calculations are based on the assumption that (a) each deposit is made at the beginning of the month, (b) interest is compounded semiannually, and (c) interest is calculated according to the actual amount of time (each whole six-month period) that a deposit has been in the account.

Regardless of the amount of income received, it will be consumed by expenses unless one plans to save some of it each month. We are able to save each month only by controlling our expenses. Though a person's income may be small, usually if he really wants and needs something, he can plan to get it by saving a little at a time.

Compound interest tables are available at banks and savings companies and in some books, showing how much must be deposited each month at a given rate of interest in order to have a specific amount such as $1,000 available in five years, ten years, twenty years, or any other period of time.

A Summary of Saving Procedures

1. Determine what you want most in the future, such as more education, a home, a business, an income for retirement; establish these things as goals for saving.

2. Most people need an income for retirement. We need to plan for retirement income throughout the entire period that we earn, which means saving for retirement income should be started as early as possible in one's career.

3. Consider every expenditure, especially those for luxuries, very carefully before making it. Decide if you really can afford to buy the article or spend the money; consider how it will affect your savings.

4. Have a plan for saving. Usually separate funds or accounts are desirable—one for each of the goals you have decided upon.

5. From time to time check the effect of changes in economic conditions, that is, changes in the general price levels, upon the value of your savings.

6. Make your savings work for you by investing them at compound interest. Study interest tables to determine how much you must save a month to accumulate the amount you want at some future time.

Make Money Work for You. Very few people realize the cumulative power of compound interest. Interest is a very diligent and faithful worker, but it will work for one only if one has savings. This fact explains why many rich people have no difficulty in making a living. Although they cease to work, their money continues to work for them by earning interest. If a person lends his money or places it in some institution that uses it for making loans, the money will produce an income. Lending money is one way of sharing wealth with others. Because the lending of the money renders a service to someone who needs to borrow, the lender is entitled to interest.

The following table shows the rate at which money accumulates when interest is compounded semiannually. If the interest is compounded quarterly or monthly, the increase is greater.

INTEREST RATE	DOUBLED IN	QUADRUPLED IN	MULTIPLIED IN 47 YEARS (AGE 18 TO 65)
2 %	35.00 YEARS	70.00 YEARS	2 1/2 TIMES
2½%	28.00 YEARS	56.14 YEARS	3 1/5 TIMES
3 %	23.28 YEARS	46.58 YEARS	4 1/20 TIMES
3½%	19.98 YEARS	39.96 YEARS	5 1/10 TIMES
4 %	17.50 YEARS	35.00 YEARS	6 2/5 TIMES

If a person eighteen years of age invests one dollar at 4 per cent interest, compounded semiannually, the investment will be worth two dollars when he is thirty-five and a half years old, four dollars when he is fifty-three years old, and six dollars and forty cents when he is sixty-five years old.

The cumulative power of compound interest.

Let Savings Earn Interest As They Accumulate. The average individual saves only a few dollars a month. Hence, he needs a place to put his savings month by month, until a sufficient amount accumulates to invest in bonds, stocks, real estate, or for some other form of permanent investment. In deciding upon a place to put savings where they will earn income, the following questions should be considered:

(a) Will the account be safe?
(b) Will it pay a reasonable rate of interest?
(c) Will the savings be available at any time?
(d) How often is interest compounded?

Of the many institutions where savings will earn interest as they accumulate, banks, building and loan associations, postal savings, United States Savings Bonds, and credit unions are most commonly used.

Banks. There are two general types of banks in which savings may be deposited. The first is the commercial bank with a savings department, and the second is the savings bank.

A savings account may be opened either in a commercial bank or a savings bank.

Ewing Galloway

Banks usually are conveniently located, making it easy to deposit savings at the time of cashing a pay check. The interest may be credited quarterly, semiannually, or annually. Some banks require thirty days' notice before withdrawing a deposit. This right is not always exercised, but it may be if necessary. Rates of interest on savings accounts are fairly uniform among banks. The rules and regulations of banks with regard to opening an account, making deposits, crediting interest, and withdrawing savings may influence the selection of a place to deposit savings. The deposits in all national and in many other banks are insured by the Federal Deposit Insurance Corporation to the extent of $10,000 for each depositor. However, some banks not having the insurance may be just as safe as those having it.

Most commercial banks and regular savings banks are owned by stockholders and pay a fixed rate of interest. A *mutual savings bank* is a slightly different type of bank because it is owned by the depositors. The depositors are not promised a fixed rate of interest. If there is a profit, each depositor is paid a dividend instead of interest. But, if there is no profit earned on the operations of the bank, the depositors do not get a dividend. In most other respects, however, a mutual savings bank is operated the same as any other bank.

Building and Loan Associations. Building and loan associations serve essentially the same purpose as savings banks,

453

and many of them operate in much the same way. Although such associations have relatively uniform procedures, each is regulated by the laws of the state in which it is located. There is considerable difference in the laws of the various states.

The building and loan association is organized for the purpose of lending money to people who do not have enough money to buy or build a home. The money that the association lends is accumulated from depositors. In many states, when a person makes deposits in a building and loan association, he really buys *shares* and becomes theoretically a part owner. These shares usually earn a fixed rate of income, which generally is a slightly higher rate than interest on a savings account in a bank.

All Federal building and loan associations are members of the Federal Home Loan Bank and operate under regulations established by the Federal Government. The accounts of these associations are insured with the Federal Savings and Loan Insurance Corporation. All other building and loan associations may have their accounts insured with the Federal Savings and Loan Insurance Corporation if they are members of the Federal Home Loan Bank and if they pass rigid insurability tests. It may also insure the accounts of homestead associations, and of co-operative banks organized and operated according to the laws of the state, district, or territory in which they were chartered or organized. Any institution in which the accounts are insured provides an extra margin of safety for the person who places his savings in it.

Postal Savings. Many people who do not have ready access to a bank or who do not have faith in their local bank buy postal savings certificates at the local post office. The United States Postal Savings System was established in 1910 and has served many depositors, especially those having small amounts to invest.

A person desiring to open a postal-savings account should apply at the nearest post office or station. Any person ten years of age or over is eligible under this plan. No person may have more than one account, and all accounts must be of a personal nature.

Deposits are acknowledged by postal-savings certificates in denominations of $1, $2, $5, $10, $20, $50, $100, $200, or $500, which are made out in the names of the depositors. These serve as receipts and are valid until paid. The certificates are not negotiable or transferable. If a certificate is lost, stolen, or destroyed, a new certificate will be issued. No depositor may have an account in excess of $2,500, exclusive of accumulated interest.

Interest accumulates at the rate of 2 per cent for each full year that a certificate is outstanding. It accumulates for a partial year at the rate of one-half per cent for each full quarter. Interest is not compounded, but a depositor may withdraw it and use it for making a new deposit. Therefore, it is advisable to withdraw interest when it has been earned.

A depositor at any time may withdraw all or any part of his postal savings by presenting a certificate for redemption. Withdrawals may be made in person, through a representative, or by mail.

No person connected with the Post Office Department is permitted to disclose the name of a depositor or to give information about an account to any person other than the depositor.

United States Savings Bonds. Several types of government bonds may be purchased by investors; however, the most popular among people who are saving small amounts regularly are the Series E Bonds. These bonds are available at the prices indicated in the following table and are payable in ten years at the prices indicated in the right-hand column.

COST		REDEMPTION VALUE
$ 18.75	increases in 10 years to	$ 25.00
$ 37.50	increases in 10 years to	$ 50.00
$ 75.00	increases in 10 years to	$ 100.00
$150.00	increases in 10 years to	$ 200.00
$375.00	increases in 10 years to	$ 500.00
$750.00	increases in 10 years to	$1,000.00

Any person may purchase up to, but not more than, $10,000 worth (maturity value) of bonds issued during any calendar year. In each subsequent year, however, additional bonds not exceeding the same maximum value may be purchased. Other series may be purchased in larger quantities.

The individual owner of bonds may name only one beneficiary, to whom payment will be made upon the death of the owner. A co-owner may also be named so that either or both may cash the bond.

If a savings bond is lost, stolen, or destroyed, a duplicate will be issued upon satisfactory proof. The Treasury Department, through the Federal Reserve Banks, provides means of safekeeping that are available without charge. To take advantage of this service, one should apply in person at the nearest Federal Reserve Bank or branch bank, or write and obtain an application blank. The owner of the bond must sign the application. If there is a co-owner, both of the owners must sign. The bond with the application should then be presented personally or by mail to the Federal Reserve Bank. A receipt is then issued.

While the rate of interest earned on United States savings bonds is not high, it is reasonable in comparison with the rate of earnings on some other savings. If a bond is held until maturity, it has an equivalent yield of 2.9 per cent interest, compounded semiannually. After sixty days from its date of issue, a savings bond may be redeemed at the established cash redemption value. The table on page 457 shows the redemption values.

Credit Unions. Credit unions are co-operative associations operating both as savings and lending institutions for the benefit of members. In most states credit unions have operated and are authorized to operate under state laws. With the passage of the Federal Credit Union Act, approved on June 26, 1934, Federal credit unions may be organized and operated under a Federal charter issued by the Farm Credit Administration.

Credit unions are usually formed by large groups of people with common interests. For instance, they may be

Table of Redemption Values
of United States Savings Bonds

Series E

ISSUE PRICE	$18.75	$37.50	$ 75.00	$375.00	$ 750.00
Redemption values after the issue date:					
First ½ year	$18.75	$37.50	$ 75.00	$375.00	$ 750.00
½ to 1 year	18.75	37.50	75.00	375.00	750.00
1 to 1½ years	18.87	37.75	75.50	377.50	755.00
1½ to 2 years	19.00	38.00	76.00	380.00	760.00
2 to 2½ years	19.12	38.25	76.50	382.50	765.00
2½ to 3 years	19.25	38.50	77.00	385.00	770.00
3 to 3½ years	19.50	39.00	78.00	390.00	780.00
3½ to 4 years	19.75	39.50	79.00	395.00	790.00
4 to 4½ years	20.00	40.00	80.00	400.00	800.00
4½ to 5 years	20.25	40.50	81.00	405.00	810.00
5 to 5½ years	20.50	41.00	82.00	410.00	820.00
5½ to 6 years	20.75	41.50	83.00	415.00	830.00
6 to 6½ years	21.00	42.00	84.00	420.00	840.00
6½ to 7 years	21.50	43.00	86.00	430.00	860.00
7 to 7½ years	22.00	44.00	88.00	440.00	880.00
7½ to 8 years	22.50	45.00	90.00	450.00	900.00
8 to 8½ years	23.00	46.00	92.00	460.00	920.00
8½ to 9 years	23.50	47.00	94.00	470.00	940.00
9 to 9½ years	24.00	48.00	96.00	480.00	960.00
9½ to 10 years	24.50	49.00	98.00	490.00	980.00
Maturity value	25.00	50.00	100.00	500.00	1,000.00

Redemption values of U. S. savings bonds.

formed by such groups as teachers in a large school system, workers in a large factory, store employees, and church or fraternal organizations.

While the credit unions established under the laws of the various states are by no means uniform, there is uniformity in the organization of Federal credit unions. A member of a Federal credit union must agree to subscribe for at least one five-dollar share, payable in one sum of cash or in periodic installments. He may subscribe for a larger number of shares if he desires. He must also pay an entrance fee of 25 cents. Members who are in arrears in their payments are subject to a small fine unless they are excused by the directors.

When a member has paid for one share, he is eligible to his proportionate share of the annual dividends that may be declared by the members. These dividends represent interest on the savings deposited with the credit union. A credit union is a true co-operative in that its members share in the earnings. The maximum rate that may be paid, however, as a dividend is 6 per cent.

Savings and Investments. Usually a savings program provides for the accumulation of savings from month to month. While savings accounts bear interest, many people prefer to use accumulated savings to purchase permanent or long-term investments on which the yield may be greater than on savings accounts of temporary nature. Investing is putting savings to work. For the average individual there can be no investing unless it has been preceded by saving. The principles of investment will be discussed in the next chapter.

TEXTBOOK QUESTIONS

1. Name the four guides for personal and family saving.
2. Name at least three important goals of saving.
3. How does the possibility of a change in the purchasing power of the dollar affect savings plans for retirement?
4. Give an example of how one must evaluate his expenditures in order to carry out a savings program successfully.
5. What do you recommend as a policy of paying as you go?
6. From the table given on page 452, find out (a) how long it takes to double your money at 2 per cent compound interest, (b) how long it takes to double your money at 3 per cent compound interest.
7. Why must savings precede investments?
8. What facts should be considered in selecting a place to open a savings account?
9. What are the two general types of banks in which savings may be deposited?
10. What is the difference between a mutual savings bank and a regular savings bank?
11. Is a building and loan association a bank?
12. For what purposes is a building and loan association organized?
13. What is the Federal Savings and Loan Insurance Corporation?
14. What is the interest rate on postal savings?
15. How may deposits be withdrawn from the Federal Postal Savings System?
16. What is the redemption value of a $25 (issue price $18.75) United States savings bond at the end of one and a half years? at the end of eight years?
17. Give examples of groups of persons who may organize credit unions.

DISCUSSION QUESTIONS

1. If a person has built up a reserve cash fund, what are some of the ways in which he can utilize this fund? (Do not include the ways mentioned in this chapter.)
2. A man says, "What is the use of saving? I always have to spend my savings for emergencies." Discuss this statement.
3. Why is it necessary to correlate budgeting, saving, and buying a home?
4. Suppose that a man is able to save $20 a month. He has accumulated $500 and uses this amount as a down payment on an automobile. It will cost him $20 a month to complete paying for the automobile. Is he justified in buying it? Discuss the situation.
5. Some people borrow money and also buy on account and on the installment plan in order to have furniture and luxuries comparable to those of people with larger incomes. They follow this plan because they feel that they deserve these things. What advice would you give to a person of this kind?
6. A particular loan company is liberal in lending on mortgages and offers a high rate of interest to depositors. If you were seeking a place to accumulate savings, would you select this loan company or one that is conservative in making loans and offers a rate of interest that is ½ per cent less?

PROBLEMS

Note: For Problems 1 and 2 use the following table, which shows the value of monthly deposits of one dollar at interest rates of 2, 3, and 4 per cent, compounded semiannually.

END OF YEAR	2%	3%	4%
1	$ 12.13	$ 12.20	$ 12.26
2	24.51	24.76	25.02
3	37.13	37.70	38.29
4	50.01	51.04	52.10
5	63.14	64.78	66.46
6	76.54	78.93	81.41
7	90.21	93.51	96.96
8	104.26	108.54	113.14
9	118.49	124.01	129.97
10	133.00	139.96	147.49
11	147.80	156.38	165.70
12	162.90	173.30	184.66
13	178.30	190.74	204.38
14	194.02	208.70	224.90
15	210.05	227.20	246.25

1. A person deposits $10 in a savings account at the beginning of each month. The interest rate is 3 per cent, compounded semiannually. How much will be in the savings account at the end of thirteen years?
2. If $2 a month is deposited in a savings account on which 3 per cent interest is compounded semiannually, how much will be available (a) in five years? (b) in ten years?
3. Using the table on page 452 showing the cumulative power of compound interest, assume that you have $1,000 to invest at 18 years of age at 2 per cent interest, compounded semiannually. How much will this amount to at age 65?
4. Assume that one U. S. savings bond is purchased for $18.75 at the end of each month for ten years. Using the table of redemption values in this chapter, what will be the value of all the bonds at the end of ten years?

COMMUNITY PROBLEMS AND PROJECTS

1. Make a study of the cost of attending some particular college or several colleges. From the college or colleges obtain information with regard to tuition, laboratory fees, room rents, and cost of meals and laundry. Add to these amounts the cost of clothing, amusement, transportation, and any other items that you believe should be included in the cost of a college education. Make an estimate of the total cost for each of the four years of a college education. Prepare a report showing how you believe it will be possible to finance this education through (a) income from parents or relatives, (b) loans, (c) scholarships, (d) personal savings, (e) earnings made while you are in school.
2. (a) Calculate your yearly requirements for clothes. (b) Compute the amount of regular weekly savings that must be accumulated to provide for buying the clothes as they are needed. Assume that the amount you will need for clothes will be provided through weekly allowances.

Chapter 26

Principles of Investing Your Savings

Purpose of the Chapter. A planned system of investment is the logical outcome of systematic saving. All investments should be made with, first, safety of the principal and, secondly, certainty of the income in mind. As a general principle, the safety of an investment depends upon the certainty, not the size, of the income as indicated by past and present records and future possibilities.

Most individuals have only a limited amount of money to invest. This money is usually accumulated by hard work and careful saving. Very few, if any, individuals are justified in speculating. Their money should be truly invested with the idea of earning an income for some future purpose. The purpose of this chapter is to state the more important principles that an individual should follow in investing his funds.

Savings and Investments. Several principles of investments should be observed in planning the kinds of investments one makes. *Saving* refers to the accumulation of earnings over expenses, month by month, usually deposited in accounts that bear interest. *Investing* is putting savings to work through the purchase of assets, such as long-term securities, real estate, or a business, from which a substantial income may be expected.

Differences between Investing, Speculating, and Gambling. *Investing* is buying assets, such as securities, with the expectation of receiving a certain, though maybe small, income over a long period of time. *Speculating* is buying securities or other assets with the hope that the value of those securities or assets will increase in a relatively short period of time. *Gambling* is taking an unnecessary risk of losing the money paid for a lottery ticket or for a chance of extraordinary, unearned gain.

For most families investment should wait until a home has been purchased.

Federal Housing Administration

In all three cases there are risks, but the risks increase as the possibilities of large gains or losses increase. Investment and speculation both serve worthy economic functions in the business world. Gambling does not.

When Is a Family Ready to Invest? Ordinarily, a person or a family should not make investments in securities, such as stocks and bonds (except Government Savings Bonds), or in real estate (other than a home) until after an emergency savings fund has been established, a reasonable amount of life insurance has been planned, and a home has been secured. However, a person having a few hundred dollars to invest may be wise if he invests it in a small business that he expects to operate and manage.

Important Points in Selecting Investments. Speculations are often disguised as sound investments. Because of this fact, the prospective investor should rely on someone who is capable of giving sound advice. The banker in a small town may or may not be able to do so, although any banker is usually more capable than the average investor. Large banks have experts qualified to analyze securities and to give advice. Brokerage businesses have similar experts. The opinions of bankers and brokers are, however, sometimes biased by personal interest. Taking these facts into consideration, the prospective investor should investigate the following points with regard to a security:

462

(a) Suitability of the investment.
(b) Safety of the principal.
(c) Satisfactory and certain income from the investment.
(d) Marketability of the security.

Suitability of the Investment. A bond, a stock, a note, or a mortgage may prove to be safe as an investment, but it may not fit into the investment program of a particular person. The suitability of a certain investment is therefore important. The following are important considerations in determining the suitability:

(a) *Acceptable amount.* Bonds are usually available in denominations of one hundred, five hundred, or one thousand dollars, although the market value may vary. Sometimes a thousand-dollar bond can be purchased for five hundred dollars or less. When a bond sells far below its stated value, there is a cause for the loss in value that should be carefully investigated before the bond is purchased.

Stocks may have stated values from one dollar to one hundred dollars, although the market value may be widely different from the stated value. Stocks with no stated value also have a wide price range.

The number of units of a bond or a stock to be purchased will be regulated by the amount that can be invested.

(b) *Diversification of the investment.* There is an old saying, "Don't put all your eggs in one basket." There is, on the other hand, a contradictory saying, "Put all your eggs in one basket and watch the basket."

The first rule is probably the better one for the average investor. It means that he should diversify his invest-

Diversify your investments. Don't put all your eggs in one basket.

ment. By diversifying his investment, he diversifies his risks. If a person puts all his money into one type of security and that security decreases in value or becomes totally worthless, the loss will probably be severe. On the other hand, if a person invests his money in ten different securities and only one of them decreases in value or becomes worthless, the loss is not so severe.

Each security should be selected carefully. It is better to confine the investment to a few good securities than to purchase several questionable securities.

(c) *Period of the investment.* An investment in a bond, a mortgage, or a note continues a definite period of time before the obligation matures. For instance, a bond may mature in six months or in forty to one hundred years. If a person wants to make an investment for a long period of time without the trouble of reinvesting, he should consider the date of maturity.

(d) *Value of the security as collateral.* Frequently an investor may want to use a security as collateral in obtaining a loan. If the need for obtaining a loan is a possibility, he should buy a security that will be acceptable to a bank as collateral. Securities that do not have a ready market are not desirable as collateral.

(e) *Income periods.* Bonds have definite dates on which interest is payable. The interest may be calculated quarterly, semiannually, or annually, and the specific dates of payment are set. Stocks may have quarterly, semiannual, or annual dividend dates. The person who has a diversified investment program may want to buy securities that have interest and dividend dates that fit into the complete investment program and assure a relatively steady income.

Bonds in some cases are callable before maturity. In such a case the corporation or other institution that issued the bonds may call them in and pay the owners at a specified rate. If a person wishes to invest his money in bonds for a definite length of time without the bother of reinvesting, he will want to determine whether the bonds are callable. A good income-producing bond may soon be called in unexpectedly.

Safety of the Principal. Any good investment involves the protection of the principal. If there is any question about the safety of the principal, the investment should not be made. The following are some tests of the safety of the principal of corporation securities:

(a) *Ability of the management of the corporation issuing the security.* Competent management is indispensable to the success of any business. Before purchasing a stock or a bond, the investor should make certain that those who manage the business have ability. Ability should have been demonstrated through successful previous operations, through the standing of the enterprise, and through the personal records of the managers.

(b) *Reliability of the managers of the corporation and of the investment promoters.* The integrity of the managers of the business and the promoters of the sale of the security should be investigated thoroughly. No one should buy a security issued by an unknown company. The statement of an unknown person should not be accepted without investigating through a person of known integrity and ability.

(c) *Past performance of the corporation.* The past performance of the business should be measured by the assets and the earning record. The outstanding bonds and the outstanding stock should have a very conservative relation to the assets. Any well-established company with securities listed on the open market can be investigated through the stock exchanges and banks, or through such listings of securities as those given in *Poor's Manuals* and *Moody's Manuals.* From these same sources information can be obtained with regard to the earning performance of the corporation.

(d) *The future earning position of the corporation.* Some investments in once well-established companies have been lost because of technical developments, changes in consumer buying habits, or loss of markets. Although there is no way of judging the future earnings of a given company except by the past performance of the company, consideration must be given to whatever will likely affect the future of the company.

Comparisons should be made between different companies. If a company has found it difficult to pay operating costs and interest on indebtedness and still have a comfortable margin for dividends, it is not advisable to purchase a bond or a stock of this company. At least there is no reason to believe that the investment is conservative.

As was explained in Chapter 6, the Federal Government, through the Securities and Exchange Commission, regulates the sale of securities through registered security exchanges. A good policy for any investor is to buy only a security that is registered and approved in his own state, and registered and approved by the Securities and Exchange Commission. If one is buying a security through an exchange, the safest practice is to purchase through an exchange registered by the Securities and Exchange Commission.

The safety of the principal is also involved in any other kind of investment, such as in a government bond or in real estate. Your investment in a government bond is as safe as the government itself. Cities, counties, and states have credit and financial ratings just the same as businesses.

There are three main factors to be considered as to the safety of the principal when one invests in real estate. First is the question of whether you get a good and legal title to the property, second is the question of location, and third is the question of economic conditions. Checking on the title involves legal assistance, and in checking on the location one should make sure that it is in a location that will not decrease in value. For instance, some residential neighborhoods are going down in value gradually while others are increasing in value principally because of the location. Economic conditions affect the value of real estate just as they affect the value of all other investments. These factors will be discussed in more detail in later chapters.

Satisfactory Income from the Investment. The safety of the principal is more important than a satisfactory income. If the principal is lost, there will be no income. The following are considerations with regard to the income:

(a) *Rate of return.* It should be remembered that a sound investment does not have a yield that is higher than the average rate of interest used to attract investors. A conservative rate of interest on a good bond will be determined by the conditions that exist at the time the bond is offered for sale. A high-grade bond sometimes pays no more than 2 or 3 per cent interest on the face value. If the bond sells below its face value, it may, however, pay a higher rate on the basis of its actual selling price. When the rate of return offered on a bond is ½ per cent to 2 per cent above the rate of interest on high-grade government bonds, special care should be taken in investigating the quality of the security. If some of the tests of quality cannot be met by the bond, the reason for this failure should be determined.

(b) *Guaranteed rate of return.* A bond assures a definite rate of interest. If the company fails to pay the interest, the bondholder has a legal right of action to obtain the property (or income, in the case of debenture bonds) that has been pledged by the issuer of the bonds. Preferred stock also carries a stipulated rate of dividend and has preference in the distribution of earnings to stockholders. The earnings on common stock are regulated in many ways. A corporation is not obligated to pay any established rate of dividend on such stock. There may be two or three grades of common stock, one of which has preference with regard to sharing in the profits of the company. Before buying common stock of any kind, a person should investigate the stipulations regarding dividends. As owners of stock are part owners of the company that has issued the stock, they are paid out of the earnings of the company after the bondholders and other creditors have been paid.

(c) *Regularity of the income.* Most investors are interested in having a steady and reliable income. The continuous payment of interest or dividends is therefore one of the first considerations in evaluating a security. The prospects of future income from the security can be judged on the basis of the records of past earnings of the company. In most cases it is very simple to determine whether a company has paid its interest and dividends regularly in the past. Unless the prospects of future income can be judged, the purchase of the security on the basis of the return is largely a speculation.

(d) *Margin of safety.* The margin of earnings regulates not only the safety of the income that is paid to the investor but also the safety of the principal. If past records show that the company has had difficulty in earning enough to pay interest and dividends, it is questionable whether it could pay interest and dividends under any unusual circumstances.

Marketability of the Security. Although an investor, in the true sense of the word, is not interested in buying a security with the thought of selling it immediately, he must give consideration to this possibility. No one can foresee every emergency that may arise.

With regard to the marketability of an investment, one may ask the question, "Is there a market?" Unless a security can be disposed of by some satisfactory means, it may have to be sold at a sacrifice in an emergency, or perhaps it cannot be sold at any price. A security that is *listed* on an organized exchange is usually salable. If there are no buyers who want it, however, it may prove to be an undesirable investment for a person who wants to be able to convert his investment quickly into cash. A security that is not listed on an exchange may be handled by certain exchanges and brokers without being listed. This is called an *unlisted* security. If there is no ready market for such

---

Factors in Determining the Marketability of a Security

1. Is there a market for the security? Where could one sell it?
2. Is the security listed on an organized exchange?
3. What is the possibility that the security may have to be sold at a discount?
4. What effect may the maturity date or the date callable have on the market price?

Securities regularly sold through brokers have a ready market.

Harold M. Lambert

a security, however, it is questionable whether this security should be considered as an investment. A security may meet all the regular tests of quality, but unless it is well known there may be no demand for it.

Sources of Information about Investments. The main sources of information for the inexperienced investor are:

Banks	Investment services
Investment brokers	Local better business bureau
Newspapers and financial journals	Local chamber of commerce
State securities commissions	Securities and Exchange Commission

If one is in doubt about any corporation in which he is considering investing money, he should write to the Federal Securities and Exchange Commission and his state securities commission. From these sources he can determine whether the corporation is properly registered, and he can obtain information in regard to the organization, the capitalization, and the indebtedness.

Bankers and long-established and reputable investment brokers are in a position to give sound advice about the desirability of securities. However, having securities for sale, they may be biased in their judgment.

Many newspapers and journals publish information regarding investments. This information should always be verified by comparing it to that available from other sources. Other investment data are available in weekly and monthly bulletins and periodicals. Some of these services are expensive; others are not.

469

Using Good Judgment in Selecting Investments. A prospective investor should always remember the slogan of the National Better Business Bureau: "Before you invest, investigate."

Questions to Be Asked of Persons Selling Securities

(Suggested by National Better Business Bureau)

1. What are the names and the addresses of your employers, and how long has your company been in business?
2. With what bank does your company do business, and what are its other references?
3. What was the net worth of your company on the date of organization, and what is the net worth now?
4. What are the liabilities of the company?
5. What are its earnings?
6. How many times has the interest [or the dividend] on this security been earned in the past five years?
7. Who are the officers of the company, and what is their record of business activity?
8. What experience have these officers had in the business in which the company is engaged?
9. Is this security accepted as collateral for loans at banks?
10. What is the market for this security?

Methods of Deception Used by Investment Promoters. In spite of the fact that most of our financial transactions are conducted in an ethical and honorable manner, everyone must recognize the fact that some people try to make their living by defrauding others. Most of the fraudulent promoters prey upon people who desire to "get rich quick." The National Better Business Bureau has issued a bulletin entitled *What an Investor Should Know.* The following paragraphs are quoted from that bulletin:

Beware of "get rich quick" investment schemes.

"The swindler relies for success upon the universal human desire to make money—as much money as possible, as quickly as possible. The average salesman in order to make a sale has to convince his prospects of two things: first, that they want something and, second, that what he has to offer will satisfy that want. For the swindler, the task is simplified. Everyone wants to make money. The swindler needs only to convince his prospects that his particular proposition will enable them to do so. To accomplish this end, he appeals to their greed, prejudices, and self-esteem. He takes advantage of their lack of investment knowledge. Above all, he tries to prevent them from making an investigation or, when this is impossible, to discredit what he knows in advance will be the outcome of that investigation.

"Thus, if a hesitant investor suggests that he would like to consult his banker, the swindler will seek to discourage him. 'Don't ask your banker for advice,' the glib-tongued salesman will argue. 'Don't tell him why you're drawing out your money. He'll be sure to tell you not to do it. And why not? He's paying you 2 per cent on your money and investing it to bring him in five times that much. Be smart and put your money in that kind of proposition yourself— the kind I'm offering you.'

"Sometimes the argument works. And suppose the investor does consult the banker and the latter disapproves of the 'investment.' Wasn't that what the salesman predicted? And isn't the banker acting from selfish motives?

"Another favorite trick is to attempt to discredit the banker, better business bureau, or other source of disinterested information by trying to tie it up with the 'interests.' 'The Better Business Bureau is the tool of Wall Street,' the swindler rants. 'The monopolies don't want us to go into production because they know we'll cut into their profits. The big shots tried to buy us out and failed and now they're trying to throw suspicion on us. They want to keep the gravy for themselves. We believe in giving the little fellow a chance.'

"The prospect, being a little fellow himself, is likely to lend a sympathetic ear to this fantastic tale of persecution.

He may not know that 'little fellows' or small stockholders
own a majority of the stock of most large corporations.

"Under different circumstances, however, the dishonest
promoter is far from reticent in claiming endorsement of
his proposition by 'big names.' This financier owns 5,000
shares in the company, that prominent industrialist has
bought 10,000, he assures his listener. (An examination of
the list of corporation stockholders would tell a different
story.) Or he will exhibit an imposing list of directors.
Frequently such names may have been used without consent. Sometimes prominent men do lend their names
thoughtlessly to promotions of dubious merit without making any substantial investment themselves.

"Unfounded comparisons with successful companies are
also part of the sharper's stock in trade. 'Look at Home-
stake!' he urges. 'A few hundred dollars put in that company originally would be worth millions now. Our mine has
even better prospects today.' He fails to state that, for
every successful mining company, there have been thousands of failures—all with marvelous 'prospects.'

"Flattery is often an effective weapon in dulling the sus-
picions of the investor. 'We're limiting this offer to a few
important people like you.' 'You're one of the first to have
a chance to take advantage of this opportunity. You're
right in on the ground floor.' 'This is strictly inside information. I wouldn't take a chance of passing the tip along
to everyone.' These timeworn arguments are calculated to
make the investor feel important and put him in an amiable
frame of mind to part with his money.

"Promises are cheap but effective—promises that a stock
will be listed on a stock exchange; promises that a dividend
will be declared at an early date; promises to redeem the
stock whenever the investor wants to surrender it; promises that are beguiling but fail to materialize. Sometimes
the promise is made in the form of a guarantee. But a
guarantee is only as strong as the company behind it.
Guarantees may be worthless and often are.

"Claims of Government approval are also made with
marked success. 'If our offering were not strictly on the

level,' the swindler argues, 'the Government would put us out of business. We couldn't use the United States mails unless we were all right.' If this argument were true, there would be no such thing as fraud.

"One point in common to all these arguments which swindlers have used so successfully is that the arguments have practically no bearing on the intrinsic value of the investment offered. The value can be determined only on a basis of facts."

Guides to the Sound Investment of Savings

1. Your investment program should be built in the following sequence:
   (a) Accumulate several hundred dollars in bank savings accounts and in United States savings bonds for emergency use.
   (b) Buy life insurance for protection and for future income.
   (c) Buy a home as soon as possible.
   (d) If you wish to work for yourself, invest in a business enterprise for profit.
   (e) Buy high-grade stocks and bonds or real estate for income purposes.

2. In selecting investments consider:
   (a) The suitability of the investment as a part of your investment program.
   (b) The safety of the principal.
   (c) The certainty of income from the investment.
   (d) The marketability of the security, that is, the ease with which it can be sold if necessary.

3. Investigate every possible source of information about the security before buying. Be sure to obtain the rating of the corporation in standard manuals. Consult the Securities and Exchange Commission if in doubt.

4. Become acquainted with the protection to investors provided by state and Federal laws.

5. Select the type of investment (real estate, bonds, stocks, investment trust shares, or a business) to fit your investment program, considering the date you may need your funds and the amount of time you have available to manage your investments.

TEXTBOOK QUESTIONS

1. Make a distinction between saving and investing.
2. Explain the differences between investing, speculating, and gambling.
3. What elements in the financial plans of a family should come before investing?
4. What are the four points that an investor should consider in regard to any investment?
5. What are the five points that determine whether a security is suitable for a particular investment program?
6. Give the four tests of safety for a corporation security.
7. Name some factors that you should consider as to the safety of your investment in real estate. *f, l, e*
8. What are the four factors that help to determine whether an investment will pay a satisfactory income?
9. What factor determines the marketability of a security?
10. What are some of the sources from which the inexperienced investor can obtain information on investments?
11. Give at least two questions that the better business bureau recommends should be asked of persons selling securities.
12. What devices does a swindler use to convince his victims?
13. What does the swindler often tell the victim when the latter desires to obtain advice from his banker?
14. What argument do fraudulent promoters sometimes use against the better business bureau as a source of investment information?
15. What is the fallacy of comparing a new venture with a profitable existing venture of a similar type?
16. What is meant by "being let in on the ground floor"? Why should an investor be cautious when such an assurance is made?

DISCUSSION QUESTIONS

1. If a friend of yours tells you about a stock that is not paying dividends but that he has heard will soon begin to pay dividends, would the buying of this stock be a speculation, an investment, or a gamble?
2. "A bond is an investment; a stock is a speculation." Discuss this statement. Is it true or false?
3. A person wants to invest $1,000 for an indefinite period of time. He prefers purchasing a bond, and finally selects a good first-mortgage bond of an outstanding utilities corporation. The bond is marked "callable." Do you think this bond will be satisfactory as an investment?
4. Would you reject a stock because it is not sold actively on a market?

5. Which do you think would pay the higher rate of interest:
(a) a good bond with poor marketability, or (b) a good
bond with good marketability? Why?

6. How do you think you could test the collateral value of a
security?

7. A person who is earning 2 per cent interest on a savings
account considers buying bonds that pay interest at a net
rate of 4 per cent. Discuss the merits and the demerits of
this plan.

8. On what basis of reasoning can you condemn an investment
tipster sheet that comes to you unsolicited?

9. (a) What is your opinion of the securities of mining corporations? (b) Is the average person justified in buying such
securities? (c) Who should buy these securities?

10. Why should an investor not consider solicitations made by
telephone?

11. Why would it be absurd for you to believe a stranger who,
in trying to sell you a certain stock, stated that you were
one of the few invited to participate in the investment?

12. If a promoter tells you something over the telephone or in a
personal interview, why would it be advisable to have him
verify his statements in writing by mail?

13. Just because stock in a seemingly legitimate oil venture is
offered for sale in the producing region, is there assurance
that the oil property is valuable?

14. Suppose a young man just finishing high school receives
$1,500 from the estate of his uncle who died. How would you
recommend that he invest this money? Explain your reasons.

PROBLEMS

1. A stenographer who had saved $1,000 asked her banker what
investments he would recommend. He recommended a United
States Government bond. She purchased it for $1,045. She
obtained $30 a year as interest. (a) What was the rate of
yield? (b) Was there any relation between the yield and the
chance of loss?

2. A man considers paying $12,000 cash for a house for invest-
ment purposes with the idea of renting it. (a) The house is
now occupied by a family that is paying $80 a month rent.
This amount is considered reasonable compared with the rent
on other similar homes. (b) The statistics of real-estate
agents show that, on the average, rented houses are vacant
one month out of every year. (c) The house will require
immediate repairs costing $250 and annual repairs of about
$120. The taxes on the property amount to $108 a year; there
are no assessments. (d) The loss from depreciation each year

is estimated to be $400. (e) The commission of the real-estate agent in buying the house, and the cost of transferring and recording the title, will amount to $150. (1) Calculate the total cost of the house, including both the property and the cost of having the title transferred and recorded. (2) Calculate the total operating costs, the net income, and the percentage of net income based on the original investment. (3) Do you think the purchase of the house would be a good investment?

3. Mr. Stinson has ten shares of each of ten different preferred stocks. The total value amounts to $6,323. He also has ten different bonds valued at a total of $1,116. Ten shares of stock valued at $46 a share become worthless. Mr. Brown has fifty shares of stock in three different corporations, the total value of which are $5,200, and ten bonds, the total value of which are $1,046. Fifty shares of Mr. Brown's stock are the same kind as the ten shares of Mr. Stinson's stock that became worthless. (a) Figure Mr. Stinson's percentage of loss on his total investment. (b) Figure Mr. Brown's percentage of loss on his total investment. (c) Can you draw any conclusions?

COMMUNITY PROBLEMS AND PROJECTS

1. Select as an investment some local piece of residential real estate that is offered for sale. (a) Make a study of the total cost of the property, including the costs of purchasing it and the expenses of upkeep and depreciation. (b) Compute the amount of income that can be expected from the property and the percentage of income based on the cost.

2. Obtain financial statements of a bank, a building and loan association, and an insurance company. (a) Compare the types of securities owned by the various institutions. (b) Draw some conclusions as to the conservativeness of the investor.

3. From a daily newspaper select ten stocks and ten bonds, or follow the instructions of your teacher in selecting the securities. Determine the current market prices and dividend and interest rates. (a) Record the market price quoted Monday through Friday on each stock and on each bond for a period of two months. (b) Average the prices of the stocks and those of the bonds for each day of the period. (c) Draw a graph that shows a comparison of the fluctuation in the average prices of the stocks and of that in the average prices of the bonds. (d) Draw some conclusions with regard to these price fluctuations.

Chapter 27

Information You Need About Investments

Purpose of the Chapter. For most individuals and families savings are accumulated by hard work over a long period of time. To carry out an investment program as outlined in the previous chapter, we need to know more about the different kinds of investments. This chapter will, therefore, give you a better background for carrying out an investment program.

Real Estate. When real estate is purchased as an investment, the following points should be considered carefully after the desirability of the location and the quality of the property have been determined:

(a) Can the property be rented?
(b) At what price can the property be rented?
(c) What will be the annual cost of repairs?
(d) What will be the taxes and assessments?
(e) What will be the yearly loss from depreciation?
(f) During what percentage of time will the property be vacant?
(g) What will be the approximate net earnings from the investment?

Real estate is subject to fluctuations in price. The current cost of a piece of property is therefore no indication of the future value. The community may change rapidly with a resulting decrease or increase in the value of the property. Because of a change in business conditions, the value of the property may be raised or lowered.

Unimproved real estate (with no buildings) is usually a speculative investment made in the hope that it can be sold at a profit. A person well acquainted with managing property may find real estate more suitable than any other type of investment; but if one is not in a position to manage real estate with buildings on it, it may not prove to be a desir-

477

able investment. Other kinds of investments may be much easier for such a person to manage.

Business Enterprise. People with money are frequently tempted to buy an interest in a partnership, or stock in a small corporation in which a friend is interested or in a small close corporation, or to lend money to a friend or a relative in business. Such investments should be made with the utmost care.

Investing in a partnership involves complicated legal responsibilities in most states. Even though one of the partners may not be actively engaged in the business, under the laws of many states he is equally responsible with the other partners. For instance, suppose that you become a part owner of a business and allow your partner to operate it. The business fails to make a profit, and the creditors demand payment. As your partner cannot pay, the creditors demand payment from you.

Many people with experience will advocate not investing in the enterprise of a friend or a relative. The friend or the relative usually feels that he has the right to operate

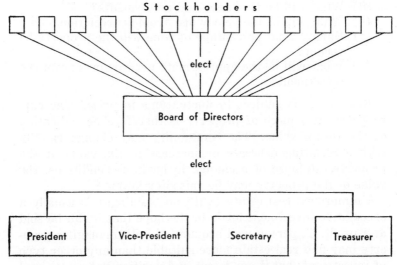

Chart of the organization of a corporation.

the business as he sees fit. He may legally have the right, but sooner or later trouble may arise.

A *close* corporation is one in which the stock is owned usually by a small group of people, and sometimes by only one or two families. Those who own the greater share of the stock are generally the managers. Those who own the minority share of the stock have practically nothing to say with regard to the management, but take what dividends are allotted to them on the basis of their holdings. Those who operate the business may pay themselves large salaries and thus leave very little for distribution as dividends.

The most common type of corporation is an *open* corporation. The stock of this type of corporation is available for public sale.

Mortgage Notes and Mortgage Bonds. The illustration below shows a *mortgage note,* which is a written promise to pay with interest the specified sum that is secured by the specific property described in the mortgage. A mortgage makes it impossible to sell the property on which the mortgage is given without payment of the loan that it secures. In some states mortgage bonds are used instead of mortgage notes.

$2500.00 Youngstown, Ohio, March 15 19 –
Three years after date for value received, I
promise to pay Jerome A. Burkhart or order,
the sum of Twenty-five Hundred 00/100 DOLLARS,
with interest thereon at the rate of 6 per cent. per annum, payable semi annually
This note is secured by a mortgage of even date herewith. executed and delivered by R. M. McDonough
and which is a 1st lien on land situated in Youngstown, Mahoning County, Ohio, fully described in said mortgage. If any installment of interest or principal be not paid when due, or within three days thereafter, or if default be made in the performance of any of the agreements or conditions of said mortgage, the entire principal shall become immediately due and payable at the option of the holder hereof.
Notice of said option is hereby waived.
R. M. McDonough
Due Mar. 15, 19 –
No. 1

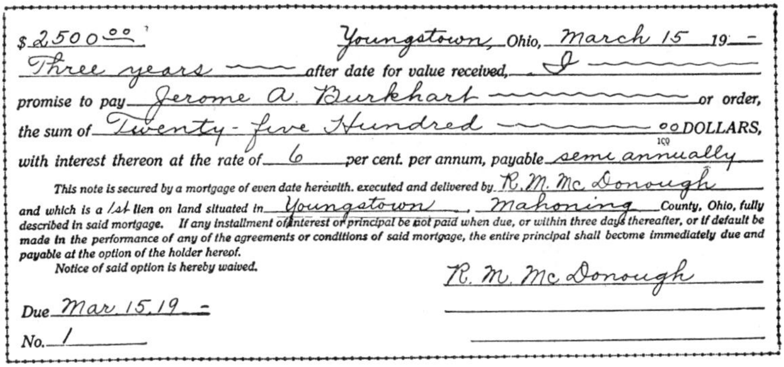

A mortgage note.

When a person borrows money on real estate, he usually signs (a) a mortgage and (b) a note or series of notes. He gives both the mortgage and the note or notes to the one from whom he is borrowing the money. The *mortgage* is a written contract giving the lender permission to dispose of the property to satisfy the debt in case the debt is not paid.

There are first-mortgage notes, second-mortgage notes, and third-mortgage notes. The first-mortgage note is the most common. The loan that it represents should not exceed 50 or 60 per cent of the appraised value of the property.

A first mortgage has first claim against the assets. The holder of the second mortgage cannot be paid until the claim of the first mortgage is settled. Interest rates are lower on first mortgages because these mortgages have first claim. Interest rates on second and third mortgages are higher because greater risk is involved.

Mortgage bonds are usually issued in one of the following three ways:

(a) The mortgage company acquires the mortgage on a particular piece of property, issues a bond, and sells it to an investor.
(b) The mortgage company acquires a large mortgage; issues bonds in denominations of fifty, one hundred, or one thousand dollars; and sells these to investors.
(c) The mortgages on several pieces of property are pooled. One large bond or a number of bonds in smaller denominations are issued against these mortgages and sold to investors.

The value of mortgage bonds is measured by the value of the property behind them and the ability of this property to provide funds for the payment of the interest and the principal on the due dates.

Stocks. A *share* of stock represents part ownership in a corporation. The two general types of stock are common stocks and preferred stocks. Ordinarily, the *common stock* entitles the owners to management of the business, whereas the owners of *preferred stock* do not have management control of the business but they have certain preferred claims. The primary difference between the two kinds is that the latter usually is preferred as to dividends; that is, the owner of the preferred stock receives his stipulated share of profits before the common stockholder receives any share.

Sometimes the stock is preferred as to assets in case of
dissolution of the corporation. In other words, the owner
of the stock preferred as to assets would receive the amount
of his investment before common stockholders would receive
anything.

A common-stock certificate.

A preferred-stock certificate.

There is such a great variety in each class of stock that it is difficult to distinguish between the different grades. The provisions governing a stock should be read carefully to determine one's rights and obligations. For instance, the purchase of a stock may carry with it the right to purchase at a certain price additional stock of a new issue that may be made. This right may or may not be valuable. The holders of one grade of common stock may have voting power, whereas the holders of another grade may not. When there are various grades or classes of a common stock, the public is usually urged to buy the least desirable class. The better classes are often reserved for those who are promoting the sale of the stock.

Dividends on Stock. Under the laws of most states, dividends cannot be paid on either preferred stock or common stock unless all interest has been paid on outstanding bonds. It is also a general rule that dividends cannot be paid on common stock unless those on preferred stock have been paid.

In other words, bondholders have first claim on earnings, before preferred stockholders; preferred stockholders have second claim on earnings, before common stockholders; and common stockholders receive dividends only to the extent that there are sufficient earnings to pay them. They are never promised or guaranteed. In poor years the preferred stockholders are therefore more likely than common stockholders to get their dividends; in good years, however, common stockholders have the possibility of getting much more than is paid to preferred stockholders.

Cumulative and Noncumulative Preferred Stock. The preferred stock of most companies carries with it a specified dividend rate, but the dividends may be discontinued if the corporate earnings dwindle. There is, however, one type of preferred stock that is issued under the agreement that back dividends will be paid to the holders of the stock at the regular rate if the dividends are ever discontinued temporarily. This type of preferred stock is called *cumulative*. For example, if the dividends on a preferred stock are discontinued for one year, the preferred stock-holders will receive those dividends as soon as the company earns enough profits to pay them. These back dividends must be paid before any other dividends are declared.

Preferred stock may also be *noncumulative*. If the stock is noncumulative, the preferred stockholders are not guaranteed their income in case the corporation ceases temporarily to pay dividends. If the corporation does not earn a profit, dividends may not be declared. When profits are earned again, the preferred stockholders begin to receive dividends again, but they do not receive dividends for the time when no profits were earned.

Participating Preferred Stock. Some preferred stocks are classified as *participating*. In the case of such stocks, if excess earnings are still present after the regular dividend on preferred stock and a specified dividend on common stock have been distributed, the preferred stockholders will participate with the common stockholders in the surplus earnings. For example, the regular dividend rate on a preferred stock may be 6 per cent. If the earnings of the company, however, become large enough to pay a dividend at a specified rate on the common stock, in addition to the 6 per cent dividend on the preferred stock, the preferred stockholders will share with the common stockholders in the surplus earnings.

Par-Value and No-Par-Value Stocks. Stocks are also designated as *par-value stocks* or *no-par-value stocks*. Par value means very little to the average investor or even to the expert, for the par value of a stock has no specific relation to the actual value. A stock may bear a par value of one hundred dollars, but may be sold for only sixty-five or seventy-five dollars. The use of a definite par value for a stock was probably intended originally to indicate the worth of the stock, but the practice of assigning par values to stocks has resulted in many abuses. For instance, there have been cases in which promoters have sold stock to unsuspecting investors on the assumption of the latter that the stock was worth approximately the par value assigned to it. Inasmuch as shares of stock represent ownership in a corporation, the stock of one person represents that part of the ownership equal to the percentage that his shares bear to the total number of shares issued. The use of no-par-value stock is intended as a means of avoiding the inference that the stock is worth a certain amount. A no-par-value stock bears no designated value. Its value, like the value of par-value stock, is regulated by what the investing public believes the stock is worth.

The stock of a corporation is either *listed* or *unlisted* on a stock market. That which is listed is more easily salable than unlisted stocks.

Bonds. *Bonds* do not represent a share in the ownership of an enterprise; they are evidence of a debt owed by the enterprise. When a business or a government issues bonds, it acknowledges that it owes the holders a certain sum of money and agrees to repay the sum on a certain date and under certain conditions. It also agrees to pay interest at a specified rate and at specified intervals.

A *short-term bond* is frequently referred to as a note and serves the same purpose as a note. A *mortgage bond* usually extends for a relatively long period of time and is essentially the same as a mortgage note. The bond shown in the illustration on page 485 is a *coupon bond*. Anyone who owns a coupon bond can tear off each coupon as it becomes due and present it to his bank for the collection of interest. A *registered bond* is a bond that is recorded by the issuer in the name of the person to whom it has been sold. The interest on the bond will be paid only to the registered owner. From the point of view of theft, a registered bond is therefore safer than a coupon bond.

When a bond is issued, the issuing corporation usually pledges some security, such as specific property, mortgages on property, or the right to certain earnings. A railroad may pledge some of its equipment or real estate. A municipality or a county may pledge its water system or light system. A *debenture bond* is one for which no security is pledged to guarantee the safety of the principal.

Although certain property or rights are pledged to insure the safety of the principal of a mortgage investment,

A coupon bond.

various difficulties are encountered if the bondholders are forced to take over the property or the rights in case the interest is not paid. It is therefore desirable to investigate bonds from the following points of view:

  (a) Record of past earnings of the company and likelihood of future earnings.

  (b) Record of past market prices of the bonds.

  (c) Competitive and general business conditions.

  (d) Marketability of the bonds.

The same general investigation should be carried on in connection with bonds of a governmental unit. The taxes of a governmental unit are comparable to the earnings of a business. The economic conditions within such a unit are comparable to the competitive conditions within an industry. Such factors have a definite effect upon the ability of the issuer of the bonds to pay interest and to repay the principal on the maturity date. State and national legislation also has a definite bearing upon the value of governmental bonds. For instance, state legislation allowing a governmental unit to postpone interest payments on bonds would have the effect of reducing the value of the bonds.

Some bonds are designated as convertible. There are so many possible stipulations in relation to convertible bonds that any particular bond should be investigated and studied carefully. A *convertible bond* is one in which there is a stipulation that permits or forces the bondholder under certain conditions to accept stock in exchange for his bond. The bondholder may therefore change in status from a creditor to a stockholder.

As a general rule, bonds are more stable than stocks because a corporation is required to pay the fixed interest on the bonds as long as it is solvent, that is, as long as it has the money with which to pay the interest. However, except in the case of cumulative preferred stock, the corporation may skip dividends on stocks for one or more years without incurring any obligation to pay the back dividends.

Bonds are usually sold in denominations of fifty, one hundred, five hundred, one thousand dollars, or more. Different issues bear varying rates of interest, the rates depending upon the prevailing investment rates, the time of sale, and the desirability of the investment.

The amount appearing on the face of a bond is called the *par value*. The interest is based on the par value. If, for various reasons, bonds cannot be sold at their par value, they are sold at less than par value; and the difference between the par value and the selling price is called *discount*. If the bonds are in demand by the investing public, they will be sold at a rate above par value; and the difference between the two values is called *premium*. The selling of bonds below par or above par is not necessarily an indication of their value. The selling of bonds below par may result from (a) unsatisfactory security that has been pledged by the issuer of the bonds, (b) an interest rate that is low in comparison with interest rates on other similar securities, or (c) unfavorable economic conditions that result in a lack of demand for bonds.

Comparisons of Bonds and Stocks. In order to illustrate different types of bonds and stocks, let us consider a corporation with $100,000 of 3 per cent first-mortgage bonds outstanding; $100,000 of 4 per cent debenture bonds; $200,000 of noncumulative 6 per cent preferred stock (2,000 shares at $100 par); and 20,000 shares of common stock. If the corporation makes a profit of $50,000 after taxes have been paid, the mortgage bondholders will get $3,000 in interest, the debenture bondholders will get $4,000 in interest, and the preferred stockholders will get $12,000 in dividends, leaving a remainder of $31,000 available for the common stockholders. At the discretion of the board of directors, all or part of the amount available may be declared as a dividend to common stockholders. If a dividend of $1 a share is declared, the common stockholders will get $20,000, leaving $11,000 to be added to the surplus of the corporation.

Let us assume, however, that in another year the corporation makes only $9,000 net profit after paying taxes, but has some money in the bank. The mortgage bondholders are entitled to their interest at 3 per cent, amounting to $3,000. The debenture bondholders have a first claim on whatever earnings there are left. They are therefore paid $4,000, leaving $2,000 to be divided among the preferred stockholders. The common stockholders get nothing.

Investment Trusts. The investment trust is an outgrowth of modern finance and is usually subject to considerable regulation by state laws. It is established for the purpose of accepting funds from investors and reinvesting them in a variety of securities. Thus small sums are combined and used to purchase business and governmental securities of a wide diversification.

The investment trust, if operated honestly and efficiently, has two great advantages for the small investor. These are:

(a) Wide diversification of the investment.

(b) Expert analysis in the purchase of securities.

The person with a small sum of money to invest cannot buy securities in any great number of companies and usually cannot obtain satisfactory expert advice. An investment in a good investment trust is therefore usually more desirable for him than an attempt to invest money on the basis of his personal opinion.

It is especially important to investigate the investment trust in which one is interested. Although investment trusts are fundamentally excellent outlets for the small investor's funds, there have been many badly managed investment trusts. It is therefore important to get unbiased information on the character, the history, and the management of the trust in which one is considering an investment.

TEXTBOOK QUESTIONS

1. When real estate is to be purchased as an investment, what are some of the factors that should be investigated in determining its desirability?

2. Why should a person not buy real estate as an investment unless he has the time and the energy to take care of it?

3. Why do some people advise against investing in an enterprise managed by a friend?

4. What is a close corporation?

5. Why is it sometimes inadvisable to buy stock in a close corporation?

6. Express briefly the difference between a mortgage note and a mortgage bond.

7. In what ways are mortgage bonds usually issued?

8. What are the two general types of stocks?
9. Do all stocks have the same voting power?
10. Distinguish between cumulative stock and noncumulative stock.
11. What is meant by participating stock? To what general type of stock does the term apply?
12. Does the par value of a stock indicate the true value?
13. What is a listed security?
14. In what ways does a bond differ from a stock?
15. (a) If a $100 bond is selling for $90, is it selling at a premium or a discount? (b) What are some of the reasons why bonds sell below their par value?
16. What are some of the advantages of an investment trust that is operated efficiently and honestly?

DISCUSSION QUESTIONS

1. Discuss the merits of real estate as an investment for an elderly woman.
2. You have an opportunity to invest some money with two other men in a partnership in a neighboring town. You expect to continue your work and to allow the other two persons to operate the business. Discuss the disadvantages of this plan.
3. In some states it has been difficult, if not impossible, during financial depressions, for mortgage holders to foreclose on the property pledged as security for the payment of the interest and of the principal due them. How do you think such a condition affects (a) the mortgage holder; (b) the future market for mortgages; and (c) the interest rates?
4. If a stock is issued by a reliable corporation, is there any need for reading the provisions that are printed on the stock certificate?
5. Some people believe that, if a person is going to buy stock, he should buy common stock instead of preferred stock. Why do you think that they are of this opinion?
6. Assume that you are contemplating buying some common stock in either of two outstanding corporations of approximately equal size. Both corporations have good reputations and good records of past earnings. They have issued approximately the same number of shares of stock. One has cumulative preferred stock and one grade of common stock; the other has noncumulative preferred stock and one grade of common stock. From your point of view, which common stock would be more desirable? Why?
7. What kind of preferred stock combines some of the features of a preferred stock and a common stock?

8. How well do you think an investor is protected if he buys a municipal bond on which the security is the sewage system of the city?

9. In what way might a callable bond disrupt one's investment program?

10. Can you explain why shares in investment trusts are placed ahead of or given preference as an investment over mortgages, preferred stocks, common stocks, and improved real estate?

PROBLEMS

1. There is more involved in bonds and stocks as investments than it is possible to describe in this chapter. From a library or some other source, obtain a book on investments that discusses bonds and stocks. Write a report of at least 500 words in which you present additional information about stocks and bonds that is not included in this chapter.

2. Obtain from a library, or some other source, one of the important financial services that provides investment information. Write a report of at least 500 words describing the kinds of information available, and include in your report some specific information quoted from the financial service pertaining to a particular corporation.

3. From a library obtain copies of the reports from one of the investment services and write a report of at least 500 words in regard to municipal bonds, including some specific information about a particular municipal bond issue.

COMMUNITY PROBLEMS AND PROJECTS

1. (a) Make a list of the ways in which it is possible to invest money in your local community. (b) For each type of investment indicate whether it is suitable for the small investor or the large investor, and whether it is conservative or not conservative.

2. From a local newspaper, your local banker, or a financial journal, obtain the price quoted (at the close of the previous day) on some stock specified by your teacher. (a) Determine the rate of the latest dividend. (b) Calculate the cost of buying one hundred shares. (c) Using the rate of the latest dividend, compute the rate of net income on the basis of the cost.

PART VIII
BUYING INSURANCE PROTECTION

Chapter 28
How Insurance Protects You

Purpose of the Chapter. Risk is the possibility of loss, cost, or damage. Some individual or business risks are unavoidable, but others can be avoided by various means. Many risks are uncertain not only as to the amount of the possible loss, but also as to the time of the loss. When a risk is transferred to an insurance company, it ceases to be a risk on the part of the insured person but it becomes a definite cost.

The purpose of this chapter is to study the organization and the development of insurance, the types of risks covered by insurance, the types of insurance companies, and to point out specifically how certain types of risks are covered by insurance. It will also serve as a general introduction to the two chapters on life insurance that follow.

The Nature of Insurance. Whenever one person transfers to another the risk of loss due to fire, theft, death, injury, or damage of any kind, he is insuring himself against loss. The major risk-bearing agency in modern society is the insurance company. An insurance company can bear the risks that individuals cannot afford to bear because it spreads the losses of a few persons over the entire group insured.

An insurance company can estimate in advance the probable losses it must bear by applying the *law of averages,* also called the *law* or *theory of probability.* Strange as it may seem, a large number of uncertainties may be combined to form certainties that can be predicted with reasonable accuracy. The mortality experience of individuals is a good example. For many years insurance companies have compiled statistics regarding the number of deaths of individuals. From a study of these figures it is possible to determine very nearly the exact number of people in a given group who will die each year. The insurance companies, of course, cannot predict who will die, but they can estimate with reasonable accuracy how many will die. It is on the basis of these figures that life insurance rates are calculated.

It may seem strange at first that a fire insurance company, for instance, can assume the risk of paying all losses and yet charge each policyholder only a small fee. Frequently the total yearly fee is as low as one tenth of 1 per cent of the possible loss. The reason why insurance companies can follow this practice is that they know from the theory of probability what losses can be expected. They can therefore keep in a reserve fund a sufficient amount to pay each loss as it occurs. It is true that unusual circumstances, such as an exceptionally large fire, may cause unforeseen losses; but, over a long period of time, losses are predictable. The surplus fund that an insurance company keeps is used as a protection against unusual losses.

The theory of probability is based upon a study of experiences in the past. For instance, a fire insurance company finds that three out of every one thousand houses in a certain city have burned each year. The company can therefore reasonably assume that this average will continue; that three houses in every thousand will burn during the succeeding year. There may be various factors, however, that change this condition. One large fire may cause an unusual loss; or, on the other hand, the use of new fire equipment may reduce the loss from fires.

The law of probability cannot be based upon a study of a comparatively small number of houses—one hundred, for example—because such a group of houses might be subject to many unusual conditions. Furthermore, the loss in one city may decrease in one year, whereas that in another city may increase in the same year. When the number is increased to many thousands of houses in several communities, the average chance of unusual disasters is decreased. In other words, the chance of loss per house is less. Insurance companies therefore try to spread their risks over a wide area to protect themselves.

Here is an example of how insurance companies can help individuals to protect themselves from losses that they cannot afford. Let us assume that the Midland Insurance Company carries fire insurance on 100,000 homes; each home owner pays an average of $25 a year for insurance. The company would collect $2,500,000 from the owners of the property with which to pay its operating expenses and losses due to fires. The rates charged are based on past experiences so that the insurance company should take in enough money to pay losses when they occur. The insurance company takes a calculated risk; while each property owner pays a certain amount each year so that if his home is burned, he will be reimbursed by the insurance company. Most property owners can afford to pay $25 a year, but they cannot afford a $5,000 fire loss. In a sense, therefore, the 100,000 home owners are pooling or sharing their risks, and the insurance company is the agent that handles the financial matters.

Each state is usually taken as a unit when fire insurance rates are to be established on the basis of losses. Some states are divided into sections. Cities are rated by classes, ranging from one to ten. A first-class city has the lowest rate, for it has the best fire protection. A tenth-class city has the highest rate because it has no fire protection. The following factors are considered in classifying cities:

(a) Water supply.
(b) Fire department.
(c) Fire-alarm system.
(d) Police system.
(e) Building laws.
(f) Hazards.
(g) Structural conditions.
(h) Climatic conditions.
(i) Correlation between the water supply and the fire department.
(j) Fire-sprinkler system.

Some Important Insurance Terms. An insurance agreement is a form of contract. An insurance contract is called a *policy*. The person who buys an insurance policy pays periodically what is called a *premium*. He is known as the *insured* or *assured*. The party from whom he buys the insurance and who agrees to make good the loss is called the *insurer* or *underwriter*. The possibility of a loss is called a *risk*, and the maximum amount that is to be paid in case of a loss is called the *face value*. The person to whom the proceeds of an insurance policy are payable in case of loss is called a *beneficiary*. If there is no beneficiary of a life insurance policy, the money becomes a part of a fund called an *estate* (composed of all the deceased's property) which is disposed of according to law or according to the provisions of a will left by the insured.

Organization of Insurance Companies. Premiums are paid weekly, monthly, quarterly, semiannually, or yearly, the time of payment depending upon the kind of insurance, the type of policy, and the nature of the company. The funds collected from policyholders are used by the companies in somewhat the same manner as cash deposits are used by banks. In other words, insurance companies use the funds paid by policyholders in making investments that will earn an income. The insurance companies must, of course, keep a reasonable amount of cash available to pay the claims of policyholders in case of fire, accident, death, ill health, or other similar happenings.

There are two general types of insurance companies. One is known as the *stock company*; and the other, as the *mutual company*. The stock company is a corporation that is formed according to the laws of the particular state. The stockholders own the company and elect directors, who in turn hire executives to run the business. The stockholders are, however, not necessarily policyholders. An insurance company of this type obtains money from the purchase of stock by stockholders, as well as from the collection of premiums from policyholders. The profits of the company are paid to the stockholders, who are the owners of the business.

A mutual company must also be organized under the laws of the particular state. The policyholders in such a company are, however, the owners. Each person or business concern that is insured in a mutual company becomes a member of the company and is entitled to a share in the

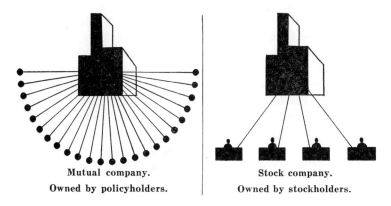

Mutual company.

Owned by policyholders.

Stock company.

Owned by stockholders.

ownership, the control, and the earnings. There are no stockholders as in a stock company.

Insurance companies are also classified as to *participating* or *nonparticipating*. A policyholder of a participating company receives dividends, which are shares in the earnings of the company. Some stock companies are participating and some are nonparticipating. All mutual companies are participating. Policyholders pay premiums at a predetermined rate; but if there are any profits during the year, each policyholder receives a dividend in proportion to the amount of his policy.

In case a mutual company loses money, it may, if it has reserved the right to do so, assess policyholders a certain amount on each policy to cover the loss. In such cases the maximum assessment usually cannot exceed the original premium. However, most life insurance policies in mutual companies are nonassessable.

Regulation of Insurance. Insurance is such an important factor in the stability of modern business that all states have found it necessary to place some regulation upon insurance companies. All insurance policies are contracts that call for the fulfillment of conditions at some future time. The states therefore believe it their duty to protect the interests of those who buy insurance.

Each state has a special insurance law and usually designates some official whose duty it is to administer and enforce the law. The most important function of state regulation is to make sure that all insurance companies are able to pay all obligations as they become due. The payment of all obligations is the paramount duty of an insurance company, for it involves the fundamental purpose of insurance.

State regulation also protects insurance buyers from fraud. Most states require reports from insurance companies, as well as inspection of the securities, accounting records, and business methods of the companies. In most states, insurance companies are regulated as to the ways in which they can invest the money collected from policyholders. These investments are usually confined to high-grade bonds of the Federal Government, of states, utilities, and cities, and high-grade real-estate mortgages and mortgage bonds. If an individual followed the example of a good insurance company in investing funds, he would be following an investment policy that is far above the average.

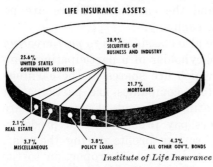

LIFE INSURANCE ASSETS

38.9% SECURITIES OF BUSINESS AND INDUSTRY

25.6% UNITED STATES GOVERNMENT SECURITIES

21.7% MORTGAGES

2.1% REAL ESTATE

3.7% MISCELLANEOUS

3.8% POLICY LOANS

4.2% ALL OTHER GOV'T. BONDS

Institute of Life Insurance

How insurance companies invest their dollars.

Although special bureaus provide information for establishing insurance rates, the state governments retain the right to regulate these rates. Court rulings have established the principle that fire insurance is subject to regulation because it is a matter of public interest.

Kinds of Insurance. In the United States there four principal divisions of insurance: life, fire, marine, and casualty. Among these four types of insurance there are variations and overlappings.

Life Insurance. There are various uses of life insurance. Besides using life insurance for family protection, a person may have his life insured so that when he dies his debts can be paid. The partners in a business may insure each other so that, upon the death of either partner, the surviving partner will have funds with which to continue the business. Many business executives are insured because of the possible loss that may result from their death. Suppose, for example, that the success of the Central Manufacturing Company is due largely to the peculiar ability and popularity of its president, Mr. J. W. Cook. The directors of the corporation decide that it is wise to insure Mr. Cook's life for $500,000. They are reasonably certain that, if Mr. Cook should die suddenly, it would be difficult to make adjustments in the business to replace him. It is reasonable to expect that the profits of the business would be less for a considerable time until someone would be able to take his place. The $500,000 payable upon Mr. Cook's death can therefore be used to protect the company against any unfavorable circumstances following his death. The proceeds of this insurance will reduce the risk of failure of the business after the death of Mr. Cook. In other words, the money can be used to keep the business running until necessary adjustments are made.

Fire Insurance. Fire insurance provides funds to replace buildings or materials destroyed by fire. Many business concerns carry fire insurance on buildings, furniture and equipment, machinery, raw materials, and finished goods. Insurance on a building usually does not cover the machinery, stock, and equipment. Ordinarily separate policies are required to give full protection from fire loss. The owner of a building should be interested in fire insurance to protect his investment. The occupant of a rented building should be interested in such insurance to protect his business. In buying fire insurance, one should know just what is covered by the policy.

The actual loss in property destroyed by fire is not the only loss to a business concern. The interruption to business until a new place can be obtained and operations can be resumed will result in a loss of profits and considerable incidental expense. Special types of insurance can be obtained to cover the costs caused by the inconvenience of the fire.

In case of total loss the face value of the fire insurance policy is paid if this does not exceed the value of the property destroyed.

Ewing Galloway

Standard fire insurance policies provide that, if a building which is occupied at the time the contract is made becomes unoccupied or vacant for a specified length of time, the policy becomes void. It is, therefore, important for a policyholder to read a policy carefully. Even if the original contract does not provide protection during vacancy, one can make arrangements with the insurance company for such protection. For example, if you expect to be on a vacation longer than the amount of time allowed for vacancy, you should notify the insurance company and obtain in writing a statement to attach to your policy so that you will be assured of proper protection.

Extended coverage is also an important feature of many fire insurance contracts. For a small additional premium, a property owner may obtain, with his regular policy, protection against damage from wind storms, tornadoes, rain storms, explosions, falling aircraft, riots, smoke, or damage from motor vehicles.

How Fire Insurance Operates. A person usually insures his property for a specified amount. For example, Mr. Thompson's property may be valued at five thousand dollars. If there is a garage on the property, the insurance company will require a separate valuation for the house and the garage. Suppose the lot is valued at one thousand dollars; the house, at thirty-eight hundred dollars; and the garage, at two hundred dollars. Mr. Thompson decides to insure his house for thirty-eight hundred dollars and his garage for two hundred dollars. If the house is burned completely, he can collect the maximum amount of his policy, which is thirty-eight hundred dollars, if the face of the policy is not more than the value of the house. If it is not burned completely, the insurance company has the privilege of replacing it as nearly as possible in its original condition. Suppose, however, he insures his house for only two thousand dollars. If it is completely destroyed, he can collect only two thousand dollars.

Proof of Loss. A person who carries any kind of insurance should protect his policy carefully, for it is the first evidence of claim in case of loss. If possible, life insurance policies should be kept in safe-deposit boxes. If they are stolen, destroyed, or lost, they can be replaced only through a tedious process. Even if a policy cannot be presented, however, as evidence of claim in case of loss, the claim will usually be paid after sufficient identification has been made.

When property is insured against fire or theft, it is extremely important to keep a record of the property that is insured. In case of loss the insurance company will require some kind of evidence to serve as the basis for paying the loss. The insurance company will frequently accept a sworn statement as to the loss. The safest practice, however, is to keep some type of inventory record of the insured property.

Living Room				
No.	Article	Date of Purchase	Cost	Description
	Carpets,			
	Chairs,			
	Clock,			
	Couch,			
	Curtains,			
	Cushions,			
	Jardinieres,			
	Lamps,			
	Mirrors,			
	Piano,			
	Stool and Cover,			
	Rugs,			
	Shades.			
	Window Fixtures,			
	Tables,			
	Tapestry,			
	Pictures.*			
	Vases.			
	Smoking Stand,			
	Draperies,			
	Radio,			

* See Special List

A sample record for household furniture that is insured.

A record of insured property should be kept in a place where it will not be destroyed in case the property that is insured is destroyed. A safe-deposit box is a good place. A policy may contain a clause that makes it mandatory for the insured person to maintain an inventory record and to keep this record in a place where it cannot be destroyed.

How Coinsurance Operates. Coinsurance is a type of insurance commonly used in business, but it does not apply to insurance on a home, household furnishings, or any personal possessions in any building. A home is considered to be a one- or a two-family house. Coinsurance may be used, however, on an apartment building housing three or more families and on the household furnishings or the personal property contained in such a building.

In the case of coinsurance, if the insured carries more insurance than he ordinarily would carry, usually 80 per cent of the value, the rate is lower and the insurance company will pay all losses up to the amount carried.

Marine Insurance. Marine insurance is often called *transportation insurance.* This type of insurance has many uses. If a shipment is sent by water, the person who owns the goods will want protection against damage, theft, and loss. The person who owns the goods may obtain this insurance, or the company that transports them may provide it as a part of the cost of transportation. The transportation company may carry its own insurance and pay its own losses, or it may insure its shipments with another company.

Shipments hauled by express companies are usually insured, and the cost of the insurance is included in the transportation charges. Railway freight shipments may be sent insured or uninsured. Parcel-post packages may also be sent in either way.

Casualty Insurance. Casualty insurance is a term that applies to several different kinds of insurance, such as burglary insurance and automobile insurance.

Burglary Insurance. Insurance may be obtained to cover loss due to theft or embezzlement. Theft insurance may cover specified items such as money, or it may cover all the merchandise and equipment of a company. Insurance of this type is frequently referred to as *burglary insurance*, although the theft may be performed by an employee of the company. Banks and companies that handle large amounts of money carry insurance against robbery. Many businesses carry insurance that protects them from loss in case of theft or embezzlement by dishonest employees. Some employees who handle large sums of money are covered by *surety bonds*. If such an employee proves dishonest, the company can recover from the surety company the loss to the extent of the bond. A surety bond is one form of insurance.

Automobile Insurance. Automobile insurance is one of the most common types of casualty insurance. It may cover potential loss caused by fire, theft, collision, property damage, bodily injury, a tornado, a windstorm, rain, flood, or the like involving the insured automobile.

Kinds of Automobile Insurance

1. Fire and theft insurance.
2. Comprehensive insurance, including fire and theft coverage, and providing protection against tornadoes, hail, flood, lightning, wind storm, earthquake, riots, glass breakage, robbery, and pilferage.
3. Collision insurance, covering damage to one's own car.
4. Property-damage insurance, covering damage done to other people's property.
5. Bodily-injury insurance, covering damage to other people.

Almost every owner of an automobile agrees that *fire and theft insurance* is desirable. There are relatively few automobile owners who do not carry this protection. The insurance rates are low because the risks are low and they are spread among a great number of automobile owners. It formerly was the custom for companies to issue policies in which they agreed to pay a fixed amount in case of the loss of the automobile by fire or theft. The most common practice now is to issue policies that state that the market value

BUYING INSURANCE PROTECTION

of the automobile at the time of loss will be paid. Most policies are worded in such a manner that the insurance company may replace the car with a similar one or pay the market value at the time of loss, regardless of the amount of insurance carried on the car. When there is only a partial loss, the insurance company repairs the damage or pays the amount of cash equivalent to the cost of the repairs. Most policies include protection against loss due to fire and theft while an automobile is being transported on a boat or a railroad.

Comprehensive insurance is an inclusive coverage against fire and theft and such other hazards as tornado, windstorm, and rain. It is used less frequently although the rates for such protection are low. The rates are low because the chance of loss from these hazards is relatively small.

Collision insurance is usually meant to be protection against loss arising from damage to one's own car. This type of insurance is unpopular because the cost is high. The cost is high because of the many minor damages to automobiles. Most people feel that it is less expensive to assume the risk of loss from collision than it is to carry a collision insurance policy. The rates on this type of policy are considerably less if one is willing to assume the risk on minor injuries and hold the insurance company liable only on major damages. For instance, a policy may have a deductible clause, such as a $25 or $50 deductible clause. In the case of the $25 deductible clause, the owner of the car would stand the loss from damages up to $25 on any one collision. The insurance company would pay the loss from damages above that amount.

Property-damage insurance provides protection against loss resulting from damage to an automobile or some other property of another person, while *bodily-injury insurance* provides protection against loss arising from the injury of any living person. These two forms of insurance are often sold jointly in the same policy, although they can be bought separately. They are important because the hazards of not carrying them are unknown and potentially great. On the other hand, the hazards from fire and theft are definitely known and are not particularly great. Another important reason for carrying these two types of insurance is that the insurance company will take care of all details in case of a claim. In case of accident the insurance company will take charge of the case. The car will be released and the owner can go on his way.

Although fire and theft insurance are the most widely used forms of automobile insurance, property-damage and bodily-injury insurance are probably the most important. Some states have passed legislation that makes it necessary for automobile owners to take out these types of insurance before they can obtain licenses for their cars.

Ordinarily bodily-injury insurance should be carried for not less than ten thousand dollars in case of the injury of a single person, or not less than twenty thousand dollars in case of the injury of more than one person. Most claims can be settled within the limits of these amounts. If ten thousand dollars' worth of bodily-injury insurance is carried as protection against loss due to a single injury, the person who is injured can collect from the insurance company an amount not exceeding ten thousand dollars. In the case of injury to more than one person, the maximum pro-

Bodily injury can result in large claims for damages.

Harold M. Lambert

tection is twenty thousand dollars. The extent of the injury must be determined by a court or established by an agreement between the injured person and the insurance company. A good insurance company will take care of all legal details. If the amount of damages exceeds the amount of insurance, the insured person will have to pay the difference.

Ordinarily it is considered wise not to carry less than five thousand dollars' worth of property-damage insurance. If an automobile driver who carries five thousand dollars' worth of property-damage insurance damages the automobile of another person or the front of a store, for instance, the person whose property has been damaged may collect damages from the insurance company to the extent of five thousand dollars.

Health and Accident Insurance. One may obtain at low cost policies covering accidents and sickness. Some of these policies provide payments as a result of lost time due to an accident or sickness. The policies that provide payments only in case of loss of a leg, loss of an arm, or some other specified injury are of very little practical value to most people because these types of accidents seldom occur; however, the costs are low and for persons in hazardous occupations such insurance may be desirable.

Special clauses are sometimes included in regular insurance policies that provide some protection against accidents and sickness. For instance, there may be a waiver of the premium in case of disability, or there may be a payment of twice the face value of the policy if death results from an accident.

Features of Health and Accident Insurance

1. May provide a specified income while the insured is ill or disabled.
2. May provide a lump-sum payment for specified types of injuries or illnesses.
3. May provide money to pay medical or hospital bills or other special expenses due to accidents or illnesses.

Hospital Care. Another type of insurance that is now commonly in use in all major cities is the hospital service plan, commonly known as *hospital care.* Under this system everyone who is a member of the plan pays a specified rate, for which he receives certain hospital privileges. These privileges vary, but they usually include all hospital services under certain limitations, but do not include services of a private physician. The theory of this plan is that everyone can afford a definite, small payment monthly, quarterly, or yearly, but he might not be able to pay a large hospital bill in an emergency.

Personal Liability Insurance. Several companies write at a very low cost a comprehensive personal liability policy covering claims resulting from injuries to temporary help in the home, from hitting someone with a golf ball, from damage caused by children, from injuries caused by a dog, and from numerous other types of accidents that might result in claims and law suits.

Can You Carry Multiple Insurance? Insurance covering the same property may be carried in more than one company. Multiple insurance has no advantage if you carry full protection in more than one company, however, because one can collect only the amount of his loss. If the policies of two or more companies cover part or all of the value of the property, both insurance companies will share in the loss. For example, if you carry $4,000 worth of fire insurance in one company and $2,000 in another and if the loss amounts to $3,000, the first company will pay $2,000 and the second company will pay $1,000 of the loss.

Assignment of Insurance. If you carry an insurance policy on property that you sell, you cannot transfer the insurance policy to the new owner without the approval of the insurance company. The insurance company need not contract with the new owner, but with the approval of the insurance company the policy can be assigned or transferred to the new owner. The transfer is called an *assignment.*

Insurable Interest. Insurance may be secured only by persons having what is known as an *insurable interest*. Everyone has an insurable interest in his own life. Whether a person has an insurable interest in the life of another depends upon whether he will be deprived of some benefit by the death of the other. One need not be a relative of a person in order to insure that person's life. A creditor, under some circumstances, may insure the life of a debtor. Close kinship is often, but not necessarily, sufficient to constitute an insurable interest.

When property is insured against loss due to fire or other causes, the purpose of the insurance is considered to be the protection of the interest of the person who buys the insurance. The policyholder must have an insurable interest in the property. A person is considered to have an insurable interest in property if there is a reasonable expectation that he will derive a financial benefit from the existence of the property or will suffer a loss from the damage or the destruction of the property. For instance, both the owner of a home and the person who holds a mortgage on the home have an insurable interest. If the property is not insured and is later destroyed, the owner will lose the money he has invested in it, and the person who owns the mortgage may lose the money that is due him on the mortgage.

In the case of property the insurable interest ordinarily must exist at the time of the loss; otherwise, the contract is not enforceable. For example, a person might carry some insurance on property that he rents and occupies. If he moves out of the property without canceling the insurance, he could not collect for a fire loss in case the building burns after he moves.

Most mortgages contain a clause that requires the owner of the property to carry enough insurance to protect the *mortgagee*, the person lending the money. If this insurance is carried in accordance with the agreement, the mortgagee is entitled, in case of loss resulting from fire or some other cause, to enough money from the proceeds to equal the unpaid balance on the mortgage. The remainder of the proceeds goes to the *mortgagor*, the one who borrows money.

If there is no such agreement between the mortgagor and the mortgagee, the mortgagee may protect his interest by purchasing enough insurance to cover the unpaid balance on the mortgage. Many variations exist with regard to the rights and the liabilities of the mortgagee, the mortgagor, and the insurance company in cases of insurance on property that is mortgaged. The laws of the particular state, the clauses in the mortgage, and the clauses in the insurance policy should therefore be studied carefully.

If there is any change in the title to insured property, the protection under the policy usually becomes void. For instance, if a house is insured by Mr. Smith and is sold to Mr. Howard, the insurance policy taken out by Mr. Smith becomes void, for it was written to protect the latter's interest and cannot be transferred without the consent of the insurance company. An exception to this rule arises in case of the death of the person who has purchased the insurance. If such person dies, his heirs are protected under the insurance.

Automobile insurance is essentially the same as fire insurance with regard to a change in the insurable interest. If an automobile is sold, the insurance company should be requested to transfer the policy immediately in order to assure protection to the new owner. As insurance policies differ, their clauses should be read carefully to determine one's rights and the nature of the protection.

Life insurance does not become void if there is a change in the insurable interest. For example, a policy taken out by a corporation on the life of its president is still valid even though he retires or is discharged.

Analysis of Insurance Needs. Nearly everyone is interested in some kind of insurance. He is therefore confronted with the problem of choosing what insurance to buy, how much to buy, and from whom to buy. In some cases the person does not have any choice as to whether he will carry insurance or not. If he has purchased a home, and a bank or a loan association holds a mortgage on the home, he will be required to insure the home. In an increasingly large number of states, a person cannot obtain an automobile license without buying bodily-injury and property-damage insurance.

The mere fact that a person has never suffered a loss is no reason to believe that he will continue to be so fortunate. One cannot assume the attitude, "It has not happened to me thus far. What reason is there to expect it to happen?" One must look upon the buying of insurance from the point of view of (a) the cost of carrying insurance, (b) the results of not carrying insurance, and (c) the benefits of carrying insurance. It is just as foolish to carry too much insurance as it is not to carry any. For instance, a person would be foolish to use all his surplus income for buying life insurance. He would not have any money left for emergencies, for investment, for acquiring a home, or for personal advancement.

A person who has a million dollars and who owns a large estate might not find it desirable to insure a small building on that estate or a motor boat that he owns, for the loss of either of these would not cause him any special handicap. On the other hand, a person who owns his own home and has only a small amount of additional savings should, by all means, insure the home. If he did not carry insurance and the home were destroyed, he would have difficulty in replacing it.

If a person owns a small cottage that he uses during his summer vacation, he may debate whether to insure it. The loss of the cottage would be inconvenient, but it would not impose upon him a great financial loss. If the insurance rate on a cottage of this type is high, the insurance will not be justified. On the other hand, if the same man owns a small building that he uses for a workshop in making a living, he will want to insure it even though its value may not be equal to that of the summer cottage. The destruction of the workshop would result in a severe handicap.

The use of insurance should be looked upon as a means of enabling one to carry out fixed plans through life without the hazards of uncertainty. Insurance makes plans certain, whereas the lack of it makes plans uncertain. A sudden large loss might disrupt an otherwise good plan.

TEXTBOOK QUESTIONS

1. Explain briefly how losses, such as those due to fires, deaths, accidents, or the like, are predictable.
2. In determining the probability of fire insurance losses, why is it necessary to use a large number of houses?
3. Give an example of how an insurance company collects money, from individuals in small amounts to protect each individual from a major loss.
4. How do fire-prevention activities affect insurance rates?
5. What factors are considered in classifying cities for the purpose of determining fire insurance rates?
6. (a) How many classes of cities are recognized for the purpose of establishing basic fire insurance rates? (b) In what respect does the highest rate differ from the lowest rate?
7. What is an insurance contract called?
8. Who is the insured or the assured?
9. Who is the beneficiary?
10. Explain the fundamental difference between a stock company and a mutual company in the insurance business.
11. (a) What kind of insurance company makes assessments against policyholders? (b) Under what circumstances are assessments made?
12. What is meant by extended coverage on fire insurance policies?
13. Explain briefly how regular fire insurance operates on a residence as to the amount carried and the payment of claims.
14. What precaution should be used in order that proof of loss can be provided in case insured property is stolen, destroyed, or lost?
15. Is coinsurance available on a regular residence?
16. Under the agreements in most automobile insurance policies, what options does the insurance company have if the automobile is destroyed by fire?
17. If an automobile on which you have a fire insurance policy is damaged by fire while it is being shipped, are you protected from the loss?
18. If a person has a collision insurance policy on an automobile with a $25 deductible clause, how much will the insurance company pay if the car is damaged in an accident to the extent of $35?
19. (a) What is bodily-injury insurance on an automobile? (b) What is property-damage insurance?
20. Indicate the three principle features that may be found in health and accident policies.
21. What kind of insurance will give you some protection against a claim resulting from an injury caused by your dog?

22. If you carry full fire insurance protection on your house in each of two different companies, can you collect the full amount of fire loss from each of these companies?

23. What is meant by an insurable interest?

24. On what basis is a person considered to have an insurable interest in the life or the property that is insured?

25. Explain how one may have an insurable interest in property at the time the property is insured but may not have an insurable interest at the time the property is destroyed.

26. Explain the difference between the insurance needs of the wealthy person on a small cottage that he uses for his vacations and the insurance needs on a small workshop used by another man in making a living.

DISCUSSION QUESTIONS

1. (a) How could an insurance company determine rates for insurance against loss due to rain? (b) Do you think such rates would be high or low as compared with the rates for automobile insurance? Why?

2. Two companies of equal size and financial standing insure farmers against the risk of crop losses. Company A operates nationally, and Company B operates in a section that comprises ten states. (a) From your consideration of these facts only, draw some conclusion as to the relative merits of these companies. (b) In which one would you take out insurance?

3. If a city has strict building ordinances and strict inspection of buildings, how would you expect the fire insurance rates to be affected?

4. If you were buying automobile insurance, what consideration would you give to the type of policy and the general attitude of the company in paying claims?

5. What, in your opinion, represents the more serious risk of an automobile owner: (a) the risk of property damage or (b) the risk of injury to a person? Why?

6. If your automobile insurance policy provides $10,000 protection against injury to a person and the court awards damages of $12,000 to the injured person, how is the claim settled?

7. What do you think of an accident policy that provides protection against such risks as loss of one leg, loss of both arms, loss of one eye, and other similar hazards?

8. Explain why you do or do not have an insurable interest in (a) the life of your brother, (b) your neighbor's house, and (c) a house on which you are holding a mortgage.

PROBLEMS

1. Assume that the straight fire insurance rates on a home are $5 a thousand and that a new fire alarm system and fire department in a city will reduce this rate to $3.50 a thousand. (a) What will be the savings in insurance on a house valued at $6,000, assuming that the entire value of the house is covered? (b) If these improvements will increase the tax rates $1 a thousand on all real estate, what savings will there be to the same owner, assuming that the house and lot combined are valued at $8,000?

2. A fifty-dollar deductible collision insurance policy on an automobile has cost Mr. Fall an average of $42 a year for ten years. At the end of the tenth year he had a wreck costing $650 to repair his car. How much has he saved or lost by carrying the insurance as compared with assuming his own risk and paying all of his own damages?

3. In a certain city the hospital care plan costs a family with two children $6 quarterly for the semiprivate plan. During the past three years the hospital bills of the Harrison family have amounted to $70, $65, and $120. Assume that under the hospital care plan all these bills would have been reimbursable. Figure to what extent the hospital care plan would have saved the family money annually. Use the average amount of the hospital bills per year in making the comparison.

COMMUNITY PROBLEMS AND PROJECTS

1. Obtain a policy for fire insurance on a home. Study its clauses and regulations. Write a report on it.

2. Make an investigation of the local rates for bodily-injury and property-damage insurance on automobiles and for fire and theft insurance. Compare these rates with those in other communities. Write a report summarizing your findings.

3. Obtain an automobile insurance policy of some kind. Study its clauses and make a report on its features. Point out some of the ways in which the automobile owner may not be protected adequately by the policy.

Chapter 29

PART VIII _____

Features of Life Insurance Contracts

Purpose of the Chapter. In the last chapter the general principles of insurance and the most common types of insurance were described. This chapter is devoted to a study of the nature and the specific features of different kinds of life insurance contracts. The study of this chapter will help you to distinguish the advantages and disadvantages of certain types of policies, to determine some ways to plan a life insurance program, and to understand some of the important provisions of policies.

What Is Life Insurance? *Life insurance* is a voluntary plan through which people set aside portions of their income during their earning years to make provision for the time when their income will cease by death, declining health, or retirement. It is a risk-sharing plan that provides for each member of a group protection that would be impossible for each individual to provide for himself.

Life insurance involves a specific plan or contract (the *policy*) between the insured and an insurance company in which the company promises to pay a sum of money to the person or corporation named in the policy (the *beneficiary*) at the time of the insured's death. If the insured is alive at a future date specified in the policy, a certain sum or periodic sums of money are usually paid to him, except in the case of term insurance. The promise on the part of the insurance company is given in return for the payment of a sum of money (the *premium*) to the insurance company.

Since insurance is a sort of co-operative plan through which individuals pay the same rates under similar conditions, most general forms of insurance require a physical examination and the meeting of other requirements. This is done so that the cost of the insurance and the protection of all members of the insured group will be fair. For instance, if there were no physical examinations required, a

person in poor health and likely to die soon would not pay
any higher rate than one in good health; or a person 25
years of age would have to pay as high a rate as one 50
years of age. A physical examination determines eligibility,
therefore; and the age, sex, and other conditions determine
the rate. Sometimes persons with impaired health or in
extra hazardous occupations can obtain insurance but at
higher rates than normal.

Legal-Reserve Insurance. *Legal-reserve,* or *level-premium,*
life insurance constitutes the chief type in force today. Approximately 90 per cent of the life insurance is of this kind.

The probability of death increases at a rapid rate as the
age of the individual increases. If this increased risk were
reflected in the annual premium, the cost would increase
steadily, becoming more and more burdensome and finally
impossible to pay. The practice in legal-reserve insurance
is to determine a level premium that, because it is more
than enough in the early years, will provide a reserve for
the later years when the cost of protection exceeds the level
premium. The reserve really may be called a savings fund,
or investment element. It accumulates with interest at a
guaranteed rate until the insurance policy matures under
its own terms or is paid at the death of the insured person.
It is the practice of legal-reserve life insurance companies
to regard this investment element as the property of the
insured person and to make it available for his use with
certain restrictions.

Insurance Contracts. There are many types of life insurance contracts, usually referred to as policies. Some of
them are simple; others involve a combination of elements
that cannot be explained without considerable detail. The
following are the more or less basic types of policies: term,
ordinary life, limited-payment life, single-premium life,
endowment, combination, and annuity. These types of policies are explained in the following pages.

Term Insurance. Term insurance, as the name implies, is
insurance that covers a specified period of time and is usu-

ally obtained to cover a specific need. For example, if a man has a debt that he expects to pay off in ten years, provided he lives, he can buy a ten-year term policy for the amount of the indebtedness. This insurance will protect his family from the debt in case he dies.

Term insurance is often referred to as "pure insurance" because it provides protection only. It does not have (a) a cash-surrender value, (b) a loan value, or (c) an investment or savings value. One of the major advantages of term insurance is the low cost compared with that of other types. Although this type of insurance is considered primarily as temporary insurance, some individuals prefer to obtain insurance protection entirely through it and to establish a savings plan independently of the insurance program. Term insurance therefore has some advantage for those who can successfully save and invest.

The most common periods covered by term insurance are five years and ten years, but it may cover any period of years. Such policies are usually convertible into other types of contracts that provide protection over longer periods of years and involve the accumulation of reserves. For instance, a man may wish a large amount of protection at a low cost while he is educating his children. After they have been educated, he may convert the term insurance into some other type of insurance at a higher cost and thereby create an investment value in the insurance.

Ordinary Life Insurance. The ordinary life plan may be called the basic life insurance policy for protection over a long period of years. This type of insurance is sometimes called *whole-term life* or *straight life insurance.* If one has dependents and is anxious to provide primarily for their protection in the event of death, the ordinary life plan is ideal. The premium rate is lower than that for any other type of permanent insurance. When the premium is calculated, a substantial reserve is created over a long period of years so that the costs of protection for the maximum estimated period of the life of the insured person are "leveled off." This reserve is usually made available to the policy-

KINDS OF LIFE INSURANCE

	AMOUNT	PAYMENTS	TYPE OF PAYMENTS	PHYSICAL EXAM	COST
ORDINARY	$500—UP	MONTHLY QUARTERLY SEMI-YEARLY YEARLY	MAIL	YES	MEDIUM
INDUSTRIAL	$100—UP	WEEKLY	COLLECTED BY AGENT	NO	HIGH
GROUP	SMALL	DEDUCTION FROM WAGE	COLLECTED BY EMPLOYER	NO	LOW
SAVINGS BANK	$250—UP	MONTHLY QUARTERLY YEARLY	MAIL OR AT BANK	YES	LOW

PICTOGRAPH CORPORATION

holder as a loan or a cash-surrender value. It is customary for the insured person to continue paying premiums for the entire length of his life or to age 96, at which time he is paid the face value of the insurance policy.

Limited-Payment Life Insurance. A limited-payment life insurance contract is the same as an ordinary life contract except that premiums are paid for a limited time, such as ten, twenty, or thirty years, instead of for life. Because premiums are paid only for a limited time, the rates are somewhat higher than for ordinary life insurance. When these premiums have been paid, the insurance policy is said to be fully paid. If the face value of the policy is, for example, ten thousand dollars, the insurance company will pay this amount whenever death occurs.

Such a contract is desirable when the earning years are limited. If a person is reasonably sure that his earning days will cease when he is fifty-five years of age, he certainly will not want to continue to pay premiums after that age. This type of policy is therefore based on the idea that the payment of premiums should cease when the person's earnings dwindle. As it is assumed, in calculating the premium rate for a limited-payment policy, that there will be fewer annual payments than in the case of the ordinary life policy, each annual payment must be larger than it would be for the ordinary life policy.

Endowment Insurance. The company that issues an endowment policy agrees to pay a definite sum of money at a specified time to the insured person or, in the event of death, to the beneficiaries of this person. An endowment policy costs more than a limited-payment policy for an equivalent number of years. The face amount is available, however, as cash at the end of the period; whereas, in the case of the limited-payment policy, it is available only in the event of death or at age 96.

An endowment policy is an excellent means of accumulating a definite amount for a future need. Short-term endowments for periods of from five to twenty years are ideal to create sums of money that will be needed to educate children, to start a child in some particular profession or business, to purchase a home, or to pay off a debt.

Frequently, and particularly in the case of young people, the short-term endowment policy should not be used. In such a case the amount of insurance that can be purchased may be limited by the comparatively high premium rates. For example, with one particular insurance company, a young man at age 20 could purchase ordinary life insurance at an annual rate of $18.01 a thousand, twenty-payment life insurance for $27.78 a thousand, twenty-year endowment insurance for $47.54 a thousand, or endowment at age 65 for $21.03 a thousand. If one is seeking maximum protection at the lowest price, ordinary life insurance is the cheapest. Often in the case of young people who purchase ten- or twenty-year endowment policies, the money becomes available too early in life and the protection against death ceases, although the insured person will have a great need for the protection in later life. When the policy matures, he may even find himself physically impaired and thus uninsurable.

It is usually most desirable to obtain a long-term endowment policy so that the money will become available at about the age of sixty or later. At this stage in life the insured person may have little or no earning power. If the policy matures at that time, its face value will be available to provide comfort during the later years of life. Many estimates and surveys that have been made indicate the need for old-age income.

Combination Insurance. Many contracts in force today involve combinations of various types of life insurance. For example, one particular type of combination policy provides a low rate for the first four or five years and a higher rate in later years. The same insurance plan would be carried out if an individual purchased a term insurance policy and then, at the end of four or five years, converted it into an ordinary life, a limited-payment life, or an endowment policy.

Annuity Insurance. Many people purchase an *annuity* by turning over to an insurance company a specified sum of money. In return for this sum of money the insurance company agrees to pay a specified monthly or yearly income over a definite period of years or until the death of the insured. Some insurance contracts that are paid up can be converted into annuity contracts. In this way a specified income is assured to the person who is insured or to his beneficiaries after his death.

Annuities are not limited to wealthy people. They can be purchased for as low as one thousand dollars. An annuity fund in a life insurance company can be accumulated through annual savings of as little as twenty-five dollars. Under the terms of the contract the insurance company distributes this fund in regular payments to the one who accumulated it, or to his beneficiaries.

There are numerous types of annuity policies. However, the principal feature of an annuity is guaranteed income starting at a certain age. Therefore, through an annuity one may, during his earning years, provide for an income after his retirement.

Industrial Insurance. Industrial insurance is the type that requires small weekly, or sometimes monthly, payments. It is commonly sold to the industrial or wage-earning group. The payment required each week is usually five cents or some multiple of five cents. This type of insurance furnishes varying amounts of protection, according to the age of the insured person and the plan selected. A fairly large proportion of industrial insurance is on the lives of children and women. The medical examinations are usually not stringent. In fact, this type of insurance is sometimes issued without a medical examination.

The rates reflect the high cost of collecting the small premiums and the high rates of mortality resulting from the lack of rigid standards in medical examinations. Since its cost is high in proportion to the protection provided, no one who can obtain other types of insurance should consider industrial insurance.

This type of insurance serves essentially the following useful purposes: it reaches many people who would other-

WHAT HAPPENS TO INDUSTRIAL POLICIES
(HOW 16,804,595 INDUSTRIAL POLICIES WERE TERMINATED, 1949)

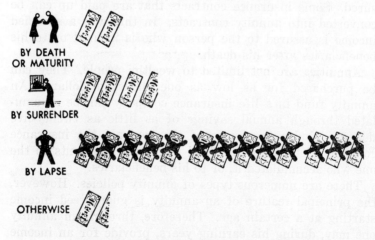

BY DEATH OR MATURITY

BY SURRENDER

BY LAPSE

OTHERWISE

Each symbol represents 5 per cent of all policies terminated

wise not buy any insurance; it teaches these people to save and to guard against unfavorable possibilities; it enables many people who are not insurable under most of the other plans to obtain insurance.

Group Insurance. Group insurance is best used to protect the workers of a common employer. Under this plan many employees can be insured through one policy and without medical examination. The cost is determined by an analysis of the group and is based on the losses indicated by the ages, environment, occupation, and general health of the members. The rates may be increased or decreased, but they are usually low. Employers ordinarily pay part of the premiums.

There are two types of group insurance: one is *group term insurance* that does not build up any cash value; the other is *group straight life insurance* that does build a cash value.

When an employee, covered by a group term policy, leaves the employment in which he has been insured, his policy is canceled unless he chooses some permanent plan of insurance. Under most policies he may become reinsured at a rate covering his existing age without being required to take a physical examination. If the employee is covered by a straight life group policy, he has the privilege of carrying on this policy himself after leaving his employment. By notifying the insurance company of his intentions, he may assume responsibility for paying the premiums and continuing the policy in force.

Savings-Bank Insurance. For many years the state of Massachusetts has had in operation a plan of selling savings-bank insurance. Under that plan savings banks accept payments for insurance policies in the same way as they accept deposits in savings accounts. Premiums are not collected by solicitors. Savings-bank insurance was intended to supplant industrial insurance sold largely to wage-earners. It is contended that the savings-bank insurance plan saves 20 to 50 per cent because commissions, as well as much of the other overhead, are eliminated.

New York and Connecticut also permit the sale of savings-bank insurance. In all cases there are certain restrictions on the amount that a person can buy. For instance, in the state of New York no person can buy more than $1,000 from a single bank or more than a total of $3,000; in Massachusetts the limit is $25,000.

Endowment Feature of All Legal-Reserve Contracts. The fact has been established that out of every one hundred thousand persons starting at the age of ten, only three will reach the age of ninety-five and they will die before the age of ninety-six. The last age is therefore considered as the extreme of life. If, for instance, any person who has an ordinary life policy reaches that age, he will be paid the proceeds of his policy just as if he had originally purchased an endowment policy to mature at the age of ninety-six. Basically, therefore, any life insurance policy in legal-reserve companies, except a term contract, is an endowment contract that will pay to the insured person the previously determined amount if he lives to reach a designated age. If he dies before that time, the company will pay the amount to his beneficiary.

Insurance as a Form of Saving. In considering insurance as a form of saving, one must compare it with at least two other forms of saving utilized by individuals: (a) the deposit of savings in a bank and (b) the purchase of government bonds. There are advantages to each of the three forms. Certain types of insurance policies, such as the endowment policy, are in reality insurance plus the savings element. Of course, insurance savings may not accumulate so rapidly as bank savings because, in the case of insurance, payment must be made for the protection involved. A comparison of the difference between saving by making deposits in a bank and saving by means of insurance may be made by computing the amount that must be deposited annually in a bank account in order to accumulate a given sum, for example, one thousand dollars, and the insurance premiums that must be paid on a thousand-dollar policy over the same period of time.

Bank savings offer no financial protection beyond the amount of the deposits and the accumulated interest. These savings can, however, be readily withdrawn. The cash value of an insurance policy can also be withdrawn. If funds are borrowed on an insurance policy, interest must be paid. Government bonds offer an excellent medium of savings because they can be bought in small denominations and pay a fair rate of interest.

Incontestable Clause. The purchaser of life insurance should understand the meaning of the *incontestable clause* in his policy. The essence of such a clause is that, if the insurance company and its agents have not discovered within a specified time (usually one or two years) that the insured person intentionally or unintentionally made misstatements of fact with regard to diseases or other information required in the application, the insurance company cannot contest the validity of the policy. In other words, if any error has been made or if there has been any fraud in obtaining the insurance policy by giving false information, it is the responsibility of the insurance company to discover such a fact within the time limit specified in the incontestable clause.

Some contracts make a misstatement of age a basis for contesting the claims of the insured. When a misstatement is made in the age of the insured, the policy is not canceled, but the amount payable under the contract will be the amount that could have been obtained at his true age by the actual premiums paid. For instance, if the insured has understated his age five years, each premium payment is less than the premium for his true age. He is entitled to protection equal only to the amount that his premium payments based on his true age would have purchased.

Some contracts have specific war clauses limiting the liability of the insurance company, but some contracts do not have these clauses. War restrictions may apply to death, disability, and accident benefits.

If one fails to live up to his contract by failing to pay the premium within the grace period (usually thirty-one days after the due date), the policy lapses. It can be reinstated only by presenting proof of continued insurability and by paying the past-due premiums with interest.

All standard policies permit the insured person to ride in a licensed airplane on an established route; but if one has ridden in an airplane or expects to ride in an airplane, he should give these facts in his insurance application. If he fails to give this information and rides in an airplane before the expiration of the time limit set in the incontestable clause, the insurance company may choose to cancel the policy. Some of the policies written during the early days of the airplane forbid the policyholder to ride in an airplane under any circumstances. Insurance companies will, however, without charge, grant such policyholders, upon application, a supplementary clause that can be attached to their insurance policies. This clause permits those policyholders to ride in airplanes without jeopardizing the validity of their policies.

The Use of Dividends. Mutual companies and some stock companies pay dividends to policyholders as a sort of profit-sharing plan. Such policies that earn dividends are referred to as *participating*. Dividends are distributed in proportion to the amount of insurance owned by each policyholder. There are different ways in which these dividends may be used, but the following are the most common:

(a) They may be obtained in cash.
(b) They may be used to reduce the amount of the next premium payment.
(c) They may be used to purchase additional insurance.
(d) They may be left with the company to accumulate at an interest rate prescribed by the company. This accumulated amount may be used later for any purpose, or it may be withdrawn in cash. If the insured dies before using the accumulated dividends, the beneficiary will be paid the face amount of the policy, plus the amount of the accumulated dividends and interest. When dividends accumulate, ordinary life policies may be paid up eventually, and other policies may be paid up faster than normal.

Nonforfeiture Values. There are certain cash, loan, paid-up, or extended term-insurance values available to policyholders, except in the case of term insurance. These are technically called *nonforfeiture values*. All legal-reserve life insurance companies provide a choice of nonforfeiture values to a policyholder who stops paying premiums on any policy except term insurance. These are cash value, extended term insurance, paid-up insurance, and automatic premium loans. The following is an explanation of these nonforfeiture values:

(a) Each policy states the *cash value*, which is the amount of money that will be paid to the insured if the policy is canceled. It is stated in his contract or required by law.

(b) If one wishes to continue the maximum amount of insurance protection without paying premiums, he may accept *extended term insurance*. This is usually the face value of the policy, which is continued as long as the accumulated cash value will pay the premium.

(c) Under the *paid-up insurance* plan, the cash value is used to pay up the policy for a reduced face value.

(d) If one elects the *automatic premium loan plan*, the company will automatically pay any overdue premiums by means of a policy loan. If you make no further choice and do not pay any further premiums, the policy will be continued in force until such time as the total indebtedness equals the cash surrender value. At that time the policy is terminated without further value.

If one is not able to keep up the payments on his insurance policy, he may also arrange to exchange the policy for one with a lower face value or for a different type of policy that he can afford to carry.

Time of Premium Payments. Read your insurance policy carefully concerning your obligations in regard to premiums. Premiums are due on the date mentioned in your policy. They must be paid to the home office or to an authorized representative in exchange for an official receipt.

You may change the frequency of your premium payments upon written request to the insurance company. For example, you may have been paying premiums quarterly, but upon written request you can arrange to pay premiums annually, thereby saving a little money.

Life insurance policies generally allow what is called a *grace period*. This is a period ranging from twenty-eight to thirty-one days after the date the premium is due. If the premium is paid during this grace period, there is no penalty to the policyholder. However, if you die within this period, the unpaid premium will be collected from the amount paid to the beneficiary.

If the premium is not paid during the grace period, the policy *lapses*. This means the termination of the contract and the loss of protection. However, if you stop payments of premiums, you may reinstate your insurance policy provided you have not surrendered your policy for a cash settlement. In order to reinstate it, you must take a new physical examination and pay all the overdue premiums with interest. Some policies also have other requirements for reinstatement.

Change of Beneficiary. When anyone buys a life insurance policy, he names a beneficiary or his policy becomes payable to the estate upon his death. If you decide to change your beneficiary, you may do so at any time by filling out forms furnished by the insurance company. This may be done provided you have reserved this right in your policy. If you have not reserved the right to change your beneficiary, you must get the written consent of the original beneficiary before naming a new one.

If the beneficiary you have named should die before you do, your insurance will be paid to your estate. Because of this possibility, you may name secondary and tertiary beneficiaries so that if the first one dies, the estate will be paid to the next in order.

Assignment of Your Policy. If you have reserved the right to change the beneficiary of your life insurance policy, it can be assigned as security for a loan. Banks will lend money on some life insurance policies provided the policy is assigned to the bank as protection to the bank until the loan has been paid.

Some Limitations in Insurance Policies. Some life insurance contracts contain limitations on travel in foreign countries, travel by air, and war risks. If you have an insurance policy, it is well to study the special clauses providing limitations. These are usually inserted in the back of your policy as *riders*.

The risk of suicide is usually not covered by an insurance policy if it occurs during the first year or two of the contract. If suicide occurs during that time, however, the insurance company will return the premiums.

Special Clauses. Some insurance policies have provisions whereby it is not necessary to pay the premiums if a person is permanently disabled. Still others have clauses that provide twice the amount of death benefit if the insured dies as a result of an accident instead of from natural causes. There are many other such clauses that may be found in insurance policies.

Each company sets its own standard practices. However, the clauses in policies of the same type issued by one company in different states may not always be alike, for the various clauses must conform to the laws of the states in which the company operates and the policies are issued.

TEXTBOOK QUESTIONS

1. What is life insurance?
2. In life insurance, who is the beneficiary?
3. What is meant by the premium on a life insurance policy?
4. How could a mutual life insurance company or a stock-company that pays dividends to policyholders reduce its net rates by selecting carefully the best risks?
5. Why is legal-reserve insurance sometimes referred to as "level-premium insurance"?
6. Why does not the premium on a legal-reserve insurance policy increase as one grows older and the risk of death becomes greater?

7. What are the recognized basic types of life insurance policies?
8. What is the most important merit of term insurance?
9. Is ordinary life insurance recommended for permanent or temporary insurance?
10. In what ways does a limited-payment life policy differ from an ordinary life policy?
11. What is the difference between endowment insurance and limited-payment life insurance?
12. What is one good use of an endowment policy?
13. Why is a short-term endowment policy sometimes not desirable for a young person?
14. As compared with a limited-payment life or an endowment policy, does an ordinary life policy have a lower or a higher premium rate for protection?
15. Describe an annuity in a few words.
16. Why are the rates on industrial insurance high?
17. Do group insurance policies require a medical examination?
18. What is the asserted advantage of savings-bank insurance?
19. If a person has dependents and wants to buy permanent insurance that will provide the maximum amount of protection for the minimum amount of money, what type of policy is recommended?
20. What is the incontestable clause in a life insurance policy?
21. In what way may a policyholder use dividends?
22. What are the four common nonforfeiture values of legal-reserve life insurance?
23. Explain what is meant by the grace period and tell what happens if the premium on a life insurance policy is not paid during that period.
24. If you have not reserved the right to change your beneficiary in your life insurance policy, what must you do in order to change the beneficiary?
25. How can an insurance policy sometimes be used to obtain a mortgage from a bank?
26. Do all life insurance policies provide protection against the risk of air travel or war?

DISCUSSION QUESTIONS

1. "Insurance is the opposite of gambling." Explain this statement.
2. If you borrow some money to buy a home and want to obtain a life insurance policy at the lowest possible cost as a pro-

tection until the loan is paid, what kind of insurance will you buy?

3. While he is in school, a student obtains some assistance from his widowed mother. Most of her savings are needed for financing his education, but he earns some of his own money. He hopes to finish school and then to support his mother. He believes that he should carry some insurance to protect his mother. What kind of insurance do you recommend? Why?

4. Under certain circumstances is a limited-payment policy similar to an ordinary life policy?

5. What is the advantage of a limited-payment life policy to a person whose earnings can reasonably be expected to cease at some definite time?

6. Mr. Brown has no dependents, but he wants to buy some insurance so that he can accumulate the maximum amount of savings with reasonable protection and at the same time save some money that can be used to buy a home in ten years. What kind of policy will best suit his needs?

7. Explain why it is necessary to pass a physical examination to qualify for most regular insurance policies. Is there any difference in the case of group insurance?

8. If you want to obtain an insurance policy that will provide permanent protection, become paid up eventually, and have a cash-surrender or a loan value, what kind of policy will you obtain?

9. Which type of policy provides the greatest element of saving but the least element of protection in proportion to the premiums?

10. If one has purchased a twenty-payment life insurance policy from a company that pays dividends, what practice would you recommend if it is desired to pay the policy up before the end of twenty years?

11. Explain how the automatic premium loan plan works with legal-reserve life insurance.

12. Assume that you have been sixty days delinquent on paying a premium on a life insurance policy. Is there anything you can do to reinstate it?

13. Describe a circumstance in which the beneficiary of a life insurance policy would have a right to object to changing the beneficiary.

14. (a) In what way may riding on a regular commercial airline jeopardize most insurance policies? (b) In what way will riding in a private plane or operating a private plane jeopardize an insurance policy?

PROBLEMS

1. According to the life insurance contract of one company, it will pay to the widow of the insured for each $1,000 of insurance, a monthly income of the following amounts for at least ten, or at least twenty years, and for as long thereafter as she lives:

AGE OF WIDOW	10 YEARS CERTAIN AND FOR LIFE	20 YEARS CERTAIN AND FOR LIFE
35	$3.11	$3.07
40	3.34	3.27
45	3.61	3.50
50	3.95	3.76
55	4.37	4.05
60	4.87	4.35

On a $10,000 policy (a) how much will the widow at the age of 40 receive each month on a ten year certain basis? (b) a widow at age 55 on a twenty year certain basis?

2. A certain insurance company sells a twenty-year endowment policy at age 25 at the premium rate of $51.28 per year per thousand dollars. The average dividends on policies of this company in recent years have been $4.18 per thousand dollars. Assuming that the dividend rate will continue and that the dividends will be used to reduce the premium, how much will be paid into the insurance company on a $1,000 policy in twenty years?

COMMUNITY PROBLEMS AND PROJECTS

1. Obtain a copy of a form used in applying for an insurance policy and fill out the form for yourself.

·2. Obtain an insurance policy at home or from some insurance agent. Examine it carefully in regard to rates, dividends, and special clauses. Make a list of the facts that you learned from an examination of this policy.

Chapter 30

_____

How to Buy Life Insurance

Purpose of the Chapter. In buying life insurance, it is important to select the right kind of company and the right kind of insurance policy or contract. It is also important to purchase insurance in the proper amounts to provide the kind of protection that is desired. Some insurance policies involve both protection and savings. One should study his insurance program carefully to be sure that he gets the proper protection or the proper savings elements or both. The purpose of this chapter is to point out the simple guides in buying life insurance as a means of providing protection and building an estate.

Selecting a Company. To sell life insurance, a company must be licensed in each state in which it operates. From the point of view of the buyer of insurance, the best insurance laws and the strictest supervision are in the states of New York, Massachusetts, and Ohio. If you are planning to buy insurance from a company that is licensed to do business in any of those states, you therefore have assurance that the company has passed a rigorous inspection. You should also be sure that the company is licensed to do business in your particular state.

In evaluating the cost of a policy, a person should determine the basic rates on the equivalent type of policy in other companies. He should then investigate past earnings and dividends. If a company does not grant dividends, the basic rate is the premium that must be paid. If the company does grant dividends, the average dividend that has been granted may be used as a reasonable basis for computing the deduction to be made from the premium in order to determine the actual net cost. The tables on the following page show the rates on various policies of two typical companies. After deducting the average dividends of Company

B, the rates of that company may or may not be lower
than those of Company A.

Annual Premium Rates

AGE OF INSURED AT ISSUANCE OF POLICY	ORDINARY LIFE ($1,000)	20-PAYMENT LIFE ($1,000)	20-YEAR ENDOWMENT ($1,000)	5-YEAR TERM CONVERTIBLE ($1,000)
20	$14.44	$22.35	$40.93	$ 8.40
25	16.16	24.21	41.31	8.71
30	18.38	26.49	41.64	9.15
35	21.38	29.41	42.44	9.82
40	25.38	33.08	43.76	11.40
45	30.94	38.17	46.23	13.94
50	38.63	44.94	50.33	18.60
55	49.33	54.20	57.30	26.78

Company A, nonparticipating.

AGE OF INSURED AT ISSUANCE OF POLICY	ORDINARY LIFE ($1,000)	20-PAYMENT LIFE ($1,000)	20-YEAR ENDOWMENT ($1,000)	5-YEAR TERM CONVERTIBLE ($1,000)
20	$18.00	$27.76	$48.92	$10.23
25	20.14	29.98	49.21	10.61
30	22.85	32.62	49.64	11.15
35	26.35	35.82	50.36	11.96
40	30.94	39.77	51.62	13.28
45	37.08	44.82	53.88	15.57
50	45.45	51.54	57.89	19.95
55	56.93	60.79	64.71	27.61

Company B, participating.

Some participating companies set their original rates
higher than do other participating companies. The extent
to which policyholders may participate in earnings is not
the same in all companies. There are, however, tables
published each year that show the rates of each company
and the prevailing dividends. Every insurance salesman
should be prepared to give such information to a prospective
purchaser of an insurance policy.

Let us assume, for example, that the average dividend
on each $1,000 of ordinary life insurance in Company B is
$3.50 on a policy issued at the age of twenty. The net rate
after the dividend has been deducted is $14.50. This rate
is still slightly higher than that of Company A.

Publications are available providing up-to-date comparisons of the different policies and different rates of all insurance companies. One of these is a book entitled *Life
Insurance from the Buyer's Point of View*, published by

Compare insurance
companies and poli-
cies before buying.

Ewing Galloway

the American Institute for Economic Research of Great
Barrington, Massachusetts. The comparisons in this book
will help in making a selection of a company.

The operating expenses of new companies are often very
high as compared with those of old companies. On the other
hand a company that has just started or that has been in
business only a short time will have low mortality expenses
as compared with a long established company because the
new company will be insuring relatively young people and
will not have had time to start paying many death claims.

Guides in Selecting an Insurance Company

1. Select a company that is licensed to do business in states
   where the laws are the strictest. Be sure the company is
   licensed to do business in your state.
2. Compare rates between companies, including dividends.
3. Consider favorably an old company with a good record.
4. Compare expense ratios of companies—their expense per
   $1,000 of insurance.
5. Compare the investment yield of different companies—the
   percentage earned on its investments.
6. Deal only with an intelligent, authorized agent.

Selecting an Insurance Agent. As a general rule, insurance salesmen are honorable and consider seriously the
needs of clients. The buyer of insurance should bear in
mind that even an honorable insurance salesman may be
so eager to sell that he may make recommendations some-

times just to please the person who is buying the insurance, even though it may not be the best possible recommendation. The buyer of insurance must therefore learn the first principles of insurance. Even though he cannot be expected to be an expert, he should know enough to be able to judge the merits of an insurance salesman's recommendations.

A reliable agent who is working for a reliable company will give good advice to prospective purchasers of insurance. In making application for an insurance policy, the individual is usually required to indicate the amount of insurance he already owns. This information gives the insurance company an opportunity to determine whether the applicant is justified in purchasing additional insurance. In the insurance field there are many agents who have been approved as *chartered life underwriters*. These men have made a study of life insurance and are qualified to give advice to applicants.

Selecting a Policy. In buying insurance and in comparing one policy with another, one must consider: (a) the uses for which the insurance is intended, (b) his present and expected income, (c) the cost of the insurance, and (d) his willingness and capacity to save.

In examining any policy, one should compare the cash-surrender value, the paid-up insurance, and the extended insurance with those of other policies. The next problem is to choose the best policy for one's individual needs.

Planning Your Program. No one can decide how much insurance to carry on a particular life without knowing all the circumstances surrounding the person and his family. The amount of an expenditure for insurance should be governed by the budget.

Three Key Objectives

1. Adequate protection for specific needs.
2. Adequate savings through insurance.
3. Expenditures at the time of life when income is available.

Guides as to Types of Policies

1. Term policies should be used when it is essential to obtain immediate protection for an amount as large as possible or to cover a special need for a short period.

2. Ordinary life or limited-payment life policies should be used when future obligations will probably be as important as or more important than present ones. For example, a young husband should be especially interested in these types of policies for the protection of his wife and children.

3. Ordinary life policies, rather than limited-payment life policies, should be used if it is more important to get protection for a large amount than to avoid the payment of premiums in old age.

4. Endowment insurance should be used when the accumulation of funds is the main objective. Caution should be taken, however, not to buy an excessive amount of endowment insurance in early life.

5. The best solution should be determined; it should then be followed, changes in the plan being made only as circumstances require them.

In the case of most insurance policies a part of the expenditure constitutes a saving, while the remaining part of it constitutes an expense for the protection obtained. The saving is a result of the gradual increase in the cash value or the loan value of the policy. Expenditures for insurance should therefore be considered from the point of view of savings and expenses.

Life insurance should be designed primarily to replace income lost to a family when the husband and father dies. Except for certain sums that may be needed at the time of death, the proceeds of the insurance should be looked upon as an income that will be paid regularly under some prescribed plan to the family of the deceased husband and father. A total of $10,000 may sound like a large sum of money, and it really is, as you will find when you try to save that sum. But at 2 or 3 per cent interest; $10,000 will only provide $200 or $300 a year of income from interest. Life insurance policies can be arranged to provide monthly

Insurance is mainly for the protection and support of dependents.

checks consisting of both principal and interest instead of a lump-sum payment or instead of just interest.

For example, the proceeds of a $10,000 insurance policy will pay $100 a month for nine years and six months. The proceeds of a $20,000 policy will pay $100 a month for twenty-two years and ten months. Other methods of payment may enable a person to work out almost any desired program of income for his family after his death. His life insurance agent should be quite helpful in arranging the details of adequate protection and proper payments.

When the head of a family dies, the scale of living must be lowered in most cases. Many families are entitled to social security benefits, but these are seldom sufficient to take care of all the needs; however, they do supplement the insurance program and should be taken into consideration. Unless an insurance program is planned, the family will have to depend upon its own earning power or upon the income from other property already accumulated. Most families are not qualified to manage investments.

The following chart illustrates the readjustments that are necessary upon the death of the father and husband. At the time of death there are certain unusual expenses involved. Then comes the readjustment period when the family may have to move into a smaller house and prepare for living on a smaller income. In many families there is

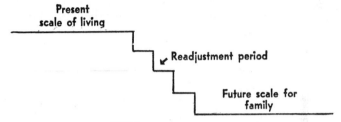

The insurance program should provide for a gradual readjustment in the scale of living.

a problem of educating the children until they are self-supporting, and then providing for at least a modest income for the widow.

An Example of a Planned Insurance Program. Let us take for an example the Nelson family. Assume that Mr. and Mrs. Nelson are both forty years of age, and that they have two children, thirteen and fifteen years of age. Mr. Nelson wants to plan his insurance program so that, if he should die, his family will have a reasonable income based upon his maximum ability to provide this income through insurance. He feels that he can afford to spend about $50 a month for insurance premiums and then proceeds to build his program based upon this expenditure.

Mr. and Mrs. Nelson feel that at least $1,000 will be necessary to take care of funeral and other expenses. They do not have any mortgage or other substantial debts that will have to be paid.

Under the present social security laws, if Mr. Nelson died during the current year, Mrs. Nelson would receive, unless she remarries or dies, a monthly income for five years, or until the youngest child reaches age eighteen. She will receive for each child a monthly income until that child reaches eighteen, marries, quits school, or dies. Assuming that Mr. Nelson has paid social security taxes on the maximum income for social security purposes and is fully covered under the new law, the benefit payments will be $150 a month for three years (until the first child reaches eighteen), and then $120 a month for two more years (until the other child reaches eighteen). Mrs. Nelson will not receive any further social security benefits until age sixty-five, at which time she will receive $60 a month for life. If she remarries, those benefits will cease.

Obviously the Nelsons must supplement these probable benefits, for they will not be sufficient for the needs of the family; and, if Mrs. Nelson or the children are forced to go to work, they will lose all or part of the benefits. Income will be badly needed while the children are in school. Furthermore, after both the children reach eighteen, Mrs. Nelson will need an income to replace the social security benefits.

Mr. Nelson owns a $10,000 straight life insurance policy bought at age twenty-five. He and Mrs. Nelson decide that a $1,000 straight life policy, payable in a lump sum, would be desirable for a cleanup fund at the time of death. They also feel that for approximately a year following his death she will need extra income to carry her through the readjustment period. They find that a policy with a face value of approximately $1,189 will provide an income of $100 a month for twelve months following his death.

The big problem is to provide a satisfactory monthly income after the first year and through the years when Mrs. Nelson will not have any social security benefits. The $10,000 policy already owned will pay $100 a month to Mrs. Nelson for nine years and six months after his death. After consulting an insurance agent, it was decided to purchase another $10,000 straight life policy with certain unusual features about it. Under the provisions of this policy Mrs. Nelson will be paid $100 a month to age sixty-five and thereafter will be paid $56.10 a month. The premium payments on this policy for the first twenty years are $401.80 a year and thereafter are $255.60.

The following table shows the amount, the purposes, and the annual cost of this program:

AMOUNT OF INSURANCE	PURPOSE AND AMOUNT OF PROTECTION	ANNUAL PREMIUM*
$ 1,000	$1,000 cash for cleanup fund	$ 32.18
1,189	$100 a month for readjustment period of 12 months	41.25
10,000	$100 a month for 9 years and 6 months for education of children	210.20
10,000	$100 a month until age 65, then $56.10 until death	401.80
$22,189	Total Insurance Required	$685.43

* The dividends will reduce the total annual premium.

A sample insurance plan.

Now let us see how this program works out from the point of view of monthly income for Mrs. Nelson's family until the death of Mrs. Nelson. The following table shows the monthly income from insurance and social security benefits, with the total monthly income given in the last column.

YEAR	MONTHLY PROCEEDS FROM INSURANCE	MONTHLY PROCEEDS FROM SOCIAL SECURITY	MONTHLY TOTAL
1 *	$300.00 *	$150.00	$450.00
2	200.00	150.00	350.00
3	200.00	150.00	350.00
4	200.00	120.00	320.00
5	200.00	120.00	320.00
6	200.00	none	200.00
7	200.00	none	200.00
8	200.00	none	200.00
9 (and six months)	200.00	none	200.00
10–25	100.00	none	100.00
26 to end of life	56.10	60.00	116.10

* And a lump-sum payment of $1,000.

Proceeds from Mr. Nelson's insurance and Social Security benefits.

Amount of Insurance Based on Income. When a married person's income is small, he needs insurance because he must have some protection for his dependents. The amount that is set aside for insurance should be budgeted in the same manner as his other expenditures. As a person's salary increases, the amount spent for insurance should also increase. The only people who do not need life insurance are those who have investments which provide a certain income sufficient to support the dependents.

The amount of insurance that should be bought is a special problem in the case of each individual. It must be determined by considering the income, the necessary expenditures, the accumulation of a cash savings fund, and the care of dependents. There are, however, reasonable percentages that have proved to be satisfactory. The following table shows the percentages of insurance expenditures recommended for individuals with incomes ranging from one thousand to five thousand dollars:

ANNUAL INCOME	PERCENTAGE	ANNUAL OUTLAY
$1,000	2–3½	$ 20 to $ 35
1,200	3–4½	36 to 54
1,500	3½–5	52 to 75
1,800	4–5½	72 to 99
2,000	4½–6	90 to 120
2,500	5–6½	125 to 162.50
3,000	5½–7	165 to 210
3,500	6–8½	210 to 297.50
4,000	6½–9	260 to 360
4,500	7–9½	315 to 427.50
5,000	7½–10	375 to 500

The amount of income to spend for life insurance.

An analysis of this table discloses that a person earning three thousand dollars a year should expect to spend from 5½ to 7 per cent of his income for insurance. Obviously, the percentage expended in any particular case will depend upon (a) one's standard of living, (b) one's sense of responsibility, (c) the cost of living, (d) the number of dependents, and (e) the type of insurance that is bought.

The amount and the type of insurance that is purchased should be based upon a carefully thought-out insurance plan and should be taken into consideration in the family budget. Unless one is able to continue payments on an insurance policy, it is not wise to buy the policy.

Amount of Insurance Required for a Future Income. Another way to determine the amount of insurance that should be purchased is to determine the amount that one wants to accumulate to provide a future income. An income from insurance can be provided in any one of three ways:

(a) By creating a cash estate, which will be reinvested to provide an income.

(b) By buying sufficient insurance to yield a fixed amount of income for life after a certain age.

(c) By arranging with the insurance company to use the proceeds of the insurance policy for paying a fixed income to dependents after the death of the insured.

Under the first plan the person can consider his insurance and his other savings in computing the amount of income that will be available. Suppose, for example, that a person has planned his insurance program so that the cash proceeds available at his contemplated retirement age of sixty will amount to $25,000. If this amount is invested at 3½ per cent, it will pay an annual income of $875. This income, plus the income from other savings and investments, will represent the sum that the person may expect for use after he retires, provided he does not use part of the original principal.

Under the second plan it is possible for a person to make a contract with an insurance company whereby the proceeds of insurance are to provide (a) a guaranteed income for life or (b) a guaranteed income for life with a cash settlement if death occurs within a certain period. The following table shows the monthly income guaranteed by one insurance company for each $1,000 of the proceeds from insurance. The payments given in this table are guaranteed for life. Tables such as this vary, of course, according to the companies with

BEGINNING AT AGE	GUARANTEED MONTHLY INCOME FOR LIFE FOR EACH $1,000 IN INSURANCE FUND
50	$4.51
55	5.07
60	5.80
65	6.75
70	8.02

Monthly income for life.

which the contracts of life insurance have been made.

For example, if a person has, under this plan, a $10,000 matured endowment policy at the age of fifty, he will receive from the insurance company $45.10 a month for the rest of his life. Some settlement options guarantee such payments for a certain number of years, such as fifteen or twenty years, and for life thereafter if the person lives longer. If he does not live beyond the fixed number of years, his beneficiary will get a specified cash settlement.

Under the third plan the person who is insured can provide for the proceeds of his insurance to be left with the insurance company after his death so that his dependents can be paid a fixed income for a specified number of years. The following table shows the proceeds that must be left with the company in order to provide fixed monthly payments of from $50 to $150 for a period of from five to fifteen years:

NUMBER OF MONTHLY PAYMENTS	MONTHLY PAYMENTS FROM CASH VALUES INDICATED BELOW							NUMBER OF YEARS PAYABLE
	$50	$70	$75	$90	$100	$125	$150	
60	$2,792	$ 3,909	$ 4,188	$ 5,026	$ 5,585	$ 6,981	$ 8,377	5
72	3,303	4,624	4,954	5,945	6,606	8,277	9,909	6
84	3,799	5,318	5,698	6,838	7,598	9,497	11,396	7
96	4,280	5,992	6,420	7,704	8,560	10,700	12,840	8
108	4,748	6,646	7,121	8,546	9,495	11,869	14,242	9
120	5,201	7,281	7,801	9,362	10,402	13,002	15,603	10
132	5,642	7,898	8,462	10,155	11,283	14,104	16,924	11
144	6,069	8,497	9,104	10,924	12,138	15,173	18,207	12
156	6,484	9,078	9,727	11,672	12,969	16,211	19,454	13
168	6,888	9,642	10,331	12,398	13,775	17,219	20,662	14
180	7,279	10,190	10,918	13,102	14,557	18,197	21,836	15

The cash value needed to provide a fixed monthly income for dependents for a certain number of years if 3 per cent interest is paid.

From this table it is apparent that, when a person dies, the proceeds from his insurance policy must amount to $5,201 to guarantee a payment of $50 a month to his dependents for a period of ten years. The cash values vary, of course, according to the companies with which the contracts have been made.

The buying of insurance should be just one part of the plan of building up savings and providing for the protection of dependents. In deciding how much insurance to buy, a person should consider his entire financial program.

Summary of Insurance Buying Suggestions. Almost everyone needs some form of life insurance. Life insurance is not, however, the solution to every problem. The following precautions should be observed in handling one's life insurance program:

1. Remember that there is no single form of insurance that is best for everyone. After an insurance plan is

started, it should be studied carefully each time a new policy is purchased.

2. Study the policy carefully before any insurance is purchased.

3. Do not buy more insurance than can safely be kept in force. One always suffers a financial sacrifice when insurance is canceled.

4. Do not buy insurance that is too high in price for you. For instance, a young man who buys an endowment policy may be making a mistake, for the probability is that he will marry and require lower-priced protection in a larger amount for his family, or that his parents as they grow older will need protection. Endowment policies may subsequently be changed to lower-priced policies for larger amounts, but evidence of insurability is required before the policy can be changed.

5. Do not surrender old insurance or change to a cheaper policy in order to obtain new insurance unless you are sure that the change will be to your advantage.

6. If you are approached by an insurance consultant, be sure that he represents a bona fide and honest organization. Be cautious if he tries to frighten you into believing that endowment policies steal money from the insured or that term insurance is the only good type of insurance.

7. Have no dealings with an unintelligent agent who is not conscious of his relationship with his client and his company. If the agent is a stranger, it is advisable to determine whether he is an authorized agent of the company being represented. Advance no money to an agent unless a receipt authorized by the company is obtained.

8. If you cannot pay the first premium in cash, avoid, if possible, paying it by signing a premium note unless you are sure you can pay the note when it falls due. The signer becomes indebted to the insurance company for the amount of the premium. Do not purchase new insurance if the first premium on such insurance will be paid by borrowing on the old policy.

9. Remember that an agent has no authority to make, alter, or discharge any contract in the name of the com-

pany, or to bind the company by any promise or statement, except upon the company's previous written consent.

10. A beneficiary should be named in each insurance policy. If one is not named, the insurance is left to the insured's estate. The proceeds of the insurance and all other assets of the deceased person will then be distributed to the heirs according to the law of the state in which the policyholder lived, and delays and extra cost will occur in settling the estate.

From time to time the insured person should consider the advisability of changing the beneficiary because of marriage, deaths in the family, or the birth of children. When a new policy is purchased, there should always be a recheck of the beneficiaries on previous policies. All previous policies and the new policy should be studied to see what changes may be desirable.

11. Premiums should be paid when due. Companies ordinarily permit a period of twenty-eight to thirty-one days of grace before the policy goes out of force. Unless premiums are paid when due, the insured person may not be covered by the necessary protection and may be required to reinstate the policy by proving insurability.

12. If money is borrowed on an insurance policy, it should be repaid as soon as possible. If it is not repaid, the beneficiary does not have the protection that was originally planned.

13. Buy insurance only from a legal-reserve company.

14. Insurance should be bought primarily on the life of the breadwinner of the family.

15. In arranging an insurance program, take into consideration the benefits payable under social security.

16. For straight protection at the lowest rate, take advantage of group insurance if it is offered by your employer.

17. If savings-bank life insurance is available in your state, you should consider that type of insurance in your program.

Insurance, Estates, Wills. As you have learned through your study of life insurance, a beneficiary may be named to

collect the proceeds of a life insurance policy. If no beneficiary is named, the proceeds go into what is called an
estate, which includes money and other property of the
deceased. An estate must be administered according to the
laws of the state. The distribution of money or other property can therefore be regulated, to a certain extent, before
one's death by designating beneficiaries of life insurance
policies and by making a will.

A *will* consists simply of instructions that a person gives
before his death as to the distribution of his property after
his death. It may be changed or revoked at any time during
the maker's life. Even though there is a will, creditors
must be paid; and a will may not deprive the wife or husband from his rightful share in property according to the
laws of the state.

Because of the difference in laws in various states and
the fact that the basic rules have certain exceptions, a
lawyer should be consulted in making a will.

Should You Make a Will? Many people in moderate circumstances do not feel that it is desirable to make a will.
They feel that wills are only for rich people. However,
if you own only a moderate amount of property, your heirs
will have less trouble and less expense if you make a will;
and you are more likely to have your wishes carried out
with a will than you are without it.

Reasons for Making a Will

1. The distribution of property is less expensive with a will
   than without it.

2. Provided the will does not conflict with the laws of the
   state, the property may be distributed according to the
   wishes of the maker of the will.

3. If a husband dies, leaving a wife and children, without a
   will, someone must administer the estate. Even though
   the wife administers the estate, she usually will have to
   provide a bond and make regular reports as to the handling of the estate for the children.

TEXTBOOK QUESTIONS

1. On what points should an insurance company be judged?
2. When the listed premium rates of companies are compared, what should be considered in computing the net rates?
3. What is a chartered life underwriter?
4. What four factors should be considered in selecting an insurance policy after a good company has been chosen?
5. What types of policies would you use for the following purposes: (a) when a special need must be covered for a short period; (b) when future obligations will be more important than present obligations; (c) when it is more important to get protection for a large amount than to avoid the payment of premiums in old age; (d) when the accumulation of a savings fund is the main objective?
6. What are the three key objectives of a life insurance program?
7. In the case of a family, who is the main person whose life is insured and why?
8. Why is it considered desirable to have a set amount of life insurance. paid in cash immediately on the death of the insured?
9. From the table on page 539 determine the guaranteed monthly income of a person who retires at the age of sixty if he has $12,000 in an insurance fund. $69.60
10. From the table on page 540 determine how much the cash value of insurance must be to pay the dependents of the insured a monthly income of $90 a month for 108 months. $8,546
11. What are some of the disadvantages if a young man buys all the endowment insurance that his income will permit?
12. If your employer offers you protection under a group insurance policy, is it desirable for you to participate in this kind of insurance?
13. What is a will?

DISCUSSION QUESTIONS

1. If you start buying life insurance at age thirty and there is inflation (a general increase in prices and the cost of living), what happens to the value of the money that is paid to you in your old age or to a beneficiary on your death? In other words, explain the effect of inflation on insurance.
2. If the situation in the previous question is reversed and there is deflation, what is the effect on insurance?
3. (a) Why do insurance companies spend considerable money each year in publishing health advertisements and in conducting health campaigns? (b) Why does an insurance com-

pany go to the expense of offering free medical examinations to policyholders?

4. (a) When a person applies for an insurance policy, why does the insurance agent ask how much insurance the person already owns? (b) Why is it desirable for the person to tell how much he owns?

5. A man forty years of age knows that in the position in which he works he must retire at the age of sixty. He would like to buy an ordinary life policy, but he wants all premium payments to cease by the time he retires. What options are open to him?

6. A man plans to go into business. He knows that he needs insurance protection, but he wants to buy insurance that will provide the maximum loan value. What kind of insurance would you recommend?

7. What kind of insurance program would you recommend for a young unmarried man of seventeen years of age who expects to finish a college education and go into business for himself?

8. In the case of Mr. and Mrs. Nelson discussed in this chapter, what would you recommend as an improvement in the program provided additional insurance could be afforded?

9. (a) Why is it undesirable for a person to carry too much insurance? (b) What is too much insurance?

10. Explain why one should avoid borrowing money to pay the first premium on a life insurance policy.

11. Give your reasons why it is better to name a specific beneficiary than it is to leave the proceeds of insurance payable to the estate.

PROBLEMS

1. Suppose Company B, the rates of which are listed on page 530, has been paying an average dividend of $6.42 a thousand on an ordinary life policy. Is the net rate lower or higher than the rate on the equivalent policy of Company A? (Base your figures on the rates for a person who is thirty years of age.)

2. A man thirty-five years of age has two children, aged four and eight. He has a good position and has almost paid for his home. He has $500 in a savings account, an endowment policy of $2,000, and an ordinary life policy of $5,000. His budget provides for a yearly saving of approximately $200. He decides that he wants to spend $100 of this amount for insurance that will provide the maximum amount of protection, but will become paid up before he is sixty years of age.

What kind of policy and how much insurance can he buy from Company A, the rates of which are listed in the table on page 530?

3. A man, age twenty, who is planning to marry, has $200 a year available for insurance. He wants to be assured of having $2,000 to use as a payment on a home by the time he is forty years of age. He also wants the maximum amount of protection from his insurance. Outline a plan of insurance for him based on the rates of Company A (page 530).

4. On the basis of the table, page 537, showing the proceeds from Mr. Nelson's insurance and social security benefits, prepare a new table showing the monthly income available to a mother, age thirty-five, with one child, age twelve, taking into consideration the following insurance and social security benefits: a $10,000 policy providing monthly benefits of $100 for nine years and six months; a $10,000 policy with monthly payments for life, beginning at age fifty (see the table on page 539 for a monthly income for life); a $5,000 policy with monthly payments for life beginning at age sixty-five (see table on page 539 for monthly income for life); social security benefits of $80 for six years; and social security benefits of $37.50 at age sixty-five.

COMMUNITY PROBLEMS AND PROJECTS

1. If your parents are paying insurance premiums monthly, quarterly, or semiannually, calculate the amount of savings that would be accumulated if the money were deposited in a savings account and used to pay the premiums annually.

2. If your family will permit you to do so, analyze their present insurance program and then give your recommendations as to changes or improvements in the program, including the use of dividends, the authorized beneficiary, and the settlement provisions.

3. Consult an insurance agent and ask him to give you the figures in regard to the types of policies, amounts, first-year premiums, and recommended use of the proceeds for a program for your family. The program should be based upon a stipulated yearly premium that can be afforded in the family budget.

Chapter 31

PART VIII _____

Social Security

Purpose of the Chapter. In general, social security legislation is that which involves the social or economic welfare of the citizen. We specifically use the term *social security* to refer to various state and Federal laws that were enacted to provide protection against such social hazards as unemployment, old age, disability, and accidents. The most important of these are the Federal social security laws in conjunction with certain state laws related to them. The purpose of this chapter is to explain the benefits, rights, and privileges under the social security laws.

Reasons for Social Security Laws. Economic insecurity has always been one of the basic problems of life, but in an industrialized, money-dependent society there are certain new factors that increase this insecurity. In the early history of our country, as explained in the beginning chapters of this book, the home was an independent unit taking care of old people and young people alike through good times and bad times. But our society has become more complicated. Old age is a more critical problem in an industrialized society. Money savings would take care of old age if they were large enough and if they were safely invested, but many among our population are not able to save enough for old age. Unemployment, depressions, accidents, and sickness cause other economic risks.

Our society, in total, is wealthy enough and productive enough to be able to take care of all individuals. Legislation, therefore, has been enacted to protect and aid those who cannot help themselves. Some of the first social legislation involved workmen's compensation for accidents and illness. One of the first states to enact old-age pension laws was the state of Arizona. We now have social security legislation on a much more comprehensive basis. The comprehensive Federal plan is the one that will be discussed in detail in this chapter.

The Federal Social Security Act. The Federal Social Security Act involves two phases, (a) benefits for unemployment, and (b) benefits for old age, death, the needy aged, dependent children, and the blind. The first phase of this program is handled primarily through state agencies with Federal assistance. The second phase of this program is administered directly by the Federal Government, and the taxes for it are collected by the Federal Government.

Wages and Taxes. Under the current social security laws, a worker's wages are taxable for old-age benefits to the extent of the first $3,600 earned each year at the rate of 1½ per cent. For purposes of unemployment insurance the first $3,000 earned in a year is taxable, but in most states the employee is not taxed.

Who Are Covered by Old-Age Insurance? Generally speaking, old-age insurance benefits have applied to workers in factories, offices, stores, mines, shops, mills, and other places of business and industry. Under the 1950 amendments to the Federal social security laws, other persons are also covered. These persons include regularly employed agricultural and domestic workers; transportation workers and Federal employees not covered by other retirement systems; state and local governmental employees on a voluntary basis if not covered by other retirement systems; workers for religious, charitable, and other nonprofit institutions on an optional basis; and certain types of agents and salesmen.

Self-employed workers are also covered. Self-employed workers include independent contractors; independent businessmen; partners in business; independent commission salesmen and agents, life insurance agents, commission truck drivers, newspaper and magazine distributors over 18 years of age, and other similar workers.

Who Are Not Covered by Federal Old-Age Insurance? Many workers still are not covered by Federal laws that apply to old-age benefits and unemployment benefits. Part-time agricultural workers and odd-job workers, and domestic workers who work only a limited amount of time are not included. Employees of nonprofit organizations are excluded unless the employer certifies that the organization desires to have the old-age and survivors' insurance system extended to services performed by its employees and unless at least two thirds of the employees concur in filing the application. Obviously, these classifications may be changed from time to time by changes in the Federal law.

Some other types of workers specifically excluded are workers in the fishing industry, employees of foreign governments or international organizations, newspaper workers under eighteen, members of the clergy, student workers employed by schools, student nurses, interns, doctors, lawyers, dentists, public accountants, and other professional practitioners.

How to Apply for Social Security Coverage. When one accepts his first job in an occupation covered by the Social Security Act, he should fill out an "Application for Social Security Number." This can be obtained from the employer or the nearest social security office. He will then be issued a social security card with a number on it. The Federal

Application for social security number.

A social security card.

Government keeps a separate account for each individual listed under the account number shown on the card. This account is credited for all payments made by the employer into the fund and for all deductions that the employer makes for this purpose from the employee's wages.

Record of Deductions. Every individual who is subject to social security taxes should keep a record of his wages and the amount of taxes paid. The employer is required by law to furnish regularly to each employee a written statement or statements showing the wages paid to the employee during the year. Each statement must be suitable for permanent retention. It may cover one, two, three, or four quarters of the year.

Whenever an employee changes employment, he should see that his new employer has his correct social security number so that he will receive credit for any wages that are earned.

Check Your Social Security Account. Mistakes may be made in one's social security account. The regulations provide that any insured person may check his account for accuracy, but any mistake more than five years old will not be corrected. Therefore, any person with a social security account should check it for accuracy and compare it with his own records at least once every five years. A convenient card usually obtainable at the post office is provided for this purpose. A sample of this card is shown at the top of the next page.

Unemployment Insurance. Under the Social Security Act each state has set up its own law providing for an unemployment insurance system. This plan is operated in co-operation with the Federal Government. In most cases the tax is levied directly against the employer, but in some cases the employee also shares in the tax. The table on page 552

```
Form OAR-7004 (2-48)
FEDERAL SECURITY AGENCY        ACCOUNT NUMBER  [    |    |    ]
SOCIAL SECURITY ADMINISTRATION
Bureau of Old-Age and Survivors Insurance,
Baltimore 2, Md.                DATE OF BIRTH   [    |    |    ]
                                              (Month)   (Day)   (Year)
        Please send me a statement of the wages recorded in my Old-Age and Survivors
Insurance Account.
          Miss
          Mrs.
Name  Mr. ------------------------------------------------------------)  Print or
                                                                          Type
Street and number ----------------------------------------------------)  Name
                                                                          and
                                                                          Address
City, P. O. zone, and State ------------------------------------------)  Use Ink

Sign your name as usually written -----------------------------------------
                                                    (Do not print)
WARNING:  Sign your own name only.  Whoever falsely represents that he is
the person whose name and account number appear above is subject to $1000
fine or 1 year imprisonment or both.

        If your name has been changed from that shown on your account number card,
please copy your name below exactly as it appears on that card.        16—8289-4
```

A card for checking the accuracy of social security entries.

provides a summary of the laws in various states applicable to unemployment insurance compensation.

Who Are Covered by Unemployment Insurance? The Federal and state unemployment insurance that is operated under the social security laws applies to workers in factories, offices, stores, mines, shops, mills, and other places of business and industry. However, these laws do not cover farmers, domestic help, Federal employees, teachers and other professional workers, and several other groups.

Unemployment Compensation. An unemployed person is entitled to compensation if he has been engaged in a specified occupation for a specified length of time prior to his unemployment.

In order to obtain unemployment insurance benefits, the worker must meet the following qualifications, besides those previously specified:

(a) He must be unemployed through no fault of his own.

(b) He must register at a public employment office for a job.

(c) He must make a claim for benefits.

State	No. of Employees	Rate and Source of Contributions	Benefits			
			Waiting Period (Weeks)	Maximum per Week	Minimum per Week	Duration (Weeks)
Alabama	8 or more	Employer .5%–2.7% *Employee .1%–1%	1	$20	$ 4	20
Alaska	1 or more	Employer 2.7%	2	25	8	25
Arizona	3 or more	Employer .5%–2.7%	1	20	5	12
Arkansas	1 or more	Employer .3%–2.7%	1	22	7	16
California	1 or more	Employer 0%–2.7% *Employee 1%	1	25	10	26
Colorado	8 or more	Employer 0%–2.7%	2	22.75	7	20
Connecticut	4 or more	Employer .25%–2.7%	1	24	8	26
Delaware	1 or more	Employer .2%–3%	1	25	7	26
District of Col. ..	1 or more	Employer .1%–2.7%	1	20	6	20
Florida	8 or more	Employer .1%–2.7%	1	15	5	16
Georgia	8 or more	Employer .5%–2.7%	2	18	4	16
Hawaii	1 or more	Employer 0–2.7%	1	25	5	20
Idaho	1 or more	Employer 1.1%–2.7%	1	20	10	20
Illinois	6 or more	Employer .5%–3.6%	1	20	10	26
Indiana	8 or more	Employer .1%–2.7%	1	20	5	20
Iowa	8 or more	Employer 0–3.6%	1	22.50	5	20
Kansas	8 or more	Employer .7%–2.7%	1	25	5	20
Kentucky	8 or more	Employer 0–2.7%	1	20	7	22
Louisiana	4 or more	Employer .9%–2.7%	1	25	5	20
Maine	8 or more	Employer .9%–2.7%	1	25	6	20
Maryland	1 or more	Employer .2%–2.7%	none	25	6	26
Massachusetts ...	1 or more	Employer .5%–2.7%	1	25	6	23
Michigan	8 or more	Employer 1%–4%	1	24	6	20
Minnesota	1 or more	Employer .3%–3%	1	25	10	25
Mississippi	8 or more	Employer .9–2.7%	1	20	3	16
Missouri	8 or more	Employer 0–3.6%	1	20	3	20
Montana	1 or more	Employer .1%–2.7%	2	20	7	16
Nebraska	8 or more	Employer .2%–2.7%	1	20	6	20
Nevada	1 or more	Employer .1%–2.7%	none	25	8	26
New Hampshire .	4 or more	Employer .5%–2.7%	1	25	6	23
New Jersey	4 or more	Employer .3%–3.6% *Employee 1%	1	22	9	26
New Mexico	2 or more	Employer .3%–3.6%	1	20	5	20
New York	4 or more	Employer 2.7% *Employee .5%	4 days	26	10	26
North Carolina ..	8 or more	Employer .1%–2.7%	1	25	6	20
North Dakota ...	8 or more	Employer .5%–2.7%	1	20	5	20
Ohio	3 or more	Employer .3%–2.7%	1	25	10	26
Oklahoma	8 or more	Employer .3%–2.7%	1	22	6	22
Oregon	4 or more	Employer .5%–2.7%	1	25	15	26
Pennsylvania ...	1 or more	Employer .5%–2.7%	1	25	8	24
Rhode Island	4 or more	Employer 1.3%–2.7% *Employee 1.5%	1	25	10	26
South Carolina ..	8 or more	Employer .25%–2.7%	1	20	5	18
South Dakota ...	8 or more	Employer 0–2.7%	1	20	6	20
Tennessee	8 or more	Employer .5%–2.7%	1	20	5	20
Texas	8 or more	Employer .5%–2.7%	1	20	7	24
Utah		Employer .8%–2.7%	1	25	7	20
Vermont	8 or more	Employer .6%–2.7%	1	25	6	20
Virginia	8 or more	Employer .3%–2.7%	1	20	5	16
Washington	1 or more	Employer 2.7%	1	25	10	26
West Virginia ...	8 or more	Employer 0–2.7%	1	25	8	23
Wisconsin	6 or more	Employer 0–4%	2	26	9	26.5
Wyoming	Annual Payroll of $500	Employer .5%–3.5%	1	25	7	20

* Disability or unemployment contributions.

The column "No. of Employees" shows that many of the states apply the unemployment compensation law to employers having fewer than 8 employees, the minimum number required in the Federal law. Utah does not specify the number of employees but includes all businesses paying wages of $140 or more in a calendar quarter.

The rate of contributions varies because in some states it depends upon the amount of unemployment compensation received by the employees of a business. In addition to the contributions paid to the various states, .3 per cent of the payrolls must be paid by the employers to the Federal Government. The tax is applicable only to the first $3,000 of each employee's wages in one year.

The final column, "Duration," shows the maximum times the weekly benefit is payable in one period of 52 weeks.

Laws for unemployment compensation.

(d) He must be able and available for work.
(e) He must be totally unemployed for the amount of time specified in each state, as indicated in the table on page 552.

Causes for Denying or Forfeiting Unemployment Benefits

1. Participating in a strike. (Some states have exceptions to this rule.)
2. Voluntarily quitting work without a good cause. (The waiting period is usually longer, and the number of weeks of benefits is usually less.)
3. Being discharged for misconduct. (The waiting period is usually longer, and the number of weeks of benefits is usually less.)
4. Refusing to apply for or to accept suitable work. (Usually the waiting period is longer, and the benefits may be cut off entirely.)
5. Intentionally misrepresenting facts. (Payments are usually forfeited for the remainder of the current year.)
6. Being discharged for theft and found guilty.

Old-Age Insurance. Under the Social Security Act a reserve fund is accumulated as in the case of life insurance. The employer and the employee must contribute regularly to the Federal Government a certain percentage of the employee's wages. This contribution is computed on the first $3,600 of income paid to the employee during any calendar year. The part contributed by the employee is deducted by the employer from the employee's wages. The percentage is subject to change by law; but, regardless of the rate in effect in any particular year, the employer pays a certain percentage as a payroll tax and the employee pays the same percentage as a portion of his wages that is laid aside for old-age benefits.

Old-Age Benefits. Because the Social Security Act is subject to change by new legislation, it is impossible to predict exactly what benefits a person may expect when he attains the age of sixty-five. Nevertheless, the following illustration shows old-age benefits that have been computed on the basis of existing rates and the present plan of figuring such benefits.

Old-Age and Survivors' Benefits for a Fully Covered Worker Starting After September 1, 1950

STATUS OF RETIRED OR DECEASED WORKER OR OF FAMILY	AVERAGE MONTHLY WAGE $100	AVERAGE MONTHLY WAGE $150	AVERAGE MONTHLY WAGE $200	AVERAGE MONTHLY WAGE $250	AVERAGE MONTHLY WAGE $300
	MONTHLY BENEFITS	MONTHLY BENEFITS	MONTHLY BENEFITS	MONTHLY BENEFITS	MONTHLY BENEFITS
Worker—no dependents	$50.00	$ 57.50	$ 65.00	$ 72.50	$ 80.00
Worker and wife, 50 years old	50.00	57.50	65.00	72.50	80.00
Worker and wife, 65 years old	75.00	86.30	97.50	108.80	120.00
Worker, wife 50, one child	*80.00	115.10	130.00	145.10	*150.00
Worker, wife 65, one child	*80.00	115.10	130.00	145.10	*150.00
Widow, one child	75.00	86.40	97.60	108.80	120.00
Widow, two children	*80.00	115.20	130.20	145.20	*150.00
Widow 50	0	0	0	0	0
Widow 65	37.50	43.20	48.80	54.40	60.00
Parent	37.50	43.20	48.80	54.40	60.00

* Maximum is $150 or 80% of average wage, whichever is less.

The benefits to which a worker himself is entitled are referred to as *primary benefits*, and they apply to a person whose income has been derived from an occupation covered by social security laws. They depend upon an average monthly wage. The original Federal social security laws were passed in 1935 and operated without any fundamental changes up to September 1, 1950, when they were changed considerably. Some people are covered under the original law, some are covered by both the original and the amended law, and many workers are covered only by the new law. The example on page 555 shows a formula for computing the benefit of a young person starting to work after the new law of 1950 went into effect.

Upon reaching sixty-five years of age, Mr. Newton will receive this benefit for the rest of his life, provided he is not working at the time of his retirement or, if working, is not earning more than $50 a month in a covered occupation.

Besides the primary benefit, Mr. Newton may be entitled to certain *supplementary benefits* for dependents. Supplementary benefits are based upon primary benefits under the following conditions:

Example

Frank H. Newton became twenty-two years of age on January 15, 1951. He will be eligible for retirement benefits at age 65. Let us assume that he will have forty-three years of service consisting of ten years at $1,800 a year, ten years at $2,000 a year, ten years at $2,500 a year and thirteen years at $3,000 a year. Frank is employed in a covered occupation. How can we figure his primary benefit?

FORMULA FOR FIGURING PRIMARY BENEFIT FOR PERSON FULLY INSURED AFTER SEPTEMBER 1, 1950

Computation of Average Wage

(1) Add all wages earned in a covered occupation, not exceeding $3,600 a year $102,000.00

(2) Divide this sum by the number of months in which the income was earned (516) to get the average monthly income .... $ 197.00*

* When the average wage does not work out to an even multiple of $1, it is reduced to the next lower multiple of $1.

Computation of Primary Benefit

(1) Take 50 per cent of the first $100 of his average monthly income .... $ 50.00

(2) Add 15 per cent of the balance of the next $200 ($97.00 x .15) .... $ 14.55

(3) Primary benefit .... $ * 64.55

* Regulations require raising each benefit that is not a multiple of 10 cents to next higher multiple of 10 cents .... $ * 64.60

1. One half the primary benefit is allowed for wife sixty-five years of age or older.
2. The wife must not be earning more than $50 a month in a covered occupation.
3. The wife must not be entitled to primary benefit of her own because of previous employment.
4. One half the primary benefit is allowed for each child under eighteen.
5. Benefits for children are not allowed if the child is earning more than $50 a month in a covered occupation.

6. The total allowed for any family may not be more than 80 per cent of the worker's average monthly wage or $150, whichever is less, but in no case less than $40.

Example

Assume that Mr. Newton has a wife fifty-five years old at the time he retires. He has two children, age sixteen and seventeen, who are attending school and are not employed. The supplementary benefits will be figured as follows:

FORMULA—SUPPLEMENTARY BENEFITS FULLY COVERED AFTER SEPTEMBER 1, 1950

(1) Primary benefit .... $ 64.60

(2) Benefit for wife (one half primary benefit) .... $ 32.30

(3) Benefits for children (two times one half of $64.60) .... $ 64.60

(4) Total primary and supplementary benefits $161.50

(5) Total amount of benefits paid $150.00
(The total benefit cannot exceed $150 or 80 per cent of the worker's average monthly wage, whichever is less. In this case the former amount is less because 80 per cent of $197 is $157.60.)

Various other rules and regulations determine the exact status of people who are entitled to old-age benefits. In order to collect these benefits you have merely to apply to the nearest social security agency office.

Benefits for Survivors. Under the Federal Social Security Act, if an employee dies before reaching the age of sixty-five, his widow will be provided for. A widow sixty-five years of age or more, whose husband was insured, is entitled to three fourths the benefits that her husband would have received if he had lived.

Lump-Sum Survivor Benefit. Under the 1950 amendments to the social security laws, the survivor of a fully covered or of a currently covered worker or the person paying the funeral expenses is entitled to a lump-sum death benefit. This benefit will be paid regardless of other benefits that may go to survivors. It amounts to three times the deceased worker's primary benefit. For example, if Mr. Newton were to die at age 65 with a primary benefit of $64.60, his widow, children, or other heirs would receive a lump-sum payment of $193.80. Application for this payment must be filed within two years after the death of the insured individual.

Summary of Benefits to Survivors

After the death of a worker at any age, if he has the necessary "quarters of coverage," benefits go to:
  —his widow, if she is sixty-five or over, or when she reaches sixty-five;
  —his children until they are eighteen;
  —his widow of any age if she has such children in her care;
  —his dependent parents if they are sixty-five or when they reach sixty-five, provided he leaves no widow or child under eighteen;
  —lump-sum benefit to anyone who pays funeral expenses.

A widow, regardless of her age, who has one or more children under eighteen years of age will receive three fourths the monthly benefits to which her husband would have been entitled. If only one child is left, the monthly benefit for that child is three fourths of the worker's primary benefit. However, if there are two or more children, the benefit is figured differently. In such cases, each of the children is entitled to benefits equal to one half of the primary benefit, plus one fourth of the primary benefit divided by the number of children. (For example, in the case of a father of four whose primary benefit was $64.00: 1/2 of $64 equals $32; 1/4 of $64 divided by 4 equals $4; $32 plus $4 equals $36 or the benefit for each of the four children.)

As each child reaches eighteen years of age or becomes employed in a covered occupation earning more than $50 a month, the benefit for the child will cease.

Example

Let us assume that Frank Newton, on whom previous examples are based, dies after reaching the age of 65. Since his primary benefit was $64.60, the following is the way the benefit will be computed for the widow and two children:

FORMULA—SURVIVORS' BENEFITS FULLY COVERED AFTER SEPTEMBER 1, 1950

Survivors' Benefits

(1) Widow's benefit, three fourths of primary benefit .... $ 48.50

(2) Benefits for two children (each child gets one half of $64.60; plus one fourth of $64.60 divided by 2) .... $ 80.80

(3) Total benefits to family $129.30

If the wage earner leaves no widow or unmarried children under eighteen years of age, but does leave parents who are wholly dependent upon him, each of the parents will receive a monthly payment equal to three fourths of the payment to which the wage earner was entitled at the time of his death. To receive these benefits, the parents must be sixty-five years of age or older. These payments will be made to the parents until they die.

Any widow will lose all her own benefits if she works in a covered occupation for more than $50 a month. The widow will lose the benefit for a child if that child works in a covered occupation for more than $50 a month.

Other Social Security Assistance. The preceding discussion on social security has dealt with the benefits that are paid as a result of deductions from wages and on the basis of previous earnings. Under the Social Security Act, however, the Federal Government has made provisions for assistance to other needy groups. In general, the plan provides for funds to be furnished for (a) needy aged, (b) needy dependent children, (c) needy blind, (d) maternal

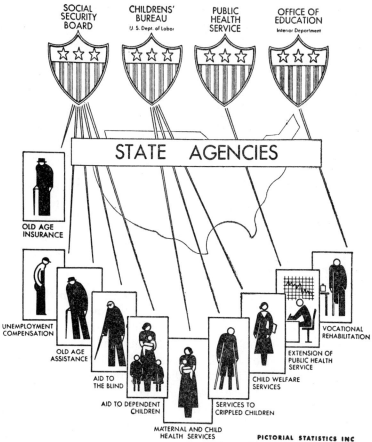

SOCIAL
SECURITY
BOARD

CHILDRENS'
BUREAU
U. S. Dept. of Labor

PUBLIC
HEALTH
SERVICE

OFFICE OF
EDUCATION
Interior Department

STATE   AGENCIES

OLD AGE
INSURANCE

UNEMPLOYMENT
COMPENSATION

OLD AGE
ASSISTANCE

AID TO
THE BLIND

AID TO DEPENDENT
CHILDREN

MATERNAL AND CHILD
HEALTH SERVICES

SERVICES TO
CRIPPLED CHILDREN

CHILD WELFARE
SERVICES

EXTENSION OF
PUBLIC HEALTH
SERVICE

VOCATIONAL
REHABILITATION

PICTORIAL STATISTICS INC
Prepared for the Social Security Board

How the social security program is administered.

welfare of infants and mothers, (e) crippled children, (f) child welfare, (g) vocational rehabilitation, and (h) public health. If a state has a plan satisfactory to the Federal Government, that state may obtain from the Federal Government a contribution up to 50 per cent of the state expenditures, provided those expenditures do not exceed a certain amount. For example, if a state that has an old-age assistance plan acceptable to the Federal Government pays $40 a month or more as a pension to the needy aged, the Federal Government will contribute as much as $20 a month.

Need for Other Insurance. Some persons have gained the impression that the Social Security Act makes it unnecessary for a person to carry other insurance. An examination of the second table on page 537 indicates the limitations. If a person wants to have more income when he retires at the age of sixty-five, he must provide that income through other insurance, an investment, or savings. Furthermore, he may want insurance to provide a certain fixed sum for his dependents upon his death. He will have to use regular insurance to provide for this type of protection.

A relatively new development in recent years has been in the field of special retirement plans sponsored by employers and unions, sometimes separately and sometimes jointly. In planning for one's total program of savings, insurance, and retirement plans, all of these factors must be taken into consideration.

Workmen's Compensation. As was mentioned in the first part of this chapter, workmen's compensation sponsored by various states is another form of social security. The laws providing protection against accidents and sickness are quite variable. For an interpretation of these laws one should become familiar with the plan in operation in his particular state. These laws have no connection with the Federal Social Security Act.

TEXTBOOK QUESTIONS

1. Explain briefly the reason for social security legislation.
2. What types of insurance and benefits are provided under the Federal Social Security Act?
3. Which part of the Federal social security program is dependent upon laws enacted by the individual states?
4. Besides workers in factories, offices, stores, mines, shops, mills, and other places of business, what types of persons were included under old-age social security benefits through the amendments of the Federal law in 1950?
5. Name some of the workers who are still not covered under the Federal old-age social security laws.
6. How does one apply for a social security number?

7. How is one informed of the amounts withheld from his wages for social security taxes?

8. How can you determine whether your social security account kept by the Federal Government is correct?

9. How many years do you have to make a correction if you find a mistake in your social security account?

10. Who are covered by the social security unemployment benefits?

11. What are the qualifications for a person to receive unemployment compensation?

12. Give at least two causes for denying unemployment benefits to a worker or causes for forfeiting these benefits.

13. Look up the rates charged the employer and the employee in your state for unemployment insurance and give these rates.

14. What is the age of retirement under the Federal Social Security Act?

15. What is a primary benefit under the old-age social security laws?

16. How do you compute the primary benefit for a retired person who began working after the new law went into effect with an average monthly income of $150?

17. What is the maximum benefit that will be paid to any family?

18. If a wife of a retired person is sixty-five years of age, to what old-age benefit is she entitled?

19. What benefits are allowed for children under eighteen of a retired worker?

20. (a) If a fully insured worker is dead, what benefits go to his widow if she is sixty-five years of age? (b) What benefits go to the widow if she is fifty years of age?

21. Some aged and dependent persons are not covered by the Social Security Act. How may these persons receive some assistance?

DISCUSSION QUESTIONS

1. Can you point out any reasons why the changes in economic conditions make social security benefits more necessary today than they were in 1700?

2. Explain how the provisions for old-age benefits under the Federal Social Security Act are a device to eliminate economic risks.

3. If a person earns $4,000 a year, how much of this income is subject to social security taxes for old-age benefits?

4. Employees of railroads are not included under the Social Security Act. Can you think of any reasons why?

5. Why does unemployment insurance differ in the various states although it is a part of the Federal social security program?

6. Can one withdraw the amount accumulated for him in an old-age pension fund?

7. If a worker is fully covered when he dies, can anyone collect any benefits for funeral expenses?

8. Does the Federal Social Security Act make it unnecessary to buy various forms of life insurance?

9. What is the purpose of so-called "Workmen's Compensation Laws"?

PROBLEMS

1. On the basis of a 1½ per cent deduction from wages for old-age benefits and the rate shown in the table on page 552 for unemployment and sickness deductions in California: (a) How much will be withheld from the payroll each year for a man earning $300 a month if the withholdings for unemployment and sickness benefits are based upon the first $3,000 a year earned? (b) How much for a man earning $400 a month?

2. From the example on page 555 for the computation of primary benefits, prepare a similar table from the following figures: wages earned, not exceeding $3,600 in any year, $90,000; number of months in which income was earned, 450.

3. From the example in this chapter on page 556 showing the benefits of the wife, fifty-five, and two children, under eighteen, compute the new table if the primary benefit is $60.

4. From the example in this chapter on page 558 showing the survivors' benefits, compute the benefits for a widow with two children under eighteen if the primary benefit is $60.

COMMUNITY PROBLEMS AND PROJECTS

1. Obtain a copy of your state law pertaining to unemployment insurance. Make a report on it, and figure out specifically how an unemployed person is compensated.

2. Make an investigation of the laws in your state affecting workmen's compensation. These laws usually cover industrial accidents and sometimes sick and death benefits. Make a written report of the important features of this law and list the occupations covered.

3. Investigate the laws in your state pertaining to assistance for the blind, and write a report explaining the aid that is available to the blind.

PART IX

OBTAINING A HOME

Chapter 32

Renting or Buying a Home

Purpose of the Chapter. Everyone must have some means of shelter. The problem of the family is to decide whether to rent or lease a house or an apartment, or whether to buy or build a house. To own a home or not to own a home is the question to be decided. Most people have an inborn desire to own a home; but not everyone is justified in buying.

The purpose of this chapter is to show the advantages and the disadvantages of renting, buying, and building a home. In studying this chapter, you will find ways of determining how to decide these questions.

Renting with or without a Written Lease. The first consideration in renting a home, whether a house or an apartment, is to determine the advisability of renting for a shorter, indefinite period or for a longer, definite period. Renting a home from month to month gives a person greater freedom to move and to take advantage of decreases in rentals as conditions change. A person who may find it necessary to move at an uncertain future date because of a change in his work should try to avoid signing a lease, particularly one covering a long period.

In some communities it is very difficult under normal circumstances to obtain a home without a written lease. Property owners naturally do not want to run the risk of the property being vacant frequently. They therefore prefer the protection of a written lease for a specified length of time.

A person who rents for an indefinite period is subject to the necessity of moving if the owner wants the prop-

---

Things to Investigate in Renting

1. Is the location desirable?
2. Is the external appearance good?
3. Is the internal appearance good?
4. Are the number of rooms and their size and arrangement satisfactory?
5. Are the lighting and heating adequate?
6. Are the laundry, plumbing, and sanitary facilities satisfactory?
7. Does the building have shades, awnings, or other similar equipment?
8. Will the landlord paint and redecorate where necessary?
9. Will the landlord take care of the necessary repairs?
10. Is the character of the neighborhood satisfactory for the family?
11. In the case of an apartment, are yard privileges granted?

---

erty for some other purpose. In most states, however, the custom or law requires the property owner to give at least thirty days' notice. If legal action is necessary to force the renter to move, still more time will be required before the property must be vacated.

Length and Expiration of the Lease. A period when rentals are going down is a bad time to obtain a long lease. A period when rentals have reached a low level or have started to rise is a good time to obtain a long lease.

In some communities most leases expire at the same time, usually at the end of April or May. You can see the desirability of having your lease expire when other leases are expiring. You will have a better opportunity to obtain another home.

Many families find that it pays them to select a home carefully with the intention of occupying it for several years. By leasing for a long period, they can reduce moving costs and become better established in the community. By staying in one place a long time, a family has an opportunity to develop a garden and to improve the property. Landlords are usually willing to keep property in good repair if the tenants indicate a desire to stay a reasonable length of time. People who lease property will therefore usually find it advantageous to obtain a lease for one year with the privilege of extending the lease one or more years.

Who Should Own a Home? Regardless of the advantages that are claimed for owning a home, one should consider the problem carefully. Even though owning a home may appear desirable, it may be economically unwise to buy or to build a house. For instance, if one expects to move soon to another town, if property values are declining, if insufficient capital is available to make the down payment, or if there is any likelihood that payments on the home cannot be made, buying a home would be unwise.

When You Should Rent, Not Buy

1. When you expect to move soon to another town.
2. When prices are declining.
3. When you do not have enough money for a substantial down payment.
4. When your budget will not allow for the payments and other expenses involved.

When You Should Own, Not Rent

1. When you expect to stay in the community.
2. When prices of real estate are stable or increasing.
3. When you have enough money to make a substantial down payment.
4. When your budget will allow for necessary payments and other expenses involved.

Advantages of Owning a Home

1. It will give you a sense of security and a home in your old age.
2. It will force you to establish a purpose and a plan of saving.
3. It will add prestige, improve your credit rating, and add stability to the family.
4. It will give you enjoyment and pride.

When to Buy. A person who is planning to buy a house should consider the following four factors in determining when to make the purchase:

(a) The economic and financial status of the family.
(b) General economic and business conditions.
(c) The community and its stage of development.
(d) The season of the year.

Success in acquiring a home depends not only upon selecting the right kind, but also upon choosing the right time to buy. In Chapter 39 there is a discussion of the business cycle and price changes that will provide a clearer understanding of when to buy.

The price of property is governed largely by the cost of building and by supply and demand. In times of prosperity, when many people are eager to buy, property sells at high prices. Calm judgment will warn a person not to "follow the crowd" in buying a home and going into debt during times of prosperity and high prices. When prices and wages drop, it is difficult for the average family to finish paying for a home. Ordinarily the best bargains in property can be obtained during periods of decreasing prices. A person who hopes to buy a home should therefore save during periods of prosperity and buy when property sells at more reasonable prices.

Sometimes property in a newly developed community is sold at an excessive price. If you want a bargain, it is not advisable to buy a home in such a community; on the other hand, it is not wise to buy in an older community that is declining.

As people ordinarily move in the spring, much property is offered for sale at that time; therefore the spring is a good time to buy.

Capacity to Pay. If a person buys a house for cash, he should not invest so much that he must use all the funds that he has laid aside for use in an emergency. For instance, if he uses all his cash to purchase a house, he may not have any reserve to use in case of a serious illness or some other emergency. A person who acquires a house by means of borrowed money makes a serious mistake if he buys beyond his capacity to pay the interest charge and to repay the loan. When one borrows money to buy a home, the loan must be repaid in installments. These payments are referred to as payments on the *principal*. One must also pay *interest* on the unpaid balance.

If the loan is too great, he may become discouraged because of the necessity of cutting down the level of living and thus depriving his family of necessities that are required to maintain health. He may even lose the house through foreclosure proceedings, which are explained in Chapter 34.

In buying a house or renting, many young people gamble to the extent of assuming that their earnings will increase. They therefore undertake a greater obligation than they should. If future earnings do not become greater, or if they become less, discouragement inevitably results. One of the first questions that should arise in the mind of a prospective renter or purchaser is the percentage of earnings to be expended in providing the home.

The amount that a person may spend as the interest and the principal on a loan on a home is always a question. The amount of the expenditure must depend upon the family budget, which should always be prepared before any plan for buying a home is accepted. Studies have been made to determine reasonable amounts that should be spent in acquiring a home. The President's Conference on Home Building and Home Ownership has shown that builders, realtors, and lenders of money estimate that about 23 per cent of the assured income of a family may safely be spent in buying a home. This total should include both interest and principal.

The Home as an Investment. Regular payments on a house include interest and scme of the principal. Besides these payments, the owner of the house has certain other expenses, such as taxes, insurance, and repairs. The total outlay may be greater than payments for rent, but the payments on principal represent an investment.

If a person who has been renting a house decides to buy it, he will be required to make greater expenditures than those required formerly in renting. If it has not been possible for him to save money regularly in the past, it will probably not be possible to finance the purchase of the home. Some people do, however, undertake such a purchase because they are then forced to follow some definite plan of saving. The purchase of a home may result in systematic saving in order to pay for the investment.

Minimum Cash Investment. As will be explained in Chapter 33, there are many ways of financing the purchase of a home, but usually a person must pay part of the original price in cash.

Conservative financial advisors recommend that a person who buys a home should pay 20 to 25 per cent of the purchase price in cash. It is frequently impossible to obtain a first-mortgage loan of more than 50 or 60 per cent of the value of a house. The plans developed under the Federal Housing Administration permit a minimum cash investment of from 10 to 20 per cent. The difference must be paid in cash, or an additional loan must be obtained from another source.

During times of national emergency the Federal Government regulates the amount of down payment that must be made on a home. The purpose of this type of regulation is to discourage the buying and building of homes so that materials will be available for other purposes and so that credit and therefore purchasing power may not be unduly expanded.

Causes of Default on Loans. Regardless of its advantages the ownership of a home should be undertaken with careful forethought. The President's Conference on Home Building and Home Ownership made a study of the reasons why people have been unable to pay for their homes. Some of the most important causes for default on loans are as follows:

(a) A decrease in income caused by depression, sickness, or death.

(b) Assuming more obligations for payments than the family can afford to continue.

(c) Failure to allow in the budget enough to take care of upkeep and depreciation of the property.

Some people invest too much money in a home and consequently do not have enough money for other purposes. Others assume a debt that is more than they can afford to pay. In such cases the installment payments on the home are more than can be made from the income. Other people are so eager to pay off the debt rapidly that they pay more than is necessary on the principal and find themselves without funds in an emergency. Sometimes the debt incurred is to be paid off in a few years, whereas it should be distributed over a longer period of years. A house may depreciate so rapidly that it requires unusual repairs and replacements. Instead of a neighborhood improving in character, it sometimes becomes undesirable and the value of the property consequently decreases.

Analysis of Financing Costs. The table on the next page shows the first-year cost of financing a home. This information was collected for prospective home owners by the Bureau of Standards of the United States Department of Commerce. The various income groups are listed according to the approximate cost of the home that a person in each income group can afford. This table assumes that an initial cash payment of 20 per cent of the total value will be made when the home is purchased.

The fact is recognized that families having the same annual income may not be able to devote the same amount toward purchasing a home. For example, a family having four or five children and living in a city may not be able to put much aside for buying a home; but another family with only one or two children and located possibly in a small village can afford to apply a larger proportion of its income for the same purpose.

The following is an explanation of the items in the table:

Item 1. Value of house and lot. The value of the house and the lot is the basis upon which the expenses in this table

	$5,000	$6,000	$7,000	$8,000	$9,000	$10,000
1. Value of house and lot	5,000	6,000	7,000	8,000	9,000	10,000
2. Annual income	2,000 to 3,000	2,400 to 3,600	2,800 to 4,200	3,200 to 4,800	3,600 to 5,400	4,000 to 6,000
3. First cash payment (20% of value)	1,000	1,200	1,400	1,600	1,800	2,000
4. Amount of loan (80% of value) ..	4,000	4,800	5,600	6,400	7,200	8,000
5. Amounts of yearly payments (10% of total value)	500	600	700	800	900	1,000
A. Interest (6%)	240	288	336	384	432	480
B. Payment of principal	260	312	364	416	468	520
6. Taxes and assessments (2%)	100	120	140	160	180	200
7. Insurance (.5%)	25	30	35	40	45	50
8. Upkeep (1.5%)	75	90	105	120	135	150
9. Total first-year cost (5 plus 6, 7, 8)	700	840	980	1,120	1,260	1,400
A. Expense (5-A plus 6, 7, 8)	440	528	616	704	792	880
*B. Saving (9 minus 9-A)	260	312	364	416	468	520

The first-year cost of financing a home.

* Although this amount represents the apparent monetary saving, there is a hidden expense called depreciation because of the wearing out and the increase in age of the house. A 2 per cent allowance for depreciation on the value of the house itself would be a fair estimate of the loss from this cause.

have been computed. The value of the lot will usually be from 8 to 20 per cent of the total amount.

Item 2. Annual income. Because of the wide variation the incomes have been grouped. No rule can be set that will apply to all classes. It is assumed in this table, however, that the value of the house and the lot will be between 1⅔ and 2½ times the annual income. For example, a family with an income of $3,000 could expect to pay from $5,000 to $7,500 for a home. The average amount to pay for a home will be about double the annual income.

Item 3. First cash payment. The cash payment should not be below 20 per cent of the value of the house and the lot. It should be much higher if possible. The greater the down payment, the better, for the financing is then simpler and the cost is less. Occasionally a home can be purchased with a down payment of less than 20 per cent, but even under normal conditions a down payment of 20 per cent is dangerously low for many people. It is unwise to make so small an initial payment unless there is a good margin for saving. When there is a shortage of money for lending purposes, the loan is difficult to obtain if only a small down payment can be made. Furthermore, the interest charge at such a time is high.

Item 4. Amount of loan. After the amount of the initial cash payment has been deducted from the value of the house and the lot, the difference represents the amount of the loan.

Item 5. Amount of yearly payments. In this table the yearly payments are the same in amount. Under some plans of financing, however, the payment is reduced as the loan is paid off. Item 5A represents the amount of each payment that is applicable as interest; and item 5B, the amount that is applicable as amortization of the principal. With a small down payment the interest rate is usually higher than with a large down payment. If it is necessary to obtain a second mortgage, the interest rate is less favorable.

The interest rate will depend upon local conditions at the time the loan is made. It is generally considered best to pay off a loan on a home within fifteen years or less. If interest rates are unfavorable at the time the loan is to be made, the loan can be obtained for a short time in the hope that it can be renewed later at a lower rate.

Various plans of financing require weekly payments, semimonthly payments, monthly payments, semiannual payments, or annual payments. The plan of payment should be fully understood before any contract is signed.

Item 6. Taxes and assessments. Local taxes on real estate usually range from 1½ to 2½ per cent of the market value of the property. Occasionally there are assessments against the property for a sidewalk, a street, lights, or other facilities; but ordinarily the assessments on residential property are not high. In this table 2 per cent has been allowed for taxes and assessments.

Item 7. Insurance. Fire insurance rates rarely amount to more than ½ per cent of the value of the house. The allowance made in this table is liberal because it has been figured on the basis of the value of the house and the lot.

Item 8. Upkeep. The cost of maintaining a home will vary considerably, depending upon the condition of the property, the age of the house, and the type of construction. The yearly cost of maintenance may, however, be estimated reasonably at 1½ per cent of the total value.

Item 9. Total first-year cost. The total first-year cost of the home includes the total annual payment plus taxes, assessments, insurance, and upkeep. Item 9A represents the yearly expense. The difference between the total cost for the year and the total expense is the saving (item 9B). In other words, this is the amount of investment that the buyer has accumulated during the first year. The rest of his money has been used for interest and the various expenses of maintaining the house. Item 9A is therefore equivalent to the rent of the house.

Buying Compared with Renting. Whether to buy or to rent a home is the problem of each individual. A person frequently rents because (a) he desires freedom of movement, (b) he is unable to arrange a plan of financing a home, (c) he believes that it is cheaper to rent, (d) he doubts the investment value of owning a home, or (e) he does not care to assume the obligation of paying for a home. If a person needs a permanent home and can buy it, the following table will serve as a guide in comparing the cost of buying a home with the cost of renting one:

1. Value of house and lot	$5,000	$6,000	$7,000	$8,000	$9,000	$10,000
2. Annual income	2,000 to 3,000	2,400 to 3,600	2,800 to 4,200	3,200 to 4,800	3,600 to 5,400	4,000 to 6,000
3. First-year cost of buying a house ..	700	840	980	1,120	1,260	1,400
Expense	440	528	616	704	792	880
Saving	260	312	364	416	468	520
4. Annual cost of renting a house						
A Example	360	420	480	540	600	660
B Example	450	540	530	720	810	900
C Example	480	570	660	750	840	930
D Example	540	630	720	810	900	990

For instance, if one is considering an $8,000 house and is paying $750 a year rent (Example C), there would be a cash expense saving of $46 a year by owning a house ($750 − $704 = $46).

Comparison of cost of buying with cost of renting.

This table does not tell the whole story because it does not take into consideration the matter of depreciation. The tables on the next page show how one may compare renting with owning a home. Let us assume that the family is paying a rent of $70 a month and that it would cost $8,000 to buy a home of equal quality. Basing the first-year cost of owning a home on the table on page 570, it will be observed that in this particular case it costs $40 a year more to own a home than to rent. In this example it is assumed that there is a down payment of $1,600 and that interest is paid at the rate of 6 per cent on the unpaid balance. Since the family has an investment of $1,600 in the home, it is assumed that they are losing interest at the rate of 2 per cent, which they could be earning on this money if it were in a savings account. It is also assumed that the house is worth $7,200 and the lot is worth $800 and that the depreciation rate on the house is 2 per cent a year.

Not all of the costs of owning a home are cash expenditures. The depreciation represents a loss in value of the home each year based upon 2 per cent of the value of the house itself. Of the total cost, $32 represents the loss of

COST OF RENTING	COST OF OWNING	
Rent $840	Interest	$384
	Taxes	150
	Assessments	10
	Repairs and Upkeep	120
	Depreciation	144
	Insurance	40
	Interest Loss on Investment	32
Total $840	Total	$880

Cost of renting compared with the first-year cost of owning a home.

interest that could have been earned if the down payment were in a savings account earning 2 per cent interest; in a sense this is equivalent to a cash outlay of $32. The family pays an additional amount of $416 a year to apply on the principal. For budgeting purposes the family therefore needs to compare the total cash outlay with the cost of renting to determine whether or not the family can afford to buy. This will be figured as follows:

RENTING	OWNING	
Rent $840	Interest	$ 384
	Taxes	150
	Assessments	10
	Repairs and Upkeep ...	120
	Insurance	40
	Interest Loss on Investment	32
	Payment on Principal ..	416
Total Cash Outlay $840	Total Cash Outlay	$1,152

Cash outlay for renting compared with the first-year outlay for owning a home.

The difference between the cash outlay for rent and the first-year cash outlay for owning a home is $312. This illustrates the fact that even though a person is able to pay rent, an additional sum may be needed each year to buy and

There are many things to consider when you build.

maintain a home, although part of it represents an addition to the investment.

To Build or Not to Build. It is just as common to make errors in building a house as in buying one. Eagerness to own a new house should not be allowed to interfere with one's good judgment in evaluating the purchase of a house that has been used or one that has been recently built and is being offered for sale.

The same principles involved in buying a home should be considered in deciding whether to build. In other words, the first element is to decide whether it is possible to carry the financial burden.

Whom to Consult. Unless the prospective builder knows a contractor in whom he has considerable confidence, the plans and specifications should be drawn up first and then submitted to more than one contractor for competitive bids. The obtaining of several bids will guard against excessive cost. It is not always wise, however, to accept the lowest bid. The reputation of the contractor should play an important part.

575

Placing a Contract. A contract for a finished house may be placed with a single contractor, who will be responsible for the entire job; or contracts for separate portions of the work may be given to various contractors. The latter plan requires some definite scheme of supervision. Letting one contractor assume responsibility for the entire job is usually considered more satisfactory because it relieves the builder from most of the responsibility of supervision and gives reasonable assurance as to the final cost of the home.

Cautions in Building

1. That the plans are well designed and the finished house will be satisfactory to the entire family.
2. That the plans meet the requirements of building codes and local restrictions.
3. That the specifications are complete and that there will be no extra charge for additional work.
4. That the contractor has a reputation for good work, financial responsibility, and fair dealing.
5. That the contract specifies clearly the amount of the payments and the conditions under which the payments are to be made.
6. That the contractor is responsible for loss due to fire or to personal injury during the construction period.
7. That the property is subject to final inspection before acceptance and final payment.
8. That all agreements are in writing and have been approved by a lawyer.
9. That you have worked out a plan of financing a home that you can afford.
10. That it is a good time to build.

TEXTBOOK QUESTIONS

1. When is it desirable to make (a) a short-term lease? (b) a long-term lease?
2. What are some of the things to be investigated when a person is contemplating renting a home?
3. What are some of the advantages of a long lease?

4. What are the advantages of renting as compared with those of owning a home?

5. (a) Indicate some circumstances under which it is better to rent than to own a home. (b) When is it better to own instead of renting?

6. What are some of the cautions against buying a home at the peak of prosperity when the prices of property are high and incomes are high?

7. What percentage of income is considered the maximum amount that one may safely spend a year in buying a home?

8. What is the minimum down payment that conservative financial advisors recommend for a person who buys his home?

9. Name at least one major cause for failure of families to keep up the payments on loans on homes.

10. What is a safe ratio between one's annual income and the amount that is paid for a home? *1 ⅓ to 2½ × annual income*

11. What is a reasonable estimate of the cost of fire insurance based on the cost of a house? *½ % value of house*

12. What is a safe estimate of the cost of upkeep based on the total value of a home? *1½*

13. Explain why depreciation needs to be taken into consideration in figuring the cost of owning a home.

14. If one invests $1,000 in the purchase of a home, explain why the loss of interest on this investment is part of the cost of owning the home.

15. From the point of a cash outlay, why does owning a home and making regular monthly payments require more expenditure than renting?

16. Indicate at least three of the most important cautions in building a home.

DISCUSSION QUESTIONS

1. Give your opinion as to whether each of the following individuals should own or rent a home, provided each can afford to buy: (a) a traveling salesman, (b) the owner of a retail store, (c) the sales manager of a district office, (d) the office manager in a local manufacturing plant. Give reasons for your answers.

2. (a) Why is location an important factor in selecting a house to rent or to buy? (b) Are the considerations the same in both cases?

3. Mr. Moore, who is considering the purchase of a house, finds in an old community a house that is better constructed and

otherwise more desirable than a newer one in a recently developed community. The two houses are offered at the same price. What do you think are some of the factors that he should consider in determining which house to select?

4. Discuss what you consider to be the merits of buying a home on the assumption that one's income will increase to such an extent that the debt can be paid off.

5. Which consideration in planning for the purchase of a home should come first: (a) the actual selection of the home or (b) the development of a plan for financing the purchase?

6. Real-estate agents sometimes advertise the sale of a house on easy terms with the statement that the buyer can "pay like rent." (a) Why do they advertise in this manner? (b) Can they sell on these terms at the same price that would be charged if the buyer paid cash in full? Why? (c) Does the buyer make a poor investment if he "pays like rent"?

7. Explain how one's budget should be the controlling guide in buying a home.

8. A young couple finds that it is possible to make a down payment on a home and to pay the principal, the interest, and the taxes with the money that is ordinarily spent for rent and the additional amount that is placed in a savings account each month. They consider that they can save more by investing in a home than they can by paying rent and accumulating a savings fund. Do you agree with them? Give your reasons.

9. Under what circumstances do you think a person would be justified in making a down payment of only 5 or 10 per cent of the purchase price of a home?

10. If one has been renting a home and has been taking care of the repairs, painting, and papering of the house under the rental agreement, how should these figures be taken into consideration in making a comparison of the cost of renting and the cost of owning a home?

11. (a) Why will an agency that lends money to you for use in having a house built be interested in examining your contract with the contractor? (b) Will the agency have any right to see the contract?

PROBLEMS

1. Using the table on page 570 as a guide, compute the first-year cost of financing a home under the following conditions:

(a) the value of the house and the lot is $9,500; (b) the first cash payment is $1,900; (c) a first mortgage is obtained on the balance of the indebtedness at 6 per cent interest, to be charged annually in advance; (d) the yearly payments of the principal and the interest are $950; (e) the taxes are 1.8 per cent of the value of the house and lot; (f) the insurance is .4 per cent of the value of the house ($8,000); (g) the upkeep is 1.5 per cent of the value of the house. Indicate what part of the first-year cost constitutes expense and what part constitutes savings. Note that the principal is adjusted at the end of the year.

2. Mr. Herbert French owns a house and a lot that cost $5,000. The lot is valued at $800. Assume that, over a period of twenty years, the valuation of the property for assessing taxes will remain at $5,000; the tax rate will stay at 2.1 per cent; the yearly cost of insurance on the house will be .35 per cent of the cost of the house; the annual cost of upkeep will be 1.5 per cent of the cost of the house; the house and the lot will be worth $4,000 at the end of the twenty years (the loss in value to be distributed equally over the twenty years); the money invested in the home would have earned a yearly income of 3.5 per cent if it had been invested in good bonds. Determine whether it is more economical for Mr. French to own his home than it would have been for him to pay a monthly rental of $40. Assume that all other costs of owning the home or of renting are negligible and that the rental rate would have remained the same.

3. Mr. Boland is paying $80 a month for rent for a house valued at $10,000. He has $2,500 that he can use for a down payment on a house valued at $10,000 and he can borrow the balance of $7,500 at 4½ per cent interest, computed semi-annually on the unpaid balance. His monthly payments on this new house would be $65, including principal and interest. Taxes would amount to $165 a year. There are no assessments; repairs and upkeep are estimated at $130 a year; depreciation is estimated at 2 per cent of the value of the house after deducting the value of the lot, which is figured at $1,000. Insurance would cost $42 a year. He would lose the interest on the $2,500 down payment because this amount is now in a savings account earning 2 per cent, compounded annually. (a) Construct a table like the one shown in this chapter, showing the cost of renting compared with the first-year cost of owning a home. (b) Construct a table similar to the one in this chapter showing the cash outlay for renting compared with the first-year outlay for owning a home.

COMMUNITY PROBLEMS AND PROJECTS

1. If you are renting your home, prepare a table similar to the one on page 574 showing the first-year cost of buying it. You can make a down payment of $1,000. Obtain the latest and most accurate information that you can in regard to interest rates, taxes, insurance, and estimated repair costs, and figure depreciation on the value of the building at 2 per cent a year. Set a reasonable value on the house according to prevailing real-estate values. If your family is the owner of the house, construct the same table and estimate the amount of rental that could be obtained from it in order to make the same comparison.

2. Analyze the total cost of rent that your family or another is paying. Compare this with the monthly cost of acquiring a home that would fit the requirements of the family. Use an actual piece of property as the basis of your study, and consider the income of the family in making the computations. Use the actual tax rate and the prevailing interest and insurance rates. Make your other computations on the basis of the tables shown on pages 570 and 574.

Chapter 33

PART IX _____

Financing the Purchase of a Home

Purpose of the Chapter. Nearly every person who buys a home has to borrow money. Money for this purpose can be borrowed from several sources. You should, therefore, become acquainted with these sources so that you will know how to get money under the most favorable terms when you need it. The conditions under which loans are obtained involve interest rates, length of the term of the loan, special charges, the amount that can be borrowed, the amount of the down payment, the method of computing interest, the method of repayment, and other factors. The purpose of this chapter is to acquaint you with the methods of financing the purchase of a home.

Sources of Loans

Building and loan associations	Trust companies
Life insurance companies	Mortgage companies
Banks	Private investors

Federal Regulations. The regulations of various lending agencies discussed in this chapter apply under normal conditions. In times of emergency the Federal Government places special regulations on down payments and other borrowing activities.

Building and Loan Associations. A building and loan association is an organization created for the promotion of thrift and home ownership. Associations of this type use various plans for accumulating funds to be used in lending. The members of an association usually subscribe for shares and make regular payments on their subscriptions until the sum of these installment payments, added to the dividends obtained through the lending operations, equals the matured, or face, value of the shares. Some associations require no subscription but accept deposits of any amount. The money obtained by building and loan associations from its subscribers and depositors is used for the purpose of making loans to persons buying or building homes.

Building and loan associations are relatively liberal in their lending. They extend loans for reasonably long periods, usually about twelve years. They frequently appraise property at a value equal to the full market price. First-mortgage loans are sometimes made on property to the extent of from 60 to 80 per cent of the valuation. The liberality in lending depends largely on local and general business conditions and on the availability of funds.

Life Insurance Companies. In recent years life insurance companies have invested considerable money in loans on real estate. The loans of such a company are commonly placed through local agents, such as banks, trust companies, mortgage companies, and individuals. The applicant for a loan is required to supply the agent with information as to the risk. Special forms are usually filled out for this purpose. The illustration on page 583 shows a sample form.

The appraiser for an insurance company will usually be very conservative in setting a value as the basis of the loan. The loan usually will not be granted for more than 50 per cent of the appraised value of the property. The loans of insurance companies run for periods as long as fifteen years. Interest is charged at the rate prevailing in the locality in which the loan is made, and is usually payable semiannually. In some cases payments on the principal can be made semiannually; in others they can be made monthly. Provision in many cases is made for allowing the borrower to pay off the loan after the third year. The person who wishes to transfer his property after a loan has been made must obtain permission from the insurance company.

Banks. An important source of borrowing on homes is a bank, especially a savings bank. When application is made for a loan, an officer of the bank or a committee

APPLICATION FOR LOAN

— TO —

THE WESTERN AND SOUTHERN LIFE INSURANCE COMPANY

OF CINCINNATI, OHIO

M. L. No. 13560   June 2   19 51

The undersigned hereby applies to The Western and Southern Life Insurance Co. for a loan of $4,000.00 for a period of 5 years at 4½ per cent interest, and offers as security therefor a first mortgage on the following property:

Location Lot 12, Block 3, Rosedale Subdivision, Cincinnati, Ohio

Size of lot 50 feet front by 130 feet in depth.

Improvements consist of Brick and stucco house and brick garage

When built? 1933

Fee simple: Yes   Leasehold-99 years, renewable forever.

Value: Land, $1,800.00   Improvements, $10,000.00

Tax value, land, $1,200.00   Improvements, $6,000.00

Gross rental?   Net income?

Amount of Fire Insurance in force? $9,500.00

In whose name is title now? Charles K. Ritchie

If now mortgaged, to whom and in what amounts? None

Purpose of loan To purchase the property

If buying the property, how much is being paid for same? $11,800.00

I agree to pay on account of the principal of this loan 10 % thereof annually, as well as all charges for examination of the title and incidental expenses.

Harold G. Knight

Address 2970 Washington Ave., Cincinnati, Ohio

Business Knight's Grocery, 1250 Main Street

Full name of wife or husband Mary Clark Knight

APPRAISAL

We, the undersigned resident owners of real estate in Hamilton County, State of Ohio certify under oath that we are well acquainted with the property described in the foregoing application, and appraise the same as follows:

Land—exclusive of improvements, $1,800.00

Improvements, $9,500.00

Total, $11,300.00

Name *Edwin S. Summers*   Name *M. B. Dane*

Address 1369 Vine St., Cincinnati   Address 1706 Plum St., Cincinnati

State of Ohio   County of Hamilton

Sworn to and subscribed before me this second of June, 1951, by Edwin S. Summers and M. B. Dane this second of June, 1951.

Walter Gibson

(Notary Public)

An application for a loan.

usually visits the property and makes an appraisal. The size of the loan that such a bank can make is generally restricted by state law (or Federal regulations in the case of national banks) to a certain percentage of the value of the property. In some states this is 50 per cent, but in others it is as high as 60 per cent. State laws do not, however, restrict the banks with respect to making liberal or conservative appraisals. A liberal bank in a state that limits loans to 50 per cent of the property value might lend more than a conservative bank in a state that limits loans to 60 per cent of the property value.

Some banks extend loans for only short periods, such as three, five, or ten years. Short-term loans can usually be renewed, but a charge may be made for the privilege of extension. Unless the property has been taken care of satisfactorily, it is difficult to renew the loan.

Trust Companies. Trust companies and the trust departments of banks usually have funds available for real-estate loans. The lending policies and methods of trust companies are similar to those of savings banks.

Mortgage Companies. In many large communities mortgage companies are an important factor in home financing. There are two classes of these companies. One class lends on first, or senior, mortgages; and the other lends on second, or junior, mortgages. There is a great lack of uniformity in the policies and the methods of these companies. They are usually not placed under such legal restrictions as are banks, trust companies, and insurance companies. They ordinarily do not lend in excess of 50 per cent of the valuation of the property. When a higher amount is lent, a commission may be charged.

Private Investors. Private investors, who are unorganized, are free to operate as they please so long as they keep within the bounds of state laws on lending. They usually follow the methods of the lending institutions in their communities. They are frequently willing to lend a higher percentage of the property value than are banks, trust com-

The terms of the mortgage should be read carefully.

Ewing Galloway

panies, or insurance companies. They do so especially when it is possible for them to get a slightly higher rate of interest.

The person who borrows from a lending institution can usually depend on being able to renew his mortgage if he has been prompt with his payments. When he borrows from an individual, however, there is nothing but personal assurance that the loan can be renewed. Such unforeseen circumstances as the death of the lender may cause an embarrassing situation for the borrower.

Second-Mortgage Borrowing. In communities where there are no building and loan associations and in those where such associations and other agencies are unwilling to make loans equal to from 60 to 75 per cent of the value of the home, borrowers who can make a down payment of only 25 to 40 per cent of the price find it necessary to use two loans, a first mortgage and a second mortgage.

The following example shows the relationship between a first and a second mortgage: A person purchases a house valued at $12,000. He pays $3,000 in cash and is successful in obtaining a first-mortgage loan of $6,000. He obtains the loan by signing a series of notes that will become due at specified intervals. The interest on the notes is 4½ per cent. To protect the lender, he gives a real-estate mortgage.

585

A second-mortgage loan is negotiated for the remainder of the purchase price, $3,000. The borrower signs a series of notes and a second-mortgage contract. The interest on the second mortgage is at a higher rate (5½ per cent) than the interest on the first mortgage because the holder of the second mortgage has a greater risk of loss. The lender holds the second-mortgage contract. If the payments are not made when they become due, the first-mortgage holder or the second-mortgage holder, or both, depending upon the laws of the particular state, have the option of suing for the disposal of the property to satisfy the claims against it. The first-mortgage holder has first claim on the proceeds from the sale; the second-mortgage holder has second claim on such proceeds.

Land Contracts. A common form of financing used by home buyers who can make a down payment of only 10 to 15 per cent involves a *land contract*. This plan is popular in the central part of the United States. It is an agreement between the buyer and the seller of the property, under the terms of which the buyer usually makes a small down payment and agrees to pay the full purchase price in installments. The seller does not give the buyer legal ownership of the property, but agrees to convey the title to him when a certain percentage of the purchase price (usually approximately 50 per cent) has been paid. When the title is transferred, the seller usually accepts a first-mortgage note or the buyer either takes care of the unpaid balance or obtains a loan from someone else.

This type of borrowing makes the purchase of a home possible for a large number of people who might be unable to buy in any other way. It is advantageous to real-estate operators because it enables the seller to hold the title of the property until the buyer has invested a sufficient amount in the home to indicate that he can satisfactorily complete payment and assume the obligation of ownership. In case the buyer fails to live up to his agreement, the seller has a better opportunity to take possession of the property than if the title had been transferred.

Renewing a Mortgage. In obtaining a loan on a home, the borrower should take into consideration what will happen to the mortgage obligation at the time it matures. Sometimes difficulty arises because the loan cannot be paid at maturity. Some mortgages require regular payments of the principal and interest, whereas others require payment of the interest regularly and payment of the entire principal at a specified date.

A mortgage that extends for a long period is safest. If a mortgage extends for only three, four, or five years, the person who borrows the money should obtain some assurance that the mortgage can be renewed or that a new loan can be obtained from some source. Suppose, for example, that a person will require ten years to pay for a home, but that he obtains a loan that will be due in three years. During the three years he will not be able to repay much of the principal. At the end of that period he must either have the loan renewed or obtain a new loan. He otherwise will run the risk of foreclosure on his property. The cost of the renewal of the loan should be predetermined, for this expense must be considered as part of the total cost of financing the home.

Figuring Rates. The final decision in choosing an agency to finance the purchase or the building of a home should be based upon the reputation of the agency and the economy with which the home can be financed. The method of calculating the interest charges and the expenses involved in obtaining the loan should be investigated.

Different types of financial institutions have considerable variation in their plans of charging interest. For instance, some loan companies calculate interest annually; others calculate it semiannually or quarterly. Occasionally the interest is figured on the basis of the original amount of the loan, extended over the entire time during which the loan is being paid off. This method results in the borrower's paying an unusually high rate of interest on the outstanding amount of the loan, provided periodic payments are made on the principal. The table on page 588 shows how a $1,000 loan at 5 per cent interest is partially retired during the first year by monthly payments of $10 each, the interest being calculated monthly on the unpaid balance.

MONTH	MONTHLY PAYMENT	PART OF PAYMENT APPLIED TO INTEREST	PART OF PAYMENT APPLIED TO PRINCIPAL	PRINCIPAL DUE AFTER INSTALLMENT PAYMENT
1	$ 10.00	$ 4.17	$ 5.83	$994.17
2	10.00	4.14	5.86	988.31
3	10.00	4.12	5.88	982.43
4	10.00	4.09	5.91	976.52
5	10.00	4.07	5.93	970.59
6	10.00	4.04	5.96	964.63
7	10.00	4.02	5.98	958.65
8	10.00	3.99	6.01	952.64
9	10.00	3.97	6.03	946.61
10	10.00	3.94	6.06	940.55
11	10.00	3.92	6.08	934.47
12	10.00	3.89	6.11	928.36
	$120.00	$48.36	$71.64	$928.36

How a $1,000 loan is reduced during the first year, with interest at 5 per cent, when the interest is computed monthly on the unpaid balance.

Extra Charges. When loans are obtained, special care should be used to detect any extra charges. Premiums, commissions, and bonuses on loans result in higher interest rates for the borrowers. When a loan is obtained from some sources, the lender charges a commission for granting it. If, for example, a $40 commission is charged on a $1,000 loan that will extend for ten years, the actual amount of cash available from the loan is $960. The interest, however, must be paid on the $1,000. The actual rate of interest is therefore greater than the nominal rate.

There are other additional charges that must be considered in obtaining a loan. In some states a tax is levied. In practically every state there is a fee for having the deed recorded. The cost of having the title examined is usually from $25 to $80. The cost of an appraisal should not exceed $10 to $25. Some lenders require title insurance, which is also charged to the borrower. Ordinarily these costs are borne by the person who obtains the loan, but occasionally they are paid by the company granting the loan.

Federal Housing Administration. The Federal Housing Administration is commonly known as the FHA. The FHA provides Federal insurance on loans that are obtained

These homes were financed by means of FHA loans.

through an approved lending agency. If the FHA approves the loan, the money can be borrowed from the regular lending agency. The lending agency is protected because the FHA insures the loan, guaranteeing its payment. Money may be borrowed for repairing or improving a home, buying or building a new home, buying an existing home, or buying a multiple-family dwelling, such as an apartment building.

From the point of view of an individual seeking a loan, an FHA loan is usually no better than many other types of loans, except that a qualified person who can make only a small down payment can sometimes obtain an FHA loan, when he might not be able to make a sufficient down payment to obtain any other kind of loan.

Where and How to Apply for FHA Loans. Any regular lending agency, such as a building and loan association, life insurance company, bank, trust company, mortgage company, or private investor, can help an individual apply for an FHA loan. A contractor, an architect, or a real-estate agent can also help a buyer of a home to apply for an FHA loan. If a loan is desired for repairing or improving a home, assistance can be obtained through a contractor or a dealer in building supplies.

The lending institution is permitted to charge its usual fees, such as those for examining the title and having the

deed recorded. The loan will not be guaranteed by the FHA
unless it is approved first by the lending agency.

Charges and Payment Plans of the FHA. A loan obtained under the FHA may be repaid over periods of fifteen,
twenty, or twenty-five years, or in a lump sum at any time.
If a new home is being purchased, the minimum down payment is 10 per cent and the mortgage insurance is one half
of 1 per cent on the decreasing annual balance of the loan.
If an existing home is being purchased or refinanced, the
minimum cash down payment is 20 per cent and the mortgage insurance charge is one half of 1 per cent on the decreasing annual balance. The interest rate in each case is
4½ per cent a year on the decreasing monthly balance. In
other words, the monthly payments remain the same, but
in each successive month more is applied to the principal
and less to interest and mortgage insurance.

The following illustration is a schedule of typical monthly
charges on insured FHA loans on newly constructed homes.

TYPICAL MONTHLY CHARGES	ON A $5,000 LOAN		
	15 YEARS	20 YEARS	25 YEARS
Principal and Interest	$38.25	$31.65	$27.80
Mortgage Insurance Premium ..	.97	1.00	1.01
Subtotal	39.22	32.65	28.81
Taxes (Estimated)	7.00	7.00	7.00
Fire Insurance (Estimated)	1.88	1.88	1.88
Total	$48.10	$41.53	$37.69

Typical monthly charges on insured FHA loans.

G. I. Loans. For persons who performed service in the
Armed Forces during World War II, special privileges are
granted under the Servicemen's Readjustment Act. These
privileges are similar to those obtainable under FHA loans.
The loan must be obtained through a regular lending
agency. It is then guaranteed by the Federal Government.
This privilege enables veterans to obtain real estate and
borrow money for business or agricultural purposes on
very favorable terms.

Life Insurance and Real Estate. When one borrows money to buy a home for his family, he likes to feel sure that the loan will be repaid and that his family will have a home even though he dies. The lender also likes to have some assurance that the loan will be repaid even though the buyer dies. Although the lender will have a mortgage claim against the property, he probably will not like to take the property away from a family if the head of the family dies. Therefore, life insurance serves an important function in the field of real estate. A buyer of real estate may purchase term life insurance sufficient to repay the amount of the loan on the real estate if he should die. Some lenders require the buyers to obtain life insurance for this purpose. Then if the buyer dies, proceeds from his life insurance will repay the loan. The lender is happy, and the family has a home without any debt on it.

TEXTBOOK QUESTIONS

1. What are the most common sources of loans on real estate?
2. (a) What is the purpose of a building and loan association? (b) How much will such an organization usually lend on property? 60 -80
3. What is usually the maximum percentage of the appraised value of real estate that a savings bank can lend?
4. In financing the purchase of a home, how can a person use a loan that will extend for only three years?
5. Explain the typical policies of mortgage companies in lending on real estate.
6. Explain how money can be borrowed on more than one mortgage on the same piece of property.
7. Which is the safer type of mortgage from the point of view of the borrower: (a) a mortgage that extends for a short term of three or four years or (b) one that extends for a long term of from ten to fifteen years? Why?
8. If a person does not make a sufficient down payment on a home to enable him to obtain the remainder of the price from a bank or a building and loan association, what other sources of borrowing are open to him?
9. What are the principal features of a land contract?
10. What happens when a mortgage matures or expires?

11. What are some of the extra charges that must be paid by the borrower of money?
12. For what purposes may FHA loans be obtained?
13. Who can assist a person in obtaining an FHA loan?
14. Over what period of payment may an FHA loan be extended?
15. What are the minimum down payments under FHA loans?
16. What items, besides payments on principal and of interest, are included in the monthly payments under FHA loans?
17. How is life insurance sometimes used in connection with borrowing to buy a home so that the family will be protected if the husband and father dies?

DISCUSSION QUESTIONS

1. If you want to borrow the greatest possible amount of money on a particular piece of real estate, from what source would you most likely obtain that amount, assuming that all sources of loans are available to you? Give your reasons.
2. Give the advantages and disadvantages of second mortgages from the point of view of (a) the borrower and (b) the lender.
3. If a person has bought a home and has agreed to pay off the mortgage at the rate of $50 a month, (a) can you see any advantage in his paying $60 or $70 a month if this amount is available? (b) Under what circumstances might there be such an advantage?
4. If a person is considering an FHA loan as compared with an ordinary loan from a building and loan association or a bank, what factors in relation to the monthly payments must be taken into consideration to determine which is the more economical method of purchase and which is the more desirable?
5. Some insurance companies that make loans on real estate include as part of the interest or the service charge an amount that is sufficient to pay for insurance on the life of the borrower during the period in which the loan will be repaid. Can you see any advantages or disadvantages in this plan? Discuss them.

PROBLEMS

1. Mr. and Mrs. Osborne have $1,000 in a savings account which has been earning 2 per cent interest, calculated annually. They buy a $6,000 home, using the $1,000 as a down payment. They succeed in obtaining a first mortgage for $3,000

at 4½ per cent interest and a second-mortgage loan for the remainder of the purchase price at 6 per cent interest. Considering the loss of the interest on their savings as a part of the cost, figure the total interest cost during the first year if the interest on the loans is computed annually.

2. (a) In this chapter is a table on page 588 showing how a $1,000 loan is reduced during the first year with interest at 5 per cent when the interest is computed monthly on the unpaid balance. Prepare a similar table for a $1,000 loan at the same rate of interest computed quarterly on the unpaid balance. (b) What is the difference in the interest charged between this method and the one shown in the chapter?

3. (a) On the basis of the table on page 590, compute the total amount (principal payments, interest, mortgage insurance, taxes, and fire insurance) paid on a $5,000 loan covering fifteen years. (b) Subtract from the total amount paid (the answer to the preceding part) the amount of the loan in order to determine the total expense. (c) Divide the total expense by the number of months in the loan period to determine the average monthly expense. (Your answer to this part is not the total monthly expense, because it does not include such items as depreciation and repairs.)

COMMUNITY PROBLEMS AND PROJECTS

1. Investigate the various local sources of loans on real estate. For each type of source find out (a) the percentage of the appraised value of property that will be lent, (b) the rate of interest, (c) the length of time during which a loan may extend, (d) the method of payment, (e) the dates on which interest is computed, and (f) any additional charges in obtaining a loan.

2. Obtain a sample form required by a bank, a building and loan association, or an insurance company for making an application for a loan. Fill out the blank, basing your figures on some particular piece of property, preferably your own home.

3. Investigate to see if there are any special emergency Federal regulations governing loans on homes. Write a brief report indicating what these regulations or restrictions are.

Chapter 34

Legal Problems of Obtaining a Home

Purpose of the Chapter. Renting or buying real estate involves many legal problems. You do not need to be a lawyer to understand some of these problems, but you may need a lawyer for advice and guidance. If you understand some of the simple legal problems, you can avoid worry and mistakes.

The purpose of this chapter is to point out the legal rights and responsibilities of the landlord, the tenant, the purchaser, the seller, and the borrower. An additional purpose is to point out the areas in which legal advice may be needed.

Renting or Leasing

Relations of Landlord and Tenant. If you are the owner of a house and, by agreement, allow this property to be occupied and controlled by another, you are a *landlord*. The one who occupies the property is the *tenant*. The tenant has the right of possession and use of the property although he must respect the rights of the landlord. After the expiration of the agreement, the landlord has the right to regain possession of the property.

Tenancy. The agreement between the landlord and the tenant is known as a *lease*. The landlord is the *lessor*, and the tenant is the *lessee*. The lease may be oral or written, the form depending upon the laws governing the form. A written lease is desirable in many cases because it clearly defines the rights of the landlord and the tenant. As we have noted, the period of occupancy may be definite or indefinite. In some states the lessor and the lessee must sign their names before a witness, such as a notary public. The formal type of lease usually embodies the following information:

594

(a) The date.
(b) The names of the landlord and the tenant.
(c) A description and an identification of the property.
(d) The length of the tenancy period.
(e) The amount of the payment.
(f) The manner of payment.
(g) A statement of the conditions and the agreements.
(h) The signatures of the tenant and the landlord.

The lessor grants the lessee the privilege of using the property without interference, provided the terms of the contract are carried out. The lease may state specifically the rights of each party to the contract, but some of the legal rights of the lessee and the lessor may not be mentioned in the lease.

Is Leasing the Same as Renting? Generally speaking, leasing and renting mean the same thing, but some people think of *renting* as meaning occupying property without a written agreement and of *leasing* as meaning occupying property with a written agreement. The term *renting*, however, is properly applied to the occupation of property both with and without a written agreement.

A person may occupy property under an agreement covering an indefinite period; he may occupy property for an indefinite period, the agreement being terminable at the will of either party; or he may occupy property under an agreement covering a definite period. Any of these agreements may be written or oral, but the first two are more likely to be oral agreements.

Rights and Duties of the Tenant. The tenant of a piece of property is entitled to peaceful possession of it. If he is deprived of that, he may sue for damages. The tenant is also entitled to use the property for any purpose for which it is adapted, unless he is forbidden certain uses by the agreement. The property may not be used for unlawful purposes.

The tenant is under obligation to make repairs, but not improvements. For example, if the child of a tenant breaks a window, it ordinarily is the responsibility of the tenant

This Lease Witnesseth:

THAT John G. Turner does HEREBY LEASE TO William F. Goodall *the premises situate in the* City *of* Portland *in the County of* Multnomah *and State of* Oregon *described as follows:* Dwelling House, No. 1229 Melbourne Road, Portland, Oregon

with the appurtenances thereto, for the term of two years *commencing* April 2, 1951, *at a rental of* eighty-five *dollars per* month *, payable* monthly.

    SAID LESSEE AGREES *to pay said rent, unless said premises shall be destroyed or rendered untenantable by fire or other unavoidable accident; to not commit or suffer waste; to not use said premises for any unlawful purpose; to not assign this lease, or under-let said premises, or any part thereof, or permit the sale of.* his *interest herein by legal process, without the written consent of said lessor ; to not use said premises or any part thereof in violation of any law relating to intoxicating liquors; and at the expiration of this lease, to surrender said premises in as good condition as they now are, or may be put by said lessor reasonable wear and unavoidable casualties, condemnation or appropriation excepted. Upon non-payment of any of said rent for* ten *days, after it shall become due, and without demand made therefore; or the bankruptcy or insolvency of lessee or assigns, or the appointment of a receiver or trustee of the property of lessee or assigns or if this lease pass to any person or persons by operation of law; or the breach of any of the other agreements herein contained, the lessor may terminate this lease and re-enter and re-possess said premises.*

    SAID LESSOR AGREES *(said lessee having performed* his *obligations under this lease) that said lessee shall quietly hold and occupy said premises during said term without any hindrance or molestation by said lessor ,* his *heir or any person lawfully claiming under them.*

Signed this second *day of* April   A. D. 1951

IN PRESENCE OF:

Gene Rainier   }   *John G. Turner*

Carl Noble   }   *William F. Goodall*

A lease.

to replace the window. He must pay his rent when it is due. Unless the lease states otherwise, the rent is not due until the end of each month.

If the lease is for a definite period of time, the tenant is not obligated to give notice when he vacates the property. The lease may be terminated, however, before the expiration of the period if an agreement is reached with the landlord. If the lease is for an indefinite period of time, the tenant must notify the landlord of his intention to give up the lease. The form and the time of notice are regulated by the customs or the laws of the community.

Auburn, Maine, June 1, 195–

Mr. Harry Becker:

I hereby give you notice that I will quit and deliver possession, July 1, 195–, of the premises at No. 417 Reading Road, in the city of Auburn, Maine, which I now hold as tenant under you.

Robert Mason

A tenant's notice of intention to terminate a lease.

The tenant should inspect carefully the property that he rents or leases. In the absence of any agreement with the landlord, he accepts the property with the risk of defects, except those hidden, being present. For example, if a tenant accepts a house with an obviously defective screen door, the landlord may not be responsible for fixing it except by agreement. However, if the tenant accepts the property in the summer and finds that the furnace will not function in the fall, the landlord is probably responsible because this is a hidden defect that could not easily be determined in the summer. In most states the tenant is liable for injuries to guests resulting from defects that he should have known and remedied.

Rights and Duties of the Landlord. A landlord does not have the right to enter the premises of a tenant except to do what is necessary to protect the property. He must not interfere with the tenant's right of possession. If the ten-

The tenant has the right to the undisturbed use of the property. The landlord has no right to enter the property to show it to a prospective buyer.

ant abandons the property, however, the landlord may take possession. At the expiration of the lease the landlord is entitled to take possession of the property. If the tenant refuses possession, the landlord may force him to give possession through legal proceedings.

The landlord is entitled to receive the rent as specified in the lease. In some states, through legal proceedings, he may seize personal property of the tenant and have it sold to pay the rent that is in arrears.

In some states the landlord is under no obligation to make repairs or to pay for improvements on the property unless such an agreement has been made with the tenant. In most states, however, he is obligated to keep the house in habitable condition. Unless the lease specifies otherwise, taxes and assessments must be paid by the landlord.

When a tenant occupies property for an indefinite period of time, the landlord may obtain possession of it by giving notice. The form and the time of the notice are regulated by local customs or laws.

                                    Cleveland, Ohio, April 30, 195–
Mr. Ronald Cramer:

I hereby notify you to surrender possession of the premises at 5942 Ridge Avenue, Cleveland, Ohio, on or before June 1, 195–. Your lease of the said premises expires on June 1, and I shall take possession of the property on that date.

                                    James Royalson

A landlord's notice requesting a tenant to vacate property.

When the landlord retains control over a part of the property—as in the case of a landlord who leases part of a building to a tenant—he is liable for certain injuries caused by the defective condition of the part of the property over which he has control. For instance, Mr. Adams owns a two-story building. He lives on the first floor and retains control over the porch and the yard, but he rents the second floor to Mr. Brown. If Mr. Brown or a member of his family is injured as a

Unless there are specific laws to the contrary, the tenant is responsible for injuries arising from defective conditions of the property.

result of the defective condition of the porch or the sidewalk, Mr. Adams is liable for the injuries. The landlord is also liable, in most cases, for injuries to any friend or guest of the tenant who may have been injured because of defects in the property which the landlord controls and therefore is obligated to maintain.

Improvements and Fixtures. In the absence of an agreement to the contrary, the improvements that are attached to the property become a part of the property and therefore belong to the owner. For instance, if a tenant builds a shed or a garage upon the lot belonging to his landlord, he cannot tear it down or take it away without permission. If a tenant constructs shelves or cupboards in the house that he has rented or leased, he ordinarily cannot take them away when he leaves. In some cases, however, courts have held that such fixtures attached with nails become a part of the property, whereas fixtures attached with screws may be removed.

Buying Real Estate

Agreements Must Be in Writing. State laws require that most agreements relating to the purchase and sale of real estate be in writing in order to be effective or legally binding on the parties involved. Therefore, in buying or selling real estate the safest practice is to have all agreements in writing and properly signed.

Title to Real Estate. The *title* to real estate is the ownership of the property. If a person has a clear title to a piece of real estate, there are no other claims against that property. To establish evidence of a clear title involves an investigation that will prove the true ownership of the property by tracing the history and the legality of the previous transfers of the title. Usually a loan on a piece of property cannot be obtained until the lender is certain that the title is satisfactory. The charge for examining the title is usually added to the loan or is paid as a special charge.

Each legal transfer of the title to a piece of property is recorded in a register of deeds, usually kept in the courthouse. It is therefore advisable to have a competent lawyer examine the records and determine whether there is a clear title to the property. In some states, individuals and companies specialize in the practice of making examinations of the titles to property. A condensation of the information taken from the recorded history of the property is referred to as an *abstract*. The report of the individual or the company making the abstract is called an *opinion of the title*. This report is sometimes, however, referred to as the abstract. It is also possible to obtain a *title-guarantee policy* from such a company. This policy guarantees that the title is clear and no claims are against it.

In order to eliminate uncertainties and to reduce the expense of transferring the titles to property, some states have established a special system of registering titles. This is known as the *Torrens System*. For instance, the owner of land applies for a registration of the title to his land. An officer then examines the records, and, if the title is good, he issues a certificate of title. Each time the title is transferred thereafter, a new certificate is issued. Under this system an abstract is usually not necessary.

Deeds, the Written Evidence of Title. There are two general types of deeds: (a) the warranty deed and (b) the quitclaim deed. The *warranty deed* is the more common. It is written evidence of the ownership of a piece of real property and serves as a means of conveying the title from one person to another. The one who transfers the title to the property is called the *grantor* of the deed, and the one to whom the title is transferred is called the *grantee* of the deed. Such a deed not only purports to convey the interest of the grantor to the grantee, but also involves stipulations that certain facts relating to the title are true. A warranty deed is shown in the illustration on page 602.

A *quitclaim deed* merely relinquishes the interest that the grantor may have in the property. The grantee assumes the risk that the title may not be good. In some communities a quitclaim deed is used instead of a warranty deed.

Consider this example: Mr. Allis desires to transfer real estate to Mr. Bush. He grants a warranty deed as evidence of the transfer of the title. In investigating the title, Mr. Bush discovers that a former owner, Mr. Carter, at one time had a claim against the property. Mr. Bush is therefore not quite sure that the claim has been settled fully. To protect his rights that are granted in the warranty deed, Mr. Bush gets Mr. Carter to grant a quitclaim deed relinquishing any rights that the latter may have had in the property.

The important elements in a deed are the description of the property, signature, seal, witnesses, acknowledgment, delivery, and acceptance. The laws in different states vary in some respects. To assure a clear title, the person executing the deed should become familiar with local laws. For instance, the laws in various states differ with regard to the ownership of property by man and wife. Some states require the signatures of both, whereas others require only one signature. In some states the witnesses must sign in the presence of one another, whereas in others they may sign only in the presence of an authorized public officer. Because of the many technicalities, the average person should obtain legal advice in granting a deed or taking the title to real estate. It is best to let a lawyer write all the legal papers.

Sales Contract. Often before the actual transfer of the title of real estate, an agreement is reached between the buyer and the seller. This agreement, which should not be

Know all men by these presents:

That __Joseph Bentley and Marie Bentley, his wife__
in consideration of __One thousand dollars ($1,000)__
to __them__ paid by __Walter Rathburn__
the receipt whereof is hereby acknowledged, do____hereby Grant, Bargain, Sell
and Convey to the said__Walter Rathburn, his__ heirs and assigns forever:)
Lot sixteen (16) block three (3) in the Avonlea subdivision
and all the Estate, Title and Interest of the said ____Grantors____
either in Law or Equity, of, in and to the said premises; Together with all the privileges
and appurtenances to the same belonging, and all the rents, issues and profits thereof;
To have and to hold the same to the only proper use of the said __Grantee__
__his__ heirs and assigns forever.
And the said __Joseph Bentley and Marie Bentley__
for __themselves__ and __their__ heirs, executors and administrators,
do____hereby Covenant with the said __Walter Rathburn, his__ heirs and assigns,
that __they are__ the true and lawful owner_s_ of the said premises,
and ha_ve_ full power to convey the same; and that the title so conveyed is Clear, Free
and Unincumbered; And further, That__they do____Warrant and Will Defend
the same against all claim or claims, of all persons whomsoever;

In Witness Whereof, The said __Joseph Bentley and Marie Bentley__
who hereby release__all their__right and expectancy of Dower in the said premises,
ha_ve_ hereunto set __their__ hand_s_ __this__
__fourteenth__ day of__October__ in the year
of our Lord one thousand nine hundred __fifty.__

Signed and acknowledged in presence of—

P M Davis   _Joseph Bentley_
E R Hall   _Marie Bentley_

State of __Virginia__, County of__Norfolk__, ss.
Be it Remembered, That on this__fourteenth__day
of__October__in the year of our Lord one thousand nine
hundred_and fifty__before me, the subscriber, a
__Notary Public__in and for said county, personally came
__Joseph Bentley and Marie Bentley__
the grantor_s_ in the foregoing Deed, and acknowledged the signing
thereof to be__their__voluntary act and deed.

In Testimony Whereof, I have hereunto subscribed
my name and affixed my__official__seal
on the day and year last aforesaid.

E. R. Stern
Notary Public.

A warranty deed.

confused with a deed, is referred to as a *contract of sale,* a *contract to convey,* or a *land contract.* It is a contract in which the seller agrees to sell under certain conditions and the buyer agrees to buy under certain conditions.

What Is Meant by Escrow? In bringing the sale of real estate to a conclusion, the seller sometimes will prepare a deed transferring ownership of the property to the buyer. He will then place this deed in the hands of a third party who is authorized to deliver the deed to the new owner when certain conditions have been fulfilled. This process is called placing the deed in *escrow.* For example, a deed may be placed in escrow until the buyer submits a certified check or bank draft in complete payment. Then the deed is turned over to the buyer. Money may also be placed in escrow to pay for work when it is completed.

Joint Ownership. In most states a husband and a wife may own real estate together. When property is owned under such a condition, the husband and the wife are considered to own it *jointly,* neither being the owner of any particular part. Our law in this respect is fashioned after the English law that considers a man and his wife to be one person.

Under the laws of joint ownership, when either dies, the survivor becomes sole owner of the property. In such

---

Legal Steps in Buying Real Property

1. Writing and signing a contract of sale.
2. Making a survey of the property to determine its exact size, location, and shape to be sure that the property is exactly as described.
3. Making a title search to determine whether the seller has a clear title to the property.
4. Obtaining a clearly drawn and legally accurate deed from the seller.
5. Recording the deed in the proper place of registration in the county in which the land is located.

a case the survivor is said to become a *tenant by entirety*. In some states, however, the manner in which the title will pass to the survivor must be indicated in the deed.

There are laws in most states that grant what is called a *dower right* or *dower interest*. This right is conferred upon the wife, who has a legal right to share in the property of her husband. A similar right is granted to the husband, who shares in the property of his wife. This right is known as *curtesy*. Some of these rights have been abolished in certain states, and the laws are not uniform. The laws of many states, however, prohibit either the husband or the wife from selling property unless the signatures of both appear on the deed. This rule holds good even though the property may be recorded in the name of only one.

In many states when property that has been owned jointly by a husband and a wife becomes the sole property of the survivor, it is not subject to an inheritance tax or a state tax, for the survivor is not considered to inherit the property.

Mortgages. When most people buy a home, they do not have enough money to pay for it. How do they go about borrowing the money to buy or to build a home? When you buy your first home, you will be confronted with this problem. If you borrow money to buy or to build a house, you will have to sign a mortgage and give it to the person from whom you borrow the money.

Mortgages are not the same in all states, although they have similar characteristics. Every mortgage should be in writing, and usually the signature should be witnessed. The correct wording can be found in statute books, and a special legal form on which to draw up the mortgage can be obtained.

In most transactions involving mortgages, at least two legal papers are required: (a) a mortgage note and (b) a mortgage. In some states a mortgage bond is commonly used instead of a mortgage note. In other states the instrument is referred to as a mortgage contract. Regardless of its title the legal instrument that is used specifies the amount of the indebtedness and the method of payment.

The mortgage is given as security for the payment of the debt. In some transactions in which a mortgage is issued, the borrower must sign a series of notes that will become due on certain dates.

In most states the laws require that a mortgage, in order to be effective protection against subsequent buyers or mortgagees, must be recorded in the county in which the property is located. This procedure enables other interested people to discover any claims against the property.

Rights and Duties of the Mortgagor and the Mortgagee. Any person who owns an interest in land, buildings, or even crops raised on land, may mortgage that interest. A mortgage on real estate includes equipment that has become so permanently attached to the real estate that it is considered a part of it. If a piece of land is mortgaged, and a house is later built on the land, the house will be included in the mortgage, for it has become a part of the land.

In the eyes of the law the mortgagor is the owner of the property. The property is merely pledged as security for the payment of a debt. It remains his property to use as he pleases, unless he allows the mortgagee to take possession or he is forced to give up the title to the property through legal procedure. If he fails to perform the agreements specified in the mortgage contract, he can be compelled by the law to relinquish the title to the property to the mortgagee.

The mortgagor is under duty to refrain from destroying or damaging the property. The mortgagee must not interfere with the occupancy of the property except through agreement with the mortgagor or through legal procedure. If a mortgagee sells a mortgage to a third person, he should give the mortgagor a notice of transfer.

When the indebtedness is paid, the mortgage is automatically canceled. It is wise, however, for the mortgagor to obtain the mortgage, the mortgage note, and a statement acknowledging the discharge of the obligation. The notice acknowledging the discharge of the obligation should be recorded in the proper place of registration, usually the county courthouse.

Mortgage Foreclosure. Although a mortgage contract usually specifies that the mortgagor loses all rights to the mortgaged property if the obligation is not performed at a specified time, the laws in most states permit the mortgagor to regain his interest in the property by fulfilling his contract at any time before the *foreclosure* of the mortgage.

If the mortgagor fails to fulfill his obligation, the mortgagee has the right of foreclosing, that is, of bringing a legal suit to obtain possession of the property and title to it. Foreclosure may consist in (a) a court order that transfers the title to the property from the mortgagor to the mortgagee, or (b) a court order that requires the property to be sold to pay the mortgagee. The procedure is, however, different in various states.

If the proceeds from the sale of the property exceed the total of the indebtedness and the expenses incident to the sale, the mortgagor gets the difference. If the proceeds are less than the amount of the indebtedness, the mortgagee has a right, in most states, to obtain a judgment against the mortgagor for the difference. This judgment is referred to as a *deficiency judgment.* Because of the possibilities of a deficiency judgment, the mortgagor does not release himself, under the laws of some states, from his obligation merely by giving up his property. For example, Mr. and Mrs. Charles purchased a home. They paid $2,000 in cash and borrowed $8,000 on a mortgage to pay for the home. They failed to repay the money as agreed. The person who loaned the money and held the mortgage foreclosed through the proper legal proceedings. The property was sold to settle the claim, which at the time of the foreclosure amounted to $7,500. The property was sold for $7,000, which was paid to the holder of the mortgage (mortgagee), leaving a deficiency of $500. The court granted a deficiency judgment of $500 against Mr. and Mrs. Charles, which they are required to pay to the mortgagee.

One piece of property may have as many as three mortgages. If it is sold through foreclosure proceedings, the mortgagees must be protected according to the preference given to their respective mortgages. The first mortgage

---

Things to Investigate in Buying Real Estate

1. What unsettled claims are there against the property?
2. Are any assessments or taxes due?
3. Are any street, sidewalk, or sewer improvements likely for which there will be future additional assessments?
4. Are there any unfavorable zoning laws affecting the property?
5. Is the property mortgaged? If so, can the mortgage be transferred to the new owner?
6. Have arrangements been made for the proper insurance on the property at the time of purchase?
7. Have you checked the fees to be charged by the lawyer?
8. Are all agreements in writing, including the settlement of old claims against the property?

---

ranks first; the second ranks second; and the third ranks third.

In many states a mortgagor who has defaulted in his obligation is given a certain time (usually one year) in which he may redeem or recover his property after the foreclosure. The property may be redeemed by paying the amount due plus interest at a stipulated rate.

Lien. Any encumbrance, or claim, on real estate that arises from a debt is referred to as a *lien*. A mortgage

is one type of lien. A *mechanic's lien* is another. For instance, a contractor who has constructed a building may hold a lien against the property for the payment of the amount due him. A *judgment* rendered by a court as the result of a lawsuit is still another kind of lien. The judgment repre-

A mechanic who has done work on the property can get a court order giving him a direct claim against the property. This is known as a "mechanic's lien."

sents a claim that must be paid by the property owner.

TEXTBOOK QUESTIONS

1. (a) Who is a landlord? (b) Who is a tenant?
2. (a) Who is a lessor? (b) Who is a lessee?
3. Why is a written lease desirable?
4. What information is usually embodied in a formal lease?
5. What is the distinction between renting and leasing?
6. May a tenant use the property for any purposes that he wishes?
7. In the absence of any agreement, when is rent usually due?
8. Under what circumstances must a tenant notify the landlord of his intention to give up the use of the property?
9. Is the landlord or the tenant liable for damages if an invited guest of the tenant is injured on the property?
10. May the landlord enter the premises of a tenant any time he wishes?
11. If the tenant fails to pay his rent, what may the landlord do in order to ensure payment of the amount that is due as rent?
12. Must the landlord make repairs and improvements that are demanded by the tenant?
13. A tenant who intends to move wishes to tear down and take with him any improvements he has made. May he do so?
14. Are oral agreements in regard to purchasing or selling real estate enforceable?
15. Through what process is it possible to determine who is the legal owner of a piece of real estate and what claims, such as a mortgage, are held against the property?
16. What protection can one obtain against the possibility that the title to a piece of property may not be good?
17. What is the advantage of the Torrens System of registering land?
18. (a) What are the two general types of deeds? (b) In what ways do they differ?
19. What is the difference between a contract of sale and a deed?
20. What is meant by escrow?
21. Is it always true that, if property is recorded only in the name of the husband, he alone has the right to sell it?
22. Name the legal steps in buying real property.
23. What is meant by joint ownership of real property?
24. (a) What is a mortgage? (b) Who is a mortgagor? (c) Who is a mortgagee?
25. If a mortgage covers a vacant lot, and a house is later built on the lot, does the mortgage cover only the lot or does it also include the house?
26. If the mortgagor fails to pay the claim against the mortgaged property, what right has the mortgagee?

27. After the mortgage on real estate has been foreclosed, is there any means by which the mortgagor may recover the property?

1 28. What is a mechanic's lien?

29. What are some of the things that must be investigated in buying real estate?

DISCUSSION QUESTIONS

1. (a) Name some of the advantages of a written lease to a lessee. (b) Name some of the disadvantages.
2. (a) Name some of the advantages of a written lease to a lessor. (b) Name some of the disadvantages.
3. (a) May a tenant change the property that he has leased by making physical alterations? (b) May he repair it without the consent of the owner?
4. When Mr. Brown visited Mr. Cooper, he injured himself on a broken step. Mr. Cooper has rented the house from Mr. Thompson. Who is responsible for the injury?
5. In most states why is it not possible for a husband to sell real estate without the signature of his wife?
6. Is a refrigerator or a stove considered part of a house or an apartment that is mortgaged? Explain your answer in detail.
7. If a mortgage on a home is foreclosed: (a) Who gets the extra money if the property is sold for more than the mortgage claim? (b) What may happen if the amount obtained from the sale is not sufficient to pay the mortgage? (c) What, if anything, can be done by the mortgagor to get his property back again?
8. When banks or other lending agencies lend money on a new home that has just been completed, why does the lender often require the builder to give proof that the plumber, the carpenter, and other types of workers and suppliers have been paid or that arrangements have been made to pay them?
9. Explain the status of a bill owed to a plumber for work performed on a house if the plumber obtains a lien.

PROBLEMS

1. Mr. Woodburn, who has rented a house to Mr. Sears, wants to sell the house. In the absence of the Sears family he unlocks the door and shows the house to a prospective buyer. When Mr. Sears learns what Mr. Woodburn has done, he objects and insists that Mr. Woodburn had no right to enter the house. Mr. Woodburn insists that he did have the right to enter his own house. What is your opinion? Why?

2. Mr. Simmons rents a house to Mr. Baker and later sells the property to Mr. Jackson. Mr. Jackson wants immediate possession of the property. Mr. Baker insists that he has an agreement with Mr. Simmons to the effect that he may stay on the property as long as he wishes. This agreement is, however, not written. (a) Do you think Mr. Jackson can obtain possession of the property? (b) In what way do you think he can obtain possession?

3. Mr. Duggan granted a mortgage on his house and lot in favor of the Central Building and Loan Association, to which he owed some money. The mortgage was not recorded. Mr. Trees accepted a deed from Mr. Duggan in good faith and without knowing that a mortgage had been granted to the Central Building and Loan Association. The Central Building and Loan Association insisted that it still had a legal claim against the property. Mr. Trees insisted that the property was free from a mortgage. Who was right? Why?

COMMUNITY PROBLEMS AND PROJECTS

1. Obtain samples of all the legal forms used in obtaining a loan on a home. Fill out all these forms, using an imaginary piece of property or some piece of property with which you are familiar. Write an explanation of the procedure and the purposes of these forms.

2. Investigate the procedure in your community for recording a deed, a mortgage, or a lease. Find out the place of recording, the details of procedure, and the fee.

3. Obtain copies of your state laws pertaining to the foreclosure of mortgages. Write a report on the legal rights of the mortgagor and the mortgagee. Point out whether there is any possibility of repossessing property after the mortgage has been foreclosed.

PART X
ECONOMIC PROBLEMS OF THE CONSUMER

Chapter 35

Money, Wealth, and Income

Purpose of the Chapter. The term *wealth* is commonly misunderstood. Many people confuse money and wealth. A study of the real nature of wealth and income, as well as of the production and distribution of wealth, aids the individual in understanding his own relationship to the economic and business system. A knowledge of the problems of money, wealth, and income helps him to understand taxation, the nature of real wages as contrasted with money wages, and the earning and the saving of income, as well as general current problems. This discussion of money, wealth, and income serves as an introduction to some of the individual management problems of the consumer.

Meaning of Money, Wealth, and Income. Usually we speak of a person with considerable money as being wealthy. Actually *money* is a convenient means of measuring wealth and is a medium of exchange; but money in itself is not wealth, except the metal in metallic money or the small amount of paper in paper money. In the economic sense, one is wealthy, not because he has money, but only because his money enables him to buy the goods and services he wants. The goods that he owns or buys are wealth. Likewise, a nation is not wealthy in terms of its money, but rather in terms of its resources.

Wealth consists of useful, tangible goods. This book is wealth. The factory in which the book was printed is wealth. Wealth consists of goods that satisfy human wants directly or indirectly.

Wealth has other characteristics; it must be scarce enough to be wanted by people and must therefore have value. Air is so free that it is not wealth, but elements taken from the air become wealth.

Income is the product of wealth; it results from the wise use of goods and services to satisfy the desires of people. Therefore, *income* is one's share of new wealth that he has helped to create by using his labor or his stored-up wealth. The baker through his labor and by the use of his equipment converts flour and other ingredients into bread. People want bread; therefore the baker, by satisfying the desire of people for bread, earns income. Income, whether of individuals or nations, results from combining wealth, that is, material goods having value, and the physical or mental work of people.

Ordinarily income is measured in terms of money, but it may be in the form of goods and services. A farmer on a completely self-sufficient farm would have an income because he would produce certain goods that he would consume and some that he might save; however, he might not have any money income.

Wealth and Money. The concepts of wealth and income given here are basic to an understanding of many other phases of business and economic life. National and individual welfare depend upon the amount of tangible wealth and income that are available for use. Minerals at the bottom of the ocean are of no practical value unless they can be recovered and used to produce goods to satisfy human wants. The miser's hoarded money is unproductive of wealth or income simply because it is not used.

One might be on a barren island with millions of dollars in money, but without any tangible goods. The money would be useless, for it could not be used to procure food or clothing, or to satisfy other needs. If this same person had jewels or several automobiles, or a hundred new suits of clothes in addition to the money, these goods would be of little value to him, for he could not use them. They would not be wealth so far as he is concerned, for they would not be useful. If his money could be used, however, to obtain goods to satisfy his needs, it could be exchanged for wealth.

The jewels would represent wealth if they satisfied a need. The automobiles would also be wealth if they satisfied a need. From this explanation we can see that wealth is comprised of usable goods and that money is of no value unless it can be used to buy the goods and services we want.

Some of the soldiers on the islands in the Pacific in World War II learned some lessons in regard to money and wealth. They usually had plenty of money, but there was very little that could be bought with the money. A story was reported of a shipment of ice cream reaching a group of soldiers on an island. There was only enough for a small helping for each soldier. Some soldiers bought the "ice cream rights" of other soldiers for ten dollars a tablespoonful. They had learned that their money was of no particular value on that island except to satisfy a human want.

Natives on some of these Pacific islands also learned some lessons in regard to money and wealth. When the soldiers first arrived, they were anxious to send grass skirts home to their friends. In a few minutes a native could make a grass skirt that he could sell for two dollars; but when the natives accumulated handfuls of paper money and found that there was nothing to buy with the money, they discovered that their labors were useless. Barter then became the basis of exchange for the grass skirts. Any soldier who had a knife, cigarettes, food, or a trinket was able to barter it for a grass skirt, but the natives did not want paper currency. Thus money decreased in value because it would not buy the goods the natives wanted; it was plentiful. The other goods used in exchange, such as the knives and cigarettes, had value because they were relatively scarce and people wanted them.

Money in itself is of no value unless it can be used. It is possible to imagine a condition of *barter*, such as existed in earlier periods of time, in which various products and services were exchanged between individuals. A person's wealth and relative prosperity depended upon what products or services he could exchange for other things. Under such conditions one's wealth directly depended upon what he could produce so long as people wanted the goods or services produced. This condition is equally applicable to-day. The more one produces of goods and services wanted by others, the greater his wealth becomes. In other words, the more one produces, the higher his standard or level of living may be.

Such is not the case with money. If the Federal Government doubled the amount of money in existence, the amount of wealth, that is, tangible goods and services, would remain unchanged. There would be twice as much money, but not twice as much goods. Prices of products and services would rise, and some producers and consumers probably would actually be poorer than they were before.

Producing Goods. Producing goods consists in part of changing their form or location to make them more useful in satisfying the desires and wants of people. To make goods more useful usually requires a combination of labor, the use of equipment, and the knowledge and skill of management. A person who makes goods more useful is a producer of wealth.

Anything that makes goods more useful in satisfying wants is said to create *utility.* In order that a commodity may have the power to satisfy a desire or a want, it must be in the proper physical form; it must be at the place where it is needed; it must be available when needed; and usually it must be owned or capable of being owned by the person who wants it. The most common types of *utilities,* therefore, are (a) *form utility,* (b) *time utility,* (c) *place utility,* and (d) *possession utility.* A producer of goods is one who helps to create the goods in the proper form, at the proper time, and in the proper place so that the goods can be used.

From this description of the production of goods, it is evident that the man who works with his hands, the man who operates a machine, the bank which finances business activity, the railroad which transports the goods, the telegraph company which facilitates business transactions, the wholesaler and the retailer which handle the goods, the salesman who sells the goods, and many others contribute to the production of goods.

The welder creates
form utility.

Ewing Galloway

Some business or economic activities can scarcely be said to be productive. The salesman who sells you something you do not need is not productive. Someone engaged in producing goods that may impair health is not engaged in productive activity. Some few types of business activities that are essentially gambling in nature are not productive. Such cases are contra-productive, rather than truly productive, from an economic point of view.

Performing Economic Services. Another type of producer is one who performs services that satisfy human wants directly. These people are producing economic services, but these services do not relate to any economic activity dealing directly with the production of wealth.

An opera singer is a producer, not because he creates any utility in wealth, but because he satisfies a human want directly. Teachers, lawyers, physicians, and actors are also producers because they satisfy human wants directly. A stenographer who works for a doctor is performing an economic service that directly satisfies a human want. This stenographer is not a producer of goods or wealth, but there is no doubt that her services are useful. Another type of stenographer may be indirectly a producer of wealth, as, for example, a stenographer in a wholesale grocery firm. She is performing a service that is one step in creating place utility in goods. Without her help, the distributor would be unable to create place utility.

It should be observed that one may produce a desirable economic service that satisfies directly a human want; but in doing so, that person is not producing wealth because this type of service is not tangible goods.

Factors of Production. The five elements of production are considered to be: (a) *natural resources,* or land; (b) *man*; (c) *capital,* or tools and machinery; (d) *management*; and (e) *government.* Some refer to these elements as nature; labor, including both physical and mental; capital; management; and government.

Clearly, men cannot produce anything without the aid of nature, for nature furnishes all raw materials with which we work, such as mineral and vegetable resources. Very little wealth is produced except through the application of physical and mental labor to natural resources. The term *capital* is applied to tools and machinery because the economist uses it to designate any kind of goods used for producing wealth. Government is considered a factor in production because it provides such services as protection, regulation, and information. The function of management in production is to integrate the other four factors, natural resources, labor, capital, and government services in such a manner as to produce usuable goods desired by people.

In an actual enterprise, such as a factory or a store, these elements of production cannot always be seen separately. Natural resources, such as minerals, may be utilized at the same time as labor, capital, management, and government. It is only for convenience that the economist separates the factors of production into these five divisions. Clearly, any productive situation involves the use of all five at the same time. In some types of enterprise the labor element may play a very important part, whereas in others it may not. In the production of Irish laces, for example, capital and management play a very small role, but hand labor, aided by nature, plays an important role. In modern industry, capital, in the form of machinery and equipment, becomes increasingly important, although labor plays a great part in producing the machinery and equipment.

The oil industry uses a great amount of capital.

United States Steel Corporation

In our present industrial society, man cannot produce efficiently without the aid of technical equipment, such as tools and special knowledge. As the wealth of a nation is measured by its ability to produce goods, the more goods the individual can produce, the greater the wealth of the country and the individuals in it. In the United States the use of tools and machinery has reached a relatively high stage of development. It has been estimated that the average amount of capital equipment used in United States factories is almost eight thousand dollars' worth for every worker. In some countries, industrial development has been retarded, and national and individual wealth and income are low.

Machine production doubtless increases individual income. It must be remembered, however, that machines are necessary to make machines. A vacuum cleaner makes the housewife's work easier and more efficient, but a factory and the labor of many people are required to produce the vacuum cleaner. The saving in labor and the increase in productivity, due to machines, can be overestimated, for most people overlook the fact that machinery and equipment must first be produced.

The problem of the business manager is to develop an effective combination of the right proportions of natural resources, labor, capital, management, and government. This combination will, of course, vary from one industry to another; but the problem of the proper adjustment of these five factors is a basic one by which the efficiency of the business manager is determined.

Specialization and Production. Specialization, sometimes referred to as *division of labor,* is one of the outstanding characteristics of large-scale production. The trades, crafts, all phases of skilled labor, and the professions have been developed by dividing large tasks among several special occupational workers in order that each one might do only the small part in which he is a specialist.

Under a plan of specialization of labor no one attempts to produce everything that he needs to satisfy his wants. Consequently, there are now hundreds of different kinds of occupations, and most workers specialize in some particular type of work. There was a time when one person with one or more helpers could do all the work in constructing a house. Now a house is constructed by specialized carpenters, bricklayers, plumbers, painters, and plasterers. Even the lathing, the laying of the floor, the roofing, and the concrete work are done by specialized workmen.

In reality, specialization has two major phases. It is not one thing, as commonly thought, but two. Specialization involves, as has been noted, the breaking down of a task into several parts. The second step, frequently overlooked, is the tying together or co-ordinating of the various parts of the task. When a house is constructed, the work of carpenters, plumbers, or bricklayers must be related to the work of all others. Co-ordinating the work of the various specialists is as important as breaking down the task into its several elements. Much waste may result if the work is badly co-ordinated.

Advantages of Specialization. Some of the advantages of specialization are: (a) it increases production, hence the amount of wealth and income; (b) it encourages the development of greater skill; (c) it saves time; (d) it lowers production costs; (e) it makes possible the employment of

persons who may otherwise be unemployable; (f) it permits
the continuous and economical use of tools and equipment;
and (g) it develops a spirit of interdependence.

Disadvantages of Specialization. Some of the disadvantages of specialization are serious, but they do not necessarily affect the production of wealth. Among the disadvantages are: (a) workers become greatly dependent upon
one another; (b) work may become monotonous and deaden-
ing to the worker; (c) a worker finds it difficult to change
from one occupation to another; (d) a worker may not
have as much pride in his workmanship; (e) the efficient
worker does not have an opportunity to learn how to perform other tasks; and (f) a worker who loses his position
may have difficulty finding another or may find other employment difficult to adjust to because it may require other
skills and knowledges.

Limiting Production. Periodically in our economic history various groups—including government, labor, farmers,
manufacturers, and others—have attempted to restrict
production in order to maintain prices and personal profits.
Certain individuals have been afraid that machines would
take the place of men. Some leaders feel that the constant
reduction of the length of the working day or the working week is a solution to the problem of distributing income
and wealth. A common practice for some producers of
food crops has been to destroy part of the crops rather than
to market them because the marketing of large surpluses
would depress the prices. For them, the marketing of a
small quantity at a good price is profitable, whereas the
marketing of a large quantity at a low price might be
unprofitable.

Any restriction on production by any particular group
may be of temporary advantage to that group. Temporary
restriction and control of production may be necessary and
helpful to our whole society in order to correct maladjust-
ments in our economic system. However, if several groups
or all groups restrict production in the same manner, we
all suffer because we have less goods to consume. The maxi-

mum prosperity can come about by maximum production of every individual so that his goods are available at a low price to everyone else and so that, in turn, the goods that other people produce are available to him at low prices. Permanent advantage cannot be realized by a group, whether it be a producer of agricultural products, machines, or clothing, by restricting production to make prices high. Not only will such a course of action contribute to forcing prices of all commodities and services higher, a policy from which no one benefits, but it also will encourage the development of substitutes for the product which is being controlled. In other words, maximum prosperity depends upon maximum production rather than on restriction of production.

The principle that maximum prosperity depends upon maximum production rather than upon restricted production is applicable to the individual worker as well as to an industry or a business enterprise. The employee who produces as much as he can each day and week consistent with his physical strength and health helps to raise the level of living for all people—for the nation as a whole. The worker who produces less than he is capable of producing, yet draws compensation for a full day's work, automatically contributes to higher price levels, which means that wages received will buy less. As a result, the level of living falls.

The standard of living can be raised only when workers produce more than they consume and when their production is at least in proportion to the wages they receive.

Men, Machines, and Productivity. Productivity is the key to prosperity. A nation improves its standard of living through increases in productivity; it increases its wealth through productivity. Future progress depends upon raising the output of each man. Greater production for each man-hour is possible through the increasing use of machine power. Machines are now the helping hand of men in modern industry. A man with his hands alone can make a very limited quantity of any product. With the aid of a few tools he can increase his production. With the

Machines increase man's productivity many times.

aid of machinery he is often able to multiply his production
ten or twenty times or more.

Three distinct advantages can arise from the use of machines in production, and as a general rule these results
have been obtained as follows:

(a) *Increased leisure on the part of the worker.* The
forty-hour week has become the recognized standard
work week. The shorter work week was brought
about by the fact that workers have been able to
produce increased quantities in a shorter amount
of time.

(b) *Wages that increase faster than the cost of living.*
Increased purchasing power is brought about largely
by increased productivity, which makes cheaper
goods available for everyone.

(c) *Increased output per man.* This increased output
per man is largely responsible for the first two ac-
complishments. It may also be responsible for an
undesirable result known as "technological unemployment," which will be discussed next.

Most of us fail to realize the advantages that we have
gained from the use of machines. It is estimated, for instance, that thirty years ago it required approximately 9
hours of a factory worker's wages to buy a pair of shoes.
Today it requires approximately 3½ hours. Thirty years
ago if a factory worker wanted to buy an electric light

bulb, he would have had to spend the wages that he would have earned in about 105 minutes. Today he can buy an electric light bulb with the wages he has earned in 12 minutes.

Effects of Technological Changes. There are two important aspects of so-called *technology* in business, or the use of machines. The first problem is the displacement of men from jobs. This is called *technological unemployment*. The second aspect is the increase in the productive capacity of each individual. If employees who are displaced by machinery obtain other employment, no serious problem develops. If the machinery is used to produce a greater quantity of goods more efficiently and at lower costs, everyone in society benefits from the introduction of the machinery. Workers in general benefit from the introduction of machinery by being relieved of a certain amount of physical labor. For instance, a simple derrick or a hand truck will relieve a worker from physical strain, but an electric derrick or an electric truck will make the work even more simple.

When major inventions are introduced, there is usually a certain amount of unemployment as a direct result of the introduction of the new machinery. In the long run, however, most new inventions not only provide more goods for all of us to use, but also create new types of jobs and thus eventually take care of persons displaced from previous jobs. For instance, the invention of the automobile displaced many employees who had manufactured wagons and other horse-drawn vehicles; but the automobile has created new jobs in automobile factories and filling stations, in the oil industry, in the steel industry, and in the rubber industry.

Many workers are fearful of machines because they look upon them as competitors. In individual cases a machine may be a competitor of a man for a particular job. When we take a larger view of industry, however, we find that the machine is not the competitor of man; it is man's helper. There is no question of the economic soundness of the use

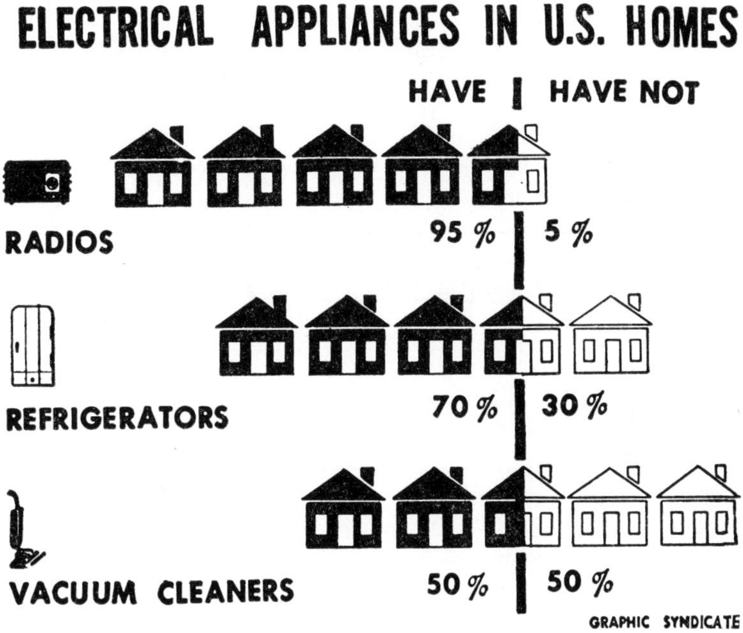

ELECTRICAL APPLIANCES IN U.S. HOMES

HAVE | HAVE NOT

RADIOS   95 % | 5 %

REFRIGERATORS   70 % | 30 %

VACUUM CLEANERS   50 % | 50 %

GRAPHIC SYNDICATE

of machines in producing wealth, but the great problem arises when men are temporarily thrown out of employment by new inventions. One would not think of giving up an electric sweeper or an electric washer in his home after having these appliances. None of us would want to do away with electricity in the home because of its many advantages. Likewise, we would not want to give up machinery in our factories or to prevent the development of new machinery. To do so would retard progress and reduce our ability to purchase the comforts we now enjoy.

National Wealth. *National wealth* is comprised of all the useful material things owned either by private persons or by units of government. This wealth is the source from which all income flows. It consists of factories, farms, horses, cattle, machinery, automobiles, houses, furniture, and numerous other types of goods.

A nation may be wealthy in economic goods; but unless the goods are shared among all individuals, there can be

MINUTES OF WORKING TIME REQUIRED FOR PURCHASE PER POUND OF SELECTED FOODS

Source: U. S. Bureau of Labor Statistics.

FOOD	UNITED STATES MAR. 1949	CHILE DEC. 1948	FRANCE APR. 1949	GERMANY MAY 1949	GREAT BRITAIN MAY 1949	ITALY MAR. 1949	SWEDEN FEB. 1949	U. S. S. R. APR. 1949
Flour, wheat	4	13	20	12	5	22	8	52
Pastes (spaghetti, macaroni)	8	…	35	…	21	14 [1]	…	78
Rice	8	18	40	…	17	21	…	145
Bread	6	16	10	9	5	17	11	25
Beef, average	29	…	108 [2]	…	…	136	33	254
Pork, chops	32	…	124	…	29	133	54	407
Lamb, leg	30	83 [3]	…	…	45	…	73 [4]	288 [3]
Chickens	26	…	…	218	…	…	49	305
Fish	19	…	41 [5]	…	…	74	19	294 [6]
Butter	32	182	146	120	34	222	58	542
Cheese	26	103	122	85	25	151	36	…
Milk, fresh (grocery) [7]	9	23	22	…	16	28	8	59
Eggs [8]	27	122	106	298	57	112	55	158
Fresh apples	7	…	…	51	…	…	20	141
Cabbage	4	3	…	5	…	…	3	9 [9]
Potatoes	2	6	3	4	3	6	2	6 [9]
Dried navy beans	7	18 [10]	32	…	21	18 [10]	…	…
Coffee	23	88	124	640	76	191	62	706
Tea	56	241	…	…	72	…	…	1,506
Lard	9	102	56	…	23	108	…	…
Sugar	4	15	27	27	10	46	9	141

[1] Corn meal. U. S. working time 4 minutes. [2] Loin. [3] Lamb, average. [4] Steak. [5] Cod, salted. [6] Herring, salted. [7] Quart. [8] Dozen. [9] Prices for Nov., 1948. [10] Kidney beans. U. S. time 8 minutes.

1961 Information Please Almanac.

no prosperity. The extent to which an individual shares in this wealth is controlled by his earnings or other income, such as pensions. The per capita wealth of the nation means very little in determining the prosperity of the nation. Even the average income of the citizens does not determine the prosperity of the whole country. A nation may be very wealthy and, in total, may have a large income; but unless this income is divided reasonably over the entire population, there will be a lack of purchasing power.

Comparative Wealth and Purchasing Power. The only way of stating national wealth is in terms of dollar values, which, of course, change from time to time according to the price level. According to available information the per capita national wealth of the United States exceeds that of every other nation in the world. When our per capita national wealth is compared with that of countries, such as Brazil, we find that ours is as much as four times as great. One reason is that much of our production is performed by high-speed machinery, whereas production in countries such as Brazil is performed largely by hand.

The real test of the efficiency of a country in producing wealth and prosperity is to determine the relative prosperity of the individuals in various countries. The table on page 624 shows the number of minutes of working time required for the purchase of one pound of selected foods in eight different countries. This table shows the purchasing power of labor. We think prices are high in our country, but observe as an example that one has to work much longer in most other countries to buy a pound of butter. In fact, in Russia a worker must work almost seventeen times as long as in the United States to buy one pound of butter.

These figures naturally change from time to time, but they do give a general indication of the prosperity or the level of living in other countries as compared with our own.

Other interesting means of comparison are automobiles, radios, telephones, and other products. Many more of these are owned per one hundred persons in the United States than in any other country. They can also be bought with

fewer hours of work in the United States than they can
be bought in any other country.

Real Wages. It is impossible to determine whether a
person is earning a high or a low wage without a knowledge
of the prices that he has to pay for the goods and services that he uses. The amount of money that one earns
does not determine one's *real wages*. Real wages are measured by their purchasing power. For instance, assume that
a man is earning forty dollars a week and paying certain
prices for food, clothing, and rent. Suppose the prices of
necessities increase 50 per cent, and his wages increase 25
per cent. He has had a substantial increase in wages, but he
still is not earning real wages that are equal to his former
wages of forty dollars. His increased wages of fifty dollars
will not buy so much as his former wages of forty dollars
did.

Let us take another example. Let us assume that one's
wages are increased from $40 a week to $46 a week. Let

**Real wages are not money; they
are what money will buy.**

us also assume that the cost
of living increases from $30
a week to $35 a week. Is
the wage earner any better
off financially? No. His real
wages have not increased,
although his monetary wages
have increased. Of course, it
is easier to pay off any debts
that he has incurred because
he is paying off the debts with dollars that are worth less
than they were when he incurred the debts. However, if
he has saved money in the bank or through insurance, this
money is worth less than when he saved it because the
dollars will buy less now than they would have bought
when he saved the money.

Still another example will help to illustrate real wages.
Let us suppose that a man has been earning $40 a week.
This person's cost of living drops from $37 a week to $33
a week. His real wages have increased, although he re-

ceives the same monetary wages. He can buy more with what he gets. If he has previously saved money, his savings are now more valuable than when he originally saved his money because they will now buy more.

What We Need to Know About Money, Wealth, and Production

1. Wealth is comprised of material goods that have the following characteristics: tangible, useful, scarce in relation to the needs of people for them, capable of being valued in terms of money, and capable of being owned.

2. Money is not wealth (except the metal in coins), but it may be used to acquire wealth. It has no value unless it can be used to obtain the goods we want.

3. Income results from the production and use of goods to satisfy human wants. Just to possess wealth will not result in income; but to use the materials, of which wealth is comprised, to satisfy the wants of people may produce income.

4. Production of goods consists primarily of making goods more useful in satisfying wants. The goods are made more useful by: (a) changing the form, (b) making them available when needed, (c) making them available where needed, and (d) making them desirable as a possession. Some people perform economic services that directly satisfy the wants and needs of people.

5. The factors in production are: natural resources or land; labor, including physical and mental; capital, or tools and machinery; management, or the process of co-ordinating the other elements of production; and government, which provides protection, regulation, and information.

6. Large-scale production is based on specialization in employment, sometimes referred to as division of labor. Advantages and disadvantages of specialization of labor to both the worker and the business enterprise are present.

7. Maximum prosperity and maximum level of living depend upon maximum production by every individual who is employed and by every business enterprise or industry, not on restricted production.

8. The real measure of a nation's wealth and prosperity is determined by the amount of goods and services an hour's wages will buy.

9. One's real wages are determined not by the amount of money one earns but by what the money will buy.

TEXTBOOK QUESTIONS

1. What is money?
2. Is money wealth? Explain.
3. What is wealth?
4. What is income?
5. Why may a native on an isolated island in the Pacific prefer to accept some kind of goods instead of money?
6. Explain what makes money valuable.
7. Name and explain the four most important types of utilities created by a producer.
8. Give an example of a strictly nonproductive activity.
9. Explain the two types or classes of producers.
10. What are the five elements of production?
11. What is capital?
12. What are the advantages of specialization?
13. What are the disadvantages of specialization?
14. Why do some producers of food crops destroy part of the crops rather than sell them?
15. Upon what does maximum prosperity depend?
16. What have been the three general good effects of the use of machines in production?
17. Give an example of how the productiveness of machinery helps us to buy more with each hour of labor.
18. What is meant by technological unemployment?
19. How does the United States rank with other nations in respect to the buying power of one hour's wages of the average individual?
20. What is meant by real wages?
21. If one's wages are increased 10 per cent and the cost of living is increased 10 per cent, what happens to real wages?

DISCUSSION QUESTIONS

1. A man is said to be worth a million dollars. Does this statement mean that he has a million dollars in cash?
2. Can new wealth be produced by labor or by wealth alone, or must the two always join forces?
3. Of what value is ten thousand dollars in cash to an individual alone on an island?
4. Does the production of harmful narcotics represent the production of wealth?
5. Some people criticize the use of the term *nonproductive activities* to designate the activities of organizations such as banks, stock exchanges, and wholesalers. Are the activities of such organizations nonproductive?

6. Why are the services of some people more valuable than the services of others?

7. If a large machine is installed in a factory to do the work of ten men, what will be the result from the point of view of the total production of wealth?

8. What are some of the advantages that nature provides for production?

9. Has specialization in production increased the average standard of living?

10. Some producers have been known to destroy part of their products in order to raise prices. They have obtained more for the small supply that they sold than they would have received for the entire quantity. What is the result of such a practice?

11. In what way has the automobile increased both employment and the production of wealth?

12. In times of war people are usually very busy. Does this fact mean that the production of wealth is increasing rapidly?

13. If the machine has made a forty-hour week possible, do you think it would be advisable to continue to decrease the working week to as low as ten or twenty hours a week?

14. Is technological unemployment a permanent type of unemployment?

15. Does the fact that our per capita wealth is greater than the per capita wealth of other countries indicate that we have a smaller percentage of poor people?

16. Some people are greatly concerned over the concentration of wealth. What do you think of this problem from a strictly economic point of view?

PROBLEMS

1. (a) If the production of everyone, including farmers, factory workers, store operators, transportation workers, and everyone else concerned in the productive processes, were increased 20 per cent, what do you think would be the general result from the point of view of individual and national welfare? (b) What would be the result if there were a 20 per cent decrease in the efficiency of production?

2. Point out the functions that each of the following three factors performs in the production of an automobile: (a) nature, (b) man, and (c) machinery.

3. The following are the approximate figures for national income, national debt, and total population in the United States for 1946 and 1948. On the basis of these figures compute to the nearest dollar (a) the per capita income in 1946 and 1948, and (b) the per capita national debt in 1946 and 1948.

If the average interest on indebtedness costs 2 per cent, calculate (c) the interest cost in 1948, and (d) the per capita interest cost in 1948.

	1946	1948
National Income	$179,562,000,000	$226,204,000,000
National Debt (Federal, State, and Local)	$243,300,000,000	$232,700,000,000
Population	141,229,000	146,571,000

4. The amount of money of all kinds in circulation in 1948 totaled $28 billion while the income for that year totaled $226 billion. Explain how it is possible for everyone to earn a cash income when there is less than a month's supply of cash in circulation.

COMMUNITY PROBLEMS AND PROJECTS

1. Compare the average income of your community with that of your state. Your local chamber of commerce may be able to supply you with the figures.
2. From your personal observation and investigation, make a list of ten examples of producers of each of the following types of utilities: (a) form utility, (b) time utility, (c) place utility, and (d) possession utility.
3. Make a study of the natural resources available in your state. Give as much information in regard to each resource as possible. If you can get the figures, compare the resources of your state with those of others.

Chapter 36

PART X _____

How We Share Our Income

Purpose of the Chapter. As a group, we continuously produce a gigantic stream of wealth in the form of goods and services. Each of us shares to a small extent in this great wealth through the income we receive. The income we receive may be in various forms. Not all of us, of course, receive equal amounts. It is difficult to conceive of a perfect system of distributing wealth and income; but man through the experience of centuries has developed laws, customs, and economic practices on the basis of which the income of a nation is divided among the individuals who compose that nation. The purpose of this chapter is to show how we divide our national wealth and income.

Who Shares in Income? The _national income_ for a given period of time consists of the net total of goods and services produced by all of the people. The value of these goods and services is measured in terms of money, which in turn serves as the medium for distributing to those who contributed to the production of the wealth the share to which each is entitled.

In industry the results of production are divided among those who represent the factors involved in the production of goods and services. These factors, usually classified as natural resources, labor, capital, management, and government have been discussed before. The results of productive effort are divided in the form of wages, interest, rents, profits, and taxes. These are various forms of income. Wages go to the workers; interest goes to those from whom funds have been borrowed; rents go to the owners of land or other resources; profits go to the owners of business or industrial enterprises; and taxes go to government for the services it performs.

The owner of a business may own the land on which his business is located. He therefore may pay no rent. If he owes no money, he does not pay any interest. The only two elements involved in such a case are wages and profits. Society as a whole, however, shares in the income of the business through the taxes that are paid. It may be said, therefore, that the results of productive effort are divided into wages, interest, rents, profits, and taxes.

Sharing in Several Forms of Income. One may share in several of the forms of income from production. For instance, Mr. Jones, the owner of a garage, has a house that he rents. In this way he shares in rent. He has some money in a savings bank and gets interest on it. In this way he

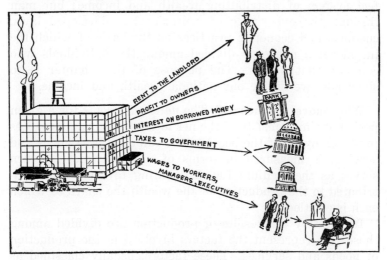

The results of production are divided through wages, interest, rents, profits, and taxes.

shares in interest. From the business that he operates, he probably draws a weekly or monthly salary. In this way he shares in wages. Since he owns the business, he earns profits, if there are any after all the expenses of operating the business have been paid. If he owns some stock in a corporation, he shares also in the profits of that business.

Illustration of Sharing in Income. Studying the income and the expenses of a business provides a concrete picture of the ways in which those who represent the various factors of production share in the income from production. The Eureka Manufacturing Company, a corporation, is organized to produce electric fans. The corporation is owned by the stockholders. The stockholders, through their board of directors, hire a manager to operate the business. The manager rents a building and land. He borrows money from a bank in order to buy equipment and to help pay the expenses that will be incurred in making sales. He also hires people to do the work in the factory and in the office, and to sell the goods.

At the end of the first year the manager prepares for the stockholders a statement to show how those who represent the various factors of production will share in the income. The income and expense statement of the Eureka Manufacturing Company is shown below.

EUREKA MANUFACTURING COMPANY

Income and Expense Statement for the Year 195–

Income from Sales	135,000	00		
Cost of Merchandise Sold	97,000	00		
Gross Profit			38,000	00
Rent of Land and Building	2,800	00		
Wages of Clerks and Factory Workers	11,800	00		
Salary of Manager	4,200	00		
Interest on Borrowed Money	3,900	00		
Taxes	2,500	00		
Other Expenses (Supplies, Insurance, etc.)	9,300	00		
Total Expenses			34,500	00
Net Profit (to Owners)			3,500	00

Statement showing the sharing in the fruits of production.

This statement briefly illustrates how rent, wages, interest, profits, and taxes represent the distribution of the income of the Eureka Manufacturing Company. After all other deductions have been made, the balance of the income, or net profit, goes to the stockholders, who own the business. If there is nothing left after the other items have been deducted, the owners do not get any share of the income. If there is a loss, the owners are the ones who lose.

Individual Income. One's individual income depends upon (a) his earning power, that is, his skill and ability together with the market demand for it, and (b) the amount of money and other resources he has and allows to be used for productive purposes. Wages, salary, or fees depend not only upon the skill of the individual, but also upon his ability to market his skill. Sometimes highly skilled persons receive relatively low incomes because they have failed to sell their skills in the best markets, or because they are engaged in highly competitive occupations. The drive and enterprise of the individual as well as good fortune may also be important factors in one's ability to market his skill. Skill is developed through education or training. A high degree of skill developed in such a way, however, does not always mean a large income. Earning power is a relative matter. If a high degree of skill has been developed through education or training, but if at the same time too many others have been trained in that particular skill, and hence the marketability of the skill has been diminished, earnings will necessarily be low.

Individual Wealth. The accumulation of wealth depends upon the ability to save and to acquire resources that will bring additional income. Saving often depends upon the ability to spend effectively. If a person earns and saves, he can share in rent, interest, or profits by various means. He may, for instance, buy real estate and rent it; or lend money at interest; or acquire a share in the ownership of a business enterprise and thus receive profits.

Differences in the amount of wealth people have and in the income they receive are due largely to differences in individuals. Some produce more than others; some use the wealth they have more wisely than others in producing income; and some have greater ability to earn than others. Opportunity is also a factor in determining the amount we may produce. Of course, some wealth is obtained as the result of inheritance or luck. Even if incomes were equal, the distribution of wealth would not long remain equal simply because of the differences in human nature. When wages are high, some workers spend freely and unintelligently; and when wages are low, these same people find it difficult to buy the necessities of life.

Wages, Labor's Share of Income. Wages constitute that part of the national income which belongs to those who perform either mental or physical labor. *Wages* are the prices paid for the services of labor. The price of labor in terms of money places a value on labor.

The price of labor is determined in the same manner as the price of any product. In the absence of any control, the price is determined by the supply and the demand. The supply consists of the workers who are offering their services for sale. The demand consists of the needs of employers for workers. The principle of supply and demand of labor is as effective for an occupation as for all labor taken collectively. For example, except when there are wage controls, the ratio of the available supply of stenographers seeking employment to the demand affects the wages stenographers may receive.

An employer can pay a wage based on the value of the worker's product. He must take into consideration the price that he can obtain for his goods and how much the worker can produce. The price for which a product will sell can be determined reasonably well from the prices at which other similar products are selling. In order to produce goods that can be sold in competition with others, the employer must estimate accurately the cost of rent, the cost of wages, and amounts of other expenses. The cost of materials can be computed with reasonable accuracy. The financial statement on page 633 is an example of the kind of analysis that an employer must make. He will have to pay the prevailing rates of wages, just as he will have to pay the prevailing prices for materials. He may not always be able to make a profit.

If the manager of a factory contemplates hiring more employees at the existing price that is being paid for labor, his problem is to decide whether the additional goods that will be produced by the new employees will earn additional profit. If more goods are needed for sale, and if the labor can be hired at a wage that will allow a profit on the additional production, new workers will be employed.

The Supply of Labor. As there are thousands of occupations, various classifications may be made of them. A common classification is that based on the kinds of labor required by the occupations: (a) unskilled, (b) semiskilled, (c) skilled, (d) clerical and semiprofessional, and (e) professional. The first three groups represent manual labor; the last two, work of a service type. The occupations in the last two groups are sometimes referred to as "white-collar" occupations. The requirements of the various occupations differ greatly. Consequently, a worker may not be able to transfer from one type of occupation to another. An unskilled day laborer could scarcely become an engineer; but many engineers could serve, if need be, as day laborers.

The supply of labor is indicated by the number of workers who are seeking employment in each kind of work at each of the wage rates offered in the occupation. If the wage rate for an occupation is low, a relatively small number of workers will be available; but as the wage rate increases, the larger will be the number of workers who will seek employment in that occupation.

The fact that there are many occupations for which a large number of persons can qualify affects the supply of labor. The attractiveness and the working conditions of certain occupations also affect the supply. Many persons prefer clerical occupations, even at low wages, because they believe the working conditions in such occupations are more desirable than those in occupations requiring manual labor. The desire to live in certain sections of the country or in a city affects the supply of labor. Many other factors influence the supply of labor, such as minimum age at which employment may begin, economic condition of older workers who may wish to retire, amount and cost of training, and the policies of organized labor.

The Demand for Labor. The demand for labor is the result of the demand for the products of labor. If, for any

INCOME PER PERSON

$ 5,630 $ 5,350 $ 3,350 $ 3,260 $ 2,570 $ 2,407

MANAGERS   PROFES-SIONALS   SKILLED WORKERS   CLERICAL & SALES   FARMERS   LABORERS

SOURCE: FEDERAL RESERVE BOARD   GRAPHIC SYNDICATE

reason, the demand for a product or a service declines or disappears, the demand for the labor that produces it will likewise decline or disappear. The worker will therefore become unemployed unless he is able to shift to a new type of work. The development of a demand for a new product or service may result in abnormally high wages for the comparatively few workers able to produce the product or provide the service.

Wage rates are determined by demand and supply; but many conditions may affect either factor. Demand may fall off because of the lack of purchasing power on the part of consumers. Supply, too, may be affected in many ways. One common method of regulating supply is through the unionization of workers. Other factors that may affect demand and supply are the substitution of other types of labor and an increase in the use of machines.

Training and Wages. As we go up the scale from unskilled labor to other types, we find that education and training become more and more important. Any person with a normal mind and a good physique can do unskilled work in farming, building roads, or handling goods for storage or shipping. To be a skilled mechanic, however, a person needs more education; and to be an engineer, still more. Usually, if there is a choice between the person who has no high school education and one who has, the employer will take the one with a high school education. The person with a limited education therefore has a relatively limited choice of occupations and usually receives relatively lower wages.

It should not be assumed, however, that more education always results in higher wages. With increases in high school and college enrollments, the competition for certain occupations has become keener. Furthermore, the educated person may not be trained for any particular occupation and must compete with the uneducated. Some skilled mechanics, with relatively little formal education, earn more than some college graduates. Usually the reason for this situation is that they have a specific skill for which there is a market demand.

Wage Inequalities. How is it possible to explain why one worker gets six dollars a day and another gets fifteen dollars a day? Why are those who do some of the more disagreeable work of the world rather poorly paid? Without having evaluated the reasons for this condition, one might assume that every person who is earning only six dollars a day would quit his position and try to get one in which he could earn fifteen dollars a day. There are, however, definite reasons for these wage inequalities.

Education and training are two of the most important factors causing wage inequalities. Natural ability is another. The supply of people who can handle the low-paying positions is greater than the supply of those who can handle the better positions. If a certain kind of work demands more training and knowledge than another, an employer is willing to pay more for someone to do this work. Essentially, however, the wages in each group are determined according to the supply of labor in that group. The supply of labor becomes smaller as we progress from the lowest group to the highest. The supply in the highest group is often very limited. Why does a baseball star or a radio performer get fifty thousand dollars or more a year, even though either occupation may be rather pleasant? Clearly, the answer rests in the matter of supply and demand. If the public refused to pay for (or did not demand) such services, or if the persons who render those services could be found with ease, the salaries in that group would, of course, decline.

The value of the worker's product is also another factor that determines wages. In certain industries the profits of the business will allow only certain low wages; but if the worker transfers to another type of production where the value of his product is higher, he may be able to earn a higher wage.

Legislation Affecting the Wages of Labor. After considering the regulation of wages and hours of labor for many years, Congress in 1938 passed the Fair Labor Standards Act, commonly known as the Wage-Hour Law. The law directly regulated the extent to which children may be employed in industry, fixed the minimum rates of pay for labor, and limited the standard work periods a week.

The Wage-Hour Law defines as "oppressive child labor" the employment of children under 16 years of age subject to certain conditions and under 18 years in hazardous occupations. The minimum wage rate per hour was to change gradually from 25 cents in 1938 to 40 cents by October, 1945, and the maximum standard work week was to change gradually from 44 hours in 1938 to 40 hours by June, 1940.

Congress amended the Wage-Hour Law, effective in 1950, by increasing the minimum hourly rate to 75 cents, and provided 150 per cent of the regular hourly rate as compensation for the hours a week in excess of 40. The Wage-Hour Law applies only to interstate industries; however, it tends to influence minimum wages and maximum hours in all industries. Furthermore, the law encourages state labor legislation; many states have now enacted labor laws patterned generally after the Federal law.

In 1950, the Walsh-Healey Act authorized the Secretary of Labor to determine the prevailing minimum wage in a particular industry and set that as the lowest wage an employer can pay for work on government contracts of $10,000 or more. The effect of this Act is to increase the minimum hourly wage for thousands of workers in American industry. Steel manufacturers were ordered to pay a minimum hourly wage of $1.23 in most areas, woolen mills $1.05, and soap manufacturers at least 95 cents.

Minimum wage rates and maximum work periods a week are protections to employees, especially when wages are dropping. The effect is to force industry to operate efficiently enough to meet the wage-hour standards or to discontinue business.

In addition to the wages and hours legislation for the protection of labor, several other kinds of laws enacted by states and the Federal Government regulate collective bargaining in labor-management negotiations, child labor, employment of women, and employers' liability and workmen's compensation in the event of accidents.

Interest, Capital's Share of Income. Funds are borrowed to serve three purposes: (a) to enable individuals to buy goods and services before having accumulated sufficient savings to pay for them, (b) to enable individuals and business firms to increase their productive capacity, and (c) to provide governments with funds to be used in both production and consumption. The amount paid for the use of borrowed funds is *interest*. Another concept of interest is that it is that portion of national income attributable to the use of capital, not including land. Usually, however,

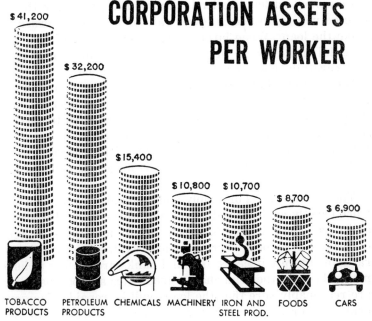

CORPORATION ASSETS
PER WORKER

$ 41,200

$ 32,200

$ 15,400

$ 10,800 $ 10,700

$ 8,700

$ 6,900

| TOBACCO PRODUCTS | PETROLEUM PRODUCTS | CHEMICALS | MACHINERY | IRON AND STEEL PROD. | FOODS | CARS |

NAT'L CITY BANK 1949   GRAPHIC SYNDICATE

interest is considered the payment for the use of money borrowed.

The interest that one must pay to obtain the use of money is the price at which the services of the money can be obtained. The rate of interest is established by supply and demand in the same way that wages are determined by supply and demand. However, government agencies, such as the Federal Reserve Board and the U. S. Treasury, also influence interest rates as described in Chapter 18.

Suppose, for example, that Mr. Jacobs, the owner of a department store, needs to borrow five thousand dollars to buy a stock of goods for his fall season. He goes to an individual or a bank and inquires about the rate that is being charged on loans made at that time. If the rate quoted him is too high, he may go to another individual or bank. Frequently the rate of interest asked by one bank may be the same as that asked by another in the same community. In some cases, however, one bank may have more money on hand to lend than another, and may therefore be willing to take a lower rate of interest in order to make the loan. When large loans are being negotiated, the bargaining for rates of interest is frequently prolonged and carefully considered on a competitive basis.

When banks have available plenty of money for which there is no immediate need, they are usually anxious to lend it. If there are very few business firms that wish to borrow money, there is a lack of demand. As a result the rates on loans are low. When, on the other hand, banks have already lent most of their funds and there is an active demand for loans, the rates are high.

These simple laws of supply and demand, however, do not work exactly as described because of governmental controls and psychological factors. When profits and the prospects of profits are good, borrowers are willing to pay higher rates of interest if necessary, and banks are willing to lend money because they can charge good rates and because they are reasonably sure that the loans will be repaid. The government, through its monetary controls and lending activities, may cause low interest rates and a plentiful supply of money when prospects of business are good.

In times of depression, there is usually plenty of money lying idle in banks; rates are low; but loans are hard to get because banks and others are afraid to lend money in view of the risk involved. The interest rate is important because it determines the amount of national income that is distributed to those who supply capital.

Why Is Interest Paid? Essentially, interest is paid because money controls that form of wealth known as capital goods, which are productive goods. If capital goods did not increase productivity, interest could not be paid. When money is borrowed for use in operating a business, the borrower hopes to increase production and therefore profits. If interest rates are high, businessmen are less likely to borrow, but they will borrow if there is a sufficient chance for a profit. Interest rates are sometimes high simply because the risk of the loan is high. Low interest rates, however, encourage borrowing and business activity.

If money is to be borrowed for business purposes, the amount that can be paid for its use is determined by the amount of profit that can be made from business operations. The amount that will be paid on other types of loans is determined by the productivity of those forms of wealth that the money will buy and the amount that the borrower is willing to pay. The borrower's willingness is dependent upon the intensity of his needs and what other alternatives he has. For example, if one had to pay 20 per cent interest on a loan to finance the purchase of a home, the borrower would probably find it far less expensive to rent a home.

Risk in Lending Money. The person who lends money takes a risk just as does the person who rents an automobile to another. If the automobile is damaged and there is no means of collecting money to pay for the damages, the owner will suffer a loss. The person who owns the automobile has a right, therefore, to charge for its use and for the risk that he takes in renting it. Likewise, if a person lends money and it is not repaid, he suffers a loss. A person who lends money is entitled to a reasonable rate for the services performed by his money and also as compensation for the risk that he is taking. If the risk is great, the rate should be high; if the risk is negligible, the rate should be low.

Rent, Landowners' Share in Income. In an economic sense, land includes all natural resources. Thus it includes farms, urban building sites, minerals, forests, water, and even air, because all are natural resources. In many instances, land has man-made improvements, such as buildings, permanent equipment, or dams. These and similar improvements increase the usefulness of the land and hence its value.

In the popular sense, *rent* is the price paid for the temporary use of land, including the improvements. Strictly speaking, *pure economic rent* is the price for the use of land without the improvements, and the additional amount paid for the use of the improvements is similar to interest. The former concept of the meaning of rent is the one with which we are primarily concerned here.

What Regulates the Cost of Rent of Land? Why should some farm land rent for one dollar a year an acre while other farm land rents for ten dollars an acre? Why should a building on one street in a city rent for twenty-five cents a square foot while a building on another street rents for one dollar a square foot?

Rent in such cases depends upon the usefulness, the productivity, and the desirability of the property. For example, a piece of land that will produce fifty bushels of wheat to an acre is theoretically worth at least twice as much as land that will produce only twenty-five bushels to an acre. Richness of the soil, mineral deposits, and location with regard to water or transportation facilities are a few of the many factors that have their bearing on the value of land. In buying land for investment, all these factors should be taken into consideration. If an individual has land available for rent, he can obtain a rent only in proportion to the productivity of the land measured in comparison with that of competing land. The law of supply and demand applies to land just as it does to wages and interest.

Rent and Prices. Only a slight relationship exists between the rent that a producer pays for the use of the land in production and the price that he charges for his product. For instance, one who produces chickens for sale in a large city does not govern the price of his chickens by the cost of the rent on his land. The price is determined by competition and by the supply of chickens, as well as by the demand for them. A producer of chickens close to the city will probably pay higher rent than one farther away, but the one close to the city will have a lower transportation cost than the one farther away. If the rent on any particular piece of land becomes so high that a reasonable profit cannot be made by the renter, this land will go out of use unless the rent is lowered, or it will have to be used for another purpose for which it is better suited.

Merchants sometimes advertise that, because their rent is lower, they can sell merchandise at a lower price than other merchants. Their statements are sometimes, but not always, true. Other factors, such as the quantity that can be sold, affect the price at which merchandise can be sold. The fallacy of the argument that low rents make it possible to sell at low prices lies in the fact that the rent of land is determined by supply and demand.

The merchant in the center of a large city pays a high rent, but he has many times as many customers as the merchant in an outlying district. He probably sells his goods faster and therefore needs less borrowed capital to finance his purchases. The person in an outlying community or a small town has fewer customers and sells his goods more slowly. His rate of profit is not any higher, and frequently is lower, than that of the city merchant.

Profit, The Owner's Share of Income. *Profit* is the share of income from an enterprise remaining for the owner after distributing the shares to which all others have claim. The rent share is paid to the owner of the land and permanent equipment leased; the interest share, to the one from whom funds have been borrowed; the wages, to laborers and employed management; and taxes, to local and Federal governments. Anything left over out of income after these claims have been paid is the property of the owner. It is his profit. If the income in a given period is not large enough to pay the claims of rent, interest, wages, and taxes, the loss must come out of previously accumulated surplus or must be paid by the owners.

Net profit as computed by the accountant does not make allowance for deductions from income for the rent value of land and equipment owned by the enterprise, for the interest on investment in the enterprise, and sometimes for the total wages or services of the management, if the owner or part-owner devotes his time to management. The economist makes deductions from the accountant's net profit for these items and considers the amount remaining as *pure profit*. In the corporate form of enterprise, the wages of management usually are considered by accountants in computing net profit.

In order to induce men to invest in a business enterprise and to devote their time and energy to its management and operation, the business must hold the possibility of profit after allowances are made for normal return on investment and for the wages of management.

Competition and Profits. On the average, the profits of a business are limited to a fair return on the investment and a reasonable compensation for risk. Sooner or later competition retards the increase in profits. New competition always tends to develop when someone makes a success of a business.

If one businessman has a secret that will enable him to operate at a profit that is greater than the profits of competitors, he has an important advantage. If his competitors learn the secret and become as skillful as he, the latter will lose his advantage.

In difficult times, when there is little profit to be made, many concerns voluntarily go out of business and others are forced out. The workers in these businesses then become idle and increase the supply of labor. When profits are again possible in business, many people start in business for themselves. Estimates made by businessmen indicate that the average businessman does not earn as a regular salary any more through the profits of his business than he would earn if he became an employee in a similar capacity. As a result of the risks that he takes, he sometimes receives an additional earning; but these risks, on the other hand, cause many businessmen to become bankrupt. As a business manager, the man of much ability and wide training receives a higher rate of income than a man of lesser competence. Likewise, an employee who is well trained and has much ability receives a higher rate of income than a less capable employee.

Risks and Profits. A business must build up a surplus to take care of times when there will be no profits. In times when there are profits, the businessman must receive a reasonably high rate of profit so as to have the means to protect his business during adverse times. It is by this plan that the businessman can take risks. He is entitled to a greater income than a paid employee.

Many people who work for wages or a salary think that the man who owns or manages a business has an easy life and that his profits are far greater than they rightfully should be. They overlook the fact, however, that the average owner or operator of a business must make many sacrifices of his physical energy and his resources. He often works long hours in his place of business and at home. He risks not only his money but also his health. He must plan ahead when the employed person is resting or is enjoying recreation. He must often meet acute competition. To become successful, he must be a leader; but relatively few people are good leaders. Many businessmen succumb to the physical and mental ordeals of managing a business. These are some of the reasons why many men are willing to take positions and to let their employers do the worrying and planning.

Businessmen are entitled to a profit for the risk of losing on their investment and for performing the arduous tasks of ownership and management. Estimates indicate that 60 per cent of those who enter business fail or quit.

Actual Distribution of National Income. The national income varies from year to year according to the amount of productivity of the industry of the nation, and it is influenced by business conditions in general. Since 1929, the national income has ranged from a low of a little less than 40 billion dollars in 1933 to a high of more than 224 billion dollars in 1948. The following table shows how this national income was divided in 1948.

HOW THE NATIONAL INCOME IS SHARED
(Billions of Dollars)

Wages	139.4	
Professionals, Farmers and Proprietors.	43.5	
Total Wages		182.9
Interest		4.9
Rent		7.4
Corporation Profit		29.2
National Income		224.4
Federal Taxes (all kinds)		41.9

U. S. Department of Commerce, 1948.

In 1949, the national income was approximately 217 billions dollars which, if equally divided among all men, women, and children in the United States, would have given each one an income of approximately $1,441 for the year or about $28 a week.

Of course many people received more than the average share of income and many received less. In some sections of the country average personal income is higher than in other sections. For example, in 1948 the average income per person in the United States was $1,410, while in the state of New York it was $1,891 and in Mississippi, $758.

Numerous factors account for the inequality of income distribution among people. Among these factors, personal traits, habits, and abilities are among the most important. We are just not alike in our earning ability. Other factors, such as general economic conditions in the geographical area in which one lives and works, education, accumulated savings, and employment opportunities also affect the amount any one person may earn.

The table below was prepared by the President's Council of Economic Advisors. This table shows the relative distribution of our national income among families. The average family probably is comprised of two to three persons. During the year 1948, a fifth of our families received 4.2 per cent of the national income, which gave these families an average income of $893 for the year; the second

MONEY INCOME RECEIVED BY EACH FIFTH OF FAMILIES AND SINGLE PERSONS, 1935-36, 1941, and 1948

FAMILIES AND SINGLE PERSONS RANKED FROM LOWEST TO HIGHEST INCOME	PERCENTAGE OF MONEY INCOME			AVERAGE MONEY INCOME IN DOLLARS OF 1948 PURCHASING POWER [1]		
	1935-36	1941	1948	1935-36	1941	1948
Lowest fifth	4.0	3.5	4.2	$ 534	$ 592	$ 893
Second fifth	8.7	9.1	10.5	1,159	1,546	2,232
Third fifth	13.6	15.3	16.1	1,810	2,597	3,410
Fourth fifth	20.5	22.5	22.3	2,734	3,816	4,711
Highest fifth	53.2	49.6	46.9	7,083	8,418	9,911
All groups	100.0	100.0	100.0	2,644	3,396	4,231

[1] Current dollars divided by the consumers' price index on the base 1948 = 100 to give a rough measure of changes in purchasing power of income.

Sources: National Resources Planning Board (1935-36), Department of Labor (1941), and Council of Economic Advisers (1948).

fifth received 10.5 per cent of the income or $2,232 a year; and the highest fifth in income received 46.9 per cent of the income or $9,911 a year.

How Do We Share in Income?

1. The national income consists of the total of goods and services produced by all of the people. It belongs to those who helped produce it.

2. The claims to a share of the national income are represented by:

   (a) Wages, for the services of the laborer, manager, and executive.

   (b) Interest, for the lender of funds borrowed by the producing industry.

   (c) Rent, for the landowner whose land was leased for use in production.

   (d) Profits or losses, for the owner of the business.

   (e) Taxes, for governmental units that provided protection, information, and services to the producing firm.

3. The share each person receives for his contribution to the production of income depends upon many factors. Supply of and demand for land, availability of money for loans, and supply of labor affect the distribution of income to persons representing these three claims; other factors also affect each of the three. Inequalities of distribution of income among people are due in part to the differences in the education, training, and ability of the people; in part to geographical or regional conditions; and to several other economic causes.

TEXTBOOK QUESTIONS

1. In what sense do all share in the national wealth?
2. Of what does the national income consist?
3. In what five forms are the results of productive effort of industry distributed?
4. How may a person share in more than one form of income?
5. According to the statement of the Eureka Manufacturing Company on page 633, how much profit is available for the owners?
6. Upon what does individual income depend?
7. What determines whether an employer will hire additional workers?
8. The price of labor is said to be determined to some extent by the supply and the demand. What is meant by (a) the supply? (b) the demand?

9. What does a shortage of workers tend to do?
10. What factors tend to cause wage inequalities?
11. As amended, the Wage-Hour Law now provides for what minimum hourly rate?
12. What is the justification for paying interest?
13. What factors besides the law of supply and demand affect interest rates?
14. What determines the value of land?
15. Why is the rental rate on a piece of business property in the center of a city higher than in an outlying district?
16. What is profit?
17. Explain how competition tends to control profits and prices.
18. About what percentage of the people who enter business either fail or quit?
19. What was the average income for the American people in 1948? in 1949?

DISCUSSION QUESTIONS

1. In how many forms of income may a farmer who owns and works his own farm share?
2. Explain how a manager of a small business shares in different kinds of income, although his total income is the profit from his business.
3. Why do wages depend not only on the skill of an individual but also on his ability to market his skill?
4. Why are there differences in the amount of wealth individuals have and in the amount of income they receive?
5. What is a fair wage for a man? Upon what does it depend?
6. Why will the wages of unskilled workers always be low in comparison with those of other workers?
7. Does higher education result in higher wages always? usually?
8. Trace the Wage-Hour Law from 1938 to 1950.
9. Why do reduced interest rates on loans encourage borrowing?
10. Sometimes when there is plenty of business activity and good profits can be made, how are interest rates affected by a program of the Federal Government of lending large sums of money to corporations at low interest rates?
11. A merchant in the downtown section of a city advertises that he sells a large volume of goods and that he therefore can sell at lower prices than competitors. Discuss this statement.
12. Assume that there is only one hardware store in a city of 10,000 population. Since there is only one store, the owner charges very high prices and makes an exceptionally large profit. What natural economic controls are likely to remedy this situation? Explain.

13. Does a dividend paid to a stockholder represent a share of income in the form of wages, rent, interest, or profits? Explain your answer.

PROBLEMS

1. In one particular state a proposed new law would increase a tax $20 on each $1,000 of valuation of city real estate. If a piece of property were worth $7,000 and were being rented, how much would the landlord have to increase the monthly rent in order to pay the additional tax?
2. A person has $300,000 invested in the Eureka Manufacturing Company. This amount represents all the stock of the company. On the basis of the financial statement shown on page 633, compute the percentage of income earned on the investment.
3. A businessman finds that he can borrow $5,000 for three months at 4 per cent and make a gross profit of $100 on the transaction in which the $5,000 will be used. After deducting the $50 interest charge, he will make a net profit of $50. If the interest rate were 6 per cent, what would be the profitableness of the transaction?
4. In 1948 Federal taxes took what per cent of the national income?
5. In 1948 total wages represented what per cent of the national income?

COMMUNITY PROBLEMS AND PROJECTS

1. Wages vary according to occupations and localities. For your own community investigate (a) the wage rates for various classifications of local workers and (b) the minimum wage rates that have been established for various classes of workers. Compare the wage rates in your community with those in other communities. Compare the wage rates with the costs of living in order to determine the real wages.
2. Investigate the prevailing interest rates in your community for (a) loans on real estate, (b) loans on securities, (c) commercial loans, and (d) other types of loans. Find out how they compare with the rates of the year before, of five years ago, and of ten years ago. Give a report to indicate the reasons for the variations.
3. Compare rental rates on two similar pieces of property, either residential or business, each in a different section of your community. Explain these differences in rates.
4. Make a list of as many as possible of the risks of making profits in business.

Chapter 37

PART X_____

The Functions of Money and Credit

Purpose of the Chapter. Modern business would be impossible without money and credit. Practices in production, exchange, distribution, and consumption are all based upon money and credit. In fact, all phases of economic activity are dependent upon the functions of money and credit. As individuals we deal with money from early childhood to old age. We must use it constantly. It is so important to us that we should understand what money is and what it does. Credit is so closely related to money that it is important that money and credit be studied together. Banks must also be studied in their relation to the supply of money and credit. The purpose of this chapter is to provide an understanding of money and credit and of how banks perform functions in the use of money and credit.

Functions of Money. Anyone is willing to take money in payment. A person may accept goods as payment, but not so willingly. If you have canned vegetables and want to trade them for clothing, you may have some difficulty in finding a person who will be willing to make the exchange of goods. Nevertheless, you probably can find someone eventually. Today, in many rural communities, eggs are brought in by farmers and traded for clothing or other food or products.

The use of money has arisen because of the need for some medium that will be accepted in exchange for any product or service. Money is therefore defined as a *medium of exchange*. Money serves as a medium of exchange, for the person who has one type of goods can sell the goods for money and can use that money for buying what he wants. In this way money simplifies the process of exchange. In the selling of goods for money and the buying

652

of other goods for money, the value of each type of goods is established in terms of money. Money is therefore also a *measure* or *standard of value*. The following illustration shows how money functions in serving all members of society.

True wealth consists of goods. Through the use of money it is possible to accumulate wealth (or the means of obtain-

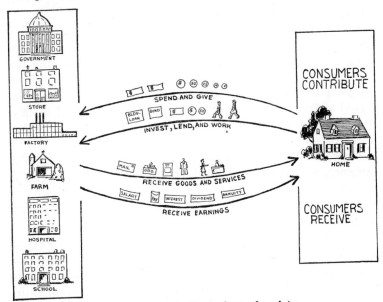

How money serves all members of society.

ing wealth, that is, purchasing power) without having to amass and store actual goods. Money, except metallic money, is therefore only a right or claim to wealth. All the money in the world would not be of any value to a person if he could not use it in exchange for goods and services. To have value, money must therefore be readily exchangeable for goods and services. Whenever anyone has accumulated money, he is wealthy as long as money is exchangeable for goods and services. If money ceases to be of value, he is no longer wealthy. In such a case only those who have in their possession actual goods are wealthy.

Kinds of Money. If one were to trace the matter back through history, he would find many varieties of money. Gold and silver have been used frequently for making money, largely because of the fact that the coins made of these metals have a value in themselves.

The money of most civilized countries can be classified essentially as standard money, representative money, credit money, and token money.

Standard money is the term applied to money that obtains its value from the standard metal contained in it—the metal selected as the measure of value in the country issuing the money. The value of a gold coin, for example, is based on the gold that is in it if the country issuing the coin is on a gold standard. Since gold in this case is standard money, it serves as the basis for establishing the value of other kinds of money.

Representative money consists of paper certificates. For instance, a silver certificate is representative money; it is not standard money, but merely a claim to standard money. The reason for using representative money is to keep metallic money out of circulation. Paper money is usually considered more satisfactory for circulation and less costly to use. These paper certificates serve the same purposes as coins. Each piece of representative money certifies that the government is holding in its treasury enough actual metallic money to pay every holder of a certificate if that holder wishes metallic money instead of the certificate. Under the plan of issuing representative money, the government must keep in its vaults exactly the same amount of metallic money as the total value of the certificates it issues.

Theoretically, under this system of issuing money, the holder of a certificate can obtain standard money on demand. A government may, however, under special laws *nationalize* the metallic or standard money, such as gold or silver. In the United States gold has been nationalized, which means that it is not legal for any individual to possess gold coins, gold bullion, or gold certificates. These gold items are held by the Federal Government and the Federal reserve banks. By nationalizing this money, the

MONEY IN THE U.S.A.

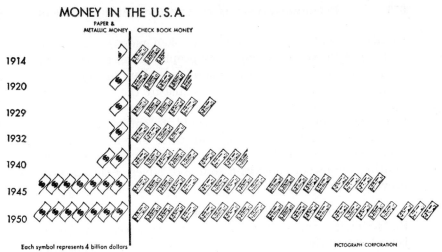

PAPER &
METALLIC MONEY | CHECK BOOK MONEY

1914

1920

1929

1932

1940

1945

1950

Each symbol represents 4 billion dollars

PICTOGRAPH CORPORATION

Government prevents the hoarding of it and gains certain controls.

While the holder of a certificate may be assured that the issuing government has in its vaults metal equal in value to the amount of the certificates issued, he cannot always obtain the actual metallic money. The security behind the certificate is, however, just as good as ever. All people who hold the certificates within their own countries are in the same relative position. Actual metallic money is therefore used largely only for exchange between nations.

Credit money is actually not money in the sense of standard money or representative money. It represents the promise of a government or of a bank to pay money on demand. Neither the government nor the bank that issues the credit money is required to keep on hand an amount of standard money equal to the total value of the notes in circulation.

Token money consists of coins that contain metal of less value than that indicated by them. These coins are usually made of silver, nickel, or copper. Token money is used largely for making change and is not available in large denominations. Inasmuch as gold coins are no longer in circulation, all coins that are now in circulation are token money.

The theory of issuing token money is that it may be exchanged on demand for standard money. When monetary

655

metals are nationalized, however, token money cannot be exchanged for standard money by people within the country.

The actual value of the metal in token money must always be less than the value indicated by the coin. If, for instance, the actual silver in a twenty-five cent piece were worth fifty cents, silver coins would go out of circulation and would be hoarded because of their silver content, or would be melted and sold as uncoined silver. Laws prohibiting the use of coins as a source of silver could scarcely prevent such action.

Paper Currency Now Being Issued. In the United States the following types of notes, or paper money, are being issued currently: (a) United States notes, (b) silver certificates, and (c) Federal reserve notes. The United States notes are commonly referred to as "greenbacks." Upon them will be found an inscription similar to the following: "The United States of America will pay to the bearer one dollar." Silver certificates in denominations of $1, $5, and $10 are issued by the United States Treasury against standard silver dollars held in the Treasury. Federal reserve notes are issued by Federal reserve banks in denominations of $5, $10, $20, $50, $100, $500, $1,000, $5,000, and $10,000. These are secured by deposits of gold certificates and other securities held by the Federal reserve banks.

Standards of Money. The money values of the civilized world are based upon either gold or silver. Most countries are on either the gold standard or the silver standard. A few countries follow a bimetal policy; that is, both gold and silver are used in one country as the standard, or measure of value, of money.

In a country on the gold standard, the value of standard money is based upon the actual gold content. Under an act of May, 1933, amended in January, 1934, the President was given the authority to change the gold content of the dollar. Under the President's proclamation the gold content of a dollar was reduced from $25\frac{8}{10}$ to $15\frac{5}{21}$ grains of gold, nine-tenths fine. The law further provided that the lowest limit to which the gold content could be reduced was

U. S. Treasury Department

United States bullion depository, Fort Knox, Kentucky.

50 per cent of the original amount, or 12.9 grains of gold, nine-tenths fine.

The intended result of changing the gold content of the dollar was to reduce the value of the dollar in terms of goods offered for sale. Prices would consequently rise in terms of dollars. This condition is referred to as *inflation*. Although inflation from a cause such as this is not always immediately noticeable within a country, the effect is immediately noticeable in the buying and selling between nations. When the United States dollar was devalued and prices were inflated, the people in the United States had to pay more for imported goods in terms of dollars than they were accustomed to pay before the change in the gold content of the dollar. This result was due to the fact that the foreign person who sold goods to someone in the United States expected to be paid for his goods in terms of gold. When the dollar became worth less in terms of gold, the American buyer had to pay more dollars for the goods that he imported.

The primary effect on the consumer of devaluing of the dollar and the consequent inflating of prices is that the purchasing power of his dollars of income and savings decreases. The effect on foreign trade is that it is more difficult to import goods but easier to export them. When the dollar of the United States becomes worth less in terms of foreign money, foreign money will buy more after inflation than it did before inflation.

Some countries use silver as the standard. Unless the prices of gold and silver are established by governmental control, the relative supply of and demand for gold and silver regulates the ratio of the values of these metals.

Purchasing Power of Money. Prices of commodities and services vary inversely with the purchasing power or value of money. In other words, when general price levels are high, we say that the value of money is low. When prices are high, it takes more money to buy the same amount of goods than it did when prices were low. If prices begin to fall, we say that the purchasing power of money increases, for the dollar will buy more than it would formerly buy at the higher prices. The purchasing power or value of money is measured by the quantity of goods that a given amount of money will buy. Of course, the quantity of goods a dollar will buy depends upon the price of the goods.

The purchasing power of the dollar at one time is frequently compared with the purchasing power of a dollar at another time by a device known as a *price index number*. The U. S. Department of Commerce and the Bureau of Labor Statistics prepare price index numbers on many groups of commodities.

PURCHASING POWER OF THE DOLLAR
Index, 1935-1939 = 100

As Measured by:	May, 1950
Wholesale prices	51.6
Consumer prices	59.3
Retail food prices	49.9

Source: U. S. Department of Commerce.

The above figures mean that on an average a dollar would buy 51.6 per cent as much goods at wholesale prices in May, 1950, as it did in the 1935 to 1939 period, and that in consumer goods a dollar would buy 59.3 per cent as much as during the base period of 1935-1939. This decrease in the purchasing power of the dollar gave rise to such expressions as the "fifty-nine cent dollar."

The relative value of the dollar is affected by (a) the supply of and the demand for commodities that money will buy, and (b) the forces that affect money itself. The control of these forces presents a delicate and complicated problem that has never been solved completely by economists because of the presence of many uncontrollable factors. It is unquestionably true, however, that supply and demand help to regulate the prices of commodities and the relative value of money.

The *quantity theory of money* assumes that the value of money varies inversely with the quantity of money or credit in existence and the rapidity of its turnover. In other words, if the quantity of money is doubled, prices double; and the value of a dollar is cut in half, provided the rate of turnover remains constant.

When prices are controlled through governmental regulation or by other means, the quantity of money may have little, if any, effect on prices. For instance, if the government puts a ceiling on prices, as in World War II, an increase in the quantity of money will not cause an increase in prices in the same ratio.

What Is Credit?   The word *credit* has many meanings. We ordinarily think of credit as the privilege extended to a person who buys on account with a promise to pay the amount due under the usual terms of the sale. In this sense credit involves capacity to pay and implies character. The most important meaning of credit relates to the transfer of goods or funds with a promise of future payment. When goods are exchanged on credit, not money, but a promise to pay, is given for the goods. These promises are usually stated in terms of money. It is estimated that from 85 to 90 per cent of all business transactions involve the use of credit.

Credit may be classified as producers' credit and consumers' credit. *Producers' credit* is used for productive operations, such as a manufacturer buying more machinery so he can produce more or a farmer buying grain and other feed to fatten cattle. Both of these and similar uses of credit increase the borrower's productivity and earning power. *Consumers' credit* is used to buy automobiles, fur coats, furniture, and sometimes consumable commodities such as food. Consumers' credit does not increase the borrower's productivity or his earning power.

Credit also involves an element of time and some tangible evidence of the indebtedness. The evidence of the indebtedness is referred to as a *credit instrument*. There are many forms of these instruments. For instance, a dealer in New York sells a shipment of imported rugs to a merchant in Chicago. The dealer in New York believes that the merchant in Chicago can pay for the rugs and that he will pay when the amount is due. By making the sale on credit, the New York dealer shows his belief in the capacity to pay and the character of the Chicago merchant. An ordinary invoice is one type of credit instrument that can be used in a transaction of this kind.

Credit Instruments. Any instrument that is used instead of metallic or paper money is a *credit instrument*. The most common type of credit instrument is the *bank check*. A person accepts a check with the confidence that it will be honored by the bank when it is presented for payment.

Checks are also used in transactions between banks. These are called *bank drafts*. The illustration on page 351 is a bank draft. Checks of this type are also sold to individuals who might have difficulty in transferring money by their personal checks. A bank draft is an order in which one bank directs another bank to pay a certain sum of the money it has on deposit in the latter. Suppose, for example, a person in St. Louis wishes to pay one thousand dollars to someone in San Francisco. He can go to a bank in St. Louis and buy a draft drawn on a San Francisco bank and made payable to his creditor. When the person in San Francisco receives the draft, he can collect the amount from any bank in San Francisco. If the man in St. Louis sent his personal check, it might not be honored because he is not known there. The bank draft will be honored, however, because the bank is known.

Bill of exchange is a general term that includes commercial *time drafts* or *sight drafts*, *trade acceptances*, and

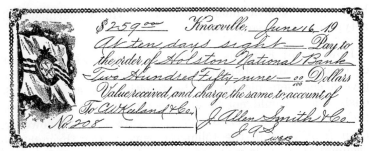

A commercial time draft.

checks. Three original parties are involved in a bill of exchange: (a) the party who gives or issues the bill of exchange is called the *drawer*; (b) the party who is ordered to pay is called the *drawee*; (c) the party to whom payment is to be made is called the *payee*.

In the case of a bank draft, Bank A issues an order for Bank B to pay a certain sum of money to a third party, Mr. C. In the case of an ordinary check, Mr. A orders Bank B to pay a certain sum of money to a third party, Mr. C. In the case of a time draft or sight draft, the drawer orders the drawee to pay a certain sum to the payee, usually a bank. The forms shown in the illustrations on page 344 and on this page are a check, a time draft, and a sight draft.

A *note* is a promise to pay to another a certain sum of money for value received. The time and the method of payment are indicated in the note. Interest may or may not be involved. Promissory notes are issued by individuals and

A commercial sight draft.

businesses. Credit money issued by the Government is a type of promissory note.

How Credit Expands the Use of Money. The expansion of credit through banking is presented here in order to give a complete picture of the functions of credit. Obviously, there would not be enough metallic money to serve the needs of business. Business operations have, however, been facilitated in the following ways: (a) through the accumulation of deposits of money in banks, (b) through the process of lending money on the basis of these accumulated deposits, (c) through the issuance of notes (money) by Federal reserve banks, (d) through various other forms of credit. From this outline it is evident that banks perform an important function in expanding the use of money.

The following simple bank statement shows the status of the Central National Bank at a specific time:

Balance Sheet of Central National Bank

ASSETS:
Cash ....$ 80,000
Bonds 120,000
Deposits in Federal Reserve
  Bank 20,000
Equipment 20,000
Building 60,000

Total Assets $300,000

LIABILITIES AND OWNERSHIP:
Amount Due Depositors $100,000
Capital Stock 150,000
Surplus 50,000

Total Liabilities and
  Ownership $300,000

The American Manufacturing Company, a customer of this bank, obtains a loan of $10,000 for three months at 6 per cent and gives as security its promissory note. The bank deducts (discounts) its interest in advance and gives the customer credit for $9,850 in its account. The latter may use this credit by writing checks to the extent of $9,850. The note, which is a credit instrument, has become an asset of the bank, for it represents a promise of the American Manufacturing Company to pay $10,000 at the end of three months. After the loan has been made, the statement of the bank appears as shown on page 663.

It is evident that there has been no increase in the amount of money, but there has been an increase in the use of money. The deposits are almost 10 per cent larger than they were previously.

Balance Sheet of Central National Bank

ASSETS:		LIABILITIES AND OWNERSHIP:	
Cash	$ 80,000	Amount Due Depositors	$109,850
Bonds	120,000	Capital Stock	150,000
Deposits in Federal Reserve		Surplus	50,000
Bank	20,000	Undivided Profits (Interest)..	150
Loans to Customers	10,000		
Equipment	20,000		
Building	60,000		
		Total Liabilities and	
Total Assets	$310,000	Ownership	$310,000

Since this bank is a member of the Federal Reserve System, it can sell the note of the American Manufacturing Company at a Federal reserve bank. When the note is sold to the Federal reserve bank, it is *rediscounted*. The Federal Reserve Bank Board regulates the rediscount rate. Suppose, for example, the note is rediscounted in this case at 3 per cent. The bank accepts Federal reserve notes (lawful money) for $5,000 and leaves the remainder on deposit in the Federal reserve bank. The statement of the Central National Bank then is as follows:

Balance Sheet of Central National Bank

ASSETS:		LIABILITIES AND OWNERSHIP:	
Cash	$ 85,000	Amount Due Depositors	$109,850
Bonds	120,000	Capital Stock	150,000
Deposits in Federal Reserve		Surplus	50,000
Bank	24,925	Undivided Profits	75
Equipment	20,000		
Building	60,000		
		Total Liabilities and	
Total Assets	$309,925	Ownership	$309,925

This process of expanding the use of money by means of credit could continue indefinitely. The outstanding loans and the deposits of the average bank change from day to day and week to week. The relations between the member bank and the Federal reserve bank also change constantly. A member bank is not required to maintain a certain cash reserve for its deposits, but it must keep a minimum reserve in the Federal reserve bank of the district in which it is located. Under present laws the expansion of credit can continue until the reserve in the Federal reserve bank drops to a specified percentage of the bank's deposits.

Credit is also expanded in other ways. Let us assume that individuals go to a store and buy on account. The merchant obtains credit from the wholesaler to buy new merchandise; the wholesaler obtains credit from the manufacturer to buy merchandise; the manufacturer borrows money from the bank. He does not receive actual cash, but receives credit to his account on which he can write checks. Most of these transactions, from the individual consumer's credit through to the manufacturer, are handled by the use of checks, making it necessary to use little currency in the transactions. When merchants, manufacturers, and banks curtail credit, business transactions decline in volume.

The illustration below shows how people place their money in various institutions and how this money is loaned out again. For example, when one buys life insurance he actually becomes a creditor of the life insurance company. The life insurance company lends the money to others.

Idle money does not stimulate business; but if money is used to buy goods or is lent for productive purposes, production is increased, more workers are needed, and business is improved. The illustration below shows how the money of individuals is lent to various institutions and is then used for various productive purposes.

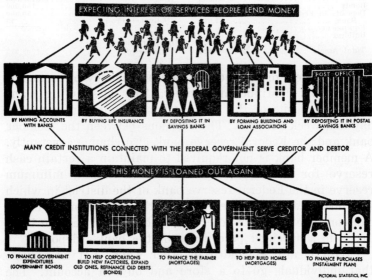

From Maxwell S. Stewart, *Debts—Good or Bad?*
The Public Affairs Committee, Inc., New York City

Creditor and debtor relationships in expanding the use of money.

Advantages and Disadvantages of Credit. After a system of credit is established, it is impossible for an economic system to operate on its existing scale without the use of continued credit. The following are some of the advantages of credit:

(a) Credit reduces the use of precious metals in coins.
(b) Credit saves time and expense by providing a safer and more convenient means of completing transactions.
(c) Credit facilitates production by making funds available for productive enterprises. For instance, a person without funds, but with ability and character, can obtain credit to use in producing new wealth.
(d) Credit facilitates the accumulation and the use of money for productive processes. An individual may not be able to use his savings funds for productive purposes, but he can safely put them to use by lending them to some productive enterprise.

We cannot overlook the disadvantages of credit. These disadvantages are not inherent in the system, but arise from the abuse of the system. They are as follows:

(a) Credit sometimes encourages speculation. Those who have charge of the savings of other people sometimes become careless and unscrupulous in their eagerness to expand credit and thereby make a profit. Federal and state controls have been designed to prevent such loose practices. The most common safeguards are (1) restrictions as to types of loans that can be made by banks and other savings institutions, (2) requirements as to the amount of cash that must be kept available to pay depositors, (3) regulation of interest rates, (4) inspection of financial institutions, and (5) insurance of deposits.
(b) Credit sometimes causes extravagance and carelessness in the people who obtain it. Since the person who obtains credit is not using his own money but is using the money of other people, he should not fail to appreciate the trust of credit.
(c) Credit may expand certain industries so much that they become relatively too large or experience "mushroom" growth. Certain industries may grow too

rapidly on the basis of installment or other types of credit. Industrial expansion that takes place largely on the basis of consumer credit depends upon the consumer's *future* earning power. Should this future earning power fail to materialize, these industries are likely to experience a severe contraction of their business. If an industry bases its expansion on a large proportion of cash business, it is not likely to grow so rapidly, but is also not likely to experience a serious contraction of its business because of the curtailment of consumer purchasing power.

(d) Because business can be expanded rapidly or contracted rapidly through the use of credit, businessmen are quite susceptible to confidence or pessimism. Credit causes one businessman to be dependent upon others. In order to extend credit, he must have faith in other businessmen and faith in the future. If credit relations become strained, however, many businesses may fail and a business recession may set in.

Flow of Money. Money and credit give life to business. Without the use of money or credit, business could not use its machinery, could not hire workers, and could not buy transportation facilities. When money circulates normally, the economic system operates smoothly. When something interrupts the flow of money in any particular direction, the economic system is thrown out of balance. If people draw off money from the economic system without putting money or credit back into it, the system is retarded and sometimes broken down.

The illustration on page 667 shows the flow of money. It indicates the income and the expenditures. When too small a part of the income goes into the pockets of those who need commodities or when those who receive the income hoard it instead of spending it or lending it to others to spend, the essential flow of money is dried up. This condition helps to cause an economic depression.

This particular chart does not represent the exact amounts or proportions of money which flow through the

various channels. It does, however, show how the money
flows. For example, in recent years there has been an increasing amount of money drawn off through government
agencies. As taxes draw off money for governmental agencies, there is a less proportion available for other purposes.
Credit plays a prominent part in this flow of money. Ex-

THE ROUND FLOW OF MONEY—INCOME AND EXPENDITURE

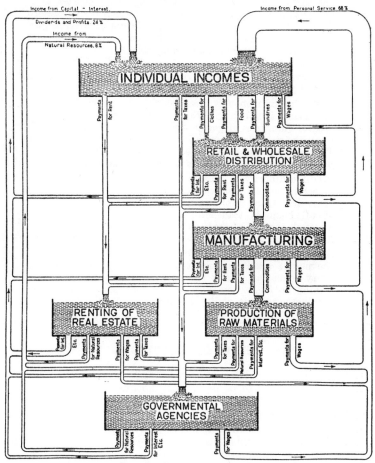

Reproduced from "Some Problems in Current Economics,"
M. C. Rorty, McGraw-Hill Book Co.

The circulation of money is the lifeblood of business.

pansion and contraction of credit therefore tend to regulate
the flow of income and expenditure.

What We Need to Know About the Functions of Money and Credit

1. Money serves as a medium of exchange (that is, it enables
   one to exchange his labor in a factory for groceries without working for the grocer); as a measure or standard
   of value; and as a means of accumulating or storing purchasing power for future use. Modern business could not
   be carried on without money and credit.
2. Several kinds of money are in circulation. They are:
   standard, representative, credit, and token. The Federal
   Government controls the monetary system.
3. The value of money is measured by the amount of goods
   or services it will buy. When the value of money is high,
   greater quantities of goods can be purchased with a dollar;
   when the value is low, smaller quantities can be purchased.
   Thus, an inverse relation exists between the purchasing
   power of money and prices of commodities and services.
4. Credit ordinarily is considered to be the power or ability
   to secure money, goods, or services on a promise to return
   equivalent value in the future. Approximately 90 per cent
   of all business transactions involve the use of credit.
   Through the use of credit instruments, banks and business
   firms expand the use of money.
5. An understanding of the advantages and disadvantages of
   the use of credit is important to every producer and to
   every consumer. Many consumers do not realize that obtaining credit on the purchase of consumable goods does
   not increase their ability to earn.

TEXTBOOK QUESTIONS

1. Why has the need for money arisen?
2. If money ceases to be of value, who are the only persons to
   possess wealth?
3. What is standard money?
4. What is representative money?
5. Under what circumstances can a person who possesses representative money obtain silver coins for it?
6. What is credit money?
7. What is token money?
8. What are the two most common standards of money?

9. How does a change in the gold content of a dollar affect prices?
10. What is the relation between value of money and prices?
11. What is meant by a "fifty-nine cent dollar"?
12. What is the quantity theory of money?
13. What use is made of producers' credit?
14. What use is made of consumers' credit?
15. Explain what is meant by a credit instrument.
16. What is the most common type of credit instrument?
17. When a business borrows from a bank, how does the transaction affect the financial statement of the bank?
18. What can a national bank do with notes that it obtains from businesses and individuals that borrow from it?
19. What are some of the advantages of credit?
20. What are some of the disadvantages of credit?
21. With what can the flow of money be compared?

DISCUSSION QUESTIONS

1. "Money is a standard of value." Explain this statement.
2. (a) Is a bond wealth? (b) Is a silver certificate wealth?
3. Why do you think it would not be desirable to use iron as a standard of money?
4. What is the difference between standard and representative money?
5. Why are postage stamps sometimes accepted as money?
6. What are the types of paper money currently issued in the United States?
7. From the point of view of foreign trade, what, in your opinion, would be the effect of a sudden decrease in the value of the United States dollar?
8. Why did the purchasing power of a dollar fall from 1939 to 1950?
9. In what way does the use of credit act just as an increase in the amount of money?
10. What is the difference between a bank check and a bank draft?
11. Study the balance sheet of the Central National Bank that is shown on page 662. Explain what would be the effect on the depositors (a) if $10,000 worth of additional stock were sold, and (b) if the bank used $50,000 of its cash to buy an equal amount of its own stock from its stockholders.
12. Why do you think some bankers need to keep more cash than others in order to be sure that they have enough to pay depositors on demand?

13. Explain the function of banks in expanding credit.
14. From a study of the chart on page 667 showing the round flow of money, what will happen to our economic system if the amount of flow of income from personal services is reduced as much as 50 per cent?

PROBLEMS

1. Make a chart of the purchasing power of a dollar from 1914 to 1950. Figures may be obtained from the *World Almanac* or government publications.
2. List and define as many credit instruments as you can find.
3. There is about 28.2 billion dollars worth of money now printed and coined. Bank deposits total 155.2 billion dollars. How can there be on deposit more than five times as much money as there is in existence?
4. Refer to the first balance sheet of the Central National Bank on page 662. Make a new statement, assuming that depositors have withdrawn $70,000 in cash.
5. Refer to the first balance sheet of the Central National Bank on page 662. This bank lends $100,000 to customers at 6 per cent for thirty days and deducts the interest in advance. Prepare a new balance sheet showing the conditions of the bank at this particular time. Assume that the customers receive the loans in the form of credits to their accounts.

COMMUNITY PROBLEMS AND PROJECTS

1. From a bank, a Federal reserve bank, your local chamber of commerce, the United States Treasury, or from any other source, obtain the latest information in regard to foreign exchange rates. If it is possible, make a comparison with the rates ten years ago. Report your conclusions.
2. Take some local example, such as a retail store, and trace the flow of credit back through to the source of raw materials. Illustrate your report with a sketch showing the various hands through which the product has traveled and the various persons and institutions that have probably provided credit.
3. From your school or public library, or any other source, find out how payments are made between the businessmen in one country and the businessmen in another. Write a report based on your findings.

Chapter 38

How Values and Prices Are Established

Purpose of the Chapter. Every person is affected by prices. Prices affect wages, interest rates, savings, the buying of commodities, the making of investments, and many other activities. A study of this chapter will, for instance, show how a person may receive an increase in wages, but because of an increase in the prices of goods he may not be able to buy so much with his wages as he formerly was able to obtain. Few people realize the full significance of prices and why they change. In fact, there are so many influences on prices that even our experts in economics and finance sometimes have difficulty in determining how prices will change and what effect prices will have on other interests. Nevertheless, there are certain fundamentals that do not change. These should be understood by everyone. The purpose of this chapter is, therefore, to present a background of information about prices that will be useful to everyone, especially in the process of buying.

Barter System Versus Price System. In the days of barter, the person who produced wheat traded his wheat to the person who made saddles. The person who raised cows traded his cows to the person who raised flax. The person who made shoes traded his shoes to the farmer who produced potatoes. There was no single medium of exchange. A person enjoyed a variety of the necessities of life in proportion to his ability to produce and to exchange what he had produced for other things that he needed and wanted.

In the days of barter the value of wheat as compared to that of shoes depended largely upon the supply and the degree of usefulness of each product. When wheat was plentiful and shoes were scarce and difficult to produce, a considerable amount of wheat was required in return for shoes. When people found that a great many others had

671

wheat to trade, but very few people had shoes to trade, more people began to produce shoes. As the supply of shoes increased, more shoes were required in return for wheat. Under the barter system, therefore, the supply of products regulated to a large extent the relative values of products. When the demand for a product was great, the product could be traded easily for other products. As the demand decreased, trading became more difficult.

Under the *price system,* the product one makes or one's labor is exchanged for money, and the money is used to buy goods and services. *Price* is the exchange value of goods or services stated in terms of money. For example, the price of wheat is the amount of money that is required to buy a bushel of wheat. All prices are stated in terms of money. Thus money serves not only as the medium for exchanging one kind of goods or services for another, but it is a measure or standard of value by which prices are determined. Under the price system, a general rise in all prices or a general fall in all prices may occur. A general rise or fall in prices means that the purchasing power or value of money has changed. Inflation results in higher prices in general, which means that the value or purchasing power of money has decreased.

Price is a powerful influence in our lives. In periods of rising prices, the man who has plenty of money can pay the prices of goods and services. A man whose expenses are almost as great as his income, however, will find that he must choose the goods and services he wants and needs most. He probably will continue to produce as much goods as he did before the increase in prices; but until his money income is increased, he will be unable to buy as many goods and services as he did before the general price rise.

Relation Between Production and Price. No businessman wishes to produce unless he receives enough money to pay all his costs. Costs include wages, raw materials, insurance, rent, interest, transportation, and many other items. Some businessmen will continue temporarily to produce goods without profit in the hope that they will eventually make enough profit to repay them for their previous losses.

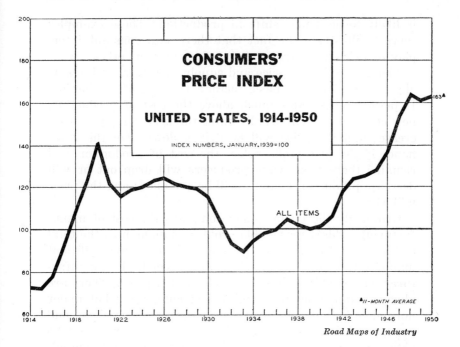

CONSUMERS'
PRICE INDEX

UNITED STATES, 1914-1950

INDEX NUMBERS, JANUARY, 1939=100

ALL ITEMS

▲ 11-MONTH AVERAGE

Road Maps of Industry

Since many producers have certain unavoidable fixed costs, continuing to produce, even at a loss, may involve less loss than stopping altogether. For example, a wheat farmer may lose money if he gets only seventy-five cents a bushel for his wheat, but he cannot afford to quit work and let his wheat stay unharvested in the field because he would lose much more. Production without profit cannot, however, be continued indefinitely.

Price tends to govern production. For instance, if the price of wheat goes up while the price of corn and hogs remains the same, as many farmers as possible will shift to the production of wheat. Then the production of wheat will rise, while the production of corn and hogs will decrease.

Production, in turn, tends to govern price. If too many farmers have shifted to the production of wheat, as indicated above, the supply of wheat will increase and the price will go down. Because of the decrease in the supply of corn and hogs, the price of corn and hogs will rise. Then there is likely to be a new shift in production. These examples serve to illustrate the fact that there is a constant interplay of price and supply, each influencing the other.

The fluctuation in price and supply, however, will generally be steadied by a basic factor: the cost of production. If price long remains much above the cost of production, new competitors will usually enter the field; supply will increase; and the price will be driven down. On the other hand, if the price falls below the cost of production and remains there long, some producers will drop out or will decrease production; supply will be curtailed; and the price will rise.

Ordinarily the businessman computes the cost of manufacturing, adds a reasonable profit, and announces the total as the price of his goods. If the price is based upon efficient manufacture and if conditions are normal, the manufacturer will be able to sell the goods at that price. There are always competitors who will sell at cut prices; but under normal conditions efficient manufacturers can go ahead and produce without lowering prices because the person who cuts prices and thus eliminates profit for a temporary advantage cannot long endure such a situation.

Production cannot be continued indefinitely unless the selling price is greater than the costs of production. More efficient methods of production permit the lowering of the selling price. It is for this reason that the first producers driven out of a field are those who are the least efficient. Their departure may cut the supply enough to steady prices above the production costs of the more efficient.

As a summary: high prices stimulate production, low prices discourage it; high production tends to depress prices, low production tends to raise prices.

Our Federal Government has influenced both the price and the quantity of production of agricultural products through subsidy and guaranteed prices. A *subsidy* is a direct payment to the producer. There is a further discussion of government controls later in this chapter.

Relation Between Price and Goods Offered for Sale. The amount of goods and services offered for sale is governed considerably by the price. If the price is favorable, the producer will offer large quantities of his product for sale. If the price is not favorable, he will not produce. Similarly, a farmer may have harvested 10,000 bushels of wheat. If the price of wheat is $2.30 a bushel, he may sell all of his wheat; but if it it is only $1.50 a bushel, he may sell only enough to supply him with sufficient cash until he can dispose of the rest at a better price. A southern cotton-grower may have harvested 1,000 bales of cotton. If he can get 30 cents a pound for his cotton, he may sell all the bales; but if he can get only 12 cents a pound, he may be willing to sell only 500 bales. Price therefore tends to regulate supply.

Theoretically, *supply* represents the quantity of *goods offered for sale*. If the supply increases—in other words, if more goods are offered for sale—the price tends to be lowered. If the supply continues to increase, the price will eventually reach a level that closely approximates the cost of production. When the price goes below this point, producers frequently fail and go into bankruptcy, for they cannot continue to produce without profit. The supply then tends to decrease, and the price becomes more stable. As the supply decreases, the price rises.

An opportune time to buy is when the supply is great and the demand is low. This condition is called a *buyer's market*. When the demand is high and the supply is low, the condition is referred to as a *seller's market*. In the first case the buyer has the bargaining advantage; in the second the seller has this advantage.

How Consumption Is Influenced by Prices. The study of the effect of prices on production throws some light on the effect of prices on buying. The person who buys goods wants to pay the lowest price possible. While, in general, the consumer may recognize that it is best for all producers to receive a fair price, in a specific case he is probably not particularly interested in whether the price he is paying is less than the cost of production. This is because he is selfishly interested in getting all he can for his money.

As a general rule, a person will buy a commodity when that commodity will be more useful to him than some other commodity or service that the money would buy. For instance, a person may admire a rare, imported vase. He may not buy it for personal use, however, because he feels that the money he would have to spend could be used more wisely in some other manner. Suppose, however, that the price of the vase is lowered considerably. He may then decide that he can afford to buy the vase at the lowered price.

As the price of a commodity increases, the number of people who buy that commodity at the price asked decreases. Take the example of clothing. Normally an increase in the price of clothing will reduce the amount of clothing bought unless the incomes of people are increased. As a general rule, the quantity of the article that is sold will decrease as the price rises, and will increase as the price drops. This general principle is, however, subject to modifications because of the influence of demand, supply, competition, monopoly, money, credit, and various other factors.

Relation Between Demand and Price. From the discussion of supply and demand, it will be seen that *demand* is the amount of goods that people will buy at a particular price and under a particular set of circumstances. The desire for or the demand for goods may be influenced by factors of utility, seasonal changes, advertising, changes in personal taste, social position, habits, training, earning power, wealth, sex, and age. The demand for some goods responds considerably to price changes. This kind of demand is called *elastic*. The demand for some goods changes very little as the price changes. This kind of demand is called *inelastic*.

As an example, elastic demand is the type in which the amount of goods and services bought increases readily as the price decreases, as in the case of automobiles. Many of the motor-car manufacturers have discovered the fact that, by reducing the price of their cars, they can sell a much larger number. The sale of a larger number will enable them to produce cars at lower per unit cost. Their reduction in price in many instances has resulted in their making more profit than they made at the previous higher price.

A hypothetical example of the elastic demand for automobiles will serve to illustrate the general principle of elastic demand. The following table shows (a) the decreasing prices of a car, (b) the number of cars that can be sold, (c) the total receipts from sales, and (d) the profits from sales:

PRICE PER CAR	NUMBER THAT CAN BE SOLD	TOTAL RECEIPTS FROM SALES	PROFITS FROM SALES
$2,400	250,000	$600,000,000	$36,000,000
2,000	375,000	750,000,000	52,500,000
1,600	500,000	800,000,000	64,000,000
1,200	750,000	900,000,000	45,000,000

The principle of elastic demand.

It is evident from this analysis that the reduction in price proves profitable up to the point where the price is approximately $1,600 a car. Any further reduction in the selling price of the car results in a decrease in the profit.

An inelastic demand is the type of demand in which the amount of goods and services bought does not change, or shows relatively little change, when the price changes. For instance, a decrease in the price of bread may cause only a slight increase in the demand. The profit becomes less at the reduced price if the cost of production remains about the same. A hypothetical example will serve best to illustrate the principle of an inelastic demand. The following table shows an example of the relation between (a) the price, (b) the quantity that can be sold, (c) the total receipts from sales, and (d) the profits from sales:

PRICE OF A LOAF OF BREAD	NUMBER OF LOAVES THAT CAN BE SOLD	TOTAL RECEIPTS FROM SALES	PROFITS FROM SALES
10¢	6,000,000	$600,000	$60,000
8¢	6,250,000	500,000	40,000
6¢	6,500,000	390,000	5,000
4¢	6,750,000	270,000	Loss, $20,000

The principle of inelastic demand.

From these analyses we see that demand and price are interrelated and that demand has an important effect on price. Demand for a commodity tends to make the price increase when the supply is limited. This tendency prevails not only for commodities having a so-called inelastic demand but in a modified degree for those having an elastic demand. If, for example, there is a scarcity of wheat as well as of bread, the price of bread rises, for the producers know that they can expect a relatively constant demand. In the case of elastic demand, however, the producers are less likely to raise the prices of products any more than necessary, for they know that when prices are raised the demand decreases.

Even in the case of an inelastic demand these rules do not hold strictly true when prices get too high. Although the demand for bread is relatively inelastic, regardless of price, yet if the price were to go high enough in proportion to the price of potatoes, poor people would shift to the buying of potatoes as a substitute. This represents *substitution* as a principle of economics.

How Competition Affects Prices. Competition is one means of protection for the consumer, for it helps to minimize prices, to promote efficiency, and to assure buyers that they can obtain what they want at the time they want it. Fundamentally we operate on the basis of a competitive system; but as will be discussed later, we also have some regulated monopolies and occasionally price controls, which set the maximum prices allowed on various goods.

Under free competition the cost of production is an important regulatory factor in determining prices. The price of goods usually fluctuates above and below the cost of production. No producer can persistently sell goods at prices that are much higher than those of his competitors. If producers make too much profit—in other words, if they charge high prices—their customers will buy from competitors that sell at lower prices. New competitors may also enter the field. As a result of this competition, the high prices that were formerly charged will be reduced.

The efficient businessman makes more profit than the inefficient. The inefficient producer who cannot succeed in keeping his costs low finds that he cannot compete with the efficient producer. When he tries to lower his prices to compete with the efficient producer, he fails to make a profit and has to quit business.

Through competition, buyers tend to get goods at the lowest prices at which the goods can be produced. Of course, there are exceptions. Some people prefer to pay more than others. Wealthy persons frequently patronize stores where prices are higher than in ordinary stores. As a general rule, however, people will buy products at the lowest prices at which the products can be obtained.

The economic principle of substitution is also an important factor in the competitive system. If prices of cotton go to a high level, there is likely to be a shift to substitutes such as rayon. In a similar manner airlines may take passengers away from the railroads.

How Monopoly Affects Prices. In a few instances, a producer free from competition may have absolute power to determine the selling price by releasing for sale a supply of his goods or services that is less than the demand, thus keeping prices high. This situation is known as a *monopoly*. As there is no competition, the person who has the monopoly may try to charge what he pleases. He usually will limit production to keep prices artificially high. He undoubtedly will attempt to create demand and maintain demand so that he can get the prices he asks. Prices do not necessarily have any relation to the cost of production; rather, as has been explained, they are determined by supply and demand. Generally speaking, the price and the supply are regulated in relation to demand so that the person controlling the monopoly will obtain the greatest aggregate profit.

The telegraph and the telephone companies provide interesting examples of monopolies, or at least partial monopolies. If one telephone company has a monopoly on the telephone service in a particular city, it has control over the supply of that service. In the absence of any legal control, the telephone company could set its own rates. A rise in the rates would cause some people to quit using the telephone. If the rates were to continue to rise, the telephone company might lose so many customers that it would not be able to make a profit. State governments, however, reserve the right to regulate the rates, or prices, charged by such companies.

The production of diamonds is controlled largely by monopoly. The monopoly governs the price and keeps it high. As a result of a restriction in the supply, diamonds are in constant demand. The volume of sales is limited, however, by the high price. At the high price at which diamonds are sold, a large profit is made. If the price were lowered, the rate of profit would decrease, although the demand would increase. If the price were lowered still more, it would eventually reach a point at which the total sales would not pay the producers as much profit as that which resulted from the total sales at the former high price.

How Money Affects Prices. Money is our medium of exchange. It also serves as the basis for establishing the relative values of goods. The value of money is determined by the amount of goods that a dollar will purchase. When the value of a dollar is low, the dollar will not buy so much as when its value is high. In other words, money is cheap if it buys little, and dear if it buys much. When money changes in value, prices in general change.

On the other hand, a change in the price of a particular product does not necessarily influence the prices of other products. For example, the price of shoes may rise, but the prices of other commodities may stay at the same level. In other words, a rise in the price of shoes does not affect the prices of clothing, bread, and other commodities, since each product is evaluated individually in terms of money.

The illustration on page 673 is a chart that shows fluctuations in consumers' prices. In other words, it shows the purchasing power of the dollar and is therefore an indicator of the cost of living. The fact that the value of money does change is evidenced by this chart. A dollar will not buy so much when the cost of living is high as it will when the cost of living is low.

Two factors that affect the price level are (a) the quantity of money and (b) the rapidity with which money is used. The amount of money in the United States is less than the total value of goods that are being exchanged at a particular time. It is estimated that the total quantity of money in the United States changes hands from twenty to forty times a year. Ordinarily the quantity of money does not increase. The quantity has, however, been increased several times during the history of the United States by the issue of new paper money in the form of representative money or credit money. When there is an increase in the money available to buy goods and this money is used rapidly, prices tend to rise (a) because the supply of dollars is greater and (b) because the increase in rapidity with which money is used has the same effect as an increase in the amount. The general rise in prices is not always in proportion, however, to the increase in the supply of money or to the increase in turnover.

As a simple example let us consider an island on which there is a certain amount of money and a relatively inelastic supply of goods. The people who have money will soon establish the values of goods. If the total supply of money is suddenly doubled, however, everyone is in the same relative position. Each person has twice as much money as he formerly had, but he cannot buy twice as much goods because all the people want the goods in the same proportion as they formerly wanted them. If he attempts to buy goods with the same amount of money that he formerly used, he will find that other people are willing to pay more because they have more money. He will therefore have to pay just as much as anyone else. Prices in terms of money will rise because of the increase in the supply of money. In other words, increasing the supply of money has caused inflation of commodity prices.

How Credit Affects Prices. Increases and decreases in credit affect prices in very much the same way as increases and decreases in the supply of money. Since credit expands the use of money, it serves to increase the rapidity with which money is used. If a person has one hundred dollars to spend and borrows one hundred dollars, he has a total purchasing power of two hundred dollars. If everyone in the United States borrows in this way, the purchasing power in terms of dollars is doubled. If, at the same time, *the supply of products and services remains unchanged*, prices will increase because there is an increased amount of money and credit with which to buy products and services. When money and credit are increased, however, *the supply of products and services may also increase*. If the purchasing power continues to increase faster than the supply of goods and services, prices will continue to rise. When credit decreases, prices tend to decrease.

The prices of goods and their relation to the amount of money, the rapidity of use of money, and the amount of credit may be likened to weights on the ends of a pair of scales. Suppose that the scales are in balance, with the goods on one end and money and credit on the other end. If the amount of money decreases, the goods will drop in price. If the amount of money increases, the goods will rise in price. The same reactions will result from a decrease or an increase in the rapidity of use of money, or from a decrease or an increase in credit. Suppose, however, that as the prices of goods rise, the supply begins to increase. This increase in supply will tend to keep the prices down. If there is, however, a sufficiently large expansion of (a) the amount of money, (b) the rapidity of use of money, or (c) the use of credit, the prices will continue to rise. These three factors usually go hand in hand.

How Taxes Affect Prices. In general, high taxes on producers and distributors tend to increase prices, for taxes constitute part of the cost of producing any article or rendering any service. If a high tax is levied on a building, it must be included in computing the rent of the building. If a sales tax is levied on any item, such as gasoline, clothing, or drugs, regardless of the person against whom it has been assessed, it constitutes part of the cost of the product. Part or all of the taxes are usually passed on eventually to the consumer, either directly or indirectly, so that the levying of a tax against a particular product will eventually cause a rise in the price of that product. Sometimes all the tax or part of it is absorbed by the producer, resulting in a decrease in his profits. In the case of a tax on real estate, the result will be a decreased net profit from rentals if the owner does not pass the tax on to the tenant.

Such taxes as state and Federal income taxes that are levied on the incomes of individuals reduce the total purchasing power of consumers and hence tend to decrease the demand for goods and services. Decreasing the demand for these goods tends to lower prices.

Control of Prices. The preceding discussion of prices has assumed that there would be no control of prices. Nevertheless, prices are controlled to a certain extent by government, by businessmen, by farmers, and by workers.

The Federal Government owns and operates some industries and sometimes sets the prices of its commodities or services at less than cost and sometimes at more than cost. Among these industries owned by the Federal Government in which prices are controlled are the postal system, the Panama Canal, and the Tennessee Valley Authority. Some states also engage in production and distribution. States and municipalities own and operate many industrial and commercial enterprises, most of which are natural monopolies because they have the characteristics of a public utility. In many government-owned enterprises, prices are arbitrarily set almost without reference to costs. Deficits are paid from funds derived from taxation.

The rates for services given by public utilities, not government owned, are usually regulated or controlled by the state or Federal Government. For example, the rates for telephone service are under the control of the government. Likewise, railroad passenger rates and freight rates are controlled.

For many years, the various states have had regulations as to the maximum interest rates that may be charged for borrowed money. In more recent years the Board of Governors of the Federal Reserve System has exercised the power of control of discount or interest rates that Federal reserve banks may charge member banks. This control influences the rates of interest that banks charge their customers.

With the enactment of laws regulating the minimum wages per hour and the maximum hours per week for labor, a control of the price of labor has been in effect. Not all workers are covered by the laws, but the wages of all are influenced.

At various times, primarily since 1930, the Federal Government has extended its powers to control prices because of either a real or purported economic emergency. In 1933, the National Recovery Administration was created primarily to establish codes designed to provide for minimum prices and some control of the volume of production of industry. About the same time, the Secretary of Agriculture was empowered to set up a quantity restriction on the production of certain farm crops. If this quantity restriction on production was agreed upon by the growers of the crop, then the Government would make parity payments to the farmers if the market price of the crop fell below the established parity figure. This agreement to limit production and this guarantee of a specified minimum price constitute, of course, control through *price supports*.

Another phase of price supports for farmers is crop insurance. If market prices are lower than parity (government guaranteed price), the farmer may store his crop in a government-controlled warehouse and borrow from the Government a certain per cent of the parity value of the crop. If the price rises above the parity price guaranteed by the Government, the farmer may sell his crop, pay off his loan, and keep the difference. If the price does not rise above parity, he may sell at market price and the Government will pay him the difference between the price he obtained and parity price.

During World War II the Emergency Price Control Act regulated maximum prices for most goods. The maximum prices allowed were called *price ceilings*. The regulations affected the producers of raw materials, manufacturers, wholesalers, and retailers but did not include farm commodities, wages of labor, or the compensation of professional workers (wages were restricted through the War Labor Board). The regulations were administered by the Office of Price Administration, commonly known as OPA.

Price control, subsidies, grants of funds to certain types of industry, and government ownership of industry are

---

What We Should Know About Prices and How They Are Determined

1. Barter is exchanging directly one product or service for another; under the price system, one exchanges his products or services for money and then uses the money to buy the things he wants whenever he chooses.

2. Price is the amount of money that is required to obtain a product or service. For example, the amount of money required to buy a pair of shoes is the price of the shoes.

3. A close relationship exists between the quantity of production and price. As prices increase, the volume of production tends to increase; and as the volume of production increases, prices tend to decrease because of the increase in supply.

4. The supply of a given commodity is represented by the quantity offered for sale. When supply is high and demand is low, we have a buyer's market; when demand is high and supply low, a seller's market.

5. The price of a commodity or service influences the quantity that will be used. Thus, if prices are high, ordinarily smaller amounts will be consumed; if prices are low, there will be a tendency to use more.

6. Commodities or services for which little relationship exists between the demand by consumers and the price are said to have an inelastic demand; those for which a considerable relationship exists, an elastic demand.

7. Competition tends to protect the consumer by forcing a reasonable relationship between costs of production and distribution and the price asked.

8. Purchasing power is influenced greatly by the supply of money and by the amount of credit. Both affect prices.

9. Taxes on producers tend to increase costs of production and hence increase prices; taxes on personal income reduce consumers' purchasing power and hence reduce demand for consumer goods.

10. With the trend of increasing government powers, Federal authority to control prices of rent, wages, interest, commodities, and services is being increasingly asserted.

among the most important economic problems with which
the American people are faced at the present time.

Organized groups representing various aspects of production, distribution, and consumption attempt to obtain governmental protection or regulation on their behalf. Labor,
professional, business, and farm groups practically all seek
some kind of Federal legislation primarily to give them an
economic advantage. Some of the legislation is undoubtedly
desirable, and some is necessary. However, from the
early days of the Roman Empire to the present, attempts
to control price and to regulate income have created many
other problems.

As citizens, we vote in state and national elections on
economic issues. It is highly important that we understand
clearly the issues having to do with prices, subsidies, and
ownership so that we may have a basis for intelligent
voting.

TEXTBOOK QUESTIONS

1. Under the barter system what was the medium of exchange?
2. Under a barter system could there be any general rise in
   prices?
3. What effect does price have on production?
4. What effect does production have on price?
5. Explain how the cost of production tends to govern price.
6. How does supply affect prices?
7. What constitutes the supply of any product?
8. What is a buyer's market?
9. What is a seller's market?
10. In general, how does price affect consumption?
11. Explain in a general way what we mean by *demand*.
12. (a) What are the two types of demand? (b) Explain each.
13. Explain the economic principle of substitution.
14. In what ways does competition protect and aid the consumer?
15. In what way does competition regulate prices?
16. What effect does monopoly have on prices?
17. If you had a monopoly, in what manner would you adjust
    your prices?
18. In what way is the value of money determined?
19. If money changes in value, what happens to prices?
20. In what way does the use of credit affect prices?
21. How do taxes affect prices?
22. Explain two different kinds of price control.

DISCUSSION QUESTIONS

1. If we are to have an ideal economic society, why is it absolutely necessary for the prices of goods and the prices of wages to remain relatively stationary or to fluctuate up and down together?
2. How do you think a general reduction in the price of coal would affect the consumption of coal?
3. The consumption of lettuce in the United States has increased rather rapidly within the last twenty years. Why do you think this increase has taken place?
4. One store in a shopping section indicates the prices on all articles displayed in its windows. Another store does not indicate any prices. How do you account for the difference in practice?
5. The history of most new products, such as the automobile, the radio, and air-conditioning equipment, shows that the products at first sold at high prices, although they were not nearly so good as they were later. How do you account for the reduction in price?
6. Some people believe that quantity production at a low price is the solution to the problem of competition. In other words, producers can master competition by increasing their production and thus cutting down their costs. Is there any limit to the practicability of meeting competition in this way?
7. What effect does a drought in a particular section of the United States have (a) on the individual farmer in that section? (b) on farmers as a group? (c) on everyone?
8. Why are the farmers in many states encouraged to diversify their production by raising a variety of crops?
9. Explain the situation in which you believe that southern cotton farmers will find themselves after two or three good years of production of cotton above the normal consumption. Assume that foreign-grown cotton can also be imported at the same or lower prices and that rayon and nylon are also competitors of cotton. Can you recommend any remedies?
10. (a) Give some examples of elastic demand. (b) Give some examples of inelastic demand.
11. (a) How may competition cause prices to rise? (b) How may it cause prices to decrease?
12. How do you think a sales tax affects prices?
13. What would you expect to happen if all apple growers were able to control the supply and maintain prices at a very high level?

PROBLEMS

1. From your library or some other source obtain figures in regard to prices quoted on some commodities today as compared with ten years ago or five years ago. Select one or more items, such as wheat, cotton, wool, eggs, cattle, poultry, or any other commodity. Submit a report explaining the differences that you find and try to explain some of the reasons.
2. From your library or any other source obtain books pertaining to the agricultural problem in the United States. Study the supply and the price problems, as well as governmental controls, and write a report based on the various principles that you have studied in this chapter.

COMMUNITY PROBLEMS AND PROJECTS

1. Make a study of local price trends by keeping a record of the prices of several commodities over a period of at least two months.
2. Investigate the national production figures for a period of five years for at least two products, such as cotton goods, shoes, iron, or any other similar commodities. Draw your conclusions as to the relative adequacy of supply, and, if you can also obtain figures in regard to prices, explain the differences in prices based upon supply and demand.
3. Telephone companies, public power companies, and railroads are examples of controlled monopolies. Investigate the Federal and state laws affecting one of these types of companies and find out how prices and rates are regulated. Write a report.

Chapter 39

PART X _____

How Business Conditions and Prices Affect Us

Purpose of the Chapter. Business conditions are almost always changing. We have periods of great activity and other periods of less activity. Both our income and the prices we pay for goods and services tend to fluctuate with business or economic conditions. As prices fluctuate, the purchasing power of our money changes. When the value of money changes, we are affected in various ways. Every individual should understand the business cycle and how price changes affect us. This knowledge will help one to understand the danger of inflation or deflation.

How to Determine Business Conditions. A businessman knows that his own business is bad when his sales and his profits are low. He knows that it is good when his sales and his profits are high. The condition of one business does not, however, determine general business conditions. In order to determine the general condition of business, it is necessary to know (a) the conditions in many businesses of a similar nature and (b) the conditions in a wide variety of businesses, such as the steel, lumber, and coal industries.

Many explanations have been given by businessmen and economists for changes in business conditions. These explanations vary widely. Some explanations credit or blame the current state of business activity on the political party in power, on labor troubles, on communism, or on conditions brought about by the weather. No one wholly satisfactory or reliable explanation has ever been given for the cyclical changes that occur in business activity.

Most people who are interested in the business cycle study statistical analyses of business conditions to discover trends and to gain an understanding of the significance of changes that take place. Several agencies prepare statistics that are available to the average citizen and businessman to indicate general business conditions. The United States Department of Commerce, the Federal Reserve Board, the Bureau of Labor Statistics, and the Department of Agriculture are governmental agencies that serve as sources of information regarding prices, wages, cost of living, volume of production, money and credit, tax payments, and other data.

The data for the chart of the *Federal Reserve Bulletin* below were taken from United States Department of Commerce figures. This chart indicates the relationship between the production of durable and nondurable goods and minerals over a twelve-year period. The table on the dollar value of sales on page 691 shows the relationship between the volume of sales of manufacturers, wholesalers, and retailers for the same years. Each of the factors shown on the chart and in the table is an indicator of business activity. The variation in the trends of the indicators is proof that more than one indicator is needed to provide evidence of business conditions.

INDEXES OF BUSINESS CONDITIONS

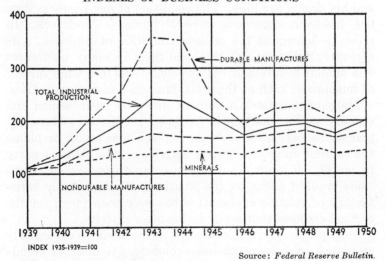

INDEX 1935-1939=100

Source: *Federal Reserve Bulletin.*

Business Cycle. By the time the average person reaches the age of maturity, he reads and hears the term *business*

Sales on an Annual Basis in Billions of Dollars

YEAR	MANUFACTURERS	WHOLESALERS	RETAILERS
1939	61.56	30.06	42.0
1940	70.25	33.48	45.96
1941	98.02	43.74	55.5
1942	124.1	48.13	57.6
1943	151.19	51.91	63.32
1944	160.77	54.02	68.8
1945	148.41	57.26	75.80
1946	144.20	73.58	100.25
1947	185.58	87.59	118.86
1948	211.05	94.35	129.99
1949	213.8	90.1	128.1
1950*	230.4	91.8	134.4

Source: *U. S. Dept. of Commerce*

* Based on the average of the first six months of 1950.

Sales of manufacturers, wholesalers, and retailers, adjusted for seasonal variation, at annual rate.

cycle. Just what is a business cycle? The business cycle is computed from the various business indicators that show the "ups and downs" of business. It usually extends over a period of from three to nine years and includes alternating periods of prosperity and depression. The average person is aware that business conditions change, but he is not always aware of the causes or of the significance of the changes. Even experts disagree on the analysis of the business cycle, but the following discussion will give an elementary understanding of the problem.

Analysis of the Business Cycle. A business cycle may be measured from the low point of one depression to the low

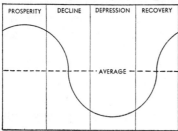

The business cycle extends from one high point to the next high point, or from one low point to another, and includes periods of prosperity, decline, depression, and recovery.

point of the next depression, or from the high point of one period of prosperity to the high point of the next period of prosperity. The illustration at the left shows the four phases of a business cycle. The four phases are referred to as (a) prosperity, (b) decline, (c) depression, and (d) recovery.

Prosperity. Starting with a period of *prosperity,* let us analyze the characteristics of the various phases of the business cycle. In periods of prosperity most people have work. Wages and prices are relatively high as compared with those in other periods of the cycle. Most businessmen are able to make profits. Businesses and consumers buy goods generously. Eventually prices begin to rise; wages begin to increase; the prices of securities rise in anticipation of increased profits from business; many people are tempted to speculate in securities, commodities, or real estate; businesses continue to expand; money is borrowed on a large scale; interest rates are reasonably low so long as money is plentiful because the lenders see an opportunity to make profits with a very little risk.

Decline. In past periods of prosperity eventually we reached a stage when there was overproduction; the selling of the merchandise became a critical problem in business; competition became keen; profits were reduced; production began to lag; gradually employers started to reduce wages and to lay off workers; lenders became fearful and quit lending money; consumers reduced their purchases; the psychological factor of fear set in; and with these characteristics the period of *decline* had started.

The decrease in production, the curtailment of expansion of business, the curtailment of loans, the demand for payment of loans, the lowering of wages, and the laying off of workers, as well as many other factors, gradually accelerate the speed of decline and cause a decrease in the demand for manufactured products and therefore a decrease in the demand for raw materials.

We cannot overlook the human element in the business cycle. Many people watch for indications of a decline in business. They then begin to cut prices, to discharge employees, to pay off their loans as rapidly as they can, and to cease borrowing. Many of these actions cannot be helped. Merchants conduct special sales and cut prices in order to pay bank loans. As soon as production in factories is curtailed, men are thrown out of work and the purchasing power of the people is therefore decreased. Wages decrease because of the drop in prices and in the demand for workers. Many businessmen fail because they cannot make profits. The pessimism of those who are in a position to continue to produce at a profit sometimes prevents them from continuing to produce.

Depression. Just when the process turns into *depression* is difficult to determine. When business in general is bad, the period is referred to as a depression. In other words, business activities are depressed. In general, depression is considered to be the low point in the cycle. Prices are greatly reduced; many people are unemployed; businesses fail and sometimes banks fail. Some banks fail because they have been unable to collect loans and to keep themselves in a position to pay depositors. Others fail because people become panic-stricken and all demand their money at once.

During the time of depression very few people start in business because there is a lack of prospect for profit. People do not buy because they want to save their money in anticipation of worse conditions. Businessmen do not buy goods in large lots because they do not want to run the risk of lower prices.

PROSPERITY	DECLINE	DEPRESSION	RECOVERY
1. Labor is fully employed.	1. Profits decline.	1. Volume of business is low.	1. There is an accumulated shortage of goods.
2. Wages are high.	2. Goods are forced on to the market.	2. Buying is only for immediate requirements.	2. Most debts are paid.
3. Costs of operation increase.	3. Prices are reduced.	3. Wages are low.	3. Outlook is favorable.
4. Selling prices increase.	4. Buying is reduced.	4. Production is efficient.	4. Sales increase.
5. Stocks of goods are large.	5. Volume of business decreases.	5. Prices are low.	5. Construction increases.
6. There is new construction and expansion of business.	6. Unemployment results.	6. Costs of operation are low.	6. Borrowing begins.
7. Banks are willing to lend money.	7. Businesses cease to expand.	7. Costs of construction are low.	7. Prices begin to rise.
8. Demand for consumers' goods increases.	8. Businesses quit borrowing.	8. Stocks of goods are small.	8. Buying begins in anticipation of rising prices.
9. Profits are high.	9. Prices decline.	9. Shortage of goods develops.	9. People go back to work.
10. Interest rates tend to increase.	10. Creditors press for payment.	10. Interest rates are low.	10. Businesses begin to operate at a profit.
	11. Failures increase.	11. Demand for loans is low.	

Characteristics of the business cycle.

Recovery. Eventually *recovery* begins. Prices and costs readjust themselves. Producers find that they can sell goods at a profit because the goods are produced cheaply. The production of cheap goods begins to stimulate buying. Banks offer low rates of interest to encourage businessmen to borrow. Wage rates slowly begin to rise as prices of commodities, prices of securities, and dividends begin to increase.

Causes of the Business Cycle. There will always be a certain amount of fluctuation in profits, in the total amount of business that is done, and in the incomes of individuals. If we could prevent the extreme fluctuations, we would have the cure for declines and depressions.

In the low periods of depression in the last thirty years, our national income was as low as 40 billion dollars. The highest it has been was 224 billion dollars in 1948. It seems probable that a national income of 200 billion dollars or more a year is needed in order to pay the interest on the national debt, to make payments to reduce the national debt, to maintain a sound business structure, and to provide individual incomes adequate to maintain a reasonable standard of living. Whenever the national income is insufficient to meet these needs adequately, we are moving toward a depression period.

Nearly everyone has an idea as to the cause and the cure of a business depression, but no one has yet been able to devise a satisfactory means of eliminating the sensational booms and the terrible slumps in business. There are, however, certain rather basic reasons on which most economists and financial experts agree as causes that lead to a depression. Some of these were mentioned in the description of the business cycle. The following factors are considered very fundamental in understanding the causes of a depression and the development of cures:

    (a) Purchasing power usually lags behind production power. Not enough of the income received from production is put back into purchasing power, and the income from production is not sufficiently widely distributed among all the population to create widespread purchasing power.

(b) At the same time that buying power has lagged behind production, surpluses are built up on the shelves of merchants, in warehouses, and at the mines. Lenders begin to get nervous. They ask for the repayment of their loans. Those who borrowed the money have to pay off the loans and curtail their businesses. They begin dumping goods on to the market and discharging their employees in an attempt to keep going.

(c) In all of this process there is usually an attempt to stabilize prices and to keep them at a high level, and also to stabilize wages; but prices usually do not come down fast enough to keep in balance with the purchasing power, particularly when large numbers of individuals are thrown out of employment. Probably the greatest problem is keeping purchasing power in balance with production and prices.

(d) Tied up with the factors mentioned above is the fact that many consumers have bought on the installment plan. They have bought more than they can pay for quickly; therefore they stop buying until they can pay their debts. Many individuals and merchants have bought more than they can use, so they stop buying until they can consume or sell what they have purchased. Many others stop buying because of the fear of what they feel is an inevitable slump.

(e) The psychological factor of fear cannot be overestimated in this whole problem, for when a decline gets started, fear accelerates it and often causes a slump that otherwise might never have happened. Fear causes scarce money and high money rates, decreased buying, discharge of employees, the calling of loans, and many other problems that push us downward.

Effects of Prices on Business Operators. For purposes of discussion business operators may be considered to be owners of individual businesses, farmers, and managers of large corporations. Their problems are largely the same in relation to price changes. In periods of rising prices business operators face increasing costs of production, such as the costs represented by labor, materials, rent, and interest. Business operators must then raise their own prices and receive more for their products; otherwise their profits will decrease.

Sometimes individual owners of various businesses find that they are gradually paying more for the products and the services that they use, but are unable to raise their own prices. This fact applies especially to farmers. There have been times when farmers have had to pay high prices for equipment, clothing, and labor, and high rates of interest and taxes; but, because of the low prices of farm products, they were unable to earn profits from their farms.

When prices drop, producers usually find themselves with a supply of goods on hand. These goods were produced at higher cost; and now, because prices have dropped, they cannot be sold at a price that will provide a profit based on the cost of production. The producer must suffer a loss.

All phases of production must be correlated closely in order to ensure a profit. For instance, in periods of rising prices, a manufacturer must watch carefully such costs as those represented by labor, materials, rent, insurance, and other expenses, in order to be sure that he will make a profit. Unless the price at which he can sell his products keeps in step with his cost of production, he cannot make a profit. In periods of falling prices he must be careful not to buy too much material or to allow his total cost to exceed his selling price. He cannot afford to pay his employees any more than his competitors pay theirs; otherwise his competitors will be able to undersell him.

Effects of Prices on People with Fixed Incomes. In times of falling prices the person with a fixed income is fortunate. A fixed income is one that does not vary in times of rising or falling prices. The income from some good investment, such as high-grade bonds, is an example. Those who were fortunate enough to have their investments in United States Government bonds during the last depression were assured a fixed income. Their real income increased, for their dollars bought more products than they did when prices were higher.

When prices rise, the person with a fixed income is in an unfavorable position. The income in terms of dollars remains the same, but these dollars will buy less in terms of commodities and services. Therefore, people who live on a pension or a fixed investment income suffer when prices rise.

Effects of Prices on Salaried Workers. In times of falling prices salaried workers are in essentially the same position as people with fixed incomes. Salaries ordinarily do not change so quickly as prices. In other words, salary changes lag behind price changes. For a while during a period of decreased prices, salaries will remain the same, but eventually they will change. As long as the salaries remain the same, the persons who receive them are in a favorable position, for their dollars will buy more than they did during periods of high prices.

When prices rise, salaried people are in a disadvantageous position. The rise in their salaries lags behind the increase in prices. Consequently, their dollars will not buy so much as they did when prices were lower.

Teachers, governmental workers, and junior executives are in the group of salaried workers. It is notably true that the salaries of teachers do not rise rapidly with rising prices; on the contrary, they rise slowly. The same fact applies to governmental workers and, to a less extent, to junior executives. Because of the slowness with which governmental bodies act, teachers and governmental workers can always expect their salaries to lag behind a general rise in prices. Fortunately, they can also expect their salaries to lag behind a drop in prices. They are at a disadvantage during times of rising prices, but at an advantage during times of falling prices. Junior executives are at a less serious disadvantage in times of rising prices, but at a less advantage in times of falling prices, for private employers may reduce salaries at will.

Effects of Prices on Wage Earners. Wage earners are considered to be those who work for hourly, daily, or weekly wages. In the absence of control through government or labor contracts, wages can usually be changed easily, often on merely a moment's notice. In the absence of such control, wage earners are therefore in an unfavorable position.

When prices begin to drop, wages also soon start to decrease. Sometimes they lag slightly behind decreases in prices, but occasionally they precede such decreases. Ordinarily, they do not lag so far behind decreases in prices as do changes in salaries. In periods of increasing prices the income of wage earners lags behind the increase in prices. Wages usually increase, however, before salaries.

Ordinarily wage agreements function advantageously for workers during periods of decreasing prices, but disadvantageously during periods of increasing prices. If a wage agreement has been made prior to a general price level decline, the wage earner is protected from lower wages. However, if the general price level rises, the purchasing power of the worker's wages decreases accordingly, and an increase in wages while the agreement is still effective may be difficult to obtain. In a few cases, wage agreements have been made for relatively long periods of time, that is, three to five years but with stipulations that adjustments be made with the rise and fall of the cost of living index. If the index rises a certain number of points, wages are increased automatically either a certain amount an hour or a certain per cent based on hourly wage rates.

During times of changing prices the monetary value of wages does not provide a satisfactory indication of their true value without a consideration of the general price level of goods and services. Real wages—that is, the amount of goods and services that the money will buy—are important. For instance, a man may be earning $50 a week. If the general price level were to rise 50 per cent, he would have to get a wage of $75 a week to have the equivalent of his former wage of $50.

Prices, Cost of Living, and Real Wages. The cost of living as compared with our monetary wages will determine real wages. The Federal Government and other agencies collect figures to establish an index of the cost of living. These indexes usually compare the cost of living of a family at one particular time with that of a previous base period to determine whether prices have increased or decreased. The table below on this page shows the index of the cost of living in large cities. The base period used for comparison is 1935-39. For instance, for all items in all cities on June 15, 1950, it cost $1.70 to buy the same items that could have been purchased for $1 during the period of 1935-39.

We can use this table to determine real wages. For instance, if the income of a family in Baltimore during the period of 1935-39 averaged $3,000 a year, it would have had to earn $5,229 in 1950 to maintain the same real wage (174.3 per cent of $3,000 = $5,229). Stating it another way, the $5,229 in 1950 would not purchase any more than the $3,000 income would have purchased during the previous period ($5,229 ÷ 174.3 per cent = $3,000).

CITY	ALL ITEMS	FOOD	CLOTH-ING	FUEL, ELEC-TRICITY AND ICE	HOUSE FUR-NISH-INGS	MIS-CELLA-NEOUS
Average: Large Cities	170.2	204.6	185.0	138.9	185.2	155.3
Baltimore	174.3	218.7	180.0	149.2	186.9	152.8
Birmingham	171.1	195.0	193.2	131.9	177.1	150.4
Boston	166.2	198.4	175.7	151.4	177.6	153.9
Chicago	176.4	211.1	190.1	133.0	168.9	158.2
Cincinnati	171.2	206.9	183.9	146.7	177.3	156.3
Detroit	174.2	205.2	181.5	149.4	197.5	170.8
Houston	173.1	207.3	194.9	98.4	183.6	158.6
Jacksonville	176.7	207.0	184.5	147.6	181.3	163.0
Los Angeles	166.7	200.3	181.5	100.1	182.2	151.8
Memphis	169.9	206.4	203.1	140.3	172.0	141.0
Minneapolis	169.2	194.9	190.6	139.1	176.2	159.6
Mobile	167.4	201.1	186.9	129.3	167.2	145.3
New York	167.0	204.3	183.2	140.2	173.8	157.7
Philadelphia	169.7	201.5	181.6	141.5	192.0	152.4
Pittsburgh	173.4	209.1	214.6	137.1	187.6	149.9
St. Louis	169.7	212.4	188.6	135.2	167.0	144.5
San Francisco	173.1	214.3	181.2	86.8	158.3	165.7

Data from Bureau of Labor Statistics.

Index is based on 1935-1939 as 100.

Index of cost of living in large cities, June 15, 1950.

Effects of Prices on Creditors and Investors. A fall in prices benefits the creditor and the investor. For instance, a person lends money on a note at a time when money is cheap in relation to commodities and services. In other words, he lends the money when prices are high. After prices fall, the person who has borrowed the money must pay interest in dollars that will buy more than they would have at the time he obtained the loan, for dollars are now more difficult to obtain. If the loan is repaid while prices are low, the dollars are more valuable than those that were borrowed. The creditor or the investor is therefore in an advantageous position. Of course, the advantages gained in this manner are not great unless the period of time is long enough to make the price differences important.

In periods of rising prices the creditor and the investor are in a disadvantageous position. If a person lends money during periods of low prices, the dollars are valuable in terms of commodities and services. After prices have risen, the creditor, or the investor, is repaid in cheap dollars. If he has made a loan of three hundred dollars during low prices, he will be repaid three hundred dollars after prices have risen. This amount will not, however, buy so much goods or services as it would have at the time he lent the money.

Effects of Prices on Debtors. In periods of decreasing prices the debtor is in a disadvantageous position; but in periods of increasing prices he is in an advantageous position. The farmer presents a good example of the position of debtors. For instance, during World War I many farmers bought farms at high prices. They contracted debts to pay for these farms and expected to pay off the debts from their earnings. When they contracted their debts, farm products were selling at high prices. As prices fell, their earnings decreased. In other words, dollars became scarce. They still had to pay the same amount on their debts, but more bushels of wheat or more hours of work were required to get the money to pay the debt. As a result many farmers lost their farms through the foreclosure of mortgages. Many other people lost their homes in this way.

Obviously, it is wise to make an investment during periods of low prices and to sell during periods of high prices. One who assumes a debt obligation during a period of low prices finds it much easier to pay off the debt when prices rise. As one's income usually increases as prices rise, more dollars are available to pay off the debt. If a person assumes a debt during a period of high prices, however, he will find it difficult to pay off the debt during a period of low prices.

Price Lag. From the foregoing discussion it is evident that interest rates and certain types of salaries and wages lag behind when prices rise or fall. There is also a lag between wholesale prices and retail prices. Wholesale prices usually change first. If all prices, interest rates, wages, rents, and taxes would rise and fall simultaneously, neither consumers nor businessmen would be adversely affected by changes in the business cycle.

Inflation. In several of the previous discussions in this and earlier chapters examples are given of what happens when we have so-called inflation. When prices are inflated or forced up beyond their normal level, the value of money decreases. The previous discussion shows what happens to all types of individuals when this continues to occur. New price levels are established and, until the earning power of individuals catches up with the cost of living, all suffer because the money that they earn will buy less than previously. When inflation continues over a long period of time, it tends to destroy the purchasing power of all kinds of savings that have been put into banks, insurance companies, and other investments, because when those savings are needed for future use, each dollar will buy less than it would have bought at the time the money was saved.

The only way to prevent inflation is to hold prices and incomes down. This is a well-recognized principle, but it is seldom put into practice. It was established by our Federal Government as a definite practice in World War II after the disastrous experiences in World War I. It was only partially successful, however, because various individuals and groups of individuals gradually succeeded in attempts to increase their incomes. During World War II, prices did not rise as rapidly as during World War I; however, when the controls on prices were lifted in 1947, the general price level of commodities and services rose very rapidly.

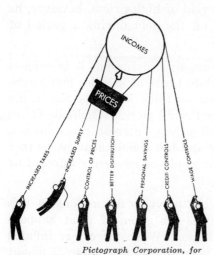

Pictograph Corporation, for
Public Affairs Committee, Inc.

**Devices which are used or can be used
to prevent inflation.**

The illustration at the left shows the common devices that may be used for controlling inflation — increased taxes, increased supplies, better distribution, personal savings, and control of prices, credit, and wages. Very few of these were used during the First World War, but most of them were used during the Second World War. Thus, we know it is possible to control inflation and to help preserve a better real wage.

Government Control of Business Activity. In some periods, such as war, the Government tries to hold prices down. We noted in the preceding paragraph that many devices were used during World War II. In periods of unemployment and low prices, the Government may attempt to stimulate business activity and to increase prices. During the depression in 1930-37 the Federal Government attempted to stimulate business activity and to increase prices by various means.

One of the early attempts of the Federal Government to influence directly business conditions was the development of the Federal Reserve System following a period of economic distress in 1907. While the primary purpose of the Federal Reserve System was to regulate the supply of money and credit and to adjust interest rates, it in effect stimulates business activity or slows it down, either of which influences the business cycle.

In general people in a democracy resist governmental control of business activity; however, extreme fluctuations in prices, sales, and employment are recognized as very undesirable. In the Employment Act of 1946, provision was made for a Council of Economic Advisers, the primary purpose of which is to recommend to the President economic policies for the maintenance of employment, production, and purchasing power and to avoid the extreme fluctuations in business activity that lead to periods of inflation and depression. The Council is required to make a report to the President on the economic conditions of the nation in December each year. The recommendations of the President

---

What We Should Know About the Business Cycle

1. The general business condition at any one time is the result of many factors. Among these factors are: volume of production, volume of sales, general price level, status of employment, money and credit, and taxes.

2. The business cycle is characterized by four distinct but overlapping phases: prosperity, decline, depression, and recovery. The characteristics of each phase are easily recognized.

3. The causes of fluctuations of business activity are not fully known; however, certain factors, such as the lag of purchasing power behind productivity, decline in sales, and increasing inventories seem always to occur in periods of decreasing business activity.

4. The business cycle has important effects on various groups of people, such as business owners, people with fixed incomes, those on salaries, wage earners, creditors and investors, debtors, and consumers. Periods of falling prices may affect one group one way and another group another way. Every person should be aware of the effects of the various phases of the business cycle on personal income, expenditures, and savings.

5. Devices to control inflation have been tried, particularly during war periods. They have been only partially successful.

6. Inflation means high prices and low purchasing power of wages and income. It affects all groups of people adversely except those who pay off debts contracted during periods of low prices.

7. The Federal Government through various means is attempting to regulate business activity to prevent extreme fluctuations in income, production, and purchasing power.

in his Economic Report to Congress are ordinarily based upon or at least substantially influenced by the report made to him by the Council of Economic Advisers. The Council thus becomes the central governmental agency for analyzing and interpreting business conditions for the guidance of Congress. The highest ambition of the Council would be to eliminate extreme fluctuations in business activity through economic adjustment. The extent to which major fluctuations in business activity can be controlled by governmental regulation is yet to be proved.

TEXTBOOK QUESTIONS

1. In order to judge the general conditions of business, what is it necessary to know?
2. What satisfactory explanation has been offered for cyclical changes in business activity?
3. What Federal agencies provide information about prices, wages, and production?
4. How many years are usually covered by a business cycle?
5. What are some of the characteristic indications of prosperity?
6. What are some of the characteristic indications of a decline in the business cycle?
7. What are some of the characteristic indications of a depression?
8. What are some of the indications that are characteristic of a period of recovery?
9. How much national income is considered necessary by experts to maintain and pay off our national debt and to assure a satisfactory income for everybody?
10. Give possible causes of changes in the business cycle, particularly causes of a decline.
11. What effect on business operators has a fall in prices? a rise in prices?
12. If a person has a fixed income, how is he affected (a) when prices rise? (b) when prices drop?
13. How are salaried workers affected (a) by rising prices? (b) by falling prices?
14. In the absence of wage-control agreements, how are wage earners affected (a) when prices rise? (b) when prices drop?
15. What attempt has been made to tie wages and cost of living together?
16. Explain the meaning of the index of cost of living.

17. (a) How is a creditor affected as prices rise? (b) How is he affected as prices fall?
18. How are debtors affected by price changes?
19. What is meant by price lag?
20. Explain why the value of money is decreased when there is inflation.
21. How may inflation be prevented?

DISCUSSION QUESTIONS

1. How is it possible to determine if business conditions are prosperous or not?
2. How is the amount of payments made by checks drawn on bank accounts an indicator of business conditions?
3. Do you think that there is a sharp dividing point when business activity makes the change from one phase to another in the business cycle?
4. Why does the overexpansion of business lead to a decline in the business cycle?
5. Name some factors in a period of decline that you believe contribute to the speed of the decline.
6. (a) How is recovery aided by the elimination of inefficient producers? (b) How are wage earners benefited by the elimination of inefficient producers?
7. How do you think the element of fear affects decline and recovery?
8. How does credit affect a decline in business?
9. Excessive installment selling is sometimes given as one of the main reasons for the beginning of a business depression. Why?
10. Why does production become efficient during a depression?
11. (a) When prices and profits increase, who has the greater advantage: the owner of bonds or the owner of stocks? (b) Who has the greater advantage during periods of decreasing prices and profits?
12. Some people yearn for the return of the days when two dollars would buy plenty of food for the average family for one week. Did people live any better in those times than they do during periods of high prices?
13. According to the table on page 699, which city shows the highest percentage increase in (a) the cost of food, (b) the cost of clothing, (c) the cost of house furnishings? (d) Can you give any reasons?
14. If a person buys a house during a period of depression and gives a mortgage, how is he affected when conditions improve?
15. Why should persons who own insurance fear inflation?

PROBLEMS

1. Assume that the cost of living index in your city today is 150 and that Mrs. James A. Barclay, a widow, has $50,000 in bonds from which she gets interest at 3 per cent. If the cost of living index is 200 per cent five years later, how is Mrs. Barclay affected?

2. Two years ago Mr. Nelson earned $45 a week. Although his wages have remained the same, the figures of the United States Department of Labor disclose that the general price level has increased 20 per cent. (a) What are his real wages now as compared with his real wages of two years ago? (b) How much would he have to earn now to buy what his wages bought two years ago? (c) How much would he have had to earn two years ago to buy what his present wages buy?

3. A person who earns $2,000 a year owes a $2,000 debt and sets aside 10 per cent of his salary each month to pay on the interest and the principal of the debt. How much should he be able to set aside each month to pay on the debt if the general price level rises 20 per cent and his salary increases accordingly?

COMMUNITY PROBLEMS AND PROJECTS

1. On the basis of the principles discussed in this chapter, make a report showing whether the present is the time to buy real estate or whether it is the time to save money in anticipation of buying later.

2. Using two or more sources of information, prepare a report on the outlook of business conditions. If you find any differences of opinion, explain these and point out why current observers of business conditions feel that such conditions are improving or are becoming worse.

3. (a) Obtain the latest figures on the cost of living in various cities of the United States. On the basis of the cost of living designated for your city or the city nearest your home, prepare a report in which you compare the present price level with the former price level and present wages with former wages. (b) From local people find out what wages are earned now in comparison with those that were earned formerly. Draw some conclusions with regard to real wages.

Chapter 40

PART X _____

How the Consumer Buys Services with Taxes

Purpose of the Chapter. Consumers and producers alike face problems involving taxes. We receive the benefits of many services that governments—local, state, and national —produce for us. We have to pay for these services just as though they were purchased from private organizations. As consumers of governmental services, we are very much concerned as to whether or not we are getting our money's worth from taxes paid. The consumer is also interested in tariffs (which are a form of tax) because they affect him both directly and indirectly and they are part of the source of income of our Federal Government.

In fact, as consumers, we are interested in all aspects of public finance, including not only governmental revenues from taxes and other sources but also governmental expenditures, debts, and administrative policies and procedures. In a democracy, one of our obligations and responsibilities is to be informed about the business management aspects of our government. We must have a knowledge of taxes and revenues, expenditures, and the debts of our government if we are to be intelligent voters. The purpose of this chapter is to give a brief explanation of taxes and tariffs.

Taxes

What Are Taxes? The average citizen looks upon taxes as a burden and as something to be avoided if possible. If there were a better understanding of the purposes and the uses of taxation, citizens would have a more kindly attitude toward being taxed.

Taxes are, in a sense, a method of distributing wealth. A discussion in a preceding chapter has shown how wealth is distributed through various persons and agencies that share in the production of wealth. Without govern-

WHAT AMERICANS WORK FOR
BASED ON PERSONAL INCOME 1949

FOOD
72 DAYS

TAXES
34 DAYS

CLOTHING
26 DAYS

SAVINGS
10 DAYS

OTHERS
26 DAYS

HOUSING
HOUSEHOLD
47 DAYS

TRANSPORTATION
23 DAYS

RECREATION
12 DAYS

250 DAYS · 1 WORK YEAR   GRAPHIC SYNDICATE

ment our present economic system could not operate. Inasmuch as government helps our economic society to operate, it must share in the fruits of production. Someone must pay the expenses of operating the government. Obviously, those who benefit from the use of governmental agencies must pay for these services.

Taxes are imposed, directly or indirectly, by the citizens of a city, a county, a state, or a country. A tax, after it is imposed, requires a compulsory contribution of money to be made to the government in payment for services for the common good. Taxes therefore have no specific application to special benefits conferred on individuals. They are for the common good, and they are compulsory.

This definition distinguishes taxation from other payments to governmental agencies. For instance, a postage stamp pays for a service, but its use is not compulsory unless the service is desired. Citizens who violate laws have to pay fines as penalties. The fines are compulsory, but they are not taxes; they are penalties. Every person in a state may pay a tax for some general improvement in the state, but an assessment on certain property for the construction of a street or a sewer does not constitute a tax. It is a payment for the improvement of the property. In most cases assessments are voluntary. The majority of property owners who are to benefit from the improvement agree to the assessment.

Purposes of Taxes. Taxes levied to provide revenue come under the taxing power of the government. In the past, most taxes have been for the purpose of raising revenue to pay for the costs of government. Taxes levied for regulatory purposes come under the government's right of police power. As a rule, our Government has not used taxation as a means of removing inequalities in wealth among people.

Our governmental bodies must first determine what services should be provided at public cost. They must then decide the problem of assessing each citizen to pay for these services. In the levying of taxes, exact justice can never be attained. Even the simplest tax is frequently purely arbitrary. In general, there have been attempts to levy taxes so that each citizen would contribute in proportion to his ability and to the benefits that he derived. No tax can be levied, however, without affecting some particular interest of citizens and without falling more heavily on one group than on another.

When governmental agencies need new sources of revenue, they must devise new taxes or raise the rates of the existing taxes. Because of a general feeling among taxpayers that all taxes are bad, there is a constant effort to shift the burden of taxes from one class of taxpayers to another. In the early history of the United States, the Federal Government was supported largely by import duties. It is reported that at one time Congress considered distributing a surplus of money that had been collected from these taxes. As our country has developed, the multiplicity of governmental units and services has caused a need for increased revenues. New forms of taxation have consequently been created.

Governmental Income and Expenditures. The income of local governments and state governments is principally from taxes, but also from borrowing. The income of the Federal Government is principally from tariffs, taxes, and borrowing. Borrowing is necessary when there is not sufficient income from regular sources to take care of expenditures.

The gross debt of the Federal Government increased from approximately 17.5 billion dollars in 1929 to 257.9 billion dollars in 1948. During the same period the increase in the combined debts of local and state governments was relatively small, 17.2 billion dollars in 1929 and 18.7 billion dollars in 1948. When money is borrowed, it must be repaid out of regular current income or by borrowing additional money. Interest on the borrowed money must be paid out of current income. Obviously, a program of borrowing cannot be continued indefinitely.

Benefits of Taxes. In a primitive civilization there is little need for taxes because few services are expected. As civilization develops, greater demands are made for public services. Citizens rarely realize, however, what additional tax burdens these demands cause. Services, whether produced by governments or private enterprises, cost money. Any

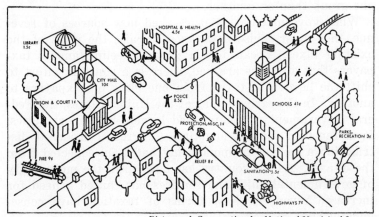

Pictograph Corporation for National Municipal League
The way in which the average local tax dollar is spent.

additional service rendered by a government must be paid for by some group of citizens. The real question to the consumer is, How can I get the service most economically and effectively? Does my tax money produce more service in the hands of government than it would in the hands of private enterprise? The question is not answered easily. Most taxpayers consider only how much they pay in taxes. Equally important is a consideration of how effectively the tax money is utilized.

Few realize the benefits of taxation and the uses of the tax dollar. The following is a brief list of some of the services that are provided through taxation. Not all these services may be furnished in a particular community, but many of them are available in all communities.

Services Provided Through Taxes

1. Police, fire, military, and coast-guard service.
2. Legal title records.
3. Health protection.
4. Garbage collection and sewage disposal.
5. Inspection of weights and standards.
6. Schools, universities, and research laboratories.
7. Legislative and executive services.
8. Postal service.
9. Transportation service.
10. Courts, prisons, and jails.
11. Welfare and relief agencies.
12. Water, electric, and gas systems.
13. Street lighting and cleaning.
14. Maintenance of streets, sidewalks, highways, and waterways.
15. Parks and recreational activities.
16. Civic museums, auditoriums, and libraries.
17. Harbor and terminal facilities.
18. Unemployment insurance and old-age pensions.
19. Inspection of building construction.
20. Regulation of admission requirements for professions.
21. Forestry and reclamation service.
22. Employment service.
23. Price supports and subsidies.
24. Grants to other countries for economic, political, and protective purposes.

When new services are added, new sources of income must be discovered by governmental agencies. If one type of tax will not provide the income, another type must be tried.

People who vote for taxes should first weigh the advantages of the services that will be provided by the taxes. The advantages should be evaluated in the light of the benefit to the entire community. It should be remembered that no public service is free; someone has to pay. The person who ultimately bears the burden is the taxpayer.

Direct and Indirect Taxes. Taxes are frequently classified as direct and indirect. This distinction is not entirely accurate. A *direct tax* is one that is levied upon a particular group of persons or organizations without the possibility of the cost of the tax being passed on to others. An *indirect tax* is one that is levied upon a group of individuals or organizations but that can be passed on indirectly to others.

A tax on real estate is usually considered to be a direct tax because it must be paid by the owner of the real estate. Nevertheless, the tax on real estate can be passed on to the renter by charging higher rent. From this point of view it may be considered as an indirect tax.

Some sales taxes are direct, and others are indirect. If a sales tax is charged on the total sales of a merchant, it will probably be passed on indirectly to the individual customers through increased prices; whereas if the tax is added to each sale, it is direct because it is paid by the consumer.

A number of states have a *poll tax.* In some cases it is imposed on every voter; in others, it is imposed on every male person who is of voting age. A poll tax is one tax that cannot be escaped and cannot be passed on to anyone else.

There are many excise taxes, some of which are direct and others, indirect. An *excise tax* is one that is levied upon the commodities, facilities, privileges, or occupations within a country. It should be distinguished from an import tax. Some excise taxes are supposed to be direct, but many of them become indirect. For example, a Federal excise tax on cigarettes is imposed as a direct tax upon the merchant, but he includes it in his selling price. The consumer therefore pays the tax. This process is referred to as "shifting the tax burden." Whenever the cost of a product is increased to include a tax, the tax is being passed on to the buyers.

Many of the taxes on gasoline were supposed to be direct taxes on the producers or the distributors, but they have become indirect taxes by being passed on to the consumers through an increase in the retail price. They thus resemble many other taxes that are supposed to be direct but that result in being indirect. Legislators have discovered that the least "painful" taxes are the ones that arouse least opposition. Indirect taxes are considered in this class.

Hidden Taxes. Many of the so-called *indirect* taxes are referred to as *hidden* taxes because most people are not aware of the fact that they are paying those taxes. For instance, one may pay a sales tax when he purchases a new radio. The purchaser is aware of paying that tax, but he is not aware of paying many others that are included in the selling price. For instance, taxes have been paid on the labor that was required to produce the radio or on raw materials that were needed in manufacturing the radio. Taxes have been paid on the factory in which the radio was manufactured. Transportation costs have been included in the selling price. The transportation companies that handled the radio have included a certain amount of taxes in their charges. Most of these taxes cannot be traced definitely to their original sources, but it has been estimated that hidden taxes represent almost 20 per cent of every dollar of retail sales.

Property Taxes. A *property tax* is one levied upon real estate or any personal property that has value and that may be bought or sold. The property tax is one of the oldest forms of tax. Until recent years it provided the greatest source of revenue; and, although it does not represent an ideal form of taxation, it is still one of the main sources of revenue in most taxing districts. The illustration at the top of the next page shows a typical form of tax bill for real estate.

It is difficult to bring about changes in methods of property taxation because rents have been adjusted to the property taxes. In some states different types of property are taxed at different rates. Some forms of personal property are exempt entirely. A new form of property tax is the tax on intangible property, such as money, deposits, and securities.

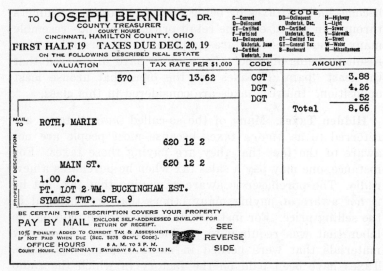

A real-estate tax bill.

One of the most important arguments for a property tax is that, since property receives protection from the government, the owners should be required to pay for the protection. In the early days when our tax system was established, the ownership of real estate was a reasonably good index of the ability to pay taxes. Now, however, there are many persons who do not own real property but who have much greater incomes than some other people who own real estate. The ownership of real estate, therefore, should not be the only means of determining one's ability to pay taxes.

Property tax rates may be stated in terms of mills, dollars per thousand, percentages, or other units. For instance, a tax rate may be specified as 18 mills, 18 dollars a thousand, 1.8 per cent, or .018. The total tax rate on property is the sum of the separate rates on property imposed by the various units of government that are empowered to levy a tax. The following is an example of how the total tax rate on property is comprised of the sum of the separate rates levied by different units of government:

```
State unit .............................. .003
City unit ............................... .008
County unit ............................. .002
School district ......................... .005
Total tax rate .......................... .018
```

Property valuations are not always computed fairly, for they are based on judgment. Judgment is sure to vary. If one person's piece of property is evaluated conservatively and another person's property is evaluated liberally, the latter person pays a greater tax in proportion to the actual value of his property. The table on page 716 shows comparisons of tax rates and differences in property valuation.

Who Pays Property Taxes? A property tax is supposed to be a direct tax. If a person lives on the real estate on which he is paying taxes, the tax is reasonably direct. If the property is rented, however, and the tax is figured in the cost of maintaining the property, the renter actually pays the tax. In some cases it may be shared by the owner and the renter.

Sales or Consumption Taxes. There are two principal forms of the sales tax (sometimes called excise tax) : (a) general and (b) selective.

General sales taxes are of several different kinds, among the most common of which are: the retail sales tax, levied on retailers; the wholesale tax; the gross income tax, usually levied on all income from sales both of commodities and of services; the gross sales tax, which is applicable to all sales including manufacturers'; and the gross profit tax, levied on gross profit. Taxes on luxuries, amusements, and gasoline are good examples of selective or commodity taxes.

An argument in favor of the sales tax is that many who do not pay other taxes are thus required to contribute to the support of government. Many people argue also that this tax meets one of the basic requirements of taxation not only by charging those who have the ability to pay, but also by charging them in proportion to the ability to pay. The general sales tax is obviously open to many criticisms. For instance, it places a heavy burden especially

TAX RATES OF AMERICAN CITIES FOR 1950

Compiled by the Detroit Bureau of Governmental Research from Data Furnished by the City Officials and Members of the Governmental Research Association

NO.	CITY	ACTUAL TAX RATE AS LEVIED PER $1,000 ASSESSED VALUATION					ESTIMATED RATIO OF ASSESSED VALUE TO CURRENT MARKET VALUE (PER CENT)	ADJUSTED TAX RATE ON 100% BASIS OF ASSESSMENT
		CITY	SCHOOL	COUNTY	STATE	TOTAL		
	Group I Population 1,000,000 or over							
1	New York, N.Y.	30.80				30.80	100	30.80
2	Chicago, Ill.	17.12	11.98	3.40		32.50	100	32.50
3	Philadelphia, Pa.	17.00	11.75			28.75	63	18.03
4	Los Angeles, Calif.	17.86	23.04	24.40		65.30	50	32.65
5	Detroit, Mich.	21.19	11.90	6.07		39.16		.....
	Group II Population 500,000 to 1,000,000							
6	Baltimore, Md.	28.80			1.24	30.04	100	30.04
7	Cleveland, Ohio	17.50	11.00	4.20		32.70	100	32.70
8	St. Louis, Mo.	17.70	9.10		.60	27.40	100	27.40
9	Washington, D. C.					21.50	70	15.05
10	Boston, Mass.	41.83	15.81	3.34	2.02	63.00	100	63.00
11	San Francisco, Calif.	47.27	15.63			62.90	50	31.45
12	Pittsburgh, Pa.	19.84	11.75	10.88		42.46	54	22.93
13	Milwaukee, Wis.	16.67	14.02	12.90	.28	43.87	69	30.19
14	Houston, Tex.	19.75	12.70	12.90	7.20	52.55	24	12.63
15	Buffalo, N.Y.	23.85	6.96	14.30		45.11	95	42.86
16	New Orleans, La.	23.78	10.00		5.75	39.53	100	39.53
17	Minneapolis, Minn.	27.85	33.25	27.82	8.08	147.00	34	49.98
18	Cincinnati, Ohio	11.72	11.09	3.29		26.10	50	13.05
	Group III Population 250,000 to 500,000							
19	Seattle, Wash.	20.40	12.50	14.40	2.10	49.40	45	22.23
20	Kansas City, Mo.	14.80	16.80	7.10	.60	39.30	35	13.76
21	Newark, N. J.	37.50	21.70	9.20		68.40	60	41.04
22	Dallas, Tex.	18.50	12.30	8.60	7.20	46.60	31	14.35
23	Indianapolis, Ind.	20.48	14.30	7.84	1.50	44.12	30	13.24
24	Denver, Colo.	21.60	25.00		3.86	50.46	35	17.66
25	San Antonio, Tex.	20.20	10.60	8.80	7.20	46.80	40	18.60
26	Memphis, Tenn.	11.50	6.50	9.70	.80	28.50	70	19.86
27	Oakland, Calif.	26.20	24.78	24.72		75.70	23	17.41
28	Columbus, Ohio	5.90	11.10	3.00		20.00	35	7.00
29	Portland, Oreg.	17.90	20.30	13.30		51.50	61	31.42
30	Louisville, Ky.	15.00	14.70	5.00	.50	35.20	50	17.60

Note: Data applies to 1949 tax year.

upon those who scarcely can earn a living. Some of these objections are overcome, however, by the selective sales tax.

Some sales taxes are supposed to be levied on producers and wholesalers and not to be passed on to consumers. The consumer, however, usually pays the tax because it is passed on to him indirectly through a rise in prices. In many cases a sales tax is without question a direct tax on the consumer. The retail price is quoted, and the tax is added to it. For instance: retail price, 25 cents; sales tax, 1 cent.

Business or Service Taxes. Business or service taxes can rightfully be called privilege taxes. They are sometimes also referred to as benefit taxes. Those who pay them derive a privilege from Federal, state, or local governments. Franchise taxes, occupational taxes, and severance taxes come within this classification. The tax on gasoline is sometimes classed as a benefit tax, for it is usually levied to pay for the construction and maintenance of roads.

Franchise taxes are those charged to public utilities and certain other companies that are granted concessions or privileges. In most states all corporations must pay a franchise tax for the privilege of doing business within the state.

The occupational tax has been the subject of controversy and legal action in many communities. In some states and in some cities, it has been ruled illegal. An *occupational tax* is that levied on businesses for the privilege of "occupying" a location within the city for the purpose of doing business. In some respects it serves as a license tax. Occupational taxes vary in rate.

A *severance tax* is levied by a state as a charge against the consumption of natural resources. For instance, certain states charge a percentage on the oil that is pumped, the ore that is mined, and the timber that is cut. These taxes are levied on the assumption that the state is granting the privilege of a profit to be derived from the consumption of natural resources.

Other good examples of service taxes are those imposed on corporations, particularly on life insurance companies.

Since a corporation is an artificial being created by the state, it is subject to the regulations of the state and must pay for the privilege of its existence. Life insurance companies usually pay on the basis of their gross income or their net income.

Business or service taxes are direct taxes for those on whom they are imposed, although they frequently result in indirect taxes on the consumers. In some states certain taxes have been imposed on public utilities without the possibility of the taxes being passed on to the consumers. For instance, a state may impose a 2 per cent tax on the sale of electricity and gas. The public utility may be restrained from passing this charge on to the consumer since the rates have already been established and cannot be raised. The corporation must therefore pay the tax without passing it on to the consumers.

Inheritance and Gift Taxes. During the twentieth century the growth of inheritance, estate, legacy, or succession taxes has been very rapid. Such taxes, commonly referred to as death taxes, are now levied under Federal and state laws. The theory behind the legislation is that wealth should not be allowed to accumulate, through successive generations, in the hands of a few people, and that large estates should be broken up. Two general types of inheritance taxes are: (a) the estate tax and (b) the share, or inheritance, tax. The Federal Government largely employs the estate tax, whereas most states employ the share tax.

The *estate tax* is calculated on the entire amount of the net estate, regardless of the interests of the beneficiaries. A *gift tax* is levied upon a gift from one person to another. Ordinarily, gift taxes are levied to prevent avoidance of estate and inheritance taxes.

The *inheritance tax* may be taken out of each share of the will, provided the will so specifies. In the absence of a specification in the will, the tax is taken out of the part of the estate remaining after specific bequests have been distributed. The rate of this tax may vary according to the individuals who share in the estate. Under most state laws the portions of an estate that go to distant relatives are subjected to higher taxes than the portions going to close relatives.

Under this type of taxation the beneficiaries of an estate are the ones who bear the tax burden. In other words, the state deprives them of part of the estate. This type of tax is a good example of a tax that cannot be shifted to someone else.

Those who argue against inheritance and gift taxes assert that an estate is built as the result of one's business skill, foresight, and labor; descendants therefore have a natural right to the proceeds of the estate. It is also contended that such taxes tend to discourage initiative and thrift. Those who argue for inheritance taxes assert that there is no natural right of descendants, that property rights cease with death, and that the state merely confers a favor upon descendants by permitting a person before his death to make a plan disposing of his property in their favor. The administration of inheritance taxes is therefore a social and an economic problem.

Income Taxes. The income tax is the principal source of revenue for the Federal Government. In theory the income tax is sound and just. It is one of the fairest direct taxes because it is levied in reasonable proportion to one's ability to pay. While property is considered as evidence of ability to pay, it may not be good evidence. An actual income is, however, good evidence of the ability to pay. Although the theory may be correct, the particular rates charged on various incomes are nevertheless subject to debate. Most authoritative economists approve of the income tax, although they do not agree as to the method of its application. One of the weaknesses of the income tax is that, in times of reduced earnings, the revenue from it shrinks rapidly. Property taxes are not subject to such violent fluctuations.

The income tax is also imposed in many states. The state income-tax laws are patterned largely after the Federal law, although they are usually not so complicated and the rates vary. The legal accounting procedure governing the operation of the Federal income-tax law has become quite com-

plicated. The interpretation of many of the stipulations of
the law has been clarified through court decisions. The
law may be changed by Congress, but the principles remain
the same.

Who Pays Income Tax? The Federal income tax applies
to both business firms and individuals. The rates of tax
and the regulations relative to exemptions, methods of payment, and the items constituting deductible expenses are
different for business firms than for individuals. Practically all business and professional firms must file income
tax returns. Usually business firms have tax accountants
or attorneys compute their taxes for them.

Every individual who has a gross income of $600 or more
for the taxable year must file a return. Age is no factor,
and it makes no difference whether the individual is single
or married. The amount of the net income is immaterial.
Even if the deductions and the credits are such that no tax
is payable, a return still must be filed. Failure to file a
return when required to do so may result in certain penalties being imposed.

When computing income tax, individuals are permitted
to deduct from their total income an amount known as an
exemption. For example, a man having a wife and a six-
teen-year-old daughter may claim three personal exemptions if he is filing one income-tax return for the income
of the entire family. An exemption is not applicable to a
member of the family, besides the taxpayer, whose personal
income has exceeded $500. The amount of the exemption
varies from time to time. In 1950 exemptions of $600 were
permitted for husband, wife, and each dependent; in 1913,
an exemption of $3,000 was allowed a single person and
$2,000 each for husband and wife living together.

Tax Payments Withheld from Wages. Since January 1,
1943, employers have been required to withhold a percentage of the wages paid to their employees for Federal income
tax purposes.

Each employee is required to furnish his employer with
a signed withholding exemption certificate setting forth the

number of income tax exemptions that he claims. The employer may use either a percentage method or a wage bracket (table) method in determining the amounts to be withheld each payday. The amounts withheld by the employer must be paid to the collector of internal revenue or a bank designated as a U. S. depositary. At the end of each year the employer must furnish each employee with a written statement showing the amount withheld from his wages during the year. If the amount withheld is more than the actual amount of the tax, the excess will be refunded; if it is less, the employee will be required to pay the difference to the collector of internal revenue.

Having the Federal taxes withheld and paid by one's employer does not relieve a person from filing an income tax return. Persons whose income is primarily from wages and not over $5,000 a year may file Form 1040A known as *Employee's Optional U. S. Individual Income Tax Return,* which virtually means that the collector of internal revenue computes the tax for you. It is estimated that about 40 million taxpayers may use the short form of return. Persons having income other than from wages and in excess of $5,000 a year are required to file a more detailed statement (Form 1040) of their income and the items that are deducted from income as deductible expenses.

A declaration of estimated income tax for the year must be filed by March 15 by persons who expect to receive wages in excess of $4,500, plus $600 for each exemption claimed, or by persons whose total income is $600 or more and whose income from sources other than wages will exceed $100.

Social Security Taxes. Under the Social Security Act the Federal Government collects Federal pay roll taxes for (a) old-age benefits and (b) unemployment insurance. These are often called social security taxes. Employers and employees make payments to the Federal Government for old-age benefits. The Federal unemployment insurance tax does not provide for the payment of unemployment insurance benefits, but imposes on employers a tax against which credit is allowed for payments that the employers make to state unemployment compensation funds. Every state has an unemployment compensation act. In some cases the employers pay all the tax, but in others the employees as well as the employers contribute to the tax.

The Federal payroll taxes do not cover all forms of employment. There are various exemptions, and these may be changed from time to time by amendments to the law.

Special Taxes. Various special taxes are levied by the Federal Government, state governments, and local governments. Many of these, such as the tax on legal papers (deeds, notes, and mortgages), are *stamp taxes;* that is, they are collected through the use of revenue stamps. Some are customs taxes on imports; others, excise taxes in the form of automobile, dog, and hunting and fishing licenses; and still others, special licenses for conducting certain types of businesses. These licenses vary in cost.

State Trade Barriers. The Federal Constitution theoretically regulates the commerce among the states. State taxing systems and the so-called port-of-entry systems of taxing goods as they enter states have, however, resulted in tariffs on imports of goods into the various states.

These various state trade barriers tend to nullify the provisions of the Federal Constitution that provide for free trade among states. The products made in one state are so regulated by taxes that it is extremely difficult, if not impossible, to sell them in other states. Any increased tendency in this respect will serve to work to the serious disadvantage of consumers and businesses.

Tariffs

Purposes of Tariffs. *Tariffs,* sometimes known as *customs duties,* are taxes levied on exports or imports, usually the latter. Tariffs are levied on two bases, *ad valorem* and *specific.* The former is a percentage of the value of a commodity; the latter is a given payment on a unit of the commodity, as per bushel or per ton. Tariffs may be levied for purposes of (a) revenue, (b) protection of an industry or of labor, or (c) both. While tariffs produce a revenue, the amount of revenue from tariffs is relatively insignificant in relation to the total amount of income that is necessary to run the government. Most of our tariffs are intended to protect business interests and labor. They are sometimes used to protect industries that are vital in our national defense. Tariffs are also used to protect infant industries and certain other industries that might be destroyed by competition of foreign goods.

How Tariffs Affect Marketing. The common practice of placing tariffs on foreign products is the result of the desire of domestic producers to have the national market to themselves. While a tariff on an import gives the domestic producers some control over the market, it also tends to limit their foreign markets because foreign countries tend to retaliate and place tariffs on products produced in a country with high tariffs like the United States. Of course, our high tariff policy affects various producers differently. From the point of view of a manufacturer whose entire market is in this country, a high tariff is desirable; from that of a manufacturer whose main business is abroad, a high tariff may be unfortunate.

How Tariffs Affect Prices. From the consumer's point of view a tariff on a foreign product is simply a tax. Tariffs, although they protect certain manufacturers or other producers, necessarily result in higher price levels. Most consumers are quite unaware of the fact that they daily have to pay high prices for certain commodities or have to accept similar inferior products at lower prices simply because of the existence of tariffs. A tariff is a hidden tax. For example, woolen blankets are manufactured in certain foreign countries and sold at prices much lower than the prices prevailing in the United States. If a person in this country wishes to purchase a woolen blanket that was produced abroad, he must pay the foreign price of the blanket plus the tariff. He may, however, purchase a similar blanket produced in this country, but he will have to pay a price that is approximately the cost of the foreign-produced blanket plus the tariff. Or the consumer has the alternative of purchasing a lower-grade blanket at a price approximately the same as the price of the foreign blanket without the tariff.

How Tariffs Affect Labor. One of the most frequent statements favoring a high tariff is that such tariffs protect workers from the competition of foreign countries where labor is cheap and standards of living are low. Whether or not this argument has a basis of fact depends upon (a) the purchasing power of the worker's dollar and (b) whether or not the benefits of the tariff accrue to the manufacturer or the worker. If a general high tariff results in a high price level, obviously the worker's wages will not purchase so much as they would if the price level were lower.

It is generally maintained by economists that tariffs tend to reduce the productivity of labor because they restrict the amount of specialization possible in a particular country. In the United States this argument is not serious because the domestic market is so large.

Most students of tariff problems agree that a sudden reduction in tariffs would not be desirable, although they believe that tariffs should be reduced over a long period of time. A sudden reduction in tariffs would result in unemployment and the decay of certain industries that have been artificially built up by a high tariff policy. These results would have a serious effect on our economy.

How Tariffs Affect Agriculture. Tariffs affect farmers in two ways. They affect the things the farmers must buy that are manufactured products; and they affect, in some cases, the products the farmers sell. In the United States the major farm crops have been protected by high tariffs, although the tariffs on some agricultural products have been reduced. There have also been tariffs on clothing, machinery, and other products that a farmer must have. Thus the advantages that a farmer might gain from higher prices on his crops are offset by higher prices he must pay for the products he buys.

The farmer is not always protected by tariffs on his crops. In the case of large staple crops for which the production is greater than the domestic market, some of the surplus must be exported. It would make little difference therefore whether or not there was protection for such crops because the prices would fall on the basis of domestic competition alone. In the case of specialized crops like olives, rice, citrus fruits, and certain types of vegetables and other fruits, tariffs do give actual protection because the demand for these products in the domestic market exceeds the domestic supply.

How Tariffs Affect Manufacturing. Very early in the history of the United States, certain manufacturers, notably in the textile field, sought governmental protection by the encouragement of high tariffs. They argued that infant industries would be protected and encouraged and that in case of war certain industries were necessary; they also defended the idea that high tariffs brought about high standards of living. Not all manufacturers have, however, sought tariff protection. One of our major industries, the automobile business, has, in the main, grown without the protection of tariffs. Manufacturers whose market is largely domestic are the chief gainers from tariffs. Other manufacturers may actually be injured and their foreign market destroyed when foreign nations react against our tariff policies.

How Tariffs Affect the Consumer. Although an individual as a producer may gain from tariffs, as a consumer he suffers because high tariffs are generally injurious. From the consumer's point of view solely, tariffs result in (a) high prices and (b) a narrower range of choice. In some few instances tariffs may protect a consumer from cheap and shoddy goods. In general, the competition of foreign products would necessarily make domestic manufacturers more efficient so that they could compete with foreigners and not have to withdraw from the market. As productive efficiency is always to the consumer's advantage, tariffs indirectly serve to discourage efficiency and therefore penalize the consumer. In general, it may be said that high tariffs decrease the consumer's purchasing power.

Conflicting Theories. The tariff problem has long been a source of political and economic debate. Economists have generally agreed that low tariffs or no tariffs are desirable from a national and a consumer point of view, but political representatives have usually been powerful enough to overcome the opposition to tariffs. There are many pros and

---

What the Consumer Needs to Know About Taxes and Tariffs

1. A tax is a compulsory contribution to be made in payment for governmental services for the common good without regard to the specific benefit the taxpayer may derive from it.

2. Most taxes are levied to raise revenue to pay the cost of government; some taxes are levied to regulate certain aspects of business or business transactions.

3. Public finance is concerned with governmental income, expenditures, and public debt. Tax problems and public finance problems are interrelated.

4. Many of the services we use daily are provided through taxation. These services include police, fire, and national defense protection; education; postal service; courts; welfare; highways, bridges, and streets; and many other similar services which we tend to take for granted, but which must be paid for from public funds.

5. A direct tax is one that cannot be passed on to others; an indirect tax is one that can be included in the cost of a service or a commodity and thus passed on to the consumer. Many indirect taxes are hidden.

6. The common types of taxes are: property taxes, on both real estate and personal property; sales taxes and commodity taxes; business or service taxes; death taxes, including estate and inheritance; gift taxes; income taxes; and payroll taxes.

7. Tariffs or customs duties are levied usually on imports to protect labor and certain kinds of domestic business. Tariffs tend to increase the general price level within the country that levies them. The effects of tariffs are widespread, some of which are beneficial but many of which are of doubtful value.

cons with respect to tariffs. The tariff advocates point out that tariffs keep out cheap foreign products made by low-paid labor; that they maintain industries necessary in case of war; that they promote young and weak industries; and that they help to make the nation self-sufficient. Economists and others point out that tariffs reduce productivity by limiting specialization and markets; that they penalize the consumer; that they help, not labor, but only particular groups; that they create international animosities and ill will.

The dominant point of view seems to be that tariffs are undesirable; but in a world in which national rivalries are increasing, it is difficult to reduce them. Then, too, if tariffs are reduced, certain industries, especially those in which foreign competition is strong, will be affected adversely.

TEXTBOOK QUESTIONS

1. Why should consumers be concerned with taxes?
2. It is easy to demand new public services, but it is not always easy to pay for them. What should be considered before establishing a new public service?
3. What is (a) a direct tax? (b) an indirect tax?
4. What do we mean by "shifting the tax burden"?
5. What is meant by the term *hidden taxes*?
6. Give an example of (a) a tax on tangible property; (b) a tax on intangible property.
7. How much money is a mill?
8. (a) Who pays the property tax on real estate that is rented? (b) Is such a tax direct or indirect?
9. What are the most common kinds of general sales taxes?
10. Why is the franchise tax of a corporation sometimes called a privilege tax?
11. What is a severance tax?
12. What are the two types of inheritance taxes? Explain each.
13. (a) Is the income tax a direct tax or an indirect tax? (b) What is its principal weakness from the point of view of government?
14. Who must file Federal income tax returns?
15. What is an exemption?
16. Explain how a worker pays his income tax as he earns his wage.

17. For what two purposes are taxes collected under the Federal Social Security Act and the various state acts relating to it?
18. How do the state trade barriers, such as taxes on goods made outside the state, affect the consumer?
19. What are the main purposes of levying tariffs on imports?
20. From the consumer's point of view what is a tariff on a foreign product that is imported?
21. From the point of view of labor what is the advantage of a tariff?
22. Why is not the farmer particularly concerned with tariffs on large staple crops such as wheat?

DISCUSSION QUESTIONS

1. (a) Distinguish between a tax on gasoline to pay for roads in all parts of a state, and an assessment on adjoining property to pay for the paving of a new street. (b) What are the benefits derived in each case? (c) Why is one a tax and the other not a tax?
2. A new viaduct and an arterial boulevard are constructed from the center of a city into an outlying district. Part of the cost is paid from a general tax fund, and part is obtained through the assessment of adjoining property owners. Some taxpayers believe that the entire cost should be paid by the adjoining property owners. Would this plan be fair or unfair?
3. Give your arguments against a policy of continued governmental borrowing to take care of deficits.
4. If a government spends more than it receives, where does it secure money?
5. (a) What do you think would be one of the most "painful" taxes to a man who owns considerable real estate? (b) What would probably be one of the least "painful"?
6. The statement is frequently made that rents adjust themselves to taxation. What do you think is meant by this statement?
7. Suppose a sales tax of 2 per cent were levied by a state on all commodities and services. If this tax were the only state tax, why would it be fair or unfair?
8. What is the theory or purpose of inheritance taxes?
9. From the point of view of the ability to pay, which type of tax do you think is most fair—a sales tax, an income tax, or a property tax? Why?
10. (a) In terms of the ability to pay, who bears the greatest percentage of a sales tax in proportion to his earnings? (b) Who bears the least?

11. Why are there many conflicting opinions on the subject of tariffs?

12. The statement is often made that high tariffs mean high prices. Why is this statement true?

PROBLEMS

1. If a real-estate tax rate is listed as .0224, what is the total tax for a half year on real estate with an assessed valuation of $6,430?

2. The tax valuation of the real estate in a certain city is approximately 80 per cent of the actual value, and the tax rate is .0189. Mr. Allison builds a new house that costs $8,000. What is a reasonable estimate of the taxes on this property that he will have to pay each year?

3. The real property in City X is listed at a tax valuation of $812,446. The rates for the various taxing bodies that share in the income from the tax are as follows: state unit, .002; county unit, .003; city unit, .018; school unit, .013. (a) What is the total tax rate on the real property in the city? (b) What is the estimated yearly income from the tax for each of the taxing bodies?

4. Assume that 1½ per cent of a worker's yearly wage of $3,500 is deducted for social security taxes. (a) How much is withheld for social security taxes? (b) If the employer must match a worker's social security contribution and contribute an additional 3 per cent of wages paid for unemployment insurance, how much do wage taxes cost the employer?

5. Assume that the withholding income tax rate for a single worker with no dependents is 15 per cent on all weekly wages over $13. What amount is withheld from a worker's wage of $45?

COMMUNITY PROBLEMS AND PROJECTS

1. Make a list of the specific types of taxes in your community.

2. Make a study of some particular tax in your community and find out (a) the rates of taxation, (b) the basis on which the taxes are levied, (c) how taxes are collected, and (d) for what purposes the tax money is used.

3. Determine how much it costs your community to provide education for each high school pupil a year.

Chapter 41

Your Interest in Your Government

Purpose of the Chapter. Every phase of life is affected in some way by government. Our level of living, for example, is affected greatly by governmental policies; and the role of government in the personal, occupational, and economic lives of people is becoming increasingly significant. It is essential for all people as citizens and consumers to have a clear understanding of their relationships to government. Those relationships are discussed in this chapter.

Government and Consumers. If you were the only person who lived in the United States, you would be entirely independent; your work, your actions, and even your thoughts would not affect anyone else. At the same time you would be wholly dependent upon yourself. You would have to protect yourself. You could turn to no one for help, nor could you exchange commodities with others. No need would exist for laws or regulations. In other words there would be no need for government.

In a society people help each other. They co-operate in making and doing things that would be difficult or impossible alone. Under a system of specialization or division of labor people become dependent upon one another and upon government to supply the services and the goods they want. The greater the number of people, the more complex are the problems of working and living together, and the greater is the need for government.

Government serves citizens in many ways. It protects them from many dangers, such as invasion by a foreign nation; loss of property by fire; personal injury; infringement upon their personal and civil rights; and harmful or inferior products that may be offered for sale. In addition to giving protection to citizens, government also gives other services needed by its citizens, such as the postal

730

By exercising their right to vote, citizens help to make decisions of government in economic matters.

Harold M. Lambert

service, development of natural resources, and the building of public works as roads, bridges, and dams.

While all governmental services are intended to serve society in general, some groups of citizens benefit directly from certain services and others only indirectly. Old-age assistance, unemployment insurance, and price supports for eggs and cotton are examples of services or benefits to special groups of citizens.

There is a tendency for state governments to take over services previously given by local governments and for the Federal Government to take over or contribute substantially in providing services formerly rendered by state governments. For example, road building and maintenance were at one time almost wholly functions of local government. In recent years, they have been practically absorbed by the state governments with the financial assistance of the Federal Government.

When relatively few services and benefits are requested by citizens and consumers, the costs of government are low. However, the more services that a government provides for its citizens at public expense and the more special benefits that are provided for special groups of citizens or consumers, the more complex and costly government becomes.

As citizens we participate in making the regulations and rules by which we are governed by voting for legislators whose points of view about government we approve. We also pay for the costs of government. As consumers we use the services provided by government. Our interests as citizens and our interests as consumers in government are almost identical.

Once a governmental service is provided at public expense, all consumers help pay for it through taxes and often through higher prices even though many of them may not need or want the service. Our interest, therefore, is to see not only that our government provides services for the general good of people but also that the government does not provide services and special benefits that are nonessential.

Governmental Operations Are Extensive. To provide services and benefits for citizens, our governmental units operate the world's most extensive business. The combined operation of local, state, and Federal governmental units in the United States requires millions of public employees and billions of dollars annually to pay the total costs. Every person working for the government is one less to help pay the costs of government.

Of approximately 58 million people who were gainfully employed in 1949, 7 million were employed by the Federal, state, and local governments. This means that of every eight persons gainfully employed one was working for the government. In 1900, one of every 23 gainfully employed persons was employed by the government. From 1900 to 1949, the total number of persons employed increased from 27 to 57.9 million, an increase of 114 per cent; governmental employment increased during the same period from 1.2 to 7.3 million, an increase of approximately 508 per cent.

The combined expenditures of Federal, state, and local governments in the United States in 1949 were a little less than 60 billion dollars or approximately $400 for every adult and child. Approximately $275 a person was spent by the Federal Government, and $125 by state and local governments combined. Since the average consumer had an income of approximately $1,400 in that year, governmental services cost the average consumer from 25 to 30 per cent of his annual income. Consumers, therefore, have a deep interest in the business affairs of government.

Protection of Citizens by Government. No governmental service or activity is more important to its citizens than protection. We must feel secure not only from physical harm and discomfort but from injustices to our personal rights and freedoms.

National defense and internal police protection are among the most important protective services given by government. The army, navy, and air corps provide protection from invading foreign powers and protect our possessions located in other parts of the world. This protection we take for granted in times of peace, but it is of vital importance to us in times of world unrest and war. In times of war the amounts spent on national defense are much greater. In 1949, approximately 12 of the 40 billion dollars spent by the Federal Government were spent for national defense. This was 30 per cent of the total amount spent. The 12 billion dollars did not include approximately 5 billion dollars expended for interest on the public debt incurred during war or 7 billion paid for services and benefits for veterans. The annual expenditures for national defense comprise the largest item in the Federal budget. The money spent for defense comes from taxation.

The Federal Bureau of Investigation, state police departments, and local police protect us from physical harm and injustices from people within the country. Protection from fire, flood, storms, and other disasters is provided by the Coast Guard and local agencies. The total amount spent for national defense and internal security is reflected not only in direct taxes but in higher prices of commodities wanted by consumers.

In addition to the services of governmental agencies to protect consumers discussed in Chapter 6, the government indirectly protects its citizens in other ways. Illustrations of legislation to protect consumers are state and Federal laws dealing with such matters as fair trade practices, licenses and permits to engage in certain types of businesses or professions, sanitation and health practices, control of interest rates, wage-hour provisions, old-age benefits and unemployment insurance, and insurance on bank deposits.

Most of the protective services furnished by government cannot be provided economically or cannot be provided at all by consumers themselves. Therefore, as consumers we have an interest in the kinds and extent of the protective services provided by government. We want those services provided efficiently and economically.

Governmental Aid to Education and for Handicapped Persons. Many families cannot afford to send their children to private schools. Therefore, public education is very important to them. Consumers are interested in good schools that are operated economically and in an efficient manner.

Education has always been considered a responsibility of government in the United States. The Federal and state governments recognized early in the history of the United States that education contributes to the productivity of its citizens and hence to the economic welfare of the entire country. While a major portion of the cost of education has been borne by local and state government, the Federal Government stimulated and encouraged education, first through land grants, the income from which was to be used for educational purposes, and later through direct grants of funds. The Federal funds were to be used primarily to stimulate the development of special types of education, such as agriculture and home economics, until the state and local governments would recognize the value of them, and, therefore, support them. However, once Federal funds for a particular kind of education have been granted, there is reluctance to have the Federal funds discontinued.

Handicapped persons, such as the sightless, deaf, and physically impaired, are given special training; and in some cases partial financial support is provided by government. Persons who have been injured in their occupations or by accident may receive training to rehabilitate them or fit them for a job again.

Government Produces for Consumer Use. Ordinarily we think of commodities and services as being produced under competitive conditions by individuals and by private enterprises for profit. Upon examination, however, we find that many services and some commodities are produced by government without profit and under noncompetitive conditions. Whether consumers actually pay less through taxes for a service provided by government without profit than they would pay for the same service provided by a private enterprise that makes a profit is an unsettled question.

Many of the services provided by government are financed wholly through public taxation. No direct charge is made to the persons using them; however, in some cases the person using a service pays a portion of the cost. Electricity generated by the Tennessee Valley Authority is paid for in part by the user. Of course, in cases in which the user pays only a portion of the cost of the service, the remainder is paid from public funds raised through taxation.

Some of the services provided by government are not used by individuals but are provided for all of the people collectively. Inspection of food processing plants to insure clean and wholesome food is an example of services for the good of all people. The use of many governmental services by consumers is voluntary; however, a few, such as provisions for social security, are compulsory for those persons to whom the laws are applicable.

In some cases the government has become a producer in order that, through research and experimentation, a new product may be developed and made available to consumers. Aluminum, synthetic rubber, and synthetic gasoline are examples of products that have been developed experimentally and produced at least in the initial stages by the government.

The majority of people believe that government should produce only those services that are not and cannot be provided by individuals and private enterprise. Illustrative of the services that cannot be provided by private enterprises are national defense, police and fire protection, conservation of natural resources, general hospitals, public health,

Our Government
helps to develop
natural resources.

Ewing Galloway

education except college, and institutions for unfortunate people. Those persons who lean strongly toward socialism, however, believe government should assume the responsibility for providing as many services and for producing as many commodities as possible.

The Relation of Government to Business. The relation of government to business has manifested itself in two ways, aid to business and regulation of business. Let us consider aid to business first.

Government Aid to Business. • The Federal Government has aided business in many ways. One type of service to business is the gathering, compiling, and distributing of statistics and information relative to payrolls, wages, prices, volume of production, finance, costs, and many similar aspects of business. These data are collected by such agencies as the Department of Commerce, the Bureau of Labor Statistics, and the Federal Reserve Board.

The Bureau of Standards has given an invaluable service to business by testing materials and establishing standards. Many divisions of the Department of Interior and the Department of Agriculture primarily serve producers. Following World War II the Reconstruction Finance Corporation loaned millions of dollars to railroads, banks, insurance companies, and manufacturing companies when

736

loans from other sources would have been almost impossible. During the Second World War many industries engaged in war production were subsidized by the Federal Government. Air lines and steamship companies have in some cases really been subsidized in the form of very liberal compensation for carrying mail. The aids to business by the Federal Government are often overlooked or taken for granted. The foregoing examples are only a few of the specific ways in which business has been stimulated and helped by government.

The aid of government to some phases of business is more direct and more concrete than that of providing statistical information and determining standards. For example, in an effort to guarantee a substantial income to the producer of such commodities as potatoes, eggs, butter, and cotton, the government may regulate the prices of these commodities by buying and storing or otherwise disposing of sufficiently large quantities of the products to keep prices at a level satisfactory to the producer. Without governmental control, if potatoes or eggs are plentiful, the market price drops; consequently the consumer is able to buy at a relatively low price; however, the return to the producer is also low. Under governmental control of prices, the market price is maintained at a relatively high level, from which the producers of the commodity benefit by realizing a better income. On the other hand, the consumer pays not only a higher price for the commodity he wants, even though it is plentiful, but through taxes he also pays the cost of the product bought by the Federal Government in order to keep prices up for the producer.

In other instances, the Federal Government regulates the amount of a product produced or grown, as the case may be. Regulation of the number of acres of wheat planted is a typical example. By reducing the amount of wheat grown, the market price of that product is forced up by the demand for it. Consequently, the wheat farmer may have a return as great by planting 85 per cent of his land in wheat as he would have had without governmental regulation if he planted 100 per cent of his land in wheat. In order to

induce the wheat farmer not to plant too much wheat, the
Federal Government may make a direct payment to him
for reducing the amount of wheat he grows. These payments are based upon the estimated net income that might
have been earned if the unused acres had been planted and
the crop had grown.

Price supports and subsidies for special groups of producers, whether farmers or manufacturers or distributors,
are of vital interest to consumers. They are beneficial to
consumers in that some of the products and services would
not be available to them if the producers were not protected
by price supports or did not benefit from subsidies. They
are not beneficial if some groups of producers through
political pressure are successful in obtaining the benefits
of price supports or subsidies even though their products
could be produced and distributed satisfactorily without
governmental aid. A situation of this kind results in un-
fairness to the producers of other products for whom
governmental aid is equally justifiable but who do not seek
governmental aid. These producers help pay for the subsidies and other aids given to the business firms that receive
them.

The issue of vital importance to consumers is, What
kinds of products and services should be subsidized or protected by price supports, and to what extent?

Government Regulation of Business. The state and Federal governments have exercised control over business from
the early days of the United States. The various regulations controlling business activities and practices have been
authorized by specific state and Federal laws. The regulations are administered by state and Federal agencies already existing or by new agencies created for the purpose.
The methods used by government in regulating business
have taken many forms.

Government regulations of business activities and practices are imposed to achieve certain desirable goals, some
of which change from time to time as business changes and
as the points of view of government officials change.

Methods Used by Government to Regulate Business

1. Control of entry into business by requiring licenses, permits, and certificates.
2. Government ownership and operation of businesses that are difficult to control when privately owned and operated.
3. Conducting periodic and special investigations of business practices by the officials of governmental agencies that are authorized by law to make such investigations.
4. Requiring businesses to file detailed and summary reports of business transactions revealing business practices.
5. Regulation of prices and rates.
6. Regulation of advertising practices.
7. Control of business and professional activity by requiring licenses and permits to be renewed periodically.
8. Stimulating or curbing business activity through taxation.
9. Regulation of interest rates and credit.
10. Labor legislation regulating employee-employer relations, hours, wages, safety, and health.
11. Regulation of the amount of production of industries dealing with natural resources, such as oil, coal, metals, and wood.
12. Governmental aids to business sometimes have conditions attached that amount to partial regulation or control.

While businessmen generally regard government regulation of business as interference, they recognize that certain regulations are necessary and desirable. The primary concern of the businessman is that only the regulations that are absolutely necessary shall be authorized, that these regulations shall be reasonable, and that they shall be administered in a fair manner.

How Foreign Policy May Affect Consumers. Foreign policy is a dominant factor in determining the political and economic relations between the United States and other nations. Our political and economic relations with the other nations of the world may have either favorable or unfavorable effects on domestic economic conditions. The economic

Why Government Regulations of Business Activities and Practices Are Imposed

1. To curb monopolistic trends; to regulate and control prices, rates, and services of enterprises that can operate effectively only as monopolies; and to prevent practices in restraint of trade.
2. To control quality of products and services, primarily in protection of consumers.
3. To regulate prices on products and services as protection for consumers and to prevent unfair trade practices among businesses.
4. To protect business owners and managers from unfair methods of competition and unfair trade practices.
5. To protect investors by controlling the practices of financial institutions in issuing stocks, bonds, and other securities.
6. To control public utilities, which usually are monopolistic in nature, especially as to rates, services, and managerial policies.
7. To promote some aspects of business by curbing others.
8. To promote safety, health, and good working conditions.

welfare of individual consumers is directly dependent upon economic conditions within the United States.

Foreign policy is a significant factor in establishing and maintaining completely friendly relations with other nations. When friendly, cordial relations exist between nations, we have not only a two-way flow of economic goods but also an exchange of cultural, scientific, and technical information between the nations from which both benefit. If there is mistrust, jealousy, or a feeling of ill will between nations, commerce and the exchange of information are reduced, if not eliminated.

Foreign trade enables us to obtain many raw materials and products that we need and want. It also provides a market for the raw materials and products that we produce. Generally speaking, good foreign trade relationships with other nations has a favorable effect on economic conditions in the United States. Foreign policy thus has an indirect but significant effect on business and hence on consumers.

The foreign policy of the United States in protecting our economic and political interests influences the attitudes of other nations toward the United States. Whether these attitudes are cordial and friendly or hostile determines the extent to which preparation for national defense is necessary. Many times hostile relations and war between nations have resulted from economic and political misunderstanding and conflict. The wisdom of our foreign policies is reflected in the need for national defense. The costs of national defense and wars are borne by consumers through taxes.

The effects of the foreign policy of our government on consumers are indirect, but they are important.

Consumers' Interest in Public Finance. The management and control of the financial aspects of government are referred to as *public finance*. In other words, public finance deals with the revenues, expenditures, and debts of government. It is clearly a phase of economics that is of significance to consumers.

The sources of government income are taxes, fees and fines, special assessments, and revenue from government-owned industries. One of the major problems of legislators is to keep costs of government as low as possible and at the same time provide the services needed. Another problem is to devise ways by which the revenue may equal or exceed the expenditures of government. It is practically impossible to conceive of any source of revenue for the government that does not directly or indirectly affect consumers. The burden of most taxes, fees and fines, and special assessments ultimately is on consumers.

Government expenditures have increased almost continually since the early days of the United States. In war years Federal expenditures are exceedingly high.

From 1929 to 1949 Federal expenditures increased approximately 1,462 per cent and state and local expenditures, 167 per cent.

Consumers, businessmen, and legislators have expressed great concern over the increase in expenditures of the local, state, and Federal governments. One may legitimately

Expenditures of Federal, State, and Local
Governments for Selected Years *

YEAR	FEDERAL EXPENDITURES (MILLIONS)	STATE AND LOCAL EXPENDITURES (MILLIONS)
1929	$ 2,648	$ 7,689
1934	6,393	8,055
1939	8,955	9,303
1940	10,094	9,095
1941	20,545	8,974
1942	56,150**	8,732
1943	85,979**	8,353
1944	95,559**	8,504
1945	84,929**	9,130
1946	36,584	11,200
1947	31,113	14,669
1948	35,493	18,100
1949	41,370***	20,565

* Source: Survey of Current Business, Table 9, Office of Business Economics, U. S. Department of Commerce.
** World War II.
*** Net Federal expenditures excluding transfer payments, $39,785 million.

ask, why are the total expenditures of government increasing at such a rapid rate?

Several factors have contributed to the steady increase in the costs of government.

How far can the trend of increasing cost of government go without making us an insolvent nation? What percentage of national income may be paid to the government in taxes without seriously impairing our standard of living? What will be the effect on business and economic conditions if the cost of government and the amount of public debt continue to increase? What can be done to curb the trend of higher costs of government? Every consumer and taxpayer, and that includes all of us, has much at stake in the answers to these questions. Our standard of living, the possibility of accumulating personal savings, and the opportunities for employment all are dependent upon the issues raised by these questions.

Public debt results from governmental expenditures exceeding revenue. In only two of the years from 1930 to 1950 did the Federal revenue exceed expenditures. Those years were 1947 and 1948. During this same period from 1930 to 1950 the public debt increased from approximately

Factors Contributing to Increases in the Cost of Government

1. The population of the United States in 1930 was approximately 123 million; in 1940, approximately 132 million; in 1950, approximately 151 million. This increase is almost 23 per cent in a period of 20 years. It is natural that as population increases the costs of government also increase.

2. Military expenditures account for a very large part of the increase in the expenses of the Federal Government. In 1948, approximately one third of the total expenditures of the Federal Government was for national defense and pensions to veterans of wars. If the interest on the national debt, a great part of which was incurred by the cost of war, is considered as a military expenditure, almost one half of the Federal expenditures for 1948 was for national defense and payments on obligations incurred during war.

3. When economic depressions occur, farmers, businessmen, and others demand relief. For example, during the years following the depression which began in 1929, large sums of money were appropriated by the Federal Government to give assistance to business groups. When the business conditions improve, the tendency is to continue the assistance that was started in depression days.

4. Expenditures for social security and welfare increase almost annually. The demands of relatively small but persistent groups of producers and consumers for special appropriations are increasing.

5. The services of government are expanding. Many services formerly performed by private agencies have been taken over wholly or in part by the Federal Government. Education, road building and maintenance, and recreational facilities such as national parks are examples.

6. As the purchasing power of money decreases, the cost of government increases in terms of dollars. In 1950, approximately $1.85 was required to buy articles and services that cost $1 in the 1935-1939 period.

16 billion dollars to more than 257 billion dollars or more than 1500 per cent. This debt increased from $131.51 to $1,696.11 per person. The interest on the public debt in 1950 was more than 5 billion dollars. This amount for interest alone is greater than the total annual cost of the Federal Government for any year prior to 1934 except the

years during and immediately following World War I. The increase in the cost of government and in public debt since 1930 is almost too great for one to comprehend.

Every citizen has an obligation to learn all he can about the financial affairs of government. An understanding of the problems of public finance is essential for every consumer if he is to vote intelligently on economic issues.

Our Economic Interest in Government. The primary purpose of government in a democracy is to provide the services its people want. By expressing our opinions and points of view and by voting, we determine the kinds and extent of the services and benefits our government shall provide. Directly or indirectly we give 25 to 30 per cent of our income to pay for the cost of government. Not only is it our right and privilege as consumers to participate in determining the kinds and extent of the services and benefits our government shall provide and how our money given for taxes shall be used, but also it is our obligation as citizens to exercise that right and privilege.

To fulfill this responsibility we must understand as well as we can all aspects of the economic problems and issues affecting consumers. Intelligent voting on economic issues is possible only when we clearly understand the problems involved. This understanding can be obtained through alertness to and study of the economic problems confronting government. To formulate our points of view about economic problems and issues affecting consumers is not sufficient. We must express our points of view in public forums and discussions; we must convey our views to our legislators and governmental officials; and above all we must register our views by voting.

TEXTBOOK QUESTIONS

1. Name some governmental services from which certain groups of people receive the primary benefits.
2. How may consumers have a voice in determining what governmental services shall be given and what regulations shall be made?

3. What per cent of increase was there (a) in the number of people employed in the United States from 1900 to 1949? (b) in the number of persons employed by the local, state, and Federal governments combined? (c) What per cent of the people who were working in 1949 were employed by government?
4. What was the combined cost of local, state, and Federal governments in 1949?
5. What percentage of the 40 billion dollars spent by the Federal Government in 1949 was spent directly for national defense?
6. Why is the responsibility for education considered a responsibility of local, state, and Federal governments?
7. How do services produced by government differ from those produced by individuals and business firms?
8. In what ways does government aid business?
9. Explain how consumers pay for price support programs in two ways.
10. What methods are used by government to regulate business?
11. What are the primary reasons for government regulation of business activities and practices?
12. How may foreign policy affect the economic welfare of consumers?
13. Explain how the relation of foreign policy to national defense is of importance to consumers.
14. What is meant by public finance?
15. What are the primary sources of government income?
16. Explain why the costs of government are increasing.
17. How much did the public debt increase from 1930 to 1950?
18. How much greater was the public debt per person in 1950 than in 1930?

DISCUSSION QUESTIONS

1. Explain why laws and regulations are necessary when people live together in a community or state.
2. Explain why the more services a government provides for its people the more complex and costly government becomes.
3. In what way do consumers have a financial interest in the business affairs of government?
4. Why do not consumers protect themselves individually from injury or physical loss instead of depending upon government?
5. Discuss the various ways that the people of your community are protected by the local, state, and Federal governments.
6. What would be the arguments against a plan for education in which public funds would not be used for education and

parents would use the taxes thus saved to provide education for their children?

7. If the Federal Government should increase materially the kinds and extent of the services it now offers to consumers, what would be the effect upon business firms that produce services and commodities for profit?

8. The postal rates for letters and other classes of mail do not provide sufficient income to pay the costs of the Postal Department, and the Federal Government bears the remainder of the cost. What are the arguments against eliminating postal charges entirely and permitting all mail to be carried free of charge?

9. Explain how the Federal Government has regulated the price of such commodities as potatoes, eggs, and butter.

10. Explain how the Federal Government regulates the price of a commodity by regulating the quantity produced.

11. Give some examples of government regulation of business activities from which consumers benefit.

12. Discuss how business firms are affected by foreign policy.

PROBLEMS

1. Make a list of the services provided for you by each unit of government under which you live.

2. In your school or public library obtain the file of the local and state newspapers for the past month. Make a list of the items of economic importance of interest to consumers in your community that are featured in editorials and news stories.

3. Using a reference, such as the *World Almanac and Book of Facts* or the *Information Please Almanac,* which probably will be found in your school library, determine: (a) What was the per capita income for the average person in your state for the latest year for which such data are available? For the average person in the United States? For the average person in the region in which you live? (b) What has been the trend in income per capita in your state for the past five years? For the United States? (c) Compare the receipts and expenditures of the United States Government for each of the last 20 years showing the deficit or surplus.

COMMUNITY PROBLEMS AND PROJECTS

1. What are the three or four major problems of general economic nature confronting the Federal Government and the people of the United States now? In order to discover these problems read the issues of the past month of magazines

dealing with national problems, such as *Newsweek*, *U. S. News and World Report*, and *Time*. Also read editorials and news stories dealing with economic problems in leading newspapers. It is suggested that while scanning the magazines and newspapers for topics dealing with problems of economic nature, you make a list of all of those that you find. Those occurring on the list the most frequently during the past month and those given the greatest amount of space may be considered among the most important current problems.

2. The Federal Government of the United States spent more than 39 billion dollars in 1949. The main items for which this amount was spent are as follows:

EXPENDITURES
(MILLIONS)

National defense	$11,914
Veterans' services and benefits	6,669
International affairs	6,462
Social welfare, health, and security	1,907
Agriculture and agricultural resources	2,512
Natural resources	1,512
Transportation and communication	1,622
General government	1,170
Interest on the national debt	5,352
Other (including education and research)	665
	$39,785

a. Compute the percentage that each class of expenditure is of the total Federal expenditures for 1949. Construct a bar chart showing the percentage spent for each main item of the total expenditure.

b. Payments to veterans and payments for interest on the public debt are primarily costs of past wars. Assuming this statement to be true, what per cent of the total Federal expenditures for 1949 resulted from past wars and from outlays for national defense?

c. Which of the classes of items of expenditures are for services or benefits to the citizens and business firms of the country?

d. What per cent of Federal expenditures for 1949 was spent for items of special or direct benefit to the citizens and business firms of the country?

INDEX